# Anti-Semitism
### AND
# Early Christianity

# Anti-Semitism

## AND

# Early Christianity

## *ISSUES OF POLEMIC AND FAITH*

Edited by
**Craig A. Evans**
and
**Donald A. Hagner**

*Foreword by James A. Sanders*

**Fortress Press**                    **Minneapolis**

ANTI-SEMITISM AND EARLY CHRISTIANITY
Issues of Polemic and Faith

Interior design: ediType
Cover design: Ned Skubic
Cover image: Relief sculpture from the Arch of Titus depicting Roman soldiers marching with booty from the Temple of Jerusalem in 70 C.E. Photo by Philip Gendreau.

---

Library of Congress Cataloging-in-Publication Data

Anti-semitism and early Christianity : issues of polemic and faith /
    edited by Craig A. Evans and Donald A. Hagner.
        p.   cm.
    Includes bibiliographical references and indexes.
        ISBN 0-8006-2748-2 (alk. paper)
    1. Jews in the New Testament.  2. Bible.  N.T.–Criticism,
interpretation, etc.  3. Antisemitism–Biblical teaching.
4. Christianity and antisemitism–History.  5. Judaism (Christian
theology)–History of doctrines–Early church, ca. 30–600.
I. Evans, Craig A.  II. Hagner, Donald Alfred.
BS2545.J44A58  1993
261.2'5'09015–dc20                                    92-44701
                                                     CIP

---

The paper used in this publication meets the minimum requirements of American National Standard for Information Sciences–Permanence of Paper for Printed Library Materials, ANSI Z329.48-1984                                    ∞™

---

Manufactured in the U.S.A.                                    AF 1–2750

97    96    95    94    93    1    2    3    4    5    6    7    8    9    10

*In Memory of Robert A. Guelich*

*Colleague and Friend*

# Contents

Foreword, by James A. Sanders     ix

Preface     xix

Abbreviations of Periodicals and Serials     xxi

Introduction. Faith and Polemic:
The New Testament and First-century Judaism     1
    *Craig A. Evans*

## Part One
### Antecedents of New Testament Polemic

1. A Hammer That Breaks Rock in Pieces:
   Prophetic Critique in the Hebrew Bible     21
       *Mary C. Callaway*

2. Jesus and the Question of Anti-Semitism     39
       *Bruce Chilton*

## Part Two
### Anti-Semitism and the New Testament Writings

3. A Loyal Critic: Matthew's Polemic with Judaism
   in Theological Perspective     55
       *Scot McKnight*

4. Anti-Semitism and/or Anti-Judaism in Mark?     80
       *Robert A. Guelich*

5. "Fighting against God": Luke's Interpretation
   of Jewish Rejection of the Messiah Jesus     102
       *David L. Tiede*

  6. Anti-Semitism and the Gospel of John                    113
         *Robert Kysar*

— 7. Paul's Quarrel with Judaism                              128
         *Donald A. Hagner*

— 8. Anti-Semitism in the Deutero-Pauline Literature          151
         *James D. G. Dunn*

  9. Polemic in Hebrews and the Catholic Epistles             166
         *Robert W. Wall and William L. Lane*

 10. Polemic in the Book of Revelation                        199
         *Peder Borgen*

## Part Three
### Anti-Semitism and Post–New Testament Christian Writings

— 11. Anti-Judaism in the Early Church Fathers               215
         *Lee Martin McDonald*

 12. Anti-Judaism in the New Testament Apocrypha:
     A Preliminary Survey                                     253
         *James R. Mueller*

 13. Anti-Semitism in Gnostic Writings                        269
         *R. McL. Wilson*

Epilogue                                                      291
         *Joel Marcus*

Index of Ancient Writings                                    297

Index of Modern Authors                                      323

Contributors                                                 327

# Foreword

In the mid-1960s a number of concerned scholars met at Union Seminary in New York to review the text of the Oberammergau passion play. The drama was soon to be presented again in Austria in the text and manner conceived centuries earlier in faithfulness to a vow made in gratitude to God's delivering the village from a plague that had ravaged much of Europe. The vow was conceived in faith and executed in deep piety. Viewed from the context of that village and its history one could not imagine its decennial performance as anything but an expression of the goodness of God and the abiding gratitude of the heirs of those who had been delivered.

As long as only Christians witness such expressions of faith and obedience, they might themselves be encouraged in faith and heartened that humans were capable of such faithfulness. The problem was that the post-Holocaust world beyond the village of Oberammergau began to listen in, and what had surely been piety in its purest form for Christians only now began to be seen as the focused expression of parochial Christian anti-Semitism and anti-Judaism.

The group of Christian scholars who gathered to discuss the text of the play and to try to excise the anti-Jewish elements found that the text was simply faithful recital, for the most part, of biblical scenes pieced together for continuity of story line under the sole demands and requirements of dramatic presentation. There was no way to excise the apparent anti-Jewish dimension of the play without rewriting the Gospels themselves! The text has since been somewhat revised but still is basically perceived as anti-Jewish if not anti-Semitic, because of the texts of the Gospels themselves. The experience was disturbing to say the least, coming as it did at the height of the ecumenical movement within Christianity, given impetus by papers issuing from Vatican II, and in the context of tensions in the Near East leading to the June 1967 Six Day War.

## Ecumenism and the Bible

Ecumenism had begun to take on broader meanings than simply attempts at unifying the worldwide Christian witness to God's work in Christ. As a former

student of Sam Sandmel's, I perceived that the Gospels themselves, like the
Oberammergau play, had to be read in a much broader context than their own,
indeed broader than the context of the New Testament alone. My own work at
the time on the Dead Sea Scrolls brought me in many ways sharply to have to
deal with ancient ecumenism, and I was beginning to realize that genuine and
true ecumenism could not stop short of a global dimension.

I also began to realize that one had to view concepts of the biblical canon in
an ecumenical perspective. Not only did the concept in modern times depend
on which community of faith one had in mind in referring to a biblical canon,
but the same was true in antiquity. What later became the rabbinic biblical
canon simply did not fit Qumran's views of authoritative Scripture; nor did
Greek translations of Scripture adhere to any single understanding of canon.
The limiting of the canon of the Sadducees and the Samaritans to the Torah
had to be reckoned with as well.

Early manuscripts of the developing Second Testament canon vary in content and order. Ecumenism was not just a desirable goal of mainline Christians
in the 1960s; it was a necessary perspective in understanding the development
of the various forms of Judaism and Christianity. It is interesting how often
the phrase "the canon" is still used among some theologians as if there were
only one canon. It is comparable to the use of the expression "late Judaism"
(*Spätjudentum*) in New Testament scholarship to refer to early Judaism (sixth
century B.C.E. to the first century C.E.); but fortunately one seldom hears that
anymore.

In-group thinking, even in conservative circles of Jews and Christians, has
become more and more tempered by larger if not yet global perspectives. What
is piety to one group, like the folk at Oberammergau, may appear quite evil to
another. Realizing that fact can be painful to a community striving for righteousness according to a received tradition. Light from another tradition may
expose the dark aspects of the best of human efforts. Reinhold Niebuhr called
this the ambiguity of reality. Robert A. Heinlein, a U.S. science fiction writer
(1907–88), has been quoted as saying that "goodness without wisdom always ac-
complishes evil." That thought may be more than many of us want to hear. Yet
it can hardly be denied if one tradition's notion of doing good is not tempered
with wisdom and circumspection, it may contain evil when perceived from a
different tradition.

## Wisdom and the Prophets

Wisdom pervades biblical literature from beginning to end. There was a time,
not too long past, when study of wisdom in the Bible was limited to the so-called
wisdom books (Job, Proverbs, Ecclesiastes). Now wisdom thinking is seen as
evident even in the prophetic corpus of the First Testament, which past schol-

arship sometimes saw as antithetical to wisdom; and some prophetic thinking is now seen as present by allusion and echo in the so-called wisdom books. In the mid-1950s, Samuel Terrien, moving against the stream, argued that wisdom rhetoric and thinking informed the book of Amos, indeed the very passages attributed by scholarship to the eighth-century B.C.E. prophet from Tekoa; and Hans Walter Wolff has enshrined Terrien's work in his important commentary on Amos now in English in the Hermeneia series. On hearing Terrien's paper first read at a conference of the Society of Biblical Literature, Robert Dentan aptly reminded the hearers of the wise woman of Tekoa in 2 Samuel 14.

Wisdom thinking has an international dimension. On the simplest level, wisdom describes human skills—the techniques involved in raising crops, flocks, and children—and how to relate to others to the benefit of society as a whole. Such skills and customs cannot be defined by national borders; they involve the experience of survival and development at the most basic human levels. Legal *corpora* exhibit wisdom thinking. And wisdom may involve the cleverness of the wise courtier in the halls of a foreign king, serving the king's interests while sponsoring those of his or her own people and even serving their god without the king's suspecting it. Joseph, Esther, and Daniel in the Bible provide wonderful examples of how wisdom provides the perspective necessary to ask crucial questions of one's community's traditions about good and evil and look at them from other angles. Job and Qoheleth provide in-depth probings of this sort.

How did Amos arrive at the hermeneutic by which he "read" Israel's most sacred traditions (2:9-11; 3:1-2) in such a way as to claim them as the authority by which he challenged the official theology of Northern Israel—a quarter of a century before that challenge became manifest in history through the destruction of Northern Israel by the Neo-Assyrian Empire? The Northern Israelites claimed a unique relation to God based on the very precious identifying traditions of exodus–wanderings–entrance (which we know from the Pentateuch and Joshua), and Amos was able to read those traditions as the authority for his claim that God was nonetheless free to judge God's own people. The same observation can be made in the case of all the preexilic judgmental prophets.[1]

Wisdom thinking lies at the center of the prophetic corpus in the sense that its international aspect brought an ecumenical dimension to prophetic theological thought. God was creator of all as well as redeemer of Israel. The threat of falsehood in prophetic conflict and debate was present when God was viewed as redeemer only or as committed to Israel's view of the divine promises. Deutero-Isaiah read the traditions of Israel and Judah by the same hermeneutic when the challenge needed was something like the opposite; God, being creator of heaven and earth and all that in them is, could appoint the foreign monarch, Cyrus, as messiah (45:1) for salvation in his time in the same manner that an

---

1. See J. A. Sanders, *From Sacred Story to Sacred Text* (Philadelphia: Fortress, 1987) 61–73, 87–105.

earlier Isaiah had said that Sennacherib was the instrument of God's judgments
(10:5) of Judah and in the same way that Jeremiah had said Nebuchadnezzar
was God's servant (27:6) in judgment of God's own people.

In reading the prophets today one must at some point attempt to identify
not with the prophets but with the good, responsible religious folk of their day
who—like those at Oberammergau—were doing their very best, to the best of
their in-group thinking, for their people. The goodness they pursued, according to the very prophets who eventually became "canon" in some sense for all
time to come, was without the wisdom the prophets brought to bear in reading
and applying the same traditions to the same situations as the leaders. There
are always three factors that need to be taken into account: the tradition or
text being reapplied, the new sociopolitical situation where reapplied, and the
hermeneutics by which the tradition or text was being "read" in the new setting.

## An Experiment

One then cannot but ask if such lessons learned in recent study of true and false
prophecy in the First Testament might not be brought forward in reading the
Second Testament. To engage in such an experiment one needs to read the text
of the Gospels as received without bias with respect to source criticism as it has
developed in Gospel study. That does not mean, even for the experiment, an
uncritical reading of the Gospels; it does mean, however, a focus on the function
of the First Testament in the Second without assumption as to provenance, especially according to recent formulations of the two-source hypothesis. It means
in effect allowing the First Testament, whether in fluid translations in *koiné*
Greek in Mark and John, or in its more Septuagint guise in formal citation in
Matthew and Luke, to be a source of Gospel formation as important as Q and
Mark. It means taking seriously the Gospels' claim that it was the way Jesus
applied Scripture in his day that offended the official views of Scripture and its
meaning for Jews in the first third of the first century.

It means reading the Gospels intertextually, that is, as exhibiting midrashic
readings of Scripture. To "search" (*darash*) Scripture and tradition means reading them seeking light from them on new situations—precisely what the prophets,
psalmists, and historians did, as well as their heirs who wrote early Jewish literature (Apocrypha, Pseudepigrapha, etc.). Some scholars are apparently unwilling
to entertain or understand midrash in its broad sense and prefer rather to limit
it to the Qumran or rabbinic literary forms.[2] Reading the Second Testament

---

2. Such as R. E. Brown, "Gospel Infancy Narrative Research from 1976 to 1986: Part I
(Matthew)," *CBQ* 48 (1986) 468–83, esp. 477. The broad sense is found in the works of R. Bloch,
G. Vermes, R. LeDéaut, myself, and so on; and see now the brilliant discussion in D. Boyarin,
*Intertextuality and the Reading of Midrash* (Bloomington and Indianapolis: Indiana Univ. Press,
1990) 12.

intertextually and midrashically is a serious challenge to seeing Scripture in the Second Testament as largely *dictum probantium.*

Dating the Nag Hammadi "Gospels" earlier than the canonical Gospels has skewed perception of the vital role Scripture plays not only in the Gospel texts but in their formation. All Jewish literature, beginning in the exile, was written scripturally. Even the book of Job is full of paraphrases of prophetic thought, rather dogmatically rehearsed in the speeches of the friends, but also reflected upon in those ascribed to Job. Under the surface of the text of Qoheleth lies a great deal of earlier biblical thought. The rest of canonical early Jewish literature is clearly written scripturally.[3] The Apocrypha, Pseudepigrapha, Qumran nonbiblical literature, Philo, Josephus, and so on are all scripturally written.

The literature of early Christians was also scripturally written, and their earliest oral formulations of what they thought had happened, and was happening, were undoubtedly shaped by Scripture (pre-Masoretic Hebrew or fluid Greek translation [so-called LXX]). They searched the Scriptures for light on their experiences, and then they recited (and later wrote down) the experiences in scriptural terms and cadences. Scripture guided and helped them shape their understanding of what happened and then their recitals of it. This is quite different from deciding what happened and then supplying the recital of it with scriptural underpinning. And they did it in the way they understood the teacher had taught them to do it. This is the picture the Gospel narratives convey.

The so-called criteria of similarity and dissimilarity can be misleading to the extent that they are developed aside from seeing the formation of Christian thought and literature in its typically Hellenistic Jewish contemporary mode of writing scripturally. The idea that most of the citations of Scripture in the Gospels were added as *dicta probantia* gives a false and misleading picture of Gospel formation. The early Christians did not search scripture primarily for support of what they already thought; they searched it *to find out how to think* about what had happened and was happening.

The hermeneutic of the search was essentially theocentric. The gentile Christians who came into the fold did so in part out of the general respect the Septuagint already had in the non-Jewish Hellenistic world; and they became Christians largely because of experiences of Christ and the Holy Spirit that were apparently strong enough to overcome the ridicule doing so must have induced. Then remaining Christian and not reverting after the persecutions became intense, and after the apparent failure of the parousia on the fall of Jerusalem in 70 C.E., induced further searching of Scripture to understand how to live in the tension between God's promises and their apparent lack of fulfillment, or later dissolution—precisely the dominant theme of the Torah and the Prophets (early

---

3. See M. Fishbane, *Biblical Interpretation in Ancient Israel* (Oxford: Clarendon, 1985); idem, *The Garments of Torah: Essays in Biblical Hermeneutics* (Bloomington and Indianapolis: Indiana Univ. Press, 1990).

and later)! But searching Scripture had begun with the founder, according to the narrative, and Jesus' mode of doing so was in large part what had gotten him into trouble with his fellow Jews in the first place.

## Midrashic Intertextuality

"Every text is absorption and transformation" of other texts, according to Julia Kristeva.[4] Midrashic intertextuality expresses the depths of community identity and the effort to overcome all threats to it.[5] To the student who arrives at study of the Second Testament fresh—without bias as to source-critical hypotheses but fully acquainted with early Jewish literature from the exile on through to the first century of the Common Era—the Second Testament is replete in intertextuality and ripe for this kind of midrashic study. It demonstrates sincere and honest search of Scripture to clarify what happened in the first third of the first century in the Gospels, and then in the second third in Acts and the Pauline corpus. The first third would be marked by the crucifixion/resurrection account, the second by the fall of Jerusalem to the Romans, with the final third reflected in redactional activity and the composition of some of the rest of the epistles and the Apocalypse.

If one reads the Gospels afresh—trying to take at face value the larger, overall picture of Jesus' preaching, teaching, and healing—and with constant reference to Scripture, one gets the impression of a Hellenistic version of what the prophetic books conveyed, of a maverick challenging the established views of the meaning of Scripture and what it says of relevance to the ongoing human situation. Sure, passages appear here and there to address the second third or final third of the century somewhat more clearly than the first third, with a few appearing to address a situation other than Hellenistic Palestine, but the overall picture conveyed is that of an Amos or Jeremiah of the first century informed by the international wisdom of the Hellenistic period just as the prophets had been informed by the international wisdom of the Iron Age.

Then as one focuses on the so-called anti-Jewish passages, one is rather impressed by how similar the woes and laments directed in the challenge against authorities are between the earlier wisdom-prophetic teachers and this wisdom-prophetic teacher Jesus. And they fall within a range of hermeneutical agreement: God is always bigger than you think; God is not only the redeemer-guarantor of divine promises but is also the creator of all the world and hence free to challenge denominational interpretations of Scripture. If God is the God of all, then the earlier command to love one's neighbor is ready for the maturity of a command to love even one's so-called enemy (Matt 5:44). And if God is the

---

4. J. Kristeva, *Semeiotike: Recherches pour une semanalyse* (Paris: Editions du Seuil, 1969) 146 (cited in Boyarin, *Intertextuality*, 22).

5. See Boyarin, *Intertextuality*, 135 n. 2.

God of death as well as of life (e.g., Deut 32:39 et passim), then one is ready
to hear of a holy war not against earthly enemies but against the last enemy,
Death, and to hear that God is now ready to raise the warrior from the dead.
Of considerable interest at this point is the realization that despite the strong
monotheizing thrust of the First Testament and its insistence that there never
was a god of death (*Mot* in Canaanite mythology), Jewish literature had to reaf-
firm his nonexistence in numerous ways throughout its development, as indeed
by the myth of Jesus' holy war against *Thanatos*.

The important point is to remember that Jesus was a Jew,[6] a member of
the Abraham-Sarah family, who like the wisdom-prophets of old challenged the
thinking of the establishment, just as they had, and on the same authority they
had—the authoritative traditions of Israel and Judah, the regular recital of which
continually provided both identity and life-style, faith and obedience. And he
got into trouble for doing so, just as they had. Pondering both, one then comes
to realize that if such a wisdom-prophetic teacher should arise today, he or she
would get into the same kind of trouble with most church managerial bodies as
the prophets and Jesus did! Why? Is it because such leaders are somehow more
sinful than others might be? No! Rather, it is because organized religion over the
world is made up of human beings who, like all those in the numerous biblical
accounts from all the ages covered, tend to box God or reality into manageable
dimensions.

## The Monotheizing Process

But the monotheizing process continues; it never stops despite the needs of
religious authorities of any age who at each new stage invariably view new developments in the process as blasphemous, heretical, and even seditious. This does
not mean that we have thereby a rule of thumb to identify true prophets: not
all blasphemous, heretical, and seditious preaching is monotheizing in thrust.
That thrust can be described in its pilgrimage from tribal views of Yahweh to
global views of God—all informed by the infinite patience of God, who has tolerated all kinds of tribalism and denominationalism in the centuries-old process
of judgments/redemptions on the pilgrimage that Abraham and Sarah began.[7]

Now, if one is willing, even if only for a moment, radically to assume
that much of what is reported of Jesus' preaching and teaching that looks like
anti-Jewish polemic actually had its inception in Jesus' ministry in the wisdom-
prophetic pattern, then one can understand how the early churches would
be interested in hearing those teachings repeated and recited—but for totally
other reasons! To them, suffering rejection and persecution by the synagogue, it

---

6. See, e.g., J. H. Charlesworth, ed., *Jesus' Jewishness* (New York: Crossroad, 1991), and more
recently J. P. Meier, *A Marginal Jew: Rethinking the Historical Jesus* (New York: Doubleday, 1991).

7. See M. Smith, *The Early History of God* (San Francisco: Harper and Row, 1990).

sounded, in "rereading" the Jesus traditions, as though Jesus had rebuked Jewish leaders generally, including all such synagogue leaders and decision makers, well before those Jewish leaders rebuked and rejected Christians. Then when the churches turned to being more gentile than Jewish, the same Jesus teachings, continuing to be repeated/recited, would be heard as rebuke of Jews who had rejected Jesus and were now rejecting those still faithful to him and the messianic message. By this hypothesis one would not need to alter or edit much of any of Jesus' wisdom-prophetic challenges in the first third of the first century to make them fit the quite different situations of either the second third of the century or the final third.

This would mean that scholarship would have to accept again, but this time in an area of particularly high sensitivity, the well-established principle of historical research that precious historical material is sometimes repeated/recited, even possibly accurately, for reasons entirely other than its original intention. It might mean reviewing all those passages in the Gospels that appear to be inserted as later anti-Jewish polemic and seeing if they might not fit just as well in the first third of the century in the mouth of a first-century Amos—that is, in the mouth of someone who knew Scripture quite well but, like Amos long before, found himself "rereading" it midrashically in a way apparently no one around him was reading it.

Those who through the ages have been blessed/cursed with such a hermeneutic of the wisdom-prophetic view of reality have generally had to pay for it personally, and Jesus did. The differences between Jesus and Amos, or Jeremiah or the others, were that Judaism had become Hellenized to some degree generally, and the Jewish-Christian churches had begun to include more and more non-Jews who also began to experience rejection at the hands of synagogue leaders. This gave the appearance of an interracial dimension that has skewed the gospel message ever since.

If this hypothesis has validity it would mean entertaining more of the Gospels as Jesus' contribution to Gospel formation than usual. Even those passages, as in Luke, that indicate acceptance of Jesus' message on the part of Samaritans and other foreigners, but failure to understand on the part of the disciples, would need to be reread in the light of similar passages in the First Testament in which those who could lay claims on God's promises were more in danger of misunderstanding them, according to the prophets, than outsiders who could make no such claims. It would mean bringing forward to the Second Testament also the observation that God works as well with *agnosis* (even ignorance) as with *gnosis* and understanding. "Who is blind as my servant Israel?" asked the Isaiah of the exile (42:18-19). It would mean reading the New Testament intertextually, midrashically—and canonically—and not only in terms of its synchronic, sociopolitical context.

Much in the history of humankind has been preserved for reasons other than those originally intended. Jesus' wisdom-prophetic strictures against his fellow

Jews in his day, while inducing rejection by them in the first third of the century, could easily by this hypothesis have been read—in many instances without changing a single word—by later rejected Christians as the encouragement they felt they needed to remain in God's Israel as the Way, and persevere in the faith.

A theocentric, monotheizing hermeneutic applied intertextually and midrashically to all the Bible will someday bring us to see that the Bible, as canon and as parable, is ultimately not about Jews and non-Jews in any of its parts, but reflects normal, human protagonists and antagonists in many kinds of situations on this rapidly shrinking globe.

JAMES A. SANDERS

# Preface

Since World War II and the exposure of the Jewish Holocaust, New Testament scholars have become increasingly sensitive to the presence of anti-Semitic thinking in their research and writing. Several studies in the last twenty-five years have explored the alleged presence of anti-Semitism in the New Testament writings themselves. Some of these studies have detected the presence of passages, even theologies, that are opposed to and highly critical of forms of Judaism that reject Jesus and the Christian proclamation. But does this criticism and polemic constitute anti-Semitism? Some scholars, both Jewish and Christian, think so. A number of years ago Samuel Sandmel concluded that "the New Testament is a repository for hostility to Jews and Judaism. Many, if perhaps even most, Christians are completely free of anti-Semitism, yet Christian Scripture is permeated by it."[1] Even more pointedly, Jack T. Sanders has argued that the evangelist Luke despised the Jews and felt that the world would be better off without them. Is this interpretation correct?

It is our contention, along with a number of other scholars, that this conclusion is erroneous and rests upon a failure to appreciate the historical context of religious conflict and polemic within Judaism of the first century. The New Testament is not, we believe, a collection of writings that reflect an antagonism between gentile Christians and Jewish non-Christians. Rather, it is a collection of writings that reflect a primarily Jewish intramural struggle. New Testament polemic, we believe, parallels to a large degree the polemic that existed among various competing religious groups within Judaism. On the basis of comparative study, the essayists in this volume conclude that New Testament polemic, for all of its harshness, even abusiveness at times, is not anti-Semitic.

The present volume is made up of fourteen essays, the first three of which (including the Introduction) attempt to trace the origin of the rhetoric of bitter criticism, while the middle eight seek to show how the respective New Testament writers engaged in this intramural struggle. Three concluding essays, by way of contrast, detect and discuss examples of undisputed anti-Semitic statements and

---

1. S. Sandmel, *Anti-Semitism in the New Testament?* (Philadelphia: Fortress, 1978) 160.

tendencies that emerged in the post–New Testament era, after the church had become overwhelmingly non-Jewish. The editors wish to express their gratitude to the contributors, whose labors have made this book possible.

We dedicate this volume to the memory of our late colleague and friend, Professor Robert A. Guelich. His contribution to the present volume is one of the last things he wrote before his untimely death. The world of New Testament studies has been made poorer by the loss of an exceptional scholar.

# Abbreviations of Periodicals and Serials

| | |
|---|---|
| AB | Anchor Bible |
| AnBib | Analecta biblica |
| ANF | The Ante-Nicene Fathers |
| *ANRW* | *Aufstieg und Niedergang der römischen Welt* |
| *ASTI* | *Annual of the Swedish Theological Institute* |
| ATANT | Abhandlungen zur Theologie des Alten und Neuen Testaments |
| *ATR* | *Anglican Theological Review* |
| BBB | Bonner biblische Beiträge |
| BETL | Bibliotheca ephemeridum theologicarum lovaniensium |
| BFCT | Beiträge zur Förderung christlicher Theologie |
| *Bib* | *Biblica* |
| BibS(F) | Biblische Studien (Freiburg) |
| *BJRL* | *Bulletin of the John Rylands University Library of Manchester* |
| BJS | Brown Judaic Studies |
| *BTB* | *Biblical Theology Bulletin* |
| *BZ* | *Biblische Zeitschrift* |
| BZAW | Beihefte zur *ZAW* |
| *CBQ* | *Catholic Biblical Quarterly* |
| CRINT | Compendia rerum iudaicarum ad novum testamentum |
| EKKNT | Evangelisch-katholischer Kommentar zum Neuen Testament |
| *ETL* | *Ephemerides theologicae lovanienses* |
| *EvT* | *Evangelische Theologie* |
| FBBS | Facet Books, Biblical Studies |
| FFNT | Foundations and Facets: New Testament |
| FRLANT | Forschungen zur Religion und Literatur des Alten und Neuen Testaments |
| GCS | Griechischen christlichen Schriftsteller |

| GOTR | *Greek Orthodox Theological Review* |
| HBT | *Horizons in Biblical Theology* |
| HDR | Harvard Dissertations in Religion |
| HNT | Handbuch zum Neuen Testament |
| HNTC | Harper's NT Commentaries |
| HTKNT | Herders theologischer Kommentar zum Neuen Testament |
| HTR | *Harvard Theological Review* |
| IBS | *Irish Biblical Studies* |
| ICC | International Critical Commentary |
| IDB | G. A. Buttrick (ed.), *Interpreter's Dictionary of the Bible* |
| Int | *Interpretation* |
| JAAR | *Journal of the American Academy of Religion* |
| JAC | Jahrbuch für Antike und Christentum |
| JBL | *Journal of Biblical Literature* |
| JES | *Journal of Ecumenical Studies* |
| JR | *Journal of Religion* |
| JSNT | *Journal for the Study of the New Testament* |
| JSNTSup | Journal for the Study of the New Testament–Supplement Series |
| JSOT | *Journal for the Study of the Old Testament* |
| JSOTSup | Journal for the Study of the Old Testament–Supplement Series |
| JTS | *Journal of Theological Studies* |
| KD | *Kerygma und Dogma* |
| LB | *Linguistica Biblica* |
| LCL | Loeb Classical Library |
| NCB | New Century Bible |
| NedTTS | *Nederlands theologisch tijdschrift* |
| NHC | Nag Hammadi Codices |
| NHLE | *Nag Hammadi Library in English* |
| NHS | Nag Hammadi Studies |
| NICNT | New International Commentary on the New Testament |
| NIGTC | The New International Greek Testament Commentary |
| NovT | *Novum Testamentum* |
| NovTSup | Novum Testamentum, Supplements |
| NPNF | Nicene and Post-Nicene Fathers |
| NTAbh | Neutestamentliche Abhandlungen |

| | |
|---|---|
| *NTS* | *New Testament Studies* |
| *OTP* | J. H. Charlesworth (ed.), *The Old Testament Pseudepigrapha* |
| *PG* | J. Migne, *Patrologia graeca* |
| *RelSRev* | *Religious Studies Review* |
| *ResQ* | *Restoration Quarterly* |
| *RevExp* | *Review and Expositor* |
| RNT | Regensburger Neues Testament |
| *RSR* | *Recherches de science religieuse* |
| SANT | Studien zum Alten und Neuen Testament |
| SBLDS | SBL Dissertation Series |
| SBLSBS | SBL Sources for Biblical Study |
| SBLSP | SBL Seminar Papers |
| SBLTT | SBL Texts and Translations |
| SBT | Studies in Biblical Theology |
| *SE* | *Studia Evangelica* |
| *SEÅ* | *Svensk exegetisk årsbok* |
| *SJT* | *Scottish Journal of Theology* |
| SNTSMS | Society for New Testament Studies Monograph Series |
| SPB | Studia postbiblica |
| TBei | Theologische Beiträge |
| *TDNT* | *Theological Dictionary of the New Testament* |
| THKNT | Theologischer Handkommentar zum Neuen Testament |
| *TLZ* | *Theologische Literaturzeitung* |
| *TRev* | *Theologische Revue* |
| *TS* | *Theological Studies* |
| TU | Texte und Untersuchungen |
| *TynBul* | *Tyndale Bulletin* |
| *TZ* | *Theologische Zeitschrift* |
| *USQR* | *Union Seminary Quarterly Review* |
| WBC | Word Biblical Commentary |
| WMANT | Wissenschaftliche Monographien zum Alten und Neuen Testament |
| WUNT | Wissenschaftliche Untersuchungen zum Neuen Testament |
| *ZNW* | *Zeitschrift für die neutestamentliche Wissenschaft* |
| *ZTK* | *Zeitschrift für Theologie und Kirche* |

# – Introduction –

# Faith and Polemic:
# The New Testament
# and First-century Judaism

## Craig A. Evans

Several years ago I addressed a group of university students on the subject of the origins of Christianity. During the course of my talk I frequently referred to "Jewish Christians." After the lecture a Jewish student came up to me and expressed wonder at this expression. "Don't you realize," she asked, "that 'Jewish Christian' is a contradiction in terms?" To this student's way of thinking I might as well have referred to "Jewish Gentiles." Scholars of Jewish and Christian origins will smile at this confusion, but I wonder if most are completely free of it themselves. In my judgment much of the debate concerned with New Testament polemic tends to assume that first-century Christianity is basically gentile and that the New Testament itself is largely a gentile book, though perhaps dressed in Jewish garb. Seen in this light New Testament disagreement with and criticism of particular Jews and forms of Judaism appear anti-Judaic (i.e., opposed to Judaism as a religion), perhaps even anti-Semitic (i.e., opposed to the Jewish people). Consider the bigoted tone that the following passages have if we assume that the New Testament is a gentile book expressing criticism of the Jewish people:

> You brood of vipers! Who warned you to flee from the wrath to come? Bear fruit that befits repentance, and do not presume to say to yourselves, "We have Abraham as our father"; for I tell you, God is able from these stones to raise up children to Abraham. Even now the axe is laid to the root of the trees; every tree therefore that does not bear good fruit is cut down and thrown into the fire. (Matt 3:7-10)

> Woe to you, scribes and Pharisees, hypocrites! for you are like whitewashed tombs, which outwardly appear beautiful, but within are full of dead people's bones and

1

all uncleanness. So you also outwardly appear righteous to people, but within you are full of hypocrisy and iniquity. Woe to you, scribes and Pharisees, hypocrites! for you build the tombs of the prophets and adorn the monuments of the righteous, saying, "If we had lived in the days of our fathers, we would not have taken part with them in shedding the blood of the prophets." Thus you witness against yourselves, that you are sons of those who murdered the prophets. Fill up, then, the measure of your fathers. You serpents, you brood of vipers, how are you to escape being sentenced to hell? (Matt 23:27-33)

Therefore I send you prophets and wise men and scribes, some of whom you will kill and crucify, and some of whom you will scourge in your synagogues and persecute from town to town, that upon you may come all the righteous blood shed on earth, from the blood of the innocent Abel to the blood of Zechariah the son of Barachiah, whom you murdered between the sanctuary and the altar. Truly, I say to you, all this will come upon this generation. (Matt 23:34-36)

O Jerusalem, Jerusalem, killing the prophets and stoning those who are sent to you! How often would I have gathered your children together as a hen gathers her brood under her wings, and you would not! Behold, your house is forsaken and desolate. (Matt 23:37-38)

Jesus said to them [i.e., the "Jews"], "If God were your Father, you would love me, for I proceeded and came forth from God; I came not of my own accord, but he sent me. Why do you not understand what I say? It is because you cannot bear to hear my word.

"You are of your father the devil, and your will is to do your father's desires. He was a murderer from the beginning, and has nothing to do with the truth, because there is no truth in him. . . . He who is of God hears the words of God; the reason why you do not hear them is that you are not of God." (John 8:42-47)

You stiff-necked people, uncircumcised in heart and ears, you always resist the Holy Spirit. As your fathers did, so do you. Which of the prophets did not your fathers persecute? And they killed those who announced beforehand the coming of the Righteous One, whom you have now betrayed and murdered, you who received the law as delivered by angels and did not keep it. (Acts 7:51-53)

And Paul and Barnabas spoke out boldly, saying, "It was necessary that the word of God should be spoken first to you. Since you thrust it from you, and judge yourselves unworthy of eternal life, behold, we turn to the Gentiles. . . ." And when the Gentiles heard this, they were glad. (Acts 13:46-48)

And when [the Jews] opposed and reviled [Paul], he shook out his garments and said to them, "Your blood be upon your heads! I am innocent. From now on I will go to the Gentiles." (Acts 18:6)

So, as [the Jews] disagreed among themselves, they departed, after Paul had made one statement: "The Holy Spirit was right in saying to your fathers through Isaiah the prophet: 'Go to this people, and say, You shall indeed hear but never understand. . . .' Let it be known to you then that this salvation of God has been sent to the Gentiles; they will listen." (Acts 28:25-29)

As regards the gospel [Israelites] are enemies of God. (Rom 11:28)

For you, brethren, became imitators of the churches of God in Christ Jesus which are in Judea; for you suffered the same things from your own countrymen as they did from the Jews, who killed both the Lord Jesus and the prophets, and drove us out, and displease God and oppose all men by hindering us from speaking to the Gentiles that they may be saved—so as always to fill up the measure of their sins. But God's wrath has come upon them at last! (1 Thess 2:14-16)

I know your tribulation and your poverty (but you are rich) and the slander of those who say that they are Jews and are not, but are a synagogue of Satan. (Rev 2:9)

Behold, I will make those of the synagogue of Satan who say that they are Jews and are not, but lie—behold, I will make them come and bow down before your feet, and learn that I have loved you. (Rev 3:9)

After surveying many of these passages and others like them Samuel Sandmel concluded that "the New Testament is a repository for hostility to Jews and Judaism. Many, if perhaps even most, Christians are completely free of anti-Semitism, yet Christian Scripture is permeated by it."[1] Some theologians and biblical scholars agree with Sandmel; some do not.

Is the assessment of Sandmel and others accurate? Is the New Testament "permeated" with anti-Semitism? What is it about these passages that makes them anti-Semitic? Is it the harsh criticism that they express? Is it their dogmatic exclusivism? If we affirm either of the last two questions, we then have to explain the same dogmatic exclusivism and harsh, and at times even harsher, criticism that we encounter in the Old Testament. Consider the following sampling:

Ah, sinful nation,
    a people laden with iniquity,
offspring of evildoers,
    sons who deal corruptly!
They have forsaken the Lord,
    they have despised the Holy One of Israel,
they are utterly estranged. (Isa 1:4)

For they are a rebellious people,
    lying sons,
sons who will not hear
    the instruction of the Lord;
who say to the seers, "See not";
    and to the prophets, "Prophesy not to us what is right;
speak to us smooth things,
    prophesy illusions,
leave the way, turn aside from the path,
    let us hear no more of the Holy One of Israel." (Isa 30:9-11)

---

1. S. Sandmel, *Anti-Semitism in the New Testament?* (Philadelphia: Fortress, 1978) 160.

But you, draw near hither,
   sons of the sorceress,
   offspring of the adulterer and the harlot.
Of whom are you making sport?
   Against whom do you open your mouth wide
   and put out your tongue?
Are you not children of transgression,
   the offspring of deceit,
   you who burn with lust among the oaks,
   under every green tree;
who slay your children in the valleys,
   under the clefts of the rocks? (Isa 57:3-5)

All the house of Israel is uncircumcised in heart. (Jer 9:26)

These prophetic oracles speak of Israelites as a "sinful nation," "offspring of evildoers," "rebellious people," "sons of the sorceress," "offspring of the adulterer and the harlot," "children of transgression," and "uncircumcised in heart." This kind of language certainly approximates the language found in the New Testament: "brood of vipers," "sons of the devil," and "uncircumcised in heart and ears." One of the most offensive metaphors of prophetic criticism is the comparison of Israel to a harlot:

How the faithful city has become a harlot
   she that (once) was full of justice. (Isa 1:21)

The Lord said to me in the days of King Josiah: "Have you seen what she did, that faithless one, Israel, how she went up on every high hill and under every green tree, and there played the harlot?" (Jer 3:6)

When the Lord first spoke through Hosea, the Lord said to Hosea, "Go, take to yourself a wife of harlotry and have children of harlotry, for the land commits great harlotry by forsaking the Lord." (Hos 1:2)

Sometimes the prophets reviewed Israel's history—all of it, not just a particular generation—casting it in a very negative light:[2]

Zedekiah . . . did what was evil in the sight of the Lord his God. . . . He stiffened his neck and hardened his heart against turning to the Lord, the God of Israel. All the leading priests and the people likewise were exceedingly unfaithful. . . . The Lord . . . sent persistently to them by his messengers, . . . but they kept mocking the messengers of God, despising his words, and scoffing at his prophets, till the wrath of the Lord rose against his people till there was no remedy. (2 Chr 36:11-16)

From the day that your fathers came out of the land of Egypt to this day, I have persistently sent all my servants the prophets to them, day after day; yet they did

---

2. For the best study of this tradition see O. H. Steck, *Israel und das gewaltsame Geschick der Propheten: Untersuchungen zur Überlieferung des deuteronomistischen Geschichtsbildes im Alten Testament, Spätjudentum und Urchristentum* (WMANT 23; Neukirchen-Vluyn: Neukirchener Verlag, 1967).

not listen to me, or incline their ear, but stiffened their neck. They did worse than their fathers. (Jer 7:25-26)

For I solemnly warned your fathers when I brought them up out of the land of Egypt, warning them persistently, even to this day, saying, Obey my voice. Yet they did not obey or incline their ear, but every one walked in the stubbornness of his evil heart. (Jer 11:7-8)

Jeremiah's prophecies express no more than what is found in the Deuteronomistic tradition:

And Moses summoned all Israel and said to them: "You have seen all that the Lord did before your eyes in the land of Egypt, to Pharaoh and to all his servants and to all his land, the great trials which your eyes saw, the signs, and those great wonders; but to this day the Lord has not given you a mind to understand, or eyes to see, or ears to hear." (Deut 29:1-3 [2-4E])

The prophetic oracles often went beyond description. Sometimes they called for, even demanded, judgment and punishment. An angry Isaiah enjoined God: "Forgive them not!" (2:9). Similarly, a bitter Jeremiah at one time pleaded with the Lord:

> Forgive not their iniquity,
>> nor blot out their sins from thy sight.
> Let them be overthrown before thee;
>> deal with them in the time of thine anger. (18:23)

According to Hosea: "She conceived again and bore a daughter. And the Lord said to [Hosea], 'Call her name Not Pitied, for I will no more have pity on the house of Israel, to forgive them at all' " (1:6). Jeremiah goes even further and says that God commanded him not to pray for his people:

As for you, do not pray for this people, or lift up cry or prayer for them, and do not intercede with me, for I do not hear you. (7:16)

Therefore do not pray for this people, or lift up a cry or prayer on their behalf, for I will not listen when they call to me in the time of their trouble. (11:14)

Do not pray for the welfare of this people. Though they fast, I will not hear their cry, and though they offer burnt offering and cereal offering, I will not accept them; but I will consume them by the sword, by famine, and by pestilence. (14:11-12)

After abandoning hope that Judah will repent, Jeremiah petitions God:

> Therefore deliver up their children to famine;
>> give them over to the power of the sword,
>> let their wives become childless and widowed.
> May their men meet death by pestilence,
>> their youths be slain by the sword in battle. (18:21)

The prophetic tradition even speaks of the rejection of Israel:

For thou hast rejected thy people,
the house of Jacob. (Isa 2:6)

Hast thou utterly rejected Judah?
Does thy soul loathe Zion? (Jer 14:19)

My people are destroyed for lack of knowledge;
because you have rejected knowledge,
I reject you from being priest to me.
And since you have forgotten the law of your God,
I also will forget your children. (Hos 4:6)

And the Lord rejected all the descendants of Israel,
and afflicted them, and gave them into the hand of spoilers,
until he had cast them out of his sight. (2 Kgs 17:20)

There are no statements in the New Testament that approximate these angry expressions. Unlike Isaiah and Jeremiah, Jesus commanded his disciples to forgive (Matt 6:14-15). Unlike Jeremiah, Jesus teaches his disciples to pray for their enemies (Matt 5:44). Indeed, according to Luke (23:34), Jesus prayed that those who called for his death be forgiven. Never does Jesus ask God to deliver up to death Israelites or any people (see Luke 9:51-56). He warns of coming judgment and weeps because of it (Luke 19:41-44; cf. 13:34; 23:28-31). Never does Jesus or any of the writers of the New Testament say that Israel has been rejected. Indeed, Paul proclaims the precise opposite: "I ask, then, has God rejected his people? By no means!" (Rom 11:1). Consider also the polemic of Qumran. Like Jesus and the writers of the New Testament, the people of Qumran quote, comment on, and draw upon the Old Testament for their faith (i.e., who they are and what they believe) and for their polemic (i.e., where they disagree with others and on what basis). The author of the Hymns of Thanksgiving describes his enemies, the teachers and authorities of the Jerusalem establishment, in the following terms:

And they, they [have led] Thy people [astray].
[Prophets of falsehood] have flattered [them with their wor]ds
and interpreters of deceit [have caused] them [to stray];
and they have fallen to their destruction for lack of understanding
for all their works are in folly. (1QH 4:6-8)

And they, interpreters of falsehood and seers of deceit,
devised plans of Belial against me,
bartering Thy Law which Thou hast graven in my heart
for flattering words (which they speak) to Thy people.
And they stopped the thirsty from drinking the liquor of knowledge. (1QH 4:9-11)

As for them, they are hypocrites;
the schemes are of Belial which they conceive

and they seek Thee with a double heart
and are not firm in Thy truth. (1QH 4:13-14)[3]

This thinking is also expressed in the community's Manual of Discipline:

And let him undertake by the Covenant to be separated from all perverse men
who walk in the way of wickedness.
For they are not counted in His Covenant:
For they have not inquired nor sought Him concerning His precepts
in order to know the hidden matters in which they have guiltily strayed;
and they have treated with insolence matters revealed that Wrath might rise unto
    judgment
and vengeance be exercised by the curses of the Covenant,
and solemn judgment be fulfilled against them unto eternal destruction,
leaving no remnant. (1QS 5:10-13)[4]

The Qumranians call their opponents "prophets of falsehood," "seers of deceit," and "hypocrites," who have "devised plans of Belial [i.e., Satan] against" God's true teacher. This polemic obviously parallels that found in the New Testament Gospels, where Jesus calls Pharisees hypocrites and sons of the devil, who have strayed from the truth.

Apparently the people of Qumran did not wish outsiders (i.e., non-Qumranian Jews) to discover the error of their ways. They were strictly enjoined not to reveal their distinctive teachings:

And let him not rebuke the men of the Pit nor dispute with them;
let him conceal the maxims of the Law from the midst of the men of perversity.
And let him keep true knowledge and right justice for them that have chosen the
    Way. (1QS 9:16-18)[5]

The people of Qumran, as had some of the classical prophets centuries earlier, prayed that their enemies might never be forgiven:

And the Levites shall curse the men of the lot of Belial, and shall speak and say:
Be thou cursed in all the works of thy guilty ungodliness!
May God make of thee an object of dread
by the hand of all the avengers of vengeance!
May He hurl extermination after thee
by the hand of all the executioners of punishment!
Cursed be thou, without mercy,
according to the darkness of thy deeds!
Be thou damned
in the night of eternal fire!
May God not favor thee when thou callest upon Him,
and may He be without forgiveness to expiate thy sins!

---

3. Trans. based on A. Dupont-Sommer, *The Essene Writings from Qumran* (Gloucester, Mass.: Peter Smith, 1973) 211–12.

4. Trans. based on Dupont-Sommer, *The Essene Writings*, 83.

5. Trans. based on Dupont-Sommer, *The Essene Writings*, 95.

May He lift His angry face to revenge Himself upon thee,
and may there be for thee no (word) of peace
on the lips of all who cling (to the Covenant) of the Fathers! (1QS 2:4-9)

(May there be) everlasting hatred for the all the men of the Pit. (1QS 9:21-22)[6]

The high priest is referred to regularly as the "Wicked Priest" (see 1QpHab
8:8; 9:9; 11:4; 12:2, 8; 4QpIsa^c 30 i 3; 4QpPs^a 1-10 iv 8), perhaps also as the
"Man of Lies" (see 1QpHab 2:1-2; 5:11) or "Preacher of Lies" (1QpHab 10:9).
The teachers of the religious establishment are called the "builders of the (white-
washed) wall" (see CD 4:19; 8:12, 18; cf. Ezek 13:10-11). In what is probably
a wordplay between *halak* (to walk—i.e., legal interpretation) and *halaq* (to be
smooth), the Pharisees are referred to as the "seekers of smooth things" (see
4QpIsa^c 23 ii 10; 4QpNah 1-2 ii 7; 3-4 i 7; 3-4 ii 4). The elect of Qumran will
take an active part in punishing the faithless of Israel (see 1QpHab 5:3-5).

The polemic found in the writings of Qumran surpasses in intensity that of
the New Testament. In contrast to Qumran's esoteric and exclusive posture, the
early church proclaimed its message and invited all to join its fellowship. Never
does the New Testament enjoin Christians to curse unbelievers or opponents.[7]
Never does the New Testament petition God to damn the enemies of the church.
But Qumran did. If this group had survived and had its membership gradually
become gentile over the centuries and had its distinctive writings become the
group's Bible, I suspect that most of the passages cited above would be viewed as
expressions of anti-Semitism. But the group did not survive, nor did it become a
gentile religion, and so its criticisms have never been thought of as anti-Semitic.
There is no subsequent history of the Qumran community to muddy the waters.
We interpret Qumran as we should. We interpret it in its Jewish context, for it
never existed in any other context, and thus no one ever describes its polemic
as anti-Semitic.

The polemic in Josephus oftentimes assumes a very harsh tone. In a recent
study, Luke Johnson documents how common harsh polemic is in Josephus, as
well as in other Jewish texts.[8] In the texts Johnson cites, Josephus's polemic
against fellow Jews outstrips anything found in the New Testament.

That real bigotry and racism eventually emerged within the church sadly
cannot be denied. One of the first expressions of bigotry appears in a Christian
addition to the *Sibylline Oracles* (early to mid–second century):

And then Israel, intoxicated, will not perceive nor yet will she hear, afflicted with
weak ears [cf. Isa 6:9-10]. But when the raging wrath of the Most High comes upon

---

6. Trans. based on Dupont-Sommer, *The Essene Writings*, 75, 96.

7. Paul's anathema in Gal 1:8-9 could be cited as an exception. It is not directed at outsiders,
however, but at *insiders*. It is directed against Christians who insist on the observation of many
elements of Jewish faith that, in Paul's way of thinking, contravene the spirit of the gospel.

8. L. T. Johnson, "The New Testament's Anti-Jewish Slander and the Conventions of Ancient
Polemic," *JBL* 108 (1989) 419–41. For discussion of Josephus see pp. 436–37.

the Hebrews it will also take faith away from them, because they did harm to the Son of the heavenly God. Then indeed Israel, with abominable lips and poisonous spittings, will give this man blows. For food they will give him gall and for drink unmixed vinegar, impiously, smitten in breast and heart with an evil craze [cf. Deut 28:28], not seeing with their eyes, more blind than blind rats [cf. Isa 29:9-10], more terrible than poisonous creeping beasts, shackled with heavy sleep [cf. Isa 29:9-10]. (1:360-71)[9]

What places this sentiment on the path that leads to anti-Semitism is not the severity of the criticism (e.g., "abominable lips," "poisonous spittings"), but the distinction the author makes between himself and "Israel" or "the Hebrews." Gone is the perspective of in-house criticism. The words of the prophets alluded to in this passage are used to bludgeon outsiders, which is untrue to the hermeneutics of in-house criticism. This writer believes that the evil done to the Son of God was something that Israel alone did, which, from the New Testament point of view, is bad theology. According to New Testament theology, the human race—not Israel—put Jesus to death.

This us-against-them mentality underlies the following judgment uttered by Tertullian:

It was the merited punishment of their sins not to understand the Lord's first advent: for if they had, they would have believed, they would have obtained salvation. They themselves read how it is written of them that they are deprived of wisdom and understanding—of the use of eyes and ears [cf. Isa 6:9-10; Jer 5:21-23; Ezek 12:1-3]. As, then, under the force of their prejudgment, they had convinced themselves from his lowly guise that Christ was no more than a man. (*Apology* 21.16-17)

Again the obdurate language of the prophetic tradition is invoked. The problem here is that the dynamic, in-house, prophetic criticism of Israel's classical prophets has been misapplied. In its original setting prophetic criticism is directed against one's own community. It is a challenge to assumptions that God is always on our side, or what James Sanders has called the theology of blessed assurance.[10] In-house prophetic criticism is not racist or bigoted. But Tertullian's (mis)use of it is. When he, as a gentile Christian ("us"), applies the critical words of the prophets against Israel ("them"), he has applied a false and alien hermeneutic. The words of the prophets are now made to speak against a particular race of people, something that the prophets themselves never intended. If Tertullian had applied the words of the prophets properly, in keeping with their original intent and canonical context, he would have applied them to his own community.

---

9. Trans. based on J. J. Collins, "The Sibylline Oracles," in J. H. Charlesworth, ed., *The Old Testament Pseudepigrapha* (2 vols.; Garden City, N.Y.: Doubleday, 1983-85) 1.343.

10. See J. A. Sanders, *From Sacred Story to Sacred Text: Canon as Paradigm* (Philadelphia: Fortress, 1987) 61-73, 87-105.

In the New Testament the hermeneutic of prophetic criticism is at work. John the Baptist, Jesus, and Paul challenged assumptions about election. The Baptist warned that physical descent from Abraham was no guarantee of salvation. Jesus taught, contrary to widely held opinion, that the poor and various social and religious outcasts would have an easier time getting into heaven than the wealthy and ostensibly pious. Paul argued that Israel's hardness toward the gospel was God's wise way to open the door to the Gentiles. All of these are expressions of the hermeneutic of prophetic criticism.

Consider, for example, this hermeneutic at work in Isaiah, when he interpreted and applied the sacred tradition to the crisis of his time. He tells the scoffers of Jerusalem to hear the word of the Lord (28:14, 22), a word that has decreed destruction upon the whole land (28:22):

> For the Lord will rise up as on Mount Perazim,
>     he will be wroth as in the valley of Gibeon;
> to do his deed—strange is his deed!
>     and to work his work—alien is his work! (28:21)

Isaiah refers to two of Israel's great victories over its enemies. "Mount Perazim" alludes to David's defeat of the Philistines (2 Sam 5:17-21). David declared that the "Lord has broken through [perazim] my enemies before me, like a bursting flood" (2 Sam 5:20). Therefore the place became known as Baal-Perazim, or later Mount Perazim. "Gibeon" alludes either to David's second victory over the Philistines (2 Sam 5:22-25; see 1 Chr 14:13-16) or to Joshua's victory over the Amorites (Josh 10:6-14). In alluding to these wonderful triumphs preserved in Israel's sacred tradition and warning that God plans to do a "strange" and "alien" deed, Isaiah is saying that God will once again be victorious on the field of battle—but Israel is God's enemy! It will not be Israel's enemies who will be defeated, but Israel itself. This is a classic example of the hermeneutic of prophetic criticism. Far from finding assurance in the sacred tradition that God is obligated to bail Israel out of trouble, as no doubt Hezekiah's court prophets and counselors tried to assure the king, the prophet Isaiah finds evidence of God's sovereignty, power, and freedom.[11]

Paul does the same thing. When he reviews the principles of divine election at work in the stories of the patriarchs (Romans 9; cf. Genesis 12–25), he concludes that a sovereign God could also summon the Gentiles and make of them God's people too. Moreover, if apostate Israel, utterly rejected by God and called "Not My People" (Hos 1:9), can out of God's grace be restored and once again be called "Sons of the Living God" (Hos 1:10), then why cannot God by the same principle make a people of the Gentiles? God can, says Paul (Rom 9:22-26). But what of those Israelites who reject and oppose the gospel? To them apply Isaiah's

---

11. See C. A. Evans, "On Isaiah's Use of Israel's Sacred Tradition," *BZ* 30 (1986) 92–99.

fateful words of obduracy (Rom 11:8; cf. Isa 29:10) and even more shockingly David's angry words of imprecation against his enemies (Rom 11:9; cf. Pss 35:8; 69:22-23). If Romans 9-11 had been penned by a Gentile, I suspect many would see the passage as anti-Semitic. But the passage was written by a "Hebrew of Hebrews." It is no more anti-Semitic than Isaiah's interpretation of 2 Samuel 5. Paul's hermeneutic, like that of the classical prophets before him, was the hermeneutic of prophetic criticism.[12]

Unfortunately, later generations of Christians, by this time predominantly non-Jewish, misunderstood (innocently in some instances, maliciously in others) the hermeneutic of prophetic criticism. No longer understood as challenge from within the community of faith, it was understood as condemnation of a particular people outside of the faith—the people who had rejected Jesus, his apostles, and the church. In the light of this false hermeneutic, polemicists of the church could cite Scripture from both Testaments as a weapon against the Jewish people.

But this was not what Jesus and the writers of the New Testament did. Theirs was the hermeneutic of prophetic criticism. As members of Israel, they challenged their own people to think differently. Thousands did, and the early church had its beginning.

In my judgment viewing the New Testament and the first two generations of early Christianity as anti-Semitic is hopelessly anachronistic. It is not only anachronistic in that second- to twentieth-century categories and definitions are imposed upon the writings of the New Testament; it is also fundamentally erroneous. Early Christians did not view themselves as belonging to a religion that was distinct from Judaism. New Testament Christianity was Judaism—that is, what was believed to be the true expression of Judaism.[13] Just as Pharisees, Essenes, Sadducees, and who knows what other teachers and groups believed that their respective visions of religious faith were the true expressions of what God promised Abraham and commanded Moses, so also early Christians believed that in Jesus, God had fulfilled all that the prophets had predicted and all that Moses required. Early Christianity was one Jewish sect among several.[14] The title of a recent collection of studies, *Judaisms and Their Messiahs*, captures this reality

---

12. See C. A. Evans, "Paul and the Hermeneutics of 'True Prophecy': A Study of Romans 9-11," *Bib* 65 (1984) 560-70.

13. W. D. Davies ("Paul and the People of Israel," *NTS* 24 [1978] 27) has correctly stated: "Paul was not thinking in terms of what we normally call conversion from one religion to another but of the recognition by Jews of the final or true form of their own religion." This way of thinking, I might add, was not limited to Paul but in all probability was the common understanding of the early church.

14. Significantly, Luke refers to Pharisees (Acts 15:5; 26:5), Sadducees (Acts 5:17), and Christians (Acts 24:5, 14; 28:22) as "sects" (*haireseis*). And just as the Pharisees, Sadducees, and Essenes had priests among their ranks, so too did Christians (cf. Acts 6:7). In other words, the Jesus movement's claim to legitimacy, by virtue of the makeup of its membership, is equal to the claim of any other religious sect within Judaism.

well.[15] For this reason not only is viewing the New Testament as anti-Semitic anachronistic,[16] so is describing it as anti-Judaic.[17] To say that early Christianity opposed Judaism is to say that there was a clearly defined Judaism of the first century and that early Christians saw themselves as outside of and separate from it. Both assumptions are erroneous. Judaism was diverse and pluralistic, and early Christians viewed themselves as the righteous remnant within it (e.g., Mark 4:11-12; Rom 9:27; 11:2-5). Just as the Essenes had before him (1QS 9:18), the evangelist Luke (probably a Gentile) calls his movement the Way (Acts 9:2; 19:23; 22:4; 24:14, 22). And as with the Essenes, this self-designation may very well have been inspired by Isa 40:3, a passage of eschatological restoration: "Prepare the way of the Lord, make straight in the desert a highway for our God" (cf. 1QS 8:14; 9:19-20; and cf. Matt 3:3; Mark 1:3; Luke 1:75; 3:4-6; John 1:23). Such a self-understanding provides one more indication that the early Christian movement saw itself as a movement within—and not opposed to—Israel.

If this is true, then why did Christianity eventually emerge as an essentially non-Jewish religious movement? The answer lies primarily in Christianity's radical views of proselytization.[18] Further developing Jesus' remarkable practice of extending messianic invitations to the apparently disenfranchised (i.e., the uneducated, the rabble, tax collectors, and "sinners"), the early church all but did away with the halakic prerequisites for proselytization. Belief in Jesus as Israel's Messiah whom God raised from the dead and who will return in glory was all that was required. Circumcision and observation of food laws, though not relinquished without hot debate, were no longer required. Who then was a real Jew? Paul, a Hebrew of Hebrews and a former Pharisee (see Phil 3:5-6),

---

15. E. S. Frerichs, W. S. Green, and J. Neusner, eds., *Judaisms and their Messiahs at the Turn of the Christian Era* (Cambridge: Cambridge Univ. Press, 1987).

16. S. J. D. Cohen (*From the Maccabees to the Mishnah* [Philadelphia: Westminster, 1986] 46–48) has pointed out that anti-Semitism, understood as hatred based on race alone, did not exist in antiquity.

17. In one of the better essays of the collection, B. Przybylski ("The Setting of Matthean Anti-Judaism," in P. Richardson, D. Granskou, and S. G. Wilson, eds., *Anti-Judaism in Early Christianity*, vol. 1: *Paul and the Gospels* [Waterloo, Ont.: Wilfrid Laurier Univ. Press, 1986] 181–200) rightly concludes that Matthean polemic reflects "internal Jewish dispute" (p. 198). Nevertheless, he still speaks of "Matthean anti-Judaism." I find this confusing. This would be akin to describing the polemic of one ecclesiastical faction or another as "anti-Christian." An internal dispute should not be defined as polemic against the group as a whole. Essenes were anti-Pharisaic, and the Rabbis later would express much antipathy toward Sadducees and various ruling priests and priestly families of the Herodian-Roman period. But none of this polemic—and much of it is as harsh as or harsher than anything found in the New Testament—can be described as anti-Judaic. The New Testament contains polemic that targets particular groups. There is polemic against Sadducees, Pharisees, Christian "Judaizers," gentile Christians, and gentile non-Christians. If by "anti-Judaic" one means criticism of or opposition to the Jewish religious leadership, which had rejected the Messianists, then it is appropriate. See D. A. Hagner's discussion of this point at the beginning of his chapter on Paul, below.

18. It is often thought that High Christology (i.e., regarding Jesus as God incarnate) was principally responsible for Christianity's break from Judaism. This was probably a factor. But the earliest sources indicate that the real cause of the rift was the role of Torah.

followed the lead of the prophetic tradition (see Deut 10:16; Jer 4:4; 9:26; Ezek 44:9) and averred:

> For he is not a real Jew who is one outwardly, nor is true circumcision something external and physical. He is a Jew who is one inwardly, and real circumcision is a matter of the heart, spiritual and not literal. His praise is not from people but from God. (Rom 2:28-29)

Pressed to its logical conclusion, this line of thinking suggests that anyone could become a "Jew" by confessing Jesus as Messiah and Lord. Christian proselytizing stretched the parameters of Jewish self-definition too far, with the result that the messianic movement that had centered itself around Jesus (what later becomes "Christianity") and the other expressions of Jewish faith (what later become "Judaism") went their separate ways. Steven Katz has argued that Christianity and Judaism did not separate until after the defeat of Simon ben Kokhba in 135 CE.[19] He observes that there is no evidence of an official anti-Christian policy before this time. Katz may be right. The expulsion passages in the Fourth Gospel (e.g., John 9:22; 12:42; 16:2) probably reflect only a local situation, not a widespread policy (*pace* Louis Martyn).[20] The angry polemic that emerged in subsequent centuries became increasingly racial and ugly.

Luke's ambiguous portrait of the Pharisees, an item of scholarly debate, is probably best explained against this scenario. On the one hand, the Pharisees are treated favorably because they believe in the resurrection and therefore are sympathetic to the Easter proclamation (Acts 23:6-9). On the other hand, the Pharisees have strict halakot for proselytization, and therefore they are portrayed, both in the Gospel of Luke and in Acts, as opponents of Jesus and the early church. They grumble when Jesus associates too freely with tax collectors and sinners (e.g., Luke 7:36-50; 15:1-2). They later object when Gentiles are admitted into the community without being compelled to submit to circumcision (Acts 15:1, 5).

In the first century the requirements for proselytization were an open question. What constituted a real Jew? One who had the faith of Abraham (see Romans 4)? Or one who was a physical descendant of Abraham? What made Abraham chosen in God's sight? His faith (see Gen 15:6), which is the line of interpretation taken by Paul, or his merits, which is the line of interpretation taken by some Jewish interpreters (see *T. Naph.* 8:3-9:5; Ps.-Philo *Bib. Ant.* 6.1-18; *Jub.* 12:12-14; *Tg. Ps.-J.* Gen 11:28)?

It is against these questions that the writings of the New Testament should be read. And when it is read from this perspective, the anachronistic assumption that its polemic is anti-Semitic or anti-Judaic will rightly be abandoned.

---

19. S. T. Katz, "The Separation of Judaism and Christianity after 70 CE," *JBL* 103 (1984) 43-76.

20. J. L. Martyn, *History and Theology in the Fourth Gospel* (2d ed.; Nashville: Abingdon, 1979).

Before concluding this essay, I would like to comment briefly on some of the relevant literature. In the last three decades numerous books have appeared that address the question of Christian anti-Semitism and Jewish-Christian relations. There were few precursors to these recent studies. Prior to World War II comparatively few serious books dealt with the problem of anti-Semitism in the Christian church. The works of James Parkes were a notable exception.[21] Following the war Jules Isaac attempted to persuade Christians to reexamine the teaching of the New Testament.[22] He pointed out how in places Christian thinking, including the liturgy, was infected with expressions of anti-Semitic contempt that neither derived from the New Testament nor reflected its higher ideals. The negative and at times anti-Semitic bias of European scholarship has been well documented in a collection of studies and excerpts edited by Charlotte Klein.[23] Fortunately, positive Jewish-Christian dialogue has now emerged in Germany.[24] Franz Mussner's *Tractate on the Jews*, which offers a thoughtful study of Romans 9–11, is certainly one of the most positive contributions.[25] In North America constructive dialogue has also taken place.[26] Two recent collections edited by James Charlesworth should not be overlooked.[27]

Several books have appeared that treat the more specific question of anti-Semitism in the New Testament. Gregory Baum was one of the early pioneers who addressed this problem.[28] Although initially persuaded that the New Testament was not itself anti-Semitic, Baum changed his mind when he encountered Rosemary Ruether's controversial *Faith and Fratricide*.[29] Fully persuaded that in many places the New Testament itself is anti-Semitic, Ruether asserted that anti-Semitism is at the very heart of the Christian gospel: to believe in Jesus

21. J. Parkes, *The Conflict of the Church and the Synagogue: A Study in the Origins of Anti-Semitism* (London: Soncino, 1934; reprinted, Philadelphia: Jewish Publication Society of America, 1961); idem, *Jesus, Paul and the Jews* (London: SCM, 1936).

22. J. Isaac, *Jésus et Israël* (Paris: Albin Michel, 1948); Eng. trans.: *Jesus and Israel* (New York: Holt, Rinehart and Winston, 1971). See also idem, *The Teaching of Contempt: Christian Roots of Antisemitism* (New York: Holt, Rinehart and Winston, 1964).

23. C. Klein, *Anti-Judaism in Christian Theology* (Philadelphia: Fortress, 1978).

24. W. P. Eckert, N. P. Levinson, and M. Stör, eds., *Antijudaismus im Neuen Testament? Exegetische und systematische Beiträge* (Munich: Kaiser, 1967); M. Barth et al., *Paulus–Apostat oder Apostel? Jüdische und christliche Antworten* (Regensburg: Pustet, 1977); P. Lapide et al., *Was Juden und Christen von einander denken: Bausteine zum Brückenschlag* (Freiburg: Herder, 1978); idem, "Das christlich-jüdische Religionsgespräch," in A. Baudis et al., eds., *Richte unsere Füsse auf den Weg des Friedens* (H. Gollwitzer Festschrift; Munich: Kaiser, 1979) 40–48.

25. F. Mussner, *Traktat über die Juden* (Munich: Kösel, 1979); Eng. trans.: *Tractate on the Jews: The Significance of Judaism for Christian Faith* (Philadelphia: Fortress, 1984).

26. M. H. Tannenbaum et al., eds., *Evangelicals and Jews in Conversation on Scripture, Theology and History* (Grand Rapids, Mich.: Eerdmans, 1978).

27. J. H. Charlesworth, ed., *Jews and Christians: Exploring the Past, Present, and Future* (New York: Crossroad, 1990); idem, ed., *Jesus' Jewishness: Exploring the Place of Jesus in Early Judaism* (New York: Crossroad, 1990).

28. G. Baum, *Is the New Testament Anti-Semitic?* (Glen Rock, N.J.: Paulist, 1960; 2d ed., 1965).

29. R. R. Ruether, *Faith and Fratricide: The Theological Roots of Anti-Semitism* (New York: Seabury, 1974).

is to be anti-Semitic. This claim has been challenged,[30] though Ruether is not without her supporters.[31] The problem here again is the assumption that belief in Jesus in the first century was somehow un- or anti-Jewish. The earliest Christians *were* Jews, and they believed that acknowledging Jesus as Israel's Messiah was the appropriate *Jewish* thing to do. Ruether's unnuanced view leads her to the illogical position that finds Paul himself as anti-Judaic.[32]

Others of a more scholarly bent have argued essentially the same position. Samuel Sandmel, mentioned above, examines several New Testament passages and concludes that anti-Semitism is pervasive. However, his work similarly suffers from anachronisms. He projects talmudic Judaism into the first century and seems to assume that the separation of gentile Christians and Jewish Christians had occurred before much of the New Testament was written.[33] Norman Beck's more recent work is hardly an improvement.[34] He examines the New Testament, book by book, and passage by passage. He too believes that he has found anti-Jewish polemic throughout. Unfortunately, like so many others, he fails to do comparative study of intramural polemic. He too apparently assumes that the writers of the New Testament either perceived themselves as non-Jewish or understood their faith as something different from and opposed to Judaism (as if an orthodox "Judaism" existed in the first century).

It is encouraging to observe that better contextualized and hence more nuanced studies have appeared in recent years. Gerard Sloyan has rightly challenged the simplistic and erroneous assumption that "law" and "grace" were antithetical in Judaism.[35] The trilogy edited by E. P. Sanders and others rightly focuses on how various groups defined themselves (as opposed to how their op-

---

30. J. Oesterreicher, *Anatomy of Contempt* (South Orange, N.J.: Seton Hall Univ. Press, 1974); T. A. Idinopulos and R. B. Ward, "Is Christology Inherently Antisemitic?" *JAAR* 45 (1977) 193–214.

31. A. T. Davies, ed., *Anti-Semitism and the Foundation of Christianity* (New York: Paulist, 1979). The contributors to this volume are in essential agreement with Ruether, but they do attempt to refine some of her views. See also J. Koenig, *Jews and Christians in Dialogue: New Testament Foundations* (Philadelphia: Westminster, 1979). Koenig examines the polemical passages of the New Testament.

32. Related to this is the notion, often asserted, that Paul was an "apostate" from Judaism. Again, I think this is anachronistic thinking. That Paul had apostatized from Pharisaism is certainly true (as Josephus had from Essenism, as well as from Pharisaism), but in no sense did he abandon his Jewish identity or his sense of being an Israelite. For recent discussion, with which at points I disagree, see L. Gaston, *Paul and the Torah* (Vancouver: Univ. of British Columbia Press, 1987) 76–79, and the notes on pp. 211–12.

33. It is surprising how many fail to perceive the oddness of the assumption that the New Testament and early Christianity were anti-Semitic. Should it not strike us as hard to explain how a first-century Jewish sect, centered around a revered Jewish teacher thought to be Israel's Messiah, God's Son, and fulfillment of Israel's Scriptures, within one generation of its founding could mutate into an anti-Jewish, perhaps even anti-Semitic, movement? Surely this is improbable. I suspect that scholars have unconsciously and uncritically read the New Testament through the eyes of the patristic church, which, sad to say, did give vent to anti-Semitic expressions.

34. N. A. Beck, *Mature Christianity: The Recognition and Repudiation of the Anti-Jewish Polemic of the New Testament* (Selinsgrove, Pa.: Susquehanna Univ. Press, 1985).

35. G. S. Sloyan, *Is Christ the End of the Law?* (Philadelphia: Westminster, 1978).

ponents defined them).[36] The two-volume collection edited by Peter Richardson, D. Granskou, and Stephen Wilson certainly represents one of the best efforts.[37] The distinction between anti-Semitism and anti-Judaism has clarified the discussion. John Gager's study is on the whole a competent treatment.[38] He rightly emphasizes the intra-Jewish dimension of most of the New Testament's polemic. Nevertheless, he too speaks of anti-Judaism, even a "gentilizing anti-Judaism" in the case of Acts. Terrance Callan has argued that the liberal branch of the early church, composed almost entirely of Jews, held a positive view of Judaism and held that gentile converts did not need to become Jewish proselytes.[39] And quite recently Jeffrey Siker has probed the important role that interpretation of the Abraham narratives played in Christian self-understanding and Christianity's movement away from Judaism.[40] Faith

These studies bear witness to the progress of recent years,[41] but confusion and faulty exegesis have not been eclipsed entirely. Exegesis, if it is truly exegesis, must be securely anchored in history. By "history" I mean a given document's full context—the meaning of its language as seen against social, historical, religious, and traditional factors. This means, therefore, that exegesis in context must be comparative.

Herein lies the problem with the recent study offered by Jack Sanders.[42] Concerned with the portrayal of the Jews in Luke-Acts, Sanders undertakes a detailed analysis of virtually every pericope of Luke-Acts (though with some significant omissions). He thinks that he finds evidence everywhere of the evangelist's hatred of the Jewish people. But his results are not convincing because he

---

36. E. P. Sanders et al., eds., *Jewish and Christian Self-definition* (3 vols.; Philadelphia: Fortress, 1980–82).

37. Richardson, Granskou, and Wilson, eds., *Anti-Judaism in Early Christianity*.

38. J. G. Gager, *The Origins of Anti-Semitism* (New York and Oxford: Oxford Univ. Press, 1983).

39. T. Callan, *Forgetting the Root: The Emergence of Christianity from Judaism* (New York: Paulist, 1986).

40. J. S. Siker, *Disinheriting the Jews: Abraham in Early Christian Controversy* (Louisville: Westminster/John Knox, 1991).

41. A few other studies should be mentioned. In his first chapter (pp. 1–13) M. Saperstein (*Moments of Crisis in Jewish-Christian Relations* [London: SCM; Philadelphia: Trinity Press International, 1989]) offers a brief but helpful survey of the history of Jewish-Christian relations. E. J. Fisher and L. Klenicki (eds., *In Our Time: The Flowering of Jewish-Catholic Dialogue* [Studies in Judaism and Christianity; New York: Paulist, 1990]) have assembled a collection of essays that trace the positive developments in Jewish-Catholic dialogue in recent years. Fisher provides a very useful annotated bibliography on pp. 107–61. L. Swidler (et al., *Bursting the Bonds? A Jewish-Christian Dialogue on Jesus and Paul* [Faith Meets Faith Series; Maryknoll, N.Y.: Orbis, 1990]) has given us a book divided into two parts: Jewish-Christian dialogue on Jesus (L. Swidler and L. J. Eron); Jewish-Christian dialogue on Paul (G. Sloyan and L. Dean). A variety of topics are treated, followed by responses. J. Neusner (*Jews and Christians: The Myth of a Common Tradition* [London: SCM; Philadelphia: Trinity Press International, 1991]) explores the reasons why there has been so little dialogue and what might be done to foster it. Finally, D. Novak (*Jewish-Christian Dialogue: A Jewish Justification* [New York: Oxford Univ. Press, 1992]) probes the theological and philosophical dimensions of Jewish-Christian relations. For additional bibliography see Charlesworth, ed., *Jews and Christians*, 242–47; idem, *Jesus' Jewishness*, 271–79.

42. J. T. Sanders, *The Jews in Luke-Acts* (Philadelphia: Fortress, 1987).

has not placed Luke's polemic and self-understanding in full context. Sanders's exegesis, like that of many today who have embraced the various literary approaches, offers a close reading of the text, but the text is never studied in the light of contemporary texts left behind by writers struggling with the same questions and issues. For example, nowhere is comparison made with the polemical language of Israel's prophetic tradition. Given the nature of Luke's polemic and its indebtedness to the prophets, this is an extraordinary oversight. Nowhere is comparison made with writings that offer sectarian polemic, as seen, for example, at Qumran. Because no comparative study has been undertaken, we are left without a point of reference. How was Luke understood in the first century? Would his polemic be perceived as anti-Semitic, as Sanders thinks, or as in-house prophetic criticism? Without comparative study no reading of the text can be close enough to answer this question.[43]

The studies that follow offer interpretations in full context. They attempt to discern the antecedents of religious polemic and its forms of expression in times roughly contemporaneous to those in which the respective writings of the New Testament took shape. The conclusion that is reached again and again is that these writings, though at times highly critical of Jews and Gentiles who for various reasons rejected the Christian proclamation, are not anti-Semitic.

---

43. For an assessment of Sanders's *The Jews in Luke-Acts,* see C. A. Evans, "Is Luke's View of the Jewish Rejection of Jesus Anti-Semitic?" in D. D. Sylva, ed., *Reimaging the Death of the Lukan Jesus* (BBB 73; Frankfurt am Main: Anton Hain, 1990) 29–56, 174–83.

*Part One*

# Antecedents of
# New Testament Polemic

# -1-

# A Hammer That Breaks Rock in Pieces: Prophetic Critique in the Hebrew Bible

## Mary C. Callaway

One of the remarkable aspects of the Hebrew Bible is the theme of self-deprecation that persists throughout its diverse traditions. As a national epic, Israel's story is surprisingly sparse in the language of self-glorification; it is a story told in the voice of a relentless critic rather than a proud heir. In the literature of national epics, this is unusual and even somewhat discomfiting. How are we to read a work whose shape at first so closely resembles a national epic promising the proud history of a noble people, but whose content and voice are so insistent on exposing flaws? It is as though the biblical authors were consciously confounding expectations and compelling their readers to see that Israel's story was different from others in the most fundamental way. The story's purpose was not, as would be proper to a national epic, to portray Israel as a great nation and to build a monument to its heroes, but to make clear that Israel had achieved nothing in the way of statecraft by its own abilities. In that sense it is YHWH's story rather than Israel's.

There are no real heroes in the Hebrew Bible, at least not in the sense of one who struggles against great odds and by wits or strength emerges victorious. Nor are there moral paragons; the only characters described as *tam*, perfect, are the non-Israelites Noah and Job.[1] Moses, who in another kind of national epic would surely be the central hero, is unsure of himself, fails in his negotiations with the pharaoh, is unable to inspire the people in the desert to keep faith with YHWH, and is himself forbidden from entering the land of Canaan because he angered YHWH. Although the legend of his birth suggested by its genre that he was to be a hero, and the assessment at the end of Deuteronomy elevates him as a prophet

---

1. Jacob is called *tam* in Gen 25:27, but here the word has a different sense.

unlike any other, the record of his deeds in Exodus and Numbers is not a hero's story. The texts continuously assert that the acts of Moses worth recording were really acts of YHWH; power did not flow from Moses but through him.

The Deuteronomistic Historians' portrait of Israel's history is an unrelenting catalogue of idolatry, poor management, duplicity, and failure. The older traditions preserved by these redactors demonstrate that other readings of Israel's history were possible. The optimism of the early traditions about Saul, for example, or the hints at the achievements of the house of Omri suggest the lineaments of a different kind of history of Israel. But the Deuteronomistic Historians' version became the dominant voice of Israel's official history, and the view that Israel was unable to keep faith with its God and to hold up its end of the covenant was fixed as an important part of Israel's identity.

The narrators of the history consistently assume YHWH's point of view rather than Israel's, not explaining or excusing Israel's actions, but simply judging them by the standards of the covenant. Modern scholarship, in its desire to be fair to all parties and to understand the other side of every story, is able to provide cogent sociological explanations for Israel's behavior, thereby mitigating the harsh judgments of Israel's own historians.[2] No such rationalizing can be found in the Hebrew Bible; military failures are a result of YHWH's judgment on a sinful nation, while victories are credited to YHWH's judgment on other nations or his gracious protection of Israel, but not to Israel's prowess. There is no attempt to explain Israel's affinity for Baal in terms of the sociological dynamics of life in a new culture or to describe the activities of Israel's kings in terms of the political necessities of religious tolerance that went with international diplomacy. There is only the vocabulary of theology: apostasy, idolatry, not walking in the ways of YHWH, breaking covenant, not remembering, and so on. The persistent theme of Israel's sinfulness occurs in the larger context of YHWH's plan to bring blessing to all the families of the earth through this people. Were Israel to be portrayed as deserving and upright, the story would lie by suggesting that Israel's goodness had brought blessing to the world.

## The Language of Prophetic Critique

Nowhere is Israel's tendency toward self-criticism so apparent as in the tradition of prophetic critique. Obscure in its origins, biblical prophecy owed much to the prophetic traditions of Mesopotamia, Canaan, and Syria, yet developed according to its own internal dynamic.[3] Israel clearly adopted from its neighbors the practice of prophecy as well as many of its speech forms, but the heavy emphasis

---

2. See, for example, the discussion of Ahab in J. Bright, *A History of Israel* (Philadelphia: Westminster, 1972) 236ff.

3. R. Wilson, *Prophecy and Society in Ancient Israel* (Philadelphia: Fortress, 1980) 89–124. For a useful discussion of the similarities in prophecy at Mari and Israel, see A. Malamat, "Prophetic

on critique and judgment in Israelite prophecy is not found elsewhere. Whether Israelite prophets were influenced by the strain of self-criticism already present in the early Israelite Yahwistic and Elohistic epics is difficult to say. Because at least some of the Torah was shaped in prophetic circles, or at least influenced by prophetic ideas, it is impossible to be certain about the direction of the influence.[4] In any case, the critical view of Israel presented in the prophetic literature is on the whole consistent with the Torah's emphasis on YHWH's grace over against Israel's failings.

Prophetic criticism occurs in a variety of literary genres, each of which shapes the language of critique according to its particular tradition and format. Language sounding harsh or exaggerated to our ears was often standard for the genre in which it occurred, although the prophets sometimes seemed to cross over the line of acceptable rhetoric. Three main genres in which prophetic critique occurs are woe-oracle, covenant lawsuit, and invective.[5] A brief examination of these will be helpful to understanding the language of prophetic critique.

The woe-oracle is found almost exclusively in the prophetic books, but the form may have originated in the context of funerals. The woe-oracle is introduced by the word *hoy*, an onomatopoetic representation of mourning. Usually aimed at individuals or particular groups, described in some detail by the characteristics responsible for their impending doom, the woe-oracle may represent a kind of prophetic mourning for those whose fate the prophet announces.[6]

The prophets sometimes employed imaginative descriptions and playful uses of language that made the listener see the object of the woe in a new way:

> Woe to those who draw iniquity with cords of falsehood,
>    who draw sin as with cart ropes. (Isa 5:18)

Sometimes the woe-oracle consisted of two parts, a description, in the form of "woe to those who . . . ," and a set of consequences, which are usually linguistically related to the crimes of the evildoers:

> Woe to those who join house to house,
>    who add field to field,
> until there is no more room,
>    and you are made to dwell alone in the midst of the land.

---

Revelation in New Documents from Mari and the Bible," in *Mari and the Bible: A Collection of Studies* (Jerusalem: Hebrew Univ. Press, 1975) 62–82.

4. Clear examples of prophetic influence are the account of Moses' call in Exodus 3 and the molten calf episode in Exodus 32–34. On the earliest Israelite prophets, see Wilson, *Prophecy*, 146–66.

5. For a full discussion see C. Westermann, *Basic Forms of Prophetic Speech* (Philadelphia: Westminster, 1967), and G. Tucker, "Prophetic Speech," in J. L. Mays and P. J. Achtemeier, eds., *Interpreting the Prophets* (Philadelphia: Fortress, 1987) 27–40.

6. See E. Gerstenberger, "The Woe Oracles of the Prophets," *JBL* 81 (1962) 249–63, and W. Janzen, *Mourning Cry and Woe Oracle* (BZAW 125; Berlin: de Gruyter, 1972).

> The Lord of hosts has sworn in my hearing:
> "Surely many houses shall be desolate,
>      large and beautiful houses, without inhabitant." (Isa 5:8-9)

The usurping landowners are portrayed in the extremity of their greed; owning all the land, they live alone in the midst of a land that yields practically nothing.

The format suggests an intimate link between the deeds of those described and their consequences—what the Rabbis later called measure for measure. Those who seize the land of others will have their land divided up among their captors; those who drink and feast but do not regard the deeds of YHWH will die of hunger and thirst, becoming a feast for the appetite of Sheol. Although the inventive and graphic language of the woe-oracles directs attention to the crimes of Israel's leaders, the structure of the oracles suggests that the deeper interest of the poet is in revealing the exquisite justice of YHWH.[7]

A second form in which prophetic judgment on Israel occurs is the covenant lawsuit, or disputation.[8] While all prophetic critique is founded on an understanding of the covenant as basic to Israel's existence, and the violation of covenant obligations is presented as cause for YHWH's withdrawal from Israel, in the covenant lawsuit genre the relation between covenant and judgment is seen most explicitly. Covenant lawsuits occur in full form in Jer 2:4-13 and Mic 6:1-5. The prophet brings YHWH's suit against Israel, usually employing the term *rîb*, controversy or lawsuit, and appealing to all of creation as the jury:

> Arise, plead your case before the mountains,
>      and let the hills hear your voice.
> Hear, you mountains, the controversy of the Lord,
>      and you enduring foundations of the earth;
> for the Lord has a controversy with his people,
>      and he will contend with Israel. (Mic 6:1-2)
>
> Therefore I still contend with you, says the Lord,
>      and with your children's children I will contend....
> Be appalled, O heavens, at this,
>      be shocked,
> be utterly desolate, says the Lord. (Jer 2:9, 12)

The plaintiff presents what he did for the people:

> O my people, what have I done to you?
>      In what have I wearied you: Answer me!
> For I brought you up from the land of Egypt,
>      and redeemed you from the house of bondage;
> and I sent before you Moses, Aaron, and Miriam. (Mic 6:3-4)

---

7. See K. Koch, *The Growth of the Biblical Tradition* (New York: Scribner, 1969) 97.

8. See Westermann, *Basic Forms*, 191ff.; J. A. Sanders, *Torah and Canon* (Philadelphia: Fortress, 1972) 54–90.

> What wrong did your fathers find in me
>> that they went far from me,
> and went after worthlessness, and became worthless? ...
> And I brought you into a plentiful land
>> to enjoy its fruits and its good things. (Jer 2:5, 7)

The plaintiff then lays out the accusation against the defendant:

> But when you came in you defiled my land,
>> and made my heritage an abomination. (Jer 2:7)

> Can I forget the treasures of wickedness in the house of the wicked,
>> and the scant measure that is accursed?
> Shall I acquit the man with wicked scales
>> and with a bag of deceitful weights?
> Your rich men are full of violence;
>> your inhabitants speak lies,
>> and their tongue is deceitful in their mouth. (Mic 6:10-12)

Finally the judgment is rendered:

> Therefore I have begun to smite you,
>> making you desolate because of your sins.
> You shall eat, but not be satisfied,
>> and there shall be hunger in your inward parts;
> you shall put away, but not save,
>> and what you save I will give to the sword. (Mic 6:13-14)

Perhaps more than any other form of prophetic critique the covenant lawsuit highlights the prophet's role as covenant mediator. Like a lawyer speaking on behalf of a client, the prophet brings YHWH's case before Israel and demonstrates the legal basis for YHWH's claims against the people. Not YHWH's anger, but his justice, dominates the covenant lawsuit.

The woe-oracles and the covenant lawsuit are recognizable literary forms, but most prophetic critique occurs in less easily defined literary genres. The prophets used poetic and rhetorical skill in composing their oracles of invective, and understanding the theological presuppositions of prophetic critique requires some analysis of prophetic language, imagery and traditional genres. An overview of the literary characteristics of prophetic invective will serve as the basis of our reflections on the place of prophetic critique in ancient Israel and in the canon.

Perhaps the most striking aspect of prophetic speech is the extensive use of imagery to describe Israel and its crimes. The images are drawn from a variety of sources, including the natural order (the behavior of animals and the characteristics of plants), technology (agriculture, mining, pottery), the cult (especially the language of pollution), and human social relations (marriage, parenthood, commerce).

Animal imagery is used to portray Israel as grotesquely unnatural; the people are lower than the animals in their ignorance.

> Every one turns to his own course,
>     like a horse plunging headlong into battle.
> Even the stork in the heavens
>     knows her times;
> and the turtledove, swallow, and crane
>     keep the time of their coming;
> but my people know not
>     the ordinance of the Lord. (Jer 8:6-7)

> The ox knows its owner,
>     and the ass its master's crib;
> but Israel does not know,
>     my people does not understand. (Isa 1:3)

> Do horses run upon rocks?
>     Does one plow the sea with oxen?
> But you have turned justice into poison
>     and the fruit of righteousness into wormwood. (Amos 6:12)

Animal imagery also describes Israel's leaders as predatory:

> Her officials within her
>     are roaring lions;
> her judges are evening wolves
>     that leave nothing till the morning. (Zeph 3:3)

> They hatch adders' eggs,
>     they weave the spider's web;
> he who eats their eggs dies,
>     and from one which is crushed a viper is hatched. (Isa 59:5)

The theme of Israel's sin as a gross deformity of nature is elaborated also in agricultural metaphors:

> Yet I planted you a choice vine,
>     wholly of pure seed.
> How then have you turned degenerate
>     and become a wild vine? (Jer 2:21)

This is reminiscent of Isaiah's Song of the Vineyard (Isa 5:1-7) describing Israel as the carefully cultivated vineyard that unnaturally produced sour grapes rather than the proper fruit of the vine planted in it. In such inexplicable circumstances the owner's only recourse is to plow the plants under and destroy the vineyard.

The books of Isaiah, Jeremiah, and Ezekiel are full of sexual imagery, often portraying Israel as a woman engaged in illicit or depraved sexual activities. In some cases the reference to harlotry does not seem to be related to the charges:

> How the faithful city
>> has become a harlot,
>>> she that was full of justice!
> Righteousness lodged in her,
>> but now murderers.
> Your silver has become dross,
>> your wine mixed with water.
> Your princes are rebels
>> and companions of thieves.
> Every one loves a bribe
>> and runs after gifts.
> They do not defend the fatherless,
>> and the widow's cause does not come to them. (Isa 1:21-23)

Here the prophet draws on the Northwest Semitic concept of the capital city as the wife of her patron deity, and the juxtaposition of the term "faithful" with the term "harlot" succinctly contrasts what Jerusalem says she is (YHWH's own city) with what she actually has become (available to anyone who comes along). A more extensive use of this imagery occurs in Hosea 2, in which the prophet's difficult marriage to the faithless Gomer mirrors God's covenant relation with Israel. Influenced by the Canaanite practice of sacred prostitution, Hosea's portrait of Israel as an adulterous woman who pursues her lovers in vain is drawn in graphic and bitter language.

The continuity of language and imagery in prophetic critique is apparent in Jeremiah 2–3 and Ezekiel 16 and 23, in which Hosea's sexual imagery is adapted and elaborated. Jeremiah describes Judah as one of the cultic prostitutes:

> Yea, upon every high hill
>> and under every green tree
>> you spread your legs as a harlot. (Jer 2:20b)

Perhaps the most demeaning prophetic language compares Judah to a woman overcome by lust, like an animal in heat indiscriminately seeking a mate:

> Look at your way in the valley;
>> know what you have done—
> a restive young camel interlacing her tracks,
>> a wild ass used to the wilderness,
> in her heat sniffing the wind!
>> Who can restrain her lust? (Jer 2:23-24)

This prophetic language not only highlights the crime of apostasy, but also challenges the nation's view of itself, replacing the portrait of the holy city with a lewd story of a desperate whore who cannot even get lovers. The prophetic idea of uncovering the people's false identity occurs also in the form of attacks on their mother:

> Plead with your mother, plead—
>   for she is not my wife,
>   and I am not her husband—
> that she put away her harlotry from her face,
>   and her adultery from between her breasts;
> lest I strip her naked
>   and make her as in the day she was born. (Hos 2:2-3)

> Your mother was a Hittite
>   and your father was an Amorite. (Ezek 16:45b)

One lament in Ezekiel 19 portrays "your mother" as a lioness who lost both her whelps to marauders with hooks and cages, and another portrays her as a vine plucked up, stripped of its fruit and transplanted to a dry land. This form of castigating the people by insulting their mother, like the descriptions of Israel and Judah as shameless women rejected by men, undercut the people's most cherished sources of self-understanding.

Although some of the most outrageous language occurs in these descriptions of depraved sexuality, the prophets use other offensive imagery to describe Israel. They describe Israel's leaders as drunken sots, and it is not always possible to discern whether the language is metaphorical or literal:

> These also reel with wine
>   and stagger with strong drink;
> the priest and prophet reel with strong drink,
>   they are confused with wine,
>   they stagger with strong drink;
> they err in vision,
>   they stumble in giving judgment.
> For all tables are full of vomit,
>   no place is without filthiness. (Isa 28:7-8)

Since the prophets, priests, and rulers want wine, YHWH himself will provide them with the effects of drunkenness:

> Stupefy yourselves and be in a stupor,
>   blind yourselves and be blind!
> Be drunk, but not with wine;
>   stagger, but not with strong drink!
> For the Lord has poured out upon you
>   a spirit of deep sleep,
> and has closed your eyes, the prophets,
>   and covered your heads, the seers. (Isa 29:9-10)

Other explicit references to Judah being forced to drink the cup YHWH provides and reeling in a drunken stupor as a result occur in Jer 13:12-14; 25:15-16; Ezek 23:31-34; Hab 2:15-17; and Isa 51:17, 22.

Another literary characteristic found in prophetic speech is the use of sarcasm to ridicule the people's hollow theological ideas:

> Come, my people, enter your chambers,
>   and shut your doors behind you;
> hide yourselves for a little while
>   until the wrath is past.
> For behold, the Lord is coming forth out of his place
> to punish the inhabitants of the earth for their iniquity. (Isa 26:20-21)

Sarcasm is also prominent in Amos's satirical recasting of a traditional priestly invitation to worship:

> Come to Bethel, and transgress;
>   to Gilgal, and multiply transgression;
> bring your sacrifices every morning,
>   your tithes every three days;
> offer a sacrifice of thanksgiving of that which is leavened,
>   and proclaim freewill offerings, publish them;
>   for so you love to do, O people of Israel! (Amos 4:4-5)

## The Social Location of Prophetic Critique

The literary characteristics that make prophetic critique so offensive—gross exaggeration, lewd sexual imagery, sarcasm, mockery—all seem to have been acceptable as part of prophetic speech. It was expected that prophets would behave differently from everyone else, as it was understood that prophets used a particular rhetoric and style. In his study of the social location of prophecy in ancient Israel, Robert Wilson has shown that certain otherwise peculiar behavior was expected of prophets, although the particular forms of behavior could vary from one region to another.[9] We might assume that something of the same sociological phenomenon would likewise hold true for the bizarre speech forms routinely used in prophecy. In any case, there is no record of a prophet being denounced or punished for unseemly or exaggerated language. On the contrary, the instances of official censure of prophets preserved in the Hebrew Bible all report arrests of prophets speaking nonmetaphorical, rather prosaic predictions. In every case the prophet is announcing the destruction of Jerusalem, the Temple, or the king.

Official reaction to prophetic oracles is most notable in the book of Jeremiah, in which four episodes of public censure or arrest are recounted, all of which result from the prophet's plainly worded prophecies that Jerusalem is doomed. This is perhaps most clear in the account of Jeremiah's trial (Jeremiah 26), in which the prophet is condemned for prophesying against Jerusalem and the Temple, saying that they would become desolate and like Shiloh. On the one hand, during the course of the trial Micah's prophecy that "Jerusalem shall become a

---

9. Wilson, *Prophecy.*

heap of ruins, and the mountain of the house a wooded height" is recalled as a legal precedent demonstrating that Jeremiah should not be put to death for speaking the word of the Lord. On the other hand, Uriah prophesied against Jerusalem "in words like those of Jeremiah," and he had to flee for his life to Egypt, whence he was extradited by King Jehoiakim and executed. The account in Jeremiah 26 obviously intends to contrast the good king Hezekiah with the treacherous king Jehoiakim; nevertheless, the story makes clear that except in the unusual circumstance of the reign of a God-fearing king, a prophet who spoke against Jerusalem and the Temple was guilty of a capital offense. Another episode in Jeremiah's story again testifies to the offense of prophetic prophecies against Jerusalem, presumably because those prophecies had strong political implications. Just months before the fall of the city, Jeremiah was arrested for publicly urging the people of Jerusalem to surrender to the Babylonians and live. His words were couched in the language of prophetic authority ("thus says the Lord"); nevertheless, he was condemned for "weakening the hands of the soldiers left in this city, and the hands of all the people" (Jer 38:4). Apparently he was allowed, even expected, to castigate Jerusalem for moral lapses, but prophesying that those lapses would bring about the collapse of the political order brought swift reprisal.

A similar dilemma confronted Amos. Although he spoke dozens of bitterly sarcastic and offensive oracles against the rich and powerful in Israel, it was only when he said "Jeroboam shall die by the sword, and Israel must go into exile away from his land" that his words were reported to the king, and the priest Amaziah told him to go back to Judah (Amos 7:10-13). Clearly the critical words of the prophets were expected and granted their niche in Israelite society; society, however, circumscribed the limits of prophetic speech so that prophets would not pose a serious threat to the social order or the structures of power. When the prophet impinged on these, his authority as an intermediary was not recognized, and he was held accountable to the law as a political troublemaker.

## The Content of Prophetic Critique

That Israel had a niche for prophetic critique and apparently provided public fora in which prophets could deliver their oracles, while at the same time limiting the content of those oracles by forbidding certain topics, is important for understanding prophecy in the Hebrew Bible. Israel's habit of self-criticism and its willingness to tolerate the invective of prophets were balanced by a strong sense of its security in the promises of YHWH. Ironically, it was this very sense of security that the prophets saw as the heart of Israel's problem and that they tried to undermine. In the Northern Kingdom, Amos challenged the prevailing theology of the rich by saying that God did not accept sacrifices from the unclean hands of those who had gained wealth and power by grinding the faces of the poor in the dust. In Judah, Jeremiah undercut the false sense of security that allowed people to violate the commandments and then come into the Temple to appease YHWH with sacrifices. "Has this house, which is called by my name, become a den of robbers in your eyes?" Jeremiah asks them (Jer 7:11). Because the false security and corrupt behavior of the people were sometimes supported by self-serving interpretations of religious traditions, prophetic critique often took the form of alternate readings of Israel's traditions. The prophet would quote the people's interpretation, as evidenced by their words and actions, and then provide his own quite different understanding of that same tradition.[10] Whereas many understood Israel's election as a source of security, the prophets saw it as cause for judgment. The people's optimistic reading of Israel's election as God's people, for example, is challenged by Amos when he cites the election of the Ethiopians, Philistines, and Syrians (Amos 9:7-8). Those who long for the Day of YHWH as the time of their vindication are mocked by Amos, who illustrates in detail how little they understand what will happen on that day (Amos 5:18-20). When Judah had begun to be devastated by Nebuchadnezzar's army, the elders' firm belief that God would repeat for them what he had done for Abraham is dismissed by Ezekiel (Ezek 33:23-29). The people's deep faith in the inviolability of Jerusalem as a divinely protected city is undercut by Jeremiah's repeated predictions that YHWH himself would destroy it.

The prophetic view of Israel's worship—the Temple, sacrifice, the role of priests—is sometimes misunderstood. The prophets were not against religious institutions, nor did they see sacrifices and liturgies as empty formalities. Their invective is directed against those who believed that their prayers and sacrifices would cover for their crimes in the marketplace and that YHWH would protect them and their land unconditionally. Amos's invective against the sanctuary at Bethel and Jeremiah's bitter words against the Temple in Jerusalem did not signify prophetic opposition to liturgy and sacrifice, but a judgment on the assumption that God was dependent on Israel or that he could be bought off. Of course the prophetic caricature of what the people believe is not a reliable source for understanding popular religion. Nevertheless, by correcting for prophetic exaggeration and by using other texts to understand the attitudes of the people, it is possible to arrive at some sense of the ways in which Israel's traditions of the promise, exodus and conquest, Davidic covenant and Temple functioned at various times in its history. From the prophetic point of view the problem seems to have been a consistent reading of the past as a guarantee of the future. Seen from one perspective, Israel was guilty of nothing more than having faith in YHWH—faith that YHWH would deliver on his promises and protect his people because his reputation depended on it. Such was the argument

---

10. See W. Zimmerli, "Prophetic Proclamation and Reinterpretation," in *Tradition and Theology in the Old Testament* (Philadelphia: Fortress, 1977) 69–100. For a discussion of prophetic hermeneutics see J. A. Sanders, "Hermeneutics in True and False Prophecy," in George W. Coats and Burke O. Long, eds., *Canon and Authority* (Philadelphia: Fortress, 1977) 21–41.

of Hananiah against Jeremiah in the Temple, when he said that YHWH would deliver Jerusalem from the hands of Nebuchadnezzar now as he had delivered it from Sennacherib some ninety-six years earlier (Jer 27:2-4, 11). From the prophetic perspective, however, this belief represented an idolatrous faith in Israel's religious traditions and institutions rather than faith in the living God.

While the prophets condemned the legal and economic actions that led to social injustice, and the religious abuses that constituted idolatry, they seemed to see the root of Israel's problem as a deeply flawed self-understanding. Because it was defined by its relation with YHWH, Israel's failure to know YHWH (Hos 4:6; 5:4; 6:6) meant that it did not know itself. By seeing YHWH as a tutelary deity, bound to protect it, Israel failed to understand that YHWH was free. The prophets continually emphasized YHWH's freedom to act in the present unimpeded by his past record. YHWH was not defined by theology, nor confined in the Temple, but ineffable and holy. While Israel seemed bent on taking YHWH down to size to make him fit a theological scheme, the prophets insisted that he was a living God, not a theological idea, and that this God could be known only in the covenant relation. Isaiah's Temple vision of YHWH seated on the throne conveys this sense of YHWH not fitting into human categories, for all Isaiah can see is the hem of God's garment; the Temple—indeed the whole world—is too small to contain YHWH.

Israel's failure to know YHWH is linked with its inability to walk in his ways. The long years of following its own instincts rather than the words of YHWH had formed habits so deeply etched that Israel was not able to change them. There is a degree of sadness in the prophetic assessment of Israel's situation:

> For my people are fools,
>      they know me not;
> they are stupid children,
>      they have no understanding.
> They are skilled in doing evil,
>      but how to do good they know not. (Jer 4:22)

The epithet "a stiff-necked and stubborn people" is one way of expressing Israel's theological problem. Jeremiah portrays Judah as unable to bend its will to YHWH's even if it should want to; he expresses this when he says, "but you said, 'It is hopeless, for I have loved strangers, and after them I will go'" (Jer 2:25).

In this most devastating of all prophetic critiques, the source of Israel's sin is failure of the imagination. Faithfulness to YHWH, an invisible, imageless deity whose very name was mysterious, demanded a high degree of imagination. The stories of Israel's early history helped tutor the people in YHWH's ways, and the evidence suggests that Israelites had a highly developed and richly furnished religious imagination. If the prophets are even partially accurate in their assessment, however, years of shallow and self-serving readings of these stories had disabled the people's ability to distinguish between God and their own appetites. The priests and prophets substituted their own instincts for the teachings of Torah, and the people whom they instructed were none the wiser (Jer 8:8-12). To believe in God and remain faithful in duress requires a well-furnished imagination and a disciplined will. To the prophets for whom YHWH was the assayer of reality, Israel's squandering of these gifts of imagination and will that YHWH had provided for it constituted the sorriest of human conditions.

## Prophetic Authority

By what authority did the prophets judge Israel so harshly? We can address this question both sociologically, in terms of what the society expected, and theologically, in terms of the prophets' understanding of their role.[11] As mentioned above in the discussion of social location, the mediating role of the prophet was recognized and appreciated as an important function in Israelite society, as in all of the ancient Near Eastern states for which we have evidence. The prophet was a fellow countryman speaking with privileged information obtained through the channels open to him or her but not available to others in Israel. Even when they spoke unwelcome or harsh words, prophets were accepted because they had a vital link to divine intelligence and hence performed an important role in society. Within this context, however, they were expected to be loyal to the institutions that supported them.

Prophetic authority lay primarily in the claim of being sent, and of bearing the divine word. This aspect of prophecy as a response to a divine initiative is reflected in the etymology of the Hebrew word for prophet, *nabi,* which appears to be a passive form of the Akkadian verb *nabū,* meaning to call. The prophet is above all one who is called. His caustic words against his own people were not the product of his own astute social analysis but a description of what Israel looked like from God's point of view. The books of Exodus, Amos, Hosea, Isaiah, Jeremiah, and Ezekiel all contain references to the prophet being overpowered by God and assigned the task of communicating God's point of view to the people. The prophets often used metaphorical language when citing the source of their authority, describing themselves as auditors at a meeting of YHWH's secret council. The message they spoke was not their own, they insisted, but YHWH's. It is important to remember that the role of prophet in ancient Israel was not equivalent to that of a fiery preacher or a social reformer in modern times. Although such people are sometimes called prophets, the parallel is not entirely accurate because social reform as understood by modern societies was not the main function of biblical prophecy. Even when the prophets tried to reform the behavior of corrupt leaders and complicit followers by calling them

---

11. See B. O. Long's helpful study, "Prophetic Authority as Social Reality," in *Canon and Authority,* 3–20.

back to their senses, the purpose did not seem to be improving the quality of life of the economically disadvantaged or making Israel into a more just society, but communicating the divine message that the prophet was compelled to speak. Even in Amos, the book that speaks most clearly about social justice, the prophet does not identify with the poor or try to convince the rich to do what is right. On the contrary, Amos castigates rulers and merchants with insulting language that could only alienate them. There is no evidence that Amos, or any other prophet, succeeded in social reform; yet they are not viewed by the tradition as failures.

The matrix in which the prophets worked was not political or sociological but theological. While this may seem an arcane distinction, it is critical for understanding biblical prophecy. In his now classic study of prophecy, Abraham Joshua Heschel developed a highly original and nuanced understanding of biblical prophets as those who shared in the suffering of God.[12] In this view the prophet was neither the mystic who is united with God nor the social reformer, but one who communicated to his compatriots the pain in the heart of God. In Heschel's view the prophet resonated the divine pathos, so that what he disclosed were not concepts about God but the attitudes of God. He was not guided by what he felt about the sociopolitical situation, but by what God felt. The prophet's words of judgment against his own people originated in his sympathy with the divine suffering; hence the primary aim was not to achieve a better society or to avert historical disaster but to bring the people back into the covenant relation so that the disturbance afflicting God might depart.

Following Heschel, Walter Brueggemann suggests that the often bizarre language and imaginative imagery used in prophetic speech functioned to challenge the dominant reality and to open Israel's imagination to alternate ways of living:

> The prophet is engaged in a battle for language, in an effort to create a different epistemology out of which another community might emerge. The prophet is not addressing behavioral problems. He is not even pressing for repentance. He has only the hope that the ache of God could penetrate the *numbness* of history. He engages not in scare or threat but only in a yearning that grows with and out of pain.[13]

The prophetic sympathy with God was matched by the prophet's deep identification with his own people. On the one hand, he stood outside the community and represented God's point of view; on the other hand, he was a member of that community and was called on to represent its interests to God. Nowhere is this more clear than in the stories of Moses, who alternately intercedes on behalf of the people and castigates the people on behalf of YHWH. Being given God's vision of his community did not cause the prophet to lose his human stake in it. The confessions of Jeremiah testify to the difficulty the prophet had in speaking some of the harsh judgments he was compelled to speak. Prophetic

---

12. A. J. Heschel, *The Prophets* (New York: Harper and Row, 1962), esp. 2.1–103.

13. W. Brueggemann, *The Prophetic Imagination* (Philadelphia: Fortress, 1978) 59.

critique therefore is a complex phenomenon representing God's view of Israel as his covenant partner, communicated through the prophet who "stands in the breach." The position of the prophet as the one in the middle, standing with God over against Israel while at the same time living and identifying with Israel as his own people, is critical to his role. This is so not only because the prophet is an intermediary, representing each side to the other, but more significantly because the difficult position of being fully identified with both sides is precisely the divine dilemma. As YHWH says when Jeremiah complains that even his own family has turned against him:

> I have forsaken my house,
> I have abandoned my heritage;
> I have given the beloved of my soul
> into the hands of her enemies. (Jer 12:7)

Unlike the diplomat, who shuttles between two governments to negotiate an agreement, but whose allegiance is clearly with one side, the prophet has full allegiance in both camps: with Israel by virtue of birth and with YHWH by the experience of his call. Hence the prophet is made to live out the divine pain of having to chastise, and even destroy, what is most precious to him. The deepest prophetic critique was not in the words of judgment spoken in the Temple or marketplace, but in the way the prophet by his own life brought the anguish of divine love into the midst of Israel.

## The Effects of Redaction

Our knowledge of the social location of prophecy in the ancient Near East helps explain why prophets were tolerated in Israel, but not why the invective of these prophets should be collected, edited, and even expanded by later generations of Judahites. One obvious reason for preserving the oracles of prophets who had predicted the fall of Israel and Judah was that they had been right, and in hindsight their words helped the survivors make sense of what had happened to them. The Deuteronomistic Historians presented Israel's history as an unremitting catalogue of breaches of covenant by Israel partly in order to justify the catastrophes of 722 and 586 BCE. However, the preservation and shaping of the prophetic books involved more than retrospective justification of Judah's fall. In fact the evidence suggests that from the outset the prophetic oracles were preserved not because they explained the past but because they addressed the present. So, for example, Hosea's predictions of doom against the Northern Kingdom were reinterpreted by Judaean redactors so that they would be relevant in a new setting.[14]

---

14. See H. W. Wolff, *Hosea* (Philadelphia: Fortress, 1974) xxix–xxxii.

Whatever the reasons for the initial preservation of prophetic oracles, the result of the editing process is a remarkable collection of judgments against Israel. Several aspects of the redacted prophetic corpus are noteworthy. First, the sheer volume of words depicting Israel as corrupt and arrogant cannot escape even the casual reader. Although some editing was obviously done, apparently there was no impetus to reshape the works more in Israel's favor. Even where harsh judgments were softened by the addition of new oracles, these did not diminish Israel's guilt but enlarged the context beyond judgment.

A second aspect is the presence of commissioning scenes in which the prophet is set over against his people with a task made essentially hopeless by their inhospitable reception. The formal similarity of these scenes tends to draw the prophets together into a group called by YHWH to be over against the people.[15] The prophetic canon encourages the view that the majority of Israelites were either scheming rulers or deceived followers, while a few faithful prophets bore the weight of the divine anger. This picture is sharpened by the narratives recounting the hostile reactions of the king and the religious leaders toward the prophets.[16] Preservation and editing of the prophetic words tended to highlight the prophets as a group over against a recalcitrant Israel.

The redactors sometimes included a kind of commentary on the use of the written prophetic words. This is evident in Jeremiah 36, where the story of King Jehoiakim cutting up the scroll containing Jeremiah's words as it was read to him, and tossing the strips into the fire in the brazier at his feet, provided a warning to future readers that the words on the scroll were as potent as the words spoken with the prophet's own lips. The story seems intended to contrast with the earlier account of King Josiah's reaction when a scroll was read to him (2 Kings 22–23). Although the scroll had just been discovered by workmen renovating the Temple, and its provenance was unknown, Josiah responded as though the words were addressed to him. The two stories together suggest that the prophetic word preserved in writing demanded the same response as the living prophet, and they provided alternative models for readers of prophetic words. Later readers were held responsible for their response to the scroll as the earlier hearers had been for their response to the spoken oracles.

Another noteworthy aspect of redaction is the recontextualizing of the prophetic oracles. By removing historical markers from oracles and rearranging prophetic words according to nonchronological schema, the redactors provided new contexts in which the oracles could be interpreted. The most striking example of such redaction is Isaiah 40–55, which was "detached from its original historical moorings"[17] when it was attached to the oracles of Isaiah of Jerusa-

---

15. Exodus 3; Isaiah 6; Jeremiah 1; Ezekiel 2–3.

16. For example, 1 Kings 18–19; 1 Kings 22; Amos 7:10-15; Jer 20:1-2; 26; 37–38.

17. The phrase is Brevard Childs's; see his "The Canonical Shape of the Prophetic Literature," in *Interpreting the Prophets*, 45.

lem. The comforting words of the exilic prophet cannot be read apart from the words of judgment of Isaiah 1–39.

Perhaps the most significant result of the redaction process is the emergence of a unifying theme in the prophetic corpus. In their shaping of the prophetic books, the ancient redactors have made a theological statement about the words of judgment spoken against Israel and their fulfillment in 722 and 586 BCE: the divine judgment, announced through the prophets, was part of the divine plan for Israel's salvation. Israel was chastened so that it could return to YHWH with a new heart. This theme, already adumbrated in Jeremiah, is a central theological idea that emerges from the prophetic canon and provides the context in which all prophetic words of judgment are read.[18] Having been subsumed under this broader theme of salvation in judgment, the harsh words of the prophets take on a different nuance. In fact this theological framework of the prophetic corpus is consistent with that of the Torah, in that it tends to tell Israel's story from the divine rather than the human point of view. In the end, the redaction of the prophetic words of judgment made clear that Israel would be held accountable to YHWH, but out of judgment would come new life.

This extraordinary hermeneutic of reading Israel's story from God's point of view rather than Israel's was operative throughout the prophetic books. But while it was understood in ancient Israel, it sometimes suffered when transplanted to other soil. On the whole, the exegetes of the Second Temple period, both Jewish and Christian, tended to read the prophets in an eschatological way, expecting the fulfillment of ancient prophecies in their own day.[19] Further, a frequent feature of their reading was the tendency to apply prophetic words of judgment to their enemies rather than to their own communities. Hence the sharp edge of prophetic critique that had been part of Israel's self-understanding was often lost in the later communities that read the prophetic literature. Such readings are frequent in the literature of Qumran and are at times evident in the New Testament.

The strong strain of self-criticism that persists throughout the Hebrew Bible signifies a profound theological insight. In their historical context, the prophets continually called people away from their comfortable theological constructions. In their canonical shape, the Torah and the Prophets together consistently focus the reader's attention on YHWH, who transcends definitions and confounds expectations. Further, somewhat like the role of the slow-witted disciples in the Gospels, the picture of a bumbling Israel allows the reader to see the truth more clearly. No one could confuse the ideal Israel with the historical reality; neither could anyone miss the point that YHWH's dealings with his people were characterized more by mercy than by justice. But there are twin dangers in

---

18. See R. E. Clements, "Patterns in the Prophetic Canon," in *Canon and Authority*, 42–55; and B. Childs, *Introduction to the Old Testament as Scripture* (Philadelphia: Fortress, 1979) 306–10.

19. See J. Barton, *Oracles of God* (New York: Oxford Univ. Press, 1986), esp. 151–53 and chap. 6.

this phenomenon of portraying Israel as continually falling short of the mark, dangers that the history of exegesis shows have caused great damage. For many readers the prophetic emphasis on God's judgment has led to the conclusion that "the God of the Old Testament" is demanding and full of vengeance. Such conclusions come from atomistic readings and are not possible when the prophets are studied carefully in their historical and canonical contexts.

More serious today is the danger of Christians reading prophetic invective as accurate historical descriptions of Israel. Prophetic critique was part of Israel's language and was well understood as part of its tradition. It was a family matter.[20] When it is read by outsiders in a different context, the potential for harm to both sides is great. The Dead Sea Scrolls bear witness to the problem of applying prophetic words of judgment to one's enemies rather than to one's own community. It is one thing for Jeremiah to call his own people stiff-necked; it is quite another for a Christian to refer to Jews that way. Jeremiah's words functioned in a complex and highly developed social and theological context shared by his audience, as I have tried to show in these pages. They are not objective historical descriptions of Israel but prophetic oracles whose meaning is circumscribed by rhetorical convention. Spoken by a prophet to his own people, the words of prophetic judgment were the word of the Lord and ultimately brought life; hurled at Israel from the outside, they turn to poison in the mouth of the speaker.

---

20. Israelite prophets did pronounce words of judgment on Israel's enemies. For a thoughtful discussion of the hermeneutical problems of invective directed outside the community, see J. Levenson, "Is There a Counterpart in the Hebrew Bible to New Testament Anti-Semitism?" *JES* 22 (1985) 242–60.

# -2-

# Jesus and the Question
# of Anti-Semitism

## *Bruce Chilton*

To consider that Jesus was anti-Semitic is, on the face of the matter, an oddity. There is no indication within the sources that he ever doubted that the covenant with the patriarchs was axiomatic, and he appears to have accepted both the Hebrew Scriptures and worship in the Temple as the usual instruments of that covenant. His thematic signature was "the kingdom of God," a phrase whose meaning is apparent in the Targumim, the Aramaic paraphrases of Scripture,[1] and a primary symbol of that reality within his teaching was a meal among Jews and their patriarchs.[2]

Insofar as non-Jews have any place in Jesus' story, it is marginal, and the presence of Gentiles typically arouses his concern.[3] A later age would bring the programmatic question of how uncircumcised believers could be included within the fellowship of Jesus (see Gal. 2:11-21); the rabbi[4] himself did not deal with that issue.

The Gospels, of course, were written in an environment in which the fellowship of Jesus was already seen as distinct from, and largely competitive with,

---

1. See B. D. Chilton, *God in Strength: Jesus' Announcement of the Kingdom* (The Biblical Seminar; Sheffield: JSOT, 1987); and idem, *A Galilean Rabbi and His Bible* (London: SPCK; Wilmington, Del.: Glazier, 1984) 58–67.

2. See Matt 8:11, 12; Luke 13:28, 29; Chilton, *God in Strength,* 179–201. The underlying imagery of Matt 22:1-14; Luke 14:15-24; 16:22-24 should also be considered; a good example of the image of an eschatological feast within the Targumim is presented at *Tg. Isa* 25:6-8, and it is in close proximity to the reference to God's kingdom at 24:23.

3. See Matt 15:21-28; Mark 7:24-30. In another vignette, when Jesus does have an immediately positive response to a Gentile, the man's outstanding faith is stressed, and in Luke the centurion's sympathy with Judaism is such that he is said to have endowed a synagogue (Matt 8:5-13; Luke 7:1-10).

4. The normal, respectful address of a teacher within the Judaism of the period was "my great one," or "my master," rabbi. Jesus is so addressed in the Gospels more than by any other

Judaism. That competition resulted in apologetic tension, which Rosemary Ruether describes as the "anti-Judaic left hand" of Christology.[5] In common with a recent convention, she distinguishes the anti-Judaism that sometimes surfaces in the early church from the "racial anti-Semitism" of the modern period.[6] That distinction may be helpful conceptually, in that the relative strengths of Judaism and the non-Jewish sector of the early church were quite unlike what they have been since the Enlightenment, and the entire theory of race upon which much modern anti-Semitism is promulgated is an inheritance from quasi-scientific perspectives on the development of humanity. Yet it is as well to be clear from the outset that the conceptual distinction between an anti-Judaic argument and anti-Semitic prejudice might be lost in the hatred that both attitudes tend to exacerbate. The Matthean Jews are liars in respect of the resurrection (28:15), and willful murderers who implicate their own children in the crucifixion (27:25). That is the most prejudicial charge in all of the Gospels, but it is not unlike Mark's condescending and unique claim that "all the Jews" hold to practices of washing "cups and pots and copper vessels" (7:3, 4),[7] or Luke's unique scene of Jesus' rejection at Nazareth by his own people (4:16-30),[8] or John's uniquely anachronistic claim that "the Jews" excluded the followers of Jesus from synagogues during his lifetime (9:22; 12:42, see 16:2). The *Gospel of Thomas* has Jesus himself ironically ask the disciples whether they have become as obtuse as the Jews, in that they must ask concerning Jesus' identity, when they ought simply to recognize it (log. 43). Within all five sources, which are of primary importance in the study of Jesus, Judaism and the Jews appear more as a foil for Jesus than as the matrix of his movement.

The Pauline corpus represents the vanguard within the New Testament of the claim that the covenant with Abraham was not to be restricted to the descendants of Abraham after the "flesh" (see Rom. 4:1-15; Gal. 3:6-9), but by the

---

designation. Moreover, he had a consistent interest in purity, and a dispute concerning appropriate sacrifice in the Temple cost him his life; the twin issues of purity and the Temple were characteristically Pharisaic. That Jesus' followers called him "rabbi" (Matt 26:25, 49; Mark 9:5; 10:51; 11:21; 14:45; John 1:38, 49; 3:2; 4:31; 6:25; 9:2; 11:8) is a straightforward deduction from the Gospels as they stand; that he is most naturally to be categorized among the Pharisees of his period is an equally straightforward inference. When, during the course of the twentieth century, scholars have expressed reservations in respect of that finding, they have had in mind the danger of identifying Jesus with the rabbinic movement after 70 CE, which was more systematized than before that time, and which amounted to the established power within Judaism. Unfortunately, anxiety in respect of that anachronism can result in the far greater error of bracketing Jesus within "sectarian" Judaism (as if "orthodoxy" existed in early, pluralized Judaism), or—worse still—of locating him within no Judaism at all.

5. See R. R. Ruether, *Faith and Fratricide: The Theological Roots of Anti-Semitism* (New York: Seabury, 1974) 95; for a social description of the emergence of Christianity as distinct from Judaism, see L. M. White, "Shifting Sectarian Boundaries in Early Christianity," *BJRL* 170/3 (1988) 7-24.

6. Ruether, *Faith*, 220-21.

7. See W. L. Lane, *The Gospel of Mark* (The New London Commentary; London: Marshall, Morgan and Scott, 1974) 245-57.

8. See Chilton, *God in Strength*, 123-56, where a comparison with the reception of Paul in Acts 13 is developed.

time Revelation was written, the primary institution of Judaism that survived the destruction of the Temple could be dismissed laconically as "the synagogue of Satan" (Rev. 2:9; 3:9). Other contributions within the present volume are to explicate the increasing divide between the Judaism that emerged after the destruction of the Temple and the various forms of Christianity that developed from the movement Jesus began. But the nature of that division needs to be appreciated in order for Jesus himself to be understood, for the simple reason that we have access to the reality of Jesus, the teacher within Judaism, primarily by means of the sources of those Christianities that defined themselves largely as separated from Judaism.

That separation did not come easily, or even willingly, in many cases: church by church, it was a matter of such factors as the social constitution of the community, the sort of evangelization (for example, Pauline, Petrine, or Jacobean) that had called the congregation into being, the view taken of the gospel by local Judaism, and the attitude of civic officials toward both the particular forms of Judaism and of the emergent Christianity that fell within their jurisdictions. Because the New Testament emerged during the period of transition between the pluralism of early Judaism, whose variety is at least as obvious as the unifying concern for worship in the Temple,[9] and the growing authority of the Rabbis after 70 CE, with their distinctive approach to the Torah as Israel's center, no easy generalizations in regard to the Judaism of that time are admissible. And the pluralism of Christianity during the same period is as obvious as the rhetoric of intramural disputes—reflected in the Pauline and deutero-Pauline corpus, the Pastorals, Revelation, the *Didache* and *1 Clement*—is heated.

The problem of apprehending a rabbi's position on the basis of sources that are largely antirabbinic is at once historical and hermeneutical. The more historical side of the problem is evident when we attempt to think of Jesus in respect of Judaism and refer to "the Jewish background" of his ministry. By means of a single phrase, we have imagined that Jesus' foreground lay elsewhere than in Judaism.[10] Without reflection, we have assumed that the direction of the Christianities that emerged in response to Jesus, in their increasing separation from Judaism, was inevitable. Similarly, approaches of a philosophical nature, which posit that Jesus' program involved a systematic transformation of Judaism, appear to assume that he stood sufficiently apart from his own religious environment to reflect upon it conceptually.[11] There were certainly such teachers within Judaism during the first century; Philo and Paul are perhaps the best examples.

---

9. Even then, only the concern is the unifying factor: the Sadducees and the Essenes, for example, cherished radically different understandings of what precisely should occur in the Temple.

10. Even a recent, sophisticated treatment imagines Jesus as offering a supersession of received Judaism; see A. E. Harvey, *Jesus and the Constraints of History* (London: Duckworth, 1982) 64.

11. See J. Riches, *Jesus and the Transformation of Judaism* (London: Darton, Longman, and Todd, 1980), and J. Riches and A. Millar, "Conceptual Change in the Synoptic Tradition," in A. E. Harvey, ed., *Alternative Approaches to New Testament Study* (London: SPCK, 1985) 37–60, 49–58, where Jesus' preaching is contrasted to a "zealot" theology that is entirely a matter of speculation.

But if Jesus actually stood for a religious system distinct from the Judaism he received, the lack of unanimity within the New Testament in presenting that alternative is nothing short of remarkable. The more plausible hypothesis is that Jesus and his movement initially were essentially Judaic, and that the changing constituencies of the church over time—particularly as reflected in the Pauline corpus—transformed the movement into a systematic alternative to the rabbinic Judaism that emerged after 70 CE.[12]

Two recent approaches to Jesus have attempted to explain Jesus' position within the Judaism of his time. In *Jesus the Jew*, Geza Vermes posits a more charismatic form of Judaism, alongside the early rabbinic movement, which Jesus represented. Jesus is presented as ordinarily xenophobic in his attitude toward non-Jews,[13] but as relying more upon personal prayer than conventional rabbis,[14] and as endowed with powers of healing in response to his prayer.[15] The fundamental difficulty within Vermes's construction of Jesus is its anachronistic understanding of Judaism. The distinction between charismatic and rabbinic Judaism simply does not bear scrutiny,[16] for the simple reason that figures such as Hanina ben Dosa, cited by Vermes as the best example of a charismatic of the Hasidic type, are in fact cited in rabbinic discussion as sages.[17] Effective teaching was not taken to be abstracted from tangible blessings. Vermes appears to have fallen victim to the characterization of early Judaism, an essentially pluralistic phenomenon, on the basis of the increasingly exclusive focus on the Torah in later, rabbinic Judaism. The result, ironically, is a residual Paulinism,

---

12. Matthew may be the best illustration of the conscious emergence of such a program; see G. Strecker, *Der Weg der Gerechtigkeit: Untersuchung zur Theologie des Matthäus* (FRLANT 82; Göttingen: Vandenhoeck and Ruprecht, 1962); W. Trilling, *Das Wahre Israel: Studien zur Theologie des Matthäus-Evangeliums* (SANT 10; Munich: Kösel, 1964); R. Walker, *Die Heilsgeschichte im ersten Evangelium* (FRLANT 91; Göttingen: Vandenhoeck and Ruprecht, 1967).

13. G. Vermes, *Jesus the Jew: A Historian's Reading of the Gospels* (London: Collins; Philadelphia: Fortress, 1973) 48–52. Vermes's reference to "Galilean chauvinism" is especially surprising in the light of recent studies that have suggested that the population of Judaea was in fact the more militant in dealing with the Romans; see S. Freyne, "Bandits in Galilee: A Contribution to the Study of Social Conditions in First-century Palestine," in J. Neusner et al., eds., *The Social World of Formative Judaism and Christianity: Essays in Tribute to Howard Clark Kee* (Philadelphia: Fortress, 1988) 50–68. It is ironic that, as is observed at the close of the present chapter, the Galilean form of Judaism has also been used to argue that Jesus was essentially nonrabbinic in his Judaism, if his movement can be described as Jewish at all! Evidently, sweeping claims are being made on both sides without a clear perception of the religious complexion of Galilee during the first century.

14. Vermes, *Jesus the Jew*, 73–77.

15. Ibid., 75.

16. Vermes compounds the confusion by attempting to equate "charismatic Judaism," understood as somehow distinct from "mainstream Pharisaism," with "the Hasidim," a term of which the definition is notoriously problematic (see *Jesus the Jew*, 80–82). In fact, even Hillel was known as a *hasid*, so that any disjunction between a "charismatic" and a "Pharisee" on the basis of the application of that term (which appears quite frequently in Mishnah) is untenable; see N. N. Glatzer, *Hillel the Elder: The Emergence of Classical Judaism* (Washington, D.C.: B'nai B'rith Foundations, 1959).

17. See *Abot* 3:9, 10. It is striking, as well, that Hanina's powers are heightened in descriptions of a later period, in the texts Vermes himself cites. For further criticism of Vermes's method, see Chilton, *Galilean Rabbi*, 23, 30.

in imposing a dichotomy between charisma and Torah that is as misleading for an understanding of Judaism in the first century as the better-known antithesis between spirit and flesh. E. P. Sanders's contribution, *Jesus and Judaism*,[18] is notable as an attempt to break through such categorical dichotomies, and to focus upon the issues in respect of which Jesus was distinctive, without invoking claims of uniqueness or charisma.

The issues Sanders isolates are repentance and the Temple. In his view, Jesus called recognized sinners into fellowship without requiring repentance of them and prophesied the destruction of the Temple. In order to make his claim, Sanders must argue that the language of repentance in the Gospels that is attributed to Jesus is a relatively late formation,[19] an argument that is plausible, although not conclusive: after all, it was only natural for a community to formulate Jesus' preaching in a manner that conformed to its own catechesis. But Sanders must also claim that the demand for repentance itself was falsely attributed to Jesus. That assertion ill comports with all of the sayings involving repentance that were attributed to him and also with those parables that depict repentance approvingly, without actually using the language of repentance.[20] Sanders can show no reason for supposing that a concern for repentance was as characteristic of the early Christianities that contributed to the Gospels as it was uncharacteristic of Jesus: and that supposition is just what his hypothesis demands. Ironically, the second issue identified as crucial for Jesus by Sanders is one that demonstrably exercised the early church more than it interested Jesus. The destruction of the Temple is a watershed that occasioned documents as diverse as Revelation and Hebrews (and also called forth a literature within Judaism). The "little apocalypse" within the Gospels, an evidently synthetic formulation that can not be ascribed to Jesus as it stands,[21] shows that, whatever Jesus had taught concerning the Temple, the successful Roman siege and the burning of the newly restored edifice on Mount Zion cast a radically new light on that teaching.

Neither of the two positions identified by Sanders can be plausibly taken as characteristic of Jesus. Indeed, if Vermes is more influenced by the dichotomy of charism and Torah than the passages he cited would warrant, Sanders appears unduly influenced by "the criterion of dissimilarity." As articulated by Norman Perrin, that criterion is to be used because Jesus can best be understood in the extent to which he departed from the Judaism of his day.[22] But to seek to

---

18. E. P. Sanders, *Jesus and Judaism* (London: SCM; Philadelphia: Fortress, 1985).

19. Ibid., 109, 111, 113, 187, 199, 206, 207, 227. The remarks here offered generally are developed in detail in B. D. Chilton, "Jesus and the Repentance of E. P. Sanders," *TynBul* 139 (1988) 1–18.

20. See Matt 13:44-46; 18:12-14/Luke 15:4-7; Matt 22:1-10/Luke 14:15-24; Matt 22:11-14; 25:31-46; Mark 4:26-29.

21. Mark 13 and par.; see J. Lambrecht, *Die Redaktion der Markus-Apokalypse: Literarische Analyse und Strukturuntersuchung* (AnBib 28; Rome: Biblical Institute, 1967).

22. See N. Perrin, *Rediscovering the Teaching of Jesus* (New York: Harper and Row, 1967) 39.

construe Jesus on the basis of sayings that appear most unlike Judaism, and with meanings taken in the direction of a departure from Judaism, is simply to move with the tendency of the New Testament, away from the social realities of occupied Israel and toward the religiously competitive environment of the Mediterranean world at large. Perrin's canon might give us the portrait of Jesus that became effective in the propaganda of the early church; a more adequate criterion of the historical Jesus would demand his *continuity* with the Judaism he received as his environment and would attend to Jesus' *distinctiveness* within that environment.

Two disputes between Jesus and teachers contemporary with him that are portrayed as characteristic within the Synoptic Gospels involve the time of the kingdom and the presence of vendors of animals in the outer court of the Temple. Both issues have been taken in recent scholarship to illustrate Jesus' breach with the Judaism of his time, in eschewing a literalistic understanding of the kingdom,[23] and a commercial interest in sacrificial worship.[24] But when both of those dominical positions are placed within a context that attends to disputes among Pharisees or Rabbis, their historical meaning becomes much plainer.

A parable in which God figures as a king is attributed to Yoḥanan ben Zakkai. The parable is clearly eschatological, and it is all the more interesting from the present point of view, since Yoḥanan was a contemporary of the Temple's destruction and is regarded both in Talmud and modern, critical circles as the effective founder of rabbinic Judaism.[25] In the parable, attributed to Yoḥanan ben Zakkai in the Babylonian Talmud (*Šabb.* 153a), a king invites his servants to a feast without announcing the time of the meal. Wise servants attire themselves properly and wait at the door of the king's house. Foolish servants expect definite signs of the preparation of the feast and go about their work until they might see it is time to change. The king appears without warning and throws the doors open for the feast. The wise enjoy a fine meal, while the foolish servants are made to stand and watch in their work-soiled clothing.[26] Here we see the usage of feasting in order to convey the joys of God's kingdom; eating and eschatology are presented as related,[27] and—with the emphasis in the parable upon the necessary preparation and cleanliness of the invited guests—the characteristically Pharisaic issue of purity is also raised.[28]

---

23. See Riches, *Jesus*.

24. See R. A. Horsley, *Jesus and the Spiral of Violence: Popular Jewish Resistance in Roman Palestine* (San Francisco: Harper and Row, 1987) 286–300.

25. See J. Neusner, *A Life of Yoḥanan ben Zakkai, Ca. 1–80 CE* (SPB; Leiden: Brill, 1976) 122–24.

26. For further reflections on the relevance of Yoḥanan's parable and others for the understanding of Jesus' parabolic teaching, see B. D. Chilton and J. I. H. McDonald, *Jesus and the Ethics of the Kingdom* (London: SPCK; Grand Rapids, Mich.: Eerdmans, 1987).

27. See Matt 8:11, 12; Luke 13:28, 29; and n. 2, above.

28. See J. Neusner, *The Pharisees: Rabbinic Perspectives* (Studies in Ancient Judaism; Hoboken, N.J.: Ktav, 1984) for a general characterization of Pharisaic positions that is richly illustrated with examples.

When we compare Yoḥanan's parable to Jesus' position regarding the indeterminate time of the kingdom, for example as presented in Luke 17:20, 21, certain similarities and differences are immediately striking. On the one hand, Yoḥanan is, of course, not presented (as Jesus is) as developing an argument under questioning "by the Pharisees": the discussion in the Babylonian Talmud is implicitly intra-Pharisaic, and the use of the term "Pharisee" to mark a boundary beyond which one is in opposition to Jesus probably reflects the growing tension between the early church and the emerging authority of the Pharisees or Rabbis in the period after 70 CE. On the other hand, Yoḥanan and Jesus are presented by their respective literatures as in fundamental agreement that the king or the kingdom is to arrive without warning, and yet requires preparation. Indeed, that creative tension between an eschatology that defies all calendars and an ethical stance that demands engagement is characteristic of Jesus and a demonstrable stream of rabbinic teaching.[29]

Eliezer ben Hyrcanus, a disciple of Yoḥanan's and a renowned traditionalist, connects the expectation of God's royal rule to the statement in Zech 14:9 that "on that day the LORD will be one and his name one."[30] The text in Hebrew already speaks of God ruling (*malakh*), so that the trigger of the conception of God's kingdom (*malkhutha'*) is to be found in the text itself; but it remains notable that Eliezer had the idea in his mind to be triggered in the first place. Moreover, the connection between Zech 14:9 and the kingdom is also made in the Targum of Zechariah.[31] That chapter clearly links eschatology (see 14:1-15) and sacrifice in Jerusalem (14:16-21), particularly at the feast of Sukkoth (14:16, 18, 19). The specific requirement in an eschatologically revamped world of which Jerusalem is the center and apogee is "to feast the feast of booths" (vv. 18, 19). The festival is clearly marked out as a festival of harvest in Lev 23:33-43 and Deut 16:13-15, a feast that lasts seven joyful days (Lev 23:40, 41; Deut 16:13, 15) and that would become known in Mishnah, quite simply, as "the feast" (see *Sukk.* 4:2). In Zechariah, however, that eschatological festivity is explicitly to include non-Jews (see 14:16). Eliezer therefore permits us to trace the connection between an expectation of the kingdom and ultimate and inclusive feasting, which appears to have been characteristic of Jesus, as well (see Matt 8:11, 12; Luke 13:28, 29).

The principal elements that are commonly held to be characteristic of Jesus' understanding of the kingdom include its temporal indeterminacy, the necessity of preparedness for it, and its relatedness to a universal feast of which fellow-

---

29. See Chilton and McDonald, *Jesus and the Ethics of the Kingdom*, 31–43.

30. Biblical translations throughout this chapter are my own.

31. See B. D. Chilton, "Regnum Dei Deus Est," in *Targumic Approaches to the Gospels: Essays in the Mutual Definition of Judaism and Christianity* (Studies in Judaism; Lanham, Md.: University Press of America, 1986) 99–107; the essay first appeared in *SJT* 131 (1978) 261–70. The relationship between Eliezer's dictum (in *Mek.* Exod 17:14) and the Targum is confirmed in K. J. Cathcart and R. P. Gordon, *The Targum of the Minor Prophets* (The Aramaic Bible 14; Wilmington, Del.: Glazier, 1989).

ship at table was a foretaste. All of those elements are present, in aggregate, in the teaching of Yoḥanan and Eliezer, and are by no means peculiar to them and Jesus. Claims of Jesus' historical uniqueness, which are perhaps an echo of theological assertion in the realm of academic discourse, run afoul of a consideration of what rabbis were remembered to have taught. Of course, Jesus' distinctive approach to the issue of the kingdom may be traced in his persistent recourse to the genre of parable, in his habit of using meals as verbal and enacted symbols of the kingdom, in his relative nonuse of Scripture to speak of the kingdom, and in his exorcisms in the name of the kingdom. All of those features, it may be argued, amount to an innovatively dynamic construal of the kingdom as a force influencing the life of Israel and auguring a radical change in the near future. No doubt, such a position would and did occasion debate with other rabbis; but it was well within the realm of the sort of Pharisaic or rabbinic discourse we might expect to learn of during the period prior to 70 CE.

Moreover, we might reasonably anticipate that disagreements regarding God's kingdom might have been vehement. In a later period, Aqiba, a student of Eliezer's, supported the claims of one Simeon bar Kosibah to be the new prince of Israel, acting in conjunction with a priest named Eleazar. Simeon's supporters referred to him as Bar Kokhba, "son of a star," projecting onto him the messianic expectations of Num 24:17, while his detractors came to know him as Bar Koziba, "son of a lie." His initial success and military acumen are attested in letters he sent his commanders during his revolt and regime, which lasted from 132 until 135 CE.[32] In the shape of Hadrian, the response of the Empire was even more definitive than it had been in 70 CE. The remnants of the Temple were taken apart, and new shrines were built in the city; Jerusalem itself was now called Aelia Capitolina, Jews were denied entry, and Judaea became Syria Palaestina. The Rabbis survived by disowning the aspirations embodied by Aqiba, but keeping much of his teaching. "Aqiba, grass will grow out of your jaw, before the son of David comes" (*y. Taᶜan.* 4:7; *Lam. Rab.* 2.2.4); that is to say, the Messiah is to be of David, not of popular choosing, and his time cannot be pressed. But the Pharisees or Rabbis were by no means fixated on the question of the time of the kingdom or the Messiah: such issues as how to keep the Sabbath, what makes for culinary purity, and the manner in which sufferers from "leprosy" might be declared clean have left the marks of dispute clearly behind in the Mishnah, in tractates that deal substantively with those issues. Those are precisely the issues, of course, in which Jesus is said to have been embroiled with some of his contemporaries.

Jesus' action in the Temple is commonly portrayed as marking his great and irrevocable breach with Judaism, and the story—particularly in the Synoptics—is fodder for the homiletic dismissal of actual sacrifice as an invention of

---

32. See J. A. Fitzmyer, "The Bar Cochba Period," in *Essays on the Semitic Background of the New Testament* (SBLSBS 5; Missoula, Mont.: Scholars Press, 1974) 305–54.

self-interested priests. But here, as well, attention to Pharisaic or rabbinic disputes concerning the issue to hand suggests a fresh context for the historical apprehension of Jesus. An older contemporary of Jesus', Hillel, is reported to have taught that offerings (as in the case of his own "burnt sacrifice," *ʿôlâh*) should be brought to the Temple, where the owners would lay hands on them and then give them over to priests for slaughter.[33] His perennial and stereotypical disputants, the house of Shammai, resist, insisting that the animals might be handed over directly. One of the house of Shammai (named Baba ben Buta in the Babylonian Talmud and Tosepta), however, was so struck by the rectitude of Hillel's position that he had some three thousand animals (a number specified only in the Jerusalem Talmud) brought to the Temple and gave them to those who were willing to lay hands on them in advance of sacrifice.

Generally speaking, the haggadah concerning Hillel, Baba ben Buta, and the sheep is characteristic of the Pharisaic/rabbinic program. Moreover, the broad attestation of the story within the two Talmuds and its appearance in the Tosepta constitute an indication that it may reflect an actual dispute. Finally, although Hillel's disputants are stereotypically portrayed as followers of Shammai, it is striking that in *Beṣa* 20a, Hillel pretends the animal is a female, for a shared sacrifice (*zibḥêy šelāmîm*), in order to get it by the disciples of Shammai.[34] That is, the Babylonian Talmud's version of the story assumes that the followers of Shammai are in actual control of what worshipers do in the Temple. The haggadah is a far cry from the sort of tale, common in a later period, in which Hillel is portrayed as the prototypical patriarchate of rabbinic Judaism.

In one sense, the tradition concerning Hillel envisages a movement opposite from that of Jesus in the Temple (Matt 21:12, 13; Mark 11:15-17; Luke 19:45, 46; John 2:13-17): animals are introduced, rather than their traders expelled. But the purpose of the action by Hillel's partisan is to enforce a certain understanding of correct worship, and that is also the motivation attributed to Jesus in the Gospels. Hillel's halakah, in effect, insists upon the participation of the offerer by virtue of his ownership of what is offered, an ownership of which the laying on of hands is a definitive gesture. "The house of Shammai" is portrayed as sanctioning sacrifice without mandating that sort of emphatic participation on the part of the offerer. Although nothing like the violence of Jesus is attributed to Baba ben Buta, he does offer an analogy for a forcible attempt to insist upon correct worship in the Temple on the part of a Pharisee.

Mishnah itself reflects a concern to control commercial arrangements connected with the Temple, and such concern is also somewhat analogous to Jesus' action in the exterior court. The following story is told concerning one of the successors of Hillel:

---

33. See *t. Ḥag.* 2:11; *y. Ḥag.* 2:3; *y. Beṣa* 2:4; *b. Beṣa* 20a, b).
34. For a discussion of the versions of the story, see J. Neusner, *The Peripatetic Saying: The Problem of the Thrice-told Tale in Talmudic Literature* (BJS 89; Chico, Calif.: Scholars Press, 1985) 119–22.

> Once in Jerusalem a pair of doves cost a golden denar. Rabban Simeon ben Gamaliel
> said: By this Place! I will not rest this night before they cost but a [silver] denar.
> He went into the court and taught: If a woman suffered five miscarriages that were
> not in doubt or five issues that were not in doubt, she need bring but one offering,
> and she may then eat of the sacrifices; and the rest is not required of her. And the
> same day the price of a pair of doves stood at a quarter denar each. (*Ker.* 1:7)

Although the story requires more effort to understand than the one concerning
Hillel, it rewards the attention required. The assumption of the whole tale is that
a pair of doves might be offered by a woman as both a burnt-offering and a sacrifice for sin, in order to be purified after childbirth; the second of the two would
be offered normally, while the first—in the case of poverty—might take the place
of a yearling lamb (Lev 12:6-8). The story also assumes that miscarriages and unusual issues of blood akin to miscarriages should be treated under the category
of childbirth, from the point of view of purity. That interest is characteristically
Pharisaic, as is the issue of when the woman might be considered entitled to eat
of offerings. The Pharisees defined purity as fitness to take part in sacrifice and
in meals that—in their teaching—were related to the holiness of the Temple.

Simeon's anger, which causes him to swear by the Temple (see Matt 23:16-
22), is therefore motivated to some extent by economic considerations, and his
response is, like Jesus', to teach in the court of the Temple, to which point
such offerings would be brought. But his action there is far less direct than
Hillel's or Jesus'. Instead of importing more birds or releasing those bought at
an extortionate price, he promulgates a halakah designed to reduce the trade
in doves, no matter what their price. If a woman may await several (up to five)
miscarriages or flows of blood, and then offer a single pair of doves, and be
considered pure enough to eat of sacrifices, the potential revenue from sales of
doves would obviously decline. In effect, Simeon counters inflationary prices
with sacrificial monetarism. The political lesson was quickly appreciated (on the
very day, if we believe the story), and prices went lower even than Simeon had
intended. Presumably, there was no reason for him to continue promulgating
his view in the court of the Temple, and both he and the traders were content
with the settlement.

The exterior court was unquestionably well suited for trade, since it was
surrounded by porticoes on the inside, in conformity to Herod's architectural
preferences. But the probable assumption of rabbinic literature and Josephus is
that the market for the sale of sacrificial beasts was not located in the Temple
at all, but in a place called Ḥanuth on the Mount of Olives, across the Kidron
Valley.[35] It is conceivable that the Gospels present us with a fiction that is designed to portray worship in the Temple as distorted by commercialism. But

---

35. By association, the site was sacred; money found among the dealers, for example, was to be
considered as tithe (*m. Šeqal.* 7:2). For further discussion, see B. D. Chilton, *The Temple of Jesus:
His Sacrificial Program within a Cultural History of Sacrifice* (University Park: Pennsylvania State
Univ. Press, 1992) 91-111.

the Johannine account of the occupation does not make an objection to commercialism the point at issue; "zeal" is rather what is demonstrated (see 2:17), and particular attention is given to driving out animals and vendors, with their money (v. 15).[36] Victor Eppstein has argued that rabbinic literature attests the innovation to which Jesus objected.[37] It is recorded that, some forty years before the destruction of the Temple, the principal council of Jerusalem was removed from the place in the Temple called the Chamber of Hewn Stone to Ḥanuth.[38] Eppstein argues that Caiaphas both expelled the Sanhedrin and introduced the traders into the Temple, "an exceptional and shocking license introduced in the Spring of 30 C.E. by the vindictive Caiaphas."[39]

On the one hand, Eppstein's argument is marred by the tendency to portray Caiaphas as a villain, and it is by no means certain that he formally expelled the Sanhedrin, or even that a formal expulsion is at issue. On the other hand, the reference to the council's removal does suggest that, during the high priesthood of Caiaphas, there were disputes concerning physical arrangements at the Temple, and Caiaphas's good relationship with Pilate, under whom he served for ten years,[40] and with whose departure he was removed, would suggest that he was not held in the greatest esteem by those Jews who resisted Pilate.[41] Given that Caiaphas enjoyed the support of the Romans and that he was involved in disputes concerning the location (and presumably also the jurisdiction) of the council, the allegation of the Gospels that trade was permitted in the Temple during his tenure appears tenable.

From the point of view of Pharisaism generally, trade in the southern side of the outer court might well have been anathema. Purses were not permitted in the Temple according to the Pharisees' teaching.[42] Sufficient money might

---

36. See B. Chilton, "[os] phragellion ek schoiniōn [John 2:15]," in W. Horbury, ed., *Templum Amicitiae: Essays on the Second Temple Presented to Ernst Bammel* (Sheffield: Sheffield Univ. Press, 1991) 330–44.

37. V. Eppstein, "The Historicity of the Gospel Account of the Cleansing of the Temple," *ZNW* 55 (1964) 42–58. An alternative point of view, which posits the probability of trade in or near the Temple, was championed by J. Jeremias, *Jerusalem in the Time of Jesus,* trans. F. H. and C. H. Cave (London: SCM, 1969) 49.

38. See '*Abod. Zar.* 8b; *Šabb.* 15a; *Sanh.* 41a. The wording of *Sanhedrin* is representative: "Forty years before the destruction of the Temple, the Sanhedrin was exiled and installed in Ḥanuth."

39. Eppstein, "Gospel Account," 55.

40. He had been appointed high priest c. 18 CE by Valerius Gratus (see *Ant.* 18.2.2 §33–35).

41. In 36 CE, Caiaphas was removed by Vitellius, who also dismissed Pilate and—at the same time—released the high priestly vestments from custody in the Antonia (*Ant.* 18.4.3 §90–95). Evidently, Caiaphas had acquiesced in that arrangement and had accepted the close control of the Roman administration that it implied.

42. See *Ber.* 9:5. It may also be of interest that in *Šeqal.* 4:7, Eliezer and Joshua enter a dispute concerning what should be done with cattle that are among goods dedicated to the Temple. Eliezer holds that the males should be sold to those who want burnt sacrifices and the females to those who want shared sacrifices. But Joshua teaches that the males should themselves be offered and the females sold for shared sacrifices, with the proceeds designated for the purchase of burnt sacrifices. The unbreakable affinity between animals owned and dedicated for sacrifice, and the act of sacrifice itself, is upheld by Joshua and is somewhat analogous to Jesus' position.

be brought to put directly into the large containers for alms,[43] to purchase seals redeemable for libations,[44] and/or to exchange against Tyrian coinage in order to pay the annual half-shekel,[45] but the introduction of trade into the Temple rendered impossible the ideal of not bringing into the Temple more than would be consumed there. Incidentally, the installation of traders in the porticoes might also involve the removal of those teachers, Pharisaic and otherwise, who taught and observed in the Temple itself.[46]

From the point of view of the smooth conduct of sacrifice, the innovation was sensible. One could know at the moment of purchase that one's sacrifice was acceptable, and not run the risk of harm befalling the animal on the way to be slaughtered. It is therefore unnecessary to impute malicious motives, "vindictive" or otherwise, to Caiaphas in order to understand what was going on, although it may be assumed that additional profit for the Temple was also involved. But when we look at the installation of the traders from the point of view of Hillelite Pharisaism, for example, Jesus' objection becomes understandable. Hillel had taught that one's sacrifice had to be shown to be one's own, by the imposition of hands; part of the necessary preparation was not just of people to the south of the altar and beasts to the north, but the connection between the two by appropriation. Caiaphas's innovation was sensible on the understanding that sacrifice was a matter of offering pure, unblemished animals *simpliciter*. But it failed in Pharisaic terms, not only in its introduction of the necessity for commerce into the Temple, but in its breach of the link between the worshiper and the sacrificial action. The animals were correct in Caiaphas's system, and the priests regular, but the understanding of the offering as by the chosen people appeared—to some at least—sadly lacking. The essential component of Jesus' occupation of the Temple is perfectly explicable within the context of contemporary Pharisaism.

The second major element of the story of Jesus' occupation of the Temple—his overturning the tables of the money changers—has been the more cherished within Christian apologetic. Most recently, the argument of Robert Hamerton-Kelly has linked the monetary interest of the cultic establishment in Jerusalem with what is taken to be the implicit and systemic violence of sacrifice. Of course, as compared to such an axis of greed and destruction, Jesus is portrayed, in respect of his action in the Temple, as the prophet of reasonable love.[47] But precisely the utility and the appeal of the story of the successful rebellion against the money changers and their backers ought to make us cautious in evaluating

---

43. See *Šeqal.* 5:6; 6:1, 5; 7:1.

44. See *Šeqal.* 5:4.

45. See *Šeqal.* 1:3; 2:1.

46. See *Sanh.* 11:2; *Pesaḥ.* 26a.

47. See R. G. Hamerton-Kelly, "Sacred Violence and the Curse of the Law (Galatians 3:13): The Death of Christ as a Sacrificial Travesty," *NTS* 36 (1990) 98–118. Hamerton-Kelly is presently applying his analysis to the text of Mark in particular, and I am grateful to him for the early draft of the manuscript that he sent me.

it as an actual component of the action of Jesus. The fact of the matter is that, every year, money changing—for the sake of collecting the tax of a half-shekel for every adult male—went on publicly throughout Israel.[48] The process commenced a full month before Passover, with a proclamation concerning the tax (*Šeqal.* 1:1), and exchanges were set up in the provinces ten days *before* they were set up in the Temple (*Šeqal.* 1:3). Moreover, according to Josephus the tax was not even limited to those resident in the land of Israel (*J.W.* 7.6.6 §218; *Ant.* 18.9.1 §312), so that the procedure itself would not have been stopped by the sort of interruption the Gospels (with the exception of Luke) describe. The primary target of Jesus' action, as the stories concerning Hillel and Simeon would suggest, is far more likely to have been vendors of animals in the outer court of the Temple.

Jesus' teaching in regard to God's kingdom and his activity in the Temple lie at the heart of what made him distinctive among Rabbis of his period. But his distinctiveness should not be confused with eccentricity or complete originality: his insistence that God had commenced his rule and that Israel was to offer of its own with purity in the Temple was vehement and even violent, but not unique or bizarre. Indeed, Jesus' words and deeds were framed out of the common vocabulary of early Judaism, and were particularly resonant with the concerns that appear to have been characteristic of the Pharisees, later known as Rabbis. The change of the social and religious constituencies of the early church deeply influenced the meaning of the Gospels, however, and particularly cast Jesus' debates with his contemporaries into boundaries separating primarily non-Jewish believers from Jewish nonbelievers. His particular construal of the temporal dimensions of the kingdom, inclusive of a present aspect (Luke 17:21b), was turned into a challenge to "the Pharisees" to recognize God's power in Jesus' own ministry (vv. 20, 21a; see vv. 22-27). His incursion into the operation of the Temple, chiefly aimed at establishing the purity of Israel's worship (see Matt 21:12a, 12c, 13; Mark 11:15a, 15c, 16, 17; Luke 19:45, 46; John 2:14, 15a-c, 16, 17), was transmuted into a jeremiad against the commercial operation of the Temple itself (see the references to the "money changers" in Matt 21:12b; Mark 11:15b; John 2:15d; and his prophecies of the Temple's destruction in the "little apocalypse").

If one is aware of these two cases of transformations of meaning within the Gospels, the other disputes between Jesus and his Pharisaic contemporaries, *mutatis mutandis*, may also be approached as instances in which vehement debates concerning the issues of God's holiness and Israel's purity have been turned into markers of the boundaries separating those who believe within christological terms of reference from those who do not. Early Christians could

---

48. See B. D. Chilton, "A Coin of Three Realms (Matt 17:24-27)," in D. J. A. Clines et al., eds., *The Bible in Three Dimensions: Essays in Celebration of Forty Years of Biblical Studies in the University of Sheffield* (JSOTSup 87; Sheffield: Sheffield Academic Press, 1990) 269–82.

only be painfully aware of those boundaries, but to read them back into Jesus'
ministry is to inflict an anachronism upon the understanding of his position.
Moreover, that historical anachronism may lead, and in some cases in the past
has led, to a formal anti-Semitism in Christian theology, in which Jews and
Judaism as such are rejected on the grounds that their rejection of Jesus was
inevitable. Certain contributions have attempted to provide a greater plausibility to an overtly non-Jewish Jesus, on the grounds that Galilee was a mixed
environment, racially and culturally,[49] but continued research into the varied,
pluralistic nature of early Judaism must never become a pretext to play into
the hands of the desire to abstract Jesus from Judaism. That desire, the dark
side of the eagerness to include non-Jews that influenced early Christianity and
contributed to its classic character, can be modulated only by a properly historical approach to the question of Jesus, which addresses him and his movement
within the context of the Judaism(s) that produced them.

---

49. See W. Grundmann, *Jesus, der Galiläer und das Judentum* (Leipzig and Weimar: Georg
Wigand, 1940), and the more explicitly programmatic *Entjudung des religiösen Lebens als Aufgabe
der Theologie* (Leipzig and Weimar: Georg Wigand, 1939). Grundmann's academic leadership of the
Institut zur Erforschung des jüdischen Einflusses auf das deutsche kirchliche Leben is discussed in
Richard Gutteridge, *The German Evangelical Church and the Jews (1879–1950)* (New York: Barnes
and Noble, 1976) 196–97. Although there is no hint of an anti-Semitic sentiment or program within
it, it might be mentioned that there is a contemporary movement to construe Jesus apart from
the terms of reference of Judaism; see, for example, B. L. Mack, *A Myth of Innocence: Mark and
Christian Origins* (Philadelphia: Fortress, 1988).

*Part Two*

# Anti-Semitism and the New Testament Writings

# -3-

# A Loyal Critic:
# Matthew's Polemic with Judaism
# in Theological Perspective

## *Scot McKnight*

### Prophetic Rhetoric as a Convention

Rhetorically potent language is used throughout the ancient world to erect, fortify, and maintain the boundaries that distinguish one religious community from another or to separate, within the same religious community, the obedient from the disobedient.[1] This form of religious rhetoric is especially prevalent in the Hebrew prophetic tradition that, through this kind of communication, seeks repentance on the part of the sinful.[2] Whether we look at the potent language regularly punctuating the pages of the Hebrew Bible, like Amos (1:1–9:5), or at the heated diatribes of the books of the Second Temple period (e.g., 4 Ezra 7:22-25; see also 2:7), or at the religious fighting found in the New Testament book of James, the rhetoric of early Judaism robustly attacks opponents and heartily defends its truthfulness.

I am grateful to D. C. Allison, Jr., L. H. Feldman, and especially A.-J. Levine for their comments on an earlier draft of this essay and for the improvements they have made to my ideas. Their comments have, at times, found their way into the text and notes, and they will no doubt perceive their contributions.

1. An excellent study of the use of "labels" as sociological markers can be found in B. J. Malina and J. H. Neyrey, *Calling Jesus Names: The Social Value of Labels in Matthew* (Sonoma, Calif.: Polebridge, 1988); see also the earlier essay of M. Pamment, "Witch-hunt," *Theology* 25 (1981) 98–106. A step further in the direction of self-definition has been reached in the fine essay of S. Freyne, "Vilifying the Other and Defining the Self: Matthew's and John's Anti-Jewish Polemic in Focus," in J. Neusner and E. S. Frerichs, eds., *"To See Ourselves as Others See Us": Christians, Jews, "Others" in Late Antiquity* (Chico, Calif.: Scholars Press, 1985) 117–43.

2. James Parkes has illustrated the importance of "faith" in formulating religious rhetoric and difference; see his *Judaism and Christianity* (London: Victor Gollancz, 1948) 43–44. See also L. T. Johnson, "The New Testament's Anti-Jewish Slander and the Conventions of Ancient Polemic," *JBL* 108 (1989) 419–41; Johnson collects significant data for evaluating "Jewish rhetorical boundaries."

Accordingly, regardless of which variety of Judaism we choose, and regardless of which period we examine, we will find (what is for us) extremely volatile language expressing group differentiation and, through differentiation, identification. In this chapter I maintain that (perhaps) none of this harsh language is to be construed as racial hostility (as has often been argued); rather, the denunciations contained in this literature were a tolerable religious rhetoric designed to shock and revive. What strikes us as harsh or what may very well be avoided by us may not have been harsh to, or avoided by, first-century Jews and Christians. Such a perception of what is acceptable language is the rhetorical context of the Gospel of Matthew's polemic against the Jewish leaders and their followers. Matthew's polemic is an inheritance from Jewish polemic, and it is not to be classified as "anti-Semitic."[3] And I will argue that Matthew is arguing directly against nonmessianic Judaism and can therefore be accurately classed as reflecting "anti–nonmessianic Judaism" or "anti–disobedient Judaism." He thinks messianic Judaism is right; he thinks nonmessianic Judaism is wrong; he wants nonmessianic Judaism to turn into messianic Judaism. He believes Christian Jews are being loyal and that non-Christian Jews are disloyal to God's covenant with Israel. Whatever we think of his religious stance or his form of communication, these, I believe, are the reasons he says what he does and the reasons he says it in a certain manner.

## Defining Our Terms

In this chapter I will be using *anti-Semitism* for irrational, personal, racial prejudice against Jews because they are Jews;[4] *anti-Judaism* for the religious polemic

---

3. See the excellent analysis in Johnson, "Anti-Jewish Slander"; Johnson actually sees New Testament polemic as "remarkably mild" (!) in contrast to Hellenistic conventions (p. 441); see also the fine section of D. A. Hagner, *The Jewish Reclamation of Jesus: An Analysis and Critique of Modern Jewish Study of Jesus* (Grand Rapids, Mich.: Zondervan, 1984) 288–92. He states, "If all negative statements about Jews and Judaism are to be designated anti-Semitic, then, absurdly, we will be forced to designate the prophets of Israel as anti-Semitic" (p. 289). See also L. H. Feldman, "Is the New Testament Anti-Semitic," *Humanities* 21 (1987) 1–14, here 2–3; and also M. J. Cook, "Anti-Judaism in the New Testament," *USQR* 38 (1983) 125–37, here 125–26. Cook, however, goes on to say that some of the statements of the New Testament "exceed any rebuke of the Prophets of old" (p. 127); how one measures tolerable degrees of rebuke, of course, is more than a little problem.

4. For the problems and contours of definition, see A. T. Davies, *Anti-Semitism and the Christian Mind: The Crisis of Conscience after Auschwitz* (New York: Herder, 1968) 23–34; J. G. Gager, *The Origins of Anti-Semitism: Attitudes toward Judaism in Pagan and Christian Antiquity* (New York: Oxford University Press, 1983) 8–9; D. Berger, "Anti-Semitism: An Overview," in D. Berger, ed., *History and Hate: The Dimensions of Anti-Semitism* (Philadelphia: Jewish Publication Society, 1986) 3–14; S. J. D. Cohen, "'Anti-Semitism' in Antiquity: The Problem of Definition," in Berger, ed., *History and Hate*, 43–47.

It must be admitted by all objective historians and theologians that tolerant and civil "anti" sentiments flowing from any firm religious conviction are beyond the capacity for historians to pronounce a final verdict regarding truth. Just as an orthodox Jew, *by definition*, must think that Christianity is wrong at some level (and Jesus Christ not God's sole agent of salvation), so an orthodox Christian, *by definition*, must think that any expression of Judaism is wrong at some level

exercised especially by early Christians who thought rejecting Jesus as Messiah was abandoning God's covenant with Israel;[5] *Jew* for those who are Abraham's biological descendants; and *Israel* for God's covenantal people, whether Jewish or Christian (as might be seen in the discussion about the new or true Israel).[6] We can never emphasize enough that earliest, Jewish Christianity did not envisage itself as a new religion, but as a true manifestation of Judaism.[7]

---

if it excludes Jesus Christ as God's sole agent of salvation. So also, Hagner, *Jewish Reclamation*, 290–92; and with serious qualifications, D. R. A. Hare, "The Rejection of the Jews in the Synoptic Gospels and Acts," in A. Davies, ed., *Anti-Semitism and the Foundations of Christianity* (New York: Paulist, 1979) 27–47, here 41–42. The point I make, however, is that this kind of argument of truth falls short of final historical proof. Faith is an integral part of all religion. The problem of anti-Semitism, as I see it, is *how* Christians have expressed their disagreement with Judaism, not *that* they disagree. The right to disagree is assumed; the means of disagreement has boundaries of decency. Toleration and even civil evaluation of differences is one thing; obliteration and even the pretense of denial of differences is another. In effect, there are two possible responses: confession of pluralism (Judaism and Christianity are both truth) or the uncomfortable mutual existence of radical difference (Judaism and Christianity are not both truth). An example of the former is C. M. Williamson, *Has God Rejected His People? Anti-Judaism in the Christian Church* (Nashville: Abingdon, 1982); see also the more recent book, C. M. Williamson and R. J. Allen, *Interpreting Difficult Texts: Anti-Judaism and Christian Preaching* (Philadelphia: Trinity Press International, 1989); two examples of the latter, one Christian and one Jewish, are R. I. Vasholz, "Is the New Testament Anti-Semitic?" *Presbyterion* 11 (1985) 118–23, esp. 122–23; S. Sandmel, *We Jews and You Christians: An Inquiry into Attitudes* (Philadelphia: J. B. Lippincott, 1967).

5. I, for one, cannot understand why Samuel Sandmel, after arguing that "anti-Semitism" (as commonly understood, i.e., as racial prejudice) is not found in the New Testament, decides that "anti-Semitism" is still to be preferred over "anti-Judaism." This use of language that provokes disturbing reactions on the part of almost all Christians and certainly all Jews is most unfortunate. See his *Anti-Semitism in the New Testament?* (Philadelphia: Fortress, 1978) xxi. Throughout his book then he finds "anti-Semitism" in the New Testament (which he understands as "anti-Judaism"). The same kind of fuzziness in definition mars the otherwise helpful article of D. Patte, "Anti-Semitism in the New Testament. Confronting the Dark Side of Paul's and Matthew's Teaching," *Chicago Theological Seminary Register* 78 (1988) 31–52, esp. 32–35. The distinction made by Patte between the "intention" of a text and its "effects" is quite useful and has been explored further, from a reader-response angle, by A. Reinhartz, "The New Testament and Anti-Judaism: A Literary-Critical Approach," *JES* 25 (1988) 524–37. It is now customary to argue that the term "anti-Semitism" refers only to racial bigotry (i.e., it is "Jew-hatred") and not religious disagreement (which can be quite civil, regardless of how deep-seated the differences might be), and that "anti-Judaism" is the term preferred for Christian (or whatever) disagreement with Judaism over questions of religious truth. I prefer, however, not to speak of "anti-Judaism" because I am not sure the earliest Christians would agree with this either. The early Jewish Christians, it seems to me, thought of themselves as true Jews and saw nonmessianic Jews as false Jews. But these early Jewish Christians saw themselves, then, as for Judaism (defined messianically). Thus, they were "anti–nonmessianic Judaism" or "anti–disobedient Judaism" but not simply "anti-Judaism" (which kind?). See the helpful comments of Johnson, "Anti-Jewish Slander," 423–30.

6. Although there is dispute over whether Matthew would have agreed with seeing the church as the "true" or "new" Israel (see below), few dispute the view that the early church did eventually define itself as the true successor of Israel, effecting a clear line between the physical (Jew) and the religious (Israel). I know of no better way to express this ideological development than to use "true" or "new" Israel. "True" pertains to continuity, to remnant; "new" pertains to salvation-history fulfillment and to Christology, as well as to discontinuity. On the development of this identification, see P. Richardson, *Israel in the Apostolic Church* (SNTSMS 10; Cambridge: Cambridge University Press, 1969).

7. See G. Lindeskog, "Anfänge des jüdisch-christlichen Problems: Ein programmatischer Ent-

## Matthew's Supposed Anti-Semitism

In spite of recent (especially Jewish) scholarship's near consensus that the New Testament is generally not anti-Semitic,[8] it remains a part of critical scholarship that Matthew was surely anti-Judaistic if not anti-Semitic. At the least, some of Matthew's statements (e.g., 27:25) are for many an embarrassment to modern Christian sensitivities.[9] In fact, some scholars would contend that Matthew is "anti-Semitic" in the technical, racial sense. Lloyd Gaston has said,

> There is a great deal in Christian theology which needs to be rethought after Auschwitz, and one good place to begin is with Matthew.

---

wurf," in E. Bammel, C. K. Barrett, and W. D. Davies, eds., *Donum Gentilicium: New Testament Studies in Honour of David Daube* (Oxford: Clarendon, 1978) 255–75; see also J. D. G. Dunn, *Unity and Diversity in the New Testament: An Inquiry into the Character of Earliest Christianity* (Philadelphia: Westminster, 1977) 235–66.

8. See the abundance of positive remarks and evaluations made by Jewish scholars regarding Jesus (and the Gospels in general) in Hagner, *Jewish Reclamation*. Above all, see L. H. Feldman, "Is the New Testament?" An exception is D. Flusser, "Two Anti-Jewish Montages in Matthew," *Immanuel* 5 (1975) 37–45. A noted Roman Catholic, D. J. Harrington, concurs with the modern tendency to deny the presence of anti-Semitism in the New Testament: "It makes no sense to call Matthew anti-Semitic or anti-Jewish" (see D. J. Harrington, "A Dangerous Text: Matthew and Judaism," *Canadian Catholic Review* 7 [1989] 135–42, here 142).

9. See the fine posing of the main issues in S. Légasse, "L'antijudaïsme dans l'Évangile selon Matthieu," in *L'Évangile selon Matthieu: Rédaction et Théologie* (BETL 29; Gembloux: Duculot, 1972) 417–28, esp. 417. Including Légasse, the more recent studies dealing specifically and critically with Matthew and anti-Semitism/anti-Judaism are Sandmel, *Anti-Semitism*, 49–70; Hare, "Rejection"; Freyne, "Vilifying the Other"; E. Buck, "Anti-Judaic Sentiments in the Passion Narrative according to Matthew," in P. Richardson, S. G. Wilson, and D. Granskou, eds., *Anti-Judaism in Early Christianity* (Studies in Christianity and Judaism/Études sur le christianisme et le judaïsme; 2 vols.; Waterloo, Ont.: Wilfrid Laurier Univ. Press, 1986) 1.165–80; B. Przybylski, "The Setting of Matthean Anti-Judaism," in Richardson, Wilson, and Granskou, eds., *Anti-Judaism*, 1.181–200; V. Mora, *Le refus d'Israël: Matthieu 27, 25* (LD 124; Paris: Cerf, 1986); E. A. Russell, "'Antisemitism' in the Gospel of St. Matthew," *IBS* 8 (1986) 183–96; A.-J. Levine, *The Social and Ethnic Dimensions of Matthean Salvation History* (Studies in the Bible and Early Christianity 14; Lewiston/Queenston: Edwin Mellen Press, 1988); E. E. Johnson ("Jews and Christians in the New Testament: John, Matthew, and Paul," *Reformed Review* 42 [1988] 113–28) illustrates the importance of context in which comments about Jews and Christians function in the writings of John, Matthew, and Paul; see also Harrington, "Dangerous Text"; F. A. Niedner, Jr., "Rereading Matthew on Jerusalem and Judaism," *BTB* 19 (1989) 43–47 (the decisive weakness of Niedner's rereading is the absence of an explanation of the destruction of Jerusalem in the context of Matthew's positive perception of Judaism); G. N. Stanton, *A Gospel for a New People: Studies in Matthew* (Edinburgh: T. and T. Clark, 1992) 146–68, from whom I have learned much that forms the bases of this chapter.

See also F. W. Burnett, "Exposing the Implied Author in Matthew: The Characterization of God as Father" (paper delivered before the Literary Aspects of the Gospels and Acts Group of the SBL, Chicago, 1988). Two quotations reveal his essential positions: "The narrator and the character of Jesus, as reliable voices for the implied author, seek to manipulate the reader into a discursive position where he or she will accept the exclusiveness of Jesus' sonship and will say 'our father' with the disciples. When the reader does this, he or she is in effect cursing 'the Jews' and joining the father's cause against them" (p. 15). And, "But, most importantly, the implied author of Matthew will be exposed for what it is: an old Wizard of Oz, blowing smoke and whistles, pushing buttons, and, through the loud speaker of its reliable character, passing off as objective truth the most subjective and ideological discourse imaginable about 'the Jews'" (p. 16).

> For many, Matthew's theology of *Unheilsgeschichte* for Israel is simply unacceptable. We can be grateful to redaction criticism for underlining more clearly this theological stance [Matthew's anti-Semitism] *so that we can learn to avoid it.* Preachers expounding a Matthean pericope should ignore the context and play down the Matthean specifics in favor of the earlier Synoptic tradition. . . . If the redaction critics are right, then the redactor Matthew, as distinguished from the traditions he transmits, can no longer be part of the personal canon of many.[10]

This statement is perhaps extreme but poignantly presents us with the dilemma of this book and with a serious question facing New Testament, especially Christian (if one believes in the authority of the New Testament), scholars: Is the New Testament, here Matthew, anti-Semitic?[11]

The evidence adduced for supposed anti-Semitism in Matthew is not hard to find (either in the Gospel or its commentators).[12] One thinks of Matt 3:7-10; 6:1-18; 15:1-20; 21:33-46; 23:1–26:2; and 27:24-25 as representative of Matthew's polemic. In addition, numerous instances of Matthew's own redactional hand betray this polemic (e.g., 12:11-12; 16:2-3; 21:45).[13] Matthew's criticism of non-messianic Judaism, especially the legitimacy of the authority of the Pharisees, is

---

10. L. Gaston, "The Messiah of Israel as Teacher of the Gentiles: The Setting of Matthew's Christology," *Int* 29 (1975) 24–40, here 39–40; emphasis added. On p. 40 he speaks of Matthew "who taught the Church to hate Israel." Although Gaston surveys the motif of Israel's rejection competently, the tone of the article is rhetorically designed to set up his conclusion that Matthew is anti-Semitic.

11. It may be assumed here that anti-Semitism existed in the ancient world in some forms, though scholars differ here, especially when nuances and analogues are needed. Of the numerous studies on anti-Semitism in the ancient world, see J. L. Daniel, "Anti-Semitism in the Hellenistic-Roman Period," *JBL* 98 (1979) 45-65, who undoubtedly has overstated the amount of anti-Semitism; the most complete study is Gager, *Origins;* for his bibliographical survey of the material, see J. G. Gager, "Judaism as Seen by Outsiders," in R. A. Kraft and G. W. E. Nickelsburg, eds., *Early Judaism and Its Modern Interpreters* (Philadelphia: Fortress; Atlanta: Scholars Press, 1986) 99–116, covering both New Testament studies and pagan evidence; see also the fine collection of the evidence in L. H. Feldman, "Anti-Semitism in the Ancient World," in Berger, ed., *History and Hate,* 15–42. But see also the hard-hitting plea of Cohen ("Anti-Semitism in Antiquity"), who argues that modern scholars who see anti-Semitism in antiquity are largely retrojecting a later phenomenon onto antiquity.

12. In addition to Gaston and Sandmel, others who see Matthew as "anti-Semitic" to some degree include (here it is difficult for me to discern whether it is "anti-Judaism" or "anti-Semitism," and so I must infer on the basis of tone and the scholar's view of the moral and religious legitimacy of Matthew's stance): Hare, "Rejection," 32–46; Cook, "Anti-Judaism," 131–32; N. A. Beck, *Mature Christianity: The Recognition and Repudiation of the Anti-Jewish Polemic of the New Testament* (Selinsgrove, Pa.: Susquehanna University Press, 1985) 136-65; Flusser, "Anti-Jewish Montages"; Burnett, "Exposing the Implied Author."

13. Several scholars compare Matthew with his sources, observing Matthew's harsher treatment of the Jews; see, e.g., Sandmel, *Anti-Semitism,* 49–70; Hare, "Rejection," 32–40; Beck, *Mature Christianity,* 136–61 (a complete survey). Hare, however, minimizes both Mark's and Luke's prophetic and Jewish-Christian anti-Judaism as a foil against which Matthew may be compared. From the literary-critical angle, F. W. Burnett has argued for an essentially anti-Judaism stance; see "Exposing the Implied Author." For a detailed analysis of the Pharisees in Matthew, particularly how Matthew handles and redacts his traditions, see my "New Shepherds for Israel: An Historical and Critical Study of Matthew 9:35-11:1" (Ph.D. diss., University of Nottingham, 1986) 30–71. See also D. E. Garland, *The Intention of Matthew 23 (NovT* 52; Leiden: E. J. Brill, 1979).

certainly acute and active (e.g., 1:1-17; 28:11-15), and it forms the socioreligious context from which the First Gospel emerges.[14]

In spite of the numerous studies that have shown Matthew's heated reaction to the Pharisees, who are often seen as a type of Jewish leadership in general, it is not accurate to say that Matthew's only polemic is with the leadership.[15] To be sure, the bulk of Matthew's polemic is targeted at the leadership, especially the Pharisees. However true this may be, Matthew nonetheless ties larger portions of the Jewish people into his polemic against the Pharisees. As an instance, one might take 23:13-33, with its vituperative attacks on the "Pharisees and scribes," and then notice how the judgment expressed at the end is directed at an even larger group: Jerusalem, the Temple, and "this generation" (23:34-39; 24:34). However focused Matthew's attack might be on the Pharisees, those leaders do not exhaust Matthew's concern; disobedient Jews, understood here as those who reject Jesus as Messiah and who follow the leaders who reject Jesus, are also culpable (e.g., see 11:2-19, 25-27 with 11:20-24; 27:25).[16] Thus, it is inaccurate to infer that, since (as it is supposed) Matthew's polemic is directed solely against the Pharisees, he cannot be charged with anti-Semitism (only anti-Pharisaism). Matthew's complaint is broader.

But the crucial question that we seek to address is how this polemic is to be explained. Was it racial, social, or religious? Or was it a combination of factors?[17] Is it fair to say that Matthew reflects some "astonishing animosity" with the natural inference that animosity implies racism?[18]

---

14. See now the exceptional commentary of W. D. Davies and D. C. Allison, Jr., *The Gospel according to St. Matthew* (ICC rev.; 3 vols.; Edinburgh: T. and T. Clark, 1988-), for a thorough explanation of Matthew in this context. Many writers on Matthew and the Jewish conflict have expressed the same, e.g., Sandmel, *Anti-Semitism*, 49–51; J. Koenig, *Jews and Christians in Dialogue: New Testament Foundations* (Philadelphia: Westminster, 1979) 82–87; McKnight, "New Shepherds"; W. A. Meeks, "Breaking Away: Three New Testament Pictures of Christianity's Separation from the Jewish Communities," in Neusner and Frerichs, *"To See Ourselves,"* 93–115, here 108–14; Buck, "Anti-Judaic Sentiments," 176–79; Przybylski, "Setting"; Harrington, "Dangerous Text," 138–40.

15. So, e.g., Koenig, *Jews and Christians,* 82–96, who contends that, whereas Jesus fought only with the leadership, Matthew has let this spill over onto the entire Jewish people on a couple of occasions. This, he says, is the consequence of the bitter battles Matthew's church is experiencing. See also Cook, "Anti-Judaism," 128 (only redactional elements are unacceptable; Jesus called, in love, for repentance). An emphasis on the leaders can be seen in Levine, *Social and Ethnic Dimensions;* see also Mora, *Le refus,* 83–118, 128–32.

16. For a similar understanding of the last discourse with regard to the Jewish people, see F. W. Burnett, *The Testament of Jesus Sophia: A Redaction-critical Study of the Eschatological Discourse in Matthew* (Washington, D.C.: University Press of America, 1981), app. 1 (pp. 404–11). However, I cannot agree with his method of seeing the same referent (people in history) in each reference to "crowds" (see below, n. 64).

17. I do not mean to suggest that what may not have been "anti-Semitic" in intention became "anti-Semitic" in the hands of some (tragically) mistaken interpreters. See, e.g., the nuances brought out by D. M. Crossan, "Anti-Semitism and the Gospel," *TS* 26 (1965) 189–214.

18. These are the words of Sandmel, *Anti-Semitism,* who states: "Matthew is a mixture of sublimity and astonishing animosity" (p. 68). He then states that Matthew has reworked Mark, "openly expressing anti-Semitism." I assume that Sandmel means "anti-Judaism," but, when he uses "anti-Semitism" in the context of "animosity," the important difference becomes blurred.

## The Thesis

Matthew's polemic is with a particular form of Judaism, namely nonmessianic Judaism, especially as led by the scribes and Pharisees, and that polemic is motivated religiously and socially, but not racially.[19] In short, I contend that Matthew believes that Jesus of Nazareth is Messiah, the Son of God, who inaugurates the kingdom of heavens through his public ministry (teaching, preaching, healing; see 4:23; 9:35), and who confronts Israel in his own person with an eschatological decision. Because so much of Judaism, led as it was by the Pharisees and scribes (in Matthew's perspective), rejected Jesus as Messiah, Matthew's Jesus warns of a coming judgment by God that will be visibly demonstrated in the sacking of Jerusalem. This judgment illustrates the withdrawal of the national privilege of the Jewish people (21:43; 23:1–25:46).[20] In maintaining God's own faithfulness to his covenant with Israel, Matthew contends, God establishes a new people, the church (comprising those who obey Jesus). This new people of God is related to God through the new covenant Jesus proleptically establishes in the Last Supper and is, in Matthew's view, the new and true Israel of God.

Matthew's viewpoint, then, is that of a loyal Jew who believes that a new epoch in salvation-history dawned in Jesus Christ and that this new era called forth a decision. The consequence of this decision effects a radical separation of Jews into true and false Israel; true Israel is the new Israel. The difference between earliest Christianity and Judaism then was as much hermeneutical (how the author understands Scripture's unfolding in history) as anything.[21]

---

19. Thus, we believe that understanding the theology as well as the social and rhetorical context of Matthew alleviates the harshness and moral appropriateness of Matthew's polemic. Others have sought to alleviate Matthew's rhetoric in different ways: (1) by appealing to the inspiration of Scripture and its truthfulness; (2) by seeing Matthew's polemic as entirely directed against leaders and the elites; (3) by appealing to Jewish prophetic criticisms as the background; (4) by blaming Christians but not Christian Scriptures; (5) by positing a difference between Jesus, with his apostles, and the evangelist; and (6) most frequently by appealing to the socially charged setting of Matthew's Gospel (see especially the excellent essay of Przybylski, "Setting"; see also Harrington, "Dangerous Text"). A nuanced study of the second view can be seen in Levine, *Social and Ethnic Dimensions;* whereas Levine's thesis seeks to show that *ethnicity* moves from a Jewish, national privilege to a nonethnic universalism and that social elites are the primary focus of Matthew's criticisms, this study is more concerned with how Matthew perceives unbelieving Judaism (not Judaism as a whole). Our views, in most respects, complement one another. For an example of the fifth view, see M. Lowe, "Real and Imagined Anti-Jewish Elements in the Synoptic Gospels and Acts," *JES* 24 (1987) 267–84. See also M. J. Cook, "Confronting New Testament Attitudes on Jews and Judaism: Four Jewish Perspectives," *Chicago Theological Seminary Register* 78 (1988) 3–30; Cook expounds various Jewish readings of the New Testament.

20. This fits Hare's third degree of anti-Judaism: Gentilizing anti-Judaism. See "Rejection," 38–40.

21. Early Christian hermeneutic has been subjected to careful analysis in the last thirty years. One of the most recent studies can be found in D. Juel, *Messianic Exegesis: Christological Interpretation of the Old Testament in Early Christianity* (Philadelphia: Fortress, 1988). In spite of many overly radical statements, Rosemary Ruether correctly observes a hermeneutical foundation for the differences between Christianity and Judaism; see her *Faith and Fratricide: The Theological Roots of Anti-Semitism* (New York: Seabury, 1974) 64–66, 78–79. See also Harrington, "Dangerous Text," 140–42.

In saying this, however, I do not mean to suggest that the difference between Judaism and Christianity was simply christological or ideological. This would be a serious historical reductionism. Rather, the theological convictions of an author like Matthew led to actions that gave birth to social and religious tensions. Thus, I would like to suggest that theology (ideology) giving birth to behavior (praxis) generated the parting of the ways. Put directly, belief that God had fulfilled history in Jesus as Messiah (the christological factor)[22] and in the new people of God led to such actions as evangelism of Jews, condemnation of Jews, violation of traditional customs (e.g., Sabbath, purity laws), and the formation of splinter groups that met outside traditional Jewish authority. It was these *actions*,[23] regardless of their theological foundations, that sparked an inevitable parting of the ways.[24]

In this chapter I will examine Matthew's theological standpoint under two main categories: first, Matthew's theological foundations; second, Matthew's polemical implications. Finally, my conclusion will summarize Matthew's polemical hermeneutic.

## Theological Foundations

The most significant place to begin understanding Matthew's polemic with nonmessianic Judaism is his presupposition that God has directed history to consummate it in Jesus Messiah, son of Abraham and son of David (1:1-17; 5:17-20; 21:33-46). For Matthew, the fulfillment of salvation-history takes place in Jesus Christ, and therefore the fulfillment of the people of God realizes itself in the new people of God, the church (16:18; 18:17).[25] These twin theological foundations, fulfillment in Jesus and fulfillment in the new people of God, form the basis for Matthew's polemic with nonmessianic Judaism. I believe that Matthew sees continuity in his theme of fulfillment and discontinuity in his theme of an exclusive new Israel (i.e., the church). If God has inaugurated his salvation in Jesus and if Jesus has created a new people of God, then it logically follows

---

22. See Richardson, *Israel*.

23. It goes without saying that other movements with perhaps analogous belief systems that did not act out their views in ways contrary to Jewish traditions were not as volatile in Judaism. Thus, it is the praxis (the application of one's hermeneutic) that led to eruption. It must not be thought, however, that there were no ideas in earliest Christianity (e.g., worship of Jesus alongside God) that did not generate serious tension. In general, see Hare, "Rejection," 31–32; on the worship of Jesus and its early origins as well as the tensions it created for monotheism and Judaism, see the exceptional analysis of L. W. Hurtado, *One God, One Lord: Early Christian Devotion and Ancient Jewish Monotheism* (Philadelphia: Fortress, 1988).

24. P. Richardson is surely correct when he points out that there is both continuity and discontinuity between Israel and the church, and the issue is spelling out the lines of both. See his *Israel*, 4–8, 188–94. On p. 194 he says: "it [the church of Matthew] is very conscious of continuity between itself and the old entity. It is not a *tertium genus*."

25. On fulfillment in Matthew, see esp. R. T. France, *Matthew: Evangelist and Teacher* (Grand Rapids, Mich.: Zondervan, 1989) 166–278; see also Niedner, "Rereading Matthew," 43–44.

that to reject Jesus as Messiah and to oppose the new people of God are sins
that incur God's disapproval. In fact, for Matthew, this rejection explains the
destruction of Jerusalem in 70 CE.

In examining Matthew's theology, I begin by looking at Matthew's theme
of fulfillment in Jesus and the church. The first section will look at the Moses
motif and then at Matt 5:17-20.

## Fulfillment in Jesus

One of the fulfillment themes of Matthew is how *Mosaic* Jesus is presented.
The Moses motif in Matthew reveals one of the ways Matthew depicts Jesus
as the fulfillment of Israel's history. In particular, apart from 5:1-2; 8:1–9:34;
11:25-30;[26] 17:2-9; 28:16-20,[27] it is the birth narrative itself (1:18-2:23)[28] that
especially colors the life of Jesus in images drawn from Jewish traditions about
Moses. This motif speaks then of Jesus being a new Moses.

Thus, as the tradition has it that God appeared to Amaram(es) (Moses' father)
in his sleep to reveal his sovereign control over pharaoh's desire to exterminate
the Jews (Josephus *Ant.* 2.9.1-3 §201-16),[29] so an angel of the Lord appears
in a dream to Joseph, the father of Jesus, with a similar message of comfort
and control (Matt 1:18-21). Furthermore, the notion of Joseph naming his son
"Jesus, for he will save his people from their sins" (1:21),[30] reflects a similar
tradition about Moses. Josephus tells us that God told Amaram(es) that Moses
would "deliver the Hebrew race from their bondage in Egypt" (*Ant.* 2.9.3 §216).
This is how Matthew often describes the ministry of Jesus—as a saving mission
(8:25; 9:21-22; 14:30; [18:11]; 27:42).

As pharaoh gave orders to exterminate all the Jewish boys (Exod 1:15-22;
see Josephus, *Ant.* 2.9.2 §205-9), so Herod the Great ordered Jewish boys to be
killed (Matt 2:16-18).[31] And, as Josephus points out, the former potentate acted
when he learned of the future redemption of the Jews through a prophetlike

---

26. See esp. D. C. Allison, Jr., "Two Notes on a Key Text: Matt. XI.25-30," *JTS* 39 (1988)
472–80; W. D. Davies and D. C. Allison, Jr., *Matthew* (forthcoming), vol. 2, ad loc; I am grateful to
Dale Allison for kindly allowing me to read this portion of their commentary before publication.

27. For an older analysis, see W. D. Davies, *The Setting of the Sermon on the Mount* (Cambridge:
Cambridge University Press, 1964) 14–108; Davies-Allison, *Matthew*, contains numerous instances
of this motif; France, *Matthew: Evangelist*, 185–91. But see also T. L. Donaldson, *Jesus on the
Mountain: A Study in Matthean Theology* (JSNTSup 8; Sheffield: JSOT, 1985).

28. A neat listing of the parallels can be found in Davies-Allison, *Matthew*, 1.192–93. I am
indebted to their list in what follows.

29. Josephus, *Ant.* 2.9.1 §201-4 goes considerably beyond the text of Exod 1:8-14.

30. This popular etymology (*Yeshua, yeshua:* Yahweh is salvation, salvation) was recognized
outside Palestine (e.g., Philo [*Mut. nom.* 121] clarifies why Moses changed the name of Hoshea
["he is saved"] to Joshua ["safety of the Lord," i.e., who has been saved]). But see R. H. Gundry
(*Matthew: A Commentary on His Literary and Theological Art* [Grand Rapids, Mich.: Eerdmans,
1982] 23), who draws attention to specific Old Testament texts (Ps 130:8; see Judg 13:5). For
further support of the popularity of this etymology, see Davies-Allison, *Matthew*, 209.

31. On this incident of extreme cruelty, see esp. R. T. France, "Herod and the Children of

scribe (*Ant.* 2.9.2 §205; see *Tg. Ps.-J.* Exod 1:15); correspondingly, Herod acts when he learns through the Magi, the chief priests, and scribes that a baby destined to be king had been born (Matt 2:1-12, 16-18).

As Moses was providentially preserved from pharaoh's destruction, once through Jewish intrigue (Exod 2:1-10; see Josephus, *Ant.* 2.9.4 §217-27)[32] and once through escape (Exod 2:11-22; see Josephus, *Ant.* 2.11.1 §254-57), so Jesus was preserved by God's protection from Herod the Great (2:13-15). And, just as Moses was commanded by God to return to Egypt after the death of pharaoh (Exod 4:18-20), so an angel of the Lord appeared to Joseph in a dream and told him to return the child to Palestine (Matt 2:19-21). In particular, the wording of the LXX in Exod 4:19 and Matt 2:20 is almost identical, confirming the author's design to paint Jesus like Moses. This kind of evidence supports the conclusion that Matthew wants to portray Jesus as a new Moses.

These several examples show that Jesus is like Moses. What took place in Moses' life takes place in Jesus' life. In fact, in the scheme of Matthew's hermeneutical grid, because Jesus is the Messiah, it can be said that anything that happened to Moses can happen to Jesus because Jesus fulfills the Moses type. Matthew's hermeneutic (a typological method) permits the patterns to be found.[33] Jesus may be Mosaic; but just as he is greater than the Temple (12:6), greater than Jonah (12:41), and greater than Solomon (12:42), so also is he greater than Moses by virtue of his sonship, mighty acts, and sacrificial death.[34] In Matthew's scheme of history, Jesus completes the work of Moses.[35] In the words of W. D. Davies, "He is not Moses come as Messiah, if we may so put it, so much as Messiah, Son of Man, Emmanuel, who has absorbed the Mosaic function."[36] This theological foundation forms the basis for part of Matthew's polemic: namely, because fulfillment has taken place in the person and ministry of Jesus as Messiah, salvation is granted only to those who recognize God's hand in Jesus Messiah (see 12:28, 31-32). And this theological foundation also puts nonmessianic Judaism in a vulnerable position, virtually forcing its leaders to accuse the new movement of disloyalty to the traditions of Israel.

I turn now to a text that speaks directly of this theme of fulfillment, Matt

---

Bethlehem," *NovT* 21 (1979) 98–120; idem, "The 'Massacre of the Innocents'–Fact or Fiction?" in *Studia Biblica 1978 II: Papers on the Gospels* (Sheffield: JSOT, 1980) 83–94.

32. Josephus tells of more tales that evince God's protection; *Ant.* 2.9.6-7 §228-37.

33. On Matthew's hermeneutic, see France, *Matthew: Evangelist,* 166–205. Matthew's exegetical procedure, it cannot be emphasized enough, is a "messianic exegesis." On this in general, see Juel, *Messianic Exegesis;* C. A. Evans, "The Function of the Old Testament in the New," in S. McKnight, ed., *Introducing New Testament Interpretation* (Grand Rapids, Mich.: Baker, 1989) 163–93.

34. Though I cannot agree with J. D. Kingsbury's one-sided emphasis on the Son of God in Matthew's Christology, he is nonetheless surely accurate in pointing out that Mosaic motifs are overshadowed by Son motifs; see *Matthew: Structure, Christology, Kingdom* (2d ed.; Minneapolis: Fortress, 1989) 89–92.

35. See here D. R. A. Hare, *The Theme of Jewish Persecution of Christians in the Gospel according to St. Matthew* (SNTSMS 6; Cambridge: Cambridge University Press, 1967) 5–6.

36. Davies, *Setting,* 93.

5:17-20. Although greatly disputed, these verses reveal several facets of Matthew's concept of salvation-history and hence provide the grids through which he filters information about nonmessianic Judaism.[37] The structure of this pericope is significant for interpretation: (1) a statement of fulfillment (5:17) is followed (2) by an explanation of that statement of fulfillment (5:18). Thus, Jesus did not come to abolish the Law or the prophets because he has come to fulfill them (5:17); rather, the Law and the prophets are permanent as fulfilled by Jesus (5:18). Because Matthew's concern is not with the theoretical relationship of the Law to Jesus' teachings but with practice, Matthew moves (3) to the implication of the fulfilled Law for practical living: it must be obeyed and taught (5:19). In other words, (4) the righteousness of the Pharisees and scribes, following as it does the Mosaic, unfulfilled Law, is insufficient. The righteousness that is acceptable to God, according to Jesus, is a righteousness that conforms to the teachings of Jesus (the fulfilled Law [5:20]).

The logical workings of the conjunctions in this passage move from an anacoluthic statement (5:17) to a reason (*gar* [5:18]), to an inferential "therefore" (5:19), to a second reason (*gar* [5:20]).[38] The implication of the structure is this: because a new age has dawned in Jesus, the teacher of the fulfilled Law (5:17-18), a new ethic also is given to Israel (5:19-20). This bridges the gap about which we are concerned: salvation-historical fulfillment in Jesus' teachings brings with it a new people of God who follow those teachings.

The nature of this fulfillment requires some explanation. The evidence for *pleroo* in Matthew suggests that this term speaks not of "restating" the Law or even "clarifying," nor of "establishing" the Law or of "doing" the Law, but rather of "consummating" (see below) the Law in the person and teaching of Jesus. Jesus is saying that he, not Moses, is the focal point of the Law, and he is, does, and teaches the will of God. The Law and the prophets had as their *telos* the Messiah and his teachings. This is abundantly demonstrated in the use of "fulfill" in the Old Testament patterns drawn upon in the birth narratives (1:23; 2:6, 15, 18, 23).

By the expression "consummating the Law" I mean both discontinuity and continuity: Jesus does something permanently irreversible to the Law to the effect that his followers do not find their moral guidelines primarily in the Law of Moses. And yet, the teaching of Jesus does not abolish that Law by ripping it from the Bible. Rather, the Mosaic Law is perfected and comes to completion in the teachings and person of Jesus.[39] Moses' Law is not done away with

---

37. For an excellent survey of the exegesis in this light, see Hagner, *Jewish Reclamation*, 122–26.

38. In addition, observe that both of the "reason" propositions (5:18, 20) begin also with "I say to you."

39. A useful illustrative analogy of this is the relationship of a typewriter to a computer: whereas the computer consummates all that the typewriter ever could be, all that the typewriter could do is certainly found in a computer. And, apart from glitches and breakdowns, once one has a computer one no longer has need for a typewriter (except as found in the computer).

in Jesus; rather, it is transcended and yet preserved (9:17) in its perfection in Jesus.[40]

The implications of these conclusions are substantial. It is Matthew's conviction that the Law of Moses is no longer the final authority for the people of God because the Law of Moses has been consummated and transcended in Jesus: the Law and prophets pointed toward him; he has come; and now he has revealed God's will. The Law and the prophets are not abolished; rather, they are now completely fulfilled in Jesus. Jesus is the fulfillment of God's designs, and therefore history makes a radical step forward in Jesus. One might say at this point that Matthew sees in Jesus a *new* Israel, the remnant of God. This new Israel is in continuity with the old Israel inasmuch as it also is rooted in Moses now come to fruition in Jesus. There is no place in Matthew's mind for a "new religion"; rather, it is the old made perfect through fulfillment.

And it is this understanding of fulfillment that leads to my second point: namely, just as Jesus is the fulfillment of Hebrew history, so those who perceive him as that fulfillment form the nucleus for the new people of God. This new people Matthew calls "the church" (16:18; 18:17).[41]

## Fulfillment in the New People of God, the Church

From the outset of the Gospel, Matthew develops the theme of the establishment of the true people of God who find their salvation in Jesus Messiah. Thus, the angel of the Lord informs Joseph that Mary, his virgin betrothed, will give birth to a son and "he will save his people from their sins" (1:21).[42] In light of Matthew's *theology* of the establishment of the church (see the developments in 7:21-27; 10:5-6; 16:17-20; 18:17; 21:43), I take "his people" of 1:21 to refer to more than Jewish Israel (whatever the earlier traditions might be taken to have meant). At 1:21, then, Matthew states that Jesus has come to form a new people of God by forgiving their sins. This can imply only that Jews per se are

40. For this view, see especially R. Banks, "Matthew's Understanding of the Law: Authenticity and Interpretation in Matthew 5:17-20," *JBL* 93 (1974) 226–42; idem, *Jesus and the Law in the Synoptic Tradition* (SNTSMS 28; Cambridge: Cambridge Univ. Press, 1975); D. J. Moo, "Jesus and the Authority of the Mosaic Law," *JSNT* 20 (1984) 3–49; R. A. Guelich, *The Sermon on the Mount: A Foundation for Understanding* (Waco, Tex.: Word, 1982) 134–74; Davies-Allison, *Matthew,* 481–503.

41. D. R. A. Hare, accurately I think, points to the rejection of Jewish nationalism as the second contributing factor in the parting of the ways (see his *Jewish Persecution,* 7–8). It follows that the third factor is the inclusion of Gentiles (pp. 8–13). The logical connection between Christology and ecclesiology is shown in Freyne, "Vilifying the Other," 122–23.

42. Disputes have arisen over the referent of "his." Whereas some take it to refer exclusively to the Jewish nation as God's covenant people, and imply that this is the natural theme of Jewish expectation, others, and I agree with them, take it to refer to the new people of God, the church, comprising both Gentiles and Jews, a new people that is formed on the basis of a new covenant with Israel. For the former view, see e.g., U. Luz, *Matthew* (3 vols.; trans. W. C. Linss; Minneapolis: Augsburg, 1989) 1.121; J. Gnilka, *Das Matthäusevangelium* (2 vols.; HTKNT; Freiburg-Basel-Wien: Herder, 1986) 1.19; for the latter view, see Davies-Allison, *Matthew,* 210.

no longer the exclusive people of God; a new people is being formed by Jesus. This new people includes some Jews, but not all Jews. Those included are those who are forgiven by Jesus (his followers).

The *universal* scope of this new people of God highlights the newness of this people.[43] What was formerly essentially national and racial becomes now (at least by Matthew's time) predominantly international and interracial.[44] From the women in the genealogy (1:1-17) and the arrival of the Magi (2:1-12) to the centurion at the cross (27:54) and the command to disciple the nations (28:16-20), Matthew takes great pains to emphasize the universal dimension of salvation and the new people of God.[45] And this theme is often on the surface of redactional passages in Matthew or in passages reworked by Matthew (1:1, 2; 4:12-16; 4:23-25; 5:13-16; 6:7-8; 10:18; 12:18, 21; 13:24-30, 36-43; 13:31-32; 21:43; 22:1-14; 24:9-14; 25:31-46; 26:6-13). These passages, undoubtedly, form a contrast with some particularistic passages (e.g., 10:5-6; 15:24), but for Matthew, this kind of particularism serves a larger universalism: Jesus is sent to Israel so that the nations can be reached.[46]

Entry into the new people of God, the church, is made by coming to Jesus (11:25-30) and obeying his commands. If I was accurate in stating above that the ethics of Moses have been consummated and transcended in Jesus, then it follows that only the followers of Jesus' commands are those upon whom God's favor rests (12:46-50). And a necessary obedience to Jesus is a pervasive theme in Matthew's Gospel. Thus, Jesus calls the fishermen to follow him (4:18-22), and he charges the growing circles to follow him and obey his teachings (5:17-48; 6:33; 7:21-27; 8:18-22; 12:46-50; 16:24-28; 21:28-32). They enter into table fellowship with Jesus, share his meals, and live in communion with him (9:9-

---

43. See L. Sabourin, *The Gospel according to St. Matthew* (Bandra, India: St. Paul Publications, 1982) 70–75; see also more generally Hare, *Jewish Persecution,* 8–13. On Jewish attitudes toward Gentiles, see my *A Light among the Gentiles: Jewish Missionary Activity in the Second Temple Period* (Minneapolis: Fortress, 1991).

44. I have essayed to demonstrate that Judaism was not a missionary religion during the Second Temple period in *A Light among the Gentiles.* My statement does not intend to deny the existence of gentile proselytes to Judaism.

45. Though it cannot be worked out here, I believe the First Gospel evinces a view of gentile salvation that is predominantly future-oriented—in particular, gentile salvation comes to the fore not during the time of Jesus (e.g., 10:5-6; 15:24), but especially as a result of the destruction of Jerusalem (10:18; 21:33-46; 22:1-14; 24:29-31; 28:16-20). The Great Commission of 28:16-20, however important ideologically, is not the actual moment for full gentile inclusion. Gentiles become the focus of salvation, in Matthew's theology, not so much as a result of the cross–resurrection–commission, but as a result of the revoking of Jewish privilege that does not become visibly demonstrated until 70 CE (see 21:33-46; 22:1-14; 24:29-31). On the latter passage, see esp. R. T. France, *Jesus and the Old Testament: His Application of Old Testament Passages to Himself and His Mission* (London: Tyndale, 1971) 227–39; idem, *The Gospel according to Matthew* (Tyndale New Testament Commentary; Grand Rapids, Mich.: Zondervan, 1985) 343–46. On Matthew's salvation-history, see now the most recent study in Levine, *Social and Ethnic Dimensions.*

46. On this, see T. W. Manson, *Only to the House of Israel? Jesus and the Non-Jews* (FBBS 9; Philadelphia: Fortress, 1964); D. Bosch, *Die Heidenmission in der Zukunftsschau Jesu* (ATANT 36; Zurich: Zwingli, 1959); J. Jeremias, *Jesus' Promise to the Nations* (SBT 24; London: SCM, 1958); G. B. Caird, *Jesus and the Jewish Nation* (London: Athlone, 1965).

13; 26:17-30). The Great Commission ends with the charge to teach the new disciples everything Jesus commanded (28:20). In short, for Matthew a disciple is one who is "righteous," one whose life conforms to the will of God (5:6, 10, 20; 6:1, 33), or who "does the will of God" (6:10; 7:21; 12:50; 21:43)[47] and lives in fellowship with Jesus (11:25-30).

The disciples of Jesus are occasionally presented in such a way that one thinks of them forming the leadership of a new group.[48] One can only surmise that the call of the fishermen (4:18-22) and tax collector (9:9-13) had, as its goal, the establishment of *new leaders for Israel* (understood as leading the true Israel; see 9:36 with 10:1-15). But, even if this is not clear from the fact of a call, it becomes clearer when Jesus, according to Matthew, designates certain of his followers as "apostles" (10:2-4). Their designated leadership becomes dominant in Jesus' vision of the future: they will "rule" over the twelve tribes (19:28).[49]

But the disciples in general, and those attached to Jesus along with them, are also seen as *a distinct group* within the Jewish nation. Those who follow Jesus are singled out as a special group: "For whoever does the will of my Father in heaven is my brother, and sister, and mother" (12:50). Accordingly, Jesus gives these followers new moral guidelines that frequently enough envisage a self-conscious stance vis-à-vis Judaism (see 5:1–7:29, esp. 5:3-12, 21-48; 6:1-18; 7:15-27). And this group of Jesus' followers will be targeted for persecution (5:11-12; 10:16-38; 23:34-39; 24:9-14). For Matthew, the followers of Jesus are to be seen as a special group: Matthew calls them the "church" (16:18; 18:17), "free" from the common, even covenantal, obligations to Judaism (17:24-27),[50] and a "nation" (21:43).[51] Now it can easily be said that this group of Jesus' disciples is still *within* Israel and not a separate, new religion. This, I think, is

---

47. See B. Przybylski's exceptional monograph, *Righteousness in Matthew and His World of Thought* (SNTSMS 41; Cambridge: Cambridge Univ. Press, 1980); see also H. Giesen, *Christliches Handeln: Eine redaktionskritische Untersuchung zum dikaiosynē–Begriff im Matthäus-Evangelium* (Europäische Hochschulschriften 23/181; Frankfurt am Main/Bern: Peter Lang, 1982); see also Davies-Allison, *Matthew*, 452-53, 499-500; D. R. A. Hare, *Jewish Persecution*, 130-32.

48. On the ecclesiology of Matthew, see esp. R. Schnackenburg, *The Church in the New Testament* (New York: Herder and Herder, 1968) 69-77; France, *Matthew: Evangelist*, 206-78. On the importance of rejecting Jewish leadership for the parting of the ways, see Hare, *Jewish Persecution*, 13-15.

49. Much discussion has taken place both regarding (1) when this will take place: thus, What is the meaning of the "new world" (*palingennesia*)? Is it earthly or heavenly? and (2) what is the nature of the Twelve's responsibility: Will they "judge" in the sense of "condemn," or "judge" in the sense of "rule" or "govern"? I take the latter sense, though it may include the sense of "condemning" as well; see e.g., Gundry, *Matthew*, 393; W. Grundmann, *Das Evangelium nach Matthäus* (THKNT 1; 5th ed.; Berlin: Evangelische Verlagsanstalt, 1981) 435; D. C. Allison, Jr., "Gnilka on Matthew," *Bib* 70 (1989) 536-37.

50. See R. Hummel, *Die Auseinandersetzung zwischen Kirche und Judentum im Matthäusevangelium* (Beiträge zur Evangelischen Theologie 33; Munich: Chr. Kaiser, 1966) 103-6; E. Schweizer, *The Good News according to Matthew* (Atlanta: John Knox, 1975) 355-57. I disagree with R. Walker (*Die Heilsgeschichte im ersten Evangelium* [FRLANT 91; Göttingen: Vandenhoeck and Ruprecht, 1967] 101-3) that the present shape of the text has a political (Christians vs. state powers) and not a religious (Christians vs. Judaism) concern.

51. See Hare, "Rejection," 38-39.

quite accurate. However, the category that seems to be operative for Matthew is that of the church as expressing the "true and new Israel": for Matthew, with the Twelve as the new shepherds for the new Israel, there is a movement within Judaism that has a new leader (Jesus), new shepherds replacing the Pharisees (the twelve apostles), and a new people of God (the church), inclusive of all who follow Jesus and take up his yoke. This movement is seen as the true people of God that fulfills the old (Jewish) people of God.

Furthermore, the group following Jesus seems to be so separate that it has a *special organization* (Matthew 18).[52] In spite of the apparent "egalitarianism" of Matt 23:8-12, there remains in Matthew a stubborn commitment to a functional leadership and hierarchy, beginning with the Twelve (10:2-4), led by Peter (16:13-20),[53] and pastoral leaders among the new people of God (16:13-20; 18:12-14, 15-20; 28:16-20).[54] It can be argued that there are separate leadership functions behind such terms as "prophets" (10:41; 23:34), "righteous ones" (10:41), "wise ones" (23:34), and "scribes" (13:52; 23:34). But it must also be said that Matthew presents leadership as service, not exploitation of power.[55] Whatever the precise terms used for leadership functions in Matthew's community, and the evidence is too ambiguous to be of heuristic value, it remains a fact that Matthew envisages the followers of Jesus forming a distinct group with organization, and the evidence also lends itself to the observation that Matthew sees this group as the new people of God, replacing the Jewish nation as the true and new Israel.

## Summary

Matthew's polemic with Judaism is founded ideologically then upon two theological convictions. First, Matthew's firmest conviction is that God's plan for redemption has been consummated in Jesus as Messiah. This Messiah fulfills Old Testament promise and anticipation in his own person and ministry (teaching, healing, and saving). Second, the implication of this final revelation in Jesus as Messiah is that those who hear must respond to Jesus in faith, repentance, and obedience (4:17). Those who do respond to Jesus are the new people of God, the new Israel. The newness is rooted in the epoch-forming revelation in the Messiah. But this Israel is also the true Israel because only those who follow Jesus retain their legitimate Jewish status. Further, those who do not respond

---

52. See W. Trilling, *Das wahre Israel: Studie zur Theologie des Matthäus-Evangeliums* (3d ed.; SANT 10; Munich: Kösel, 1964) 106–23.

53. On Peter in Matthew, see the study of J. D. Kingsbury, "The Figure of Peter in Matthew's Gospel as a Theological Problem," *JBL* 98 (1979) 67–83; see also R. E. Brown et al., *Peter in the New Testament* (Minneapolis: Augsburg; New York: Paulist, 1973) 75–107. The forthcoming excursus in vol. 2 of Davies-Allison, *Matthew*, points to the unique *Tradent* rôle of Peter and compares him to the image of Abraham with great promise.

54. For a defense of Matthew's egalitarianism, see E. Krentz, "Community and Character: Matthew's Vision of the Church," in SBLSP (1987) 565–73; Levine, *Social and Ethnic Dimensions*.

55. The point is made frequently in Levine, *Social and Ethnic Dimensions* (e.g., p. 11).

to the Messiah, typified by Matthew in the Pharisees, are the false Israel. The recalcitrant are warned of imminent and eternal judgment. It is to this theme that we now turn: Matthew's supposed anti-Semitism.

## Matthew's Polemical Implications

In light of this theological understanding of salvation-history, Matthew draws out the implications of this theology for the Jewish nation and its status as the covenant people. Matthew sees at least three implications: (1) that the Jewish nation must respond; (2) that rejecting Jesus is rejecting God's salvation and incurs God's judgment; and (3) that the message is now for the whole world. These three motifs have often been taken to be evidence for anti-Semitism; I contend that they are racially acceptable religious polemic for that time. To be sure, persecution of the Christians is clear evidence that for some elements of Judaism, the Christian movement was intolerable. The point I make, however, is that nonmessianic Jews did not persecute messianic Jews for racial hatred. Instead, the persecution had other (both theological and sociological) bases. What then are the polemical implications of Matthew's theology of salvation-history?

### Israel Must Respond to the Eschatological Message of John and Jesus

The first note heard from John the Baptist is the dawn of the kingdom (Matt 3:2), and the second, also grounded eschatologically,[56] is the severe warning to the Pharisees and Sadducees that national privilege no longer counts (3:7-10): fruit worthy of repentance needs to be produced for God's approval. John, furthermore, points the hearer not only to the eschatological need for repentance but also to Jesus as the eschatological and purging-saving Messiah (3:11-12).[57] Thus, Israel must respond to the eschatological message of Jesus as well.

Baptized as God's servant who is Son (3:13-17), Jesus is tempted and demonstrates his faithfulness—in contrast to the Jewish nation of old (4:1-11).[58] On the basis of this call of God and his utter obedience, Jesus begins to summon Israel to accept the advent of the new era with its universal call to repentance (4:12-17; see 1:21). Four respond properly (4:18-22) as Jesus canvasses the area (4:23-25). His message is then declared in word (5:1–7:29) and deed (8:1–9:34).

---

56. Observe in Matt 3:7: "the wrath to come" (a note of imminency); and in 3:10: "Even now the axe is laid to the root of the tree."

57. On the purging-saving functions, see the discussion of 3:11 in J. D. G. Dunn, "Spirit-and-Fire Baptism," *NovT* 14 (1972) 81–92; Davies-Allison, *Matthew*, 316–18.

58. The story line is significant: having passed through the waters as the Jewish nation did, Jesus enters the desert to be tested for "forty" days (corresponding to Israel's forty years). Jesus' obedience, then, is in marked contrast to Israel's disobedience, making him the founder of the new people of God who leads them to a new land. See Davies-Allison, *Matthew*, 350–74.

This message of Jesus is then multiplied through the words of the twelve apostles (9:35–11:1). In short, 4:12–11:1 may be seen as Jesus confronting Israel (10:5-6; see 15:24) with the message of the kingdom of heavens to which Israel must respond with repentance and obedience. The emphasis in these several chapters on Israel's need to respond cannot be missed (see 5:3-12, 20, 48; 6:1-18; 7:6, 12, 13-27; 8:4, 5-13, 18-22, 23-34; 9:1-8, 9-13, 14-17, 32-34; 10:5-6, 17-20, 23, 34-36).

Two parables bring this theme of responding to John and Jesus to the fore: Matt 11:16-19 and Matt 21:28-32. As children who played music or sang a dirge for some unresponsive others, so John and Jesus have played "God's music" (the message of the kingdom of heavens) and warned of judgment to their contemporaries (nonmessianic Jewish people).[59] Their "deeds" (11:19) confirm their commission from God (see 12:28). The implicit message here is that John and Jesus are God's prophets but have been rejected by nonmessianic Jews, especially their leaders. This is visibly demonstrated in overt rejection and harassment (10:24-25; 11:7-15; 14:3-12).

The second parable (21:28-32) is similar: like a son who promises obedience but who fails, unresponsive Jews have not lived up to their high calling as the people of God. They have rejected the Messiah. In contrast, like a son who scorns the demand of obedience but who, after repentance, returns to obedience, so those who followed Jesus, irrespective of social and racial status, are those who are truly God's people, the true Israel. Jesus' closing words bring the message into focus: whereas the Jews, especially their leaders, have spurned the message of John (and therefore Jesus), the tax collectors and prostitutes have surprisingly responded to the kingdom of heavens as taught by John and Jesus (21:31-32).[60]

For Matthew, then, John and Jesus have been sent by God to announce the dawn of the kingdom of heavens, and, because God is uniquely and finally active in their prophetic words, even the Jews must respond to their ministries.

## Rejecting Jesus Is Rejecting God's Salvation and Incurs God's Judgment

The conviction of the presence of God in the ministries of John and Jesus has a serious corollary: rejection of their ministries is rejection of God.[61] We should observe, first, that both John and Jesus are thoroughly rejected. John, apparently for salvation-historical reasons,[62] must be off the scene before Jesus' ministry

---

59. Matthew's word for "generation" (11:16) is *genea*; it refers to "Jewish contemporaries," and, in particular, has a Pharisaic cast to it (12:39-45; 16:4; 17:17; 23:36).

60. See Levine, *Social and Ethnic Dimensions*, 203-6, and throughout for an emphasis on the marginal.

61. See France, *Matthew: Evangelist*, 213-32.

62. For Matthew, John functions as a transition from one age to the other; however, his transition makes him clearly separate from both Israel's past and Jesus' ministry (see 4:12; 11:12; 21:28-32). See also J. P. Meier, "John the Baptist in Matthew's Gospel," *JBL* 99 (1980) 383-405.

proper begins. The traditions about John have one dominant motif: John was rejected, especially by the leaders (4:12; 11:2-19; 14:3-12; 21:25, 32).

The motif of Jesus' rejection, of course, is a major theme of the entire Synoptic tradition and need not be discussed in detail here. But a few references are notable: (1) when Jesus proposes to heal the paralytic, some of the scribes contend that he is blaspheming (9:3); (2) when Jesus sits at table with tax collectors and sinners in the house of Matthew, he is opposed (9:9-13); (3) Jesus' freedom from fasting obligations is called into question (9:14-17); (4) Jesus' exorcisms are opposed as stemming from the evil one (9:32-34; 12:22-37); (5) his Sabbath practices are seriously questioned (12:1-14); (6) some of his parables imply rejection (13:1-9, 18-23), and overt statements about parables speak of rejection (13:10-17); (7) Jesus, like other prophets, is in the line of those who are rejected and so is not welcome in his home synagogue (13:54-58);[63] (8) Jesus predicts his own death at the hands of Jewish opponents (16:21; 17:22-23; 20:18-19); and (9) Jesus' teachings are hotly disputed during the final week (21:23–22:40). Jesus is opposed by Jews for a variety of reasons, most notably his attitude toward the Law, toward legal traditions, and toward the sanctity of the Jewish nation. For Matthew, Jesus is clearly a threat to Jewish (at least Jewish leaders') sacred tradition.

And, the last few scenes are peppered with Jewish and Roman rejection of Jesus: the rejecters include various kinds of leaders, both Jewish (26:3-5, 14, 57-75; 27:1-2, 20, 62-66) and Roman (27:2, 11-14, 27-31, 62-66); the Jewish crowd (27:22-23, 25, 33-44);[64] as well as Jesus' disciples (26:30-35, 36-46, 57-

---

63. See here Hare, *Jewish Persecution,* 137–41; Trilling, *Das wahre Israel,* 80–84.

64. On the Jewish and Roman rejection of Jesus, see esp. Buck, "Anti-Judaic Sentiments"; for a profile of Matthew's redactional reworking of Mark, see ibid., 166–71.

On 27:24-25, see H. Kosmala, " 'His Blood on Us and Our Children' (The Background of Mat. 27, 24-25)," *ASTI* 7 (1970) 94–126, who argues that the idiom means, "We will bear the responsibility for the execution and you [Pilate] will be innocent—no more and no less" (p. 118). The key word for Kosmala is "responsibility" not "blood guiltiness." On the "our children," see n. 79, below. See also Feldman, "Is the New Testament?" 5. See also a popular article by historian P. L. Maier, "Who Killed Jesus?" *Christianity Today* 34/6 (1990) 16–19. This latter article is both historically and religiously sensitive. The early history of the interpretation of this verse has been carefully documented in R. Kampling, *Das Blut Christi: Mt 27,25 bei den lateinischsprachigen christlichen Autoren bis zu Leo dem Großen* (NTAbh, Neue Folge 16; Münster: Aschendorff, 1984). See also V. Mora, *Le refus,* 165–73.

This text has been greatly debated (but only of late) and, more importantly, regularly abused by anti-Semitic proponents (see C. Klein, *Anti-Judaism in Christian Theology* [Philadelphia: Fortress, 1978] 92–126). This verse says no more that "all of Judaism" is culpable for the death of Jesus than that "all of the Decapolis" followed Jesus in 4:25 or that "all Gentiles" rejected Jesus along with the soldiers who scorned him; neither does Pilate's handwashing suggest "total gentile innocence" or "the acme of the exculpation of the Romans" (so Sandmel, *Anti-Semitism,* 66).

Matt 27:25 is generalization for rhetorical and dramatic effect and is a reference to a particular group of people (among whom there were certainly variations, not to say crowd pressure); see Kosmala, "His Blood," 98. It speaks as much of the suspension of national privilege and the extension of the gospel to the Gentiles as it does of Jewish guilt; see J. A. Fitzmyer, "Anti-Semitism and the Cry of 'All the People,' " *TS* 26 (1965) 670–71; Hare, "Rejection," 38. W. Trilling, on the other hand, overemphasizes the guilt of the Jews and underemphasizes how "Jewish guilt" fits

75) and Judas (26:14-16, 20-25, 47-56). Thus, the rejection of Jesus, however closely aligned with the Jewish leaders in the prepassion narrative (4:12–26:1), comprises more than one group of people and more than one race. It includes Jewish leaders, Jewish people, Jewish disciples, as well as Roman leaders and, if we can presume to think of soldiers, Roman military personnel. It is simply wrong to argue that Matthew's desire is to put the blame solely on the Jews, especially the entirety of the Jewish populace.[65] It can be fairly said that Matthew's Christology has a significant suffering (i.e., rejected) servant overlay.[66]

Second, we need to observe that Matthew logically connects rejection of Jesus' followers with rejection of God and then rejection by God. Jesus tells the Twelve to shake the dust off their feet against the city or house that rejects the message of the Twelve (10:14)—undoubtedly to be understood as a prophetic gesture of judgment. This rupturing of fellowship indicates also the creation

---

into Matthew's theological and salvation-historical frameworks; see his *Das wahre Israel*, 66–74; so also Sandmel, *Anti-Semitism*, 66; F. Mussner, *Tractate on the Jews: The Significance of Judaism for Christian Faith* (Philadelphia: Fortress, 1984) 193–97; Beck, *Mature Christianity*, 159–61.

The text, nonetheless, does show some strong animus against Jesus on the part of a considerable number of Jews (*laos* might refer to "the ethnic people of Israel"; but see Kosmala, "His Blood," 96–99). But it is morally wrong to infer from this that "all Jews" killed Jesus and are, therefore, an inferior nation for having committed deicide. At least three kinds of people were involved in Jesus' death: (1) cowardly disciples who refused to come to his defense and a betraying disciple; (2) ignorant people and leaders who did not take the time to establish justice in the case (Pilate?); and (3) some who were hostile to Jesus, whether Jews (probably some Pharisees) or Gentiles, for whatever reasons. I do not doubt that some Jewish leaders were in part the instigators. In general, see the excellent and evenhanded essay of N. B. Stonehouse, "Who Crucified Jesus?" in *Paul before the Areopagus and Other New Testament Studies* (Grand Rapids, Mich.: Eerdmans, 1957) 41–69, esp. 69. Significantly, H. Kosmala (and others after him) points out that nowhere in the early Christian writings do we find Christians citing Matt 27:25 as proof of Jewish guilt. See "His Blood," 122–23 n. 1.

As to the crowds: I do not for a moment think scholarship should speculate about the number of people involved or their representative nature, and I do not believe it should pursue lines of identity among the references to "crowds" in Matthew, whether identifying them in the real world of history or in the literary world as a "literary character." For one example of this kind of identifying disparate groups, something done quite often, see J. D. Kingsbury, *Matthew as Story* (2d ed.; Philadelphia: Fortress, 1988) 56–57. "Crowds" is a term used to cover a massive variety of individuals and groups at different locations and at different times and of different sizes; to *assume* their identity without foundation and then to trace development (i.e., from widespread acceptance to thoroughgoing rejection) and profile strikes me as a serious hermeneutical blunder. Historical probabilities must have something to say in our study of the gospel traditions! Why must we assume that the "crowds" who praised Jesus in 21:9 and sided with him in 21:46; 26:5 are the same "crowds" who pushed for his crucifixion at 27:25? I would argue that we should not assume this identification. See Crossan, "Anti-Semitism," 199–206, for a telling critique of this assumption; see also the important clarifications of Crossan in G. G. O'Collins, "Anti-Semitism in the Gospel," *TS* 26 (1965) 663–66. In particular, Crossan's neglect of Matt 27:25 was fixed by Fitzmyer, "Anti-Semitism," 667–71.

65. Studies concerned with the particular viewpoint of Matthew have sometimes done this. But see the balanced perspective of D. P. Senior, *The Passion Narrative according to Matthew: A Redactional Study* (BETL 39; Leuven: Leuven Univ. Press, 1982), esp. the summary on 338 (the responsibility of the Jews serves Matthew's Christology). See also 380–81.

66. See D. Hill, "Son and Servant: An Essay in Matthean Christology," *JSNT* 6 (1980) 2–16; idem, "The Figure of Jesus in Matthew's Story: a Response to Professor Kingsbury's Literary-critical Probe," *JSNT* 21 (1984) 37–52; France, *Matthew: Evangelist*, 300–302.

of a new people of God and a judgment by God on those who refuse to have fellowship with them (see 21:33-46; 22:1-14). To the statement about the gesture is added "an intolerable word": "Truly, I say to you, it shall be more tolerable on the day of judgment for the land of Sodom and Gomorrah than for that town [which rejects my messengers and message]" (10:15; see also 11:20-24; 12:38-42). The strongest word in Matthew in this regard must be 10:33: "But whoever denies me before men, I will also deny before my Father who is in heaven." God, for Matthew, sees rejection of his Son, Jesus Messiah, as an intolerable and unforgivable sin because he (God) is at work inaugurating the kingdom through him (Jesus) (12:31-32). To reject Jesus is to reject God. Matthew holds some (but clearly not all) Jews culpable for this very sin: the sin of rejecting God's Messiah; the consequence is judgment from God.

Third, Matthew spares no words for his warning of sin and condemnation for rejecting God's offer of salvation in Jesus Messiah. Whether it is John, criticizing the Pharisees and Sadducees (3:7), or Jesus' hot words for the Pharisees (23:1-39), a consistent theme of Matthew is threat of judgment on the Jews, especially the Jewish leaders (i.e., the Pharisees), for rejecting Jesus. Matthew's favorite word is "hypocrite," meaning both contradiction of inner reality and outward appearance as well as didactic abuse through false teaching (12:11-12; 15:7; 22:18; 23:15, 23, 25, 27, 29).[67] Matthew turns against the Pharisees (and scribes) for their inadequate righteousness (5:20), their ostentatious religiosity (6:1-18), their misguided and misguiding traditional exegesis (15:1-20; 23:13-33), and for leading people astray (21:33-46; 23:15).[68] Blame, however, is not limited to the Pharisees and scribes; those who follow them are also blamed (10:12-15; 11:16, 20-24; 26:57; 27:24-25).[69]

Matthew's stiff and persistent warning given to disobedient (nonmessianic) Judaism is not, however, to be taken to indicate that he sees only judgment and damnation for nonmessianic Judaism.[70] The most that can be said is that

---

67. On this see D. Garland, *The Intention of Matthew 23* (NovTSup 52; Leiden: E. J. Brill, 1979) 91–123, for the finest study of "hypocrite" in Matthew's redaction.

68. See also Freyne, "Vilifying the Other," 132–35, who sees three main areas of criticism: failure to understand the Law adequately, hypocrisy, and culpable blindness. He shows that these criticisms are designed to show that only the Christian scribes are the true interpreters of Scripture. Freyne, unfortunately, calls this bitter polemic the "language of annihilation" (p. 135).

69. S. Freyne, in my opinion, restricts Matthew's polemic too narrowly to the leaders and so misses the finer nuances of this polemic and their implications for the intra-Jewish nature of the setting of Matthew; see "Vilifying the Other." See the more balanced treatment in Buck, "Anti-Judaic Sentiments," 171–72.

70. So Trilling, *Das wahre Israel*, 87–96; Légasse, "L'antijudaïsme," 423–26; Hare, *Jewish Persecution*, 146–62. Hare's comments are too harsh here, although they are mitigated somewhat by his inclusion of individual Jews (pp. 153–54). His more recent breakdown of kinds of anti-Judaism (prophetic, Jewish-Christian, Gentilizing) is useful, but he retains a view that sees Matthew as too harsh; see "Rejection," 28–40. The harshest terms seem to be those of Gaston, "Messiah," 39, who sees in Matthew an "utter reprobation of the people of Israel," which he sees as "monstrous and obscene." Few have argued for this complete of a rejection of Israel by Matthew. For partial agreement with my view, see A. Schlatter, *Die Kirche des Matthäus* (BFCT 33/1; Gütersloh: C. Bertelsmann, 1929) 17–19. Matthew, for whatever reasons, does not speculate on the future of Israel (in contrast

this judgment is reserved by Matthew for only the leaders and their followers among the nation as a special, privileged body, not for individual Jews. But a better explanation is this: for Matthew, the church is the salvation-historical climax of the Jewish nation, both in continuity (true Israel) and discontinuity (new Israel). Israel is not judged as much as Israel has been fulfilled and altered. If Matthew was written by a Jew, and I agree with those who have so argued,[71] then it is a logical absurdity to think that Jews are banned from God's people. Matthew's theological perspective is not to lower the Jewish nation to the lowest rung but rather to elevate all people to the level of potential people of God.[72] The leveling process is complete and radical (Matthew denationalizes Judaism), and the process does not result in a new hierarchy. For Matthew, Jews (by race) are simply people, like Gentiles, who need to seek God's salvation in Jesus Messiah. Finally, there is evidence in Matthew of a continued dialogue with Judaism,[73] of mission to the Jews (10:5-6, 23),[74] and, above all, of Gentiles being the exception rather than the rule (2:1-12; 8:5-13). The ethic of Jesus is love of neighbor as well as enemy, whether Jewish or gentile (5:43-48; 7:12; 22:34-40), and the offer of Jesus to come to him is still present (11:28-30).[75] Israel's judgment then is not a racial judgment but a religious transference of the locus of God's activity: from a nation to the new people of God (21:43).[76] Only in this sense is Israel judged: as a people that follows false shepherds, as a people that does not follow Jesus.

Fourth, the visible demonstration of this rejection by God of the Jewish people as the people of God is the destruction of Jerusalem.[77] The sacking of Jerusalem is a sign of God's judgment (22:7). It is a fact that the traditions of Israel consistently explain destructions of cities in Israel and deportations as God's judgment (see 23:38).[78] Prefigured in the cursing of the fig tree (21:18-19)

---

to Paul's Romans 9-11), but this can be explained by seeing Israel as a people *continued in the church.* Israel has no future because Israel does not need one; Israel is present in the church and its future.

71. See most recently Davies-Allison, *Matthew,* 7-58; see also G. N. Stanton, "The Origin and Purpose of Matthew's Gospel. Matthean Scholarship from 1945 to 1980," *ANRW* 2/25/3 (1984) 1914-16, 1921; Hare, *Jewish Persecution,* 164-66; Harrington, "Dangerous Text," 136-38.

72. See Levine, *Social and Ethnic Dimensions,* 241-71.

73. Above all, see Davies, *Setting.*

74. On 10:23, see S. McKnight, "Jesus and the End-time: Matthew 10:23," SBLSP (1986) 500-520, esp. 519-20. Although I am not against seeing 10:5-6 as partly showing (for apologetical reasons) that the message was preached to the Jews and that they are therefore responsible for rejecting Jesus, I am more persuaded that the essential meaning of these verses revolves around salvation-history and (the former) Jewish privilege. W. Trilling errs in emphasizing Jewish guilt here; see *Das wahre Israel,* 99-105. See esp. the thorough defense of Matthew as still extending the gospel to the Jews in Levine, *Social and Ethnic Dimensions,* 165-239; Stanton, *Gospel for a New People,* 157-59.

75. Légasse, "L'antijudaïsme," 428; Niedner, "Rereading Matthew."

76. See Trilling, *Das wahre Israel,* 55-66; France, *Matthew: Evangelist,* 227-30.

77. Trilling, *Das wahre Israel,* 84-87; Légasse, "L'antijudaïsme," 424-26; Mora, *Le refus,* 43-81, esp. 68-73; E. A. Russell, "The Image of the Jew in Matthew's Gospel," in E. A. Livingstone, ed., *SE* 7 (TU 126; Berlin: Akademie-Verlag, 1982) 441.

78. See, e.g., J. A. Goldstein, "Even the Righteous Can Perish by His Faith," *Conservative Judaism* 41 (1989) 57-70.

and in two parables (21:33–22:14), the destruction of Jerusalem is announced by Jesus (23:1–24:36), and Matthew connects this indissolubly with rejection of Jesus as God's Messiah.[79] The pattern of the last confrontations makes this clear: (1) Jesus enters Jerusalem prophetically, the "cleansing" symbolizing its sterility (an "old wineskin") and imminent judgment (21:1-19); (2) Jesus engages the leaders in public debate, lacing each encounter with threat and condemnation (21:23–22:40); (3) Jesus finishes the encounters with a riddlelike question that exposes the spiritual blindness of his opponents (22:41-46); (4) he warns both followers and Jewish leaders of the dangers of hypocrisy, which he ties closely to the leaders and their persecution of God's prophets (23:1-36); (5) he laments over Jerusalem's imminent catastrophe for rejecting him (23:37-39);[80] and (6) he therefore predicts Jerusalem's destruction (24:1-36).[81] For Matthew the destruction of Jerusalem is to be blamed on the Jewish leaders (especially the Pharisees) and the crowds who follow them in their rejection of Jesus as God's Messiah. For the Jewish nation nothing could be more symbolic of God's displeasure than his refusal to vindicate them; instead, God allows their city, the center of their cultus, to be destroyed by gentile sinners. The destruction demonstrates that God's salvation is no longer "ethnocentric" (for Jews only). The kingdom is therefore moved from Jewish special prerogative to all the world (21:43).[82]

## The Message Is Now for the World

But the inference Matthew draws from the sack of Jerusalem is not an arrogance or lack of compassion: rather, Matthew's inference is that salvation has now been offered to all, including both Jews and Gentiles.[83] Scholars differ

---

79. Given this theological platform on which Matthew is standing, it makes most sense for Matthew if the "our children" of 27:25 literally means "the physical descendants of those urging Jesus' crucifixion," which then were those who suffered in the destruction within a generation.

80. See the lucid comments of G. Strecker, *Der Weg der Gerechtigkeit: Untersuchung zur Theologie des Matthäus* (3d ed.; FRLANT 82; Göttingen: Vandenhoeck and Ruprecht, 1962) 113–15.

81. A serious exegetical error is made when Matthew 23 and 24 are read separately; chap. 23, in fact, prepares for chap. 24 (see, e.g., 23:37-39 and 24:1-3; see also the "all this" of 23:36 with the same or similar expression in 24:2, 3, 8, 33, 34). The logical implication is obvious: Jerusalem is sacked as a visible demonstration of God's judgment on nonmessianic Judaism, especially its leaders, for rejecting the Messiah who has confronted Israel and warned Israel of imminent judgment for not responding to him.

82. S. Légasse writes: "By this, Israel erases itself from the history of salvation" ("L'anti-judaïsme," 424).

83. I disagree completely with those scholars who read Matt 28:19 as "to all the Gentiles" (excluding Jews) but do agree with the notion that it is not an offer to "the Jewish nation" as a separate body. To argue that at some particular point in history (e.g., following the *Birkath ha-Minim*, etc.) Jewish missions ended is a serious historical reductionism. In fact, local conditions (including the relation of the churches to synagogues, individual leaders to other leaders, etc.) were more crucial than some theological conviction. The best discussion, with representative scholars, can be found in Levine, *Social and Ethnic Dimensions,* 185–204. I demur, however, from her (however important) emphasis on the "alteration of time" at the Great Commission. See also Koenig, *Jews and Christians,* 88–89; Russell, "Image of the Jew," 441-42.

as to when this "gentile moment" begins in Matthew's scheme of salvation-history, but as indicated above,[84] I see a progressive inclusion that climaxes in the aftermath of Jerusalem's destruction: (1) gentile promise in Old Testament prophecy; (2) occasional inclusions (e.g., 2:1-12; 8:5-13; 15:21-28); (3) the cross-resurrection (e.g., 27:51, 54); (4) the Great Commission (28:16-20); and (5) even greater inclusion following the destruction of Jerusalem (see 21:33-46; 22:1-14; 24:14, 31).[85] Even if one disputes this position, no one doubts the universal thrust of Matthew's Gospel: the message of the kingdom is for all, and one of the major foundations for this offer is the suspension of national privilege (21:43). Suspension here, however, does not mean that Jews have become inferior to every other nation; rather, suspension of privilege means that Jews have either been reduced to the level of all nations or, as Levine has argued, all nations have been raised to their level as potential people of God.[86] The historical Israel finds its salvation-historical fulfillment in the new people of God, the church, which itself includes both Gentiles and Israel "according to the flesh" who now believe in Jesus as God's Messiah.

## Summary

Matthew's theological conviction that God's salvation-history has found its definitive new inauguration in Jesus and in the new people of God, the church, leads him to a polemical argument with Judaism: Jews are no longer the special people of God but are rather simply human beings like all others. Consequently, even Jews must respond to the eschatological message of (John and) Jesus. If they reject that message and the Messiah, they are rejecting God's definitive offer of salvation and will incur God's judgment, made visible in the destruction of Jerusalem.

# Conclusion

It is my contention that Matthew's Gospel, however harsh and unpleasant to modern sensitivities, is not anti-Semitic. It is, on the contrary, a compassionate but vigorous appeal to nonmessianic Judaism to respond to the Messiah. True to the prophetic form, however, Matthew does not hesitate to use the harsh rhetoric of condemnation for those who opt to reject Jesus. But Matthew's rhetoric is conventional, unabrasive for his time, and founded upon his theological convictions (salvation-historical and christological). It is, in effect, his Jewish hermeneutic

---

84. See above, n. 45.

85. I see both 24:14 and 24:31 to be referring to the preaching of the gospel to Gentiles largely as a result of the destruction of Jerusalem (a coming of the Lord in judgment).

86. See esp. Levine, *Social and Ethnic Dimensions*.

of fulfillment put to Christian praxis: God has fulfilled his plans in Jesus Messiah, and, because Israel has failed to respond as it should have, it has lost its national privilege and is like all nations—that is, it is potentially the people of God. Matthew is, however, decidedly against disobedient or nonmessianic Judaism. In fact, it might be inferred that Matthew saw nonmessianic Judaism as itself "anti-Judaism" because, in his view, true Judaism is messianic. Thus, Jews who were not messianic had opted out of true Judaism and were, therefore, no longer Israel. Opposing messianic Judaism, in such a context, would be perceived as "anti-Judaism."[87] Matthew's polemic against disobedience, however, is not just reserved for former Israel. Matthew is just as hard on disobedience among Christians, whether Jew or Gentile (e.g., 24:45-51).

Matthew, then, needs no apology, for he is not anti-Semitic. He is no more anti-Semitic than Amos or Jeremiah. Those who have read Matthew so, I believe, have surely misread him. His rhetoric may be unacceptable to modern sensitivities, but it was not to his Jewish world. For this reason it would be well if pastors, interpreters, and activists would distinguish between the *nature* of the disagreement (Jesus as Messiah, sociological factors, etc.) and the *means* of the disagreement (polemical tones). Above all, it is time for us to look even more deeply at knee-jerk stereotypes that foster anti-Semitism (e.g., Pharisees are bigots; Judaism is a sterile religion).[88] But, having said this, I maintain that the only apology that needs to be made is "the deeper form of apology that every Christian owes to every Jew for the part which historic Christendom has played in the shaping of modern anti-semitism."[89] This kind of apology I do offer and, to do so, I finish with a personal postscript, a memory of mine from nearly twenty years ago.

## Postscript

During the summer after my freshman year in college, on a hot, muggy day, I, with a handful of young European Christians, walked up a short hill outside a small village in Austria, called Mauthausen. On top of that hill, away from

---

87. See also Russell, "Antisemitism," 183.

88. The scholars who have made this the clearest in modern academic discussions are E. P. Sanders, *Paul and Palestinian Judaism: A Comparison of Patterns of Religion* (Philadelphia: Fortress, 1977) 33–75; J. Neusner, *From Politics to Piety: The Emergence of Pharisaic Piety* (New York: Ktav, 1979); K. Stendahl, "The Apostle Paul and the Introspective Conscience of the West," in *Paul among Jews and Gentiles* (Philadelphia: Fortress, 1976) 78–96. Their central observations have been applied in Christian scholarship with great sophistication and clarity to Romans by J. D. G. Dunn, *Romans* (WBC 38A, 38B; Waco, Tex.: Word, 1988). See also the potent paragraph of G. Baum in his foreword to Klein, *Anti-Judaism*, x, and the entire, revealing volume of Klein itself. But for Baum to speak of a "negation" of the Jews inherent in Christianity is to go too far; surely a confession of faith inevitably involves at some level a denial of other confessions of faith, but a confession does not "negate" someone else's existence. Rather, it puts it in contrast.

89. Davies, *Anti-Semitism*, 18.

the concerns of the village, were the remains of a German concentration camp. To this day I am stunned by the memory of what was preserved for future generations: the dimly lit, cramped "living quarters"; the (morally appropriate) black and white photographs, hanging in the museum, pictures taken when Americans released the prisoners; the shocking sign about "blueberry picking" (an enigmatic sign about shooting unsuspecting Jews for their supposed attempts at escape); the cruel and rugged walk up and down the rock quarry; the strong, privatizing walls that the quarry provided—day by day, hand by hand, life by life; and most gruesome of all, the crematorium sign on a lifeless, moist grey building. The crematorium was decked in utter simplicity. Its simplicity was outstripped only by the horrors it conceived and evoked. My hands shook, my throat went dry, my knees lost their strength, and my eyes swelled with tears—as they do to this day—when my being tries to cope with what remains monstrous, obscene, and unabsorbable.

I am grateful to the people of all places for their indefatigable, if at times discouraging, efforts to keep these solemn events and memorials before modern consciousness. I never want to return to such a place, due to the pain it causes, but I want my two children to see what horror can be caused when diabolical people gain the upper hand in society and culture and impose their power in the name of religion and race. My wife and I have taught our children that a person who behaves this way is "an enemy of Christianity as well as Judaism."[90]

---

90. Ibid., 33. Our teaching, I admit, does not seek to hide the embarrassing reality of Christian-conceived anti-Semitism.

# -4-

# Anti-Semitism and/or
# Anti-Judaism in Mark?

## Robert A. Guelich

John Gager in *The Origins of Anti-Semitism*[1] distinguishes between "anti-Semitism" and "anti-Judaism." The former is a "term to designate hostile statements about Jews and Judaism on the part of Gentiles" that "betray very little knowledge of Jews or Judaism, and tend to be sweeping generalizations."[2] The latter is "primarily a matter of religious and theological disagreement."[3] Furthermore, Gager generally accepts Douglas Hare's taxonomy of "anti-Judaism" that distinguishes between: (1) "prophetic anti-Judaism" as found in the invectives of the Old Testament prophets and in the writings of Qumran; (2) "Jewish-Christian anti-Judaism," which scores the Jewish rejection of Jesus' message and of God's overture of salvation but leaves the door open for the Jews through repentance and faith in Jesus Christ; and (3) "Gentilizing anti-Judaism," which emphasizes the "new" Israel, the gentile character of Christianity, and the rejection by God of the Jews as incurably apostate.[4]

Few would assign the term "anti-Semitism" to Mark,[5] and the current debate

---

1. J. Gager, *The Origins of Anti-Semitism: Attitudes Towards Judaism in Pagan and Christian Antiquity* (Oxford and New York: Oxford Univ. Press, 1983).

2. Ibid., 8. See also G. I. Langmuir, *Towards a Definition of Antisemitism* (Berkeley: Univ. of California Press, 1990), for a thorough discussion of the historical development of anti-Semitism from anti-Judaism.

3. Langmuir, *Definition*. This distinction marks much of the contemporary discussion: e.g., J. N. Sevenster, *The Roots of Pagan Antisemitism in the Ancient World* (NovTSup 41; Leiden: Brill, 1975) 3; W. Klassen, "Anti-Judaism in Early Christianity: The State of the Question," in P. Richardson and D. Granskou, eds., *Anti-Judaism in Early Christianity*, vol. 2: *Paul and the Gospels* (Waterloo, Ont.: Wilfrid Laurier Univ. Press, 1986) 2.7, 19.

4. D. R. A. Hare, "The Rejection of the Jews in the Synoptic Gospels and Acts," in A. T. Davis, ed., *Anti-Semitism and the Foundations of Christianity* (New York: Paulist, 1979) 28–32.

5. Cf. the title of S. Sandmel's *Anti-Semitism in the New Testament?* (Philadelphia: Fortress, 1978).

has focused more on the nature and extent of the "anti-Judaism" in Mark. Does, for example, Mark's anti-Judaism reflect a Gentilizing anti-Judaism that radically dissociates itself with Judaism?[6] Or does Mark reflect "only the barest traces of prophetic and Jewish-Christian anti-Judaism, and not the slightest evidence of that Gentilizing anti-Judaism that was later to dominate Christian theology"?[7] In either case, this debate assumes without question that Mark reflects at least some form of anti-Judaism. The task of this study will be to examine anew this assumption and the meaning of anti-Judaism.

The broad consensus of New Testament scholarship holds that the Gospel of Mark served as the foundational text for at least the Gospels of Matthew and Luke. As the earliest of the four Gospels, Mark gives the Christian community the first narrative portrait of Jesus and his ministry. Nevertheless, this portrait, which the evangelist calls the "gospel concerning Jesus Messiah, Son of God" (1:1), comes over a generation after the narrative time and setting of the story itself. The content and details have doubtless been shaped by the circumstances of the intervening years and most certainly by the evangelist and the concerns of his own community. Therefore, either one can use this Gospel as a primary source for early Christian tradition by seeking to delineate the texts behind the text, or one can use this Gospel as a primary source for a particular community in the emerging Christian movement in the period around the time of the Jewish War by examining it as a text in its own right.

In either case one would be examining the text in a way different from its general use through the centuries as a canonical text for the Christian church, for whom it was neither a window on the developing Christian movement (e.g., form criticism) nor a means for examining a particular Christian community (e.g., redaction criticism). Consequently, the search for the roots of anti-Semitism and/or anti-Judaism in Mark becomes much more complex. Whereas one may trace the roots of anti-Judaism *and* anti-Semitism, using Gager's definitions, to the canonical use of Mark in the life of the church, the more historically appropriate question for the community of Mark as well as its underlying traditions really involves only the issue of anti-Judaism. By design this study will concentrate on Mark solely as a sociohistorical text (where much of the current debate has been centered) and leave aside the more complex historical question of the texts behind the text as well as the difficult hermeneutical question of the text as a canonical text.

---

6. E.g., Sandmel, *Anti-Semitism*, 48: "In short, Mark is a tract on behalf of gentile Christianity, contending that Christianity has only negative connections with the Judaism into which it had been born." Similarly, N. A. Beck, *Mature Christianity: The Recognition and Repudiation of the Anti-Jewish Polemic of the New Testament* (Selinsgrove, Pa.: Susquehanna Univ. Press, 1985) 100: "The Marcan community may be described, therefore, as a sect over against Judaism, an apocalyptic, eschatological sect that put into writing its self-conscious identity in the form of connected stories about Jesus."

7. So Hare, "Rejection of the Jews," 35; similarly, J. Koenig, *Jews and Christians in Dialogue: New Testament Foundations* (Philadelphia: Westminster, 1979) 60–81.

This study has three parts. First, I shall review the identity and role of the groups and individuals who make up the characters of the story, especially the antagonists. Second, I shall examine key passages in Mark pertaining to the two crucial Jewish religious institutions, the Law and the Temple. Third, I shall look more closely at the parts of the story having to do with Jesus' death and the purported role of the Jews in it. On the basis of the data drawn from these three areas, I shall return in the conclusion to the question: Anti-Semitism and/or anti-Judaism in Mark?

## The "Jews" in Mark's Gospel

Mark's story consists of a cast of characters composed of individuals, named and unnamed, and particular groups of people. Character development plays an integral role in the thrust of a narrative. Not only do the characters inhabit the world of the story, they invite the reader to respond positively and/or negatively to them and their role in the story's plot. Therefore, character study provides at least an indirect means for tracing the author's biases and prejudices as seen in the development of the characters through what is said about them or by how they play their role in the story.

Beginning with the individuals, with the exception of the Roman rulers, Herod Antipas, his wife Herodias (6:17-29), and Pilate (15:1-15), every person identified by name is Jewish.[8] Except for Judas, each Jew is portrayed essentially in a positive light. Even Barabbas (15:6-14), arrested in conjunction with—though not accused of—murder (15:7), is set free by the Roman authorities at the request of the Jewish crowds. Furthermore, the large majority of unnamed characters from the demoniac in the synagogue (1:23-28) to the rebels crucified with Jesus (15:27) are obviously Jewish. The exceptions are rare and generally well marked. For example, the Gerasene demoniac's territory, occupation (swineherd), and diction (i.e., use of the expression "Most High God")[9] betray his gentile orientation (5:1-20). The territory and designation (i.e., "a Greek") of the Syrophoenician woman leave little doubt about her gentile background. The same is obviously true of the Roman centurion at the scene of the crucifixion (15:39).[10] Yet instead of being anti-Jewish figures, all three Gentiles actually recognize and affirm Jesus' mission above all as a Jew.[11]

---

8. E.g., Jesus (1:1); John the Baptist (1:4-8); Peter, Andrew, James, and John (1:16-20); the Twelve (3:13-19); Levi (2:13-17); Jairus (5:21-24); Bartimaeus (10:46-52); Simon (14:3); Barabbas (15:6); Simon of Cyrene, Alexander, and Rufus (15:21); Mary Magdalene, Mary, Salome (15:40, 47; 16:1); Joseph of Arimathea (15:43).

9. R. A. Guelich, *Mark 1–8:26* (WBC 34A; Dallas: Word, 1989) 279.

10. The locale may suggest that the deaf mute in 7:31-37 and the blind man of Bethsaida were also Gentiles, though nothing else in Mark indicates that.

11. Cf. the Gerasene demoniac's acclamation, "Son of the Most High God" (5:7); the Syrophoeni-

Therefore, the individual characters per se in Mark's narrative exhibit no trace of anti-Judaistic bias.[12]

It is arguable that the individuals, for the most part, play at best minor roles in Mark's story. The major characters, apart from Jesus, who move the plot along are the groups—that is, the disciples, the Jewish leaders, and the crowds;[13] and all of them are unquestionably Jewish. Do any or all of these characters as developed by the author reflect an anti-Judaistic bias or evoke an anti-Jewish response from the reader?

Next to Jesus, the disciples are the most prominent characters in Mark's story. Their prominence is borne out in the structure of the narrative. Jesus' first act of ministry, in 1:16-20, is to call four disciples: Peter, Andrew, James, and John. The final word as the Gospel now ends in 16:8 is that Jesus will meet the disciples in Galilee as he promised. Each of the three sections in the first half of Mark (1:16–8:26) opens with the disciples on stage. Jesus calls the four disciples in 1:16-20, appoints the Twelve in 3:13-19, and sends the Twelve to mission in 6:7-13. In the first section of the second half (8:26–16:8), Jesus concentrates on teaching the disciples about his coming death and the meaning of discipleship (8:27–10:52). They accompany him during his days in Jerusalem in the second section, which involves mounting conflict with the Jewish authorities in Jerusalem (11:1–13:37). Then in the third section they abandon him at his arrest (14:50), and Peter emphatically denies knowing him at the time of his trial (14:66-72). Only the faithful women disciples are on hand to see "where they laid him" (15:47) and to anoint his body (16:1). Yet they too fall prey to fear at the very end (16:8).

Mark's picture of the disciples is complex. On the one hand, discipleship, especially that of the Twelve, is a privilege. Disciples are those who respond in faithful allegiance to Jesus' call to follow him.[14] They have the privilege of Jesus' company (3:14; cf. 5:37), of special instruction (4:13-20, 33-34; 7:17-23; 8:27–13:37), and of sharing in Jesus' ministry as observers and as participants (6:7-13; 6:30-44; 8:1-9). They, in contrast to the "people," know who he is (8:27-29). On the other hand, discipleship is a struggle. Despite the privilege, the disciples are frequently shown to be uncomprehending (e.g., 4:13, 41; 6:52; 7:18; 8:14-21) and given to misunderstanding (e.g., 6:37; 8:31-33; 9:38-40). At times they are described with terms applicable to Jesus' adversaries and outsiders: they are

---

cian woman's recognition of the rights of the "children" (7:27-28); and the centurion's reference to the one crucified as the "King of the Jews" as indeed the "Son of God" (15:39).

12. One individual known by his office, the high priest, rather than by name (cf. Matt 26:57; John 18:13) plays a significant role in Jesus' death, but he does so as the leader of the Sanhedrin rather than as an individual.

13. So J. D. Kingsbury, *Conflict in Mark: Jesus, Authorities, Disciples* (Minneapolis: Fortress, 1989) 4–24.

14. Cf. the pattern in 1:16-20 and 2:13-14. See the challenge of 9:34-38.

"hard of heart" (e.g., 6:52; 8:17; cf. 3:5; 10:5),[15] blind and deaf (Mark 8:18; cf. 4:12), and a "faithless generation" (Mark 9:19; cf. 6:6). Peter is called "Satan" and accused of "thinking not divine but human thoughts" about Jesus' mission (8:33) and eventually denies even knowing him (14:71).

Though some have found in this complex portrait a polemic by the evangelist against threats of false teaching represented by the disciples,[16] there is little hint here of any anti-Judaism.[17] The fact that Jesus singled out "twelve" whom he called "to be with him and to send them out to preach and have authority over demons" (3:13-19) has nothing intrinsically to do in Mark with the twelve tribes of Israel. References to the Twelve as a group do appear throughout Mark, but they in no way represent a "new" or "true" Israel. The presence of disciples other than the Twelve[18] and the frequent singling out of one, two, or three of the Twelve demonstrate how little symbolic value the number twelve has in Mark. Furthermore, their incomprehension, misunderstanding, fear, and failure, which parallel the response of Jesus' family, adversaries, and the outsiders (cf. 4:11), make them anything but a "true" Israel. Therefore, the role of the disciples, who, in the Gospel, most likely represent Mark's own community,[19] contributes nothing by way of anti-Judaistic sentiments.

A second group distinct from the disciples in Mark is "the crowd." Appearing nearly forty times, the crowd remains as nondescript as their designation. For the most part their presence and actions underscore Jesus' popular appeal (e.g., 11:18; 12:12). When not seeking to avoid them (1:35-39; 4:36; 7:17), he frequently teaches (2:13; 4:1; 6:34; 10:1) and works miracles (3:7-12) in their presence. "The crowd," though not necessarily implying the same group of people throughout the Gospel, appears for the last time in 15:8-15. Yet here they take on for the first time the role of an antagonist by effecting Barabbas's release and the crucifixion of Jesus, "the King of the Jews" (15:11-14). Since the context here as elsewhere suggests that "the crowd" was Jewish rather than gentile, one might view this to reflect an anti-Judaistic perspective. Certainly the blaming of the Jews for Jesus' death through Christian history demonstrates such a perspective. Yet Mark's text places the responsibility for the crowd's ac-

---

15. See C. A. Evans, *To See and Not Perceive: Isaiah 6.9-10 in Early Jewish and Christian Interpretation* (JSOTSup 64; Sheffield: JSOT, 1989) 91–106, 200–208.

16. E.g., T. J. Weeden, *Mark: Traditions in Conflict* (Philadelphia: Fortress, 1971); J. B. Tyson, "The Blindness of the Disciples in Mark," *JBL* 80 (1961) 261–68.

17. Cf. S. Sandmel, *Judaism and Christian Beginnings* (Oxford and New York: Oxford Univ. Press, 1978) 351: "Whatever the full range of the purpose of Mark, the denigration of Jews, especially the Jewish disciples, is a leading motif. So extreme is this denigration that it appears to suggest a disconnection between Christianity and the Judaism in which it was born."

18. Cf. "Levi" in 2:13-14, who is not on the list of the Twelve, and "those around him with the Twelve" in 4:10; Jesus explains the parable to the latter group, as distinct from the crowds (4:13-20; cf. 4:33-34).

19. See E. Best, "The Role of the Disciples in Mark," *NTS* 23 (1976–77) 377–401; repr. in E. Best, *Disciples and Discipleship: Studies in the Gospel according to Mark* (Edinburgh: T. and T. Clark, 1986) 98–130.

tions explicitly on the chief priests who orchestrated their demands (15:11) and whose complicity is paramount in Jesus' death. Consequently, "the crowd" in Mark hardly functions as a culpable basis for anti-Judaism.

"The Jews" occurs six times in Mark, five in the designation "King of the Jews" (15:2, 9, 12, 18, 26), a designation that appropriately occurs exclusively on gentile lips, whereas "King of Israel" is used by the Jews (15:32). In 7:3 "all the Jews" does indicate that the implied reader is not Jewish and, as the explanatory parenthesis implies, is unfamiliar with the Jewish custom of ritual washings. Despite the broader context of 7:1-23 that disputes the Jewish purity laws, the use of "all the Jews," like "King of the *Jews*," is a neutral designation and does not reflect here any signs of anti-Judaism.[20]

A very different picture emerges, however, when we shift attention to the other groups that are named in Mark: the scribes, Pharisees, chief priests, elders, Herodians, Sadducees, and the Sanhedrin. Seven in all, they are surprisingly numerous in Mark, and all but the Herodians are familiar, first-century Jewish groups.[21] Each had its own sphere of influence in the life of the Jews. Thus they can be appropriately referred to as different Jewish "authorities." Indeed, they function in Mark in the context of their respective authority.

The scribes[22] appear most frequently in Mark, nearly twice as often as the Pharisees.[23] They are mentioned first (1:22) and last (15:31). Apart from the story of "one of the scribes" who Jesus said was not "far from the kingdom of God" (12:28-34), all references are to the "scribes" as a group and place them in a negative light as antagonists in the story. First, Jesus' teaching stands in contrast to theirs (1:22; 9:11-13; 12:35-37). Second, they take issue with Jesus' ministry of forgiveness (2:6), disregard for purity laws (2:16; 7:1, 5), and exorcisms (3:22; 9:14). Third, in league with the chief priests and as members of the Sanhedrin, they play an active role in Jesus' arrest, trial, and death (11:18, 27; 14:1, 43, 53; 15:1, 31). Finally, Jesus himself warns the crowd in the Temple against the pretentiousness of the scribes who "like to walk around in long robes, receive greetings in the markets, the choice seats in the synagogues and at dinners and who devour widows' homes and pray long prayers for appearance' sake" (12:38-40). At the risk of oversimplification, the conflict between the scribes and Jesus revolves around the issue of authority. This is explicit in the comparison of 1:22 and in the question of 11:28. It is certainly implicit in their charges regarding his forgiveness (2:6), his indiscriminate table fel-

---

20. See *Ep. Arist.* 305 (ca. 150-200 BCE), where a similar expression occurs: "Following the custom of *all the Jews,* they washed their hands in the sea...[offering] prayers to God."

21. For discussion of these groups, see B. Reicke, *New Testament Era* (Philadelphia: Fortress, 1968) 141-68.

22. For a redaction-critical discussion of the "scribes" in Mark, see D. Lührmann, "Die Pharisäer und die Schriftgelehrten im Markusevangelium," *ZNW* 78 (1987) 169-85.

23. Twenty-one times. Alone—1:22; 2:6, 16; 3:22; 9:11, 14; 12:28, 32, 35, 38; with the Pharisees—7:1, 5; with the chief priests—10:33; 11:18; 14:1; 15:31; and with the two other groups of the Sanhedrin, the elders and the chief priests—8:31; 11:27; 14:43, 53; 15:1.

lowship (2:16), and his exorcisms (3:22). As their capital charges (2:6; 3:22) and their part in Jesus' arrest, trial, and death indicate, this becomes a mortal conflict.

The Pharisees also appear frequently in Mark,[24] always as antagonists. Not one reference presents them in a positive light. Twice they exhibit conduct different from Jesus' disciples (2:18; 7:3), conduct that, at best, is portrayed neutrally. Usually they take issue with him over observance of the Law.[25] Jesus calls them "hypocrites" (7:6), refuses to grant their request for a sign (8:11), and warns his disciples against the "leaven of the Pharisees" (8:15). Editorial comments about their intention to "test" (10:2) or to "trap" (12:13) him with their questions reflect an adversarial tone consonant with their unsuccessful conspiracy with the Herodians to kill Jesus (3:6). Nevertheless, the Pharisees per se play no role in Mark in Jesus' actual death. Their only appearance in Jerusalem comes under the aegis of the Sanhedrin (12:13, cf. 11:27; 12:1, 12), and they do not appear in the passion predictions or anywhere else in the passion narrative.[26]

The chief priests actually appear more often than the Pharisees,[27] though their appearance comes much later in Mark and is obviously related exclusively to Jerusalem. This group, which, like the others, Mark leaves undefined, consisted of ten members including the current high priest, the captain of the Temple, five additional priests, and three other priests or laity. In addition to their special responsibilities, they also served as one of three groups comprising the Sanhedrin. They plot with the scribes about how to put Jesus to death (11:18; 14:1); they plan with Judas how to capture Jesus; they work with the scribes and elders to question (11:27) and arrest (14:43) Jesus; and as members of the Sanhedrin, they play a role in interrogating and convicting (14:53, 55) Jesus and then delivering him to Pilate (15:1). They act in consort with Pilate (15:3) and the crowds (15:11) to bring about Jesus' death. Finally, they join the scribes in mockery at the cross (15:31). In fact, the chief priests are the one Jewish group, assisted by the scribes, that appears most directly responsible for Jesus' death in Mark. Yet neither the narrator nor Jesus makes any evaluative comment about them or their behavior. Their character is developed solely by their complicity in Jesus' death.

The same obtains for the elders, who appear only in conjunction with the

---

24. Twelve times. Alone—2:16, 18 (2x); 2:24; 8:11, 15; 10:2; with the scribes—7:1, 5; with the Herodians—3:6; 12:13 (cf. 8:15); with "the Jews"—7:3.

25. The Sabbath—2:24; 3:6; purity issues—2:16; 7:1, 5; divorce—10:2.

26. Historically, the scribes of the Sanhedrin doubtless included those from the Pharisee party (cf. Acts 5:34; 23:6, 9), but Mark does not highlight this. That he identifies them at least in part may be seen by the linking of the "Pharisees" with "scribes *from Jerusalem*" on the issue of ritual purity, a special concern of the Pharisees, in 7:1.

27. Fourteen times. Alone—14:10; 15:3, 10, 11; with the elders and scribes of the Sanhedrin—8:31; 11:27; 14:43, 53; similarly with the elders, scribes, and Sanhedrin—15:1; with the Sanhedrin—14:55; and with the scribes—10:33; 11:18; 14:1; 15:31.

chief priests and the scribes,[28] the other members of the Sanhedrin. They share in the questioning (11:27), arrest (14:43), interrogation (14:53), and deliverance of Jesus to Pilate (15:1). Similarly we find an explicit mention of the Sanhedrin in the context of the interrogation or trial (14:55) and the deliverance of Jesus to Pilate (15:1). In this same context the high priest[29] appropriately comes on the scene to convene the meeting and lead the interrogation (14:53, 60, 61, 63).

Two other groups receive brief shrift. First, the Herodians are joined with the Pharisees on two occasions (3:6; 12:13). The Herodians are unknown outside the Gospel of Mark and its Matthean parallel (12:13 par. Matt 22:16), and one can only surmise from the context of these sayings that they represented Jews with connections to "Herod," possibly Herod Antipas who ruled the area of Galilee from 4 BCE to 39 CE, as a figure of Roman authority.[30] In any event, the alliance was clearly contrary to Jesus' best interests. Finally, the Sadducees make one appearance to question Jesus about the resurrection (12:18). The content, form, and context of the question indicate that the appearance was adversarial. Their question seeks to trap Jesus by the use of the Law, since, as the writer indicates to the reader, they denied the resurrection (12:18).[31] Furthermore, the question appears in a context of similar questions that challenge Jesus and his teaching in 11:27–12:34.

Without exception the various Jewish groups that are identified in Mark consistently play an adversarial role against Jesus in the narrative. They provide much of the conflict that moves the plot along. One might, therefore, argue that Mark's narrative deliberately vilifies the Jewish groups and thus reflects and deliberately evokes an "anti-Judaism." Yet one must ask which kind of "anti-Judaism"—prophetic, Jewish-Christian, or Gentilizing—while keeping in mind that antagonists in a narrative are not always villains. One needs to look carefully at how this adversarial role is developed. First, it consistently grows out of a response to Jesus' teaching and actions. With the exception of the warning against the pretentiousness of the scribes (12:38-40), Jesus never takes the initiative by speaking pejoratively about any of the Jewish groups. Any such comments come in response to something they have said or done (e.g., 3:5, 28-30; 7:6-13; 10:5). Second, the role played in the narrative by each of these groups closely corresponds to what we know about them from sources other than Mark. This role has to do with basic issues of Judaism that generally involve the Law and the Temple. One cannot fault Mark's portrait of the Pharisees' concern for the Sabbath and purity laws, the Sadducees' question about the resurrection,

---

28. Five times—8:31; 11:27; 14:43, 53, 15:1. "Elders" in "tradition of the elders" (7:3, 5) is more a qualifier of the tradition than a distinct sociopolitical group.

29. "High priest" also appears as a qualifier in 14:47 (high priest's servant); 14:54 (high priest's palace); and 14:66 (high priest's maid servant).

30. See Guelich, *Mark*, 138–39; cf. A. Hultgren, *Jesus and His Adversaries: The Formation and Function of the Conflict Stories in the Synoptic Tradition* (Minneapolis: Augsburg, 1979) 92 n. 36.

31. So Josephus, *Ant.* 18.1.4 §16; *J.W.* 2.8.14 §165.

the role given the scribes, and the jurisdiction of the chief priests. In other words, the actions and words of these groups do not seem arbitrary or contrived in order to create a villain or a caricature. Third, one must look carefully at the roles played by these groups and determine if each role represents the particular groups involved, a religious position, or more generally a people. In other words, do these groups represent: (1) various segments within Judaism, (2) Judaism, or (3) "the Jews"? Is the anti-Judaism, assuming its presence, in Mark aimed at certain segments within Judaism, or the Jews as a people? This question becomes acute when one notes the number of groups involved and the historically appropriate, discrete way the role of each is developed.

In summary, a quick review of the character development provides little basis for concluding that Mark views the Jews or the Jewish people in a pejorative manner. In general, Mark's portraits of individual Jews and of the Jewish people as a whole exhibit no anti-Judaism. By contrast, the specifically identified groups are consistently depicted in mortal conflict with Jesus. They represent power groups or "authorities" concerned about fundamental elements of Judaism like the Law and the Temple. Does their role in defense of these fundamental elements of Judaism, a role that results in Jesus' death, provide a basis for anti-Judaism in Mark? If so, at what level? Before answering, one must look more closely at the basis of the conflict (Jesus, the Law, and the Temple) and the result of the conflict (Jesus' death) in Mark.

## Jesus, the Law, and the Temple

In Mark's narrative Jesus runs into conflict with the Pharisees and the scribes over issues of the Law.[32] That these two groups should be involved comes as no surprise, since the scribes, as interpreters and teachers of the Law, may well represent Pharisaic interests. Certainly both were concerned above all about the Jewish Law. The issues of conflict have to do for the most part with the boundary markers of Jewish identity, such as the Sabbath and purity laws, that arise concretely from Jesus' or his disciples' activities.[33] Only twice is Jesus asked to comment more theoretically about the Law—once about divorce (10:2-9) and once about the greatest commandment (12:28-34).

In 2:23-28 the Pharisees query Jesus about the behavior of the disciples who pluck grain while walking through a field on the Sabbath (2:23-24). Jesus gives a twofold response. First, he refers to David's "unlawful" action of eating

---

32. See Kingsbury, *Conflict in Mark*, esp. 63–88.

33. For recent discussion of Jesus, the Law, and the Pharisees, see J. D. G. Dunn, "Pharisees, Sinners, and Jesus," in J. Neusner et al., eds., *The Social World of Formative Christianity and Judaism* (H. C. Kee Festschrift; Philadelphia: Fortress, 1988) 264–89; repr. in J. D. G. Dunn, *Jesus, Paul, and the Law: Studies in Mark and Galatians* (Louisville: Westminster/John Knox, 1990) 61–86. Mark uses tradition reflecting Jesus' and the early church's struggle with Judaism but more to highlight the element of conflict than for determining issues related to the Law.

and sharing the shewbread with his companions (2:25-26). Then he refers to the Son of man's authority over the Sabbath (2:27-28). Both responses make a christological claim. As the counterpart to David, he, the Son of man, has authority as "lord of the Sabbath"[34] to determine what was appropriate behavior for the Sabbath. For Mark the question is more christological than legal, more about Jesus' authority than about the Sabbath law.

Similarly, in 3:1-6 Jesus heals the man's crippled hand on the Sabbath, while posing the question about whether doing good or evil, saving life or taking it, is lawful on the Sabbath (3:4). That more than casuistry was at stake becomes evident both in his angry reaction at the Pharisees' "hardness of heart" (3:5) as well as in their action of conspiring with the Herodians to destroy him (3:6). By healing the man, Jesus laid claim to "saving life," not in the sense that this was a life-or-death situation, but, as seen in the larger context of the Markan narrative, by bringing to the man wholeness and a new relationship with God that befits Jesus' announcement of the coming of God's redemptive reign (1:1, 14-15).[35] Rather than redefine the casuistic limits of the Sabbath, with which the Pharisees might well have argued, Jesus lays claim to doing God's redemptive work (i.e., giving life) that knows no limits, not even the constraints of the Sabbath law. The Pharisees' extreme response in 3:6 denies his claim of doing good and also denies the implications of this claim.

In Mark, Jesus' claims and actions regarding the Sabbath do not annul the Sabbath law in principle. We have no statement that abrogates the Sabbath law. Rather both pericopes represent a christological claim about God's work in and through Jesus that is implicit in the preceding stories of his forgiving sins, healing the sick (2:1-12), sharing a table with toll collectors and sinners (2:13-17), and feasting rather than fasting (2:18-22). The Pharisees rejected this claim so totally that they sought to destroy him. Therefore, rather than an attack against the Sabbath law or against Judaism, for which the Sabbath was an issue of identity, these Sabbath controversies in Mark provide a commentary on Jesus' ministry and the Pharisees' rejection of its claim.

The purity laws first come into play when Jesus eats with sinners in 2:13-17. Here the "scribes of the Pharisees," noted for their concern about ritual purity,[36] pose the question about Jesus' table fellowship (2:16). Jesus' response in 2:17 does not reject the question of ritual defilement. In fact, nothing is stated that would indicate any desire by Jesus to denigrate their concerns. Eating with "toll collectors and sinners" was of the same cloth as calling a toll collector like Levi to follow him. "Being a friend of toll collectors and sinners" (Matt 11:19;

---

34. See Guelich, *Mark*, 117–30.

35. Ibid., 134–37.

36. See J. Neusner (*From Politics to Piety* [Englewood Cliffs, N.J.: Prentice-Hall, 1973] 83–90), who points out the Pharisees' concern for table fellowship before 70 CE. See also Neusner's *The Rabbinic Traditions about the Pharisees before 70* (Leiden: Brill, 1971) 1.303–4, for further discussion of their concern for purity laws.

Luke 7:34) went beyond friendliness. Like the explicit forgiveness of sin in the previous pericope (2:5), Jesus' table fellowship here represented the healing of the sick and the calling of the sinner (2:17), a claim about the nature of his ministry rather than a commentary on the rules of ritual purity.

Much more is at stake, however, in the question of eating with unwashed hands (7:1-23). Actually, three questions are addressed in this passage: (1) the issue of ritual defilement, (2) the issue of the "tradition of the elders,"[37] and (3) the issue of clean and unclean food.[38] As the text now stands, the Pharisees and "scribes from Jerusalem" accuse Jesus' disciples of eating with unwashed hands (7:5) contrary to the "traditions of the elders." The response of 7:6-13 rejects the very premise of the charge by dismissing the tradition of the elders as human ordinances with no binding authority. In fact, the Pharisees and the scribes from Jerusalem are accused of using the tradition of the elders to circumvent God's commandments, as illustrated by the *Corban* provision (7:6-13). Therefore, Jesus is seen, on the one hand, as categorically rejecting the tradition of the elders (not unlike the Sadducees) while holding to Mosaic Law, and, on the other hand, he is seen as rejecting the specific charge of ritual defilement without necessarily rejecting ritual defilement as such. Yet in the teaching narrative of 7:14-23, Jesus appears both to reject ritual defilement and to annul the Mosaic Law regarding clean and unclean foods by moving the focus from what enters one to what comes from within (7:15). In fact, the narrator actually declares that Jesus has made all foods clean (7:19). Consequently, one has here a rejection not only of the tradition of the elders but also of the Levitical food laws regarding things clean and unclean. At this point, 7:1-23 appears to transgress one of the crucial social boundaries between not only the Pharisees and other Jews regarding ritual defilement but also the food laws that separate the Jews from the Gentiles, a social boundary with which the early church struggled in its own mission (see Gal 2:11-14; cf. Acts 10:9-16). Therefore, what begins in Mark 7 as a dispute over ritual purity ends as a statement about the Levitical dietary laws that reflects the perspective of a community for whom not only ritual purity was no longer an issue but even the Levitical dietary laws no longer obtained. Whereas the former was directed at the "Pharisees and some of the scribes from Jerusalem" (7:1-13), the latter was given especially as instruction for the disciples (7:18-23).

In 10:2-12 the Pharisees pose the question about divorce to "test" Jesus.

---

37. A. I. Baumgartner, "The Pharisaic Paradosis," *HTR* 80 (1987) 63–77; cf. J. Neusner, *The Pharisees: Rabbinic Perspectives* (Studies in Ancient Judaism; Hoboken, N.J.: Ktav, 1973) 230–32.

38. Most likely a composite tradition reflecting several stages of development, the earliest stage pertained to ritual defilement (7:1-2, 5b, 15) that was expanded to address the question of the "tradition of the elders" (7:5a, 6-8, 9-13). Then 7:14-23 became a unit of its own built around 7:15 with commentary. Mark 7:1-23 now consists of a controversy narrative (7:1-13) and a teaching narrative (7:14-23). See Guelich, *Mark*, 361–62; R. P. Booth, *Jesus and the Laws of Purity: Tradition History and Legal History in Mark 7* (JSNTSup 13; Sheffield: JSOT, 1986) 55-114; Dunn, *Jesus, Paul and the Law*, 37–60.

Whereas the Pharisaic representatives of Shammai and Hillel debated the grounds of divorce,[39] here we find the issue raised about divorce itself. Jesus counters by asking what Moses had commanded (10:3-4). When his questioners allude to the provision of Deut 24:1-4, Jesus attributes that to "hardness of heart" and cites from Gen 1:27 and 2:24 regarding God's design at creation that antedates the onset of the "hardness of the heart" of Genesis 3. He concludes by declaring: "What God has joined, let no one separate." In so doing, Jesus does not follow the rabbinic practice of using one part of the Law to interpret another. Rather, he is assuming a new starting point from which the "hard heart" has been transformed in keeping with the dawn of the day of salvation, the new creation, revealed in his own ministry.

These relatively few incidents in Mark pertaining to the Law do set Jesus in contrast to the Pharisees and occasionally the scribes over issues of the Law. Jesus' categorical rejection in Mark 7 of the tradition of the elders as "human ordinances" and his accompanying declaration about what defiles a person—a declaration that meant, according to the narrator, that all foods were clean—might lead one to conclude that Jesus broke with the Law. Nevertheless, Mark does not portray Jesus as arbitrarily or programmatically abrogating the Law. Indeed, there is much in Mark's portrait of Jesus that affirms the Law. For example, Jesus rejects the tradition of the elders precisely because that tradition countervenes the Law. Furthermore, in 1:44 Jesus orders the cleansed leper to follow Moses' commandments, and he approvingly cites the commandments in answer to the rich man in 10:19. When queried by the scribe about the most important commandment (12:28-34), Jesus responds by citing love for God from the schema of Deut 6:4-5 as the first and love for neighbor from Lev 19:18 as the second commandment, a response that even the scribe applauds (12:32).

Yet in the cases of the rich man and the scribe, something more than the Law is involved. While the scribe was not "far from the kingdom of God" (12:34), the rich man, who had kept the commandments from his youth, lacked one thing, namely, the recognition of Jesus as the one whose ministry represented the presence of the kingdom of God (10:20-21). In Mark, this something more that is present in Jesus' person and ministry is evident in Jesus' "authority"[40] and leads to the conflict between Jesus and the Pharisees and scribes in the controversy narratives. Does this "more" of Jesus' implicit claim carry at least an implicit "anti-Judaism," especially when it leads to actions and sayings involving the very laws that serve as critical boundary markers for first-century Judaism?

In Mark's narrative Jesus also engenders and encounters conflict over the Temple. Yet apart from his instructions to the cleansed leper to offer the offerings prescribed by Moses (1:44), we have not the slightest allusion to the Temple

---

39. See Billerbeck, 1.312-20. Cf. the wording of Matt 19:3.

40. See H. Sariola, *Markus und das Gesetz: Eine redaktionskritische Untersuchung* (Annales demiae Scientiarum Fennicae Dissertationes Humanarum Litterarum 56; Helsinki: Suomalainen eakatemia, 1990) 249-50.

before Jesus' arrival there during the Passover season in 11:11. From 11:11 on, it becomes the locus for his final public appearances (11:15, 27; 12:35; 13:1; 14:49). His actions there (11:15-17), his sayings about the destruction of the Temple (13:3; 14:58; 15:29), and the rending of the Temple curtain (15:38) stand out. Nevertheless, all subsequent references to the Temple stand in the light of the Temple scene in 11:15-17.

Much ink has been spilled over the so-called cleansing of the Temple in 11:15-17.[41] This episode is qualified in Mark by the surrounding story of the fig tree (11:12-14, 20-22) and the mixed citation of 11:17. First, the evangelist employs his redactional technique of sandwiching one tradition in the middle of another[42] to use the story of the fig tree (11:12-14, 20-22) as the interpretative framework for the Temple scene. Second, the mixed citation in 11:17, which is drawn from Isa 56:7 and Jer 7:11, elucidated Jesus' actions in the Temple. Consequently, both his actions and his teaching are set in the context of the divine destruction of the Temple as prophesied by Jeremiah. Intended by God to be a "house of prayer for all nations" (Isa 56:7), the Temple had become a "den of outlaws" (Jer 7:11).[43] Rather than "God's house" where all nations could come to know and express their faith in God in prayer (11:17b; Isa 56:7; cf. 11:20-23), the Temple, under the leadership of the Temple establishment, in particular the chief priests, stood now under God's judgment as prophesied by Jeremiah (11:17c and Jer 7:11-14; cf. 11:12-14, 20). This judgment motif becomes explicit in Jesus' statement in 13:2 and is implicit in the accusations of his adversaries in 14:58 and 15:29 surrounding his death.

In Mark's narrative, the Temple scene in 11:15-17 has a dual function in connection with Jesus' death. On the one hand, it sets the stage for his eventual arrest and death. In 11:18 the "chief priests and the scribes" respond to the Temple scene by "seeking how they might destroy him." Then at the trial before the Sanhedrin, testimony is given about his claim to destroy the Temple (14:58), and reference to the same is made by those "blaspheming" him at the crucifix-

---

41. See, for example, V. Eppstein, "The Historicity of the Gospel Account of the Cleansing of the Temple," *ZNW* 55 (1964) 42–58; R. H. Hiers, "Purification of the Temple: Preparation for the Kingdom of God," *JBL* 90 (1971) 82–90; R. E. Dowda, *The Cleansing of the Temple in the Synoptic Gospels* (Ann Arbor, Mich.: University Microfilms, 1972) esp. 129–36; C. A. Evans, "Jesus' Action in the Temple: Cleansing or Portent of Destruction?" *CBQ* 51 (1989) 237–70.

42. See J. R. Edwards, "Markan Sandwiches: The Significance of Interpolations in Markan Narratives," *NovT* 31 (1989) 193–216.

43. Although seen in recent literature (e.g., D. Lührmann, *Das Markusevangelium* [HNT 3; Tübingen: Mohr [Siebeck], 1987] 193) to refer to the occupation of the Temple by the Zealots during the Jewish War (or in Jesus' time–cf. M. J. Borg, *Conflict, Holiness and Politics in the Teachings of Jesus* [Studies in the Bible and Early Christianity 5; New York and Toronto: Mellen, 1984] 171–75), the phrase most likely comes over as a piece of Jeremiah's oracle of divine judgment (see D. Juel, *Messiah and Temple: The Trial of Jesus in the Gospel of Mark* [SBLDS 31; Missoula, Mont.: Scholars Press, 1977] 132–33; Evans, "Jesus' Action in the Temple," 251, 267–69). On the perceptions of corruption in the first-century Temple establishment, see C. A. Evans, "Jesus' Action in the Temple and Evidence of Corruption in the First-Century Temple," in D. J. Lull, ed., *1989 Society of Biblical Literature Seminar Papers* (Atlanta: Scholars Press, 1989) 522–39.

ion (15:29). Yet Mark makes clear that any connection between Jesus' personal involvement with destroying the Temple and his death was unjust; he does that by noting that the charge was based on false testimony (14:58). Furthermore, despite Jesus' explicit declaration of the total destruction of the Temple in 13:2, nothing specific is said in the ensuing discourse of 13:3-37 about this coming event, not to mention his own role in it. On the other hand, Mark does provide a link between the Temple scene and Jesus' death for the reader by noting that the curtain of the Temple was rent (15:38) at the time of Jesus' death (15:37). Indeed the rending of the curtain (15:38), which is followed by the centurion's confession that Jesus is "indeed the Son of God" (15:39), stands in ironic contrast to the blasphemy regarding Jesus and the Temple (15:29) and the mockery of the chief priests and the scribes regarding his being the "Messiah, King of Israel" (15:31-32).

Does this contrasting scene in 15:29-32, 37-38 along with the Temple scene in 11:15-17 and Jesus' prophecy of the destruction of the Temple in 13:2 constitute a major break with Judaism for Mark? Some commentators have argued that it does.[44] Others would deny any direct theological implications behind the scene at the crucifixion by taking the rending of the curtain to be mainly a sign confirming and vindicating Jesus' prophecy of the coming destruction of the Temple.[45]

Mark's narrative does contain a strong, though subtle, Temple critique. Set in the redactional context of the cursing of the fig tree (11:12-14), Jesus' statement (11:17) drawn from Isa 56:7 and Jer 7:11 and his actions in the Temple (11:15-16) clearly represent a statement of divine judgment against the Temple—like the fig tree that had failed to bring forth figs, the Temple had failed to be God's "house of prayer for all nations." Mark 13:2 along with the false charges in 14:58 and 15:29 imply that Jesus saw that judgment as ultimately leading to the actual destruction of the Temple. The rending of the Temple curtain, however, could hardly be equated with the actual physical destruction of the Temple or even be a symbol of the same for Mark.[46] Rather its setting in Mark's narrative context suggests that more than the physical destruction of the Temple is involved. For Mark the rending of the curtain also declares that the divine judgment (11:17) had indeed come to the Temple in Jesus' actions in the Temple scene (11:15-16; cf. 11:12-14) because of its failure to be God's "house

---

44. E.g., W. Lane, *Commentary on the Gospel of Mark* (NICNT; Grand Rapids, Mich.: Eerdmans, 1974) 575: "Jesus' death and the destruction of the formal structures of Judaism are inseparably bound together." Similarly, E. Lohmeyer, *Das Evangelium des Markus* (Göttingen: Vandenhoeck and Ruprecht, 1963) 347; W. Schenk, *Der Passionsbericht nach Markus: Untersuchungen zur Überlieferungsgeschichte der Passionstraditionen* (Gütersloh: Gerd Mohn, 1974) 47.

45. Cf. Lührmann (*Markusevangelium*, 264), who takes the rending of the curtain in 15:38 to be a "sign" of Jesus' prophesied destruction of the Jerusalem sanctuary in 13:2. Similarly, Juel, *Messiah and Temple*, 140–42; R. Pesch, *Das Markusevangelium* (2 vols.; HTKNT 2/1-2; Freiburg: Herder, 1977) 2.498.

46. Cf. Josephus, *J.W.* 3.8.3 §351–353; *b. Yoma* 39b, where the mysterious opening of the outer Temple doors served as an omen for its coming destruction by the enemy.

of prayer for all nations" as illustrated both by the rejection of God's Messiah by the Temple establishment (15:29-32; cf. 11:18) and by the recognition of the Son of God by the gentile centurion at the cross. The actual destruction of the Temple as announced by Jesus (13:2) would simply follow as a matter of course.

In summary, Mark appears to portray Jesus, on the one hand, as affirming the Law yet addressing the Law by word and actions at points peculiar to the social boundaries of Jewish identity. On the other hand, the evangelist portrays Jesus as pronouncing divine judgment on the Temple by his words and actions, a judgment confirmed by the divine rending of the Temple curtain. Consequently, this portrait of Jesus' ministry engages the two main foci of Judaism, the Law and the Temple. By addressing the laws that most serve as boundary markers (e.g., those regarding the Sabbath, ritual purity, and food), Jesus in Mark widens the circle to include those who follow him but fail to observe such identifiers. By pronouncing God's judgment on the Temple, Jesus intends that it cease to be the cultic center and locus for God, who is seen rather to be at work redeeming in the world through the ministry of Jesus. Does this Markan portrait that speaks directly to the central matters of the Law and the Temple in first-century Judaism not constitute a form of anti-Judaism, and, if so, at what level? Before drawing final conclusions, one needs to look at the related topic of Jesus' death, particularly at the role assigned the Jewish leaders in this event.

## Jesus' Death

The theme of Jesus' death plays a major role in the plot development of Mark's story. It implicates his "Jewish" adversaries almost from the outset of the narrative. In 2:6-7 scribes accuse Jesus of the capital crime of blasphemy.[47] This charge takes on even greater significance because it is used later by the high priest to gain an indictment of Jesus from the Sanhedrin in 14:64. In 2:20 Jesus may give his own first hint of his coming death by referring to the future time of fasting when the "bridegroom is taken." Then in 3:6 the controversies of 2:1–3:5 come to a climax with the Pharisees conspiring with the Herodians to destroy Jesus.[48] Thus the evangelist uses a series of controversies (2:1–3:6) early in his narrative to set an ominous tone for the conflict between Jesus and his adversaries.

---

47. In 3:28-29 Jesus turns the tables on the "scribes from Jerusalem" (3:22) by warning them against "blaspheming the Holy Spirit," an offense whose consequences before God extend beyond that of other blasphemies.

48. On the one hand, nothing comes of this conspiracy for obvious reasons, if one assumes that the "Herodians" in Mark's narrative referred to those under the Galilean jurisdiction of Herod Antipas. Jesus' way eventually led to Jerusalem where his death occurred under the jurisdiction of Pilate. On the other hand, though the "Pharisees" do not surface again as mortal enemies in Mark's narrative, their representation among the "scribes" on the Sanhedrin is a common assumption and may explain the shift to the "scribes" in Mark's narrative (cf. 7:1; 3:20; esp. 2:16).

The motif of mortal conflict surfaces again toward the end of the story with appropriate predictions setting the stage along the way when Jesus enters Jerusalem. The fatal conflict is set in motion by his actions in the Temple (11:15-17) and reflected in the controversy stories between him and the Jewish authorities that take place in the Temple area (11:27–12:40). In 11:18 the "chief priests and the scribes sought how to destroy him." In 12:12 "they [chief priests, scribes, and elders; cf. 11:27] sought to arrest him" but "feared the crowd." In 14:1 the "chief priests and scribes sought how to arrest him by stealth and kill him" without disturbing "the people." Finally, in 14:10-11, to the delight of the chief priests, Judas Iscariot offers to betray Jesus to them at night away from the crowds (14:43-44). Intrigue and conspiracy mark these accounts and clearly place the onus on Jesus' adversaries.

The complicity of the Jewish leaders stands out in the apparent "trial" by the Sanhedrin in 14:55-65 and in their actions before Pilate (15:1, 3, 10). Despite the extended debate over whether Mark intended to describe the Sanhedrin scene of 14:55-65 as a trial or something akin to a grand jury hearing,[49] its purpose from the beginning, according to 14:55, was to find incriminating testimony against Jesus. The attempt failed, however, to establish any testimony of a capital crime of blasphemy, and the Sanhedrin condemned him to death (14:63-64) only after Jesus responded affirmatively and spoke of the coming Son of man in terms of Dan 7:13 and Ps 110:1 when asked by the high priest if he was the "Messiah, Son of the Blessed" (14:61).

Once the verdict was given (14:64), the Sanhedrin bound Jesus over to Pilate (15:1), and after that the chief priests played a continuing role. Pilate's abrupt, self-incriminating question, "Are you the King of the Jews?" (15:2), implies knowledge of the Sanhedrin's verdict given most likely by the chief priests who, as noted in the following verse (15:3), accuse Jesus of "many things" (15:3). Then they later incite the crowd to choose Barabbas over Jesus when given the alternative by Pilate (15:11).

Indeed, the responsibility for Pilate's actual sentencing of Jesus to death appears to lie with the chief priests who apparently raised the charge and influenced the crowd. When asked by Pilate if he was the "King of the Jews" (15:2), Jesus responded with: "You say so" (15:2). Yet Mark's story implies that despite the fact that Pilate eventually sentenced Jesus to death for this charge (15:26), he did not take this claim as a serious political threat. First, he offered to release Jesus to the crowd because he recognized that the chief priests had acted "out of jealousy" (15:9-10). Second, he asked the crowd what, if he released Barabbas to them, they wanted him to do with the "King of the Jews" (15:12). When they responded by calling for Jesus' crucifixion, Pilate then asked the crowd, "What

---

49. See, for example, Lane (*Mark*, 529), who takes it to have been a trial, and V. Taylor (*The Gospel according to St. Mark* [rev. ed.; London: Macmillan; New York: St. Martin's, 1966], 570), who opts for a hearing.

has he done wrong?" (15:14). Nevertheless, Pilate, who is hardly portrayed in Mark as either a victim or innocent, does give the order to execute Jesus on political grounds and crucifies him between two "bandits" (*lēstas* [15:27]) who may well have been revolutionaries (see 15:7).

When laid out in this manner, Mark's Gospel does appear to lay Jesus' death at the doorstep of the Jewish authorities, but not the "Jews."[50] Though the Pharisees and the Herodians are implicated early in the story as mortal enemies (3:6) and the "crowd" apparently leaves Pilate no choice,[51] Jesus' death comes ultimately through the forces active in the Sanhedrin, especially the scribes and above all the chief priests.[52] These two groups would have been most involved at the two points in Jesus' ministry that, according to Mark's story, raised greatest conflict with these Jewish authorities—the Law and the Temple. To that extent, Mark's story has a narrative consistency in its plot line that may well have its roots in Jesus' own ministry. At the same time, neither Jesus' actions nor his teaching regarding the Law or the Temple provided sufficient basis for condemning him to death (14:55-59). Grounds for death were found by both the Jewish authorities (14:64) and Pilate (15:26) along political lines by portraying Jesus as the "Messiah, Son of God" (14:61-62) and as the "King of the Jews/Israel" (15:2, 26, 32), for which Pilate with the support of the chief priests sentenced him to death.

Yet there is another side to Jesus' death in Mark's narrative. Instead of appearing merely to be a miscarriage of justice or the result of political conspiracy, it comes as part of God's revealed plan. The Markan narrative reaches a climax in 8:27-29 when the question of Jesus' identity in the light of his ministry is answered from the standpoint of the "people" and of the disciples. The popular opinion viewed Jesus to be a prophet (8:27-28), but Peter, speaking on behalf of the disciples, correctly declared him to be the Messiah (8:29). Yet in Mark's narrative, Jesus responds by speaking of his coming death and vindication as the Son of man (8:31). This and two subsequent passion predictions (9:31; 10:33) provide the theme and substructure for the section of Mark's narrative (8:27–10:52) that leads up to Jesus' fateful arrival in Jerusalem (11:1-11) and the ensuing passion narrative.

In this section Jesus speaks about his coming death as being according to God's plan. The "it is necessary" (*dei*) of 8:31 most likely implies that his death follows in keeping with God's will for him as found revealed in the Scriptures.[53]

---

50. See especially his use of the parable of the Wicked Husbandmen (12:1-12); cf. Gager (*Origins of Anti-Semitism*, 146), who disputes this.

51. In view of the role of the "crowd" in Mark's Gospel, one can hardly take them as representative of the Jewish people. Even so, their actions were laid to the account of the chief priests in 15:11.

52. One might argue that the scribes include the interests of the Pharisees and the chief priests as close associates of the Roman authorities include the interests of the Herodians in the power configuration of Jerusalem.

53. Pesch, *Markusevangelium*, 2.49; J. Gnilka, *Das Evangelium nach Markus* (EKKNT 2/2;

This is certainly stated explicitly by Jesus in 9:11-13 and in 14:21, 27 and is most likely prefigured in the role of the suffering righteous of the Psalms and the suffering servant of Isaiah 53. Motifs from each surface repeatedly throughout the passion narrative. For example, in 10:45 Jesus declares that the Son of man has come "not to be served but to serve and to give his life as a ransom for many," and Psalm 22 underlies much of Mark 14. Furthermore, Jesus' prayer in Gethsemane clearly indicates that his death was in keeping with the Father's will (14:36, 39). Jesus' death for Mark was part of God's plan.

Rather than a contradictory portrait of Jesus' death that attributes it to God's redemptive plan on the one hand and to the political intrigue of the Jewish and Roman authorities on the other hand, these two motifs come together in Mark's portrait of Jesus Messiah, Son of God. Indeed they merge almost at the outset in the controversies between Jesus and the Jewish authorities (3:6) occasioned by his work and message as the Messiah, Son of God (1:1) who has come to announce and inaugurate God's sovereign rule (1:14). The passion prediction of 8:31 combines them most explicitly where God's revealed plan means that the Son of man will be rejected and put to death by the "elders, chief priests, and the scribes" (cf. 9:31; 10:33), the very ones in Mark's narrative who condemn him in 14:55-65 and decide to give him to Pilate for execution (15:1).

Nevertheless, one can hardly conclude that Mark depicts the Jewish authorities as merely carrying out God's redemptive plan and thus playing an innocent if not positive role in the narrative (cf. 12:1-12).[54] As noted above, their role is that of antagonists, as seen by their rejection of Jesus' claim that he is indeed the "Messiah, Son of the Blessed" (14:61-65; cf. 15:32); it is on the basis of that claim that they lead Pilate to execute Jesus as "the King of the Jews" (15:9, 12, 26). Mark's narrative makes it clear that Jesus was indeed the "Messiah, Son of God" (1:1, 11; 3:11; 8:29; 9:7; 14:61-62; 15:39), but not in the sense of a political revolutionary who would reestablish a Davidic kingship that would overthrow the Romans (12:35-37). To the contrary, his true identity as "Messiah, Son of God," included his death and resurrection (8:27-31; 9:2-9) and could be appreciated only after his death, as seen in Mark's development of the so-called messianic secret. Therefore, the demons were silenced (1:34; 3:11-12); Peter's confession of Jesus "Messiah" was silenced and qualified by the passion prediction (8:31); and the disciples were silenced about the events of the transfiguration until the Son of man was raised from the dead (9:9). The climactic scene at the crucifixion comes when the centurion recognizes Jesus at his death to be the "Son of God" (15:39), while the "chief priests and the scribes" mock him as the "Messiah, King of Israel" (15:31-32). With a touch of irony the Jewish authorities then culpably reject Jesus as the "Messiah, Son of

---

Zurich: Benziger; Neukirchen-Vluyn: Neukirchener Verlag, 1979) 16; cf. W. Bennet, Jr., "The Son of Man Must...," *NovT* 17 (1975) 113-29.

54. See K. Snodgrass, *Parable of the Wicked Tenants* (WUNT 27; Tübingen: Mohr [Siebeck], 1983) 72-110.

the Blessed" (14:61-65), by condemning him and contributing to his crucifixion as "the Messiah, King of the Jews" (15:26; cf. 15:31-32). The Jewish authorities not only failed to recognize him to be the "Messiah, Son of God," in whom God was redemptively at work, but, according to the evangelist, the chief priests had delivered Jesus to Pilate for execution "out of jealousy" (15:10).

In summary, Jesus' death is integral to his identity and role as "Messiah, Son of God," in Mark's Gospel in two ways. First, this death was an integral part of God's redemptive plan for Jesus Messiah, Son of God (8:29-31; 9:2-9; 15:39). Second, this death was spawned by the conflict between Jesus' ministry as the Messiah, Son of God, and the Jewish authorities. This conflict ultimately led the Jewish ruling body, the Sanhedrin, to condemn Jesus to death and to deliver him to Pilate for execution (14:65; 15:1). The "trial" before the Sanhedrin (14:55-59) and Pilate's question of the crowd (15:14) show Jesus to be innocent of any capital crime. Rather his identity as the "Messiah, Son of the Blessed," provided the occasion for his death sentence (14:61-65; 15:26) as "King of the Jews." Jesus Messiah, Son of God, dies as part of God's will and plan, but his death is precipitated by the ruling Jewish authorities in Jerusalem, the Sanhedrin, led especially by the chief priests with the help of the scribes. The focus on these authorities and their agenda hardly implicates the "Jews" or "Judaism."

## Anti-Semitism and/or Anti-Judaism in Mark?

The analysis above makes very clear that nothing in Mark's narrative, when read within its historical setting of first-century Palestine, suggests any form of "anti-Semitism" if that term is taken "to designate hostile statements about Jews and Judaism on the part of Gentiles" that "betray very little knowledge of Jews or Judaism, and tend to be sweeping generalizations."[55] The broader question of whether and to what extent Mark's narrative reflects "anti-Judaism" does become an issue especially in view of Jesus' encounter with various Jewish authorities over the Law and the Temple as well as the role of the Sanhedrin and its constituent members in Jesus' death.

First of all, Mark's Gospel betrays very little interest in distinguishing between Jews and Gentiles. Once Mark refers to "all the Jews" in an explanation of an unfamiliar custom (7:3), a statement that says as much about the apparent ignorance of an implied non-Jewish audience as about the Jews. The other references to the "Jews" come in the title "King of the Jews," used exclusively and appropriately by the Romans (15:2, 9, 12, 18, 26; cf. 15:32!). Once Mark refers to a woman as a "Greek, a Syrophoenician by birth" (7:26). This suggests—and an analysis of the Gospel would support this—that unless Mark makes it obvious otherwise, the characters in the Gospel are presumably Jew-

---

55. Gager, *Origins of Anti-Semitism*, 8.

ish. In other words, the identity and roles of the characters in Mark do not appear to reflect any conscious dissociation with the Jews or Judaism (cf. 13:9a), even though Mark's audience itself was apparently non-Jewish and familiar with certain Jewish customs.

Mark does portray Jesus in mortal conflict with various Jewish groups, especially the scribes, Pharisees, and the chief priests. As noted above, these groups have special concerns and responsibilities that provide them with authority or make them "authorities" regarding the crucial institutions of first-century Judaism, the Law and the Temple. Furthermore, as seen above, this mortal conflict between Jesus and these groups almost invariably arises in Mark's narrative over the issue of authority, especially at points concerning the Law and the Temple.

The conflict over the Law involved the Pharisees and the scribes and arose primarily from Jesus' or his disciples' behavior regarding the Sabbath and purity laws, laws that served as boundary markers for groups like the Pharisees even with Judaism. In Mark 7, however, a concern for ritual purity based on the "tradition of the elders" is categorically rejected by Jesus (7:1-13); that leads to a declaration about defilement that goes so far as to set aside the Levitical dietary codes that served as a principal boundary marking a distinction between Judaism and those outside it. Yet in Mark's narrative these episodes serve more to demonstrate the conflict between Jesus and the religious authorities than to provide a guide for determining how his community was to relate to these laws, since these issues hardly concerned the evangelist's community, for whom some of the customs and implications even had to be explained (e.g., 7:3-4, 19). Rather, for Mark, on the one hand, these accounts demonstrate Jesus' authority to redefine the boundary markers as they had been set by the Pharisees and even to set aside the Levitical dietary laws, and, on the other hand, they demonstrate the religious authorities' rejection of this authoritative claim.

The conflict over the Temple arose from Jesus' actions and words (11:15-17) that declared divine judgment against the Temple for failing to fulfill God's intended purpose of a "house of prayer for all nations." In Mark's narrative this judgment was confirmed by the rending of the Temple curtain at Jesus' death (15:38) and would ultimately be demonstrated by the Temple's actual destruction (13:2). At the same time Jesus' actions in the Temple set in motion the conflict with the chief priests and scribes that eventually led to his death (11:18).

Despite the mortal conflict engendered by Jesus' words and actions regarding both the Law and the Temple, Mark's portrait of Jesus that also affirms the Law (7:1-13; 12:28-34) and the Temple cult (1:40-45) makes clear that Jesus is operating within the context of Judaism. At most one would see such words and actions as representing, in Hare's taxonomy, a "prophetic anti-Judaism" not unlike that found in the prophets, Qumran, and John the Baptist. While definitely offering a challenge to the religious authorities, Jesus hardly represented a break with Judaism in Mark.

We have seen that in Mark's narrative Jesus' words and actions pertaining to the Law and the Temple created a mortal conflict with the religious authorities. Even the conflict with the Pharisees is portrayed as a mortal conflict (cf. 3:6), despite the fact that their designs come to naught and they play no role in his death. The scribes, however, who in Mark's story share much of the Pharisees' concern about Jesus' regard for the Law, do participate actively along with the chief priests in arranging for his death. These two groups first come together to plot Jesus' death when he declares judgment on the Temple (11:18). They work together as members of the Sanhedrin to condemn Jesus (14:53-65), and they stand together at the crucifixion to mock the "Messiah, King of Israel" (15:31-32). Yet it is the chief priests who carry the final responsibility for Jesus' death by accusing Jesus before Pilate and inciting the crowd to persuade Pilate to release Barabbas rather than Jesus (15:2-11).

One might, indeed history shows that many have, read Mark's account as an attempt intended primarily to implicate the Jews or the Jewish leaders with Jesus' death. Such a reading, however, does not do justice to the narrative. Mark's portrayal of this mortal conflict focuses on a clash of authorities. From the outset Jesus is seen as "having authority" unlike that of the scribes (1:21-28). His authority is declared in response to the scribes in 2:1-12, is restated in 2:23-28, is questioned by the Pharisees in 8:11-13, and finally is questioned by the chief priests, elders, and scribes in 11:27-33. For the reader of Mark's narrative this clash of authorities is much more than a power struggle, since Jesus' authority comes from his being the "Messiah, Son of God" (1:1) who has come to announce and effect the promised good news of God's rule that calls one to turn back to God (repent) and believe this good news (1:14-15). Therefore, the conflict with the religious authorities spawned by Jesus' work and words demonstrates their failure to recognize his authority and highlights their rejection of him as "Messiah, Son of God." Ironically the rejection of him as "Messiah, Son of the Blessed," led to his death sentence both by the Sanhedrin (14:61-65) and by Pilate (15:24) as the "King of the Jews/Israel" (15:26, 32). Yet it was in his death that not only God's will was accomplished (8:31; 10:33-34, 45; 14:36), but he was ultimately seen to be in fact the "Messiah, Son of God" (15:32-39).

When this mortal conflict is viewed from the perspective of the Jewish religious leaders' rejection of Jesus, one can at most find here a form of "Jewish-Christian anti-Judaism." In Hare's terminology, Jewish-Christian anti-Judaism accents the Jewish rejection of Jesus' message and thereby God's overture of salvation. Yet in Mark this designation must be qualified because it does not obtain for the Jews in general but only for certain of the Jewish authorities who reject Jesus' claim and thereby God's overture of salvation. Furthermore, this designation does not obtain even for all religious authorities, as seen by the stories of Jairus, the president of a synagogue (5:21-43); the scribe who was not "far from the kingdom of God" (12:28-34); and Joseph of Arimathea, who was a "respected member of the council" waiting "expectantly for the kingdom of

God" (15:42-46). Despite the fact that Mark's community does not itself appear to be within Judaism, we have found no trace of any "new" Israel motif or any hint of God's final rejection of an apostate Israel.

Thus, to the extent that Mark's narrative shows Jesus to have addressed issues of the Law and the Temple from within Judaism and in a manner not unlike that found in the prophets, Qumran, John the Baptist, and even among the various groups within Judaism, one can speak of a "prophetic anti-Judaism" in Mark. To the extent that the conflict created by Jesus' words and deeds in Mark's narrative demonstrates the rejection by the religious authorities of Jesus' claim to be announcing and effecting the promised good news of God's redemptive rule in the lives of people (1:14-15) as the "Messiah, Son of God" (1:1), one can speak of a "Jewish-Christian anti-Judaism." Yet one wonders about the value of using such a broad qualifier as "anti-Judaism," which includes everything from an "intra-Jewish polemic"[56] to a "denigration" stemming from a conscious "disconnection"[57] and thus necessitates its own qualifier (so Hare's threefold taxonomy). By referring to an unqualified "anti-Judaism" in Mark, one risks the distortion of the more popular, virulent "anti-Judaism" that can lead and has led to an "anti-Semitism." History bears out that such a distorted reading—including some recent scholarly reading—can be given to at least parts of Mark's text. Yet a careful, historical, literary reading of Mark's narrative will demonstrate that one can in no way speak of "anti-Semitism" and only in a highly qualified manner of "anti-Judaism" in Mark's Gospel.

---

56. Gager's (*Origins of Anti-Semitism*, 9) preference for Hare's "prophetic anti-Judaism."
57. So Sandmel, *Judaism and Christian Beginnings*, 351; similarly, Beck, *Mature Christianity*, 95–128.

# -5-

# "Fighting against God":
# Luke's Interpretation of Jewish Rejection
# of the Messiah Jesus

*David L. Tiede*

## Offense to Jews and Hazard to Christians

Luke-Acts is either a Jewish-Christian story that fell into gentile hands[1] or a Christian tale told at the expense of the Jews.[2] Unfortunately for the Christian gospel and the Jews, it has been both of these throughout most of its history.

The irony and tragic quality of the narrative do not resolve the problem.[3] Nor can centuries of gentile Christian, anti-Jewish triumphalism be denied. Historical efforts to redeem Luke's narrative from such anti-Semitic misreading must also take full measure of Luke's central affirmation: "Let the entire house of Israel know with certainty that God has made him both Lord and Messiah, this Jesus whom you crucified" (Acts 2:36).[4] The text reflects and provokes controversy with and within Israel.

It does make a difference, however, if God's confrontation with Israel, according to Luke, has been perverted by interpreters into a gentile vindication.

---

1. D. L. Tiede, " 'Glory to Thy People, Israel': Luke-Acts and the Jews," in *The Social World of Formative Christianity and Judaism* (Philadelphia: Fortress, 1988) 327–41; repr. in Joseph B. Tyson, ed., *Luke-Acts and the Jewish People: Eight Critical Perspectives* (Minneapolis: Augsburg, 1988) 21–34.

2. J. T. Sanders, *The Jews in Luke-Acts* (Philadelphia: Fortress, 1987); idem, "The Parable of the Pounds and Lucan Anti-Semitism," *TS* 42 (1981) 660–68.

3. Note, however, the immense contribution made by recent literary studies. See R. C. Tannehill, "Israel in Luke-Acts: A Tragic Story," *JBL* 104 (1985) 69–85; D. P. Moessner, "The Ironic Fulfillment of Israel's Glory," in *Luke-Acts and the Jewish People,* 35–50.

4. Throughout this chapter, biblical translations are from the NRSV.

To steal a few lines from the apostle Paul, who was Paul the apostate according to other Jewish views,[5] the unavoidable "stumbling block to Jews" of Christian preaching (1 Cor 1:23) is the crucified Messiah. The narrative of Luke-Acts does not remove this offense, but neither does it turn the story of Christian origins into a cause of gentile "boasting" (see Rom 11:18).

Yet this is exactly the way Luke-Acts has been read through most of Christian history. The story has been understood as "the gentile gospel," testifying to gentile Christian succession or replacement of Israel in the economy of God, much as the Roman triumph was claimed to show that divine favor had passed from the Greeks. So Paul's threefold "turning to the Gentiles" (Acts 13:46; 18:6; 28:28) was thought to demonstrate that "God has hardened the Jews' hearts; salvation is now for the Gentiles."[6]

This is the stuff of anti-Semitism and anti-Judaism in Christian history. Luke's story itself is read as the foundational myth of Christian origins where the triumph of the Christian mission becomes a boast at Israel's expense. When this reading of Luke-Acts is established as definitive, some Jews will conclude that Jesus is "the Messiah of the Gentiles."

But that is impossible for Luke. Jesus is either the Messiah of Israel or he is an imposter. Luke's narrative must justify the gentile mission in order to demonstrate how this can fit with the fulfillment of God's promises to Israel in the reign of the crucified and exalted Messiah. The gentile mission is a major "problem" of the narrative, especially as this mission is invested with God's relationship with Israel and Israel's calling to be the light to the Gentiles.[7]

Historical studies of Luke-Acts must also acknowledge that the question of anti-Semitism is now filled with the heat of the furnaces of "the final solution" to "the Jewish question." Peter Haas observed, "After reading Christian accounts of Judaism, I often wish that Marcion had won. He recognized, I think absolutely correctly, that Christianity and Judaism were utterly different religions and that neither should have to explain itself in terms of the other."[8]

But Luke's narrative was written before Marcion and before "Christianity and Judaism were utterly different religions." Marcion's proposal belonged to the second century when gentile Christians were clearly dominant and the Jewish origins of Christianity had become the problem. In the wake of dire experiences since the second century of the common era, Jewish readers may conclude that the whole New Testament is anti-Jewish. But that judgment is anachronistic in the first century, the formative era of both Judaism and Christianity.

---

5. A. F. Segal, *Paul the Convert* (New Haven: Yale Univ. Press, 1990).

6. E. Haenchen, *The Acts of the Apostles*, trans. R. McL. Wilson (Philadelphia: Westminster, 1971) 729.

7. See S. McKnight's documentation of "the diversity of Jewish authors over gentile questions" in *A Light among the Gentiles* (Minneapolis: Fortress, 1991) 9 passim.

8. P. Haas, "Recent Theology of Jewish-Christian Relations," *RelSRev* 16 (October 1990) 316.

The story of Christian origins in Luke-Acts belongs within the conflict among the people of Israel about the fulfillment of God's promises. All readers of Luke-Acts, therefore, must come to terms with its depiction of "divided Israel."[9] Even those who reject Luke's uncompromising claim for the messiahship of Jesus must acknowledge the thoroughly Jewish origins of the narrative.

## Anti-Semitism: Who Decides and When?

The identity of the interpreter affects the credibility of the judgment of whether Luke-Acts is an anti-Jewish text. Christian interpreters might well consider how much credence they would give to the judgment of a member of the Church of the Latter Day Saints about whether the Book of Mormon is Christian. Trinitarian Christians could understand that the Mormons claim to be Christian and believe their sacred text to be the authoritative fulfillment of the New and Old Testaments. Nevertheless, most Christians would judge the Book of Mormon to be non-Christian or even anti-Christian.

Similarly many Jews will reject gentile Christian affirmations about Luke-Acts as a Jewish book, and the concept of Jewish Christianity will be an evident oxymoron to them. More is at stake here than social identity. To the extent that Judaism, Christianity, and also Islam are theological identities, Jews, Christians, and Muslims confront each other with differing truth claims. Mutual respect of the religious sincerity and integrity of the others is possible, but the truth about God will finally require conversion and commitment to one faith or another.[10]

Therefore, on the one hand, Jews and Christians can agree that the discussion of whether Luke-Acts is anti-Jewish has theological consequences. Christian interpreters, like myself, must affirm that this is not merely a historical question. Naïveté will not excuse or eliminate offense.

On the other hand, this is also a historical question, which deserves an answer as free as possible from the overburden of later centuries. In this light, modern academic Jewish and Christian interpreters can benefit from recent historical studies of the first century CE. When viewed within the social world of formative Christianity and Judaism,[11] Luke-Acts will appear to be a claimant to the heritage of Israel alongside others. In its historical setting, it is impossible for this narrative to be anti-Jewish, at least not anti-Jewish in the way it will later be used by a dominant culture of gentile Christianity.

---

9. J. Jervell, "The Divided People of God: The Restoration of Israel and Salvation for the Gentiles," in *Luke and the People of God* (Minneapolis: Augsburg, 1972) 41–74.

10. See the classic study of A. D. Nock, *Conversion* (Oxford: Oxford Univ. Press, 1933).

11. See J. Neusner et al., eds., *The Social World of Formative Christianity and Judaism* (Philadelphia: Fortress, 1988).

## Luke and the Judaean Conflict

In order to make a thorough historical assessment of whether this literature was anti-Jewish, two questions must be answered in greater detail than is possible in this essay. (1) How does the narrative express or construe the social/theological realities of its own era as it tells of earlier decades? (2) How does this telling compare with other Jewish (messianist and not) versions of "the events that have been fulfilled among us" (Luke 1:1)?

This approach is not merely a return to the "quest for the author" as undertaken by traditional introductions. The issue will not be resolved by a personal identification of the narrator traditionally named "Luke" as Paul's coworker and a physician, whether or not "of the circumcision" (Col 4:10-14). Nor is it simply a question of how historically reliable Luke's narrative is in relating the foundational events of Christian origins.

Precise dating and location of the composition of Luke-Acts are likely to remain elusive in any case. Such details would help specify the social and theological location of the narrative. But the description must be "thicker" to understand the "webs of significance" that humans weave to attach meaning to events around them.[12] A broader grasp of the world that shaped the first century must be coupled with a thorough investigation of the alternative renditions of Israel's faith in the period. Then the meaning and polemics of particular claims and conflicts can be explored.

It is important to note, therefore, that a century and a third of Roman rule probably preceded the composition of Luke-Acts. This narrative stands out among first-century Christian sources in drawing attention to the Caesars (Augustus, Tiberius, and Claudius), proconsuls, procurators, and Herodian client kings. This public arena fits Luke's conviction that the events of Jesus and the apostolic mission occurred in Jewish history as the center stage of God's enterprise of salvation for the whole world (Acts 1:8).

The social realities that Luke-Acts describes fit Israel's late first-century circumstance of conflict, exaggerated by the external pressures of the Roman order. With the possible exception of the stories of the greed of Ananias and Sapphira (Acts 5:1-11) and Simon the magician (Acts 8:9-24), even the episodes of conflict with the Christian community are filled with conviction about the public mission of true, restored Israel (see especially the Hellenists and Hebrews in Acts 6, Paul's call in Acts 9, and the gentile mission in Acts 10 and 15). In comparison with other early Christian literature, only the Revelation to John may be as preoccupied as Luke-Acts with the Christian conviction that "this was not done in a corner" (Acts 26:26).

Many Christian interpretations of Luke's narrative have focused on Luke's place in early Christianity with particular comparisons and contrasts to Paul and

---

12. C. Geertz, *The Interpretation of Cultures* (New York: Basic Books, 1973).

Mark. Such inner-canonical studies have produced elaborately nuanced descriptions of Luke's theology. But this is too narrow a base for determining whether or how Luke's narrative may be anti-Jewish.

Comparisons with other late first-century Jewish literature are more productive. When Josephus, *2 Baruch*, the apocalypses, and early rabbinic sources are read next to Luke-Acts, less is learned about whether Luke has a theology of the cross. But these comparisons teach much more about Luke's conviction concerning the repentance that must precede Israel's restoration in God's plan.[13]

Thus Josephus's historical narrative is also transparent as a construal of how the calamities of the destruction evidence God's just providence. As Harold W. Attridge has summarized this theodicy in the *Jewish War* and the *Antiquities:*

> God does act as an ally, according to the biblical paraphrase, but only for those who are worthy. The major difference in the positions of the two works is the basis on which aid is given. In the *Bellum* it is adherence to and maintenance of the temple cult. In the *Antiquitates* it is virtue, which is epitomized in piety, but which is more inclusive.[14]

In the wake of the Roman destruction, however, Josephus's application of this justice vindicated God and convicted Israel. Even the Romans were justified, at least as instruments of divine judgment. This is consistent with the response to the crisis that Jacob Neusner found in common among the apocalyptic writers, the Dead Sea sect, the Christians, and the Pharisees: "The response of the visionaries is, thus, essentially negative. All they had to say is that God is just and Israel has sinned, but, in the end of time, there will be redemption."[15]

Thus in *2 Baruch*, the revelation ostensibly recalled the first destruction but fundamentally vindicated God's judgment in the Roman War and called for return to faithfulness to God's law as the hope for restoration. The purpose of the theodicy was not, however, essentially negative. The revelation of judgment pointed to the repentance that would yield restoration. As Gwendolyn B. Sayler amplified by comparisons with Pseudo-Philo, 4 Ezra, the *Apocalypse of Abraham*, the Paralipomena of Jeremiah, and the Gospel of Matthew: "All of the documents anticipate some kind of eschatological restoration."[16]

How would restoration come? How long would be the "days of vengeance . . . until the times of the Gentiles are fulfilled" (Luke 21:21, 24)? As Jacob Neusner's study of Yoḥanan ben Zakkai has shown, the foundations of normative Judaism were grounded in these same questions, but now with a "detailed,

13. D. L. Tiede, *Prophecy and History in Luke-Acts* (Philadelphia: Fortress, 1980).

14. H. W. Attridge, *The Interpretation of Biblical History in the "Antiquitates Judaicae" of Flavius Josephus* (HDR 7; Missoula, Mont.: Scholars Press, 1976) 150–51.

15. J. Neusner, "Judaism in a Time of Crisis: Four Responses to the Destruction of the Second Temple," *Judaism* 21/3 (1972) 313–27.

16. G. B. Sayler, *Have the Promises Failed?* (SBLDS 72; Chico, Calif.: Scholars Press, 1984).

practical program... for the repair of the Jewish soul and reconstruction of the social and political life of the Land of Israel." This also came with a new timetable: "Yohanan offered not hope of speedy redemption, but rather a conditional promise: just as punishment surely followed sin, so will redemption certainly follow *repentance.*"[17]

Every Jewish group had the Scriptures, with great stability in the readings of at least the Torah and the Prophets. All knew the Deuteronomistic interpretation of the first destruction, which also permeated the prophetic declarations of Jeremiah, Ezekiel, and Lamentations. Even before the destruction of Jerusalem by the Roman armies, a variety of cultic, nomistic, militaristic, separatist, and cosmopolitan proposals had been advanced among the Jews for how to live faithfully. The Judaean conflict had begun long before the war, persisted in the struggles of the conflict, and continued after the conquest. But by then Israel had lost its physical identifications of Temple, priesthood, and even its puppet kingship.

In this spectrum of Judaean conflict, Luke's narrative is neither more nor less anti-Jewish than the other sources. Luke-Acts is preoccupied with the same question of divine judgment on Israel, and it offers a particular diagnosis of the sin that brought destruction and requires repentance: "because you did not recognize the time of your visitation from God" (Luke 19:44; 23:28-31); or even more directly, "because the residents of Jerusalem and their leaders did not recognize him or understand the words of the prophets that are read every sabbath, they fulfilled those words by condemning him" (Acts 13:27).

The narrative, therefore, is a call to all "the house of Israel" to repent, announcing the messiahship of the crucified and raised Jesus (see esp. Luke 2:29-35; 24:47; Acts 2:36; 3:26; 5:30-32; 10:39-43; 13:32-38; 26:19-23; 28:23-28). The content of this repentance is turning to God by acknowledging that "you acted in ignorance, as did also your rulers. In this way God fulfilled what he had foretold through all the prophets, that his Messiah would suffer" (Acts 3:17-18).

Paul's own call was depicted as a healing of blindness, more a story of repentance than conversion. Nevertheless, Paul's former mission of persecuting the "disciples of the Lord" was actually a persecution of "the Lord Jesus" (Acts 9:5). His call then set the apostle in confrontation with the Judaeans and Hellenists he once represented as a persecutor of "the Way" (Acts 9:1-29). Now as the "chosen instrument" to bring the Messiah's name before Gentiles and kings and before the people of Israel, Paul would learn "how much he must suffer for the sake of my name" (Acts 9:15-16). The repentant Paul is no longer authorized to persecute anyone, but to suffer as did the Messiah.

---

17. J. Neusner, *Judaism in the Beginning of Christianity* (Philadelphia: Fortress, 1984) 93.

## Luke's Claim on Israel's Identity

The conflict in Luke's narrative does not immediately reveal what is going on in Luke's community, and efforts to determine the author's attitude to "the Jews" consistently falter on apparently inconsistent and overlapping comparisons with "the Hellenists," "the Gentiles," "the believers," "the God-fearers," "the Samaritans," "the Galileans," and so on. Most modern interpreters are surprised to read in Acts 15:1-5 about the Christian teachers who "came down from Judaea" and "the believers who belonged to the sect of the Pharisees." Questions about who is Jewish and who is Christian receive very different answers in the world of Luke's narrative.

In broader perspective, however, Luke's story took a clear stand on the issue of who is "true Israel." Whether the author was a (Greek-speaking?) Jew by birth, a proselyte, or a Gentile, the narrative itself set the boundaries so that "everyone who does not listen to that prophet will be utterly rooted out of the people," and "that prophet" is Jesus, the prophet like Moses promised in Deut 18:15-20 (see Acts 3:17-26).

Luke-Acts is a repository of first-century Jewish lore, a major source of datable information on the synagogue in Palestine and the Diaspora, the Temple, the high priesthood, the debates between Pharisees and Sadducees, and even includes allusions to the Zealots and other contenders for Jewish identity such as Theudas and Judas the Galilean (see Luke 6:16; Acts 1:13; 5:33-39). The historical accuracy of some of this data is debated, and the narrative includes most of it in passing. But the narrative is thoroughly at home in Jewish history. Above all, Luke's narrative is filled with scriptural allusions, argumentation, and citations, and the Scriptures are Israel's.

The narrative also depicts a deep conflict within Israel. Luke's summary of Peter and John's commentary on Psalm 2 in Acts 4:27-28 presses the conflict theologically: "For in this city, in fact, both Herod and Pontius Pilate, with the Gentiles and the peoples of Israel, gathered together against your holy servant Jesus, whom you anointed, to do whatever your hand and your plan had predestined to take place."

Such opposition in the story to God's plan has been identified as a literary or plot device, which raises questions about the historical accuracy of Luke's depiction or whether the narrative plausibly reflects actual relationships in Luke's era. If the issue is whether the narrative is anti-Jewish, what counts is how the opposition is depicted and whether such conflicts are historically plausible.

Many in Israel in the story fulfill Simeon's prophecy concerning the infant Jesus; he is truly "a sign that will be opposed" (Luke 2:34). Luke's account of the rejection in Nazareth (Luke 4:14-30) anticipates the story of Jesus' arrest, trial, and execution. The responses of Herod, Pilate, and the Temple leadership are simply hostile and cynical. Like Judas, they are pictures of "wickedness" (Acts 1:18), active conspirators with Satan (Luke 22:3-6). But the story of the people of Israel is much more complex and tragic. Like the disciples and Peter, the people also turn against Jesus, almost against their will, until Pilate "handed Jesus over as they wished."[18]

In Acts, Luke portrays a divided Israel, stressing the thousands of the people who repent at Peter's preaching and are baptized. Furthermore, the narrative gives the reader a plausible idea of why others, notably various religious leaders, reject Jesus. For them, this narrative and its theological claims are intrinsically anti-Jewish.

The Sadducees arrest Peter and John at the Temple "because they were teaching the people and proclaiming that in Jesus there is resurrection of the dead" (Acts 4:2). The rulers of the people, "elders, scribes,...with Annas the high priest, Caiaphas, John, and Alexander, and all who were of the high-priestly family," then hold court, listen to Peter and John proclaim Jesus' resurrection, and release them with a warning "to speak no more to anyone in this name" (4:17). When the apostles explicitly disobey, the high priest and the Sadducees arrest them again out of "jealousy" (5:17), and they object that "you have filled Jerusalem with your teaching and you are determined to bring this man's blood on us" (5:28). The confrontation is fierce with the high priest and Sadducees, as it is again in Acts 23:1-5, where Paul speaks back to the high priest when struck and then concedes his failing at speaking evil of a leader of the people.

In these conflicts, the high priest and the Sadducean rulers regard the disciples as a threat to the peace, the public order, and their authority. If the Sadducees had prevailed as the normative form of Judaism, the question of whether Luke-Acts is anti-Jewish would have antipriestly nuances. Furthermore, the political polemic of preaching the resurrection would be clear.

In both sets of encounters, however, the Pharisees appear on the scene as protectors, if not defenders, of the accused Messianists. Luke's narrative presents a complex picture of the relationships between alternative Jewish groups, each of them laying claim to being true Israel. This diversity is historically plausible and interesting, especially as the narrative depicts the liaisons that emerge between otherwise opposed parties.

In Acts 23:6, Paul explicitly lays claim to his identity as a Pharisee, albeit a messianist Pharisee (see Acts 15:5). The episode is quite opaque as to whether either Paul's apology to the high priest or his appeal to the Pharisees was sincere. Again the issue is not the historical Paul, but whether Luke's story was a caricature or a reasonably plausible depiction. The episode is very compact, and yet the interparty strife is so well documented in Philo, Josephus, and early rabbinic sources that the resulting dissension, even its near violence, is historically credible. Thus Luke's story is not cynical or anti-Jewish. Rather it is a display of how the pressure of the Roman order, here in the presence of the tribune, further fractured the Jewish parties, pitting them against each other. Neither

---

18. See Tiede, *Prophecy and History*, 65–125.

Pilate, Gallio, Felix, nor Festus was finally interested in "matters of questions about words and names and your own law" (Acts 18:15), but these matters were the heart and soul of a scriptural people.

In Acts 5:33-40, it is again a Pharisee, Gamaliel, "a teacher of the law, respected by all the people," who stood up to speak against persecuting the Messianists. His is hardly an endorsement of the apostles' message, but a word of caution, filled with the political and theological wisdom of leaders who wish to prevent party divisions from visiting a worse wrath upon a people. The examples Gamaliel cites are both theopolitical insurrectionists, Theudas and Judas the Galilean. The Roman destruction of such efforts is interpreted as a sign that their undertakings were "of human origin" (v. 38).

Gamaliel's speech is best understood as a piece of Luke's story, reflecting the mode of Hellenistic historians of conveying their critical interpretations through credible speakers. The concluding line with its sharper warning, therefore, is a central theological affirmation that Luke will highlight in the story: "If it is of God, you will not be able to overthrow them—in that case you may even be found fighting against God" (v. 39).

Such an idea was not original with either Luke or Gamaliel. History is full of claims by those in conflict or war that "God is on our side," and such convictions had particular force in Israel's heritage with its consistent confidence in God's judgment and blessing following its faithfulness.

In 2 Maccabees 7, the seven brothers who are enduring persecution instruct the king in the ways of God, even as they are being tortured to death. They appeal to the vindication of resurrection, confess their own sins against God, and warn the king not to assume that "God has forsaken our people" (v. 16). The sixth son's dying words are, "But do not think that you will go unpunished for having tried to fight against God" (v. 19).

In Acts 5, the Messianists who have endured persecution are allowed to leave the council, apparently because of Gamaliel's speech. Then "they rejoiced that they were considered worthy to suffer dishonor for the sake of the name" (v. 41). The suffering for the name itself is interpreted as a trial, and this is directly linked with the continued boldness of proclaiming Jesus as the Messiah (v. 42; see also Acts 9:15, 27-29).

In Acts, the followers of Jesus must come to terms with the fact that they are up against various authoritative representatives of the people of Israel. Even the warning to such leaders from a respected Pharisee in the council helps legitimate the difficult but crucial claim that Jesus is Israel's Messiah. This can be true only if the religious leadership is wrong.

In Acts 10, Peter is confronted with a similarly difficult question of the inclusion of Gentiles. In Luke's narrative account of his speeches, Peter first tells God that he will not eat unclean things (v. 14), then alerts Cornelius that "it is unlawful for a Jew to associate with or to visit a Gentile" (v. 28), but is confronted at every turn with God's will. Having conceded that "God shows no partiality" (v. 34), Peter preaches about Jesus, the Holy Spirit falls on the hearers, and he must ask, "Can anyone withhold the water for baptizing these people who have received the Holy Spirit just as we have?" (v. 47).

All of this leads to the conclusion that the Messianists must themselves be careful not to be found "hindering God" (11:17). The inclusion of the Gentiles to whom God has also given "the repentance that leads to life" (11:18) must finally be conceded to seem "good to the Holy Spirit and to us" (15:28).

Compared to Luke's labored apology for the legitimacy of the messianist mission as God's program, Josephus's account in the *Jewish War* (5 §376–419) of his own speech before besieged Jerusalem is more chilling in its indictment and call for repentance. Jews and Christians alike may be grateful that Josephus's views did not receive normative reception. His need to justify himself and the Romans creates a stance that is more anti-Jewish than Luke's, but this is the postwar narrative of a Jewish general recounting his own speech to the besieged city.

The theme is again that history proves who is on God's side, and the argument is that "you are warring not against the Romans only, but also against God" (§378). The precedents that are cited are more ancient than Gamaliel's in Acts 5, leading like a sad tale of inadequate righteousness on Israel's part to the present crisis. Josephus sees no hope when "the Deity has fled from the holy places and taken His stand on the side of those with whom you are now at war" (§412). The only salvation lies in confession and repentance. The content of this repentance was simply surrender to the Roman armies (§416).

## Jews, Gentiles, and the Messianist Testimony

The Scriptures were common to all the Jewish groups described above, and the call to repentance is fundamental to the prophetic-Deuteronomistic understanding of history, especially in times of crisis in Israel. But what is the content of repentance?

Once Jerusalem had fallen, neither surrender to the Romans nor the return to Temple sacrifice was an option. A repentance of holy war was a failed venture. A return to observance of the law of God was the most enduring and evident repentance.

The repentance to which Luke calls Israel is faith in Jesus as the Messiah, and "God has given even to the Gentiles the repentance that leads to life" (Acts 11:18). Both this call to faith and the emphasis on the inclusion of the Gentiles set Luke's narrative at odds with those Jews, Pharisees and others, who did not accept Jesus as the Messiah and regarded observance of the Torah as the necessary content of repentance.

Christian interpretation of Luke-Acts has been preoccupied with distinctions about where this narrative fits in the spectrum of intra-Christian views,

Hebrews and Hellenists, Pauline and Petrine Christianity, and so on. But the conflict among Jews over the content of repentance is at least equally significant, revealing the broader world of Luke's discourse more evidently. As studies of conflict have shown, even elements of hostility are often evidence of close, intense social relationships.[19]

It may be inevitable that Jews and their Judaism whose identity was forged in the heat of the crisis of the Roman conquest will in time find Luke-Acts to be anti-Jewish. The offense is not the call to repentance, or even the indictment for sin. The whole heritage of Israel is practiced in confessing sin. Nor is the offense in the name-calling, as long as it is remembered that this was a family conflict with many parties contending for the heritage of legitimacy.

But as highly as Luke respects the Pharisees, he regards only those Pharisees who have come to faith in Jesus as repentant, and then they join a host of other Jews and Gentiles in the company of true Israel. This is the "turn to God" that leads to forgiveness of sins and brings "times of refreshing ... from the presence of the Lord ... until the time of universal restoration that God announced long ago through his holy prophets" (Acts 3:19-21).

In the generations that follow the composition of this narrative, Jews and Christians will agree that God has been at work in history, contending with a willful humanity. They will agree that God's justice and mercy will be wrought through human repentance. In time, however, they will also become two religions, contending with each other and with Islam. At times, the religious and racial bigotry and hatred will almost overwhelm these offspring of Abraham and of Sarah and Hagar with violence, and ancient conflicts will be cited to justify differences.

But perhaps some will remember that those conflicts were about faithfulness and repentance, about how God will bring salvation and restoration. Then Luke's narrative may be read as a quest for the truth (Luke 1:4), and the Scriptures may be examined "to see whether these things were so" (Acts 17:11). Perhaps even Jews and Christians can learn once again to discern true repentance and faithful dependence on the promises of God. Then Luke-Acts would no longer be anti-Jewish.

---

19. See G. Simmel, *Conflict*, trans. K. H. Wolff (Glencoe, Ill.: Free Press, 1955).

# -6-

# Anti-Semitism and
# the Gospel of John

## *Robert Kysar*

Over twelve years ago Samuel Sandmel correctly observed, "John is widely regarded as either the most anti-Semitic or at least the most overtly anti-Semitic
of the gospels."[1] Little has been done to ameliorate that harsh judgment since
it was first written.[2] While efforts have been made to soften the impact of the
tone of the Gospel of John when it comes to Jews and Judaism, the fact remains
that a reading of the Gospel tends to confirm Sandmel's judgment. Still, recent
theories for understanding the historical setting of the writing of the Fourth
Gospel do offer some ways of interpreting the harshness with which Jews and
Judaism are treated in this document. Such theories do not change the tone of
the Gospel but offer a way of explaining that tone. Whether explaining the tone
of a literary piece in fact alters the effects of the writing itself is a fundamental
question that must be confronted.[3]

The task of examining the Gospel of John in relationship to anti-Semitism

---

1. S. Sandmel, *Anti-Semitism in the New Testament?* (Philadelphia: Fortress, 1978) 101. In his
earlier introduction to the New Testament, Sandmel (*A Jewish Understanding of the New Testament*
[Cincinnati: Hebrew Union College, 1956] 269) makes much the same observation: "In its utility
for later Jew-haters, the Fourth Gospel is preeminent among the New Testament writings."

2. The tendency toward an anti-Judaistic presupposition operative in the tradition of New
Testament interpretation is well documented in C. Klein, *Anti-Judaism in Christian Theology*
(Philadelphia: Fortress, 1978).

3. See the persuasive argument of E. V. McKnight (*Post-modern Use of the Bible: The Emergence
of Reader-oriented Criticism* [Nashville: Abingdon, 1988] 58), particularly for what he terms "the
contemporary challenge of interpretation." McKnight points out, "Analysis of the various approaches
to the Bible uncovers the same basic procedure: Readers make sense of the Bible in the light of
their world, which includes not only linguistic and literary tools but also world views that influence
the sorts of meanings and the methods that are satisfying."

requires several projects. The first is to investigate the surface of the text and its implications for the question before us. The second is to explore the relevance of a theory for the historical origin of the Gospel that impacts upon our consideration. The final, and most difficult, endeavor is then to ask in conclusion if historical theories have any significance for assessing the relationship between this product of early Christianity and anti-Semitism then and now. My major thesis is that the text of the Gospel itself nurtures an anti-Semitism that is properly understood only in the light of the historical origin of the document.

## The Surface of the Text of the Fourth Gospel

When we raise the question of how the implied author[4] of the Gospel of John treats Jews and Judaism, a clear impression is possible, although one with some ambiguity. The effort here will be to observe the ways in which anti-Semitism surfaces in a reading of the text and how it is cast into shades of ambiguity by the strategies of the narrative. However, in this context we can do no more than undertake a summary of the experience of the reader in following the text of the Gospel as it stands before us without recourse to the history behind the text. This chapter will only isolate and articulate a series of impressions one gains from the reading of the text. I believe that this sort of analysis of the text of the Gospel is especially important for the issue under consideration, since it affords a way of understanding how the Johannine story of Jesus is received by careful readers (and hearers). Thus it is a way of comprehending how it is that the lay reader, untrained in biblical criticism or perhaps unsophisticated in theology, will respond to the story. Such a reader-response criticism is an avenue, I suggest, into a more popular and natural understanding of the Gospel story.

The first impression the reader gains is the way in which the narrator is detached from and consequently distances the implied reader from Judaism.[5] This is accomplished through such expressions as "the Passover of the Jews" (2:13; 11:55) and "a [the] feast of the Jews" (5:1; 6:4; 7:2). Other examples of

---

4. For definitions of the terms "implied author," "implied reader," and "narrator," as used in the following discussion, see R. A. Culpepper, *Anatomy of the Fourth Gospel: A Study in Literary Design* (FFNT; Philadelphia: Fortress, 1983) 15–18, 205–11; J. L. Staley, *The Print's First Kiss: A Rhetorical Investigation of the Implied Reader in the Fourth Gospel* (SBLDS 82; Atlanta: Scholars Press, 1988) 27–47; and S. D. Moore, *Literary Criticism of the Gospels: The Theoretical Challenge* (New Haven: Yale Univ. Press, 1989) 71–73.

5. It is interesting that, while arguing against an anti-Jewish character of the Gospel, R. Schnackenburg (*The Gospel according to St. John* [3 vols.; New York: Herder and Herder, 1968] 1.436) observes about 4:22, "The Gospel displays no hatred of the Jewish people, though it regards them with a certain aloofness."

this detachment are found in 2:6 and 3:25. The effect is to align the reader with the perspective of the narrator, who is separated from Judaism. Those who "own" the festivals are "Jews," and the narrator is neither a Jew nor leads the reader to Jewishness.[6]

A second and more complex impression is gained by the portrayal of the "Jews" (*Ioudaioi*) as characters in the narrative. The clearest impression is that these characters are antagonists of the hero of the story. The Jews consistently fail to understand Jesus (e.g., 3:1-4; 6:52; 7:35; 8:57). But most often they are cast in the role of his overt opponents (e.g., 2:18, 20; 6:41; 8:48). Very early in the narrative they are described as those who persecute and seek to kill Jesus (5:16-18; 7:1), and such motives continue to be attributed to them as the narrative proceeds (10:31; 11:8). Their hostility results in fear of the Jews among those who are interested in Jesus or believe in him (7:13; 9:22; 19:38; 20:19).

Furthermore, the Jews are presented in the narrative as untrue to their own faith and tradition. They do not keep the Torah (7:19) and are not truly children of Abraham but of the devil (8:39-44). They do not understand their own Scriptures (5:39-40; 10:31-39), and their leaders abrogate their loyalty to their God for fidelity to Caesar (19:15).

The impression the reader gains of the Jews, however, is blurred with ambiguity by several features of their portrayal. They are sometimes present in the narrative as neutral inquirers or even admirers of Jesus (7:15; 10:24; 11:36; 12:9). One of their leaders, Nicodemus, seeks Jesus out but cannot understand him (3:1-15), defends Jesus against the Pharisees (7:50-52), and eventually assists in the burial of Jesus' body (19:39). Jews are even said to believe in Jesus (8:31; 11:45; 12:11). However, in the first case (8:31), they eventually become opponents of Jesus, and in the second case (11:45), while some believe, others take action that begins the death plot against Jesus. Most confusing to the reader is the fact that at one point in the narrative Jesus himself is identified as a Jew (4:9; see also 4:22).

The reader is further kept off balance by the way in which these characters labeled Jews are distinguished from other groups in the narratives. The narrator leads the reader to think that the Jews are not to be identified with people of Jerusalem (7:25), the crowds (7:13; 12:17), the Pharisees (7:32-35; 9:13, 18), Ephraimites (11:54), Galileans (4:43-45), or other individual characters in the narrative such as the parents of the blind man (9:18), Martha (11:19, 31), Caiaphas (18:14), and Joseph of Arimathea (19:38). The reader is never given any clue that might lead her or him to recognize these groups or individuals as Jews.

---

6. Staley (*Print's First Kiss*, 82) points out how the narrator's translation of Aramaic and Hebrew words (e.g., 1:38) makes "the implied reader feel like an outsider: They separate—as nothing else could—the narrator's and characters' world from that of the implied reader." This practice might also be viewed as part of the strategy of the implied author to distance the reader from Judaism.

Out of this ambiguity the reader is led to conceive of Jews as those persons in the narrative who are most often predisposed to unbelief, rejection, and even hostility toward Jesus. The vague name, "Jews," becomes in the reader's mind representative of opposition to Jesus and his mission.[7]

Another of the reader's impressions is that the leaders of Judaism are also, in general, opponents of the Christ figure. The Pharisees are blind (9:40-41) and false leaders who guide the people away from the truth, even as do the Jews (9:40; and the discourse in 10:1-18). The Pharisees along with the council and the chief priests plot the death of Jesus (11:46-53) and seek to have him arrested (11:57), eventually succeeding in doing so (18:3). While not unified in their response to Jesus (9:13-16), the Pharisees are most often presented as opponents of the Christ figure (4:1; 7:32; 8:13; 12:42). Strangely, however, the reader is told not to confuse the Pharisees with the "authorities" (*archontes*), many of whom believe in Jesus (12:42).[8]

The chief priests fare no better in the narrative. As with the Pharisees, the narrator leads the reader to believe they are opponents of Jesus. Since the chief priests are depicted as plotting to have Lazarus killed as a way of diminishing the movement toward Jesus (12:10), cry out for Jesus to be crucified (19:6), and declare that Jesus is not their king (19:15) and that they do not want him labeled as such (19:21), the reader is left with the impression that these characters are hostile adversaries of Jesus.

One cannot read the passion story of the Gospel of John and escape the impression that the Jewish leaders alone are responsible for the arrest, conviction, and death of Jesus (18:3, 12, 19ff.).[9] In his deliberations Pilate is shown caving in to the desires of the Jewish leaders (18:31, 38-40; 19:4-8, 12-16), even though he declares no less than four times his own judgment that Jesus is innocent (18:38; 19:4, 6, 12). Even the execution itself seems to be carried out by Jewish leaders and/or their representatives (19:16, where the antecedent for "they" appears to be found in the chief priests of 19:15).

Finally the impression gained by the reader is that Judaism in general is degenerate and untrue. A number of the features of the narrative contribute either explicitly or implicitly to this impression. While the Jews and leaders of Judaism are most often opponents to Jesus, the Samaritans readily receive

---

7. Culpepper (*Anatomy,* 138) suggests that "the burden of unbelief which the Jews are made to carry is relieved in two ways. First, John affirms that belief must be given (6:37, 39). . . . Second, some of the Jews do believe . . . so John allows hope that for some at least (i.e., those who are given) belief is possible." But he concludes nonetheless that "the Jews carry the burden of the unbelief of 'the world' in John."

8. Although the antecedent is vague, the reader gains the impression from 12:37-43 that the Pharisees are prevented by God from believing in Jesus. Cf. F. Mussner, *Tractate on the Jews* (Philadelphia: Fortress, 1984) 206-7.

9. Cf. D. Granskou, "Anti-Judaism in the Passion Accounts of the Fourth Gospel," in P. Richardson and D. Granskou, eds., *Anti-Judaism in Early Christianity* (Waterloo, Ont.: Wilfrid Laurier Univ. Press, 1986) 1.201-16.

and confess him (4:39-42). Those who believe in Jesus will be put out of the synagogue (9:22; 12:42; 16:2).

In contrast to the falsity of Judaism, the message of Jesus is everywhere presented as superior to the religion of the Jews (2:1-10; 4:21; 5:39, 45; 6:58; 8:31, 58). Jesus' relation with the Temple suggests the superiority of his message (2:19-22; 7:14ff., 28). The preface to John's story of Jesus functions to give the reader those essential insights that will lead her or him properly to understand the entire story.[10] The importance of 1:17, therefore, cannot be overemphasized. The "grace and truth" revealed in Christ is superior to the Law of Moses. Consequently the use of the words "true" and "truth" throughout the narrative (e.g., 1:9; 6:32; 14:6; 18:37) causes the reader to infer that Judaism is false. While Jesus is made to stress the continuity between himself and his message and Hebrew Scriptures (5:39; 6:45; 8:56; 10:34), Judaism is depicted as a faulty understanding of those Scriptures. The "true Israelite in whom is no guile" is one who goes on to become Jesus' disciple (1:47).

This summary of impressions drawn from a reading of the Gospel of John is not without shades of ambiguity. But, on the whole, the conclusion is inescapable that the surface of the text (the narrative of the Gospel taken by itself) persuades a reader to cast Jews and Judaism in an unfavorable light. The reader is encouraged to stand detached from Judaism; to take the terms "Jews," "Pharisees," and "chief priests" as referring to Jesus' opponents; to infer that the leaders of Judaism (and perhaps even the Jewish people themselves) alone were responsible for the execution of Jesus; and to believe that Judaism is untrue and that Christ is superior in every way to that religion. The conclusion is inescapable that the text of the narrative nurtures a negative mentality toward Jews and Judaism.

## The Historical Origin of the Fourth Gospel

Attention has been paid in the previous section simply to what appears on the surface of the text of the Gospel of John. Now it is necessary to try to move "behind" the text to examine two related questions. The first is the historical identity of the expression "the Jews" in the Johannine Gospel, and the second is the historical occasion for the production of the document.

The effort to identify the historical referent for the term "the Jews" as it is used in the Fourth Gospel has occupied a good deal of Johannine scholarship. *Ioudaioi* occurs some seventy-one times in the Gospel, as compared with only sixteen occurrences in the Synoptic Gospels but more than eighty in the Acts of the Apostles. The Synoptic occurrences of the expression appear most often on the lips of gentile characters, as opposed to the Fourth Gospel where it is

---

10. Culpepper, *Anatomy*, 168.

most frequently in the comments of the narrator. In the contemporary reading of John the expression is naturally taken as a reference to the religious-ethnic group we know as modern Jews. But to whom was the evangelist referring when speaking of "the Jews"?

In the framework of the evangelist's dualism it is clear that the Jews belong most often (but not with an absolute consistency) to the "world" (*kosmos*). That means that "the Jews" are part of the realm of unbelief, the reality that opposes Jesus and the revelation of God. They are the main constituent of the negative pole of the dualistic scheme of the Gospel, the opposite of which is the Christian believer. As D. Moody Smith has observed, Johannine dualism and the theological use of the expression "the Jews" "mythologizes the distinction between two modes of existence, the believing and authentic over against unbelieving and unauthentic, by identifying them with two historically and empirically distinct communities, the Christian and the Jewish."[11]

However, when we ask to what existent, historical group the expression refers, the answer is less clear. Few, if any, responsible scholars today would argue that the reference is to the entire Jewish people, for such a view would make no sense given the fact that nearly all of the characters—and certainly Jesus and the other main characters—of the Gospel are themselves Jews. In 9:22, for instance, surely the parents of the blind man are themselves Jews, and in 20:19 it must unquestionably be assumed that the disciples are also Jews. The most frequent nominees for the position as referent of the expression are Judaeans, as opposed to Galilean Jews,[12] and the religious leaders of the Judaism contemporaneous to the fourth evangelist.[13] The former argument does not prove persuasive, as von Wahlde has shown.[14] His own argument is the more convincing. It is likely that "the Jews" in the Fourth Gospel refers to those leaders who hold some influence over their Jewish constituency in the region known to the fourth evangelist. To summarize again in the words of D. Moody Smith: " 'The Jews' is, then, a term used of a group of Jewish *leaders* who exercise great authority among their compatriots and are especially hostile to Jesus and his disciples.... It refers to certain authorities rather than to the people as a whole."[15]

But our conclusions regarding the use of the expression "the Jews" lead only to a further question: What situation would result in such a slanderous

---

11. D. M. Smith, "Judaism and the Gospel of John," in J. H. Charlesworth, ed., *Jews and Christians: Exploring the Past, Present, and Future* (New York: Crossroad, 1990) 77.

12. See, e.g., R. T. Fortna, *The Fourth Gospel and Its Predecessor* (Philadelphia: Fortress, 1988) 310–11; and idem, "Theological Use of Locale in the Fourth Gospel," *ATR* (supp. series 3: *Gospel Studies in Honor of Sherman Elbridge Johnson*) (March 1974) 58–95.

13. See, e.g., U. C. von Wahlde, "The Johannine 'Jews': A Critical Survey," *NTS* 28 (1982) 33–60; and idem, *The Earliest Version of John's Gospel: Recovering the Gospel of Signs* (Wilmington, Del.: Glazier, 1989) 31–36.

14. See the previous note.

15. Smith, "Judaism and the Gospel of John," 82. Cf. Granskou, "Anti-Judaism," 202–9.

and stereotypical reference to Jewish leaders—equating them with the force of evil? In what occasion would Jewish leaders have evoked such an attitude as that of the fourth evangelist's? In other words: What was the historical situation in which the fourth evangelist wrote?

Our second issue in the consideration of the historical origin of the Gospel of John, then, leads our inquiry to what might have been the concrete setting of the writing of the Gospel of John. Unfortunately this endeavor is fraught with numerous problems. The most important of these is the obvious fact that we must deal with imaginative historical reconstruction armed only with the explicit text, its implications, and our relatively scant knowledge of the history of the period. Hence, it is with theory that we must now deal—theory that commends itself at best with some degree of probability but never with absolute conclusiveness. Nonetheless, a theory of the historical origin of the Gospel is essential to an effort to assess the relationship between the Gospel of John and anti-Semitism. I shall summarize a theory for the historical setting of the writing of the Gospel of John that holds persuasive credibility for many Johannine scholars today[16] and then attempt to view the anti-Semitic quality of the text in the light of that theory.

Over two decades ago J. Louis Martyn and Raymond E. Brown each proposed that the occasion for the writing of the Fourth Gospel was an experience of expulsion of a Christian community from their synagogue home.[17] While they differed in the details of their proposals, each took the references in the Gospel to expulsion from the synagogue (*aposynagōgos*, 9:22; 12:42; 16:2) as indications that the Christian community of which the fourth evangelist was a part and for which the Gospel was written had been part of a Jewish synagogue but was then expelled from its religious community there. The precise reasons for the expulsion are speculative, and Brown and Martyn offered differing the-

---

16. The limitations of space do not allow for a consideration of all of the many historical settings that have been proposed for the Gospel of John even in recent years. Therefore, I have chosen here to discuss only the hypothesis that seems to me to be the most widely endorsed and (in my view) the most convincing. Other proposals have been offered in recent years. The reader is directed to my surveys of such proposals in *The Fourth Evangelist and His Gospel* (Minneapolis: Augsburg, 1975) 147–65; "Community and Gospel: Vectors in Fourth Gospel Criticism," in J. L. Mays, ed., *Interpreting the Gospel* (Philadelphia: Fortress, 1981) 265–67, 273–74; "The Gospel of John in Current Research," *RelSRev 9* (1983) 316–17; and "The Fourth Gospel: A Report on Recent Research," in H. Temporini and W. Haase, eds., *Aufstieg und Niedergang der Römischen Welt* (Berlin: Walter de Gruyter, 1985) 2/3.2425–32.

17. J. L. Martyn, *History and Theology in the Fourth Gospel* (rev. ed.; Nashville: Abingdon, 1979). Cf. idem, *The Gospel of John in Christian History: Essays for Interpreters* (New York: Paulist, 1978); R. E. Brown, *The Gospel according to John* (AB 29 and 29a; Garden City, N.Y.: Doubleday, 1966). Cf. idem, *The Community of the Beloved Disciple* (New York: Paulist, 1979). While Martyn and Brown brought this theory into prominence in recent Johannine studies, they were not the first to make such a proposal. See, e.g., K. L. Carroll, "The Fourth Gospel and the Exclusion of Christians from the Synagogue," *BJRL* 40 (1957) 19–32, and J. Parkes, *The Conflict of the Church and the Synagogue: A Study in the Origins of Antisemitism* (New York: World, 1961) 83.

ories.[18] But both understood the Gospel of John (in at least one of its editions) as a response to the experience of the expulsion.

But both Brown and Martyn further understood that the present Gospel reflects the ongoing dialogue between Jews and Christians after their separation. Martyn asserts that the Gospel "seems to reflect experiences in the dramatic interaction between the synagogue and the Johannine church."[19] The central focus of that interaction appears to have been the identity of Jesus and in particular the high christological claims made by the Johannine Christians.[20]

In the years since the proposal was offered by Brown and Martyn there have been numerous studies that embraced and attempted further to confirm and expand the theory. These have come from disparate types of works on various Johannine themes.[21] Their effect has been to offer impressive demonstration of the plausibility of what Brown and Martyn had hypothesized.

An increasingly clear picture emerges from all these studies grounded in the hypothesis that the Gospel was written in response to the exclusion of the Johannine church from the synagogue and the subsequent dialogue between these two religious parties. The subject of the picture is a defensive and threatened Christian community, attempting to reshape its identity isolated from the synagogue and its Jewish roots. The picture is trimmed in vigorous debate over issues central to both Jews and Christians. It is shaded with hostility toward the Jewish parents of this Christian offspring, hostility highlighted with sometimes violent language.[22] The center of the picture, however, seems to be the subject

---

18. Martyn's earlier contention that the expulsion should be related to the "Twelfth Benediction" (the *Birkat Ha-Minim*) and the conference of rabbis at Jamnia was countered vigorously and effectively by historical investigations. Martyn himself has modified his earlier statements in this regard, and most Johannine interpreters deny any direct link between the expulsion of the Johannine Christians and the Twelfth Benediction. See S. T. Katz, "Issues in the Separation of Judaism and Christianity after 70 C.E.," *JBL* 103 (1984) 43–76, and R. Kimmelman, "*Birkat Ha-Minim* and the Lack of Evidence for an Anti-Christian Jewish Prayer in Late Antiquity," in E. P. Sanders, ed., *Jewish and Christian Self-definition* (Philadelphia: Fortress, 1981) 1.226–44. Smith ("Judaism and the Gospel of John," 84–87) is helpful in summarizing the value of Martyn's first proposal, although he assesses it more highly than I would be inclined to do. J. Koenig regrettably makes the Twelfth Benediction the basis of his approach to the Fourth Gospel in *Jews and Christians in Dialogue: New Testament Foundations* (Philadelphia: Westminster, 1979) 122–23, as also does N. A. Beck, *Mature Christianity: The Recognition and Repudiation of the Anti-Jewish Polemic of the New Testament* (Selinsgrove, Pa.: Susquehanna Univ. Press, 1985) 250–51.

19. Martyn, *History and Theology*, 37.

20. For my own brief statement of the historical setting for the writing of the Gospel, see *John* (Augsburg Commentary on the New Testament; Minneapolis: Augsburg, 1986) 13–15.

21. Examples include the following: W. A. Meeks, *The Prophet-King: Moses Traditions and the Johannine Christology* (NovTSup 14; Leiden: Brill, 1967); J. Beutler, *Martyria* (Frankfurt: Josef Knecht, 1972); E. Grässer, "Die Antijüdische Polemik im Johannesevangelium," *NTS* 10 (1964–65) 74–90; S. Pancaro, *The Law in the Fourth Gospel: The Torah and the Gospel, Moses and Jesus, Judaism and Christianity according to John* (Leiden: Brill, 1975); J. H. Neyrey, *An Ideology of Revolt: John's Christology in Social-Science Perspective* (Philadelphia: Fortress, 1988); R. A. Whitacre, *Johannine Polemic: The Role of Tradition and Theology* (SBLDS 67; Chico, Calif.: Scholars Press, 1982); Fortna, *Predecessor*; and von Wahlde, *Earliest Version*.

22. Paul S. Minear argues that the Gospel was set within the context of a realistic fear of martyrdom at the hands of Jewish authorities. See his *John, the Martyr's Gospel* (New York:

of Christian identity. Who are the Johannine Christians now that they can no longer claim the synagogue as their home? In the background of the picture, I propose, we may dimly perceive a synagogue in which there is a not dissimilar identity crisis. It may be that the Jewish brothers and sisters who found it necessary to separate themselves from the Christians in their midst were struggling to understand themselves amid the trauma of the destruction of their Jerusalem Temple and what that might mean for the future nature of their faith. In other words, the expulsion of the Christians from the synagogue may have been an effort to declare what Judaism was when stripped of its cultic center. The picture, then, is of two sibling religious communities, each with its own identity issues.

Armed with this imaginative reconstruction of the setting for the writing of the Gospel, one returns to the text enabled to see many of its features in a new light. Foremost it is the polemic tone of the Gospel that is suddenly made understandable, and to which we shall return for more extensive discussion. But also illumined by the light of the proposed setting for the Gospel is its concentration on the identity of Christ. Since that was doubtless the primary issue under consideration in the dialogue with the synagogue, it is clear why the document would seek to clarify and stubbornly insist on its community's affirmations concerning Christ. Also illumined is the danger-fraught dualistic thought of the fourth evangelist. If basic Christian identity is at stake, in order to clarify that identity the evangelist resorts to a drastic either/or schema to define the distinction between the Christian and the Jew.

But most important for our purposes is how this hypothesis for the historical origin of the Gospel informs the anti-Jewish tone of the text. First of all, it makes clear that the language regarding Jews and Judaism is polemical in nature and typical of classical polemic. If the very existence of the Christian community is threatened by its expulsion from the synagogue, it is natural that the stance toward Judaism be polemical. It is sometimes proposed that the Gospel implies the existence of "crypto-Christians" who had renounced their Christian allegiance and remained in the synagogue. Apostasy may also have threatened the Johannine church. Consequently, the tone of the writing is hostile and argumentative.

The Jewish-Christian relationship standing within the shadows of history behind the Fourth Gospel was as much a social phenomenon as a religious one.[23] The issue at stake was the social repositioning of the Christian community. By being expelled from the synagogue they had experienced the trauma of social

---

Pilgrim, 1984) 26–27. I doubt that that conclusion is warranted on the basis of the evidence of the Gospel, although the vigorous interaction of Jews and Christians may well have involved violence.

23. Increasingly more is being written regarding the sociological setting for the Gospel of John, much of it premised on the Martyn-Brown hypothesis for the origin of the Gospel. Among the most important and influential of the published works to this date are the following: W. A. Meeks, "The Man from Heaven in Johannine Sectarianism," *JBL* 91 (1972) 44–72; B. J. Malina, "The Gospel of John in Sociolinguistic Perspective," *Center for Hermeneutical Studies in Hellenistic and Modern Culture*, Colloquy 48 (1985) 1–23; and J. Neyrey, *Ideology of Revolt*.

dislocation. Their task was now one of making a new place for themselves in a society that appeared to them to be hostile and unaccommodating of their views. The tendency was to conceive of themselves as the in-group defending itself against the out-group. Hence, so much of the tone and language of the Gospel suggest this insider-versus-outsider perspective (e.g., the negative use of the word "world" [*kosmos*] in the Gospel at such places as chap. 17).

In summary, the posture of the church was that of defensiveness amid the self-doubt of uncertain identity. The polemical quality of the Gospel of John tells the interpreter more about the evangelist and the Johannine community than it witnesses to the ontological status of the Jews or Judaism. The view of the Gospel as the result of Jewish-Christian dialogue following the expulsion of the Christians from the synagogue explains why Judaism is painted in such unfortunate colors and why Christian faith is presented as superior to Judaism. If our hypothesis is sound, the Johannine Christians occupied a precarious position. They had been *Christian Jews* who understood themselves as part of the ancient people of God. Their messianic affirmations concerning Jesus of Nazareth were made in the context of the faith of Israel. But now with their expulsion from the synagogue they were trying to affirm and express that they did not need Judaism. Their Christian faith could stand on its own without the support of Judaism, even while it appealed to the Jewish Scriptures as evidence of its truthfulness. It was a formidable (and perhaps impossible) task.[24] The approach taken to the task was to argue that Judaism was in error, degenerate, and unfaithful to its God. Christ offered the true revelation of that God, and hence Christianity apart from Judaism was the truth. The leaders of Judaism had beguiled the people into falsehood; they were the "hirelings" and "robbers" of the sheepfold (10:1-15). When confronted with the true revelation of their own God—a revelation anticipated in their own Scriptures—they executed the revealer. The vitriolic attack on Judaism is nothing more nor less than the desperate attempt of the Johannine Christians to find a rationale for their existence in isolation from Judaism.

The proposal for the historical origin of the Gospel of John advocated here makes at least two additional facts somewhat more comprehensible. These two each have to do with the reality that characteristics usually associated with Judaism before the advent of Christianity are notably absent from or diminished in importance in the form of Christian thought advocated by the fourth evangelist. First among these is the absence of any central role assigned to Torah. While Torah is invoked in the argument that Jesus' message is truth and he himself is the Son of God (e.g., 5:39), the authority of Torah plays no role in the life of the believer.[25] Its moral teachings are in no way employed as a basis for

---

24. L. Gaston ("Retrospect," in S. G. Wilson, ed., *Anti-Judaism in Early Christianity* [Waterloo, Ont.: Wilfrid Laurier Univ. Press, 1986] 2.174) correctly observes, "[The Fourth Gospel] is sectarian, even paranoiac, but it does not deny the central self-affirmation of Judaism."

25. In this way the response of Johannine Christianity is markedly different from that represented

the believer's behavior. The absence of a covenantal theology is another feature of the Fourth Gospel's thought that might be considered "un-Jewish." The word "covenant" (*diathēkē*) is entirely absent from the Gospel.[26]

But in spite of the best efforts of the fourth evangelist the basic Jewishness of the perspective of the Johannine community is visible between and behind the lines of the text.[27] Hence, an older tradition in which Jesus clearly identifies himself as a Jew and affirms Judaism as the source of salvation (4:22) slips past the watchful eye of the evangelist-redactor to confuse the reader.[28] Hence, the fundamental christological statement of the Gospel (1:1-18) is modeled on the Jewish understanding of wisdom.[29] This is to say that even in their desperate need to understand themselves over against Judaism, the Johannine Christians were not able to speak of their faith without recourse to its Jewish roots.

Finally, this hypothesis for the origin of the Fourth Gospel helps us understand the role it assigns to the Jews and the leaders of Judaism. A literary observation is needed in the midst of this discussion of the historical origin of the Gospel. An effective narrative needs an antagonist as much as it needs a hero figure. The fourth evangelist could tell the story of Jesus most powerfully only with a negative figure set over against the Christ figure in the dynamics of the narrative. The situation of the Johannine community provided such an antagonist ready at hand in the figure of the Jews. Since the opponents of the fourth evangelist's own community were members of the synagogue, it was easy to make Jews, and in particular the leaders of the synagogue, the opponents of Jesus in the narrative.[30] Martyn's insight that the Gospel of John presents a two-level drama is helpful at this point. It is Martyn's contention that, while the evangelist told the story of Jesus, the opponents of Jesus in the narrative were only thinly disguised opponents of the writer's own contemporary Christian community. Hence, the character

---

in the Gospel of Matthew, which might also have been written out of an effort to define Christian faith in relationship to Judaism. See, e.g., N. Perrin, *The New Testament: An Introduction* (New York: Harcourt Brace Jovanovich, 1974) 169–75.

26. This is true in spite of Brown's efforts (e.g., *John*, 2.614) to explicate the message of the Gospel in covenantal categories.

27. Kysar, *Fourth Evangelist*, 144–46.

28. My proposal that 4:22 represents part of an older tradition is not the most common understanding of this verse. R. Bultmann (*The Gospel of John* [Philadelphia: Westminster, 1971] 189) is an example of those who insist it was an "editorial gloss." Both Brown (*John*, 1.172) and Schnackenburg (*John*, 1.436), among others, deny that, the latter saying, "Jesus had to overcome the woman's repugnance to the 'Jews.'" Neither Fortna (*Predecessor* and *The Gospel of Signs: A Reconstruction of the Narrative Source Underlying the Fourth Gospel* [SNTSMS 11; Cambridge: Cambridge Univ. Press, 1970]) nor von Wahlde (*Earliest Version*) argues that 4:22 was an early tradition. While I cannot make a case here for the claim that it was, it does seem to me that for some of the reasons implied above it may very well represent a part of the narrative of chap. 4 that originated among the Johannine Christians while they were still part of the synagogue.

29. Brown, *John*, 1.25–36.

30. In *John, the Maverick Gospel* (Atlanta: John Knox, 1979) 57, I suggest the Jews in the Fourth Gospel are "stylized types" used as a foil to demonstrate the revelation in Jesus.

of the Pharisees in 9:13-17 could so easily become the Jews in 9:18.[31] The first readers of the Gospel were thereby enabled to identify their own struggles with the struggle of their Master. The Gospel supplied them sanction to understand their own conflict with members of the synagogue as conflict with the forces that had been responsible for the death of their Lord. It was a powerful literary tool in that historical setting, however unfortunate the consequences have become for succeeding generations of Christians and Jews.

The puzzling and perplexing portrayal of the Jews as the opponents of Jesus in the Gospel of John, therefore, owes its existence to a literary necessity and a historical accident. The fourth evangelist, I suggest, had no intention of issuing a universal indictment against Jews and Judaism (note the use of the words "Israel" and "Israelite," e.g., in 1:31, 49; and 12:13). The author was attempting to be as effective as possible in aiding the community for which the writing was intended. To insure the continued existence of the Johannine church there may have seemed no alternative to indicting the Jews. To give expression to the loss and hurt of the Christian community there may have seemed no alternative than to strike out at their former religious brothers and sisters of the synagogue. Oddly enough, the community that was founded on the sacrifice of an innocent person for their salvation now sacrificed their former Jewish brothers and sisters for the sake of their self-identity.

## Conclusions

The persuasiveness of the argument that the Gospel of John was written in the wake of the expulsion from the synagogue and in the backwash of a lively dialogue between the Christian and Jewish communities is impressive. Yet it remains a theory—at best a hypothesis that commends itself to us in a number of ways. Weighed against the evidence of the experience of reading the text itself, however, the theory of the historical origin of that text is seriously weakened. The evidence we have is the facticity of the text, on the one hand, and the plausibility of a historical theory, on the other. And the latter looks rather puny when compared with the former. Furthermore, a fundamental question lurks in the background.

Does historical contingency count for anything when dealing with the issue of the posture of a Christian document in relationship to Judaism? The answer must surely be yes in one sense but no in another. The historical origin of the Gospel of John makes its anti-Semitic tone understandable, perhaps even excusable. But it does not alter the basic reality of that tone as the Gospel is read and heard. In other words, contingency may count for something in the

---

31. Martyn, *History and Theology*, esp. 24–36.

classroom but for little in the place of worship and even less in the privacy of the individual layperson's reading of the Gospel.[32]

The reality is that an occasional writing has become canonical literature. The document we know as the Gospel of John was written within, out of, and for a very concrete and specific situation involving a particular Christian community in a given time and place. It may have served an admirable purpose in its origin. We might even conclude that this document made possible the continued existence of Christianity in a certain locale. Out of that community have come invaluable resources, woven together with others to produce the rich tapestry we know today as the Christian church and its faith. Without the preservation of the Johannine community and without its heritage to later generations of Christians there is little doubt that the church today and perhaps even the world would be the lesser. We can, therefore, be grateful to that individual (or group) who produced the Gospel.

But that occasional piece designed for a particular situation and to meet certain needs has become part of the canon of the Christian church. That means that it is read and interpreted outside of its original situation and beyond its original purpose. With the passing of centuries the historical origin becomes more and more remote, less and less known or knowable. The result is that the Fourth Gospel stands on its own in isolation from the situation that occasioned its writing. Its canonization as Holy Scripture means that the divine truth is spoken through its words regardless of the historical setting or time in which it is read. However valuable it may be as a vehicle of divine truth, canonization means that the shortsightedness as well as the insight of its author and its message may now be taken as divinely sanctioned. It is now most often read and understood without reference to its first purpose. With those results comes a dreadful danger!

The danger of which we speak is the risk of the canonization of historically contingent literature. It is a danger that is not exclusive to the Gospel of John but endemic to the principle of canon. Much of what we have said about the Gospel of John might be said of certain other documents of the Christian canon, say the "tables of household duties" found in Col 3:18–4:1, Eph 5:21–6:9, and

---

32. Various remedies to the predicament occasioned by the anti-Semitic quality of the Fourth Gospel have been proposed. Beck (e.g., *Mature Christianity*, 267–68) argues for a new translation that reflects the theory of the historical origin of the Gospel of John espoused in this article and his chapter on the Gospel. Smith ("Judaism and the Gospel of John," 96 n. 24) responds to Beck's strategy by saying, "My conviction is that we cannot resolve these issues by removing offensive aspects of Scripture occasioned by the concrete circumstances of historical origins." With Smith, I have grave reservations about such a proposal. To base a translation on a hypothesis for the origin of the Fourth Gospel is risky business, the result of which would necessitate a new translation every time a new theory gained prominence in scholarly circles. But furthermore, such a proposal amounts to an effort to deceive the lay hearers and readers and would result in more difficulty than it avoids. I find more helpful the suggestion of R. Fuller ("The Jews in the Fourth Gospel," *Dialog* 16 [1977] 37) that the problem necessitates "careful teaching" of the laity. However, I think the solution is more complicated than making historical critics out of lay readers and hearers.

1 Pet 2:13–3:7. Those passages written within one cultural setting were perhaps helpful and liberating for their first readers but now are an embarrassment and oppressive in a culture that tries to correct the sins of a tradition of slavery and subjugation of women.

In its canonical status the Gospel of John has nurtured (if not conceived) repugnant attitudes and evoked abhorrent actions on the part of Christians toward their Jewish colleagues. Shall we blame those readers who used the document to sanction their own prejudices and ignorant hatreds? Shall we blame the interpreters who know better but still allow the Gospel to speak its devilish words to others who are willing to hear them as truth? Shall we blame the principle of canon that may expect more and attribute more authority to individual pieces than is reasonable or possible? Or, shall we blame the document itself and its producers for having been so parochial in their views as not to have imagined the use to which their work might be put?

Fortunately ours is not the awesome task of placing blame. But it cannot go unstated that the Christian church and Western culture have been amiss in not understanding the dangers inherent in the process of positing universal authority in documents that were never intended to carry such weighty importance. Responsibility for a misunderstanding of the nature of canon must rest at the doorstep of those in the past and the present commissioned with the duty to nurture a proper sense of canon and the interpretation of Scripture. Rather than placing blame, perhaps, the task is to issue a challenge to those of us who would read, interpret, and place authority in the Gospel of John. That challenge is simply that its authoritative value must be seriously and carefully defined and its use meticulously controlled. The challenge is to conceive and foster a new and more precise understanding of canonical authority. But it is also to advocate that canonical authority resides only within an interpretative context.[33]

The issue and the challenge have been stated with precision by J. Christiaan Beker. He argues that we must formulate what constitutes the "coherence" of the New Testament and confess that to be the normative content of its message. The "contingent situational factors" interwoven with that normative message must be clearly and explicitly distinguished, so that we are able to differentiate between the normative and the situational.

> For Christians today, the crucial question is whether, in their present theological reflections on Judaism, they shall accord normative canonical status to those contingent factors . . . , thus elevating [them] to a normative canonical status. . . . In other words, a sensible Jewish-Christian dialogue depends on a crucial *theological* decision: Where do we locate the authority of scripture? . . . Thus the task of the Christian theologian with respect to "the Jewish question" is a foundational task.[34]

---

33. The challenge, I believe, is being addressed in such efforts as those of D. Jodock, *The Church's Bible: Its Contemporary Authority* (Minneapolis: Fortress, 1989).

34. J. C. Beker, "The New Testament View of Judaism," in Charlesworth, ed., *Jews and Christians*, 63–64.

Beker's challenge is, to be sure, fraught with risks and difficulties. Not least among those risks is the delicate question of distinguishing between the normative and the contingent. It also risks all that is involved in the classical issue of "a canon within the canon." Most certainly too the challenge can be addressed not alone in the rarefied atmosphere of scholarly discussion. It must reach the congregations and the classrooms where the Fourth Gospel is read and valued. Still, the risks and the difficulties are worthwhile. It is only in precisely the program that Beker proffers that we can find our way to a new understanding of the issue of anti-Semitism in the Gospel of John and in the New Testament as a whole, while in the process bringing new clarity to the troublesome question of the authority of Scripture for Christianity. In other words, it is in addressing the issue of anti-Semitism in the New Testament that we are forced to deal with a question on which Christian self-identity hinges. Ironically, but appropriately, wrestling with the Johannine effort to define Christian identity compels us to address the issue most fundamental to our own Christian identity.

Only in a creative and diligent response to this challenge to define more sharply and interpret more effectively the doctrine of Christian canon is there the possibility of overcoming the tragic burden of the anti-Semitic tone experienced in the reading of the Gospel of John.

# - 7 -

# Paul's Quarrel with Judaism

## Donald A. Hagner

There can be no question but that the Holocaust—that ripest and most bitter fruit of anti-Semitism—perpetrated by the leadership of an at least nominally Christian nation, constitutes a fundamental turning point in Jewish-Christian relations. It should no longer be possible for Christians to remain unaware of the evil that can be caused by an improper or insensitive use of the anti-Judaic statements of the New Testament. Christians from now on must be vigilant against every manifestation of anti-Semitism and every misuse of New Testament materials that leads to anti-Semitism. Because of the possibility of misunderstanding these texts, we have reached the point where it is now necessary for every exposition of the anti-Judaic passages of the New Testament to be accompanied by explicit statements concerning what they do *not* mean. Anti-Judaism is theological *disagreement* with Judaism, and, as we shall see, this disagreement can become polemical in tone. Anti-Semitism, by contrast, is nothing less than racial *hatred* of the Jews, a hatred that can take a variety of forms such as prejudice, injustice, slander, abuse, and even physical violence.[1]

It cannot be denied that there are clearly anti-Judaic passages in the letters of Paul and elsewhere in the New Testament. There is of course a sense in

---

1. The "criteria of anti-Semitism" listed by M. Barth in his essay "Was Paul an Anti-Semite?" refer really to anti-Judaism. Barth justifies the label by designating what he refers to as "a wolf-in-sheep's-clothing type of anti-Semitism" (*Israel and the Church* [Richmond: John Knox, 1969] 54ff.). This use of terminology, however, results in confusion rather than clarity. W. D. Davies points out that "the use of the term anti-Semitism, strictly so called, for attitudes and conduct in the early church is anachronistic" ("Paul and the People of Israel," *NTS* 24 [1977–78] 18). S. Sandmel admits that "anti-Semitism" is "a completely wrong term when transferred to the first and second centuries" and that "anti-Jewish" and "anti-Judaic" "are better because they are correct." He nevertheless decides to use "anti-Semitism" throughout his book while being "aware of how wrong the term is" (*Anti-Semitism in the New Testament?* [Philadelphia: Fortress, 1978] xxi). See too the excellent article of E. H. Flannery, "Anti-Judaism and Anti-Semitism: A Necessary Distinction," *JES* 10 (1973) 581–88.

which the expression "anti-Judaism" is itself totally inappropriate, since the Jewish Christians responsible for the New Testament, including Paul, regarded Christianity as the fulfillment of Judaism.[2] Rather than being disloyal to the faith of the patriarchs and the Bible in their new-found Christian experience, they believed they had encountered what the promises had pointed toward. It was thus not a new religion they joined but the true and perfect manifestation of their ancestral faith. What they opposed in their polemicizing was in their eyes not truly Judaism, but only a truncated version of it, which tragically rejected its Messiah and which thus remained incomplete. Although "anti-Judaism," strictly speaking, is thus itself a misnomer, the term is nevertheless retained here in its commonly used sense. None of the Jewish Christians of the New Testament, however, would have been comfortable with the expression, least of all Paul.[3]

This essay will explore key passages in Paul's letters in order to ascertain the nature of Paul's anti-Judaism and to differentiate it from anti-Semitism. I do not contest the fact that anti-Judaism can lead to anti-Semitism, as it tragically has so often in the past. What I challenge is that the latter is a *necessary* outcome of the former. The anti-Judaic passages of the New Testament are in my opinion an essential component of New Testament Christianity;[4] anti-Semitism, in contrast, is not.[5]

The problem for many, however, is not simply the anti-Judaic passages of the

---

2. J. Klausner thus correctly notes that while Paul's teaching involved an anti-Judaism, "he considered his teaching as true Judaism, as the fulfillment of the promises and assurances of authentic Judaism" (*From Jesus to Paul*, trans. W. F. Stinespring [New York: Macmillan, 1943] 591). G. Lindeskog writes: "'Anti-Judaism' therefore was from the beginning an opposition *within* Judaism. This inner-Jewish controversy is therefore not *anti-Jewish*" (*Das jüdisch-christliche Problem* [Stockholm: Almqvist and Wiksell, 1986] 158). S. Sandmel notes that Paul considered his "new convictions...to be the true and sure version of Judaism" (*Judaism and Christian Beginnings* [New York: Oxford University Press, 1978] 336). See also J. D. G. Dunn, *The Partings of the Ways between Christianity and Judaism and Their Significance for the Character of Christianity* (London: SCM; Philadelphia: Trinity Press International, 1991) 148–49.

3. Thus P. Stuhlmacher is correct when he concludes: "However, as long as the apostle is criticized for harboring anti-Judaistic tendencies, without taking into account his situation and his teaching, I consider Paul to have been misinterpreted and unrefuted" (*Paul: Rabbi and Apostle*, with P. Lapide, trans. L. W. Denef [Minneapolis: Augsburg, 1984] 61). Lapide too concludes that Paul "was neither an anti-Semite nor an anti-Judaist" (p. 54).

4. Here I agree with the conclusion of U. Wilckens in a well-known article in the extensive German discussion of the question ("Das Neue Testament und die Juden," *EvT* 34 [1974] 602–11). Wilckens's conclusion that the anti-Judaic theme in the New Testament is "in essence Christian-theological" and has as its intent the profiling of the Christian faith rather than the defaming of the Jewish faith was formulated as a part of his response to D. Flusser's article "Ulrich Wilckens und die Juden," *EvT* 34 (1974) 236–43, which criticized Wilckens's handling of certain passages in his translation and commentary, *Das Neue Testament* (Zurich, 1970).

5. It is above all Rosemary Ruether who has insisted that anti-Semitism is intrinsic to Christianity, as for example in her famous dictum that anti-Judaism (and hence anti-Semitism) is the left hand of Christology. See her influential book *Faith and Fratricide: The Theological Roots of Anti-Semitism* (New York: Seabury, 1971). Her analysis of the extent and importance of the New Testament data is, in my opinion, one of the best available. She rightly speaks only of anti-Judaism in the New Testament, but she is convinced that anti-Judaism "constantly takes expression in anti-Semitism" (p. 116).

New Testament, but the absolute claim of Christianity over against all other options, including Judaism. This claim is itself thought to be objectionable because with it seems to come an ecclesiastical triumphalism and imperialism that cannot tolerate the continued existence of Judaism. But such a conclusion greatly exaggerates what is implied by the absolutism of Christianity. In view here is nothing less and nothing more than the question of truth. Paul believed in the absolute and exclusive truth of his gospel. But he no more advocates the overthrow of Judaism and the burning of synagogues than he does of the pagan mystery religions and their sanctuaries. Not that he would ever have put the two on the same level! Indeed, as we shall see, Paul can continue to say good things of Judaism and expect good things for the Jewish people. But to be fair to his teaching, it must be said that as much as we might have liked him to do so, he does not see Judaism as a valid alternative to Christian faith.[6] I shall argue, nevertheless, that this does not mean that Paul can correctly be considered anti-Semitic.

## 1 Thessalonians 2:14–16

I begin with what is the most notorious anti-Judaic passage in the Pauline corpus, **1 Thess 2:14-16.** Paul, it must be said, comes the closest here to sounding like an anti-Semite. He parallels the suffering of the Thessalonians experienced from their compatriots to that of the churches in Judaea at the hands of the Jews (*hypo tōn Ioudaiōn*), describing these Jews further as those

> who killed both the Lord Jesus and the prophets, and drove us out; they displease God [*theō mē areskontōn*] and oppose everyone [*pasin anthrōpois enantiōn*] by hindering us from speaking to the Gentiles so that they may be saved. Thus they have constantly been filling up the measure of their sins [*eis to anaplērōsai autōn tas hamartias pantote*]; but God's wrath has overtaken them at last [*ephthasen de ep' autous hē orgē eis telos*].[7]

So repugnant is this passage to the modern mind that although there is no textual evidence supporting the conclusion,[8] many have argued that the passage

---

6. See E. E. Johnson, who in a sensitive article calls attention to arguments that "frequently go beyond Paul himself by claiming in his name that non-Christian Judaism retains abiding validity alongside Gentile Christianity." "That," she adds, "may indeed be true in ultimate theological terms—that is, in the mind of God—but it is exegetically indefensible to say Paul thinks so" ("Jews and Christians in the New Testament: John, Matthew, and Paul," *Reformed Review* 42 [1988] 127 n. 21).

7. Throughout this chapter, biblical translations, with some slight alterations, are from the NRSV.

8. The only concrete evidence of the omission of any material at all, according to the Nestle-Aland apparatus, is of v. 16c, and that in only a single Vulgate MS. Ritschl conjectured that v. 16c was an addition to the Pauline material. A late nineteenth-century Jewish author named Rodrigues argued that vv. 14-15 (and 16?) were a later interpolation. See T. Baarda, "1 Thess. 2:14-16: Rodrigues in 'Nestle-Aland,'" *NedTTs* 39 (1985) 186–93.

was not written by Paul, but constitutes a later addition to the authentic epistle.[9] A fairly strong and attractive case has been made for regarding the passage as an interpolation. Birger Pearson has marshaled arguments from the form and content of the material.[10] According to one plausible analysis, chap. 1 constitutes the opening thanksgiving, and 2:1-12 is the first section of the main body of the letter. The second thanksgiving, beginning in v. 13, is then regarded as a later intrusion together with vv. 14-16 (with vv. 15-16 being particularly irrelevant to Paul's purpose in the preceding and following material); it is pointed out that one can move smoothly from v. 12 to v. 17 without missing the intervening material and at the same time avoiding the unnatural breaks it causes. Pearson furthermore argues from the content (esp. v. 16, taken as an allusion to the fall of Jerusalem) that the material must be dated after 70 CE, and thus cannot be Pauline. Daryl Schmidt has added linguistic arguments for the inauthenticity of these verses, pointing to stylistic (i.e., especially syntactical) variations from the surrounding authentic material and concluding that the passage is "built around a conflation of Pauline expressions."[11] There is furthermore and perhaps most importantly the problem of the theological incompatibility of this material with the view of Paul in Romans 11, where, far from suggesting the final judgment of the Jews, he speaks concerning the continuing validity of God's covenant with them and indeed of their eventual salvation.

All of these arguments, however, constitute only circumstantial evidence that cannot in the end overcome the total lack of confirming textual evidence. They are well-intentioned attempts to keep Paul from saying what it seems he ought not to have said. Not only can these arguments be answered, but the objectionable material is capable of more than one explanation.[12] As we shall see, it is not at all historically improbable that Paul could have written this blistering passage.

---

9. B. Pearson, "I Thessalonians 2:13-16: A Deutero-Pauline Interpolation," *HTR* 64 (1971) 79–91; D. Schmidt, "I Thess 2:13-16: Linguistic Evidence for an Interpolation," *JBL* 102 (1983) 269–79. For further support of this conclusion, see N. A. Beck, *Mature Christianity* (Selinsgrove, Pa.: Susquehanna Univ. Press, 1985) 40–46; H. Boers, "The Form-critical Study of Paul's Letters: 1 Thessalonians as a Case Study," *NTS* 22 (1975–76) 140–58; H. Koester, *Introduction to the New Testament* (Philadelphia: Fortress, 1982) 2.113; J. Sampley et al., *Ephesians, Colossians, 2 Thessalonians, the Pastoral Epistles* (Proclamation Commentaries; Philadelphia: Fortress, 1978) 77–79.

10. Pearson, "I Thessalonians 2:13-16."

11. Schmidt, "I Thess 2:13-16," 276.

12. See especially the fine article by I. Broer, " 'Antisemitismus' und Judenpolemik im Neuen Testament: Ein Beitrag zum besseren Verständnis von 1 Thess 2,14-16," *Biblische Notizen* 20 (1983) 58–91, as well as his " 'Der ganze Zorn ist schon über uns gekommen': Bemerkungen zur Interpolationshypothese und zur Interpretation von 1 Thess 2,14-16," in R. F. Collins, ed., *The Thessalonian Correspondence* (BETL 87; Leuven: Leuven Univ. Press, 1990) 137–59, and "Antijudaismus im Neuen Testament? Versuch einer Annäherung anhand von zwei Texten (1 Thess 2,14-16 und Mt 27,24f)," in L. Oberlinner and P. Fiedler, eds., *Salz der Erde–Licht der Welt: Exegetische Studien zum Matthäusevangelium* (Stuttgart: Verlag Katholisches Bibelwerk, 1991) 321–55. Also against the view that the passage is an interpolation, see the excursus in G. Lüdemann, *Paulus und das Judentum* (Munich: Chr. Kaiser, 1983) 25–27.

The argument from formal considerations is a precarious one.[13] It is a well-known fact that Paul exercised considerable freedom in his letters so far as formal structure is concerned. It is furthermore the case that a number of scholars who have studied the structure of the epistle have had no difficulty in integrating 2:13-16 into their analyses.[14] The linguistic evidence is in itself also hardly compelling. The irregularity of the syntax may well be accounted for in part by the character of the passage as well as the use of traditional materials.[15] Nor does the content of the passage necessitate the acceptance of a post-70 date. It is thus by no means certain (*pace* Pearson, following F. C. Baur, who on this basis denied the authenticity of 1 Thessalonians) that the words *ephthasen de ep' autous hē orgē eis telos* at the end of v. 16 are an allusion to the destruction of Jerusalem in 70 CE. Even if one were to insist on the aorist verb as referring to something that had already occurred, other conclusions are possible.[16]

Although it is not necessary for our purposes to decide upon the exact meaning of the statement,[17] the following may be said. It is quite possible and in keeping with the language of the passage (especially *eis telos*) to take the aorist as a kind of "prophetic perfect" referring to a final, eschatological judgment expected in the near future.[18] At the same time, however, the aorist probably points to an aspect of judgment already experienced (cf. the practically identical statement in *T. Levi* 6:11). The context shows that Paul has in mind the unbelief of the Jews that is responsible for their persecution of Christians and their hindering of the proclamation of the gospel to the Gentiles. In their present

---

13. See W. D. Davies's conclusion: "The structural argument is not certain" ("Paul and the People of Israel," 6). It is worth pointing out that yet a third thanksgiving passage occurs in 3:9.

14. E.g., R. Jewett, *The Thessalonian Correspondence: Pauline Rhetoric and Millenarian Piety* (Philadelphia: Fortress, 1986) 72–76; T. Holtz (*Der Erste Brief an die Thessalonicher* [EKKNT; Zurich: Benziger; Neukirchen-Vluyn: Neukirchener Verlag, 1986] 94) finds a close connection between 2:1-12 and 2:13; C. A. Wanamaker (*The Epistles to the Thessalonians* [NIGTC; Grand Rapids, Mich.: Eerdmans, 1990] 108–10) regards 2:13-16 as a rhetorical digression with a paraenetic function (on this matter, see also W. Wuellner, "Greek Rhetoric and Pauline Argumentation," in W. R. Schoedel and R. L. Wilken, eds., *Early Christian Literature and the Classical Intellectual Tradition: In Honorem Robert M. Grant* [Paris: Beauchesne, 1979] 177–88).

15. See J. W. Simpson, Jr., "The Problems Posed by 1 Thessalonians 2:15-16 and a Solution," *HBT* 12/1 (1990) esp. 52–54.

16. E.g., the expulsion of the Jews from Rome in 49 CE by Claudius, as the anticipation of a broader and final judgment (see E. Bammel, "Judenverfolgung und Naherwartung," *ZTK* 56 [1959] 249–315); the massacre of Jews in the Temple court, after 48 CE (following S. Johnson, see R. Jewett, *Thessalonian Correspondence*, 37–38, where other possibilities are also mentioned: "to someone who lived before that catastrophe [70 CE], several of the other events could easily have appeared to be a final form of divine wrath"). See also J. Coppens, "Miscellanées bibliques. LXXX. Une diatribe antijuive dans I Thess., II, 13-16," *ETL* 51 (1975) 90–95.

17. I. H. Marshall summarizes the options for *eis telos* as follows: (1) "at long last" or "finally"; (2) "completely," "to the uttermost"; (3) "for ever," "to the end," i.e., "lasting for ever"; and (4) "until the end" qualifying "wrath," i.e., "the wrath (that leads up) to the End." Marshall opts for "a combination of nuances," namely "fully and finally" (*1 and 2 Thessalonians* [NCB; Grand Rapids, Mich.: Eerdmans, 1983] 81).

18. Thus, e.g., Dobschütz, Rigaux; see G. E. Okeke's correct rejection of this option, "I Thessalonians 2.13-16: The Fate of the Unbelieving Jews," *NTS* 27 (1980-81) 130.

unbelief, the wrath of God has in a sense already come upon them (see Rom 1:18 for a similar, present dimension of the wrath of God), this in anticipation of the imminent, final wrath.[19] They are filling up the measure of their sins, and God's wrath has already come upon them in a final or eschatological sense.[20]

There is no compelling reason to conclude that Paul did not write 1 Thess 2:14-16. But how could he have written such vitriolic words, and do they constitute anti-Semitism (and not simply anti-Judaism)? How, furthermore, are we to reconcile the content of this passage with the final optimism of Romans 11, where Paul speaks of the salvation of the Jews in connection with the end of the age?

The language, to begin with, is obviously both polemical[21] and highly emotional. It reflects something of Paul's own personal history as well as his present commission.[22] It is written in a moment of agonizing frustration as he remembers those who have opposed his work. It partakes furthermore of the intensity and absolutism of the apocalyptic condemnation of the enemies of God.[23] The statement is thus a generalizing one applied to the Jews as a whole, rather than just to those who killed Jesus or hindered Paul's mission.[24] Like the Old Testa-

---

19. See Wanamaker, *Thessalonians*, 117: "God's wrath has overtaken the unbelieving and disobedient Jews in that they have been hardened by God and no longer experience God's grace. That they had not believed the gospel would have been proof enough of this for Paul." F. F. Bruce, *1 and 2 Thessalonians* (WBC; Waco, Tex.: Word, 1982) 49: "The language of v. 16c implies that the end-time judgment has come upon them ahead of time." Holtz, *Erste Brief an die Thessalonicher*, 109: "Because the synagogue opposes the eschatological salvation, it has fallen into the eschatological judgment." Broer, "'Antisemitismus' und Judenpolemik," 85: "The present situation is itself the judgment of God," and more explicitly in "'Der ganze Zorn,'" 157: "so Paul sees this judgment in the removal of the fundamental advantage of the Jews over all other human beings." Cf. E. Bammel, "Judenverfolgung und Naherwartung," *ZTK* 56 (1959) 308. Goppelt finds a parallel to 1 Thess 2:15-16 in Rom 9:22; see *Jesus, Paul and Judaism*, trans. E. Schroeder from 1954 original (New York: Nelson, 1964) 159. Cf. now too Dunn, *Partings of the Ways*, 146.

20. Donfried's conclusion that *eis telos* should be taken in the sense of "until the end," although it makes the passage more compatible with Romans 11, unfortunately does not reflect the most natural meaning of the language; see "Paul and Judaism: 1 Thessalonians 2:13-16 as a Test Case," *Int* 38/3 (1984) 252. A similar argument was earlier set forward by J. Munck in *Christ and Israel*, trans. I. Nixon (Philadelphia: Fortress, 1964) 64.

21. Thus O. Michel: "At stake for the apostle are conflict and argument, not reaction or temper alone" ("Fragen zu 1 Thessalonicher 2,14-16: Antijüdische Polemik bei Paulus," in W. Eckert, N. P. Levinson, and M. Stohr, eds., *Antijudaismus im Neuen Testament? Exegetische und systematische Beiträge* [Munich: Chr. Kaiser, 1967] 51).

22. Here I have in mind the persecution suffered by Paul at the hands of Jews in his missionary work (see 2 Cor 11:24-26). See P. Stuhlmacher: "The sharp tone that recurs in Paul's letters, for example, the unfortunately formulated polemic in 1 Thess. 2:14f., can, in my opinion, be explained as a direct result of this situation of personal conflict and suffering" (*Paul: Rabbi and Apostle*, 16). S. Ben-Chorin, however, goes too far in saying that Paul's attitude reflects a deep hatred of himself as a former persecutor of the Christians (Gal 1:13; 1 Cor 15:9) ("Antijüdische Elemente im Neuen Testament," *EvT* 40 [1980] 205).

23. Thus, correctly, J. C. Hurd, "Paul ahead of His Time: 1 Thess. 2:13-16," in P. Richardson and D. Granskou, eds., *Anti-Judaism in Early Christianity*, vol. 1: *Paul and the Gospels* (Waterloo, Ont.: Wilfrid Laurier Univ. Press, 1986) 33-35.

24. A common method used to soften the impact of our passage is to see it as directed only against certain Jews, e.g., those who killed the prophets and Jesus or who persecuted Paul. See

ment prophets, Paul is righteously indignant concerning Israel's opposition to the plan and purposes of God.[25] Indeed, as I. Broer has convincingly argued, it is probable that Paul's words quite consciously reflect a Deuteronomistic-type judgment oracle directed against the Jews in general.[26] The language is furthermore reminiscent of that used in polemic between philosophical schools in the ancient world, being rhetorical in function rather than denotative.[27]

The statement is therefore anything but a calm, reasoned estimate of the present circumstances of the Jews or their possible future. The bitter material is indeed a digression—Paul is on his way to something else in the letter. In passing, then, and in the heat of the moment, he lashes out against his enemies, that is, the gospel's enemies. All of this suggests that it may be a mistake to conclude too much from this passage concerning Paul's view of Israel and its future,[28] as he might care to articulate it on another occasion and in a more reflective mood.

Since Paul stands in the critical tradition of the prophets and Jewish apocalyptic, it makes no more sense to call him anti-Semitic in this passage than it does to call the prophets anti-Semitic. There is no racial hatred here. The language, harsh as it is, is spoken by a Jew to Jews and reflects the polemical idiom of an in-house debate[29] on matters of essential importance and of great consequence.

---

W. Marxsen, *Der erste Brief an die Thessalonicher* (Zurich, 1979) 48ff.; see O. Michel, "Fragen," 53. Against this conclusion see Broer, "'Antisemitismus' und Judenpolemik," 73–77; Marshall, *Thessalonians*, 83. More recently, F. D. Gilliard has revived this argument by maintaining that in keeping with Paul's common syntactical style, the participial phrase following the noun *Ioudaiōn* is restrictive and should therefore not be set off by a comma ("The Problem of the Antisemitic Comma between 1 Thessalonians 2.14 and 15," *NTS* 35 [1989] 481–502). It is clear from the context (see v. 14) that Paul has the Judaean Jews in mind initially. But the polemical words in vv. 15-16 quickly broaden in their application (with the assistance of the unnecessary *tōn Ioudaiōn*, "the Jews") to include all the Jews who were unreceptive to the gospel and who opposed Paul's missionary work.

25. M. J. Cook points out that one source of the New Testament's anti-Judaism is Judaism's own tradition of self-criticism ("Anti-Judaism in the New Testament," *USQR* 38/2 [1983] 125). For parallel sentiments at Qumran, see 1QM 3:9; 1QS 2:15.

26. Broer, "'Der ganze Zorn'," 156; idem, "Antijudaismus im Neuen Testament?" 330.

27. F. Mussner describes 1 Thess 2:14-16 as Paul's working "with the conventional handed-on topoi" (*Tractate on the Jews*, trans. L. Swidler [London: SPCK; Philadelphia: Fortress, 1984] 153). See L. T. Johnson, "The New Testament's Anti-Jewish Slander and the Conventions of Ancient Polemic," *JBL* 108/3 (1989) 419–41. According to Johnson, "The way the New Testament talks about Jews is just about the way all opponents talked about each other back then" (p. 429). See Wanamaker's description of the passage as an example of ancient rhetoric called *vituperatio* (*Thessalonians*, 118). See too D. Fraikin ("The Rhetorical Function of the Jews in Romans," in Richardson and Granskou, eds., *Anti-Judaism in Early Christianity*, 1.91–105), who concludes that Paul's attitude to Israel was positive.

28. K. P. Donfried makes effective use of J. C. Beker's notion of "contingent" elements in the Pauline letters in order to diminish the importance of 1 Thess 2:14-16. This approach also enables him to hold this passage together with Romans 11 without having to harmonize them ("Paul and Judaism").

29. I. Broer has rightly called attention to the fact that at the early date when 1 Thessalonians was written Christianity had not yet become separate from Judaism (see, too, Johnson, "Anti-Jewish Slander"). He refers to our passage "as an example of inner-Jewish polemics" ("'Antisemitismus' und Judenpolemik," 87–89). W. D. Davies writes: "The discussions of Judaism and Jews in Paul's letters are intramural" ("Paul and the People of Israel," 19). See K. Haacker, "Paulus und das Judentum,"

It may furthermore be the case, as some have argued, that Paul makes use of traditional elements in formulating the passage.[30] Thus the reference to the Jews killing Jesus probably reflects elements that were already a part of the oral tradition (see Acts 2:23; 10:39; 13:28); the reference to their killing the prophets is found in the Synoptic tradition (Matt 23:37; Luke 13:34) and is found again in Paul in his quotation of 1 Kgs 19:10, 14 in Rom 11:3. The reference to the Jews as those who "displease God and oppose everyone," in contrast, seems to be drawn from the repertoire of anti-Semitic slander common among the Gentiles of that era.[31] It is surprising that Paul would use such language at all. Yet the rhetorical language suited Paul's purpose, and he makes it his own, ironically turning what was actually anti-Semitic slander into heated polemic against his own unbelieving Jewish brethren.[32]

It is true, finally, that in this passage Paul contemplates no future salvation of the Jews as he does in Rom 11:23, 26, 31. This has been taken by some to mean that Paul could not have written our passage, and thus has been used as important evidence to support the interpolation theory. It may be, however, that Paul changed his mind about Israel in the interim between the writing of the early 1 Thessalonians and the considerably later epistle to the Romans.[33] At least one widely accepted change in Paul—his move from the expectation of an imminent parousia to the possibility of a delayed parousia—may explain why he could write the words of 1 Thess 2:16c when he did, but not some seven years later. As indicated above, however, we may be right in not taking those words as anything more than a polemical and emotional outburst, consistent with the conventions of time and context, and contingent upon the specific pain experienced by Paul as he contemplated the unbelief of the Jews and their opposition to his mission. And even as strong as they are, these words do not entirely preclude the possibility of any future repentance, should the parousia

---

*Judaica* 33 (1977) 168–69; D. Patte, "Anti-Semitism in the New Testament: Confronting the Dark Side of Paul's and Matthew's Teaching," *CTS Register* 78/1 (1988) 44.

30. For dependence on the Synoptic Gospels or Synoptic tradition, see J. B. Orchard, "Thessalonians and the Synoptic Gospels," *Bib* 19 (1938) 19–42; R. Schippers, "The Pre-Synoptic Tradition in 1 Thessalonians II 13-16," *NovT* 8 (1966) 223–34; D. Wenham, "Paul and the Synoptic Apocalypse," in R. T. France and D. Wenham, eds., *Gospel Perspectives II* (Sheffield: JSOT, 1981) 345–75; Davies, "Paul and the People of Israel," 7. See also Lüdemann, *Paulus und das Judentum*, 22ff.

31. See Tacitus, *Hist.* 5.5.2; *Ann.* 15.44.5; and Josephus, *Ag. Ap.* 2.10 §121 and 2.14 §148 (where, as Broer ["'Antisemitismus' und Judenpolemik," 79–80] points out, the words "atheism" and "misanthropy" occur beside each other in reference to the Jews).

32. F. F. Bruce concludes that "such sentiments are incongruous on the lips of Paul; ... nor can he be readily envisaged as subscribing to them even if they were expressed in this form by someone else" (*Thessalonians*, 47). This together with the fact that Paul here addresses the words not to the ones being denounced, but to Gentiles, leads Bruce to the conclusion that the Pauline authorship of vv. 15-16 "remains *sub judice*" (p. 49).

33. Opting for this solution are Okeke, "1 Thessalonians 2:13-16," 127–36; Simpson, "The Problems," 42–72; N. Hyldahl, "Jesus og jøderne ifølge 1 Tess 2,14-16," *SEÅ* 37/38 (1972–73) 238–54. See, too, M. Barth, *Israel and the Church*, 75.

be further delayed.[34] (Romans 11 will be discussed in the fourth section of this essay.)

Although it is perhaps an extreme example, 1 Thess 2:14-16 is hardly the only passage in which Paul used very sharp language against his opponents. In passages such as Gal 5:12; Phil 3:2, 18-19; 2 Cor 11:13-15; Rom 11:8-10 and 16:18, he also engages in harsh denunciation of them. Yet since these passages criticize not Jews but Christians (in the first two instances, Judaizers), no one is troubled by them.

It is, however, not only the language of 1 Thess 2:14-16 that has brought the charge of anti-Semitism against Paul, but perhaps above all it is his repudiation of Judaism that is responsible for the charge. To this subject we must now turn our attention.

## Paul and the Law

The issue of Paul's view of Judaism is increasingly debated today. As the result of a combination of factors such as a new appreciation of Judaism that corrects the stereotyping of it as a religion of legalistic works-righteousness, the exigencies of Jewish-Christian dialogue, and perhaps a desire to protect Paul from the charge of anti-Semitism, Paul is being understood as one who had no quarrel with Judaism in itself. His quarrel was alone with those Jews who opposed his Law-free gospel for the Gentiles. Paul, it is further argued, had no desire to repudiate Judaism or to convert Jews to Christianity. His sole concern was to fulfill his mission of preaching salvation in Christ for the Gentiles apart from the necessity to keep the Law.[35] In this perspective, not only is there no anti-Semitism in Paul, there is not even any anti-Judaism,[36] and thus the problem addressed in this essay is circumvented from the start.

Those who hold this viewpoint deny that Paul broke with the Law in any fundamental way, other than in refusing to impose it upon the Gentiles. They call attention to passages where Paul speaks positively of the Law, arguing that

---

34. See Holtz: "That the perpetrators nevertheless stand under the possibility, indeed, the invitation, to faith, and therewith the repentance from their evil ways, is in no way placed in question" (*Erste Brief an die Thessalonicher,* 111).

35. Above all, see the collected essays of L. Gaston, *Paul and the Torah* (Vancouver: University of British Columbia Press, 1987); see, too, J. G. Gager, *The Origins of Anti-Semitism: Attitudes toward Judaism in Pagan and Christian Antiquity* (New York: Oxford University Press, 1983) 193-264; Beck, *Mature Christianity,* 39-79; Mussner, *Tractate on the Jews,* 133-53; E. Stegemann, "Der Jude Paulus und seine antijüdische Auslegung," in R. Rendtorff and E. Stegemann, eds., *Auschwitz–Krise der christlichen Theologie* (Munich: Chr. Kaiser, 1980); C. M. Williamson, *Has God Rejected His People? Anti-Judaism in the Christian Church?* (Nashville: Abingdon, 1982) 47-63; M. Barth, "St. Paul–A Good Jew," *HBT* 1 (1979) 7-45; idem, *Israel and the Church,* 58-78; see, too, R. Jewett, "The Law and the Coexistence of Jews and Gentiles in Romans," *Int* 39 (1985) 341-56.

36. "All of the positive things Paul has to say about the righteousness of God effecting salvation for Gentiles in Christ need not at all imply anything negative about Israel and the Torah. Indeed,

only a position such as theirs can do justice to these passages. Thus, statements in Romans such as, "Do we then overthrow the law by this faith? By no means! On the contrary, we uphold the law" (3:31; cf. Gal 3:21); "For it is not the hearers of the law who are righteous in God's sight, but the doers of the law who will be justified" (2:13); "The law [is] the embodiment of knowledge and truth" (2:20); "Circumcision indeed is of value if you obey the law" (2:25); "So the law is holy, and the commandment is holy and just and good" (7:12)—these are taken as evidence that Paul has not parted with Judaism's view of the Law.

There are, however, many passages where Paul speaks of the Law in a different tone. Thus, " 'No human being will be justified in his sight' by deeds prescribed by the law [*ergōn nomou*], for through the law comes the knowledge of sin" (Rom 3:20); "For we hold that a person is justified by faith apart from works prescribed by the law [*ergōn nomou*]" (Rom 3:28); "If it is the adherents of the law who are to be the heirs, faith is null and the promise is void" (Rom 4:14); "You are not under law but under grace" (Rom 6:14-15); "But now we are discharged from the law, dead to that which held us captive, so that we are slaves not under the old written code but in the new life of the Spirit" (Rom 7:6); "For Christ is the end [*telos*] of the law so that there may be righteousness for everyone who believes" (Rom 10:4). To these verses at least the following from Galatians should be added: "We know that a person is justified not by the works of the law [*ergōn nomou*] but through faith in Jesus Christ [*dia pisteōs Iēsou Christou*]. And we have come to believe in Christ Jesus, so that we might be justified by faith in Christ [*ek pisteōs Christou*], and not by doing the works of the law [*ergōn nomou*], because no one [*pasa sarx*] will be justified by the works of the law [*ergōn nomou*]" (2:16); "I do not nullify the grace of God; for if justification comes through the law [*dia nomou*], then Christ died for nothing" (2:21); "Now it is evident that no one is justified before God by the law [*en nomō*]" (3:11); "For if a law had been given that could make alive, then righteousness would indeed come through the law [*ek nomou*]" (3:21); "Now before faith came, we were imprisoned and guarded under the law until faith would be revealed. Therefore the law was our disciplinarian [*paidagōgos*] until Christ came, so that we might be justified by faith. But now that faith has come, we are no longer subject to a disciplinarian" (3:23-25); "You who want to be justified by the law [*en nomō*] have cut yourselves off from Christ; you have fallen away from grace" (5:4).

---

it may be that Paul, and Paul alone among the New Testament writers, has no left hand" (Gaston, *Paul and the Torah*, 34). See F. Mussner: "When looking at . . . passages on the Jews in the Epistle to the Romans, one can in no way speak of an 'anti-Judaism' of Paul" (*Tractate on the Jews*, 145). For a remarkable contrasting statement by G. Baum (whose position represents a radical change of opinion), see the preface to R. Ruether's *Faith and Fratricide*: "What Paul . . . taught is unmistakably negative: the religion of Israel is now superseded, the Torah abrogated, the promises fulfilled in the Christian Church, the Jews struck with blindness, and whatever remains of the election to Israel rests as a burden upon them in the present age" (p. 6). See, too, E. P. Sanders, who concludes that Paul "denies two pillars common to all forms of Judaism: the election of Israel and faithfulness to the Mosaic law" (*Paul, the Law and the Jewish People* [Philadelphia: Fortress, 1983] 208).

We cannot here go fully into the vexed question of Paul and the Law.[37] Although there is no need to conclude that Paul's view of the Law is simply muddled (*pace* Räisänen), it is apparent just from the statements quoted above that his view of the Law is complex. While Paul regards himself as in some fundamental sense loyal to the Law, he has at the same time clearly relativized the Law, subordinating it to the gospel. This is plain from his view of the Law as a parenthesis between Abraham and Christ (Gal 3:15-18, 23-29). But more than that, Paul's negative statements about the Law seem to leave little, if any, place for it in the life of the Christian or, more accurately, at least for the gentile Christian.[38] In practically every element of Paul's theology we have to do with aspects both of continuity and discontinuity. Any fair representation of Paul's view of the Law, even if it is unable to synthesize his disparate statements into a comprehensive "system,"[39] must at least hold them in tension and not allow one group to render the other group void.

Since our task centers on the question of anti-Semitism in Paul, we must take seriously Paul's negative statements about the Law. These statements seem to imply something about Judaism and in turn raise the important question of the nature of first-century Judaism. E. P. Sanders's well-known characterization of Judaism as a "covenantal nomism"[40] has had an enormous impact on Pauline studies over the past decade. What he means by this is that Israel's preoccupation with the Law is to be understood as occurring within the framework of election and covenant. Grace thus precedes obligation, Jews have no need to earn their way with God, and consequently the hitherto common idea of Judaism as a legalism—the establishing of one's righteousness by works of the Law—is ruled out from the start. At most Judaism is concerned with "staying in," not "getting in." Yet Paul makes statements that seem to take Judaism as involving just such a legalism (e.g., Gal 3:10-12; Rom 9:31-32; 10:3, 5; Phil 3:9).

Despite recent denials,[41] Paul opposes within Judaism what must be described as a legalistic righteousness, that is, a righteousness established by doing

---

37. Among the spate of recent works, see especially: H. Hübner, *Law in Paul's Thought*, trans. J. C. G. Greig (Edinburgh: T. and T. Clark, 1984); H. Räisänen, *Paul and the Law* (Philadelphia: Fortress, 1986); E. P. Sanders, *Paul, the Law, and the Jewish People*; S. Westerholm, *Israel's Law and the Church's Faith: Paul and His Recent Interpreters* (Grand Rapids, Mich.: Eerdmans, 1988); J. D. G. Dunn, *Jesus, Paul, and the Law: Studies in Mark and Galatians* (Louisville: Westminster/John Knox, 1990); P. J. Tomson, *Paul and the Jewish Law: Halakha in the Letters of the Apostle to the Gentiles* (CRINT 3/1; Minneapolis: Fortress, 1990). A useful bibliographical essay is provided by D. Moo, "Paul and the Law in the Last Ten Years," *SJT* 40 (1987) 287-307.

38. It is nevertheless paradoxically true that the Christian fulfills the righteousness of the Law by following the teaching of Jesus (see Rom 6:13, 15, 22; 8:4; Gal 5:13-14).

39. Sanders is of the opinion that Paul is "coherent," in that his divergent statements derive from "an identifiable 'central conviction,'" but not "systematic," in that he does not relate the divergent statements to one another (*Paul, the Law and the Jewish People*, 147–48).

40. See his influential *Paul and Palestinian Judaism: A Comparison of Patterns of Religion* (Philadelphia: Fortress, 1977).

41. See especially Gaston's chapter, "Israel's Misstep in the Eyes of Paul," in *Paul and the Torah*, 135–50.

the works of the Law.[42] But how is this to be reconciled with the understanding of Judaism as a covenantal nomism? In my opinion, the answer lies in a discrepancy between Judaism as ideally (and correctly) conceived and as generally lived out on a day-to-day basis. Judaism has always been a religion whose strength lies more in praxis than in theory (or theology). As Sanders readily admits, the covenantal framework of Judaism's nomism was most often presupposed and taken for granted, rather than actually being articulated.[43] At the same time, it is a fact that in the Jewish literature a great stress is put upon the importance of works[44] and that frequently one encounters the language of merit. It should not be surprising, bearing these things in mind, if Jews often forgot the framework of grace within which the Law had been given and ended up functioning in a legalistic mode that in reality reflected a misunderstanding of their faith. (Christians too have been known to fall into this trap!) Paul is clearly against any distortion of the Old Testament that leads to the idea that righteousness is the result of our performance of the works of the Law and that it is this that merits our acceptance by God.[45]

Paul's disagreement with Judaism, however, seems to have been even more fundamental, so that it appears that he would even have distanced himself from a covenantal nomism. It seems impossible to deny that some of Paul's negative statements about the Law inevitably involve an anti-Judaism. For despite claims to the contrary,[46] Paul at least in some sense regarded the Mosaic Law itself as abolished with the coming of the Messiah.[47] A few of the important passages need to be looked at briefly. In **Gal 3:15-29** Paul argues that the Law was intended to be temporary. Promise and faith are the operative realities that remain constant before, after, and even during (see Rom 4:6-8) the dispensation of the Law. The Law was "added because of transgressions" and was never

---

42. Thus, correctly, R. H. Gundry: "The use of the law to establish one's own righteousness is what Paul finds wrong in Palestinian Judaism, including his past life" ("Grace, Works, and Staying Saved in Paul," *Bib* 66 [1985] 16). See too the balanced perspective of S. Westerholm, *Israel's Law and the Church's Faith*, esp. 141–73.

43. Thus, e.g., Sanders, *Paul and Palestinian Judaism*, 236.

44. Even on this point there is a contrast with Paul, as Gundry points out: "For Paul good works are only (but not unimportantly) a sign of staying in, faith being the necessary and sufficient condition of staying in as well as of getting in" ("Grace, Works," 35).

45. See C. E. B. Cranfield, *The Epistle to the Romans* (ICC; Edinburgh: T. and T. Clark, 1975–79) 2:851–52.

46. Dunn attempts to demonstrate that the problem Paul confronts is not the attempted establishment of righteousness by the Law, but the elevation of the boundary markers of Judaism (e.g., circumcision, the food laws, the Sabbath) to the status of criteria that determine one's relation to God. See "The New Perspective on Paul," originally published in *BJRL* 65 (1983) 95–122, now also available in Dunn, *Jesus, Paul, and the Law*, 183–214, including an "Additional Note." See too F. Watson, *Paul, Judaism and the Gentiles: A Sociological Approach* (SNTSMS 56; Cambridge: Cambridge Univ. Press, 1986).

47. See T. R. Schreiner ("The Abolition and Fulfillment of the Law in Paul," *JSNT* 35 [1989] 47–74), who, however, makes a questionable distinction between the moral and ritual Law, arguing that only the latter is abolished by Paul. See Sanders, *Paul, the Law, and the Jewish People*, 42, 45.

meant to make possible the achievement of righteousness (see Gal 3:21; Rom 5:20; 7:10). With the coming of the Messiah, the Law is no longer binding (see Gal 4:5; 5:1). A new era has dawned in Jesus Christ, who is himself the source of righteousness to all who have faith (see Gal 2:16). All of this stands over against the viewpoint of Judaism wherein the Law remains permanently in force and the de facto means to righteousness.

The fact that Paul in Galatians argues against Judaizers (whether Jewish or gentile is of little consequence) by no means necessitates the conclusion that the arguments pertain only to gentile converts and involve no application or reference to Judaism itself.[48] In Paul's view, just as the plight of the Jew is the same as that of the Gentile, so far as the problem of sin is concerned (see Rom 3:9-20), so too the answer to that problem is the same.[49] Paul never countenanced any alternative means of salvation beyond the death of Jesus Christ (Rom 3:22-24; 10:9-13). On the contrary, the gospel is the message of salvation to be offered "to the Jew first" (Rom 1:16; see 1 Cor 1:24). In this sense Paul's gospel involves a distinct and undeniable element of anti-Judaism.

Even apart from the preceding discussion of the material in Galatians, the interpretation of **Rom 10:4,** when taken in its context, points most naturally to the understanding of *telos* as "end." There is no question but that for Paul, Christ is also the goal of the Law, and this is one reason why the translation "goal" is favored by many. But in the immediately preceding verse Paul is contrasting two kinds of righteousness, that which comes "from God" (*tēn tou theou dikaiosynēn*), to which the Jews did not submit, and "their own" (*tēn idian*), that is, that righteousness that the Jews "seek to establish" through the Law. In the verses that immediately follow, Paul contrasts the righteousness that comes "from the law" (*ek [tou] nomou*) with that which comes "from faith" (*ek pisteōs*). Christ has brought the Law to an end with the result that righteousness comes to those who believe. A few verses later Paul turns the words of Moses on their head when he applies them to the gospel rather than to the commandment. Thus what Moses said was "near you, on your lips and in your heart" (Deut 30:14) is taken to refer to confessing Jesus as Lord and believing the resurrection in one's heart. This too involves anti-Judaism.

A final passage that indicates Paul's personal break with the Law, **1 Cor 9:19-23,** is also particularly helpful in understanding the complexity of his perspective. Here he frankly admits a pragmatism that enables him to "become all things to all people." This meant, as he says, that "to the Jews I became as a Jew, in order to win Jews." Very specifically he adds, "To those under the law [*hypo nomon*] I became as one under the law (though I myself am not under the law) so that I might win those under the law." In certain contexts, then, Paul

---

48. The view that the arguments of Galatians concerning the Law apply only to gentile converts and not to Judaism is held by many. See Gaston, "Paul and the Law in Galatians 2 and 3," in *Paul and the Torah*, 64–79; Gager, *Origins*, 230–41; Mussner, *Tractate on the Jews*, 144.

49. See C. H. Talbert, "Paul on the Covenant," *RevExp* 84 (1987) 310 n. 23.

observed the Law for the sake of allowing the gospel to be heard by Jews. But he did not regard himself as principally obligated to such observance. In this respect he had made a break with the Judaism from which he had come. (On 2 Cor 3:6-11, which could also be considered here, see below.)

Another statement in this passage is especially revealing. When he indicates his practice among Gentiles, he writes, "To those outside the law [*anomois*] I became as one outside the law." At this point he inserts parenthetically "though I am not free from God's law [*anomos theou*] but am under Christ's law [*ennomos Christou*]." Although he has just asserted quite clearly that he is not under the Law—that is, he is free from the Law—in the very next sentence he states that he is not free from the law of God! The key, of course, is that in being subject to the law of Christ (i.e., the teachings of Jesus known to him through the oral tradition), he is at the same time obeying the law of God (i.e., the correct interpretation of the Mosaic Law). The pattern of righteousness taught by Jesus amounts in essence to an exposition of the Law of Moses.

Paradoxically the Law is abolished only in order to be newly established, albeit by a metamorphosis, in the ethical tradition of the church that stems from Jesus. Paul is thus an antinomian only formally; in practice he can fairly be described, like Jesus, as one who finally upheld the Law. Granted, it is the Law as filtered primarily through the love commandment (see Rom 13:8-10), but it is nonetheless the Law, and recognizably so. This is very probably how we are to explain Paul's positive statements about the Law, some of which have been mentioned above. Although the gospel meant the end of the Law, there was a sense in which the Law was *not* overthrown by the gospel. Righteous living and not merely justification, the righteousness reckoned by faith, remains after all a vitally important goal of the Christian (see Rom 8:4, referring to "the just requirement of the law").

There is a sense, then, in which Paul remains faithful to the Law, and a sense in which, despite his language about the end of the Law, he cannot properly be called an antinomian. We face here in the question of Paul's view of the Law the same problematic complexity as in the question of Paul and Judaism. That is, just as Paul regarded his faith as the true Judaism, he regarded his stance toward the Law as ultimately one of faithfulness. What he turned his back on was a distortion of Judaism and an inappropriate understanding of the Law. Paul's "anti-Judaism," so far as the Law is concerned, amounts in fact to nothing other than a new adaptation of the Jewish Law appropriate to the newly dawned age of eschatological fulfillment.

## Paul's View of Israel

We turn now to look at a few other pertinent passages under the rubric of the closely related question of Paul's view of Israel. Here too we encounter various statements that not only involve aspects of discontinuity but that also imply the displacement of Israel and that have therefore again given rise to the charge of anti-Semitism.

Paul illustrates his theological argument concerning the Law in Galatians with the so-called allegory of Sarah and Hagar (**Gal 4:21-31**). Hagar, the slave woman, bore Abraham a son described as "according to the flesh [*kata sarka*]"; Sarah, the free woman, bore him a son "through the promise [*di' epangelias*]." Paul proceeds to liken the women to two "covenants [*diathēkai*]": Hagar to Mount Sinai, "bearing children for slavery [*eis douleian*]" and corresponding to "the present Jerusalem," Sarah to "the Jerusalem above [*anō*]" that is "free [*eleuthera*]" and that is further described as "our mother," that is, the mother of the "children of the promise [*epangelias tekna*]." Paul adds that as the son of the slave persecuted the son born "according to the Spirit [*kata pneuma*]" ("Spirit" now being substituted for "promise"!), "so it is now also [*houtos kai nyn*]." Then in answer to his question "What does the scripture say?" he quotes Gen 21:10, "Drive out the slave and her son; for the son of the slave will not share the inheritance with the son of the free woman," to which he adds: "So, brethren, we are not children of the slave but of the free woman."

Although Paul has in mind primarily the Judaizers, it is very difficult to conclude that this passage does not also involve an indictment of Judaism itself.[50] Consonant with what we have seen him argue concerning the Law, Paul describes "the present Jerusalem" (i.e., contemporary Judaism) as "being in slavery" to the Law. The Jews, who thought of themselves as descended from Abraham and thus the children of the promise, are surprisingly categorized as the descendants of Hagar and as children born "for slavery."[51] The point is that they are "under the law [*hypo nomon*]," from which Christians have been "redeemed" (Gal 4:5) and to which they are no longer to be enslaved (Gal 5:1). The contrast is drawn, furthermore, explicitly in terms of "two covenants [*dyo diathēkai*]," understood as the Mosaic covenant and the new covenant established by Christ. (Although the expression "new covenant" is not actually used here, it was a part of Paul's vocabulary; see 1 Cor 11:25 and especially 2 Cor 3:6.)

---

50. Yet G. Brouwer can conclude after studying the passage, "One cannot accuse Paul of anti-Judaism on the basis of this passage, Gal 4:21-31.... He does not make the Jews the sons of Hagar. The two women are symbols of two types of existence, which are not typical of Judaism on the one side or of Christianity on the other, but which are found in both religions" ("Die Hagar- und Sara-Perikope [Gal 4, 21-31]: Exemplarische Interpretation zum Schriftbeweis bei Paulus," *ANRW* 2.25.4: 3152). See, too, Gaston, *Paul and the Torah*; Gager, *Origins*, 241–43. To the contrary, see, e.g., Hübner, *Law in Paul's Thought*, 34; Ruether, *Faith and Fratricide*, 102ff., 134. See H. J. Schoeps, *Paul: The Theology of the Apostle in the Light of Jewish Religious History*, trans. H. Knight (Philadelphia: Westminster, 1961): "The conclusion of this passage is again that the Christian community is the Israel of God whereas the old Israel has been rejected of God" (p. 234). See H. D. Betz, *Galatians* (Philadelphia: Fortress, 1979) 245.

51. According to C. K. Barrett, Paul here uses a text of his Judaizing opponents, but draws opposite conclusions from it ("The Allegory of Abraham, Sarah, and Hagar in the Argument of Galatians," in *Essays on Paul* [Philadelphia: Westminster, 1982] 154–70).

This criticism of the old covenant involves something more fundamental than merely that the Jews put such emphasis on the elements of their national distinctiveness,[52] or boundary markers, and that they thereby excluded Gentiles from salvation.[53]

A second passage, closely related to the preceding, is found in **2 Cor 3:6-17.** Here Paul uses the language "old covenant [*palaia diathēkē*]" and "new covenant [*kainē diathēkē*]." He contrasts the two covenants by referring to the old as "the letter [*gramma*]" that "kills," a "ministry of death/condemnation," and to the new as characterized by "the Spirit," a ministry of the Spirit/righteousness (*dikaiosynē*; but NRSV: "justification"). The former reflects Moses and the Law, the latter the new covenant inaugurated in Christ. The glory of the two dispensations is also set in strong contrast: "For if what was set aside [*to katargoumenon*] came through glory, much more has the permanent [*to menon*] come in glory." To be sure, Paul says, the old covenant had its glory. But that glory is now far exceeded by the glory of the new covenant, wherein we are granted "the light of the knowledge of the glory of God in the face of Jesus Christ" (2 Cor 4:6).

In this passage not only is the Mosaic Law spoken of as abolished by the establishment of the new covenant. The people of Israel, now as in the day of Moses, have hardened their minds so that when they read Moses, "a veil lies over their minds." That veil, which prevents them from a correct understanding of the old covenant, is taken away only by believing the gospel: "since only in Christ is it set aside." And a few lines later he adds that "if our gospel is veiled, it is veiled to those who are perishing" (2 Cor 4:3). Again, despite the disclaimers of a few,[54] we are confronted with an anti-Judaism in Paul that can hardly be evaded.[55]

---

52. G. Lüdemann correctly concludes: "For the Paul of Galatians, just as in 1 Thessalonians, unbelieving Judaism has no theological dignity (any longer)" (*Paulus und das Judentum*, 30). If in Gal 6:16 the church is referred to as *ton Israēl tou theou*, the point is underlined.

53. See Dunn, who in this way tries to minimize the differences between Paul and Judaism ("The Theology of Galatians," in *Jesus, Paul, and the Law*, 242–64). Gaston's attempt to deny that Gal 4:21-31 involves a polemic against Judaism seems to go against a natural reading of the passage (*Paul and the Torah*, 82–91).

54. Gaston employs a "hermeneutic of experimentation" to arrive at the conclusion that Paul in 2 Corinthians 3 argues not against Israel, but against his opponents in Corinth (*Paul and the Torah*, 151–68). This conclusion had earlier been argued by H. Ulonska, "Die Doxa des Moses," *EvT* 26 (1966) 378–88. See Gager: "Paul's language is meant to contrast not Israel and Christianity but the old and the new for Gentiles!" (*Origins*, 216). For another attempt at construing the passage positively, see T. E. Provence, "Who Is Sufficient for These Things? An Exegesis of 2 Corinthians ii:15-iii:18," *NovT* 24 (1982) 54–81.

55. Beck concludes that apart from Romans, 2 Corinthians is "our most important source of information about Paul's attitude toward the Jews who did not accept Jesus as the Messiah." He continues with these words: "Paul claimed in this epistle a new ministry, which to him was superior to the ministry of his ancestors and of his own earlier experiences. It was a ministry that in his opinion superseded the ministry revealed by God through Moses" (*Mature Christianity*, 59). See C. H. Talbert, "Paul on the Covenant," 304: "Paul thought the new covenant not only surpassed the old but also replaced it." See too M. J. Cook, "The Ties That Blind: An Exposition of II Corinthians 3:12-4:6 and Romans 11:7-10" (125–39), and G. W. Buchanan, "Paul and the Jews (II Corinthians 3:4–4:6 and Romans 11:7-10)" (141–62), both in J. J. Petuchowski, ed., *When Jews and Christians*

We look finally at several passages in Romans 9–11, where Paul addresses the question of Israel at the peak of his theological maturity. First, in **Rom 9:30-33** after Paul has stated that the Gentiles have arrived at righteousness—through faith—he continues with these words:

> But Israel, who did strive for the righteousness that is based on law, did not succeed in fulfilling that law [*eis nomon ouk ephthasen*]. Why not? Because they did not strive for it on the basis of faith [*ek pisteōs*], but as if it were based on works. They have stumbled over the stumbling stone [*tō lithō tou proskommatos*], as it is written, "See, I am laying in Zion a stone that will make people stumble, a rock that will make them fall [*petran skandalou*], and whoever believes in him will not be put to shame" [Isa 28:16; see 8:14].

Here Paul simply articulates the problem that gives rise to these chapters: the failure of Israel to believe in the gospel (see 9:1ff.). He begins his answer with what might be called "remnant theology," asserting that "not all Israelites truly belong to Israel, and not all of Abraham's children are his true descendants" (9:6-7). He had already distinguished a true Jew from a physical Jew (3:28-29) and identified the descendants of Abraham as those who share the faith of Abraham, the faith that was "reckoned to him as righteousness" (4:16, 22-25).

Although Paul appeals to God's inscrutable purpose in election and the reality of a believing remnant, it remains a fact that Israel as a whole has not believed. Rather, it has taken the wrong path and has stumbled and fallen (see 9:27-29). In turning from the general election of Israel and allowing that only the remnant of Jews who believed in the gospel were to be saved, Paul adopts a position that must again be described as anti-Judaic.

At the end of chap. 10 Paul cites Isaiah's bitter criticism of Israel: "All day long I have held out my hands to a disobedient and contrary people" (Rom 10:21, citing Isa 65:2, according to the LXX). After referring to the elect remnant (11:5) who have received the gospel, he again relies upon Scripture to describe those who remain hardened. Thus in **Rom 11:8-10** we encounter some of the harshest language used in the New Testament to depict unbelieving Jews. First Paul cites what appears to be a combination of Deut 29:3 (LXX 29:4) and Isa 29:10: "God gave them a sluggish spirit, eyes that would not see and ears that would not hear, down to this very day." This is followed by the citation of Ps 69:22-23, but according to the LXX (68:22-23): "Let their table become a snare and a trap, a stumbling block and a retribution [*antapodoma*] for them; let their eyes be darkened so that they cannot see, and keep their backs forever [*dia pantos*] bent." In Paul's use of this passage the personal enemies of the psalmist have become the enemies of the gospel (see Rom 11:28).[56]

---

*Meet* (Albany: State University of New York Press, 1988). Although Buchanan finds Paul's views objectionable, he does not try to make Paul say something other than he does. "However arrogant and offensive Paul's judgments seem to twentieth-century Jews and Christians, apparently it did not seem out of order to Jewish Christians of Paul's day" (p. 158).

56. There is no need to translate Rom 11:28 as "enemies of God," as does the RSV (and NRSV).

It is worth emphasizing that in these verses we have the language of the Old Testament and not that of Paul. Again, as in 1 Thess 2:14-16, the language exemplifies the conventional, heightened rhetoric used in polemical utterances. The point, nevertheless, is that Paul chooses to apply this language to the Jews who have not believed in the gospel. They are regarded as blind and unreceptive in both passages. Again we confront what must be called anti-Judaism. The second quotation is particularly vitriolic, with its wish for retribution and that their backs be bent forever. The last sentiment, employing the word "forever," recalls the statement in 1 Thess 2:16, which we considered above. Here we have material indeed that comes close to rivaling that passage for its anti-Judaism.

An element in these citations, especially in the first, that gives them a special character is the sovereignty of God that lies behind Israel's unbelief. Paul seizes upon this motif in order finally to resolve the problem with which he began. God has planned it this way, according to God's mysterious will, so that the gospel might go to the Gentiles (11:11-12, 15, 25, 28, 30). At the same time, Paul does not use this as a way to excuse Israel's unbelief. They are still held accountable for not receiving the gospel (see 10:21; 11:20). Now, however, their unbelief is clearly spelled out as temporary, as but the shadow side of the Gentiles' opportunity and the prelude to a turning from that unbelief. Here Paul breaks new ground that brings a quite new dimension to our subject.

## The Salvation of Israel

After the devastating passage just considered, Paul returns to his initial question,[57] which now has more edge than ever: "So I ask, have they stumbled so as to fall?" He answers the question with a very strong negation: "By no means!" (11:11). Before he indicates specifically what he means by this response, he anticipates his answer in several places. In 11:12, in contrast to Israel's "trespass" and "failure," he refers to "their full inclusion [*to plērōma autōn*]"; in 11:15, in contrast to Israel's "rejection," he mentions "their acceptance [*hē proslēmpsis*]." In the olive tree metaphor he states that the Jews, "if they do not persist in unbelief [*tē apistia*], will be grafted in, for God has the power to graft them in again" (11:23), and then he adds "how much more will these natural branches be grafted back into their own olive tree" (11:24).

But it is only in **Rom 11:25-26** that he finally comes to the "mystery" that he has been hinting at in these passages: "A hardening has come upon part of Israel,

---

In the Greek text, where there is no mention of God, "enemies [*echthroi*]" is modified by the preceding phrase, "as regards the gospel [*kata men to euangelion*]." They are enemies so far as the gospel is concerned.

57. The problem that dominates chaps. 9–11 is posed from the beginning of chap. 9. The question occurs in its most pointed form in 11:1, "I ask, then, has God rejected his people?" There too the answer is "By no means!"

until the full number of the Gentiles has come in. And so all Israel will be saved [*pas Israēl sōthēsetai*]." All of Paul's earlier statements about Israel in Romans and his other letters are relativized by this final assessment concerning Israel's future. In the final analysis, then, Paul turns out to be decidedly pro-Israel, despite all of the instances where he appears to reflect an anti-Judaism.[58]

It deserves to be pointed out that this is not a conclusion to which Paul was forced out of theological necessity in order to preserve the faithfulness of God to his promises. The question of God's faithfulness to his promises has already been answered in the existence of a remnant of Jews that has believed in the gospel,[59] Paul himself being concrete evidence of that faithfulness (see 11:1-6). The salvation of all Israel is instead a part of the extravagance of God, an example of grace that continually surprises. Paul is nevertheless happy to indicate how this abundant grace underlines election and the fact that "the gifts and the calling of God are irrevocable" (11:28-29). Israel thus retains a special place in the purpose of God that will work itself out in history.

It remains a much-debated question as to how Israel is to be saved, not to mention the nature of the salvation in view. The question is an important one for our subject. For some, only if this salvation of Israel is independent of the necessity of faith in Christ, and therefore separate from the church, can Paul finally escape the charge of anti-Judaism (and anti-Semitism).[60] For them Paul must be the advocate of a two-covenant theory wherein the old covenant is for Israel, and retains full validity in itself, while the new covenant is for only the Gentiles, of whom alone is faith in Christ required. Only the acceptance of the continuing legitimacy of Judaism can make Paul acceptable.

These issues cannot be examined in detail here.[61] I can only indicate that

---

58. See U. Luz, "Zur Eneuerung des Verhältnisses von Christen und Juden," *Judaica* 37 (1981) 206-7. With Rom 11:25-26 in mind, he writes: "Paul is the only New Testament theologian who has not finally condemned unbelieving Israel" (p. 206).

59. This point is neglected by J. C. Beker, "The Faithfulness of God and the Priority of Israel in Paul's Letter to the Romans," in G. W. E. Nickelsburg and G. W. MacRae, eds., *Christianity among Jews and Gentiles* (Philadelphia: Fortress, 1986) 10-16.

60. J. T. Pawlikowski, who admits that in Romans 9-11 Paul envisions the salvation of Israel through faith in Christ, is both fair to Paul and refreshingly frank: "This section of the epistle ends on a conversionist note that I personally find unacceptable in light of what we have come to know about Judaism and by virtue of the Jewish experience of the Nazi Holocaust." See his useful survey, "New Testament Antisemitism: Fact or Fable?" in M. Curtis, ed., *Antisemitism in the Contemporary World* (Boulder, Colo., and London: Westview, 1986) 123.

61. The bibliography is enormous. A good place to begin is with that provided in H. Räisänen's overview, "Römer 9-11: Analyse eines geistigen Ringens," *ANRW* 2.25.4: 2891-2939. This article in abbreviated form can be found in English in "Paul, God, and Israel: Romans 9-11 in Recent Research," in J. Neusner et al., eds., *The Social World of Formative Christianity and Judaism* (Philadelphia: Fortress, 1988) 178-206. A few other items may be mentioned here: J. Munck, *Christ and Israel: An Interpretation of Romans 9-11*, trans. I. Nixon (Philadelphia: Fortress, 1967); P. Stuhlmacher, "Zur Interpretation von Römer 11, 25-32," in H. W. Wolff, ed., *Probleme biblischer Theologie* (Munich: Chr. Kaiser, 1971) 555-70; O. Betz, "Die heilsgeschichtliche Rolle Israels bei Paulus," *TBei* 9 (1978) 1-21; F. Hahn, "Zum Verständnis von Römer 11:26a: '...und so wird ganz Israel gerettet werden'" in M. D. Hooker and S. G. Wilson, eds., *Paul and Paulism: Essays in Honour of C. K. Barrett* (London: SPCK, 1982) 221-34; M. Barth, *The People of God* (Sheffield:

in my opinion "the Deliverer" of Israel (11:26) can for Paul be no other than Jesus Christ, and the way of salvation for both Jew and Gentile can only be one and the same.[62] The argument of the book of Romans throughout has been that Jew and Gentile are in effect on the same ground. The "advantage" of the Jew (3:1-2) is only of a preliminary or preparatory kind. In the last analysis it avails little: "What then? Are we any better off? No, not at all; for we have already charged that all, both Jews and Greeks, are under the power of sin" (3:9). The human plight is a universal one: "Now we know that whatever the law says, it speaks to those who are under the law, so that every mouth may be silenced, and the whole world may be held accountable to God. For 'no human being will be justified in his sight' by deeds of the law, for through the law comes the knowledge of sin" (3:19-20). It is for this reason that the salvation announced in the gospel must go "to the Jew first and also to the Greek" (1:16). If the problem is common to Jew and Greek, so also is the answer to the problem. Paul makes this quite clear: "For there is no distinction, since all have sinned and fall short of the glory of God; they are now justified by his grace as a gift, through the redemption that is in Christ Jesus" (3:22-24; see 3:29-30).

The same perspective is present in chaps. 9–11. The advantages of the Israelites are enumerated in 9:4-5, culminating in the reference to the Messiah coming from them.[63] Yet these advantages have not benefited them since they have not put their faith in that Messiah. Paul intensely desires and prays "that they may be saved" (10:1). He means here nothing different from the salvation about which he has been speaking previously in his letter. This is unmistakably

---

JSOT, 1983); O. Hofius, "Das Evangelium und Israel: Erwägungen zu Römer 9–11," *ZTK* 83 (1986) 297–324; G. Wagner, "The Future of Israel: Reflections on Romans 9-11," in W. H. Gloer, ed., *Eschatology and the New Testament: Essays in Honor of G. R. Beasley-Murray* (Peabody, Mass.: Hendrickson, 1988) 77-112. Volume 4 of *Ex Auditu* (1988) is devoted to the theme of "The Church and Israel (Romans 9–11)." See now too especially, J. D. G. Dunn, *Romans 9–16* (WBC; Waco, Tex.: Word, 1988). See I. Broer, "Die Juden im Urteil der Autoren des Neuen Testaments: Anmerkungen zum Problem Historischer Gerechtigkeit im Angesicht einer verheerenden Wirkungsgeschichte" (forthcoming).

62. *Pace* Mussner: "He saves Israel by a 'special path' which apparently bypasses the gospel" (*Tractate on the Jews*, 146), and Gager: "When Paul thinks and speaks of Israel's imminent restoration *he does not construe this to imply conversion to Christianity*" (*Origins of Anti-Semitism*, 261). Räisänen does not exaggerate when he concludes: "It is quite incredible that Paul should have heeded the notion that Israel could be saved apart from Christ" ("Paul, God, and Israel," 191). Räisänen provides an effective refutation of the Gaston-Gager hypothesis on pp. 189–92. See O. Hofius, "Das Evangelium und Israel," 318–20; Munck, *Christ and Israel*, 141; Davies, "Paul and the People of Israel," 28; S. Hafemann, "The Salvation of Israel in Romans 11:25-32: A Response to Krister Stendahl," *Ex Auditu* 4 (1988) 38–58; Sanders, *Paul, the Law, and the Jewish People*, 192–98; Dunn, *Romans*, 681, 691. A recent and especially effective refutation can now be found in R. Hvalvik, "A 'Sonderweg' for Israel? A Critical Examination of a Current Interpretation of Romans 11.25-27," *JSNT* 38 (1990) 87–107.

63. Referring to Rom 9:5, C. E. B. Cranfield notes that "the Jewishness of Jesus of Nazareth is the final and irrevocable condemnation of every form of anti-Semitism, whether it be blatant and brutal or subtle and even more or less unconscious, and the unbroken bond between believing Christian and unbelieving Jew" ("Light from St. Paul on Christian-Jewish Relations," in *The Bible and the Christian Life* [Edinburgh: T. and T. Clark, 1985] 40).

clear when in the lines that follow he refers to salvation as dependent upon confessing Jesus as Lord and believing in his resurrection (10:9-10). The point is confirmed when Paul adds again: "For there is no distinction between Jew and Greek; the same Lord is Lord of all and is generous to all who call on him. For, 'Everyone who calls on the name of the Lord shall be saved'" (10:12-13). That name, according to the context (see 10:9), can be none other than Jesus. Then with their unbelief in mind, Paul struggles with questions concerning whether the Jews have "heard" the gospel and whether they have "understood" it (10:18-19). What is in view here is the kerygma that makes salvation possible, the kerygma that is absolutely essential to both Jew and Gentile. "Faith comes from what is heard, and what is heard comes through the word of Christ [*dia rhēmatos Christou*]" (10:17).

Even in chap. 11, therefore, we are to conclude that Israel is saved in the same way and on the same basis as the Gentiles. It is true that neither the name Jesus nor the name Christ occurs in this chapter.[64] But to take this to mean that another salvation is in view, one altogether apart from Christ, is to make an enormous leap in logic to explain what may be purely fortuitous and to contradict what Paul has earlier said quite clearly. There are, moreover, a couple of indirect indications in the chapter that point to a consistency in Paul's perspective. In v. 23 he writes of the branches that were broken off from the olive tree (i.e., the Jews who did not respond to the gospel) that can be grafted onto the tree again, but with the important stipulation, "if they do not persist in unbelief [*ean mē epimenōsin tē apistia*]." It is extremely difficult to imagine that this can refer to anything other than faith in Jesus Christ.

In the scriptural citation used to support the statement concerning all Israel being saved, there is an allusion to Isa 27:9 in the words "when I take away their sins." But this is precisely what Paul has earlier described as the work of Jesus Christ for Jew and Gentile alike (see esp. 3:21-26). It is hardly possible to dissociate the taking away of Israel's sins from faith in Christ's atoning death.

Finally, when Paul speaks of the future salvation of Israel, he draws his contrast in these words: "So they have now been disobedient in order that, by the mercy shown to you [*tō hymeterō eleei*], they too may now receive mercy" (11:31). If this translation is allowed (see the RSV, NRSV, NIV, NJB), that is, if the Greek phrase indicated is to be taken as part of the *hina* clause (which it precedes), then a further indication is provided that the mercy to be shown to the Jews is the same as that mercy shown to the Gentiles. Since, however, it may be more natural to take the phrase as belonging to what precedes (i.e., "so they have now been disobedient for the mercy shown to you, in order that they too may now receive mercy"), the point cannot be pressed.[65]

---

64. Much is made of this by, e.g., K. Stendahl, *Paul among Jews and Gentiles* (Philadelphia: Fortress, 1976) 4; Beck, *Mature Christianity*, 66.

65. See Cranfield for arguments in favor of the reading of the main translations (*Epistle to the Romans*, 2.582-85). For an answer to Cranfield, see Dunn, *Romans 9-16*, 688.

The fact that Paul insisted upon the necessity of Jews being saved in the same way as Gentiles, through faith in Christ, should not be allowed to detract from the true significance of his statement that a time is coming when all Israel will be saved. It is furthermore clear that Paul rejoiced in the prospect of this salvation and the sense in which it so beautifully rounded out God's initial work with the patriarchs, and substantiated even beyond the remnant the covenant faithfulness of God to his people. Paul is by nature pro-Israel and exults in the eventual fruition of Israel's faith in their arrival at the true fulfillment of Judaism. Ironically, Paul's "anti-Judaism" is for the sake not only of Gentiles, but also for the Jews,[66] and as it ultimately turns out, for the sake of all Israel.

## Conclusion

To summarize and conclude: Anti-Judaism is part and parcel of Paul's theological position.[67] Indeed, it is intrinsic to his Christianity.[68] We see it in his polemical outbursts against those who oppose and hinder his mission, conditioned as they are by the conventions of the day. We see it in his rejection of the Law as central to human salvation, and his insistence upon the necessity of faith in Jesus Christ. It is also evident in his view of contemporary Israel as being in slavery, blindness, and disobedience.

---

66. Paul has reversed a Jewish expectation that after Israel's salvation, the Gentiles would also experience the grace of God. Now it is the salvation of the Gentiles that will lead to Israel's salvation, and thus Paul, as the apostle sent to the Gentiles, has a supremely important role to play in the eventual salvation of his own people. See J. Munck, *Paul and the Salvation of Mankind*, trans. F. Clarke (London: SCM, 1959); Sanders, *Paul, the Law, and the Jewish People*, 179–90; see, too, C. K. Barrett, "The Gentile Mission as an Eschatological Phenomenon," in Gloer, ed., *Eschatology and the New Testament*, 65–75. In J. Jervell's words, "Paul regards himself primarily and in the long term as a missionary to the Jews, sent to Israel in order to proclaim salvation for the people. As apostle to the Gentiles he has the salvation of Israel in mind" (*The Unknown Paul* [Minneapolis: Augsburg, 1984] 59).

67. Ruether is right when she concludes, "Paul's position was unquestionably that of anti-Judaism.... The polemic against 'the Jews' in Paul, as in the New Testament generally, is a rejection of Judaism, i.e., 'the Jews' as a religious community" (*Faith and Fratricide*, 104). See Sandmel: "Paul's criticism, if we may use that word, is directed not so much toward Jews as it is toward Judaism.... It is thus essentially Judaism that Paul denigrates" (*Anti-Semitism in the New Testament?* 16). So, too, J. D. Levenson concludes that Paul "is not anti-Semitic, but he is profoundly anti-Judaic" ("Is There a Counterpart in the Hebrew Bible to New Testament Antisemitism?" *JES* 22/2 [1985] 244). Attempts to deny this are not persuasive. Thus, for example, Gager's argument that the only objection Paul had with the Jews was "their refusal to recognize that God had now done for the Gentiles what he had already done for Israel" (*Origins of Anti-Semitism*, 264) is hardly adequate to account for the opposition and hostility Paul experienced from the Jews. If this alone was really Paul's concern, he could have stated it more clearly and thereby avoided the wrath of the Jews. First-century Judaism, after all, had room for the salvation of Gentiles, even apart from their becoming full proselytes.

68. Cf. G. Lüdemann: "In the present, the church stands in an indissoluble theological conflict with Judaism" (*Paulus und das Judentum*, 42–43). He adds to this a positive point: "The gentile church must remain in connection with its Jewish roots."

Yet this break with Judaism, this so-called anti-Judaism, must in no sense be taken to mean that Paul had turned against his people or against his Jewish heritage. The Jewish scholar Hans Joachim Schoeps was exactly correct when he wrote: "Paul is in fact convinced that he has never seceded from Judaism, since the Christian confession means for him the completion of the Jewish faith."[69] Paul is the true Jew; his gospel the message that goes back to Abraham; his Lord the One promised in the Scriptures. Beyond these facts is the supreme affirmation of Israel in Paul's resounding statement in Romans 11 that all Israel will be saved. There is no way, with all of this in mind, that Paul can fairly be regarded as disloyal to his people.

If this is true, it is all the more inappropriate to connect Paul with anti-Semitism of any kind. It is possible to love those with whom we may disagree, even if we disagree on supremely important issues. Indeed, to do so is to practice the ethic of Jesus. Speaking of the Jews who had not accepted the gospel, Paul writes: "I have great sorrow and unceasing anguish in my heart. For I could wish that I myself were accursed and cut off from Christ for the sake of my own people, my kindred according to the flesh" (Rom 9:2-3). Paul's sentiment here is motivated by love for his people. Anyone who is tempted to misuse Pauline texts for anti-Semitic purposes ought to remember this *cri de coeur*. As much as the unbelief of his people frustrated him, Paul never stopped loving them.

If anti-Judaism is essential to the Pauline gospel, as I have argued, then those who would follow Paul must make every effort to distinguish it sharply from anti-Semitism. To understand Paul is to know how far anti-Semitism was from his thinking. Paul emphasized the importance of Israel as the servant of the Lord whereby the good news of salvation came to the Gentiles (see Rom 9:5, "from them, according to the flesh, comes the Messiah"; see also 11:18; 15:8-12).[70] The salvation of the world comes through the Jews. Israel can receive its rightful honor and anti-Semitism can be avoided without distorting Paul's theology. Any who wish to identify themselves with Pauline Christianity will be most faithful to Paul when they see to it that the connecting nerve between anti-Judaism and anti-Semitism is cut, and never allowed to grow again. Nothing would honor the memory of Paul more and nothing could be fairer to his theology.

---

69. Schoeps, *Paul*, 237. W. D. Davies: "Paul did not think in terms of moving into a new religion but of having found the final expression and intent of the Jewish tradition within which he himself had been born" ("Paul and the People of Israel," 20).

70. On this, see especially O. Betz, "Die heilsgeschichtliche Rolle Israels bei Paulus," *TBei* 9 (1978) 1–21.

# -8-

# Anti-Semitism
# in the Deutero-Pauline Literature

## James D. G. Dunn

A surprising feature of the deutero-Pauline literature is its *lack* of anti-Semitism, or, more precisely, the absence of passages that have given scope to the anti-Judaism[1] of later years. The surprise is occasioned by the fact that the deutero-Paulines are in effect surrounded by just such material. The earlier Pauline writings include the fierceness of 1 Thess 2:14-16 and Galatians.[2] The contemporary Christian writings include Matthew, Acts, and John, all of which have given more than a few hostages to fortune on this theme.[3] And (probably) following behind there come *Barnabas* and Melito, with whom Christian anti-Judaism can be said really to have begun.[4] But with the deutero-Paulines the issue of anti-Judaism hardly arises.[5] It is precisely this contrast that makes a study of the deutero-Paulines so relevant to this collection of essays, since it

---

1. In common with most writers on this theme in recent years I prefer to use "anti-Judaism" rather than "anti-Semitism." The latter is better confined to the explicit racism that came to the fore in the nineteenth century and reached its nadir in Nazism. But "anti-Judaism" is only a little better, since it begs the question as to what precisely was "Judaism" in a period when there were several forms of Judaism, or Judaisms, in play. See further my *The Partings of the Ways* (London: SCM; Philadelphia: Trinity Press International, 1991) chap. 8.

2. See above chap. 7.

3. See chaps. 3, 5, and 6.

4. The hesitation implied by the "(probably)" arises because *Barnabas* has been dated within the time span usually reckoned as covered by the deutero-Paulines, by some as early as 70–79 (see J. A. T. Robinson, *Redating the New Testament* [London: SCM; Philadelphia: Westminster, 1976] 313–19, following J. B. Lightfoot), by others in the last few years of the first century (see P. Richardson and M. B. Shukster, "Barnabas, Nerva, and the Yavnean Rabbis," *JTS* 34 [1983] 31–55). See below chap. 11.

5. The only item of any real concern mentioned by S. Sandmel (*Anti-Semitism in the New Testament?* [Philadelphia: Fortress, 1978] 124) is the reference to "*Jewish* myths" in Titus 1:14; but even so he describes it as "only an unimportant bit of name-calling"; see the section on Titus, below.

reminds us that there were different attitudes toward and ways of speaking about Jews and Judaism among the Christians in the last decades of the first century, and so prevents us from making too sweeping generalizations about Christianity at the end of the first century and beginning of the second.

What are the New Testament writings which fall under the heading "deutero-Pauline"? Almost all would include the Pastoral Epistles (1 Timothy, 2 Timothy, and Titus), and almost as many would include Ephesians. A good number of scholars would include 2 Thessalonians and Colossians, though opinion is much more divided on these two.[6] For myself, I am not convinced by the arguments in favor of the post-Pauline authorship of 2 Thessalonians and await to be convinced on Colossians, but I do share the large consensus on the rest. However, since 2 Thessalonians and Colossians are so often counted among the deutero-Paulines, they will be included here.

The time-span is also a matter of some controversy. A date in the years or decades immediately following Paul's death would seem to make most sense: the more immediate the circle of disciples from whom these letters came, the more understandable that the authors should think of themselves as belonging wholly within the authoritative Pauline tradition, and the more explicable the acceptance of these letters within the Pauline canon.[7] In my own judgment this reasoning covers all the deutero-Paulines. Several commentators, it is true, would date the Pastorals some way into the second century;[8] but it is precisely their lack of overt anti-Judaism which lessens the likelihood that they were first written in a period when Christianity and rabbinic Judaism had already pulled clearly apart with the increasing acrimony evident in *Barnabas* and Melito.

## 2 Thessalonians

A feature which immediately strikes the reader of 2 Thessalonians is that the persecution spoken of in 1:5ff. is *not* attributed to "the Jews," in contrast to 1 Thess 2:14-16. There is no attempt to identify those responsible, and the language uses broad eschatological motifs of indistinct reference. "Those who do not know God" in 1:8 will certainly be Gentiles (cf. 1 Thess 4:5; also Ps 79:6 and Jer 10:25). Which could mean that "those who do not obey the gospel of our Lord Jesus" (1:8), in distinction from the Gentiles just mentioned, are

---

6. See, e.g., W. G. Kümmel, *Introduction to the New Testament* (rev. ed.; Nashville: Abingdon; London: SCM, 1975) secs. 15, 21, 23, 24; H. Koester, *Introduction to the New Testament*, vol. 2: *History and Literature of Early Christianity* (Berlin: de Gruyter; Philadelphia: Fortress, 1982) sec. 12.1-2; L. T. Johnson, *The Writings of the New Testament: An Interpretation* (Philadelphia: Fortress; London: SCM, 1986) chaps. 11, 17-19.

7. See particularly D. G. Meade, *Pseudonymity and Canon* (WUNT 39; Tübingen: Mohr [Siebeck], 1986).

8. E.g., Koester (*Introduction*, 2.305) dates them to the period 120-60.

Jews.[9] But the parallel of Rom 1:5 points the other way; and Rom 10:14-21 shows that Paul used the language of "obedience" indiscriminatingly between Jew and Gentile.[10] At all events we can say that the author has made no attempt to single out Jews as persecutors of the Thessalonian Christians—and at the very point where the immediate precedent[11] invited just such an identification.[12] This suggests, if anything, the very opposite of anti-Judaism. The same is true of 3:2, with its possible echo of Isa 25:4 (LXX).

The most striking feature of the letter is, of course, the portrayal of the coming of "the man of lawlessness" in chap. 2. What is noticeable here too is the strongly Jewish character of the expectation. The figure in vv. 3-4 and 8-10 is obviously drawn from Jewish language and precedents. In particular, the language echoes passages such as Ps 88:23 (LXX) ("son of lawlessness") and Isa 57:3 (LXX) ("lawless sons, offspring of adulterers and prostitutes"). And the precedents include: the king of Babylon (Isa 14:12-14); the wicked prince of Israel (Ezek 21:24-25); the prince of Tyre, charged with the blasphemy of claiming "I am a god, I sit in the seat of the gods" (Ezek 28:2); the king (Antiochus) of Dan 11:36 who "shall exalt himself and magnify himself above every god, and shall speak astonishing things against the God of gods" (hence 2 Thess 2:4); not to mention Pompey, "the lawless one," in *Pss. Sol.* 17:11. To be noted also is the fact that his anticipated destruction is attributed to the royal Messiah (Isa 11:4), who "shall smite the earth with the rod of his mouth, and with the breath of his lips shall slay the wicked" (hence both *Pss. Sol.* 17:24 and 2 Thess 2:8).[13] In other words, the expectation is the wholly Jewish one of an archetypal opponent in whom the final rebellion of the nations against the one God of Israel will come to its eschatological crisis—wholly of a piece with the expectation of Mark 13:14 ("'the abomination of desolation' standing where it ought not to be"), with its deliberate echo of the same Syrian crisis (which sparked off the Maccabean rebellion) to which Dan 11:31 and 12:11 allude and which likewise provided the archetype of the final rebellion against God and his people.

Also remarkable is the fact that the (Jerusalem) Temple continues to provide the focus for this final rebellion and denouement. Within the Pauline corpus this expectation stands out, since elsewhere the Temple and its cult have been

---

9. See, e.g., J. E. Frame, *1 & 2 Thessalonians* (ICC; Edinburgh: T. and T. Clark, 1912) 233; I. H. Marshall, *1 & 2 Thessalonians* (New London Commentary; London: Marshall, 1983) 177–78.

10. See also W. Trilling, *Der zweite Brief an die Thessalonicher* (EKKNT 14; Zurich: Benziger, 1980) 56; C. A. Wanamaker, *1 & 2 Thessalonians* (NIGTC; Grand Rapids, Mich.: Eerdmans; Exeter: Paternoster, 1990) 227.

11. I take 1 Thess 2:14-16 to be part of the original text. See the review of the discussion relating to these verses in R. Jewett, *The Thessalonian Correspondence: Pauline Rhetoric and Millenarian Piety* (Philadelphia: Fortress, 1986) 37–41; Wanamaker, *Thessalonians*, 114–19; and above chap. 7.

12. Contrast the oversensitivity of N. A. Beck, *Mature Christianity: The Recognition and Repudiation of the Anti-Jewish Polemic of the New Testament* (London and Toronto: Associated University Presses, 1985) 83.

13. See further Wanamaker, *Thessalonians*, 257–58.

wholly left behind, no longer relevant now that the (final) sacrifice of Christ has been offered (Rom 3:25; 8:3; 2 Cor 5:21) and the community of faith and individual believers are the temple that matters (1 Cor 3:16-17; 6:19; 2 Cor 6:16).[14] The one exception is Rom 11:26, where Paul takes up the hope of Isa 59:20-21 for a final deliverer to come from Zion. But even there it is noticeable that Paul modifies the quotation: *his* hope is for a deliverer *from* Zion, not "for the sake of Zion," as in Isa 59:20 (LXX).[15] Once again, it is this somewhat un-Pauline reaffirmation of Jewish expectation (in 2 Thessalonians 2), albeit with reference to Messiah Jesus, which makes 2 Thessalonians stand out over against the more critical attitudes vis-à-vis Jerusalem that feature elsewhere in Paul. Once again, it is the *lack* of anything overtly or even apparently "anti-Jewish" that characterizes 2 Thessalonians.

## Colossians

As with the undisputed Paulines, Colossians assumes that its readers have entered fully into the inheritance of the promises initially made to Israel. Hence the characteristic Pauline descriptions of them as "saints" (1:2, 4, 26), who have a "share in the inheritance of the saints in light" (1:12; 3:24), "elect of God, holy and beloved" (3:12).[16] The ethical exhortation is also typically Jewish, particularly the opening warnings against sexual sin, impurity, evil desire, and the covetousness which is idolatry (3:5; cf. Wis Sol 14:12, 22-27).[17] None of this is anti-Jewish, since it is not put forward in a polemical or exclusivistic way.

The claims for Christ, of course, are peculiarly Christian, but the exposition of these claims in terms of "the mystery revealed" (1:26-27; 2:2; 4:3) is again typically Jewish. That is to say, the claim made by the Christians whom Colossians represents were like those made by many Jewish apocalypses (e.g., Dan 2:19, 28; *1 Enoch* 41:1; 103:2; 106:19; *2 Enoch* 24:3; 4 Ezra 12:36-38; 14:5; *2 Apoc. Bar.* 81:4) and by the Qumran community (e.g., 1QS 9:18; 11:3-8; 1QH 1:21; 2:13; 4:27-28; 1QpHab 7:4-5). In each case Jewish writers were claiming that they had been given a special insight (revelation) into the mysteries of the divine purpose—through a heavenly revelation or journey, or through the insights given to the Teacher of Righteousness, or in the light of Jesus the Christ.

---

14. See further my *Partings*, chap. 5.

15. The contrast would be even sharper if the "Zion" of Rom 11:26 was the heavenly Jerusalem (cf. Gal 4:26; Heb 12:22; Rev 3:12; 21:2).

16. The closest parallels in Paul are Rom 1:7 and 8:33. For the Jewish (Old Testament) background see my *Romans* (WBC 38A; Dallas: Word, 1988) 19-20, 502-3; on the theme of "inheritance" see p. 213.

17. See, e.g., P. T. O'Brien, *Colossians, Philemon* (WBC 44; Waco, Tex.: Word, 1982) 181-84. That wrong desire or covetousness was the root of all sin was an already established theologoumenon in Jewish thought (see, e.g., Philo, *Decal.* 142, 150, 153, 173; *Apoc. Mos.* 19:3; *Apoc. Abr.* 24:10; Rom 7:7; Jas 1:15).

None of these can properly be called anti-Jewish claims.[18] They were simply rival claims—coming from within the varieties of first-century Judaism—to have been given by God the key to the greatest divine mystery. The implied dispute is better characterized as intra-Jewish than anti-Jewish.

It is equally significant that the references to circumcision are surprisingly nonpolemical. There are more references to circumcision in Colossians than in any other Pauline letter apart from Romans and Galatians. But unlike these earlier Pauline letters, the references in Colossians are consistently positive. In the main passage (2:11-13), uncircumcision denotes a disadvantaged (indeed dead) state (2:13), where the presupposition is the typically Jewish one that within the covenant there is life, and outside it there is death (so regularly in Deuteronomy). Consistent with this, the means by which the transition from death to life has taken place is circumcision (2:11). Of course, the author means spiritual circumcision, "circumcision without hands, in putting off the body of flesh in the circumcision of Christ" (2:11).[19] But in Jewish thought the physical act of circumcision was intended to have just such a spiritual effect; hence the frequent reference in Jewish writings to the desirability of the heart being circumcised (Deut 10:16; Jer 4:4; 9:25-26; Ezek 44:9; 1QpHab 11:13; 1QS 5:5; 1QH 2:18; 18:20; Philo, *Spec. Leg.* 1.305). The claim in Colossians (2:11-13), therefore, is simply that faith in Jesus Christ is the effective way to fulfill that long-standing goal of Jewish piety.

It is true that Col 3:11 echoes the typically Pauline formula ("There is no longer Greek and Jew, circumcised and uncircumcised . . . "; cf. 1 Cor 12:13; Gal 3:28; 5:6; 6:15). But the assumption is that the restoration of the image of God (3:10) relativizes all human distinctions (the references to Greek, barbarian, slave, etc. are equally descriptive and nonpolemical). And the final reference to "those of the circumcision" who are his fellow-workers for the kingdom of God (4:11) shows that no polemic against circumcision as such or against "those of the circumcision" is intended (contrast Gal 2:12). The implication is that the tensions of Paul's earlier missionary work, which resulted in the more negative treatments of circumcision in Galatians and Romans, have been left behind. Circumcision functions either as a description or an as expressive symbol.

The nearest Colossians comes to what could be called anti-Jewish polemic is in the references to the Law and various regulations of the Law (2:14-17, 20-23). But in striking contrast to Romans and Galatians, "the Law" is never actually mentioned in Colossians. The reference to "the hand-written document, or bond, which stood against us, with its requirements [*dogmasin*]," is very vague, and an attempt to denigrate the Jewish Law could have been much plainer

---

18. Contrast again Beck, *Mature Christianity,* 81.

19. Both phrases ("putting off the body of flesh" and "the circumcision of Christ") could refer either to believers' "putting off the old nature" (3:9) or to Christ's death (see the review in O'Brien, *Colossians,* 116–17); but the close parallel of Rom 6:4-6 suggests that exegesis at this point should not allow itself to be boxed into an either-or conclusion.

and more direct.[20] Nor is there an attempt to equate the Law itself with the hostile spiritual powers (2:15, 20), as in Gal 3:19, 23-25; 4:2-3, 9-10, though the thought of 2:20-21 comes close.

The polemic in 2:16-17, however, does reflect Jewish emphasis on dietary laws and Jewish festivals (festival, new moon, Sabbath).[21] Moreover, the description of them as "a shadow, or foreshadowing, of what is to come, but the substance is of Christ" (2:17), while making a familiar contrast between shadow and substance (as in Philo, *Conf.* 190; Josephus, *J.W.* 2.1.5 §28), also echoes the more dismissive treatment of the old covenant and the Law in Hebrews (particularly 8:5 and 10:1). But the reference to "the elemental forces of the cosmos" (2:8, 20) and possibly also 2:18 indicate that the threat envisaged was much more syncretistic in character;[22] that is, it was not a threat from Judaism as such, but rather from a variant Judaism, a form of Jewish-Christian syncretism,[23] if not a larger syncretistic system which had drawn typically Jewish features into itself (the features that attracted most attention among the Colossians). In other words, it would be unwise to assume that 2:16-18 was directed against Jews or Judaism as such.

A similar point has to be made with reference to 2:20-23, which seems to be directed, in part at least, against typically Jewish concerns (dietary and purity regulations; cf., e.g., *Ep. Arist.* 142).[24] For these verses also reflect inner-Jewish disputes (cf. 2:21 with *T. Mos.* 7)[25] and not uncharacteristic Jewish exhortation (cf. 2:22 with Isa 29:13). Here too, then, the simple thesis of an anti-Jewish polemic is hardly adequate to reflect the complexity of the situation out of which and for which Colossians was written.

# Ephesians

In close parallel to Colossians, Ephesians too echoes typically Jewish language and themes—the same emphasis on the knowledge given of the mystery of the divine will (1:9; 3:3-4, 9; cf. 5:32; 6:19), on the recipients as "saints" (1:1, 4, 15, 18; etc.), on their share in the promised inheritance (1:14, 18; 5:5), and

---

20. The word *dogma* appears nowhere in the undisputed Paulines and is used by Luke-Acts for the decrees of Caesar (Luke 2:1; Acts 17:7) or the "apostolic decree" (Acts 16:4). The only other New Testament reference is in Eph 2:15, where it does refer to the (Jewish) Law. See further G. Kittel, *TDNT* 2.230–32.

21. Hence the typically Jewish threefold sequence (cf. 1 Chr 23:31; 2 Chr 2:4; 31:3; Neh 10:33; Isa 1:13-14; Hos 2:11); hence also Gal 4:10.

22. See, e.g., the discussion in O'Brien, *Colossians*, 129–30, 142–45.

23. See, e.g., Kümmel, *Introduction*, 339–40; Koester, *Introduction*, 264–65.

24. See below n. 43.

25. *T. Mos.* 7:9-10: "They, with hand and mind, will touch impure things, yet their mouths will speak enormous things, and they will even say, 'Do not touch me, lest you pollute me in the position I occupy.'" Insofar as the targets of this polemic can be identified, the usual inference is that it is directed against the Pharisees.

the same strongly Jewish ethics (cf. particularly 5:5 with Col 3:5). Again we cannot speak of anything overtly anti-Jewish in this. Rather, such features, and the strongly Semitic language of Ephesians,[26] suggest that the one who speaks does so quite naturally as a Jew—a Jew for whom, inter alia, God is one (4:6; cf. Deut 6:4, the *Shema*), even if the praise to the one God is offered in the name of Christ (4:20). That is to say, it is not the case of language appropriated in polemical fashion—as already later in *Barnabas,* where the inheritance is spoken of as "ours" and not "theirs" (*Barn.* 4:6-7, 13, 14). Even the echo of the older Pauline polemic against works (of the Law) and boasting (2:8-9) is hardly more than that (contrast Gal 2:15–3:14; Rom 3:20–4:6; 9:11, 32; 11:6)[27]—no longer a deeply divisive issue between Jews (that is, Jews who accepted Jesus as Messiah and those who did not), but simply an echo, with all passion spent.

This impression of a native Jewish attitude, assumed from within rather than appropriated from without, is confirmed by the author's strongly Jewish attitude to non-Jews, that is, to Gentiles—a much more marked feature in Ephesians than in Colossians. The readership envisaged is clearly gentile (2:11; 3:1).[28] So the description of their pre-Christian state is significant—"dead in trespasses and sins" (2:1, 5), under the domination of evil powers (angels) who led them astray (2:2),[29] "sons of disobedience" (2:2; 5:6), "by nature children of [divine] wrath, like the rest" (2:3), "once you were darkness" (5:8).[30] Similarly the exhortation of 4:17-19:

> This I say and affirm in the Lord, that you no longer walk as also the Gentiles walk in the futility of their minds; they are darkened in their understanding, alienated from the life of God, because of the ignorance which is in them, on account of the hardness of their hearts; they have become callous and gave themselves up to licentiousness, greedy to practice every kind of uncleanness.

In such passages the author speaks naturally as one who views the world as a Jew.

It is within this context that the key passage, 2:11-22, gains its fullest significance. It is worthwhile enumerating the most striking features.

1. The reminder to the readers of their former state is again in strongly Jewish terms:

> Gentiles in the flesh, called "uncircumcision" by those who called themselves "circumcision" hand-wrought in the flesh. You were at that time without Christ,

---

26. K. G. Kuhn (cited by Kümmel, *Introduction,* 358) notes "appearances of Semitic syntax four times more frequently than all the other letters of the Pauline corpus."

27. Similarly the contrast between "the circumcision" and "the uncircumcision" in 2:11; but see further below.

28. The point is not in dispute; see also the following texts, and 1:11-14 and 2:11-22.

29. Cf. particularly *Jub.* 15:31: "Over all of them [the other nations] he [God] caused spirits to rule so that they might lead them astray from following him."

30. The fact that the author says "we" here does not count significantly against the view that the author was Jewish. It was precisely Paul's argument in Rom 1:18–3:20 that Jews were as much under divine wrath as Gentiles. Beck (*Mature Christianity,* 82), however, comments: "It is said that for those who had not been Jews an act of reconciliation to God was necessary, but it is not said that a similar act was required for Jews."

alienated from the body politic of Israel, and strangers to the covenants of promise, having no hope and without God in the world.

The perspective is clearly Jewish—of Israel[31] standing in a privileged position as a nation before God, by virtue of the favor of the one God as expressed in the covenant(s)[32] he had made with Israel, with everyone else (Gentiles) outside the scope of that favor.[33]

2. The blessings received by these Gentiles who have now responded to the gospel of Christ are the same covenant blessings of Israel—peace, access to God as Father (cf. Rom 5:2 and 1QS 11.13-15), "no longer strangers and resident aliens, but fellow-citizens with the saints and members of God's household" (2:17-19). The point is that Israel has not been cast off; its blessings have not been taken away from them and given to others (contrast even Mark 12:9 pars.). Rather the Gentiles have been brought in to share the blessings previously confined to Israel. This is the mystery, spelled out much more explicitly than in Colossians, that "Gentiles are fellow heirs [with Jews]" (3:6; cf. Col 1:27). True, the symbolism of the (Jerusalem) Temple as the place of God's dwelling has been transposed to the community as a whole (2:18-22). But this is wholly in line with the Jewish ideal implied, for example, in Exod 19:6, Lev 26:11-12, and Ezek 37:27. And Christ is understood as the "cornerstone" (2:20), but in fulfillment of the much-quoted (in the New Testament) Isa 28:16.[34] The point once again, however, is that this is understood as an inclusive ideal, as fulfillment of the hope of the circumcised; it is not a takeover; neither Gentile nor Jew is excluded.

3. All(!) that has happened is that the barrier which had previously stood between Jew and Gentile has been broken down (2:14). In the context, where the thought immediately goes on to talk of (cultic) access and use Temple imagery (2:18-22), the image in mind might well have been the barrier within the Temple complex in Jerusalem which excluded Gentiles on pain of death.[35] This was also the function of the Law—as a palisade round Israel, marking Israel out among the surrounding nations by Jewish faithfulness to the Law, and marking Israel off from the rest as outsiders, outlaws.[36] Hence also the earlier

---

31. "Israel" is precisely the word of someone looking from inside out, whereas "Jew" (which does not appear in Ephesians) first appeared as the name used by others to denote a person from Judaea; see further W. Gutbrod, *TDNT* 3.369-72.

32. The plural ("covenants") could denote either the sequence of covenants, with Abraham, at Sinai, with David, and so on, or more likely, the covenant with Abraham, renewed to Isaac and Jacob—that is, the covenants with the fathers (see further my *Romans*, 527).

33. On Israel's sense of distinctiveness and separateness see my *Romans*, lxix–lxxi.

34. See also M. Barth, *Ephesians* (AB 34; New York: Doubleday, 1974) 317–19.

35. See, e.g., R. J. McKelvey, *The New Temple: The Church in the New Testament* (Oxford: Oxford Univ. Press, 1969) 109–10; Barth, *Ephesians*, 283–84. Those who support this view are listed by R. Schnackenburg, *Der Brief an die Epheser* (EKKNT 10; Zurich: Benziger, 1982) 113–14.

36. Classically expressed in *Ep. Arist.* 139, 142: "In his wisdom the legislator [Moses]... surrounded us with unbroken palisades and iron walls to prevent our mixing with any of the other peoples in any matter, being thus kept pure in body and soul, preserved from false beliefs, and worshipping the only God omnipotent over all creation.... So, to prevent our being perverted

disparagement ("so-called," "made with hands") of the characteristically Jewish distinction between Jew and Gentile, as summed up and focused in the act or absence of circumcision, that archetypal requirement of the Jewish Law (2:11).[37] It is precisely in this, its function as a dividing line between Jew and Gentile, that the Law has been abolished (2:15).[38]

The consequence for the writer is that what were previously two (Jew and Gentile) are now "one new human being" (2:15). The imagery is not of Jew triumphing over Gentile. But neither is it of Gentile triumphing over Jew. Nor indeed of Christians as a *tertium genus* (as in the *Epistle to Diognetus*).[39] It is rather of the new creation, the new Adam, a fulfillment of God's final purpose as creator, a fulfillment which absorbs into itself and thus relativizes all human distinctions subsequent to creation (so also 1:22, echoing Ps 8:6; and 4:22-24).[40] Is this anti-Jewish? Only if it is indispensably Jewish to assume that God's covenant with Israel cannot find fulfillment except in the Jewish people triumphing and ruling over all others in the end. But for a Judaism which recognized the universalist logic of its monotheism (as in Jonah or Amos 9:7, or indeed Paul—Rom 3:29-30), the attitude is thoroughly Jewish, being thoroughly rooted in and expressive of the creation theology of the Jewish Scriptures.

The point, once again, is that what is envisaged is an opening out to others of Israel's blessings, not a denial or a reversal of them. It is a reversal of Israel's exclusivist claims, but not a new exclusivism directed against "those who call themselves 'the circumcision' by virtue of a ritual act in the flesh." In short, what is expressed here has more the character of a *universalist* Judaism than of an *anti*-Judaism.

# 1 Timothy

I will not attempt to engage with the issue of the chronological sequence of the Pastoral Epistles,[41] and it is probably better to look at each of the three indi-

---

by contact with others or by mixing with bad influences, he hedged us in on all sides with strict observances connected with meat and drink and touch and hearing and sight, after the manner of the Law."

37. See further my *Romans*, 119–20; also *Partings*, sec. 2.3.

38. See also particularly Barth, *Ephesians*, 290–91. At this point the author is a true disciple of Paul; see my *Romans*, in the index under "law, boundary"; also my *Jesus, Paul and the Law* (London: SPCK; Louisville: Westminster, 1990) esp. chaps. 7-9.

39. See further M. Simon, *Verus Israel: A Study of the Relations between Christians and Jews in the Roman Empire* (AD 135-425) (1948; repr., Oxford: Oxford Univ. Press, 1986) 107-11; P. Richardson, *Israel in the Apostolic Church* (SNTSMS 10; Cambridge: Cambridge Univ. Press, 1969) 22-23.

40. See also Barth, *Ephesians*, 308-11.

41. The usual assumption is that the original order was 1 Timothy, Titus, and 2 Timothy; see, e.g., J. Roloff, *Das erste Brief an Timotheus* (EKKNT 15; Zurich: Benziger, 1988) 45.

vidually, despite their homogeneity, since otherwise distinctive features might
be lost.

So far as the present inquiry is concerned, the striking feature of 1 Timothy
is, once again, its lack of anti-Jewish features. In particular, we may note a
number of passages where an author with an anti-Jewish attitude might well
have used the opportunity to make snide or critical remarks about things Jewish.
The description of Paul's former life as a persecutor is couched in very personal
terms (1:12-14) and avoids any reference to his way of life "in Judaism" (as
in Gal 1:13-14). In 2:7 (cf. 3:16), rather than reinforce the more characteristic
and implicitly polemical Pauline claim to be "apostle to the Gentiles" (cf. Rom
11:13; Gal 1:15-16; 2:8), the author describes Paul simply as "a teacher of the
Gentiles," in terms that echo instead the Jewish boast of Rom 2:18-20. Likewise,
talk of the divine "mystery" (3:9, 16) lacks all reference to the Gentiles, as was
characteristic of the earlier Pauline letters (Rom 11:25-26; Eph 3:3-6; Col 1:27).
And the frequent references to "works" are all to "good works" (2:10; 3:1;
5:10, 25; 6:18) without any hint that "works (of the Law)" could be something
negative.

Perhaps most noticeable of all, the polemic in the letter is remarkably lacking
in anything that might properly be called anti-Jewish elements. "The myths and
endless genealogies" (1:4) and the "godless and silly myths" (4:7) are of uncertain provenance, though if anything, 6:20 suggests a strongly gnostic character
("Avoid the godless chatter and contradictions of what is falsely called knowledge").[42] That does not exclude Jewish elements (cf. Titus 1:14), but that the
polemic should be described as anti-Jewish is hardly warranted by anything said
in 1 Timothy. Certainly no attempt is made to identify Hymenaeus and Alexander as Jews, or as having "made shipwreck" of their faith because of reversion
to or the attraction of Judaism (1:20; contrast Ignatius, *Magn.* 8-10; *Barn.* 3:6,
and Justin, *Dial.* 47.4). Even in 4:1-5 the warning against those "who forbid
marriage and enjoin abstinence from foods which God created to be received by
those who believe and know the truth" can hardly be identified *simpliciter* as directed against Jewish convictions (the food laws), despite echoes of Rom 14:6.[43]
For the echoes of 1 Corinthians 7 (abstinence from marriage) and 1 Corinthians 8-10 (emphasis on knowledge, 8:1ff.; food as given by God, 10:26) are even
stronger; and the contribution to the problems at Corinth of distinctively Jewish
attitudes and scruples is far from clear.[44]

Not least of significance in this connection is the markedly positive attitude

---

42. See particularly the discussion in N. Brox, *Die Pastoralbriefe* (RNT; Regensburg: Pustet,
1969) 31-39. It is a weakness of most discussions of the subject that they treat the Pastorals as a
unity (e.g., Kümmel, *Introduction*, 378-80) and thus allow the more distinctively Jewish character of
the opposition in Titus to color their reading of 1 and 2 Timothy—a somewhat dubious assumption,
since Titus claims to be written to a different situation (Crete).

43. That Romans 14 has particularly Jewish sensitivities in view is clear; see my *Romans*,
799-802.

44. Asceticism was a very widespread phenomenon in the religions of the ancient world; see,

to the Law in 1:7-9: to be a teacher of the Law is something good, though it requires understanding (1:6-7); the Law is good (1:8); it is "for the lawless and disobedient" (1:9); it functions "in accordance with the gospel" (1:11). The echoes of Rom 2:12-16, 7:12-13, and 13:3-4 confirm that it is only the (to some) surprisingly positive comments Paul made on the Law which are picked up, not the more familiar polemical passages which are usually taken to characterize Paul's view of the Law (note also the use of *anomos* ["lawless"] as a negative category, uncharacteristic of Paul). At any rate, we can hardly speak of an antipathy to or polemic against the Law.[45]

We should also note the almost unconscious use of Jewish language and motifs which betray a Jewish mind-set more than the conscious takeover of Jewish categories by an outsider. Examples include: in 2:2, the expression of the political prudence learned by Jewish minorities over decades of existence in the Diaspora, often under hostile authorities (cf. Jer 29:7; Bar 1:11);[46] in 3:15, the talk of "the household of God, which is the congregation [*ekklesia*] of the living God," echoing the Jewish understanding of the community as God's dwelling place[47] and the regular LXX reference to the congregation (*ekklesia*) of Israel; and in 6:7, the reflection of sober day-to-day wisdom as in Job 1:21 and Eccl 5:15.

Finally, we should not fail to acknowledge the remarkably strong reaffirmation of Jewish monotheism which is a feature of this letter. "To the King of ages, immortal, invisible, the only God, be honor and glory for ever and ever" (1:17; cf., e.g., Jer 10:10; 2 Macc 1:24-25; *Ep. Arist.* 132).[48] "There is one God" (2:5; the central Jewish confession, the *Shema* [Deut 6:4]), from which the one mediatorship of "the man Christ Jesus" does not detract but rather confirms and (if it were possible) enhances. "The blessed and only Sovereign, the King of kings and Lord of lords, who alone has immortality and dwells in unapproachable light, whom no man has ever seen or can see" (6:15-16), again a characteristically Jewish doxology, as again the various echoes and parallels indicate (e.g., Exod 33:20; Deut 10:17; 2 Macc 12:15; 3 Macc 5:35).[49] The writer is clearly someone who speaks from well within the traditional Jewish monotheism, and precisely within the distinctiveness of that claim as against the more typical theism and polytheism of other religions of the time. What is even more remarkable, 1 Timothy was written (probably) at a period not far removed from John's Gospel or, if slightly later, Ignatius. But the tension evident

---

e.g., the material collected in J. Behm, *TDNT* 2.690, and M. Rauer, *Die "Schwachen" in Korinth und Rom nach den Paulusbriefen* (Freiburg: Herder, 1923) 138–64.

45. First Timothy 1:7 is not critical of the Law and can be viewed as directed against Jews as such only by reading it in the light of Titus (see above n. 42).

46. Cf. the similar echoes in Rom 12:15-21 of the same range of Jewish wisdom on good citizenship, echoing Sir 7:34; Prov 3:7 and Isa 5:21; Prov 3:4; Ps. 34:14, and so on (see my *Romans*, 738).

47. See above p. 158.

48. See further G. Delling, "MONOS THEOS," *TLZ* 77 (1952) cols. 469–76.

49. See further Roloff, *Timotheus*, 355–57.

in John over the high christological claims made there (particularly John 5:18 and 10:33), and the taken-for-grantedness of Ignatius that Jesus can be described straightforwardly as "God" (*Eph.* inscrip.; 18.2; *Trall.* 7.1; *Rom.* inscrip.; etc.) are both quite lacking in 1 Timothy. In short, 1 Timothy does not seem to pose much of a threat to Jewish self-understanding and indicates a distinct absence of anti-Judaism in the Christianity it represents.

# 2 Timothy

There is little to add regarding 2 Timothy, since the results of any study of the letter on the question of anti-Judaism yield similar, if not so interesting, results.[50] Jewish categories are assumed: Paul speaks positively of his ancestors—his service was like theirs (1:3); he endures "for the sake of the elect" (2:10); he affirms the central importance of the holy (that is, Jewish) Scriptures (3:15-16). The target of the warnings is no clearer than in 1 Timothy—dispute about words (2:14), "godless chatter" (2:16), "senseless controversies" (2:23). The various failures or apostates are nowhere identified as Jews or their apostasy attributed to Jewish influence: Phygelus and Hermogenes (1:15); Hymenaeus and Phile-tus, "who have swerved from the truth by holding that the resurrection is past already," a more gnostic and un-Jewish belief (2:17-18); Demas, "in love with this present world" (4:10); not to mention Alexander the coppersmith (4:14). In the case of the last named, we might note that of Paul's various opponents in Acts, it is Alexander alone who is mentioned, rather than the more regular opponents, "the Jews," or indeed "the Jews" who, according to Acts 19:33, put Alexander forward.

There are one or two clearer echoes of the earlier Paul: the christological formula in 2:8 with its close parallel in Rom 1:3-4; Christ as judge, as in 2 Cor 5:10; the importance of Paul's evangelistic ministry to Gentiles (4:17). And while 1 Timothy's emphasis on "good work" is also present here (2:21; 3:17), unlike 1 Timothy, there is also the echo of the more typical Pauline polemic against works (1:9: "God who saved us and called us with a holy calling, not in accordance with our works..."), albeit in what may be some confessional or hymnic formula preserved by 2 Timothy, and lacking all the earlier Pauline passion.

Apart from that we may simply note the scattering of passages which draw on scriptural and Jewish language and themes: 2:7 (Prov 2:6); 2:19 (Isa 28:16 again, and quotations from Num. 16:5 and Isa 26:13, which are themselves expressions of a more extensive theme in Jewish wisdom); 3:8 (Exod 7:11, 22);[51] 3:11 (Ps

---

50. Beck, *Mature Christianity*, 86: "One of the New Testament writings with the least obvious anti-Jewish material."

51. The names of Jannes and Jambres do not appear in the Old Testament, Philo, or Josephus, but Jannes is already named in CD 5:18-19. See further, e.g., *IDB* 2.800-801.

34:19; *Pss. Sol.* 4:23); 3:15 (Ps 119:98); 4:8 (Wis Sol 5:16); 4:14 (Ps 62:12; Prov 24:12; etc.); 4:17 (1 Macc 2:60). Whether we see here evidence of a still living relationship with the broader Judaisms indicated by such a spread of references, it is not possible to say. But at least the relation to these Judaisms implied by such usage cannot be called hostile or dismissive.

## Titus

Titus clearly comes from a very similar context, whatever its precise relationship with the other two Pastoral Epistles. Here we may note especially the positive affirmation of Jewish categories and faith: the addressees are "God's elect" (1:1); the purpose of God's saving act in Christ was "to redeem us from all lawlessness and cleanse for himself a people of his own zealous for good works" (2:14; the resonance with Exod 19:5; Deut 7:6; 14:2; Ps 130:8; and Ezek 37:23 is clear);[52] and there are various echoes of typically Jewish language in the hymnlike passage in 3:4-7 (particularly Deut 9:5; Ps 31:21; Joel 2:28; Wis Sol 1:6).

Somewhat surprisingly, however, here at last within this sequence of letters we come upon something which might indeed and even properly be called "anti-Jewish."[53] In 1:10-11 the author castigates "undisciplined or rebellious men, empty talkers and deceivers, especially those of the circumcision," who were, so the charge runs, upsetting whole families and teaching for sordid gain. The same group is evidently in view in the dismissive talk of "Jewish myths" and "commands of men who reject the truth" (1:14), and presumably also in warnings against "quarrels relating to the law" (3:9). It will not do simply to point out that the phrase "those of the circumcision" is also used of Christian Jews elsewhere in the New Testament (Acts 10:45; 11:2; Col 4:11; perhaps Gal 2:12); nor that the echo of similar sounding warnings against "myths" in 1 and 2 Timothy suggests at least a degree of syncretism in the teaching contested in Titus. The references to the Jewish character of this teaching are too strong to permit much watering down of the language. Even if the teaching was syncretistic, the point is that it was both dominantly Jewish in character and promulgated by (Christian?) Jews.

The probability is rather that a sharper conflict between (what is usually designated as) church and synagogue lies in the background. Or, given that Judaism seems to have been quite strongly evangelistic in the likely period of this letter,[54]

---

52. H. Preisker, *TDNT* 6.57–58.

53. Contrast Richardson (*Israel*, 159): "The criticism does not spill over and affect the author's attitude to Judaism itself."

54. See particularly Simon, *Verus Israel*, chap. 10. But see the different conclusion reached by S. McKnight, *A Light among the Gentiles: Jewish Missionary Activity in the Second Temple Period* (Minneapolis: Fortress, 1991).

we should perhaps envisage a competition for adherents and sympathizers (God-fearers) from among those who were still attracted to the various house-groups/synagogues/churches which evidently still operated in a not altogether differentiated or at least overlapping way at this time.[55] At all events we seem, for the first time, to be much closer to the situations and challenges that evoked such passages as those referred to above from Ignatius, *Barnabas*, and Justin.[56] And the more substantial echo of Pauline soteriology in 3:5-7 indicates an awareness on the part of the author of the need to recall his readers to teaching which had been forged precisely in the controversies of the gentile mission and which stressed the thoroughgoing and continuing primacy of God's mercy.

But is even this, strictly speaking, anti-Judaism? The language of 1:10 and 14 *is* disparaging. But the paraenetic and polemical language of the day was much more robust and sharp-edged than most civilized debate today.[57] We need only recall Jesus' own rebuke of Peter (Mark 8:33) and Paul's equally fierce protest against the tactics of his fellow Jewish missionaries (2 Cor 11:13-15). In terms of our own time such language is generally reckoned as too fierce, and if used in our own time Titus 1:10 and 14 would be regarded quite properly as anti-Jewish. But in terms of its own time, and that is the primary and controlling context of these words, all we can say with complete fairness is that Titus 1:10 and 14 express the vigor of the competition between two missions, both of which laid claim to the heritage of pre-70 Judaism and of God-fearing sympathy with that Judaism—one of them more clearly Jewish in character, the other already becoming something Jewish in character but no longer simply Jewish in content and membership.

The tension is probably best illustrated by the four references to "God our Savior"—evidently a favorite phrase of our author (1:3; 2:10, 13; 3:4; so also 1 Tim 1:1; 2:3; 4:10). That the God of Jewish monotheism is meant is clear (e.g., Deut 32:15; Ps 24:5; Mic. 7:7; Wis Sol 16:7; 1 Macc 4:30).[58] But the role of savior is now shared by Christ (Titus 2:13; 3:6; so also 2 Tim 1:10), and, more strikingly, Christ is now understood as "the glory of our great God and Savior" (2:13),[59] and perhaps as "the goodness and loving kindness of God our Savior" (3:4). It was such identification of Christ with the saving action of God himself that was the final straw for rabbinic Judaism in the parting of the ways.[60] But it remains unclear on what side of that parting (before or after) Titus stands.

55. See further my *Partings*, particularly secs. 12.1-2.

56. See above p. 160.

57. Though perhaps we should recall that polemic within modern scholarship can sometimes be very robust, not to say fierce and highly disparaging.

58. See further G. Fohrer and W. Foerster, *TDNT* 7.975-78, 1012-14.

59. We should note that the thought is not of Christ and God as distinct saviors; the thought is still of the glorious and saving manifestation of the one transcendent God (see V. Hasler, "Epiphanie und Christologie in den Pastoralbriefen," *TZ* 33 [1977] 193-209).

60. See further my *Partings*, chap. 11.

# Conclusion

Little need be added by way of conclusion. The opening observation has, I hope, been adequately demonstrated: the deutero-Paulines are characteristically *lacking* in overt or even clearly implicit anti-Judaism, with perhaps the one exception of Titus. The distinctiveness of this important strand of New Testament writing as compared with other, particularly contemporary, Christian writing should be underlined. The more anti-Jewish sentiment we may find in, say, Matthew and John, the more striking is its (almost) complete absence in the deutero-Paulines. Even on a strongly anti-Jewish reading of these other documents, the Christianity of the late first century cannot be described as universally or even characteristically anti-Jewish.

In contrast, the prevailing impression from these letters is twofold. The first impression is that the letters were written against and within a characteristically syncretistic background, wherein Jewish elements were often prominent—understandably so since Judaism in its various expressions was such a significant part of the Middle Eastern religious systems at that time. The second impression is of a Christianity which saw itself in continuity with and as a major (the eschatological) expression of Second Temple Judaism in its more inclusivistic and universalist strands. In such circumstances "anti-Judaism," and still more "anti-Semitism," is at best an imprecise and inaccurate charge to bring against these letters, since it hardly begins to reflect the complexity of the situations, and particularly the different forms of Judaism and Christianity which were active at that time. At worst it is simply wrong, misleading the participants in Jewish-Christian dialogue, reinforcing old stereotypes rather than countering them, and perpetuating a false understanding of Christianity's and Judaism's common beginnings in the first century of the common era.

# -9-

# Polemic in Hebrews and
# the Catholic Epistles

## Robert W. Wall and William L. Lane

In this chapter, we will survey the most liberal (or "Hellenized") form of Jewish Christianity (Hebrews) and the most conservative (or "Palestinian") form of Jewish Christianity (James), thus fashioning something like a *merism* to determine the extent of anti-Judaism in the non-Pauline letters. By providing a study of extremes, we seek to illustrate the whole problem found in this particular collection of New Testament writings.

No one disagrees anymore that Christianity evolved into a pluralistic religious movement with roots in a pluralistic Judaism. Luke's Acts (15:19-21) and Paul's Galatians (2:7-10) suggest a rather simple and too sharp division along ethnic lines to demarcate this movement into its second generation: the church consisted of Jewish and gentile missions, with different kerygmata for different audiences and distinctive membership requirements for diverse constituencies. Scholars have found it considerably more difficult to reconstruct with any historical precision the extent and nature of that pluralism;[1] indeed, one of the storm centers of modern biblical scholarship since F. C. Baur has been to understand the theological and sociological diversity within each constituency, and the relationship between these two groups and their respective apostolates.[2]

---

1. Cf. J. D. G. Dunn, *Unity and Diversity in the New Testament* (Philadelphia: Westminster, 1977). Dunn's conclusion that a unifying paradigm is found outside of the New Testament and in the great ecumenical creeds of Christendom has recently been challenged by E. E. Lemcio ("Unifying Kerygma in the New Testament," *JSNT* 33 [1988] 3–17), who has recovered a "unifying kerygma" of common themes and grammar in every substratum of the New Testament.

2. In recent years, initiated by the work of H. J. Schoeps (*Jewish Christianity: Factional Disputes in the Early Church* [Philadelphia: Fortress, 1969]), various attempts have been made to define "Jewish Christianity" in order to locate it within the history of earliest Christianity. The most notable efforts are those of J. Danielou, *Theology of Jewish Christianity* (Philadelphia: Westminster,

In particular, recent studies have attempted to reconstruct the diversity within the second-generation and second-century Jewish church, and a general consensus has now emerged. First, the theological and social boundaries of the Jesus movement and its first generation were self-consciously drawn in terms of its sectarian relationship within "official" Judaism; Christianity grew up within Judaism in the same way that Judaism sponsored other movements, some of which are reported in Hebrew scriptural and intertestamental writings. Whatever anti-Judaistic rhetoric is found in the New Testament writings (esp. the Gospels), it is similar both in kind and theme to these antecedent debates—debates over the meaning of a "true" or eschatological Israel whose borders are contested between the various groups that make up all of Israel. In the case of Christianity, the convictions of messianic Jewish faith are adapted to and given "new" meaning by the promised age of God's *shalom* that his first disciples believed began with the ministry of Rabbi Jesus from Nazareth. Whenever the memories of earliest Christianity are rehearsed in the New Testament, the theological calculus of messianic Judaism is retained. In this sense, then, Jewish Christianity was constituted by religious Jews and was in no way anti-Semitic. What did distinguish this particular messianic sect from other similar movements within Judaism was the conviction that the Messiah's identity and thus the eschaton were realized in a particular person.

Second, when one follows the trajectory of Jewish Christianity into the second generation and then into the second century, the boundaries are gradually redrawn in terms of its relationship within "official" Christianity. Fraternal differences were ultimately cast in terms of orthodoxy and heresy—a phenomenon not yet reflected by New Testament writings.[3] Even in Jewish Christianity's observance of Torah and tradition, appeals were often made to traditions about Jesus or James for justification rather than to Jewish rabbis or Judaic tradition. That is, the rhetoric of second-century, Jewish-Christian writings was unmistakably Christian and even on occasion anti–Pauline Christian (or more precisely anti–contemporary "folk" Paulinisms), but was almost never anti-Judaic. Baur's reconstruction of rival factions within the earliest church, Jewish and anti-Pauline versus gentile and pro-Pauline, transposes the second-century situation upon the first; but one cannot transform the biblical James, for example, into a hostile opponent of Paul's mission.[4] Whatever disagreements emerged between

---

1984); R. A. Kraft, "In Search of 'Jewish Christianity' and Its 'Theology,' " *RSR* 60 (1972) 81–92; A. F. J. Klijn, "The Study of Jewish Christianity," *NTS* 20 (1974) 419–31; and R. E. Brown, "Not Jewish Christianity and Gentile Christianity, but Types of Jewish/Gentile Christianity," *CBQ* 45 (1983) 74–79.

3. Cf. R. E. Brown ("Not Jewish Christianity," 75), who suggests that these distinctions often made between gentile and Jewish varieties of Christianity are more true in the second century than the first.

4. See L. Goppelt, *Theology of the New Testament* (Grand Rapids, Mich.: Eerdmans, 1981) 2.200, 208–11.

the various groups that made up the earliest church, the issues had more to do with drawing the boundaries between Christianity and Judaism.

For our purposes, it is noteworthy that the canonizing community accepted the Lukan/Pauline description of the earliest church, dividing the apostolic writings into two collections: the Pauline writings reflected the "gospel of the uncircumcised" and another collection, the "gospel of the circumcised." The superscriptions added to these writings during the canonizing process located them within the Jewish mission of earliest Christianity. Sandwiched between the anonymous Hebrews and Jude are letters whose alleged authors were the very "pillars" of the Jewish church mentioned by Paul (Gal 2:1-10) and whose order is indexed by Paul in Gal 2:9 as "James, Cephas, and John." From a canonical perspective this collection of writings records the range of theological diversity found within the early Jewish mission in order to delimit, along with the Pauline corpus, the range of diversity found in the apostolic witness to the gospel and therefore the adequate rule of faith for subsequent generations of believers.

Even though our specific interest in this chapter is to assess the anti-Judaic content found in Hebrews and James, we do not dismiss the importance of the Petrine or Johannine letters for this project. We are well aware that 1 Peter, for example, represents an interesting case study: a Jewish-Christian text written for a largely non-Jewish (and perhaps even Pauline) Christian audience, perhaps intended to foster a rapprochement between Jewish and non-Jewish believers within the early catholic Asian church.[5] Although at least one influential study of 1 Peter has recently charged the author with anti-Judaism, it has done so, we think, without any basis in the text itself.[6] Clearly, the enemy of God's people according to 1 Peter is the secular mainstream of the Roman world, and this perspective is shared by both the church and the synagogue.

We are also aware of the importance of the Johannine writings of the New Testament for this topic. In the Gospel of John, "the Jews" are portrayed as adversaries of Christ. They denied that his ministry was messianic and considered it blasphemous that he should claim himself to be the Son of God Messiah. Those who take the idiom "the Jews" to be symbolic of Judaism interpret John's Gospel to be anti-Judaic (see Kysar's discussion above). Not surprisingly, some scholars at the turn of the century contended that the adversaries to Johannine Christianity found in 1-2 John were the same "Jews" found in the Gospel.[7] "The Jews" of the Fourth Gospel also denied that Jesus is Christ (1 John 2:22; cf. John 7:25-27; 9:22; 10:24), the Son of God from the beginning (1 John 2:23; cf. John 10:36; 19:7) who has come in the flesh (1 John 4:2-3; 2 John 7; cf. John 8:31-59; 12:42-43). However, there are three problems with this thesis that combine to make it untenable. First, the unambiguous statement of 1 John 2:19 identifies the

---

5. J. R. Michaels, *1 Peter* (WBC 49; Dallas: Word, 1988) xlvi–lv.

6. J. H. Elliott, *A Home for the Homeless* (Philadelphia: Fortress, 1981).

7. E.g., A. Wurm, *Die Irrlehrer im ersten Johannesbrief* (BibS[F]; Freiburg: Herder, 1903).

adversaries as former members of the author's Christian congregation. Second, the theological (or christological) and ethical positions espoused by the adversaries do not fit a Judaic perspective. The antagonists do *not* deny that Jesus is the Messiah; they deny that he is the *Son of God* Messiah, come in human form, and that he was so "from the beginning" (cf. 1 John 4:2; 2 John 7).[8] In addition, their failure to emphasize the "life of Jesus" as an element of their Christology led them to demote the importance of a Christlike (i.e., self-sacrificial) love for other believers. This is the essential norm of Johannine ethics.[9] These issues are no doubt *intra muros* and not anti-Judaic per se. Third, the author does not appeal to Scripture to defend his views against his opponents as one would expect if his opponents were Jewish. His appeal is distinctively Christian: he was eyewitness to the earthly career of Jesus (1 John 1:1-4). Sharply put, there is no substantial evidence of anti-Judaism in the Johannine letters.

Because Christianity began as a messianic movement within Second Temple Judaism, its apologia was first focused upon its continuity and contrast with Jewish faith and history. Earliest Christianity's relationship with Judaism remained important in its every effort for religious and societal legitimacy; believers understood themselves to be faithful Jews and members of a Jewish congregation. The contested issues were parochial and *intra muros:* first-generation believers argued that they belonged to messianic Judaism—the true, eschatological Israel of God—while official Judaism constituted the rest of Israel. Only in this rather limited sense can some New Testament writings be thought of as marking boundaries between Christianity and Judaism.

During subsequent centuries, these compositions were among those preserved, collected, and then canonized to establish the distinctive theological and ethical boundaries around the church catholic. Writings once used to mark the boundaries between messianic and nonmessianic Judaism were recycled to evaluate the teachings of sectarian movements *within* Christianity. Further, during the canonization of the New Testament, the issues at stake were no longer Christianity's continuity or discontinuity with Judaism but rather Christianity's continuity or discontinuity with what was remembered as the first apostles' witness to the Christ of God. The New Testament canon taken as a whole, then, is *not* intended to function as an anti-Judaic document; rather, the church's intent for its biblical canon is to help mark off those boundaries of "one holy catholic and apostolic church" from all other religious traditions (including Judaism) and *especially* from those "heretical" movements found within the church (i.e., gnosticizing Christianity). Although the New Testament includes documents that many think to be anti-Judaic in their first *Sitz im Leben* (in the sense described above), within their canonical *Sitz im Leben* their intended meanings

---

8. R. E. Brown (*The Epistles of John* [AB; Garden City, N.Y.: Doubleday, 1982] 50–54) suspects their Christology to be a more conservative, or "low," variety, perhaps the adoptionism of other Jewish-Christian groups.

9. Brown, *Epistles*, 54–55.

are non-Judaic (i.e., Christian) rather than anti-Judaic. The ongoing function of the New Testament is to form a particular faith community rather than to polemicize against another one.

To excuse the church's subsequent anti-Semitic use of the New Testament as anticanonical would be disingenuous. Our point is simply to locate the crux of the problem more precisely with the *interpretation* of certain texts or leitmotifs within the New Testament rather than with the ongoing role of the biblical canon itself. Obviously, on the one hand, whenever interpretation is biased by anti-Semitic ideology, then anti-Semitic meanings will be advanced as historically valid or theologically canonical when in fact they are neither. On the other hand, we would tend to agree with G. I. Langmuir's verdict that whenever racial anti-Semitism is found during the modern period, especially when advanced by Christians, it is often logically related to the theological anti-Judaism found in some New Testament writings.[10] Perhaps one element of this more modern relationship between anti-Judaism and anti-Semitism derives from modern methods of biblical interpretation. Biblical criticism is a child of the Enlightenment's positivism; methods of inquiry tend to focus on the ultimate importance of the conversation between a composition's author and his or her first readers. In this sense, authorized meaning is the author's intended meaning. In our view, this modern methodological orientation not only obscures the New Testament's canonical role in forming a Christian identity; it also freezes the "true" meaning of New Testament texts at the point of their origin. And when the first *Sitz im Leben* includes anti-Judaism polemic, the *Tendenz* toward anti-Semitism is only enhanced.

This caveat is not a liberal polemic against the historicist orientation of modern biblical scholarship; nor does it intend to link current anti-Semitic sentiments within the church to critical methods of biblical interpretation. Rather this opening point underscores the need to interpret and employ biblical texts in terms of the Bible's *canonical raison d'être:* that is, any interpretation of the Bible must aid in forming meaning that continues to testify to the one God of Israel and to God's Christ, Jesus from Nazareth.[11] In the light of the Bible's current role as the church's canon, first meanings of New Testament texts, when anti-Judaic rhetoric expresses the trauma of the infant church's relationship to the synagogue, come to take on new meanings when the church—apostolic and catholic—struggles with the traumas of separating itself from the secular mainstream. Canonical hermeneutics does not disregard or deny the fundamental

---

10. G. I. Langmuir, *History, Religion, and Anti-Semitism* (Berkeley: Univ. of California Press, 1990) 275–305.

11. J. A. Sanders ("First Testament and Second," *BTB* 17 [1987] 47–49) has addressed the problem by calling for a change in nomenclature within the Christian biblical canon, from Old and New Testaments to "First and Second" Testaments. While admitting some difficulties, Sanders contends that this new terminology expresses better the theological continuity between the Hebrew and Christian Scriptures.

importance of historicist hermeneutics; however, by concentrating the hermeneutical enterprise on how biblical texts continue to function as the church's
canon, the locus of meaning shifts from the point of origin and authorial intent
to the current relationship between the church and the world in which it exists
as an ongoing (or "third") testament to God's gospel.

## Hebrews

Appeal to the history of the interpretation of Hebrews immediately focuses the
importance of the issue of faith and polemic. The argument of Hebrews has
been used and misused to polemicize against antecedent forms of Judaism. The
writer's sustained use of *syncrisis* (comparison) to demonstrate the superiority
of Jesus to the angels, to Moses, to Joshua, and to other mediators of the word
and grace of God to Israel has been cited by Christian interpreters to denigrate
Judaism. Employment of the vocabulary of shadow and type in reference to
the tabernacle and the provisions for worship under the old covenant has been
invoked to discount the sacrificial arrangement and the Levitical priesthood.
These developments underscore the difficulty of interpreting Hebrews in the
light of the fact that it has been used to discredit Judaism.

The importance of referencing the history of interpretation lies in the problematic nature of the term "anti-Judaism" when it is used to characterize New
Testament texts and themes that are pejorative in reference to Jews and to Judaism. The problematic nature of the term becomes evident as soon as one
realizes that early Christians considered themselves to a large extent part of
Judaism. For that reason New Testament statements critical of Judaism have to
be interpreted within the context of conflicts among Jews in the first century.
These conflicts were rooted in divergent attitudes toward the Torah and halakah,
with Christians formulating their positions in the light of their convictions about
Jesus. It is appropriate to talk about Christian anti-Judaism only at a later period
when statements from the New Testament were detached from their context
and were misinterpreted as anti-Judaic.[12] This is precisely what is shown by the
history of the interpretation of Hebrews.

The superscription "to the Hebrews" was not a part of the original document.[13] It was almost certainly added during the course of the canonizing
process to locate Hebrews within the Jewish mission of the early church. The
character of the Jewish Christianity represented by Hebrews must be assessed
on the basis of the text itself. A close reading of the text suggests that both the

---

12. See especially D. Sanger, "Neues Testament und Antijudaismus: Versuch einer exegetischen
und hermeneutischen Vergewisserung im innerchristlichen Gespräch," *KD* 34 (1988) 210–31.

13. The earliest attestation of the superscription "to the Hebrews" is the Chester Beatty Papyrus
(p[46]), which dates from about 200 CE. The superscription was known already by Pantaenus and to
his pupil Clement of Alexandria.

writer and his audience had been nurtured through Scripture and the traditions of Hellenistic Judaism prior to their response to the preaching of those who had heard Jesus (Heb 2:3-4; 13:7). Hellenistic Judaism in the first century was by no means monolithic, but it is convenient to use this designation to connote the varieties of Jewish piety and praxis that emerged in urban centers throughout the Greek-speaking Roman world.

There is in Hebrews a constant appeal to the normative character of the Scriptures, and more particularly of the Torah (2:2; 9:13; 10:28-29; 12:25-26). For example, the writer readily concedes that "what was once spoken by God through the angels proved to be legally valid, and every infringement and disobedience received the appropriate punishment" (2:2).[14] The accumulation of juridical expressions ("proved legally valid," "every infringement and disobedience," "received appropriate punishment") confirms that "the message delivered by angels" signifies the Law delivered to Moses at Sinai.[15] The positive role assigned to the angels and the appeal to the normative character of the Torah tend to suggest that both the writer and the community addressed continued to maintain emotional and intellectual ties with the larger Jewish community.

Throughout Hebrews the argument is developed exegetically on the basis of the wording in current Greek translations of the biblical text. This is especially evident at points where older Greek versions differ from the Hebrew text.[16] The writer read his Bible in Greek, as did those whom he addressed. He was able to presuppose their general familiarity with Scripture (e.g., 12:17, "for you know that ... ," with reference to Gen 27:30-40) and with Jewish tradition. The form of his own homily reflects the influence of Hellenistic Jewish synagogue preaching.[17] Hebrews is a Jewish-Christian writing that retains a distinctly Jewish ethos shaped by Hellenistic Judaism. Moreover, the writer's constant reflection on Scripture presupposes continuity with "old Israel."

Interpreters who see Hebrews as addressed to Jewish Christians have often assumed that the document was composed to warn the audience not to retreat

---

14. Biblical translations from WBC 47A and 47B (Dallas: Word, 1991).

15. In a passage celebrating the theophany on Sinai, Moses declares that God came with "myriads of holy ones," and the Septuagint adds, "Angels were with him at his right hand" (Deut 33:2). This appears to be the source of the conviction in Hellenistic Jewish circles that angels played a role in mediating the Law (e.g., Acts 7:38, 53; Gal 3:19; cf. John 7:19). Near the end of the first century Josephus explains to his gentile audience, "And for ourselves, we have learned from God the most excellent of our teachings, and the most holy part of our law through angels or ambassadors" (*Ant.* 15 §136).

16. E.g., Heb 3:7b-14, citing Ps 95:7b-11; 10:5-7, citing Ps 40:6-8.

17. See especially H. Thyen (*Der Stil des jüdisch-hellenistischen Homilie* [Göttingen: Vandenhoeck and Ruprecht, 1955]), who based his study on Philo's allegorical commentary on Genesis, *1 Clement*, 4 Maccabees, James, Hebrews, parts of 1 and 2 Maccabees and 3 Maccabees, the speech of Stephen in Acts 7, *Didache* 1-6 and 16, the *Testaments of the Twelve Patriarchs*, and the Wisdom of Solomon (for the discussion of Hebrews see pp. 17, 43-74). For more recent discussion see L. Wills, "The Form of the Sermon in Hellenistic Judaism and Early Christianity," *HTR* 77 (1984) 277-99; C. C. Black II, "The Rhetorical Form of the Hellenistic and Early Christian Sermon: A Response to Lawrence Wills," *HTR* 81 (1988) 1-8.

into Judaism and that the writer accomplished this by means of an anti-Judaic polemic.[18] This assumption needs to be tested in the light of the observation that in its literary structure Hebrews alternates exposition and exhortation, thesis and paraenesis. In the paraenesis there is no differentiation or separation from Judaism; the distinctively Christian perspective of the writer is expressed rather in the thesis. If this generalization can be sustained it is an important observation, since in Hebrews paraenesis takes precedence over thesis. All of the assertions made by the writer in the thesis sections of Hebrews point in the direction of paraenesis and serve to support the paraenesis,[19] where there is no differentiation from Judaism.

## The Central Theme of Hebrews

The central theme of Hebrews is the importance of listening to the voice of God in Scripture and in the act of Christian preaching.[20] The opening lines of the homily focus attention upon the God who speaks. The characterization of God as the one who intervened in Israel's history through the spoken word serves to introduce the characterization of the Son as the one through whom God has spoken the ultimate word (1:1-2a). That theme is sustained with variations throughout the homily (2:1-4; 3:7b–4:13; 5:11; 10:23, 35-39; 11:11). It is recapitulated in a climactic warning, "Be careful that you do not disregard the one who is speaking" (12:25a). The redemptive accomplishment and transcendent dignity of the Son through whom God has spoken the final word demonstrate that it will be catastrophic to ignore the word of salvation delivered through the Son (2:1-4).

The writer elaborated upon this thesis through the interpretation of Scripture and by the appeal to the reality of Christian experience. The development in Hebrews conforms to the Judaic tradition of homiletical midrash, in which key phrases of an extended quotation from Scripture are taken up and expounded for the congregation (e.g., 2:5-9; 3:7b–4:11; 8:6-13; 10:5-10, 15-18; 12:26-29). This approach to Scripture, which was developed in the synagogue homiletical tradition, served to actualize the text and to bring it into the experience of

---

18. E. Grässer ("Der Hebräerbrief, 1938–1963," *TRev* 30 [1964] 148) lists among those scholars who have adopted this position W. Manson, H. Kosmala, P. Benoit, C. Spicq, A. Snell, and T. Hewitt.

19. This was demonstrated effectively by T. Haering, "Gedankengang und Grundgedanken des Hebräerbriefes," *ZNW* 18 (1917) 145-64. The view has gained broad acceptance through the magisterial commentary of O. Michel, *Der Brief an die Hebräer*, vol. 13 (13th ed.; Göttingen: Vandenhoeck and Ruprecht, 1975).

20. There are, of course, other proposals. E.g., A. Oepke (*Das neue Gottesvolk in Schrifttum und Schauspiel: Bildender Kunst und Weltgestaltung* [Gütersloh: C. Bertelsmann, 1950] 17-24, 57-75) identified the theme of Hebrews as the concept of the people of God that is deeply rooted in the biblical conviction of election and mission. This proposal is adopted by W. Klassen, "To the Hebrews or against the Hebrews? Anti-Judaism and the Epistle to the Hebrews," in S. G. Wilson, ed., *Anti-Judaism in Early Christianity*, vol. 2: *Separation and Polemic* (Waterloo, Ont.: Wilfrid Laurier Univ. Press, 1986) 5.

an audience through preaching.[21] Both the writer and his audience were thoroughly familiar with homiletical midrash by virtue of their participation in the life of Hellenistic synagogues. When the writer employs homiletical midrash he does so in continuity with his contemporaries in Judaism. The act of reflecting on Scripture and of interpreting Scripture presupposes certain shared assumptions about how the voice of God is recovered. It presupposes that Scripture announces a promise of things to come. This is a thoroughly Jewish understanding of Scripture. The apology developed in Hebrews will necessarily focus upon the continuity and discontinuity of the new covenant community with the traditions, understanding, and supports of the larger Jewish community in which they had been nurtured. By examining this aspect of Hebrews the issue of faith and polemic will remain sharply in focus.

### The Treatment of Moses in Hebrews

In considering whether Hebrews contains any obvious polemic against Judaism it is instructive to consider initially the writer's treatment of Moses. The figure of Moses, as the mediator of Israel's covenant and cult, is of central importance in Hebrews. The writer contrasts the Mosaic era, the Mosaic covenant, and the Mosaic cult with the new situation introduced by God through Jesus. This is intimated in the opening lines of the homily, in the contrast of the word spoken to the fathers through the prophets with the word spoken through the Son (1:1-2a). It is confirmed in 2:1-4, when the Mosaic Law mediated by the angels throws into bold relief the ultimacy of the salvation proclaimed by the Lord and by those who heard him.

This approach is sustained throughout Hebrews. The extended comparison of the old and new cult (4:15–10:31; 12:18-24), with its focus upon access to God in the Mosaic era and in Christian worship, respectively, develops the parallel between Moses as the mediator of the old cult and Jesus as the mediator of the new. By creative reference to Moses and the wilderness generation the writer presents Christ as the mediator of the new covenant and clarifies the dynamic character of Christian existence. Moses is not simply one figure among several who is compared unfavorably to Jesus. Instead, Moses and Jesus are yoked throughout the homily.[22]

The authority claimed for the Son in 1:1–2:18 inevitably invited compari-

---

21. See E. E. Ellis, "Midrash, Targum and New Testament Quotations," in E. Ellis and M. Wilcox, eds., *Neotestamentica et Semitica* (Edinburgh: T. and T. Clark, 1969) 61–69 (with bibliography); A. G. Wright, *The Literary Genre Midrash* (Staten Island, N.Y.: Alba House, 1968) 52–59, 64–67; R. Bloch, "Midrash," in W. S. Green, ed., *Approaches to Ancient Judaism: Theory and Practice* (Missoula, Mont.: Scholars Press, 1978) 29–50; G. G. Porton, "Defining Midrash," in J. Neusner, ed., *The Study of Ancient Judaism* (New York: Ktav, 1981) 1.55–95; J. Neusner, *What Is Midrash?* (Philadelphia: Fortress, 1987).

22. See especially P. R. Jones, "The Figure of Moses as a Heuristic Device for Understanding the Pastoral Intent of Hebrews," *RevExp* 76 (1979) 95–107. Cf. M. R. D'Angelo, *Moses in the Letter*

son with the unique authority of Moses as the man with whom God spoke more intimately and directly than with an ordinary prophet, according to Num 12:5-8. The allusion to Num 12:7 in Heb 3:2, 5 suggests that the demonstration of Jesus' superiority to Moses in Heb 3:1-6 is already anticipated in the opening sentence of the homily.[23] In some strands of the Jewish tradition the testimony to Moses in Num 12:7 was used to prove that Moses had been granted a higher rank and privilege than the ministering angels.[24] If this interpretation may be presupposed among Greek-speaking Jewish communities of the Diaspora it clarifies the structure of Hebrews, where the Son is compared first to the angels (1:4–2:16) and then to Moses, their superior (3:1-6). It indicates that in spite of the fact that Jesus had been shown on the basis of Scripture to be superior to the angels it was by no means superfluous to continue with a demonstration of his superiority to Moses.

The comparison of Jesus and Moses in 3:1-6 has been placed strategically within the structure of the homily. There it is clearly asserted that Moses should be honored, for he was faithful in all of God's house (3:2, 5). Although the writer is concerned to demonstrate that Jesus is worthy of greater honor than Moses, there is no denigration of Moses in Hebrews.

### The Writer's Use of Comparison

The use of comparison as a rhetorical strategy is employed throughout Hebrews.[25] The comparative adjective *kreissōn* or *kreittōn* and the comparative adverb *kreitton*, in the sense of "superior" or "better," are characteristic speech forms for the writer and are fundamental to his argument.[26] He describes the possession of the community as a "better hope through which we draw near to God" (7:19). Reflecting on Ps 110:4 he exclaims, "How far superior must the covenant also be of which Jesus is the guarantor!" (7:22). Comparing the ministry of Jesus to that of the Levitical priests he argues, "In fact the ministry which he has attained is as superior to theirs as the covenant of which he is the mediator is superior to the old one, seeing that this covenant has been drawn up on the basis of better promises, for if that first covenant had been irreproachable, there would have been no occasion sought for a second" (8:6-7). The theological and pastoral climax of the homily in 12:18-29 is centered in

---

*to the Hebrews* (SBLDS 42; Missoula, Mont.: Scholars Press, 1979); T. Saito, *Die Mosevorstellungen im Neuen Testament* (Bern and Frankfurt: P. Lang, 1977) 95–108, 136–49.

23. So Jones, "Figure of Moses," 97–98; cf. Saito, *Die Mosevorstellungen*, 95.

24. See D'Angelo (*Moses*, 95–131), who calls attention to *Sipre Zuṭa* to Num 12:6-8 (ed. H. S. Horowitz, 275–76) and *Sipre Num* 103 (on 12:1-16) (ed. H. S. Horowitz, 101–2).

25. Cf. C. F. Evans, *The Theology of Rhetoric: The Epistle to the Hebrews* (London: Dr. Williams's Trust, 1988).

26. These comparative terms occur twelve times in Hebrews, three in Paul, and once each in 1 Peter and 2 Peter. W. Klassen ("To the Hebrews," 6) observes that "the sense 'to be superior' or 'to be better than,' the comparative form of the adjective, appears only in the epistle to the Hebrews with reference to the relation between Christianity and Judaism."

an elaborate comparison between the experience of Israel at Sinai and that of the audience. They have come to "Mount Zion" and stand before "Jesus, the mediator of a new covenant, whose sprinkled blood speaks of better things than the blood of Abel" (12:24).

Even when comparative terms are absent the argument assumes the form of a comparison (e.g., 2:2-4; 3:3-6a; 5:4-10; 10:27-28; 12:25). Moreover, the comparisons drawn by the writer do not concern peripheral matters. They have to do with matters "at the center: covenant, hope, promises, law, approach to God."[27] The detailed comparisons necessarily pose the question whether this is an indication of the polemical anti-Judaic character of Hebrews.

What makes this question insistent is that the writer does not restrict himself to commenting upon the preeminence of Jesus, of his priestly ministry, and of the covenant he has mediated. He goes beyond this pastoral strategy to make depreciatory statements about the resources and supports of those who rely upon the provisions of the first covenant for access to God, that is, those who continue to identify themselves with the traditional perspectives and structures of Judaism. Among the pejorative statements of Hebrews are the following:

> Now there was an annulment of a former commandment because of its weakness and uselessness (for the law perfected nothing), but the introduction of a better hope through which we are drawing near to God. (7:18-19)

> For if that first covenant had been irreproachable, there would have been no occasion sought for a second. (8:7)

> In that God says "new" God treated the first covenant as obsolete and what is obsolete and outdated will soon disappear. (8:13)

> The Holy Spirit was showing by this that the way into the real sanctuary had not been disclosed while the first compartment had cultic status. This is an illustration pointing to the present time, according to which the gifts and sacrifices being offered are unable to bring decisive purgation to the worshiper so far as the conscience is concerned only on the basis of food and drink and various ceremonial washings, regulations pertaining to the human order which were imposed until the time of correction. (9:8-10)

> For since the law possesses only a foreshadowing of the good things which were to come, and not the actual form of those realities, it can never decisively purge those who draw near by the same sacrifices which are offered continuously year after year. (Otherwise would not these sacrifices have ceased to be offered, since the worshipers, once cleansed, would have no consciousness of sins any longer? In these sacrifices there is really a reminder of sins year after year). For it is impossible for the blood of bulls and goats to take away sins. (10:1-4)

> God does away with the first arrangement in order to confirm the validity of the second. (10:9)

---

27. Citing Klassen, "To the Hebrews," 7.

Are such statements anti-Judaic?

In order to answer this question responsibly it is necessary to restore these pejorative statements to their literary context within the homily. In each instance the writer's negative comments respond to Scripture. His assessment of the old and new covenants and of the ministries of their respective mediators derives from midrash, the interpretation of the biblical text. The writer finds in Scripture hints that God intended to do something radically new. In each instance the writer interprets the new character of God's action in terms of his convictions about Jesus. Without attempting to be exhaustive,[28] this critical observation can be illustrated and tested with reference to the writer's reading of Ps 110:4; Jer 31:31-34; and Ps 40:6-8, which address the crucial matters of priesthood, covenant, and sacrifice, respectively.

## *New Priesthood*

In 7:1-28 the writer explains for the first time why he has described Jesus as a high priest "like Melchizedek" (5:6, 10; 6:20). The fullness of the explanation indicates that this teaching is new to the community. Melchizedek is, of course, a historical figure who is remembered in Scripture because of a single episode in the life of the patriarch Abraham. Melchizedek met Abraham, refreshed him, and then receded into the shadows of history (Gen 14:17-20). There is no mention of him in the subsequent history or literature of Israel until the composition of Psalm 110, where we read: "The Lord has sworn, he will not change his mind, 'You are a priest forever, just like Melchizedek'" (Ps 110:4).

This oracular statement was made at a time when the divinely established Levitical priesthood had been a highly visible presence in the life of Israel for about 350 years. Suddenly God declares something new. God will install in the priestly office an individual who will be a priest *like Melchizedek*. "Like Melchizedek" the new priest will owe his priesthood to the appointment of God. In addition, God swears he will be "a priest forever." The fulfillment of this promise is guaranteed by an oath, which serves to emphasize the unchangeable character of the divine purpose.

The unexplained reference to Melchizedek in Ps 110:4 invites a whole series of questions. Why does God specify a different priesthood at a time when the Levitical priesthood continued to exercise a felt presence in the life of Israel? Why does God reach back to the period of Abraham when identifying a model for this new priesthood? Why does God say, "You are a priest . . . just like Melchizedek"?

As the writer of Hebrews reflected upon the biblical oracle he evidently took into account an important consideration. There was a fundamental difference between Melchizedek and the Levitical priests. The appointment of the Levitical

---

28. The hint in Ps 8:4-6 (5-7 LXX), where the writer finds an allusion to the incarnation, the exaltation, and the final victory of Jesus, is explored in 2:5-9; the intimation in Hag 2:26-27 of an ultimate judgment that will impact the Christian community is explored in 12:26-29.

high priest was regulated by the Torah. According to the Mosaic Law, the high priest had to be able to trace a line of physical descent back to Aaron on his father's side. His mother had to be a pure Israelite woman. Melchizedek, however, was a priest not through legal qualification but solely through the appointment of God. The silence of Scripture concerning his parents and family line throws into bold relief the uniqueness of his priesthood. On the basis of the fact that the new priest is characterized as a priest "like Melchizedek," and not "like Aaron," the writer deduced that God was announcing a change in the Law (7:11-12).

There was a second fundamental difference between Melchizedek and the Levitical priests. There was an established line of succession to the Levitical high priesthood. For every high priest after Aaron, there was a predecessor in the high priestly office and there was a successor. The Levitical priesthood was sustained on the basis of the hereditary process. But this is not true of Melchizedek in Scripture. For the writer of Hebrews, engaged in the interpretation of Scripture, this was a crucial consideration. Scripture does not refer to any predecessor, and it is silent concerning any successor. Consequently, there were no scriptural limitations to Melchizedek's life and work. He did not require priestly ancestry or priestly succession to authorize his unique and unending priesthood. For that reason, whenever one thinks of Melchizedek in terms of Scripture, it is necessary to think of him as possessing a permanent priesthood. The new priesthood announced in the prophetic oracle will be qualitatively different from the old priesthood because it will be a fully effective priesthood.

Two considerations, then, appear to have explained to the writer why God spoke of a new kind of priesthood in Ps 110:4 when he promised the coming of one who is a priest "like Melchizedek." (1) He will be a priest who owes his appointment to God rather than to the law of physical descent. (2) He will enjoy a permanent priesthood, acknowledged in the formula, "You are a priest forever." Both of these considerations possessed significance for the writer of Hebrews. They become crucial categories when he speaks of the priesthood of Jesus, for they demonstrated to him that Jesus is a priest "like Melchizedek." They clarify why the writer read the prophetic oracle in Ps 110:4 as a solemn decree of appointment spoken by God to the Son![29]

The detail of the writer's argument by which he demonstrates that Jesus is the promised new priest is for the purpose of this essay less important than the fact that the development in Hebrews proceeds step-by-step from the interpretation of Scripture. The pejorative statements that there has been a change in the Law (Heb 7:12) and that the law that regulated the priesthood has been annulled (Heb 7:18) are not intentionally polemical. They occur as reflections on a prophetic oracle announcing a startling departure from Israel's priestly tradition. They are put forth not as anti-Judaic polemic but as deductions from

---

29. The course of the argument in Heb 7:11-25 proceeds exegetically and can be charted in four steps. For the details see W. L. Lane, *Hebrews 1–8* (WBC 47A; Dallas: Word, 1991) 177–98.

the biblical text that draw their support from the formulation of the oracle. The basis of the development in Hebrews is the interpretation and appropriation of the text of Scripture in the Judaic tradition of homiletical midrash. This conclusion is important in itself for it bears directly on the issue of faith and polemic. It is confirmed by the writer's use of Jer 31:31-34 (38:31-34 LXX) and Ps 40:4-8 (39:7-9 LXX) in Heb 8:6-13 and 10:5-10.

### New Covenant

In Heb 8:6-13 the ministry of the new heavenly high priest, enthroned at God's right hand, is associated with the new covenant. The measure of the superiority of Jesus' priestly ministry is expressed with a comparison based on the fact that Jesus, unlike the Levitical high priest, entered the heavenly sanctuary as the mediator of the new covenant. The writer presupposes that the new covenant required a new mediator. By means of his death on the cross as a covenant sacrifice, he affirms, Jesus inaugurated the new covenant of Jer 31:31-34. His entrance into the heavenly sanctuary guarantees God's acceptance of his sacrifice and the actualization of the provisions of the superior covenant he mediated.

The prophetic oracle in which God promised to establish a covenant with his people that was qualitatively new (Jer 31:31-34) is cited in full in Heb 8:8-12.[30] The writer's use of the present tense of the verb ("he says") in introducing the quotation served to make the text contemporary with the audience. The writer examines the prophetic word of censure and promise from the perspective of Jeremiah's time, when the promise was first announced.

The introductory and concluding verses to the extensive citation of Jer 31:31-34 in Hebrews (Heb 8:7-8a, 13) stress the imperfect and provisional character of "that first" covenant concluded at Sinai. The writer directs the audience's attention to the blame contained within the oracle itself (see vv. 8-9). In this context the citation of Jer 31:31-34 serves the fundamentally negative function of exposing the defective character of the old covenant.[31]

The treatment of the two covenants in Heb 8:7-8a exposes the eschatological outlook of the writer. His point of view is that the covenant mediated by Moses had developed faults on the human side and has been replaced by a better arrangement. The supersession of the old covenant, however, was not due simply to the unfaithfulness of Israel to the stipulations of the covenant. It occurred because a new unfolding of God's redemptive purpose had taken place that called for new-covenant action on the part of God. To the writer, the fact that God took the initiative in announcing the divine intention to establish a new

---

30. H. Wolff (*Jeremia im Frühjudentum und Urchristentum* [TU 118; Berlin: Akademie, 1976]) has shown that no use is made of Jeremiah's statement concerning the new covenant in Jewish sources until after the year 70 and the destruction of the Temple. Even sources that refer to the new covenant (e.g., CD 6:18-19; 8:21) make no allusion to Jer 31:31-34.

31. Cf. A. Vanhoye, *La structure littéraire de l'Épître aux Hébreux* (2d ed.; Paris and Bruges: Desclée de Brouwer, 1976) 143–44. The type of reasoning displayed in Heb 8:6-13 parallels the argument concerning the ineffectiveness of the Levitical arrangement in Heb 7:11-19.

covenant with Israel (8:8a) hints that God fully intended the first covenant to be provisional.[32] God finds fault (*memphomenos*) with the Mosaic covenant, and not simply with the people.

In spite of the censure implied in the quotation, the writer's citation and use of Jer 31:31-34 are not simply polemical. Like Jeremiah, he saw the relation between the old and new covenants in dialectical terms. Although the old covenant is to be superseded and invalidated, it receives recognition as shadow and example. God will do something new, which implies discontinuity, but between the old and the new there will also be genuine continuity.

The central affirmation of the new covenant is the pledge of the presence of the Law in the hearts of believers as the gift of God (v. 10). The mention of such a gift occurs nowhere else in the old biblical text.[33] The quality of newness intrinsic to the new covenant consists in the manner of presenting Torah, not in newness of content. The people of God will be inwardly established in the Law and knowledge of the Lord. The emphasis falls on the interior quality of the human response to God through the new covenant, not on the replacement of the Torah.

The new covenant thus brings to realization the relationship between God and his people that is at the heart of all covenant disclosure from Abraham onwards. Although the intention of the covenant at Sinai had been frustrated because of the past failure of Israel to observe the conditions for that relationship stipulated by God, it will be achieved.

As a Christian, the writer was convinced that redemptive grace had reached its zenith in the full and final realization of this promise through Jesus. Consequently, the inauguration of the new covenant with the entrance of the eschatological high priest into the heavenly sanctuary (8:6) indicates that the provisions of the new covenant are now in force.[34] But there can be no doubt that the writer's appeal to Jer 31:31-34 implies for the Christian community continuity as well as discontinuity with those who continued to regulate their lives by reference to the Mosaic covenant.

This needs to be emphasized because it provides perspective on the pejorative statement in Heb 8:13, where the accent falls on discontinuity. At this

---

32. Cf. R. A. Harrisville, *The Concept of Newness in the New Testament* (Minneapolis: Augsburg, 1960) 48–53. Harrisville demonstrates that the concept of newness is an eschatological element in the preaching of the early church. He explores this dimension under the aspects of continuity, contrast, finality, and the dynamism by which the new asserts itself against the old (pp. 19–20).

33. The closest parallel is Jer 24:7: God will give his people a new heart capable of knowing him.

34. In this immediate context it is possible that the writer applied directly to Jesus the promise that it will be unnecessary to instruct someone "to know the Lord." Cf. Heb 2:3; 7:14; 13:20, where "Lord" designates Jesus. When a second, abbreviated citation from the prophetic announcement in Jeremiah concludes the central exposition of the priestly work of Christ (Heb 10:16-17), it is clear that the oracle was vital to the writer's theological understanding. See D. G. Peterson, "The Prophecy of the New Covenant in the Argument of Hebrews," *Reformed Theological Review* 38 (1979) 74–81.

point in the homily the writer shows no interest in the promises attached to the new covenant. He focuses the attention of the community upon the implications of the key word in the cited text, "new" (cf. v. 8). The fact that God spoke to Jeremiah of a covenant that was "new" intimated to the writer that the covenant mediated to Moses was defective. The argument that by designating the covenant "new" God declared the covenant concluded at Sinai to be unserviceable and obsolete carried for the writer the corollary that God himself had canceled its validity. God intends to make no further use of the old covenant and of the forms through which it operated to achieve redemption. Consequently, the old arrangement is on the point of disappearing. The principle that a new act of God makes the old obsolete (cf. Heb 7:11-12) reflects a Jewish-Christian perspective. The perception that the Mosaic and Levitical institutions have been fulfilled and superseded by the priestly mediation of Christ is the hallmark of the Jewish Christianity of Hebrews.

Two observations are appropriate. First, the argument developed in Hebrews on the basis of Jer 31:31-34 exhibits the writer's ability to recognize a significant hint in Scripture that was overlooked by contemporary writers. His procedure in drawing from the biblical text the theological implications for his audience illustrates the character and practice of homiletical midrash as it was employed in the Jewish homiletical tradition. Second, the comparison of the old and new covenants not only here but elsewhere in the homily (e.g., 12:18-29) is not an indication of the polemical anti-Judaic character of Hebrews. For the writer this represents simply an application of a hermeneutical method by which he sought to make clear to his audience the irrevocable guarantee of the divine promise that had been subjected to questioning.[35]

## New Sacrifice

The writer's apology is carried a step further in Heb 10:5-10 when he argues that the ineffective sacrifices of the old covenant have been superseded by the sufficient sacrifice of Jesus. The cultic arrangements of the Levitical law, with its annual provision for a Day of Atonement, have been set aside. The basis for consecration of the new-covenant community to the service of God is the unrepeatable offering of the body of Jesus. In developing this point the writer of Hebrews again makes effective use of homiletical midrash, citing a portion of the biblical text and commenting upon it. He appeals to Ps 40:6-8 (39:7-9 LXX) to demonstrate that it had been prophesied in Scripture that God would accord superior status to a human body as the instrument for accomplishing the divine will than to the sacrificial offerings prescribed in the Law. The text of the oracle, the writer deduced, implied the discontinuance of the old cultus because of the arrival of the new.

The words of Ps 40:6-8 are heard as those of the Son addressed to God.

---

35. This second observation is made forcefully by Grässer, "Der Hebräerbrief," 149.

The statement "See, I have come" furnished the textual basis for attributing these verses of the psalm to the divine Son at the moment when he entered the world.[36] The detail that God had prepared a body for the speaker, who entered the world to do God's will, accounts for the writer's selection of this quotation. It not only indicated to him that the incarnation and active obedience of the divine Son had been prophesied in Scripture; it also provided the exegetical support for the thesis that the "offering of the body of Jesus Christ" was qualitatively superior to the offerings prescribed by the Law (10:8-10). The writer seized upon the term "body" (*sōma*) in the text of the psalm and made it pivotal for his interpretation of the quotation. Customarily he uses the word "flesh" (*sarx*) to refer to the full humanity of Jesus (2:14; 5:7). The use of the equivalent term *sōma* in v. 10 to designate the human body of Jesus constituted a purposeful allusion to the biblical text cited in v. 5.

God's dissatisfaction with the conventional sacrificial offerings because they failed to express a corresponding desire to obey his will is a recurring motif in the Scriptures (e.g., 1 Sam 15:22; Ps 40:6; 50:8-10; 51:16-17; Isa 1:10-13; 66:2-4; Jer 7:21-24; Hos 6:6; Amos 5:21-27). The quotation of Ps 40:6-8 in 10:5-7 indicates that the focal point of concern is the relative value of the prescribed sacrifices as a means of consecration to the service of God. The quotation attests that sacrifices in themselves are powerless to please God or to secure a proper relationship with God.

The psalmist refers to a speaker who recognizes his body as the gift that God had prepared as the means by which the divine will may be realized. Behind that reference the writer recognized the figure of the transcendent Son of God who became fully human in order to fulfill the divine purpose for the human family (2:10, 14, 17). The attribution of the words of the psalm to the Son links the incarnation explicitly to the accomplishment of the will of God.

With powerful concentration the writer divides his remarks into two parts. In the first he underscores the divine rejection of conventional sacrifices. By conflating the two parallel lines of the quotation that refer to the various types of offerings, a single, emphatic contrast emerges instead of the two implied in the psalm itself. This is an important modification for it enables the writer to distinguish sharply between "the first" (arrangement) and "the second" in v. 9b. The writer deduces that the multiplicity and repetition of the sacrifices prescribed by Law unveil their fundamental inadequacy.[37]

Apart from the rearrangement of the lines of the quotation and the alteration of the singular to the plural when the biblical text is taken up for comment in v. 8, the writer limits his interpretation of the text to a single parenthetical remark: the unwanted and disliked sacrifices are precisely those which the Law

---

36. The temporal expression, "When he comes into the world," is distinctly incarnational language. See T. G. Stylianopoulos, "Shadow and Reality: Reflections on Hebrews 10:1-18," *GOTR* 17 (1972) 229 n. 36.

37. Stylianopoulos, "Shadow and Reality," 222.

prescribed (v. 8b). This comment makes the relationship between the repetition of the sacrifices and the Law explicit and relegates the sacrifices of the old cultus to the period when God's arrangement with his people was regulated by Torah.

The writer then draws the attention of his audience to the final part of the quotation in v. 7. He abridges the text to secure the pregnant formulation, "See, I have come to do your will" (v. 9a). This represented for him the essential utterance of the Son attested by the psalm. For the writer it tied Jesus' mission to a preoccupation with the will of God and prepared for the significant deduction that the offering of Jesus is the sacrifice God desired to be made. The writer reduces the significance of the Son's announcement for salvation-history to the terse formulation of v. 9b: "he does away with the first arrangement in order to confirm the validity of the second." With that statement the writer affirmed the creation of a qualitatively new foundation for the consecration of worshipers to the service of God. The old cultus and the Law upon which it was based are set aside on the strength of an event in which there is concentrated all of the efficacy of a life fully submitted to the will of God. In v. 10 the mode of that realization is specified as "the offering of the body of Jesus Christ once for all." The term "body" shows that the contrast that the writer wished to underscore was between the ineffective sacrifices of animals and the personal offering of Christ's own body as the one complete and effective sacrifice.

On the writer's reading of the text, what has been set aside are the repeated sacrifices and the Law that prescribed them. What has been confirmed as valid is the structural link between the will of God and the effective sacrifice of Christ.[38] The writer's statement in v. 9b has rightly been characterized as one of the epochal formulations of the New Testament.[39] The lines quoted from the psalm and the event of Jesus Christ confirmed to the writer that the old religious order had been abolished definitively. In the design of God the two redemptive arrangements are irreconcilable; the one excludes the other. The suppression of the first occurs in order that the validity of the new order of relationship may be confirmed. This is essentially the same argument that was developed on the basis of Jer 31:31-34 in Heb 8:7-13. For the writer, Jesus Christ and the detail of Scripture are agents of epochal change that introduced a radically new situation for the community of God's people.[40]

From the psalm the writer looks to Jesus and to the value of his death on the cross. In the sacrifice of his body on the cross, Jesus freely and fully made the will of God his own. Consequently, his sacrifice requires no repetition. It embodied the totality of obedience and eradicated the disparity between sacrifice

---

38. See especially L. Di Pinto, *Volontà di Dio e legge antica nell' Epistola agli Ebrei* (Naples: Pontificia Universitate Gregoriana, 1976) 23–30.

39. E.g., F. J. Schierse (*Verheissung und Heilsvollendung: Zur theologischen Grundfrage des Hebräerbriefes* [Munich: Zink, 1955] 66) labels v. 9b "a revolutionary principle" and "the fundamental eschatological principle" of the writer (p. 169).

40. Di Pinto, *Volontà di Dio*, 30–33; cf. Michel, *Der Brief an die Hebräer*, 337–39.

and obedience presupposed in Ps 40:6-8. Jesus' self-sacrifice fulfilled the human vocation enunciated in the psalm. By virtue of the fact that Jesus did so under the conditions of authentic human, bodily existence and in solidarity with the human family, the writer of Hebrews deduced, the new people of God have been radically transformed and consecrated to the service of God.[41]

## Conclusion

These three examples of how the writer read his Bible and used the detail of the biblical text to minister pastorally to a community that was wavering in its convictions and in danger of abandoning its confession provide a sufficient basis for answering the questions whether Hebrews is in fact anti-Judaic. The statements that may be identified as pejorative in each case occur in a literary context in which the writer brings the witness of the biblical text to bear upon considerations that were crucial to the self-understanding of the community. They concern priesthood, covenant, and sacrifice. In each case the writer proves to be creative in his selection of texts to be brought before the community. No other writer in the New Testament cited Ps 110:4, Jer 31:31-34, or Ps 40:6-8. These biblical texts, nevertheless, establish a context for appreciating the validity of the Christian message. From the writer's pastoral perspective, the issue of adherence to the confession of Jesus the community had made was of critical importance because it would determine salvation or absolute loss (cf. 3:12-15; 6:4-8; 10:26-31, 35-39; 12:14-17, 25-29). His concern was not that members of the community would simply return to the synagogue, but that they would turn away from the living God altogether (3:12-13)!

The writer was persuaded that this matter must be decided on the basis of the word God had spoken in Scripture and through the Son. For that reason he brought before the community biblical texts that demonstrated that God announced a new arrangement that would provide decisive purgation for a defiled people and unrestricted access to the divine presence. Those announcements pointed to the unique priestly ministry of Jesus and his sacrifice by which the new covenant had been inaugurated. It is on this basis that the writer calls the new-covenant community to the worship of God (4:15-16; 7:24-25; 9:11-28; 10:19-25; 12:14, 18-29; 13:15-16). This represents a different perspective from that of Paul or of any other writer in the New Testament. Nevertheless, what the writer of Hebrews was doing was profoundly Judaic. He shares fully Judaism's understanding of the role of Scripture in the life of the faith community.

The pastoral strategies adopted in Hebrews were all designed to stir the members of a Jewish-Christian assembly to recognize that they could not turn

---

41. Di Pinto, *Volontà di Dio*, 49–52; R. Deichgräber, "Gehorsam und Gehorchen in den Verkündigung Jesu," *ZNW* 52 (1961) 119–22; A. Vanhoye, *Lectiones in Hebr. 10:1-39: De efficacia oblationis christi et de vita christiana* (Rome: Pontifical Biblical Institute, 1971-72) 61–64.

back the hands of the clock and deny their Christian understanding and experience. They must hold firmly to their Christian confession. The premise that Hebrews engages in any form of anti-Judaic polemic, however, is untenable. Certainly the writer appreciated the historical and theological lines of differentiation between Jewish Christianity and Judaism. He clearly believed that God had acted decisively in Jesus to accomplish salvation and to create the people of the new covenant. Only from such an eschatological perspective could he speak of God's final word, or of the coming of the new that made the old obsolete, or of the incarnation of the Son of God. But this is not anti-Judaism; it is the reflection of a distinctive reading of Scripture in the light of the writer's convictions about Jesus.

The writer fully recognized that God was at work in the old covenant. God's decisive action in Jesus occurred within the context of the divine intervention in the life of Israel. The word that God spoke in the past was invested with authority, even when it was fragmentary and partial. It remained normative for the writer and for those whom he addressed. The writer of Hebrews traced a line of continuity from the event of God's speaking at Sinai to the event of God's speaking at that moment. God's character remained unchanged. For the writer of Hebrews, the Christian community, like Israel at Sinai, stands before the God who is a consuming fire (12:25-29). Greater covenant privilege simply entails greater covenant responsibility. The writer of Hebrews calls the community to a costly identification with Jesus (13:12-14), whose sacrificial ministry was the culmination of God's promise to Israel. He does not set aside Jewish identity and tradition, nor the authority of the biblical text for the faith community.

## James

Attention to the canonical aspect of the problem serves as an appropriate preface to the book of James. In the history of its interpretation, James has often embarrassed Christian sensitivities not because of its anti-Judaic content but because it does not seem to be sufficiently "Christian." In fact, James is the most Jewish writing found within the New Testament, and it includes no obvious polemic against Judaism.[42] If anything, the threats to the audience's faith are internal and largely fashioned by the economic and political conventions of the Syro-Palestinian world in general. Surely the author's appeals to heavenly wisdom to guide his readers toward the eschaton of divine *shalom* were familiar features in most renewal efforts within early Judaism, whether messianic or not. The ongoing problem with James is its fit within a Christian canon, and

---

42. While biblical scholarship is not divided on this point, it has been articulated in a variety of ways. For example, in his *Der Brief des Jakobus Untersucht* (Göttingen: Vandenhoeck und Ruprecht, 1896), F. Spitta finds nothing "Christian" in James, while P. Davids finds too much that is "Christian" in his *Commentary on James* (NIGTC; Grand Rapids, Mich.: Eerdmans, 1982).

specifically its intracanonical relationship with the writings of the Pauline corpus that predominate in forming mainstream Christian (and especially Protestant) orthodoxy.

Indeed, the various references to the figure of James and allusions to "his" book in the gnostic writings from Nag Hammadi (*Apocryphon of James; 1–2 Apocalypse of James*) together with Ebionism's very different use of James in its anti-Pauline polemic provide historical antecedents to the canonical problem.[43] It is too facile to dismiss the anti-Pauline rantings or pro-Jacobean ravings of marginally Christian sects, such as Ebionism, as responses to un-Paulinelike Paulinisms. In fact, Ebionism correctly detected certain features in a Pauline calculus that would lead the church toward a glib fideism and secularized antinomianism and away from the covenantal nomism of its Judaic roots.[44]

To be sure, for some church fathers, the positive and frequent appeal to the memory of James to promote a marginal or even "heretical" Christianity exposed its deficiency in spiritual matters. Perhaps for this reason, clear allusions to James by the fathers are infrequent. In fact, it now seems remarkable that mainstream Christianity's first direct and positive citation from the canonical James occurred more than a century after its writing, and in the West it was not until the fourth century that Hilary made such a citation. Even then, references to James were invariably qualified. For example, Origen refers to James but considers its contents of marginal merit. No wonder, then, that the canonization of James was contested even into the Reformation. Luther demoted James to subcanonical status on christological and Pauline grounds: although full of practical wisdom, it did not teach about Christ, and it opposed Paul's teaching on justification by faith in Christ alone. While the Reformation constituted a different *Sitz im Leben*, Luther's concerns reflected early Christianity's objections to the Ebionite use of James in the second century: James was anti-Pauline, and in a catholicizing (or recatholicizing) church in which Pauline Christianity had triumphed, this was tantamount to being anti-Christian. James appeared to enshrine an unacceptable version of the gospel.

The modern problem, especially as it is conceived by European scholarship,

---

43. In this regard, see R. E. Van Voorst (*The Ascents of James: History and Theology of a Jewish-Christian Community* [SBLDS 112; Atlanta: Scholars Press, 1989]), who argues that the *Apocryphon of James* is a Jewish-Christian document and one source of the Pseudo-Clementine *Recognitions*. Van Voorst rightly comments that the Pseudo-Clementine literature generally reflects the more generic features of Jewish Christianity (e.g., Jewish definitions of community, promotion of James, and demotion of Paul); more intriguing is Van Voorst's contention that the Christology enshrined within this literature is based upon the "Prophet-like-Moses" motif. In that disagreements between various Jewish-Christian movements during the second century were mostly christological, Van Voorst's work on a particular Jewish-Christian community is important reading.

44. Some gnostic systems would find James appealing in justifying their *Tendenz* toward an ascetical ethos. The gnostic interest in Paul had more to do with Christology than with ethics. In this sense, the gnostic use of both James and Paul is suggestive of the sort of self-correcting interplay that one finds within the New Testament canon: James underscores the need for a distinctively Christian ethic on the one hand, while Paul underscores the need for a Christian Christology on the other.

continues the Reformation's concern.[45] James continues to be viewed as a Jewish writing that is not very useful for Christian formation. Both references to Christ (1:1; 2:1), the reference to James (1:1), and the addition of an epistolary greeting (1:1) common in Christian (i.e., Pauline) circles, it is claimed, were ingredients of a later redactor's effort to Christianize the rather traditional Jewish halakah found in James in order to make it palatable for Jewish-Christian audiences.[46] Even if one were to accept this critical consensus that 1:1 and 2:1 are later interpolations, baptizing an essentially Jewish writing into a Christian genre of literature (by the superscription of 1:1) and into christological orthodoxy (by the "in Christ" formula of 2:1), such redactional activity could very well be properties of the church's canonizing of James and thus a testimony to the current usefulness of its final (i.e., canonical) form in shaping a Christian identity. Once these features are stripped away, however, and the Jewishness of the "original" work is exposed, most scholars are unwilling to attach much worth to it as canonical literature: a pseudonymous James is simply not Christian enough.[47]

The ironical problem this section of the chapter will address has now been framed. The issue at stake is not whether James is anti-Jewish, but whether it is Christian. The contention will be that James is a Christian writing that retains a distinctively Jewish ethos, and that in doing so it functions as an intracanonical check and balance to distorted (including anti-Semitic) interpretations of Pauline preaching that have plagued the church since its founding. There is a sense in which this analysis will side with the second-century Ebionites, who also used the Jewishness of James to correct second-century interpretations of Paul that had led some segments of the catholicizing church to embrace a glib fideism and secular antinomianism to suit their own bourgeois stance. In fact, the very reasons that slowed James's reception into the Christian canon may well help us clarify the importance of its biblical relationship to the Pauline corpus and its practical relationship to the faith community that continues to hear its voice as canonical.

Asking the question of whether James is a Christian book presumes that the alternative is that it is a Jewish book. Admittedly, a few erudite scholars have argued without much success that at least two conflicts found in James (2:1-7; 4:13–5:6) reflect tensions between the Palestinian church and synagogue dur-

---

45. Cf. F. Mussner, *Der Jakobusbrief* (HTKNT; Freiberg: Herder, 1964) 56–59.

46. However, the more recent work of F. O. Francis on epistolary genre ("The Form and Function of the Opening and Closing Paragraphs of James and 1 John," *ZNW* 61 [1970] 110–26) and by W. H. Wuellner on rhetorical structure ("Der Jakobusbrief im Licht der Rhetorik und Textpragmatik," *LB* 43 [1976] 5–66) moves the composition onto a Hellenistic literary landscape and makes it more difficult to argue on literary grounds for the Jewishness of James.

47. For a recent book that challenges this critical posture, see D. G. Meade, *Pseudonymity and Canon* (Grand Rapids, Mich.: Eerdmans, 1988). In addition, B. S. Childs (*The New Testament as Canon: An Introduction* [Philadelphia: Fortress, 1985]) has argued that concerns about authorship within early Judaism and earliest Christianity were less historically and more theologically conditioned: that is, a composition's canonicity was recognized when its ongoing function corresponded with the ongoing function of its "author."

ing the first century. Their arguments have been turned back in favor of an interpretation that locates these conflicts in the milieu of Palestinian class struggle, where judicial partiality in favor of the rich and against the poor concerned all religious Jews, messianic and apocalyptical or not.[48] James responds with a polemic against the "functional atheism" of materialism that finds parallels in the "piety-poverty tradition" of Jewish literature.[49] Further, the literary expressions of political or economic marginality found throughout James reflect social conventions that belong to the world of Jewish apocalypticism—a source of the author's theological perspective.

The single most important evidence that this is a Christian writing is the phrase *echete tēn pistin tou kyriou hēmōn Iēsou Christou tēs doxēs* (hold the faith of our glorious Lord Jesus Christ) (2:1b). Some commentators, however, are quite willing to neutralize the phrase by speculating on grammatical grounds that *hēmōn Iēsou Christou* is a later interpolation—a conclusion further justified because it burdens, in Dibelius's words, "the weighty assertion that the entire document is of Jewish origin."[50] But there is no evidence in the textual history of James to justify this claim, and others have offered acceptable solutions to the various grammatical problems found in this phrase. Moreover, to rule out a text because it does not suit one's hypothesis is, of course, fallacious. The real exegetical problem is to understand this christological formula within the composition of James and the Jewish Christianity it represents.[51]

First, the use of the idiom (but not necessarily the idea) "the faith" in this formula is of Christian origin. However, it is not *Pauline* Christian for two

---

48. R. P. Martin (*James* [WBC 48; Dallas: Word, 1988] 159–62) argues that the debate was between merchants and all those opposed to their wealth either on ideological (as would be the case of those who equated piety with poverty) or on competitive grounds (as would be the case of those socioeconomic classes that deemed themselves "less fortunate").

49. Especially Davids, *James*, 41–47, 105–19, 171–80; also L. E. Keck, "The Poor among the Saints in Jewish Christianity and Qumran," *ZNW* 57 (1966) 54–78; R. B. Ward, "Partiality in the Assembly," *HTR* 62 (1969) 87–97; also P. U. Maynard-Reid, *Poverty and Wealth in James* (Maryknoll, N.Y.: Orbis, 1987).

50. M. Dibelius, *James* (rev. ed.; Hermeneia; Philadelphia: Fortress, 1976) 127. The claim that 2:1 is of singular importance in arguing for James as a Christian document inevitably demotes the importance of 1:1 in this regard. In fact, the majority of scholars understand 1:1 as a later addition, perhaps to fit it more comfortably into a collection of Christian letters. The canonical purpose of the superscription, then, is to locate the writing within a particular theological trajectory of normative value to catholicizing Christianity.

51. The Christology represented by this formula envisions a different relationship between Christology and paraenesis than is found in Pauline preaching. In Paul, the community's compliance to the demands of Pauline paraenesis is one result of the Christ-event; that is, faithfulness to God's moral law is one result of the community's faith in Christ. In James (and in the non-Pauline collection as a whole), paraenesis is supported by an exemplary Christology; that is, compliance to the moral demand of God, which is not the result of Christ's death and resurrection but the result of following his example, is the focal point of God's covenant with the faith community. The consequence of obeying the will of God, as specified by the paraenetic traditions, is the maintenance of the community's covenant with God and issues in its eschatological salvation. In the context of this particular kind of "theo-logic," the Christ-event provides the normative models of covenantal nomism, which has been challenged by the various trials of human life in an anti-God world.

reasons. "Faith" is not cast in James as an existential reality, positing a community's faith in or dependency upon Jesus' messianic work for its salvation. Nor is "faith in Christ" the essential mark for James of maintaining membership in eschatological Israel, as it is for Paul. The articular form, *tēn pistin,* suggests a corporate and public expression of faith, different in content than the deutero-Pauline use of the same formula for the "institutional" church. In the immediate context, the mark of the *thrēskeia kathara kai amiantos para tō theō* (religion that is pure and undefiled before God) (1:27a) is the wisdom the community exercises in responding to its own powerless members (1:27b; 2:8-26) and to the corrupting powers of the surrounding social order (1:27c; 2:1-7). The mark of membership in "the faith" is mercy (2:12-13), especially toward the eschatological community's "last and least"—a class whose borders are symbolized by the socioeconomic distress of "widows and orphans" for whom merciful deeds are most necessary.

Second, the use of the name "Jesus Christ" in this formula envisions his work as a "prophetic exemplar," not unlike two other prophets, Job (5:10-11) and Elijah (5:17-18), whose patience and prayerfulness also provide the believing community with examples of eschatological fitness. The genitives *tou kyriou . . . Christou* (to qualify *tēn pistin*) and *tēs doxēs* (to qualify *hēmōn Iēsou Christou*) are notoriously difficult but crucial for understanding this element of Jacobean Christology. The first genitive identifies the Lord Jesus Christ as exemplar of the kind of religion that is approved by God: the lordship of Jesus indicates divine approval of his messiahship. Commentators typically interpret the formula in Pauline terms; that is, they suppose the passage refers to faith in Jesus' glorious messianic work, by which the community is baptized into a new reality where persons are equal (cf. 1 Corinthians 12; Gal 3:28). Clearly this is a mistake, unless it is another example of the author's irony that conveys the worthlessness of mere confessions of "faith in Christ" without a complement of merciful works toward the marginal ones.[52] However, it is more natural to both the genitive and to the larger context of Jas 1:22—2:26 to view the problematical favoritism toward the rich, and its tacit denial of mercy for the poor, as antithetical to the teaching or love of Christ concerning the powerless and impoverished. The point here is that Christ is *the model of mercy for the eschatological community.* He observed "the royal law" (2:8) perfectly and was approved by God as Messiah on that basis.[53]

---

52. Cf. C. Burchard ("Zu Jakobus 2.14-26," *ZNW* 71 [1980] 27-30), who regards the phrase as a confession of faith in Christ and views it as parallel to the confession that God is one God in 2:19.

53. This conclusion extends the arguments of L. T. Johnson ("The Use of Leviticus 19 in the Letter of James," *JBL* 101 [1982] 391-401), who contends that "royal" indicates that the love commandment is authorized (perhaps even authored) by God, which makes logical James's assertion that compliance to it results in divine approval. Davids (*James,* 114-15) further argues that within a distinctively Christian setting, God's law of love is clarified by the *teaching* of Jesus. God's approval of Jesus' messianic mission is indicated not only by Jesus' definitive interpretation of Torah but also by his perfect obedience to it.

The second genitive, *tēs doxēs*, is even more difficult, reading like "an appendage without any clear connection with what precedes it."[54] The simplest solution is to take *tēs doxēs* as an adjective of quality, "the faith of our *glorious* Lord Jesus Christ."[55] How this construction makes more precise the exemplary status of the Lord Jesus Christ is more difficult for the exegete to determine. A better solution seems to be that the "glory" of faithful Jesus speaks first of his exalted reputation before God and also within the community, who both view him as "Lord and Christ" (cf. Acts 2:36). But as Davids reminds us, the term "glory" translates the Hebrew *kabod*, which is a term for God's eschatological salvation.[56] Against Davids, who views the phrase as an expression of Christ's eschatological role as "judge" (cf. 5:7-9), it seems preferable to take it as an element of his exemplary role as one who models the sort of character the eschatological community must embody to receive God's mercy at the end of time (cf. 2:12-13). Thus, like Job, whose reputation for patience, and Elijah, whose reputation for prayer, provide direction for the community, so also does the Lord Jesus Christ, whose reputation for identifying with the poor points the way to the kingdom of God (cf. 2:5). The Christology enshrined by this formula is "Christian" not because it confesses "faith in Jesus Christ" but because it confirms that Jesus has been made Lord and Christ by an approving God. But the christological argot is also "Jewish" because it views Christ as prophetic exemplar for eschatological Israel.

Two other texts in James suggest a distinctively Christian development of otherwise Jewish themes. In 5:14, James conceives of healing in terms of a gift of an elder's office—an emphasis without clear Jewish parallels.[57] Not only does the elder's place of office in the church rather than synagogue suggest a Christian setting,[58] but in this context, the catchphrase, *en tō onomati tou kyriou* (in the name of the Lord), probably refers to the Lord Jesus Christ (cf. 2:1), whose name parallels healing power in the Jesus tradition and in Acts even as God's name does in the biblical tradition.[59] The presence of this healing power is maintained in eschatological Israel through the mediation of the elders who represent the exalted Messiah by invoking his name.[60]

Finally, in 1:17-18, James builds upon Jewish wisdom tradition in distinctively Christian ways.[61] The critical problem in exegeting this passage is the

---

54. S. Laws, *A Commentary on the Epistle of James* (HNTC; San Francisco: Harper and Row, 1980) 94.

55. Suggested by Davids, *James*, 106, and followed by Martin, *James*, 60.

56. Davids, *James*, 107.

57. See Davids (*James*, 192–94), who argues that this passage describes a Christian rite of healing; for sources in Judaism, see Laws, *James*, 225–26.

58. Martin, *James*, 206–7.

59. Mussner, *Jakobusbrief*, 220–21.

60. Dunn, *Unity and Diversity*, 106–9.

61. See Dibelius (*James*, 106), who says that this passage "can be understood only in terms of the milieu of a Christian faith and life."

meaning of the birth typology employed in v. 18: To what and by what does God give birth? The conceptual framework is essentially biblical: according to Genesis, God begets a new creation by the divine word. Within Judaism, these themes were used to construct a cosmology centered on God, or to underscore the cosmic importance of Israel as God's special creation. However, within Christianity, the typology took on a soteriological cast: to be given birth by God means to be reborn spiritually, and to become "first fruits" means to be repositioned in the age to come.[62] Of course, in the Johannine and later Pauline traditions, this calculus was christologized: God begets a new creation, the church, and inaugurates a new age of eternal life through the incarnated Word. However, while James certainly has the eschatological community in view as the concrete expression of God's gift of birth,[63] it is doubtful that the "word of truth" here refers either to the incarnated Word or, as most scholars contend, to the proclaimed word.[64] James's thought world is still too Jewish for this; for him, the word is heavenly wisdom (cf. Prov 22:21; Eccl 12:10; Wis Sol 18:15; Sir 43:26), which is summarized in 1:19 and then developed in the body of the paraenesis itself in terms of Torah observance (1:22–2:26), pure speech (3:1-18), and poverty-piety (4:1–5:6).[65]

Of less importance in testing the Christian quotient of James are the parallels between James and the Jesus tradition (esp. Q and Matthew). Of recent commentators, Davids has mounted the most persuasive case that the Jesus tradition formed the underlying rule for the life of the Jacobean community.[66] Yet the allusions to the Jesus tradition listed by Davids do not include those passages that he himself says contain distinctively Christian interpretation (see above). Further, most claimed allusions to the Jesus tradition are of ethical teaching that both Jesus and James share in common with rabbinic halakoth. (The same, it would seem, is true of those parallels found in the paraenesis of James and 1 Peter.) As Laws reminds us, mere linguistic or even thematic similarity is an insufficient criterion to measure the dependency of James on Jesus' moral teaching.[67] A more substantial criterion is whether James alludes to teaching that distinguishes Jesus from rabbinical Judaism. Because of James's important use of *teleios* (perfect) and because Matthew's Jesus uses the same word (5:48) to frame his distinctive teaching that true disciples love even their enemies (5:44), one may suppose that this expression of moral perfection would be alluded to in James. Not only is the "love enemy" precept not found in James, but 2:1-7 comes close to prescribing the response championed by the opponents of Mat-

---

62. Ibid., 104–5.
63. Cf. Martin, *James*, 39–41.
64. *Contra* Dibelius, *James*, 105; and others.
65. Cf. R. W. Wall, "James as Apocalyptic Paraenesis," *ResQ* 32 (1990) 11–22.
66. Cf. Davids, *James*, 47–48; also his "James and Jesus," in David Wenham, ed., *Gospel Perspectives* (Sheffield: JSOT, 1984) 5.63–84; Mussner, *Jakobusbrief*, 47–52.
67. Laws, *James*, 13–14.

thew's Jesus (5:43)! While one is on firmer ground by arguing that the rule
instituted by Jesus (as envisioned, say, by the antitheses of Matt 5:21-48) and the
rule underlying James's community are in continuity with a common eschatological and Jewish ethos, the evidence does not justify assertions that the particular
ethical argot of the Jesus tradition is a primary source for James's paraenesis.

The concluding point of this discussion is twofold. First, based on the exegetical evidence, however marginal, James must be classified as a Jewish-Christian
writing. Second, the Christian quotient of James extends existent Jewish teaching. Neither its primitive christological formula in 2:1 nor its other Christian
embellishments, tacit or otherwise, are in any way provocative; as a whole, this
composition's Christian teaching can hardly be construed as anti-Judaic, and it
remains the most Jewish document in the New Testament.

This leads us, then, to consider a final and more important question: What
is the ongoing role of a Christian James as part of the Christian biblical canon?
We can begin answering that question by emphasizing the importance of the
intracanonical relationship between James and Paul—these two voices establish
a self-correcting and mutually informing conversation in which the church catholic continues to participate and from which we all benefit.[68] We can then get
even closer to an answer to our question by applying this notion to the perceived
problem of New Testament anti-Semitism.

The crucial issue at stake from a canonical perspective moves the interpreter beyond a concern for what the historical Paul or James taught, or what
their writings meant in their original settings. Those are important concerns;
however, the more important issue is how the Pauline and Jacobean writings
of the New Testament are subsequently used and embodied by those who consider them normative for faith. A number of Jewish and Christian scholars have
recently exonerated the historical Paul from any anti-Semitism, even from anti-
Judaism—since his understanding of gentile conversion (and even of Torah and
tradition in that context) falls within the limits of early Judaism. While those
judgments are by and large sound, it is still necessary to press the point that the
tensions and ultimately the separation between the church and synagogue were
in large measure the result of Paul's preaching and his gentile mission. On both
sides, Paul's preaching was perceived to be anti-Judaic, so that even Luke had to
defend the Jewishness of Paul for the early church.[69] Some of the post-Pauline
constructions of Paul's Torah-free and tradition-free gospel had given way to
theological anti-Judaism among some gnosticizing sects and then even among
a few of the earliest church fathers. While rejecting the Marcionite heresy in

---

68. Cf. Robert W. Wall, "Social Justice," in V. Samuel and C. Sugden, eds., *Church in Response
to Human Need* (Grand Rapids, Mich.: Eerdmans, 1988) 109–27. Also, "The Liberated Legalist,"
*Christian Century* 100 (Sept. 28, 1983) 848–49.

69. Cf. J. Jervell, *Luke and the People of God* (Minneapolis: Augsburg, 1972) 153–83; idem, *The
Unknown Paul* (Minneapolis: Augsburg, 1984) 52–76. According to Jervell (*Luke,* 185–207), Luke
even recruits James to defend Paul's Jewishness!

word, catholicizing Christianity too often embraced a "Pauline" fideism with tragic consequences to its understanding and incarnation of God's gospel.

We are simply too facile in our judgments if we dismiss these popular interpretations of Paul as contrary to the historical Paul and therefore not to be taken seriously. These post-Pauline "distortions" of Paul's preaching provide the modern interpreter with important clues about certain impulses or tendencies of Pauline preaching that lead the church to the "lunatic fringe" of true and approved religion. In this sense, it is important to underscore the prophetic importance of Ebionism's appropriation of James to check dangerous "folk" Paulinisms, which finally fell outside of apostolic Christianity; that process provides us with important clues about the ongoing role of James within the New Testament biblical canon. Sharply put, Ebionism's appeal to James intends to re-Judaize Christian faith and continues to remind us that the church must become more Jewish to become more Christian.

In their exaltation of a romanticized, idealized James,[70] their dependency upon the book that bears his name, and their accusations of moral perversion and theological apostasy leveled against Paul, conservative (and sometimes "heretical") Jewish Christians sought to correct unprofitable tendencies within catholicizing (and increasingly Pauline) Christianity during the second and third centuries. For our purposes, three emphases of this Jewish-Christian apologia, already reflected in the New Testament (especially Matthew, Luke-Acts, and James) and given full and faithful expression in second-century Ebionism, are notable as markers in determining the prophetic role James continues to play within the New Testament.[71] The first emphasis is the adoptionist Christology of these Jewish Christians. Without rehearsing all the features of adoptionistic Christology in its various expressions, it is important to underscore two christological convictions to make the point. Especially in Ebionism, God's exaltation of Jesus to his status as Son of God Messiah at his baptism resulted from God's recognition of Jesus' virtuous life. Further, Jesus' messianic status resulted from his observance of Torah and Jewish tradition; that is, Ebionism celebrated the Jewishness of Jesus. These are exactly the two convictions that stand behind the christological formula in Jas 2:1 (see above). Jesus is the messianic exemplar for

---

70. Cf. Martin, *James*, xli–lxi.

71. According to Dunn (*Unity and Diversity*, 245), their "heresy" is that Jacobean Christianity failed to adapt the beliefs of the first generation Jerusalem church to a changing situation. Perhaps the terms of the Pauline kerygma were inherently more adaptable to that situation and led to the triumph of Pauline Christianity within the catholicizing church. However, the canonizing impulse was "retrospective," and James matched up well with extant memories of the earliest Jewish church. Recently, R. A. Pritz (*Nazarene Jewish Christianity: From the End of the New Testament Period until Its Disappearance in the Fourth Century* [Jerusalem: Magnes; Leiden: Brill, 1988]) has distinguished between Ebionism and Nazarene Jewish Christianity. According to Pritz, Ebionism is a more conservative strain of Jewish Christianity that resisted the catholicizing *Tendenz* of the earliest church and could not perpetuate itself as a result. Nazarene Christianity accommodated itself more especially to the developing Christology of the church and survived at least into the fourth century.

the eschatological community of the kind of faith (or religion) that is deemed true by God and will be approved by God at the Lord's coming. Jesus' virtue is determined by his compliance with Torah's "royal law" (2:8; cf. 1:22-25) that stipulates the love of needy neighbors as the criterion of divine approval. Because he loved others, he was beloved and approved (or "adopted") by God (2:8b) as Lord and Christ. The eschatological community will be approved by God if it follows Christ's example and shows mercy to the marginal and distressed (1:27; 2:12-13).[72]

By locating messianic significance in Jesus' virtuous life, the adoptionism of Jacobean Christianity checks and balances Pauline Christology of the cross in two important ways. Paul interprets the death of Jesus theologically; it is the revelation of a faithful God's forgiving grace for lost humanity. Thus, the Christ-event reduces Jesus' entire messianic career to a single moment, already past but with continuing spiritual benefits. The *Tendenz* is to demote if not deny altogether the soteriological importance of his life and teaching; Paul himself rarely appealed to Jesus' teaching or personal character in his writings. The exemplary character of the historical Jesus, a remarkable feature of all the non-Pauline letters, serves to push Jesus' messianic significance backward from the cross into the whole of his messianic mission, beginning with his baptism. For Jacobean Christianity, Jesus exemplifies the eschatological community's wisdom; his virtue—his merciful and active concern for the needy neighbor—marks out the path that leads the wise into the eschaton of God's mercy (Jas 1:2-8, 17-21).

Of course, according to Ebionism, Jesus' virtue (and that of the eschatological community) is formed by observing Torah and Jewish tradition; the character of his virtue is particular to a discrete religious heritage. The intended meaning of the idea of Law and the role of tradition in the writings of Paul continue to be hotly debated. What is more certain is the antinomianism and anti-Judaism within Pauline Christianity that resulted from the interpretation of his teaching about the Torah and Jewish traditions (e.g., food rules, holy days, circumcision). Further, his shift to a more pneumatic law and charismatic ecclesiology shaped a more adaptable, accommodating faith. This orientation, perhaps a function of Paul's missiology as much as of his Christology, certainly removed as central the stabilizing influence of a distinctively Jewish identity, and with it the sociopolitical value of maintaining a Jewish heritage to help establish a people's social borders within a secular society's mainstream. Ebionism's ownership of Jesus' and James's Jewishness, portrayed by their observance of Torah and holy days, served this sociopolitical function: observance of Torah and tradition shapes a

---

72. Davids's reconstruction of Jacobean Christology is highly speculative. This is precisely the opposite of the concern with Baur's formulation of the problem. It is preferable to recognize that second-century Ebionism retains rather faithfully the convictions of Jerusalem Christianity; what changes is the rhetoric, the antagonism toward catholicizing Christianity that was excessively Pauline. That is, the Ebionites had lost the battle for the boundaries around Christianity, and they didn't like it!

distinctive (even sectarian) community that is less inclined to be absorbed by the secularism (or Hellenism) that the more conservative Jewish believers perceived, rightly or wrongly, to be a characteristic of Pauline Christianity.

A second emphasis is the theocentricity of Jacobean preaching. While one should not deny the theocentrism of Paul's preaching and literature and his reluctance to claim deity for Jesus, clearly the trajectory of Pauline Christianity into our own day tends the church toward Christocentrism. The deeper logic of Pauline theology inclines one in this direction because of the centrality of the Christ-event for Paul.[73] Ebionism's resistance to speaking of Jesus in the language of deification or with titles that presume his divinity is a function of its primary concern to maintain a monotheistic orthodoxy against the pluralizing and syncretistic tendencies of Hellenistic, post-Pauline Christianity.[74] Without venturing off into discussions about the implications of this point for a trinitarian theology or an incarnational Christology, it can be contended that the shift from theocentrism to Christocentrism results in distortions to a biblical understanding of God's gospel. Jewish Christianity offers important correctives to these distortions, one of which is worth mentioning as illustrative.

An intriguing contrast between Ebionism and Marcionism can be found on the margins of second-century catholicizing Christianity. Marcion's Paulinisms envisaged a radical anti-Judaism, which is focused by the gnostic doctrine of two antithetical Gods: the hateful God of Israel has been replaced by the loving God of Jesus. Marcion's gnostic theology in turn interprets and contaminates his Christology, which he constructed from Paul's Christology of the cross as well as his christological arguments against his native Judaism.[75] According to Marcion, Jesus suddenly appeared not only to reveal the true and hitherto unknown redemptive God—a story that is told in his de-Judaized Gospel of Luke—but also to redeem humanity from the spiritual (and self-destructive) conditions of Israel's God. Further, Israel's God has a past in history; according to Marcion, there can be no past in a "grace freely given." In this sense, one begins to understand the Christocentrism of Marcionism. Not only does the gnosis of saving grace and Christianity, its custodian, have its "official" beginning in Jesus rather than in Judaism, but the transcendent God, true and unknowable, does as well. Thus, Marcion not only perceived fundamental discontinuity between the Hebrew canon and his Christian canon on soteriological grounds, but between Judaism and Christianity on theological grounds as well.

Unlike Marcionism, whose canon included a de-Judaized Luke and an edited

---

73. See E. P. Sanders (*Paul and Palestinian Judaism: A Comparison of Patterns of Religion* [Philadelphia: Fortress, 1977] 154–60), who argues that Paul's critique of Judaism is christological as well.

74. See Dunn's discussion (*Unity and Diversity*, 50–54) about the collapsing of the two-clause confessional formula, God is one, Jesus is Lord.

75. H. Jonas (*The Gnostic Religion* [2d ed.; Boston: Beacon, 1958] 137–46) can thus speak of Marcion as "the most 'Christian' of all gnostics."

collection of Pauline letters, Ebionism's canon included James and a *Judaized version of Matthew's Gospel* in which Christology was interpreted by a Jewish theology.[76] The intent of Ebionism's scriptural rule was exactly the opposite of Marcion's: the Ebionite story of Matthew's Jesus is stripped bare of any suggestion of his deity (e.g., virginal conception), emphasizing his Jewishness in order to insure the continuity between the two Testaments to the God of Israel and of Jesus, between Judaism and Christianity, between God's mercy and justice, between God's creation and God's redemption, between monotheistic faith and Torah/tradition observance—a continuity that Ebionism perceived to be the legacy of earliest Jacobean Christianity. In fact, this emphasis of Ebionism aids us in recovering those motifs from James that may well balance certain Marcionite interpretations of the Pauline writings that continue to this day.

In particular, the theology of James resists the antithetical arrangement of the two biblical Testaments to God: according to James, in God there is the perfect (i.e., eschatological) integration of justice and mercy (2:12-13; 4:11-12; 5:7-9), and it is a profane, earthly wisdom that distinguishes the one true God from God's creation (3:9-12). More importantly, against the fideistic current in gnostic interpretations of Paul, Jacobean soteriology resists a monotheism that disengages "grace freely given" from those works in conformity with the will of Israel's God. According to Jas 2:14-26, the confession of a monotheistic faith of which God approves (2:19a) is distinguished from the monotheistic faith of the evil powers (2:19b) in that authentic monotheistic faith is identified by merciful deeds toward others. In the examples of Abraham and Rahab, James locates the integration of faith and works, orthodoxy and orthopraxy.

Finally, then, is the requirement of the eschatological community to respond faithfully to God. Again, we turn to Ebionism and to its central symbol of a Jewish way of life, the Law. Jesus' messiahship was indicated by his faithfulness to the Torah; his reformation's agenda was to return Israel back to the true intentions of Moses. Jesus' exalted successor in this Mosaic reformation of Israel was James, whose writing was authoritative because it continued the teaching of Jesus in this regard. Our immediate interest, however, is how Ebionism used the Law in its polemical rhetoric against the antinomian Paulinisms of its day. Clearly, the issues were both religious and political. The religious threat was an antinomian distortion of the covenant between God and messianic Israel. Ebionism's use of Matthew centers Jesus' teaching on the relationship between doing the Law and the surpassing righteousness that results in the eschatological blessing promised by God to the Law-observant people. Covenantal nomism challenges an overdependency on charisma or prophetic inspiration (Matthew 7) and contends that the covenantal relationship between God and Israel is maintained into the eschaton by Torah observance.

76. Cf. G. Howard, *The Gospel of Matthew according to a Primitive Hebrew Text* (Macon, Ga.: Mercer Univ. Press, 1987) 155–60.

J. A. Sanders describes the biblical idea of covenant as an interplay between "mythos" (the story of God's redemptive grace) and "ethos" (the demand of Israel's devotion to God in word and deed). The tensions within earliest Christianity resulted when one congregation emphasized one side while another placed primary emphasis on the other. On the one hand, according to Sanders, Pauline preaching was concerned with "mythos"—with clarifying the indicatives that inaugurated the promised new age of God's salvation through the death of God's Christ.[77] Thus, the renewing of God's covenant with Israel is the result of God's gracious initiative in which the faith community boasts and finds its hope. This particular emphasis changed the calculus by which earliest Christianity understood and embodied its faith in God: its response to God was to depend upon what God had already accomplished through Jesus Christ. To the extent that the community's ethos was constructed by the rigors of Torah observance, Christianity's continuity with Judaism only diminished the centrality of the Christ-event for the new age. Moreover, Pauline Christianity became more and more sensitive to, even critical of, other congregations where that same orientation was missing.

On the other hand, the perception of anti-Judaism in Paul's preaching is more keen in those Jewish-Christian congregations whose idea of covenanting with God is centered by "ethos" rather than by "mythos," by sanctification rather than by justification, by orthopraxy rather than orthodoxy. In these congregations, where the idea of covenant is more nomistic, the real issues have more to do with maintaining membership within the eschatological community where God's salvation has already dawned because of Christ. Repentance and obedience rather than forgiveness and faith are the catchwords of true religion; "staying in" rather than "getting in" is the measure of eschatological fitness. Ebionism's perception of anti-Judaism in the second-century trajectory of Pauline fideism stems more from its perception that "mythos" had displaced "ethos" in catholicizing Christianity's covenant with the God of Israel and Jesus.

No doubt, Ebionism's "heresy" was a distortion in the other direction—ethos without mythos—resulting in legalism rather than antinomianism and in adoptionism rather than Docetism. But the crucial point is this: Ebionism's concerns detect potential distortions inherent in the Pauline kerygma; and they help the interpreter locate in James the New Testament's built-in correctives to bring balance to the church's rule of faith. For James, the eschatological "test of faith" (1:2-4) is a test of wisdom (1:5-8), because wisdom determines those actions that lead to salvation (1:17-21). The wise thing to do is to observe Torah (1:22-27), which guides the conduct of the faith community (2:1-11) and insures its salvation (2:12-13, 14-26). The wise thing to do is observe traditional patterns of pure speech (3:1-18). The wise thing to do is worship God (4:7-12) in order

---

77. J. A. Sanders, "Torah and Paul," in J. Jervell and W. Meeks, eds., *God's Christ and His People* (N. A. Dahl Festschrift; Oslo: Universitetsforlaget, 1977) 132–37.

to resist the evil impulses of materialism (4:1-6, 13-17; 5:1-6). For James, the
ingredient of true religion is the wise response to every trial that tempts the
faith community away from a right relationship with God. God's covenant with
Israel is not unilateral and unconditional; as in any relationship, God's covenant
with Israel is bilateral and reciprocal. The emphases of Pauline *and* Jacobean
kerygmata, taken together, continue to remind readers of the whole biblical
canon that God's covenant with Israel constitutes both mythos and ethos in
equal measure.

# -10-

# Polemic in the Book of Revelation

## Peder Borgen

In the book of Revelation, the messages to the church (*ekklēsia*) in Smyrna and the church in Philadelphia use the phrase "synagogue of Satan" (Rev 2:9; 3:9). Rev 2:9 reads: " ... the slander of those who say that they are Jews and are not, but are a synagogue of Satan." In Rev 3:9 the corresponding sentence reads: "Behold, I will make those of the synagogue of Satan who say that they are Jews and are not, but lie ... " In his book *The Devil and the Jews*, J. Trachtenberg refers to these and other New Testament passages as documentation for the animosity of the early church toward the Jews.[1] He draws the line from the New Testament to the fourth and fifth centuries, when the church had established itself, using Chrysostom of Antioch as a major source. Chrysostom maintained that the synagogues of the Jews were the homes of idolatry and devils, and that the Jews did not worship God but devils.[2] Since Trachtenberg concentrates on the impact that such New Testament concepts made on people throughout the centuries, he does not enter into an analysis of Rev 2:9 and 3:9 in their own historical context.

Correspondingly, in *The American Family Bible*, published by the American Institute for the Study of Racial and Religious Cooperation, Rev 2:9 and 3:9 are among the verses that are reformulated because of their assumed anti-Semitic connotations. The reformulation of Rev 2:9 reads: "I know the blasphemy of them which say they are religious, and are not, but are the assembly of Satan." Similarly, Rev 3:9 is rephrased in this way: "Behold, I will make them of the assembly of Satan, which say they are religious, and are not, but do lie ... " In another publication sponsored by the same institute, the anthology

---

1. J. Trachtenberg, *The Devil and the Jews: The Medieval Conception of the Jews and Its Relation to Modern Antisemitism* (New York: Harper and Row, 1966; originally published in 1943) 20–21.

2. Trachtenberg, *Devil and the Jews*, 20–21.

*Jews and Christians: Exploring the Past, Present, and Future,* edited by J. H. Charlesworth, a more precise understanding of these passages is presented. In his contribution to that volume, D. Moody Smith makes the observation that the term *Ioudaioi* (Jews) appears only twice in Revelation (2:9; 3:9), in both cases in an indirectly positive sense. That is, members of the "synagogue of Satan" are said to claim to be Jews although in reality they are not. "Jew" is still used in a positive sense even if the "synagogue of Satan" means Jews in Smyrna, or Philadelphia, or even contemporary Jews generally. In that case, they have defected from proper Judaism.[3] A. Yarbro Collins entertains a similar view: the name "Jew" is denied the Jews of the local synagogues because the followers of Jesus are held to be the true Jews; thus the term "Jew" is not here derogatory in and of itself.[4]

It is debated whether those who call themselves Jews in Rev 2:9 and 3:9 are actually Jews or whether they are Christians. In the latter case, the tension reflected is an intra-Christian conflict. H. Koester, B. M. Newman, H. Kraft, and S. Sandmel assume this background for the controversy. Newman and Koester assume that those who call themselves Jews are Christians belonging to the group of Nicolaitans.[5] Elisabeth Schüssler Fiorenza takes issue with this interpretation and maintains that those who call themselves Jews are actually Jewish citizens in Smyrna and Philadelphia. John says that the *ekklēsiai* might suffer persecution from the so-called Jews; no such persecution is mentioned in the statements about the Nicolaitans. Thus, some Jews endanger the churches by persecution from the outside, while the Nicolaitans endanger the churches from the inside by advocating that Christians had freedom to become part of the syncretistic pagan society.[6]

The question of polemic in Revelation is much broader than the debate on the meaning of the polemical statements in Rev 2:9 and 3:9. All scholars recognize this fact. The view that guides the present study is that John builds on traditions, thought-categories, and outlooks held by segments of Jewish people, and that he transforms them on the basis of belief in Jesus Christ. The book reflects a situation in which Christians understood themselves to be a distinct group within a Jewish context, and even thought themselves to be the true Jews.

---

3. D. M. Smith, "Judaism and the Gospel of John," in J. H. Charlesworth, ed., *Jews and Christians: Exploring the Past, Present, and Future* (New York: Crossroad, 1990) 88–89.

4. A. Yarbro Collins, *Crisis and Catharsis: The Power of the Apocalypse* (Philadelphia: Westminster, 1984) 85–87.

5. H. Koester, "GNOMAI DIAPHOROI: The Origin and Nature of Diversification in Early Christianity," in J. M. Robinson and H. Koester, *Trajectories through Early Christianity* (Philadelphia: Fortress, 1971) 114–57; B. M. Newman, Jr., *Rediscovering the Book of Revelation* (Valley Forge, Pa.: Judson, 1968) 30; H. Kraft, *Die Offenbarung des Johannes* (Tübingen: Mohr [Siebeck], 1974) 60–61; S. Sandmel, *Anti-Semitism in the New Testament?* (Philadelphia: Fortress, 1978) 122–23.

6. E. Schüssler Fiorenza, *The Book of Revelation: Justice and Judgment* (Philadelphia: Fortress, 1985) 117–20. For a more detailed discussion of the Nicolaitans, see Kraft, *Die Offenbarung,* 72–74; D. M. Beck, "Nicolaitans," *IDB* (1962) 3.547–48.

## Jewish Traditions and Perspective

The Jewish character of the book of Revelation is obvious and commonly recognized. Although the book was written in Asia Minor on the island of Patmos and seven Asian towns are mentioned by name, it draws on and interprets a biblical and traditional Jewish geographical outlook. This is the case whether the geographical references are interpreted as symbols of a spiritual reality only or are also thought of as naming geographical locations in the external and concrete world.[7]

Accordingly, Jerusalem plays the central role in the thought-world of the book. The vision of the future centers around the new Jerusalem, the holy city that is coming down out of heaven from God (Rev 21:2; see also 3:12). It is pictured as an imperial capital: "By its light shall the nations walk; and the kings of the earth shall bring their glory into it" (21:24-25).[8] The hill of Jerusalem's temple, Mount Zion, is also mentioned: "Then I looked, and lo, on Mount Zion stood ... a hundred and forty-four thousand" (Rev 14:1). As indicated by the 144,000 (that is, 12 x 12,000), the city is the center for the people of God—Israel, with its twelve tribes. Correspondingly, on the gates of Jerusalem the names of the twelve tribes of the sons of Israel are inscribed (Rev 21:12). At this point, the question will not be raised whether John here refers to the Jews—that is, Jewish Christians of the church—as the new Israel.[9] For our present purpose, it is sufficient to say that the author bases his presentation on Jewish geographical and ideological outlook.

In agreement with parts of the Old Testament (see, for example, Isaiah 13; 47; Jeremiah 50; 51; 52; Daniel 4; 5; Micah 4:10; Zech 2:7ff.), Babylon is the main city of the enemy (Rev 14:8; 16:19; 17:5; 18:2, 10, 21). Babylon is associated with "impure passions" (14:8; 18:3), "harlots and earth's abominations" (17:5), "a dwelling place of demons," "fornication ... wealth" (18:2-3, 9, 21-23). The polemic is harsh, and the city suffers devastating destruction.

The book of Revelation remains within the context of Jewish views when this biblical conflict between Israel and Babylon is applied to the new historical situation in which Rome is seen as the evil enemy. Babylon serves then as a symbolic name for Rome, as also is the case in *Sib. Or.* 5:143; and 4 Ezra 15:43ff.; 16:1ff. The analogy between Babylon and Rome underlies the setting

---

7. Concerning the problem of spiritual and/or concrete and spatial location, see commentaries such as G. R. Beasley-Murray, *The Book of Revelation* (Grand Rapids, Mich.: Eerdmans, 1974) 23, 305ff., etc.; R. H. Mounce, *The Book of Revelation* (Grand Rapids, Mich.: Eerdmans, 1977) 39-45, 368ff., etc.

8. On the new Jerusalem, see *T. Dan* 5:12; *2 Bar.* 4:2-6; 32:2-4; 4 Ezra 7:26. As for the thought that the •ings of the earth shall bring their glory into the new Jerusalem, see Isaiah 60.

9. See commentaries such as R. H. Charles, *The Revelation of John* (2 vols.; ICC; 1920; repr., Edinburgh: T. and T. Clark, 1980) 1.188-99, 2.4, 162; Beasley-Murray, *Revelation,* 139-41, 222, 320.

of 4 Ezra and *2 Baruch*.[10] The book of Revelation tells how Babylon/Rome was destroyed: "Then a mighty angel took up a stone like a great millstone and threw it into the sea, saying, 'So shall Babylon the great city be thrown down with violence, and shall be found no more' "; correspondingly, 4 Ezra 15:43ff. says: "They shall go on steadily to Babylon, and shall destroy her."

Thus, the book of Revelation draws on Jewish traditions and perspectives in its geographical and political outlook. The same is seen within the more specifically religious realm. The polemic against participation in pagan polytheistic cults in Revelation follows Jewish traditions. According to the Torah, it was a crime for the Israelites to take part in pagan idolatry. Num 25:1-9 exemplifies this attitude: it tells that the Israelites "began to play the harlot with the daughters of Moab. These invited the people to the sacrifices of their gods, and the people ate, and bowed down to their gods." It is then told how Phinehas took a spear in his hand and pierced it through an Israelite man and a pagan woman who committed the crime together.

Balaam and Balak are not mentioned in Num 25:1ff., but a widespread Jewish exegetical tradition makes the inference from the advice given by Balaam in Num 31:16 that Balak should use Moabite women to seduce Israelites to commit adultery and idolatry: "Behold, these caused the people of Israel, by the counsel of Balaam, to act treacherously against the Lord in the matter of Peor."

Philo, in *Spec. Leg.* 1.54-57, illustrates the function of the Phinehas episode in the first century CE:[11]

But if any members of the nation betray the honor due to the One, they should suffer the utmost penalties.... And it is well that all who have a zeal for virtue should be permitted to exact the penalties offhand and with no delay.... There is recorded in the Laws the example of one who acted with this admirable courage. He had seen some persons consorting with foreign women and through the attraction of their love-charms spurning their ancestral customs and seeking admission to the rites of a fabulous religion. One in particular he saw, the chief ring leader of the backsliding, who had the audacity to exhibit his unholy conduct in public and was openly offering sacrifices, a travesty of the name, to images of wood and stones in the presence of the whole people. So seized with inspired fury, keeping back the throng of spectators on either side, he slew without a qualm him and her, the man because he listened to lessons which it were a gain to unlearn, the woman because she had been the instructor in wickedness.

In his rendering of Num 25:1-9, Josephus applies the passage to the pressures felt by Jews in his own days. In his advice to King Balak, Balaam concluded:

10. See J. H. Charlesworth, ed., *The Old Testament Pseudepigrapha* (2 vols.; Garden City, N.Y.: Doubleday, 1983-85) 1.396, 520, 557, 615-17.

11. See especially T. Seland, "Jewish Vigilantism in the First Century C.E.: A Study of Selected Texts in Philo and Luke on Jewish Vigilante Reactions against Nonconformers to the Torah" (Ph.D. diss., Trondheim University, 1991) 63ff., 85ff., 119ff., 133ff., 141ff., 167-89.

> When they shall see these youths overmastered by their passions, let them quit them and, on their entreating them to stay, let them not consent till they have induced their lovers to renounce the laws of their fathers and the God to whom they owe them, and to worship the gods of the Midianites and Moabites. (*Ant.* 4.6.7 §130; cf. 4.6.6 §§126-30)[12]

Viewpoints expressed by the pagans against the Jews in Josephus's own times are reflected in the words of the Midianite women:

> Seeing then...that ye...have customs and a mode of life wholly alien to all mankind, insomuch that your food is of a peculiar sort and your drink is distinct from that of other men, it behoves you, if ye would live with us, also to revere our gods....Nor can any man reproach you for venerating the special gods of the country whereto ye are come, above all when our gods are common to all mankind, while yours has no other worshipper. (*Ant.* 4.6.8 §§137-38)

The nonconforming Israelites defended themselves in the speech of Zambrias (Num 25:14: Zimri) addressed to Moses:

> [I]...have married, as thou sayest, a foreign wife..., and I sacrifice to gods whom I hold sacrifice to be due, deeming it right to get at the truth for myself from many persons, and not to live as under a tyranny, hanging all my hopes for my whole life upon one. (*Ant.* 4.6.11 §§148-49; cf. 4.6.11 §§145-49; this speech has no warrant in the biblical account)

Elements from such traditions are drawn on by John in the edict[13] to the *ekklēsia* in Pergamum: "But I have a few things against you: you have some there who hold the teaching of Balaam, who taught Balak to put a stumbling block before the sons of Israel, that they might eat food sacrificed to idols and practice immorality" (Rev 2:14).

The sharp polemic against participation in polytheistic cults is also found in the edict to the *ekklēsia* in Thyatira: "But I have this against you, that you tolerate the woman Jezebel, who calls herself a prophetess and is teaching and beguiling my servants to practice immorality and to eat food sacrificed to idols" (Rev 2:20).

The problem of prophets encouraging the Israelites to join the pagans in worshiping idols is stated in Deut 13:1ff. In the first century CE, Philo paraphrases this passage: "Further, if anyone cloaking himself under the name and guise of a prophet and claiming to be possessed by inspiration leads us on to the worship of gods recognized in the different cities, we ought not to listen to him and be deceived by the name of prophet" (*Spec. Leg.* 1.315).

The conclusion is that Rev 2:14, 20 formulates Jewish polemic against participation in pagan polytheistic cults, such as found in Philo and Josephus.

---

12. On this see W. C. van Unnik, "Josephus' Account of the Story of Israel's Sin with Alien Women in the Country of Midian (Num 25:1ff)," in M. S. H. C. Heerma van Voss et al., eds., *Travels in the World of the Old Testament* (M. A. Beek festschrift; Assen: Van Gorcum, 1974) 241-61.

13. Concerning the letters to the seven churches as edicts, see D. E. Aune, "The Form and Function of the Proclamations to the Seven Churches (Revelation 2-3)," *NTS* 36 (1990) 182-204.

Moreover, John's statements, just as the ones by Philo and Josephus, give evidence for the existence of a tension within the people of God between different approaches to the surrounding world. In Pergamum, Thyatira, Alexandria, and other places there were Jews/Christians who wanted to function within society at large and respond positively to the conditions set by the pagans, like the one rendered by Josephus in *Ant.* 12.3.2 §§125-26: "The Ionians agitated against them [the Jews]... and claimed that, if the Jews were to be their fellows, they should worship the Ionians' gods" (cf. the words of the Midianite women in *Ant.* 4.6.8 §§137-38, cited above). Others would follow the line of John in Rev 2:14-16, 20-23 and of Philo in *Spec. Leg.* 1.54-57, 315ff.: such participation in pagan cult was forbidden and resulted in punishment.

In both Jewish and Christian polemic, pagan polytheistic worship can be associated with demonic forces.[14] Such characterizations of pagans are found in the Septuagint translation of Ps 96(95):4: "For all the gods of the peoples are demons." Similarly, Paul says that what pagans sacrifice they offer to demons and not to God (1 Cor 10:20). Such labeling of pagan worship is not intended to suggest that pagans worship gods carrying the names of demonic powers, such as the devil, Satan, and so on; rather, such terms are labels to distinguish "us" from "them" in a dualistic manner.

Against this background one might think that the phrase "synagogue of Satan" in Rev 2:9 and 3:9 indicates that a dualistic relationship existed between the Christian *ekklēsia* and the Jewish synagogue like the one between Christianity/Judaism and the Gentiles with their pagan worship. If so the conflict is extramural. The survey of research given at the beginning of the present study showed that the two passages picture an intramural Jewish conflict. The question behind the phrase "synagogue of Satan" is: Where are the true Jews to be found, in the *ekklēsia* or in the synagogue?

With this in mind it is important to note that demonic concepts are used as characterizations of the opponents in intramural controversies, within Christianity as well as within Judaism.[15] As background for Rev 2:9 and 3:9 we therefore must look into conflicts between groups among the Jews. The Dead Sea Scrolls have given us firsthand information about a covenantal community, often called the Qumran community, that harshly criticized other Jews.[16] Israel in general is caught in "the nets of Belial," the lord of the evil forces (4QpPs$^a$ 1-10 ii 10-11). These are the traps mentioned in CD 4:14-18 as consisting of fornication, riches, and the defilement of the Temple. The Qumran community is saved from these nets and will "inherit the earth" (1-10 ii 9-11). It is waiting for the destruction of the wicked and for the moment when it will rule Jerusalem.

---

14. See J. Z. Smith, "Towards Interpreting Demonic Powers in Hellenistic and Roman Antiquity," *ANRW* 2/16/1 (1978) 425–39.

15. Smith, "Towards Interpreting Demonic Powers," 425–39.

16. For the following, see D. Dimant, "Qumran Sectarian Literature," in M. Stone, ed., *Jewish Writings of the Second Temple Period* (Assen: Van Gorcum, 1984) 483–550, esp. 508–10 and 542–43.

Although the formulations in the Thanksgiving Hymns, the Hodayot, might be poetic and general and therefore might not in the same way give concrete references to specific persons and groups, it is of interest to note that the phrase "synagogue of Satan" (Rev 2:9 and 3:9) has a striking parallel in the phrase "the congregation of Belial" (1QH 2:22). The Hebrew word that is here translated as "congregation," *ē<sup>c</sup>dāh*, might even be translated as "synagogue," since in the Septuagint the Greek word *synagōgē*, synagogue, is used most frequently to render this Hebrew term (see, e.g., Num 26:9 LXX).

Other writings also tell about the dualistic relationship between the Qumran community and other persons and communities within Judaism. "The Spouter of Lies" was the leader of a rival congregation. He is accused of "building through bloodshed his city of vanity and erecting through falsehood a congregation" (1QpHab 10:10). The "Teacher of Righteousness," in contrast, leads "the congregation of His elect" (1QpPs[a] 1-10 ii 5; 1-10 iii 5), symbolized by the eschatological Jerusalem. Another adversary is "the Wicked Priest." He profaned Jerusalem and the sanctuary and persecuted "the Teacher of Righteousness," a priest, and his followers (1QpHab 8:8-13; 8:16–9:2; 11:4-8, 12-15; 12:2-6, 7-10).

Thus, the Qumran writings exemplify how a community within Judaism understood its relationship to other Jews in dualistic terms. Within the context of Judaism, the Qumran community associated "the others" with demonic forces such as the figure of Belial. Similarly, "the others" in Rev 2:9 and 3:9 are called the synagogue of Satan.

While the opponents in Rev 2:9 and 3:9 are Jews in Smyrna and Philadelphia, in Asia Minor, the polemic in the Qumran writings is primarily against persons and groups in Jerusalem, more specifically priestly circles in the Jerusalem Temple. John's polemic also includes a polemic against Jerusalem, however, as can be seen in Rev 11:1-13. The "two witnesses" will be killed after they have finished their testimony, "and their dead bodies will lie in the street of the great city which is allegorically called Sodom and Egypt, where their Lord was crucified" (Rev 11:8). The reference to the crucifixion of Jesus shows that Jerusalem is meant. Thus, in Revelation there is a dual interpretation of Jerusalem. On the one hand, it is associated with salvation and the heavenly bliss (Rev 3:12; 21:2, etc.), and, on the other hand, it is subject to severe criticism. The historical city is under judgment and in Rev 11:8 is symbolically characterized as "Sodom" and "Egypt." Corresponding statements of criticism and judgment against Jerusalem are found in Isa 1:9-10, where those who live in Jerusalem are called "rulers of Sodom" and "people of Gomorrah."[17] The persecution of the two witnesses and of their "Lord," Jesus, corresponds to the persecution suffered in Jerusalem by the founder of the Qumran community and his followers. The

---

17. See Collins, *Crisis and Catharsis*, 86–87. Another interpretation is suggested by Mounce, *Revelation*, 226–27: "The great city" in Rev 11:8 means the power of Rome. "The inclusion of a reference to the crucifixion is not to identify a geographical location but to illustrate the response of paganism to righteousness."

conclusion is that in spite of all differences between the Dead Sea Scrolls and the book of Revelation, both reflect intramural conflicts in Jewish communities in which the adversaries are associated with evil demonic forces.

As background for the reference to a "synagogue of Satan" in the edict to the *ekklēsia* in Smyrna, it is significant that there was a strong Jewish community in the city, as documented by inscriptions and literary works.[18] The Jewish community in Smyrna played an active role in the martyrdom of Polycarp, and later in the Decian persecution they took an active part in the martyrdom of Pionius.[19] These other evidences for Jews persecuting Christians support the understanding that John had such persecutions from (other) Jews in mind when he wrote: "Do not fear what you are about to suffer. Behold, the devil is about to throw some of you in prison, that you may be tested, and for ten days you will have tribulation. Be faithful unto death, and I will give you the crown of life" (Rev 2:10). John also indicates that the superior status and power of the synagogue in Philadelphia will be changed to the effect that those in the synagogue will have to render the *ekklēsia* respect and homage: "I will make them come and bow down before your feet" (Rev 3:9).

Thus we have substantiated the view that John builds on traditions, thought-categories, and outlooks held by segments of the Jewish people. Next the task is to examine the way in which John has transformed this background on the basis of belief in Jesus Christ.

## The *Ekklēsia* of Christ as the True Jews

As seen in other chapters of this book, several writings in the New Testament offer documentation of the existence of tension and conflict between Christian Jews and other Jews, as an intramural controversy within the Jewish communities. As members of a small and growing movement, persons in the early church suffered persecution from their fellow Jews (see, e.g., Acts 4:1-31; 5:17-42; 6:8–8:3; 11:19–12:19; 17:1-10; 18:12-17; 21:27-36; 23:12-22; 2 Cor 11:23-26; cf. Gal 5:11; John 16:1-2). In a recent dissertation, Torrey Seland has placed such persecutions within the broader context of reactions by zealous persons within Jewish communities against nonconformists. Seland also discusses similar phenomena in other (non-Jewish) ethnic groups, nations, and religious communities. He further shows that passages in the Law of Moses, such as the Phinehas episode (Num 25:6-9) and the law against false prophets

---

18. E. Schürer, *The History of the Jewish People in the Age of Jesus Christ (175 B.C.–A.D. 135)* (rev. G. Vermes et al.; Edinburgh: T. and T. Clark, 1986) 2/1.20–21; M. Stern, "The Jewish Diaspora," in S. Safrai et al., eds., *The Jewish People in the First Century* (Assen: Van Gorcum, 1974) 151.

19. See Charles, *Revelation*, 1.56–57; P. W. van der Horst, "Jews and Christians in Aphrodisias in the Light of Their Relations in Other Cities of Asia Minor," *NedTTs* 43 (1989) 116–17.

(e.g., Deut 13:1-11), demanded that deviants who committed serious crimes that were understood to be of anticonstitutional character should be persecuted and killed, if necessary by fellow Jews on the spot. These actions were intramural measures against persons who were felt to seriously threaten the identity of the community and its foundations. Such persecutions should be classified as vigilante actions—acts or threats of coercion in violation of the formal boundaries or laws of an established sociopolitical order; those acts or threats, however, are intended by the violators to defend that order from some form of subversion.[20] Accordingly, the Jewish persecution of Christian fellow Jews and the polemic reactions by Christians are not to be seen as Jewish antipaganism or Christian anti-Semitism, but as an intramural conflict, parallels to which are found in many other communities and groups in the world. When this intramural controversy was in the distant past and non-Jewish Christians attacked the Jewish nation as a collective from the outside, then the conflict turned extramural and in many cases became anti-Semitic.

So far it has been shown that the polemic in the book of Revelation is to be understood within the context of Jewish traditions, thought-categories, and perspectives. Further discussion is needed in order to trace the distinctively Christian use and transformation of this Jewish heritage on the basis of which John interprets the situation of the *ekklēsiai* of Christ in Asia Minor.

One might ask if the idea of Jewish proselytism is interpreted afresh and transformed from Christian notions. Rev 5:9-10 and 7:9ff. might be understood in this way. In Rev 5:9 we read about the Lamb who was slain and by his blood ransomed human beings for God "from every tribe and tongue and people and nation." Similarly 7:9 tells about "a great multitude which no man could number, from every nation, from all tribes and peoples and tongues." From 7:14 one learns that these people have washed their robes and made them white in the blood of the Lamb. There are observations that speak in favor of regarding this multitude as Christian proselytes. They came from many (pagan) nations; they needed redemption and cleansing. Philo and Josephus do not specify that cleansing was part of becoming proselytes, but Asenath, in the process of becoming a proselyte, is told by the angel to wash her face and hands with living water and take off the black dress of mourning and dress in a new linen robe (*Joseph and Asenath* 14:12-17). Moreover, Paul states in 1 Cor 6:11 that the Corinthian Gentiles became Christian proselytes by being washed and sanctified. Thus, there is some support for suggesting that the washing of the robes in Rev 7:14 reflects ideas from Jewish proselytism. Accordingly, on the surface it seems natural to understand 7:9ff. as a reference to gentile Christians from all nations, while 7:1-8 about the 144,000 from the twelve tribes of Israel seems to refer to the Jewish Christians. There are scholars who entertain such interpretations.[21]

---

20. Seland, "Jewish Vigilantism," 3.
21. See W. Bousset, *Die Offenbarung Johannis* (2d ed.; Göttingen: Vandenhoeck and Ruprecht,

Rev 5:9-10 speaks against drawing such a distinction between Jewish Christians and gentile Christians; those who are ransomed from every tribe, tongue, people, and nation are characterized as Israel in accordance with Exod 19:6: "You shall be to me a kingdom of priests and a holy nation." The Jewish institution of proselytism might still be behind these references, since there are several sources that testify to the view that the proselytes became full citizens of God's Israel.[22]

The redemptive death of Jesus Christ is not seen only as the means by which Gentiles become proselytes, however. His death is so fundamental that it constitutes the people of God (the true Jews) as such, as is seen from Rev 1:5-6: "To him who loves us and has freed us from our sins by his blood and made us a kingdom, priests to his God [... *basilean, hiereis, tō theō*] and Father... " As in Rev 5:9-10 the basis for this characterization of Israel is Exod 19:6.[23] The idea of Israel as a priestly nation was widespread in Judaism, as can be seen from 2 Macc 2:17; *Mek.* Exod 19:6; *Jub.* 16:18; Philo, *Abr.* 56, 98; *Sobr.* 66; *Mos.* 1.149. The Jewish nation had received the gift of priesthood and prophecy on behalf of all humankind (*Abr.* 98), and this nation was destined to be consecrated above all others to offer prayers for ever on behalf of the human race (*Mos.* 1.149).[24]

According to Rev 1:5-6 the redemptive death of Jesus Christ brought this priestly people of God into being. No distinction is made here between Jewish Christians and gentile Christians. In the word "us" John includes himself and the seven churches as representatives of the true Israel founded by Christ. Thus the priestly nation consists of all those who have been freed from their sins by the sacrificial death of Jesus Christ, Jews and Gentiles alike.[25] It should be remembered that there were rabbinic traditions that stated that the conditions for the admission of Gentiles were the same as the constitutive elements of the people of Israel: just as one who is admitted to Judaism must submit to circumcision, ablution, and sacrifice, so Israel during the exodus did not receive the Torah until they had performed these three ceremonies (*Mek. Rabbi Simon* 96-97).[26] Similarly, in Rev 7:14 the washing of the robes of the multi-

---

1906) ad loc.; D. Flusser, *Judaism and the Origins of Christianity* (Jerusalem: Magnes, 1988) 449 n. 191; A. Feuillet, "Les 144,000 Israelites Marqués d'un Sceau," *NovT* 9 (1967) 197-98.

22. P. Borgen, *Philo, Paul and John* (Atlanta: Scholars Press, 1987) 207-54; A. F. Segal, "The Costs of Proselytism and Conversion," in D. J. Lull, ed., *Society of Biblical Literature 1988 Seminar Papers* (Atlanta: Scholars Press, 1988) 336-69. The proselytes receive equal rank with all the privileges of the nativeborn Jews according to Philo (*Spec. Leg.* 1.52; *Virt.* 102-3). The same rule is stated in rabbinic writings; see C. G. Montefiore and H. Loewe, eds., *A Rabbinic Anthology* (London: Macmillan, 1938) 571-73.

23. For further discussion of Rev 1:5-6 and 5:9-10, see Schüssler Fiorenza, *Revelation*, 68-81.

24. For a discussion of the wording, see Charles, *Revelation*, 1.16, and other commentaries. Concerning Philo, see P. Borgen, "There Shall Come Forth a Man," in J. H. Charlesworth, ed., *The Messiah* (Minneapolis: Fortress, 1992) 342-51.

25. For a discussion of Rev 1:5-6, see Schüssler Fiorenza, *Revelation*, 78 n. 18.

26. L. Ginzberg, *The Legends of the Jews* (7 vols.; 1909; repr., Philadelphia: Jewish Publication Society, 1968) 3.88.

tude from many nations may allude to the Israelites washing their clothes when approaching God at Sinai. Among the many varied and often conflicting Jewish eschatological ideas there were also expectations that people from other nations would convert and become proselytes, that the other nations would join Israel in worshiping the one true God and have Jerusalem as their mother city, and that they would throw away their own laws and accept the Torah.[27] Against such background ideas John has interpreted the church as the inclusive eschatological Israel that comprises both Jews and Gentiles in the one people of God. Thus, the twelve tribes of the sons of Israel (Rev 7:4-8) and the great multitude from every nation, all tribes and peoples and tongues (7:9-14), do not refer to two different groups, the Jewish Christians and the gentile Christians. The redemption through the death of Christ constitutes the true people of Israel who are drawn from the Jewish nation as well as other nations. As implied in Rev 2:9 and 3:9, they are then the true Jews, in contrast to those who say that they are Jews but are not.

Thus the thinking in the book of Revelation indeed resembles the self-understanding of the Qumran community that they were the true Israel within Judaism. In this way the polemic in both cases comes from an internal polemic between the true Jews and those "who say that they are Jews and are not" (Rev 2:9; 3:9).[28] However, the Christian Israel in Revelation has a cross-national structure that is lacking in the Qumran community, even though the Qumran community, like John, looks forward to the victory of God and God's people over the enemies—that is, over demonic forces and evil people and nations, the Roman Empire in particular.[29]

Did the general populace in the various cities involved look upon this polemic between the Christian *ekklēsia* and the synagogue as an intramural conflict? Before we answer this question, the general observation should be made that at several places in Asia Minor the interaction between Jews and Christians was so extensive that the distinctions between the groups were blurred.[30] This situation was at times felt to be such a threat to leading circles in the church that sharp polemic and conflict arose. In New Testament times Christianity grew up from within Judaism and struggled with the question of whether or not gentile converts were to be understood as Jewish proselytes. The Judaizers came to the churches in Galatia and wanted to bring the newly won Christians fully into

---

27. See Philo, *Mos.* 2.44; Tanhuma Buber, *Debarim* §2; *Sipre* Deut. §354 (on 33:18); *Midr. Ps.* 100:1; Montefiore and Loewe, eds., *Rabbinic Anthology*, 564-65.

28. See Flusser, *Judaism*, 79.

29. See F. Mussner, " 'Weltherrschaft' als eschatologisches Thema der Johannesapokalypse," in E. Grässer and O. Merk, eds., *Glaube und Eschatologie* (W. G. Kümmel festschrift; Tübingen: Mohr [Siebeck], 1985) 209-27.

30. For the following survey, see especially A. R. R. Sheppard, "Jews, Christians and Heretics in Acmonia and Eumenia," *Anatolian Studies* 29 (1979) 169-80; van der Horst, "Jews and Christians in Aphrodisias," 106-21.

Jewish proselyte status, as can be learned from Paul's Letter to the Galatians.[31] The Letter to the Colossians contains a warning against Jewish ceremonial observances and dietary laws. Thus the members of the church seemed to follow Jewish life-style, mixed with a cult of angels (Col 2:16-19).

Early in the second century Ignatius of Antioch admonished the churches of Magnesia and Philadelphia not to yield to Judaizing influence. Inscriptions that were found in the area around Acmonia and Eumenia that date to the third and fourth centuries CE display a blending of Jewish and Christian features. In Sardis in early Byzantine times, a market street with Jewish and Christian shops side by side existed behind the synagogue. After the cessation of imperial cult activities in the Sebasteion in Aphrodisias, premises seem to have been used as shops. Here both menorahs and crosses have been incised on some of the doorjambs. The intense attack by John Chrysostom of Antioch in his eight homilies preached in 386-87 CE against the Jews and against Christians who frequented the synagogue illustrates how vehement polemic could presuppose extensive interaction and some degree of practical integration between the Christians and the synagogal community. Chrysostom levels charges against Christians who go to the synagogue on the Sabbath, who receive circumcision, who celebrate the Jewish Pesach, and who keep the Jewish dietary laws and other observances, such as fasting. Moreover, in canon 29 of the Council of Laodicea, which was held in the second half of the fourth century, the following formulation occurs: "It is forbidden that Christians live like Jews and rest on Sabbath; they should work on that day. They should prefer the Lord's day to rest on, if possible, since they are Christians. If they turn out to be Judaizers, let them be accursed by Christ." Canon 38 deals also with the problem of Judaizing: "It is forbidden to take unleavened bread from the Jews or to participate in their godless acts." Canon 37 forbids Christians to participate in the festivals of the Jews, and canon 36 warns the clergy against making phylacteries, protective amulets, probably meaning Jewish tefillin, small boxes with leather straps, to be placed on the arm and the upper forehead, containing strips of parchment on which are written Deut 6:4-9; 11:13-21; and Exod 13:1-16.

How far does the book of Revelation reflect common Jewish community features and social markers that could be recognized by people from the outside? One major common characteristic between the synagogue and the *ekklēsia* was that they were both organized groups that rejected the pagan polytheistic gods and worship. Insofar as there was tension within the groups with regard to separation from or integration into the pagan surroundings, they had this struggle in common. John and some (other) Jews had in common that they opposed the Roman ideology and government on the basis of Jewish traditions. Moreover, both groups based their self-understanding in general on Jewish traditions and ideas. They also had in common certain ethical standards and life-styles. Since

---

31. See Borgen, *Philo, John and Paul*, 206-72.

John understood the true Israel to be cross-national, the *ekklēsia* comprised both Jewish Christians and gentile Christians. Nevertheless, the strong Jewish character of the book and the Jewish community features mentioned above indicate that John and the Christian congregations referred to still had their base in Jewish milieus, and the congregations had Jews as members. It is to be noticed, however, that questions of circumcision, Sabbath, and Jewish dietary laws are not discussed in Revelation apart from the prohibition against eating pagan sacrificial food (Rev 2:14; 2:20). Some of these omissions may be due to the emphasis on the polemic against pagan Rome. In any case, free attitudes toward observances did exist in some segments of the Jewish communities, as documented by Philo (*Migr.* 89–93).

Why, then, was there tension between the *ekklēsia* and the synagogue, which both claimed to be Israel, to the effect that they mutually denied the right of the other group to carry the name? On the level of theology/ideology the reason must have been that each group made an exclusive claim to be the legitimate owner of the Jewish traditions. When the redemptive death of Jesus Christ is understood to be the constitutive foundation of the true Israel and the true Jews, then from the viewpoint of John the other Jews say that they are Jews, but are not. One aspect of this Christian self-understanding was the conviction that the new eschatological era had dawned. Correspondingly, the Jews in the synagogue would make an exclusive claim on the basis of their understanding of the constitutive elements of the people of Israel, and as a result they would be inclined to persecute members of the *ekklēsia*. Implicitly, John's formulations mean then that the synagogues in Smyrna and Philadelphia are the ones that are in the process of pursuing persecutions against the members of the *ekklēsia*, the true Jews.

Theology and ideology are interwoven with politics. Although some (many?) Jews in the synagogues were sharply critical toward Rome and the local governments, still as Jews they were a recognized group who had been given several privileges by the governmental authorities.[32] Jewish Christians must have been excluded from the synagogue, and the Christians were moving into a situation where they had to face political and legal insecurity in the gray zone between the synagogal community and the society at large.[33] The *ekklēsia* was cross-national and more inclusive than the synagogue but had to struggle with a community structure that cut across legal and social boundaries. In spite of this complex situation, the polemic between the synagogue and the *ekklēsia* was intramural, and the Christians were at this stage in history the ones who lived under the threat of persecution from the synagogal communities.

---

32. See, for example, L. L. Thompson, *The Book of Revelation: Apocalypse and Empire* (New York: Oxford Univ. Press, 1990) 133–45; E. M. Smallwood, *The Jews under Roman Rule* (Leiden: Brill, 1976) 120–43.
33. See Collins, *Crisis and Catharsis*, 85–87.

## Part Three

# Anti-Semitism and Post–New Testament Christian Writings

# -11-

# Anti-Judaism
# in the Early Church Fathers

## Lee Martin McDonald

Under such titles as *Adversus Judaeos* and *Altercatio cum Judaeo*, the early church fathers produced many harsh polemical writings against the Jewish people. The frequency and intensity of this phenomenon are accompanied by the strange contradiction of its presence in Christian literature. The vast majority of these criticisms are religious in nature—that is, they are anti-Judaistic and oppose those who followed Judaism's precepts. The criticisms are not racial in their orientation, in spite of the fact that many of the writings containing them are unusually intense even to the point of condemning the Jewish people as a whole and, in some cases, even suggesting hostilities toward the Jews. Anti-Jewish sentiment was nothing new when the church was born, but Christian anti-Judaic rhetoric was different from that of the Greco-Roman world, even though it may have been influenced by it.[1] What at times may appear in the church fathers to be a reference to race—that is, Jews being condemned as a people or nation because of their race—is most often a reference to their *religious* identity rather than to their ethnic origins. We shall see, however, that a "religious" anti-Judaism could be just as hostile and dangerous to the Jews as a bias based on race. Unfortunately, in that respect, religious anti-Judaism has not been unlike racial anti-Semitism, especially during the late patristic and medieval times. The hostilities, nevertheless, were not generally racial in nature but religious. From the church's perspective, as Marcel Simon argues, "a Jew

---

1. R. Ruether, *Faith and Fratricide: The Theological Roots of Anti-Semitism* (Minneapolis: Seabury, 1974) 22–31, is correct in saying that this may have had an influence upon the Christians' attitude toward the Jews, but it was not the driving force of Christian anti-Judaism.

215

was characterized by his religion. If he was converted, he ceased to be a Jew, and the ultimate aim [of the church] was just that, the conversion of Israel."[2] In the *Dialogue of Timothy and Aquila,* for example, after Aquila (the Jew) converted to the Christian faith and was renamed Theognostos, he was then described as one who "became the receptacle of the Holy Ghost—he who was once a Jew, but now a Christian by [the grace of] God; he who was once a wolf, but now had become Christ's sheep."[3]

There is little doubt that this "theological anti-Judaism"[4] had its origins in the New Testament writings, especially those of John, where "the Jews" are seen as those who oppose Jesus (John 5:10-18; 6:41-59; 7:1, 10-13; 8:48-59), and also Paul (Rom 11:17-30; Galatians 3–4; 1 Thess 2:14-16). The anti-Jewish comments in Paul, for example, are more focused on religious matters such as the Law, its ritual, and the failure of the Jews to convert to the Christian faith than on the Jews themselves. The later charges against the Jews for their obduracy, blindness, crimes committed against the prophets, and, finally, the crucifixion of Jesus are all part of the Christian tradition from its beginning. Notice, for instance, the charges of blindness in the Jesus tradition in Matt 23:16 (cf. Mark 12:37-40), which included judgment from God for killing the prophets (23:29-36). The charge of obduracy among the Jews is similar to the charge in Acts 28:25-29 in which the author grounds his judgment in Isa 6:9-19. The charge of deicide against the Jews by Melito of Sardis (ca. 180 CE) is not far removed from the words of Paul in 1 Cor 2:8. Rosemary R. Ruether has raised the question of whether anti-Judaism is essential to Christian theology. She contends that John gives the "ultimate theological form to that diaboliz-ing of 'the Jews' which is the root of anti-Semitism in the Christian tradition," and concludes that there is no way to eliminate anti-Judaism from Christian-ity without overhauling its christological hermeneutic.[5] The charges against the Jews in the writings of the church fathers, though similar to and often paral-lel with those in the New Testament, are intensified and expanded to include God's ultimate and final rejection of the Jews. Among some of the church fathers there appears to have been a shift from an anti-Judaic stance to one that was more anti-Jewish—that is, instead of opposing the tenets of Judaism as a means of salvation, they began to reject the Jewish people themselves.[6] In time this

---

2. M. Simon, *Verus Israel,* trans. H. McKeating (New York: Oxford Univ. Press, 1986) 398.

3. Trans. in A. L. Williams, *Adversus Judaeos* (Cambridge: Cambridge Univ. Press, 1935) 78.

4. L. Poliakov, *The History of Anti-Semitism,* trans. R. Howard (New York: Vanguard, 1962) 23, uses this term to describe what he calls the strictly "doctrinal" disputes that the church had with Judaism.

5. Ruether, *Faith and Fratricide,* 116.

6. See S. J. D. Cohen, *From the Maccabees to the Mishnah* (Philadelphia: Westminster, 1987) 46, and Simon, *Verus Israel,* 395–400 for a discussion of the terms "anti-Judaism" and "anti-Semitism." Cf. also W. Klassen, "Anti-Judaism in Early Christianity: The State of the Question," in P. Richardson and D. Granskou, eds., *Anti-Judaism in Early Christianity,* vol. 1: *Paul and the Gospels* (Waterloo, Ont.: Wilfrid Laurier Univ. Press, 1986) 5–12. As these writers show, it is unlikely that anti-Semitism was present at all in the ancient world. The racial overtones that are

led to outright hostilities against the Jews as in the case of Cyril of Alexandria (ca. 414 CE), who, after trying to rid Alexandria of Novatians, tried to get the Christians to throw the Jews out of the city.[7] In order to enlist Christians in this campaign, Cyril referred to alleged provocations by the Jews, which included the slaying of Christians.[8] Cyril's success in this venture is not known, but his language against the Jews is. He calls them "the most deranged of all men," "senseless," "blind," "uncomprehending," and "demented."[9] Or consider the writings of John Chrysostom, who accused the Jews of being "bandits," "killers of the Lord," "licentious," "possessed by demons," and so on.[10] Notice also how Tertullian argued that God's grace had ceased working among the Jews because they had despised and rejected Jesus as their Messiah with an impiety that was foretold about them in the Scriptures.[11] Although there are many negative comments about the Jews in the New Testament, one does not yet see the invective added in which the Jews are completely rejected by God and permanently replaced by the Christians.[12]

Some of the most intense Christian writers against the Jews (Aphrahat, Ephraem, Chrysostom, Cyril of Alexandria, and even Augustine of Hippo) are from the fourth and fifth centuries, when the Jews were still quite active in proselytizing Gentiles and having significant successes among the Christian population. The church stopped being a Jewish sect when it ceased practicing the Law or observing the Sabbath, and its separation from Judaism, which by all accounts was not peaceful, left many bitter feelings in its wake. By the end of the patristic era,[13] the vast amount of Christian literature that mentioned the Jews at all did so, with a few exceptions, in a negative and condemnatory manner.[14]

---

more commonly connected with modern times are almost totally absent in the rhetoric of ancient times. It was the Jewish religion and manners that were called into question by the ancient pagan world.

7. R. L. Wilken has a detailed description of the circumstances surrounding the hostilities in Alexandria in his *Judaism and the Early Christian Mind* (New Haven: Yale Univ. Press, 1971) 9–38; see also Socrates, *Hist. Eccl.* 7.7.

8. Socrates, *Hist. Eccl.* 7.13.

9. Cyril, *In Lucam*, Homily 101. This reference was supplied by Wilken, *Judaism*, 61. He lists many other examples of vituperative language in Cyril on pp. 54–68.

10. Chrysostom, *Against the Jews*, Homily 8 (*PG* 48.927–42).

11. Tertullian, *An Answer to the Jews* 13.

12. Paul understood the displacement of the Jews as a temporary matter and longed for their conversion. See Rom 11:11, 15, 23-24. Unlike Paul's understanding of a temporary rejection, see Cyprian's *Three Books of Testimonies against the Jews*, Treatise 12.

13. Its golden age extends essentially through the end of the fifth century, though it may arguably be extended to the end of the eighth century.

14. R. Wilde, *The Treatment of the Jews in the Greek Christian Writers of the First Three Centuries* (Washington, D.C.: Catholic Univ. of America Press, 1949) 80–82, 173–77, 192–98, 212–16, gives several examples of favorable comments about the Jews in the church fathers starting with Clement of Rome, the author of the *Didache*, the authors of the *Ps. Clementine Homilies* and *Recognitions*, the third-century work *Didascalia*, Clement of Alexandria, Origen, and others. From the Jewish perspective, B. Pearson, "Christians and Jews in First-century Alexandria," in G. W. E. Nickelsburg and G. W. MacRae, eds., *Christians among Jews and Gentiles* (Philadelphia: Fortress, 1986) 216, has observed that Eusebius claimed that Philo in Alexandria had not only met some

In time, and partly as a result of both the Jews' opposition to the church and their failure to convert to Christianity,[15] many of the church fathers adopted a more negative stance toward the Jews, sometimes even encouraging Christians to take hostile actions against them. An example of this can be found in the story of Ambrose, bishop of Milan (ca. 339–97), who intervened with the emperor Theodosius in order to keep the Christians from being forced to repay the Jews after destroying one of their synagogues.[16] The obvious implication drawn from Ambrose's actions was that it is acceptable to do such things to the Jews, and that is what in fact happened. Similar harsh comments can also be found in Ignatius,[17] the *Epistle of Barnabas,*[18] the *Epistle to Diognetus,*[19] Melito,[20] Tertullian,[21] Cyprian,[22] and in many other patristic writers and texts. Some of these writers (Aphrahat, Chrysostom, and Cyril) evidently had frequent contacts with the Jews and maintained dialogue with them well into the fourth and fifth centuries, even after the church had won a prominent role in the Roman Empire.[23]

---

Christians, but also "welcomed, reverenced, and recognized the divine mission of the apostolic men of his day" (*Hist. Eccl.* 2.17.2), trans. by Kirsopp Lake in LCL. This could be Eusebius's fantasy or based on some tradition handed on to him, but it does show that not all Jews were considered diabolical by the Christians. It should also be noted that these "apostolic men" were, in the words of Eusebius, "of the Hebrew origin, and thus still preserved most of the ancient customs in a strictly Jewish manner" (*Hist. Eccl.* 2.17.2). See Pearson, "Christians and Jews," 210, who adds that Alexandria was first evangelized by Christian Jews, perhaps led by Mark.

15. This view will be supported below, in the section titled "The Causes."

16. When the Christians in Callinicum in Asia, led by their bishop, burned down a Jewish synagogue, the local governor required them to rebuild the synagogue at the bishop's own expense. Ambrose, upon hearing of that decision, appealed the sentence to the emperor, Theodosius the Great, and publicly refused him communion until he reversed the governor's sentence. See Ambrose, *Ep.* 40 and 41. The story is described in J. Parkes, *The Conflict of the Church and the Synagogue* (Cleveland: World, 1961) 166–68.

17. In his criticisms against the (probably Christian) Judaizers in the church, Ignatius also condemns Judaism as a whole. See his *Magn.* 8–10 and *Phld.* 5–6.

18. In chaps. 2–3 Barnabas condemns Jewish practices, and in 4:6-8 he claims that God's covenant with the Jews has been passed on to the Christians because of the Jews' sins of idolatry. Again in 6:6-8 he argues that God has rejected the Jews.

19. In chaps. 3–4 the unknown author of this letter tries to show the foolishness of the Jewish practices and how the Christians avoid the "general silliness and deceit and fuzziness and pride of the Jews" (4:6).

20. See his *Peri Pascha* (lines 732–47) in which Melito condemns the Jews for their failure both to obey the Lord (Jesus) and to accept him as Lord, as well as for their having dashed him to the ground. As a consequence of these crimes, he claims, they themselves are dead, that is, rejected by the Lord. In lines 259–79 he says that Israel, the once chosen people of God, has now been superseded by the church and the Law by the gospel. See S. G. Wilson, "Melito and Israel," in S. G. Wilson, ed., *Anti-Judaism in Early Christianity,* vol. 2: *Separation and Polemic* (Waterloo, Ont.: Wilfrid Laurier Univ. Press, 1986) 88–89.

21. In his *Adv. Marc.* 2.19.1, he says that the Law was laid down by God not because of God's hardness, contra Marcion's view, but because of the hardness of the Jews. As a result, God has punished the Jews (*Adv. Marc.* 3.23.1 ff.) and wiped out their observances (5.4.1ff.).

22. Cyprian, *Test.*

23. Simon, *Verus Israel,* 138–41, 144–45, 202–33, argues this point convincingly.

Several recent scholars advocate the position that modern anti-Semitism and the ideology that has supported the persecutions of the Jews, including the modern European Holocaust, have their roots in the writings of the early church fathers.[24] Others strongly disagree.[25] Scholars of the *adversus Judaeos* tradition also disagree over whether there was Jewish culpability precipitating this negative rhetoric from the early Christian community,[26] but there is little question that something terrible happened in the vituperative exchange that seriously affected the vitality and character of Christianity.

Because of the enormous amount of literature involved in this field of inquiry, we will of necessity have to limit our focus to just a few samples, most of which will simply be referenced in the footnotes with the hope that those with a more serious interest in this subject will examine them more critically than is allowable here. We will, however, focus on some of the more important characteristics of anti-Judaism and the likely causes for its emergence in the church fathers. Before examining the Christian side of this polemic, however, we will look briefly at the Greco-Roman anti-Jewish rhetoric, which will help bring some of our discussion into sharper focus. Finally, even though a study of the Jewish Christians and how they related to Judaism in the first and second centuries is important, we do not have sufficient space to deal with that issue here. It should be stressed, however, that they were the clear losers in the church's debate with Judaism since both the gentile Christian community and the Judaistic communities rejected them as heretics.[27]

---

24. J. Parkes, *Judaism and Christianity* (Chicago: Univ. of Chicago Press, 1948) 139 and 167, makes the Christian church ultimately responsible for the Holocaust because of its religious anti-Semitism; see also Ruether, *Faith and Fratricide,* 223–25, and A. T. Davies's introduction to *Anti-Semitism and the Foundations of Christianity* (New York: Paulist, 1979) xiii–xvii.

25. Simon, *Verus Israel,* 397, presents important objections to identifying the Christian anti-Judaic tradition with the anti-Semitism of Hitler and also rejects Christian responsibility for the atrocities at Auschwitz, which were profoundly racial.

26. See R. L. Wilken, "Judaism in Roman and Christian Society," *JR* 47 (1967) 327–28, who argues that the Christian polemic did not occur in a vacuum and that the Jews were actively involved in the issues that provoked this response. So also Simon, *Verus Israel,* 139–41, contends that the Christian anti-Judaic literature did not emerge fighting a corpse, but a very live opponent and that the fighting was fierce between the two groups, even in the first century. He asks how Christians could "ever conceive the idea of directing these [anti-Jewish] treatises against the Jews if they had not on some occasions had experience of attacks from that quarter" (p. 138). Ruether, *Faith and Fratricide,* 31, in contrast, puts the blame squarely on the Christians' shoulders. This will be explored further in the next section.

27. An excellent discussion of this subject is found in T. Callan, *Forgetting the Root: The Emergence of Christianity from Judaism* (New York: Paulist, 1986), who follows the history of Jewish Christians, their theology, and their treatment through the first four centuries. He shows how earliest gentile Christianity as represented in Luke-Acts saw it as acceptable for the Jewish Christians to continue to observe the Law, but that second-century church leaders and their successors rejected Judaizing Christians as a legitimate form of Christianity. At a later time the church even had laws passed to prevent Christians from observing the Jewish Law and practicing circumcision (see pp. 66–71).

## Anti-Jewish Rhetoric in the Greco-Roman World

Long before the birth of Jesus, anti-Jewish bias in the Greco-Roman world was around in such places as Alexandria, Egypt, and Rome, but that anti-Jewish rhetoric was different from that which later appeared in the writings of the early church fathers. The Greco-Roman anti-Jewish writers focused more on the separation of the Jews from the rest of society and what to them seemed to be the strange religious practices of the Jews—for example, circumcision, dietary regulations, and Sabbath keeping.

Herod the Great had a very positive effect upon Jewish relations with Rome because of his astutely made and shifted alliances, but before Herod and even before Pompey's conquest of Judaea in 63 BCE, many Jews were already long-time residents of Rome, and their religion was accepted not only there but also throughout the empire as a *religio licita,* an authorized, and therefore tolerated, religious corporation. The Jews were exempted from military service, were allowed to redirect some of their taxes to Jerusalem for the maintenance of the Temple, and were given a number of other privileges. Jealousy and bitterness arose from other residents of the empire as a result of these and other concessions made to the Jews by the Romans. William Klassen suggests that "exemption from military service, relaxation of taxes, special laws, temple tax protected by Rome as it made its way to Jerusalem, interdiction of intermarriage, all of these are bound to bring strong feelings of antagonism from those who do not belong to the group."[28] The rub seems to have come when the Jews requested citizenship in the empire; because the Jews neither served in the military nor paid the same taxes, other subjects of the empire became jealous and even hostile toward them. Bernard Lazare lists several other Jewish privileges and concludes that because of them the Jews had an unfair advantage over the rest of the population and thus incurred both jealousy and hatred from their neighbors.[29] The Jews were also frequently criticized not only for their antisocial behavior and strange religious practices but also because of their alleged beggarly manners,[30] and reports circulated that they would try almost anything to make a living, including the use of magic and fortune-telling.[31] These criticisms came mainly from Rome, where many Jews evidently were among the lower classes. The Romans also frequently criticized the Jewish practice of circumcision,[32] but this did not take center stage in their litany of complaints.

---

28. See Klassen, "Anti-Judaism," 11–12.

29. Bernard Lazare, *Anti-Semitism: Its History and Causes* (London: Briton's Publishing Co., 1967) 9–12.

30. E.g., Juvenal, Satires 1.3.10–16, 296; 5.14.96–106.

31. Cf. Juvenal, Satires 2.6.542–47, who offers the criticism that "Jews sell for small change any kinds of dreams you like."

32. See Tacitus, *Hist.* 5.1–13. After describing some of their practices, Tacitus concludes, "The rest of their customs, evil and disgusting, have gained ground from their depravity. For all the riff-raff who scorned their native religions used to bring to them their tribute and their offerings;

Hatred and ridicule of the Jews were commonplace in the Roman Empire,[33] but still the Jewish privileges remained intact in the empire for hundreds of years until the legislations of Theodosius the Great (379–95), who acted against the Jews under pressure from the Christians. Until then, Jewish privileges were only briefly suspended during the reign of Hadrian (135 CE). In spite of the anti-Jewish uprisings that took place in Alexandria (ca. 37–40 CE) and the trouble leading to the expulsion of the Jews from Rome in 139 BCE, in 19 CE, and again in 48–49 CE,[34] including the Jewish revolts in Palestine in 66–73 CE and in 132–35 CE, the Jews' rights as a *religio licita* were not revoked until after the Christian triumph in the empire in the late fourth and fifth centuries.[35]

Another often-overlooked factor leading to anti-Jewish sentiment in the Roman Empire is the fact that from 100 BCE until sometime after 400 CE, the Jews were fervent in their missionary zeal, proselytizing many to their faith.[36] They established synagogues all over the Mediterranean world, including the one at Sardis, the largest and most impressive synagogue ever discovered in the ancient world. One of the reasons for both a fear and a hatred of the Jews was the success of their missionary work in the empire. According to W. H. C. Frend, the Jews in the first century BCE and CE were "the single most vital religious movement in the Greco-Roman world."[37] He points out that Jewish proselytizing had also been a cause for concern in Rome leading to the unpopularity of the Jews; further, he states that many of those who opposed the Jews on account of their religion had wives who had converted to Judaism![38] It was this

---

as a result the fortunes of the Jews prospered, also because among themselves there is unswerving loyalty, ready compassion, but hostility and hatred toward all others. Eating apart, sleeping separately, though a people most prone to lechery, they abstain from sexual relations with women of another race; among themselves nothing is banned. They have instituted circumcision of the genitals, in order to be recognized by the difference" (M. Whittaker, trans., *Jews and Christians: Graeco-Roman Views* [Cambridge: Cambridge Univ. Press, 1984] 22). It should perhaps be noted that the Jews were not the only, or even the first, ancient people to practice circumcision. Its practice was known among the Egyptians long before the time of Abraham.

33. For a detailed discussion of these anti-Jewish comments, see Wilde, *Treatment of the Jews,* 32–77. He argues that Jewish exclusiveness was the chief reason for opposition to the Jews (see p. 75). See also Lazare, *Anti-Semitism,* 8–9, who argues that the causes of anti-Semitism have always resided with the Jews because of their exclusiveness and exclusionist practices.

34. Suetonius, *Claud.* 5.25.4, writes: "Since the Jews constantly made disturbances at the instigation of Chrestus, he [Claudius] expelled them from Rome" (trans. in LCL). For the sake of Jewish-Christian relations, this is probably a very important text. Whether "Chrestus" here is to be identified with Jesus Christ may be debated, yet for our purposes, this reference indicates the kind of controversies the Jews were sometimes drawn into and that, in this case, led to their expulsion from Rome.

35. See Wilde, *Treatment of the Jews,* 28–31, for a listing of the various Roman privileges granted to the Jews, which included the full practice of their religion without interference from Rome and their exclusion from having to work on the Sabbath as well as exclusion from military service. Parkes, *Conflict,* 379–91, lists the large number of legislations against the Jews that began after Christianity's triumph in the empire. See also Wilken, "Judaism," 323–24, for a summary of Christian legislation against the Jews.

36. For a detailed support of this claim see Simon, *Verus Israel,* 271–301.

37. W. H. C. Frend, *The Rise of Christianity* (Philadelphia: Fortress Press, 1984) 42.

38. Ibid., 41–42. See also 52 n. 135.

continuing growth in the numbers of adherents to Judaism that led Cicero to charge that "the practice of their [Jewish] sacred rites was at variance with the glory of our empire, the dignity of our name and the customs of our ancestors" (*Flaccus* 28.69), and consequently he urged that they be resisted. Shaye J. D. Cohen has correctly observed that regardless of these feelings about the Jews, and in spite of their separationist policies, the Jews were still quite zealous to receive and retain gentile converts.[39] The Jews were also known for worshiping in one of the most important structures in the ancient world. The Herodian Temple in Jerusalem was famous throughout the empire, and Herod himself was one of the most accomplished architects and builders of his day. The Jews were a highly visible people, but were both hated and feared because of their growing influence in the empire. It was his fear over this concern that led Dio Chrysostom to advise his readers that "as everybody else does, keep clear of the Jews."[40] Nevertheless, they had many admirers and were respected because of their monotheism, rejection of images, sense of family, and refusal to commit infanticide of unwanted babies.[41]

By and large the pagan world mistrusted and ridiculed the Jews, and such writers as Cicero, Juvenal, Martial, Galen, Tacitus, Manetho of Egypt, Seneca, Suetonius, Ovid, Plutarch, and Marcus Aurelius had little good to say about them.[42] Their criticisms show the widespread disdain for the Jews in the Greco-Roman world. Often the criticisms demonstrate ignorance of both the origins and the actual religious practices of the Jews,[43] which, of course, indicates the lack of close personal contact that these ancient critics had with the Jewish people. We can conclude that that lack of exposure may not have been entirely the Romans' fault. In this regard it is helpful to consider the following comments by Juvenal on the Jews:

> Some who have had a father who reveres the Sabbath, worship nothing but the clouds, and the divinity of the heavens [a reference to the Jews' refusal to worship idols, the sky, the earth, or anything tangible], and see no difference between eating

---

39. Cohen, *From the Maccabees to the Mishnah*, 49. He also discusses what it meant to convert to Judaism during that period, namely, circumcision, baptism, and sacrifice (pp. 50–54).

40. Dio Chrysostom, *Corpus Papyrorum Judaicorum* 152.23–25 (ca. 105–10 CE).

41. Tacitus, *Hist.* 5.1–13, states that "they take measures for the increase of the population for it is criminal to kill any of their children." Similarly, Hecataeus (ca. 300 BCE), cited by Diodorus (ca. 60 BCE) in his *World History* 4.3.8–9, claims that Moses "obliged the inhabitants [of Judaea] to rear their children."

42. For examples of this, see Wilken, "Judaism," 315–17, for a summary of the pagan objections to the Jews. For further reading, see also R. Marcus, "Antisemitism in the Hellenistic Roman World," in Koppel S. Pinson, ed., *Essays on Antisemitism* (New York: Conference on Jewish Relations, 1946) 61–78; J. N. Sevenster, *The Roots of Pagan Anti-Semitism in the Ancient World* (Leiden: Brill, 1975); Poliakov, *History of Anti-Semitism*, 3–13; and Lazare, *Anti-Semitism*, 9–28.

43. M. Whittaker, *Jews and Christians*, 16–130, has a number of examples of this. She shows that Plutarch (*Quaest. Conv.* 4.4.4–5.3) was aware of the Jews' avoidance of pork but that he missed altogether the reason for it. Dio Cassius (150–235 CE) in his *History of Rome* (37.16–17) also shows little awareness of the origins and way of life of the Jews, but that does not stop him from ridiculing them.

swine's flesh, from which their father abstained, and that of man [a reference to the Jews' abstinence from eating pork]; and in time they take to circumcision. Having been wont to flout the laws of Rome, they learn and practise and revere the Jewish Law, and all that Moses handed down in his secret tome, forbidding to point out the way to any not worshipping the same rites [a probable reference to the inhospitable practices of Jews toward Gentiles], and conducting none but the circumcised to the desired fountain [a possible reference to baptism, but also possibly a reference to their failure to help persons find the basic necessities of life, namely, water, if they were not Jewish]. For all which the father was to blame, who gave up every seventh day to idleness, keeping it apart from all the concerns of life.[44]

Interestingly, the Christians rejected many of the Greco-Roman criticisms since they also applied to them. They too refused to intermarry with pagans and to sacrifice to the pagan gods, and so the Christians raised arguments against the Jews of a different sort than did the Romans. The Christians were far more knowledgeable of the Jewish origins, practices, and Scriptures than were the Romans; hence, unlike the Romans, the Christians called into question the Jewish inheritance as the people of God, their ability to interpret their own Scriptures, their method of interpretation, and even their future as the people of God.[45] They claimed as their own the antiquity and traditions of the Jews as the people of God, including the prophets, who were called believers in Christ and were appropriated into the Christian tradition. Ignatius of Antioch, for instance, claims that the "prophets also do we love, because they have announced the Gospel, and are hoping in him [Christ] and waiting for him, by faith in whom they also obtain salvation, being united with Jesus Christ, for they are worthy of love and saints worthy of admiration, approved by Jesus Christ, and numbered together in the Gospel of the common hope."[46] It was taught that the Scriptures themselves became the sole possession of the Christians because only they could properly understand them, and their fulfillment was only found in Christ.[47] According to Justin, the Christians had become the "true spiritual Israel" because the Jews had despised and forsaken the law of God and God's holy covenant and had hardened their hearts, refusing to see and perceive the will of God given to them through the prophets.[48] He and many other Christian writers, starting with the writer of the Gospel of John (see 8:29-41a), argue from the example of

---

44. Juvenal, Satires 5.14.96–101; trans. G. G. Ramsay (LCL; Cambridge, Mass.: Harvard Univ. Press, 1950).

45. See Origen, *In Lib. Jud. Hom.* 8.2 (GCS 7.510, 14).

46. Ignatius, *Phld.* 5.2; trans. K. Lake, *Apostolic Fathers* (LCL; Cambridge, Mass.: Harvard Univ. Press, 1912) 1.243 n. 1. Lake proposes that "prophets" in this text is a reference to the Christian prophets, for example, Hermas and the author of the Didache, but his view neither squares with the context of Ignatius nor makes historical sense of the passage. The Old Testament prophets are clearly in view here.

47. Clement of Alexandria, *Strom.* 6 (c.3), 28.1

48. Justin, *Dial.* 11, 12.

Abraham for the inclusion of the Gentiles and for the exclusion of the Jews.[49]
Earlier, in Rom 11:25-27, Paul spoke of a temporary situation in Israel that allowed for the inclusion of the Gentiles and maintaining the Jews as the elect
people of God. He used the example of Abraham in Gal 3:6-9, 13-14 and Rom
4:1-18 not to exclude the Jews, but to include the Gentiles. In time, however,
the inclusion of the Gentiles was viewed as taking place in conjunction with the
exclusion of the Jews. Jeffrey Siker has noted similarly that Deut 7:1-6 was used
by the Jews as a way of including the Jews and excluding the Gentiles.[50] Justin
Martyr, however, is the first writer in the church to argue specifically that the
Christians are the "true spiritual Israel" and have replaced the Jews.[51]

Both William Klassen and J. N. Sevenster have shown that the roots of
anti-Judaism in the ancient world, beginning with Hecataeus from the fourth
century BCE, had primarily to do with the Jewish exclusionistic practices and
their privileges in the empire.[52] In terms of pagan anti-Semitism, it was the
Jewish separatist policies, which were so important in preserving Jewish identity
and heritage, that also caused some of the most severe persecutions of the Jews
and their failure to be understood by their ancient neighbors.[53]

Perhaps it is worth noting in passing that the Muslims also have traditionally
had a negative attitude toward the Jews. Franklin Littell has shown that the
language in the Qur'an is even harsher against the Jews than the New Testament
writings and frequently identifies the Jews as a disobedient people (Qur'an 2:88;
4:46, 52; 5:13, 60, 64, 78) who will be punished by hellfire (59:3). Also, like
Christianity's claim of supersession, it teaches that Muhammed assumed the
Jewish expectation of the coming Messiah and proclaimed himself the last and
culminating prophet (see 3:110 and 33:40).[54]

Whatever the pagan roots of anti-Semitism, Ruether correctly concludes that
the Greco-Roman anti-Jewish writings do not form the basis of Christian anti-
Judaic polemic in the church fathers. Rather, they provide at best the grounds

---

49. Cf. John 8:44 with Justin's *Dial.* 119. J. S. Siker, *Disinheriting the Jews: Abraham in Early
Christian Controversy* (Louisville, Ky.: Westminster/John Knox Press, 1991) 144-62, cites several
examples of this in second-century Christianity.

50. Siker, *Disinheriting the Jews,* 254 n. 13.

51. See *Dial.* 11; 123; 135. It is not clear that this was Paul's intention in Gal 6:18, especially in
light of his strong affirmation of the Jews as God's elect in Rom 11:28-29, but clearly Justin could
have taken that text in Galatians to justify his claim. A. J. Saldarini, in his "Jews and Christians
in the First Two Centuries: The Changing Paradigm" (paper delivered at the Society of Biblical
Literature meeting, Kansas City, November 24, 1991), sec. 89, has made this observation and added
further that both Justin and the writer of the *Epistle of Barnabas* tried to establish the identity of
Christianity in a particular interpretation of the Bible and Israel's history. According to his study,
they saw that Israel's history reached its conclusion in Jesus.

52. For other examples of pagan anti-Jewish sentiment, see Klassen's collection, which begins
before the time of Christ, in his "Anti-Judaism," 5-15. See also Sevenster, *Roots,* on whose work
Klassen relies heavily.

53. See Lazare, *Anti-Semitism,* 8-18, who surveys the pagan polemic against the Jews and
concludes that it came primarily because the Jews were exclusivist and their exclusiveness was both
political and religious.

54. F. H. Littell, *The Crucifixion of the Jews* (Macon, Ga.: Mercer Univ. Press, 1975) 31.

for the pagans of a later period to accept the Christian anti-Judaic tradition and eventually transform it into a justification for a social anti-Semitism.[55] Although it is possible that the Greco-Roman anti-Jewish rhetoric that followed the Bar Kokhba rebellion may have influenced Marcion's hatred of the Jews and Judaism, we cannot argue it convincingly. Whatever the case may be in that instance, the Christian anti-Judaic rhetoric was in no way similar to nor has it directly been responsible for the racial anti-Semitism of this century that formed the rationale for the Holocaust of the 1930s and 1940s.[56]

We will now focus on some of the characteristics of the anti-Judaic literature in the early church fathers and offer some accounting for its causes. Rather than listing it, which has already been done to a limited but quite useful degree,[57] we will focus instead on some of the characteristics, charges, and possible causes for that polemic.

## Characteristics of Christian Anti-Judaic Literature

### Types of Literature

It is not easy to classify the types of *adversus Judaeos* writings because of the constant overlapping of subject matter, tone,[58] and styles, and the fact that such literature does not strictly follow any chronological or geographical boundaries. Nevertheless, there are three primary literary genres of anti-Judaistic writings: dialogues, testimonies, and homilies. This is not to say that anti-Jewish sentiment is absent from other ancient Christian literature. On the contrary, a fair amount of it is found in antiheretical writings[59] as well as in the apologetic literature that was written mostly to the pagan community to answer their criticisms of Christian faith.[60] All three genres are filled with Old Testament citations pri-

---

55. Ruether, *Faith and Fratricide*, 30–31.

56. Simon, *Verus Israel*, 397–402. This is not, however, to remove appropriate guilt from Christians who have wrongfully persecuted Jews from the time of the Christian triumph over the empire.

57. See, for example, Williams, *Adversus Judaeos*; Simon, *Verus Israel*; Parkes, *The Conflict*; and Wilde, *The Treatment of the Jews*. There is as yet no complete listing of anti-Jewish rhetoric in early Christian literature. Ruether, *Faith and Fratricide*, 117–82, though not a chronological approach to this literature, nevertheless gives an excellent representative digest of its content; on pp. 181–82 she gives a helpful table of abbreviations of the works she has cited. Her treatment of both the Jewish and the Christian sides of this issue is not balanced, however, and diminishes the value of her work on the subject.

58. Both negative and positive statements are made about the Jews in the same writing; this is true of Origen, who both condemns the Jews (*In Jerem. Hom.* 9.2) and yet calls for their conversion (*In Jerem. Hom.* 5). He also defends the Jews before Celsus, yet later condemns them in the five books of *Contra Celsum*. Compare his defense of the Jews in 1.14-16, which includes flattering them, with his condemnation of them later in 4.73 and 5.8.

59. E.g., Tertullian's writings against Marcion (*Adversus Marcionem*) have more negative comments about the Jews than do his *Adversus Judaeos* treatises.

60. Cf. Origen's *Contra Celsum* and Justin's *First Apology*.

marily from the Prophets, but also from other parts of the Old Testament (or Hebrew Bible) and the New Testament writings. This scriptural prooftexting supports two dominant themes—that Jesus is the Messiah of God and that Israel is both stubborn and blind for not recognizing it. The themes against the Jews appear to have a twofold purpose. First, and to a much lesser degree, they are a call for the Jews to convert to Christianity. This was a special theme of the dialogues, which continued in the church not only through the end of the fourth century with Evagrius, but well into the Middle Ages.[61] Because of the vindictive nature of most of these writings and the imbalance in the presentation of the arguments—that is, the Jews never get equal time and the Christians always win—it is doubtful whether many Jews were convinced and converted by their arguments, though, as Simon suggests, it is possible that many Hellenistic Jews were converted as a result of this method of argumentation.[62]

In the dialogues, the Jew, who is always an orthodox Jew except in the case of Justin's Trypho, is always a facilitator for the Christian's superior argument and seldom presents unanswerable questions to the Christian, as would probably have taken place if an actual dialogue had occurred. With almost endless biblical citations and repetitious arguments, the dialogues purport to describe actual debates or interactions with Jews, who are generally convinced by the overwhelming evidence of the Christian presenter and are persuaded to convert to Christianity. Seldom does the Jew go away without converting, except in the case of Trypho in Justin's *Dialogue*. It is more likely that the dialogues were written as an encouragement and admonition to the Christians. They encouraged Christians because they presented a Christian response to some specific Jewish objections to the Christian faith, and the admonition was no doubt seen as a divine warning not only to Christians, but also to the pagan Gentiles who were tempted to convert to Judaism. That warning was a reminder of the severe judgment that awaited those who converted to Judaism. The writings have a vari-

---

61. Justin's *Dialogue* calls on the "Jews" (Trypho) to convert but without any success. This failure gives more credibility to his dialogue even though the text is not likely to have been an accurate representation of all that took place in such a dialogue. In contrast, *Prudentius* (ca. 711 CE), while purportedly calling upon the Jews to convert to Christ, is extremely negative about the Jews, and apparently Justin's vituperative language is more for Christian consumption than for the Jews themselves. Williams, *Adversus Judaeos*, 210, is correct when he states that it is often difficult to determine whether the conversion of the Jews is genuinely sought by a writer or whether the writing is designed to reassure believers that they are still the heirs of the Old Testament promises, giving them arguments against Jewish attacks. G. F. Moore, "Christian Writers on Judaism," *HTR* 14 (1921) 198, concludes that only the latter issue is at stake. He says that the conversion of the Jews is not really an issue; he contends the writings are meant to supply information to edify the Christians and to convince the Gentiles to accept the Christian faith rather than converting to Judaism. Both Ruether, *Faith and Fratricide*, 119, and Williams, *Adversus Judaeos*, in his table of contents, have a helpful listing of some of the more important and best-known dialogues.

62. Simon, *Verus Israel*, 174–76, shows that the hermeneutic employed by the church in the Hellenistic communities is precisely the kind employed by Hellenistic Judaism and would have put it at a disadvantage in answering the Christians. This may well have led to many conversions from Hellenistic Judaism, a number sufficiently large enough to get the attention and draw the criticism of the Jews, but not large enough to suggest a major turning of the Jews to the Christian faith.

ety of forms and arguments even though there is some parallel in the scriptural texts cited and the main arguments set forth, as we can see in a comparison of the dialogues between Justin and Trypho, Timothy and Aquila, and Athanasius and Zacchaeus. Although the dialogues, which Amos B. Hulen calls "argumentative" literature,[63] appear to be Christian attempts to answer Jewish objections to the Christian faith, their authenticity is questioned by most patristic scholars.

While it is true that in the dialogues the Jew is generally a "man of straw," as Moore claims,[64] it is nevertheless inappropriate to conclude, as does Ruether, that the Jews are "almost useless as sources for what Jews might actually have said about Christianity."[65] Simon is on more sure ground when he grants that even though the Jew "cuts a poor figure" in the dialogues, this genre nevertheless presents a fairly reliable record of the kinds of arguments that the Jews brought against Christianity.[66] The dialogues' primary value for research today lies in the issues they address, which were most likely brought forward by the Jews in their contacts with the Christians. In seeking to answer the Jewish objections, the dialogues not only offer Christianity's alternative to Judaism through their claims about Jesus as the true Messiah, but they also give insights into the hermeneutic employed by early Christian writers. Hulen says that the objections to the Christian faith that the dialogues answer are real objections and have parallels in the talmudic literature.[67] He has also observed that, with the exception of the dialogues of Justin and "The Controversy between Jason and Papiscus," the latter of which is known only in a few citations and both of which come from the second century, the rest associate themselves with the names of persons primarily from the fourth century, but also much later.[68]

We should note in passing that the dialogue genre was not unique to the Christian community, but as Wilde has shown, there is widespread evidence of its use some five centuries before the time of Christ, including in the writings of Plato and Cicero.[69]

The treatises, of which the *testimonia* are the most common genre, offer another important example of polemical literature against the Jews. Cyprian, for example, cites Isa 1:2-4 to speak of the Lord's indignation with the Jews. After pronouncing woes upon them, he concludes: "In condemnation of these [Jews] we Christians say, when we pray, 'Our Father,' because He now has begun to be ours and has ceased to be of the Jews who have forsaken Him."[70] Tertullian also uses this form of polemic, and, while citing many Old Testa-

---

63. A. B. Hulen, "The 'Dialogues with the Jews' as Sources for the Early Jewish Argument against Christianity," *JBL* 51 (1932) 58.

64. Moore, "Christian Writers on Judaism," 198.

65. Ruether, *Faith and Fratricide*, 120.

66. Simon, *Verus Israel*, 139–43.

67. Hulen, "Dialogues," 64.

68. Ibid., 64–65.

69. Wilde, *Treatment of the Jews*, 106.

70. Cyprian, "The Lord's Prayer," in Treatise 10.

ment and New Testament texts to support his positions, he argues that since
the Jews have failed to recognize the true Christ (Jesus), they should at least
recognize their own demise, "a fate which they were constantly foretold [in the
Scriptures] as destined to incur after the advent of the Christ, on account of
the impiety with which they despised and slew him." Further, Tertullian claims
that as a result of the Jews' rejection of Christ, "God's grace desisted [from
working] among them."[71] Typical of this type of literature is the treatise that
appears in either epistolary form, as in the case of the *Epistle of Barnabas,* or
in a doctrinal exposition, as in the case of Tertullian's *An Answer to the Jews*
(*Adversus Judaeos*). Cyprian and pseudo-Gregory of Nyssa typify the *testimonia*
genre, but both types include large collections of biblical texts that focus on the
controversies addressed.[72]

The homilies present one of the strongest forms for condemning the Jews.
The homilies of Aphrahat, Chrysostom, and Ephraem, for example, are typical of the most severe expressions of this genre. Aphrahat (ca. 290–350), who
became the bishop on the Persian side of the Tigris River (ca. 335), wrote
twenty-three homilies between 336–45 in response to an unknown inquirer. Although he appeals to the Jews directly on occasion,[73] he is primarily concerned
to strengthen the Christians with arguments to answer the criticisms of the Jews
against their faith. In his nineteenth homily he concludes that the Jews' hope for
restoration (salvation) is mistaken. In his twenty-first homily he argues that as
Sodom is not yet restored, so Jerusalem cannot be restored. A. Lukyn Williams
has observed that Aphrahat seems less interested in converting the Jews than
in giving his people arguments likely to be useful in a controversy with them.[74]
Simon notes that these sermons reveal a remarkable awareness of rabbinic methods of argumentation, "in spite of the blast they deliver against Judaism"; this
awareness strongly suggests actual contact between the Christians and the Jews
of Aphrahat's day.[75] Jacob Neusner has pointed out that Aphrahat seldom cited
the New Testament writings and tended to refer to the Hebrew Scriptures; these
references did not involve fanciful or allegorical interpretations of the passages
cited but rather involved interpretations that rested on rational arguments and
historical facts.[76]

Chrysostom's homilies against the Jews are even more intense than those
of Aphrahat and reveal not only the Christians' regular contact with the Jews,
but also betray the church's fear that Judaism presented a viable and perhaps

---

71. Tertullian, *Adversus Judaeos* 13.

72. Simon, *Verus Israel,* 140, lists these and other kinds of Christian anti-Jewish literature.

73. E.g., Aphrahat, *Homilies* 12.7; 17.1; 21.1–7.

74. Williams, *Adversus Judaeos,* 95–102, has a helpful description of the Aphrahat homilies.

75. Simon, *Verus Israel,* 141.

76. J. Neusner, *Jews and Christians: The Myth of a Common Tradition* (Philadelphia: Trinity
Press Int., 1991) 71. Neusner has an excellent analysis of the context of Aphrahat's discussion
of the relationship between Judaism and Christianity and the kind of arguments he used in the
polemic (see pp. 70–73).

a more attractive alternative to the church in the fourth century. Chrysostom shows no sympathy for the Jews in his sermons and offers no hope of salvation for them. He speaks contemptuously and in condemnatory fashion when he discusses the Jews. As Simon explains, the details of Chrysostom's sermons give one the impression that the homilies "have every reason to be considered as the products of real live controversy."[77]

Ephraem the Syrian, in his poetic fashion, also clearly uses the homily to strongly condemn the Jews for killing the Messiah. He castigates the Jews because by them "Baal was honored by sacrifices, and the Messiah was persecuted by the impure. Bats and ghosts were worshiped in her [Israel's] chamber, and He, on whose nod the earth hangs, was smitten with palms in the streets."[78]

Throughout the treatises and sermons there is a strong note of condemnation that is seldom coupled with a call for the conversion of the Jews. Ruether is quite correct in asking why the *adversus Judaeos* writings, while not denying specifically that the Jews can be saved, seem to ignore that as a possibility and instead focus almost completely on their reprobation. She observes that both the tracts and the sermons "are remarkable for their relative lack of an appeal to the Jews for conversion."[79]

## Focus and Methodology

For the most part Christian anti-Jewish writings emphasize that (1) the Jews failed to recognize Jesus as their Messiah; (2) they did that because they are obdurate and blind—that is, unable to discern the truth from their Scriptures; (3) therefore, they are condemned and rejected by God, who has rejected their ritualistic practices; (4) therefore, they have been replaced by the church as the new people of God; and (5) as a result of the Jews' blindness and inability to understand their Scriptures, the Scriptures belong to the Christians, who alone can properly interpret them. The format for substantiating these claims involved citations of Old Testament texts interpreted primarily, though not exclusively, by an allegorical and typological hermeneutic that generally was at odds with the more literalist hermeneutic of Palestinian Judaism.

One of the major problems for the church from its inception was its need to establish its own status as a continuing religious movement of long standing and not simply something new. If the church had been viewed as a new religious phenomenon, it would have had no credibility or recognition in the eyes of the ancient world. Both Christians and Jews therefore competed before their pagan audiences for the heritage of Israel.[80] As we have already shown, Ignatius of

---

77. Ibid.

78. Ephraem the Syrian, *Rhy. C. Jud.* 15; trans. in Ruether, *Faith and Fratricide,* 127.

79. Ruether, *Faith and Fratricide,* 148.

80. A. Y. Collins, "Vilification and Self-definition in the Book of Revelation," in *Christians among Jews and Gentiles,* 314.

Antioch appropriated the prophets into the Christian tradition.[81] The church fathers concluded from God's evident rejection of the Jews, demonstrated by the destruction of their Temple and their displacement from Jerusalem, that the Christians themselves now constituted the "new Israel." The author of the *Epistle of Barnabas*, who assumes the Christians' role as the new people of God, called for the Christians as the new Israel to be faithful and warned that they too, like Israel, could suffer the rejection of God. Christians should therefore be reminded, he urged, that even after great things were done in Israel, "they were even then finally abandoned;—let us take heed lest as it was written we be found 'many called but few chosen.' "[82] Cyprian taught that since the Jews have "forsaken the Lord and blasphemed the Holy One of Israel," the Christians can now call God "our Father" because "He now has begun to be ours and ceased to be of the Jews, who have forsaken Him."[83]

The frequency of references to Old Testament texts in the church fathers is paralleled by the similarity and overlap of the texts that were used, which strongly suggests the existence of a collection (or collections) of scriptural proofs handed on in the Christian tradition as in the cases of Tertullian's *Against the Jews*, Cyprian's *Three Books of Testimonies against the Jews*, and pseudo-Gregory of Nyssa's *Selected Testimonies from the Old Testament against the Jews*.[84] Williams believes that such collections may have had their origin in Jesus himself, who showed from the Scriptures that he was the foretold Messiah and that he was to suffer and die (Luke 24:44-47).[85]

Any effective argument with the Jews, whose primary authority base was the Law, had to appeal to the Scriptures if that argument was to be considered viable. The church fathers' use of scriptural support for their claims is one of the most common features of all anti-Judaic Christian literature. The Christians' primary contention was that if the Jews would come to a proper understanding of their own Scriptures, they would see that a correct interpretation of the Bible would inevitably lead them to accept Jesus as the Messiah and to convert to Christianity.[86]

As important as the appeal to the Scriptures was for the church fathers, their hermeneutical approach to the Scriptures was even more critical to their polemic. It was especially at this point in their polemic that Christians and Jews were divided and where they talked past each other. One of the major differences between Christianity and Judaism, the Christians taught, was the ability of the Christian to see from the Scriptures that Jesus was the Messiah of Israel.[87]

---

81. See the quote from Ignatius's *Phld.* 5.2 on p. 223 above.
82. *Barn.* 4.14; LCL trans.
83. Cyprian, "The Lord's Prayer," in Treatise 10.
84. For a discussion of this see Williams, *Adversus Judaeos*, 7–13, 124–28, 215–17.
85. Ibid., 6.
86. Simon, *Verus Israel*, 146–47, has a helpful discussion of this line of reasoning.
87. See, for example, the Christian (Timothy) in the *Dialogue of Timothy and Aquila*, who

Conversely, it was believed that the Jews' inability to draw this conclusion was irrefutable proof of their spiritual blindness and evidence for the justness of their punishment.[88] Their blindness, it was argued, was due not only to the hardness of their hearts (obduracy), but also to their bondage to the "letter of the law" (literal method of interpretation). The church further maintained that only by a "spiritual" (allegorical) interpretation of Scripture could the true revelation of God be discerned. The rabbis from the Palestinian Judaic tradition adopted a more literal interpretation of Scripture than did those Jews from the Hellenistic Judaic tradition, and it was the latter's methodology that informed and gave rise to the Christian hermeneutic.[89] In their first five centuries, the Christians characteristically, though not uniformly, used an allegorical or typological hermeneutic in their interpretation of the Scriptures. Origen contrasted the literalist hermeneutic with his own "spiritual" (or allegorical) hermeneutic and even condemned the Jews for their blindness to the truth of Scripture that resulted from their use of a literalist interpretation.[90] He believed that the Jews kept themselves from the truth by this method of interpretation[91] and that it left them both carnal and unable to praise the Lord. He further argued that the Law of Moses was divided into two parts: the spiritual part was for the Christians, who alone possess the "spiritual Law," and the carnal (literal) part was for the Jews, who were persecuting the Christians.[92] The primary error of the Jews, as the Christians put it, was their failure to recognize Jesus as the Messiah from their own Scriptures. Apparently Jesus was recognizable only by the use of allegorical and typological exegesis, but, unfortunately, such exegesis is controlled by only the imagination of the interpreter and offers no advance in interpretation nor any means of verifying the interpreter's conclusions. Tertullian illustrates this "spiritual" approach when he interprets Cain as representing the Jews, whose sacrifice was unacceptable to God, and Abel as the church, whose

---

is asked by the Jew (Aquila) for proof from the Scriptures that Jesus is the Messiah. Timothy accommodates his request by citing numerous Old Testament texts, including Gen 28:12; 2 Sam 12:25; Deut 21:23; Isa 6:1-3 and 7:14.

88. Justin, *Dial.* 29.2; *Barn.* 4:6-7; Cyprian, "That Idols Are Not Gods," in Treatise 12.

89. Simon, *Verus Israel*, 159–62 and 174–77, has an excellent discussion of this point.

90. Origen, *Comm. in Ep. ad Rom.* 2.14 (*PG* 14.917) and *In Lib. Jud. Hom.* 18.2. See also *C. Cels.* 1.61. This allegorical approach is also defended by Justin to Trypho when he explains the necessity of a spiritual understanding of the Scriptures and then goes on to give allegorical meaning to the "second circumcision" of the Christian, which he claims was a cleansing from idolatry and every form of wickedness. The literal circumcision of the Jews, he argued, was instituted by God because of the hardness of their hearts and because of their inability to understand the will of God. For this reason God gave the Jews a bill of divorce (see *Dial.* 114). Later he explains to Trypho that if "you had understood what has been written by the prophets, you would not have denied that he [Jesus] was God, Son of the only, begotten, unutterable God" (*Dial.* 126; ANF trans.). See also his *1 Apology* 31 and 36 where Justin chides the Jews for their inability to interpret or understand the Scriptures.

91. Origen, *In Lib. Jud. Hom.* 8.2; GCS 7.510, 14.

92. Origen, *In Levit. Hom.* 6.1 (GCS 6.359.8ff.); *In Luc. Homil.* 12 (GCS 9.88.1 ff.); *Comm. in Ep. ad Rom.* 6.12 (*PG* 14.1095C). For further examples, see Wilde, *Treatment of the Jews*, 181–83.

sacrifice was acceptable to God.[93] Justin also criticizes the Jews for their literalist approach to Scripture and admonishes them about Jesus based on a typological exegesis of the story of Joshua, underscoring the "spiritual" nature of the Scriptures that alone allows one to see that the Rock (or Stone) is really a reference to Christ.[94] Simon has observed that the use of allegorical interpretation is more pronounced in contexts where the Christian is criticizing the Jewish ritual law and its rigoristic legalism that was based essentially on a literalistic, rabbinic exegesis.[95]

The Palestinian rabbis appealed to the literal interpretation of Scripture as the foundation for biblical truth, and that drew the charge from the fathers that they followed the letter of the law instead of its spirit.[96] This charge may well have originated with Paul (2 Cor 3:3-6), who himself was a user of allegory (Gal 4:21-31), but it may also have come from the tradition of Jesus (cf. Mark 7:1-13; 8:15-21; John 5:37-47). It is only much later, in the Middle Ages, that the Christians began to employ a more literal hermeneutical defense of their faith by arguing from the Hebrew text of the Old Testament and making extensive use of grammars and dictionaries. More literal approaches were found earlier in the Syrian community at Antioch represented by, among others, John Chrysostom. Aphrahat also made more use of literal interpretation to argue his views than did most of his other Christian contemporaries. The transition to a more literal hermeneutical approach was gradual, and that approach began to be used more frequently though not predominantly in the Middle Ages.[97] The allegorical hermeneutic, though conducive to the Christian proclamation in the Hellenistic world, was ultimately a poor foundation for scriptural exegesis and had little effect on the Jews from the Palestinian tradition. Ruether is correct in her observation that such exegesis "calls for extraordinary distortion of the actual meaning of the biblical texts."[98]

Perhaps it should be stressed that the patristic use of allegory to support Christian apologetics is evidence that the church's origins had more to do with an experience with the risen Christ as well as a conviction of God's call to faith in him than it had to do with an exegesis of the Scriptures. Because the Christians from their earliest beginnings recognized the authority of the Scriptures, they were logically driven to them for support of their new-found faith. In allegory and typological exegesis they found an acceptable way to make their experience

---

93. Tertullian, *Adv. Jud.* 5; Chrysostom, *Or. C. Jud.* 1.7. Ruether, *Faith and Fratricide*, 131–40, offers several illustrations of this style of exegesis in early Christian literature from, among others, Cyprian, Chrysostom, Augustine, Aphrahat, Prudentius, Maximinus, and Ephraem.

94. Justin, *Dial.* 112–14.

95. Simon, *Verus Israel*, 176–77.

96. See Origen, *Comm. in Ep. ad Rom.* 2.14 (*PG* 14.917).

97. See, for example, the *Dialogue of Petrus Alfonsi* (ca. 1100). Moore, "Christian Writers on Judaism," 201–2, also discusses this example.

98. Ruether, *Faith and Fratricide*, 140.

and their Scriptures compatible and their apologetic scripturally supportable.[99] Neusner makes the astute observation that while both Christianity and Judaism claimed to be the heir of the Hebrew Scriptures, both groups needed more than those Scriptures in order to derive authority from them. He remarks that

> the New Testament is the prism through which the light of the Old [Testament] comes to Christianity. The canon of rabbinical writings is the star that guides Jews to the revelation of Sinai, the Torah. The claim of these two great religious traditions in all their rich variety is for the veracity not merely of Scriptures, but also of Scriptures as interpreted by the New Testament or the Talmud and associated rabbinical writings.[100]

Lazare also supports this claim when he shows how that for some Jews the Hebrew Scriptures were made subordinate to the Talmud and considered less beneficial and conducive to salvation than the Mishnah. He cites as proof a reference from the Talmud that claims that "the law is water, the Mishnah is wine."[101]

By stressing the use of allegory the early Christians minimized the importance of the fact that they had received a *new* revelation of God in Christ that was not clearly discernible through any form of exegesis of their Holy Scriptures. The result of their teaching was not so much a faithful interpretation of the Scriptures,[102] but a clarification of the substance of the gospel for the world before them. Allegorical exegesis was the best available tool at their disposal to ground their arguments in the firm authoritative soil of Scripture and to justify to their hearers God's approval of their message. Whatever weaknesses may be found in this form of scriptural interpretation—and there are many— they should not be allowed to diminish or negate the Christian message that is grounded rather in the life and ministry of Jesus and the witness of the apostolic community he left behind.[103]

We should make one final but very important observation about the church's use of Scripture, namely, that its argument was frequently dependent upon the Greek translation of the Hebrew Scriptures (commonly called the Septuagint or abbreviated as the LXX), which was started in Egypt during the Ptolemaic reign of the late third century BCE and concluded in the first century BCE. This biblical text, which was used in over 90 percent of the New Testament's use of the Old Testament, was believed by the early church to be fully inspired. As the church grew and continued appeal to the LXX for support of its gospel, the Jews by and large rejected its authority and even commissioned other translations by

---

99. This manner of using Scripture is discussed in L. M. McDonald, *The Formation of the Christian Biblical Canon* (Nashville: Abingdon, 1988) 66–68.

100. J. Neusner, *Judaism in the Matrix of Christianity* (Philadelphia: Fortress, 1986) 140.

101. Lazare, *Anti-Semitism,* 13–14.

102. There are no detailed exegeses of Old Testament texts in the New Testament writings, and even the longest Old Testament text cited in the New Testament (Jer 31:31-34, cited in Heb 8:8-12) is only four verses.

103. See Irenaeus, *Adv. Haer.* 2.35.4; 3.31.1; 3.4.1, who makes this argument.

Aquila (ca. 128 CE), and later by Theodotion and Symmachus.[104] The appeals to the Hebrew text of Scripture in the translations of Origen and Jerome in the third and fifth centuries were exceptions to the norm for that time. The LXX was almost universally believed to be the inspired biblical text for the church.[105] It is only much later, during the Middle Ages, as Moore has shown, when in support of Christian apologetics the church gave more serious attention to the Hebrew text of the Scriptures and other Jewish literature.[106] Simon has suggested that the later Christian accusations that the Jews were guilty of tampering with the biblical text may, in fact, have been earlier Christian interpolations of the LXX for apologetic purposes. He adds further that this practice of altering the text may have developed when the Christians were collecting the catenae of proof texts for apologetic purposes, a process they learned from the Jews who did the same in their mission among the Gentiles.[107]

## The Charges against the Jews and Their Punishment

The church fathers frequently warned Christians against being attracted to Judaism and identifying with the Jews, who, they claimed, were blind, stubborn, and had killed Christ.[108] This warning is especially common in the fourth century homilies of Chrysostom and Aphrahat. Cataloguing the faults and crimes of the Jews became commonplace in the *adversus Judaeos* tradition. Chrysostom, in dealing with Christians who were tempted toward Judaism in the late fourth century in Antioch, asked, "Is it not absurd to be zealous about avoiding someone who sinned against mankind, but to have dealings with those who have affronted God? Is it not folly for those who worship the crucified to celebrate festivals with those who crucified him? This is not only stupid—it is sheer madness."[109] Earlier, Ignatius of Antioch (ca. 115), fearing the influence of Judaizing Christians upon gentile Christians, wrote: "If anyone interpret Judaism to you do not listen to him; for it is better to hear Christianity from the circumcised [Jews] than Judaism from the uncircumcised [probably Christian gentile Judaiz-

104. McDonald, *Formation*, 55–58.

105. The tradition about the supernatural origins of the LXX that was set forth in the *Letter of Aristeas* was generally accepted by the early Christian community (see, e.g., Eusebius *Hist. Eccl.* 5.8.11–14) and was defended by Justin, Irenaeus, Tertullian, Clement of Alexandria, Eusebius, and others. See McDonald, *Formation*, 55–58.

106. Moore, "Christian Writers on Judaism," 200–202.

107. Simon, *Verus Israel*, 153–54.

108. A good case in point is the use of Isa 6:9-10 in the church fathers. See C. A. Evans, *To See and Not Perceive: Isaiah 6:9-10 in Early Jewish and Christian Interpretation* (JSOTSup 64; Sheffield: JSOT, 1989) 147–62, who has shown the multiple use of this passage in the ante-Nicene fathers to support an anti-Jewish bias in Christian apologetic.

109. Chrysostom, *Against the Jews*, Homily 1 (*PG* 48.850). I have followed here the translation of R. L. Wilken, in W. A. Meeks and R. L. Wilken, *Jews and Christians in Antioch in the First Four Centuries of the Common Era* (Missoula, Mont.: Scholars Press, 1978) 95.

ers]. But both of them, unless they speak of Jesus Christ, are to me tombstones and sepulchres of the dead, on whom only the names of men are written."[110]

The fathers never hesitated to underscore the sins of the Jews. Whether in the dialogues, treatises, or homilies, the anti-Judaic literature accused the Jews of stubbornness of heart and blindness because of their inability to interpret their Scriptures correctly or to discern the will of God. Justin contends that the Jews "who possessed the books of the prophets did not understand, and therefore did not recognize Christ even when He came, but even hate us who say that He has come, and who prove that, as was predicted, He was crucified by them."[111] Cyprian, illustrating the dangers of jealousy, offers the Jews as a negative model, asking: "Did not the Jews perish on this account, since they preferred to envy rather than to believe in Christ? Disparaging the great things that He did, they were deceived by a blinding jealousy and they were unable to open the eyes of their hearts so as to recognize His divine works."[112]

These accusations that the Jews were blind and hard of heart were generally accompanied by the elucidation of their "trail of crimes,"[113] which not only involved their killing of the prophets (*Barn.* 5:11), becoming idolaters and law breakers, and rejecting the will of God, but also, and most importantly, involved their murder of the Christ.[114] Melito of Sardis accuses the Jews of the ultimate crime of deicide, that is, murdering God.[115] In his accusatory poetic style, he writes: "And you killed the Lord at the great feast. . . . O Lawless Israel, what is this unprecedented crime you committed, thrusting your Lord among unprecedented sufferings, your Sovereign, who formed you, who made you, who honored you, who called you 'Israel'?" (*Peri Pascha* 72–99, lines 567–84).[116] And again he asks, "And who has been murdered? Who is the murderer? I am ashamed to say and I am obliged to tell . . . the Sovereign has been insulted; the God has been murdered; the King of Israel has been put to death by an Israelite right hand!" (lines 693–716).

---

110. Ignatius, *Phld.* 6:1 (trans. from LCL).

111. Justin, *1 Apol.* 36 (ANF trans., 1.75). See also his *Dial.* 9, 39, 126. Other examples of the obduracy of the Jews are found in Irenaeus, *Adv. Haer.* 4.14.2; 4.15.2; 4.16.4; Origen, *In Isaiam. Hom.* 6.7 (GCS 8.278.3); Hippolytus, *In Deut.* 24–26; Clement of Alexandria, *Paed. 1* (col. 5) 19.4. For examples of their blindness and inability to interpret their Scriptures, see Irenaeus, *Adv. Haer.* 4.17.2; Origen, *In Lib. Jud. Hom.* 18.2.

112. Cyprian, "Jealousy and Envy," Treatise 5 (trans. R. J. Deferrari [New York: Fathers of the Church, 1958] 36.297).

113. Ruether, *Faith and Fratricide,* 124ff., uses this term to describe the catalogue of offenses the church claimed were perpetuated by the Jews.

114. Justin, *Dial.* 98, 141; Irenaeus, *Adv. Haer.* 4.18.4, recognizes that this was in the plan of God, but that does not excuse the Jews from culpability. See also his *Demonst.* 95; Hippolytus, *In Prov.* 1.11; *In Gen.* 49.6. Ruether, *Faith and Fratricide,* 124–31, lists a "catalogue of crimes" with several examples of the primary charges against the Jews.

115. Although Melito is the first of the fathers to accuse the Jews of killing "God," this is not too far removed from Paul's accusation in 1 Cor 2:8 and is a logical deduction from the developing Christology in the second century.

116. Trans. in Wilson, "Melito and Israel," 2.91–92.

The punishment for these crimes, which was explained fairly consistently in the church fathers, was not only the rejection of the Jews, along with their practices of circumcision and the various rituals of the Law,[117] but also their replacement by the church, which was now made up of all nations.[118] The fathers disagreed, however, on whether the rejection of the Jews was temporary or final. Although Origen frequently listed the crimes of the Jews and their deserved punishment from God for them, he could not imagine the plan of God being complete without their conversion.[119] In contrast, Chrysostom, in his homilies, seems to have accepted the rejection of the Jews as final and does not leave any hope for their conversion. In his Homily 3, on 1 Thess 2:14-16, he describes their sin of persecuting the prophets and killing Jesus and concludes that "our persecutors are to be punished. And if the delay is a grievance, let it be a consolation that they will never lift up their heads again."[120] Isidore of Spain (ca. 530–636), while admittedly seeking the conversion of the Jews, nevertheless argues that their evil nature never changes. His evaluation of Jer 13:23 leads him to conclude that the Jews cannot change (*C. Jud.* 1.18). Eusebius also seems to conclude that God's rejection of the Jews is irrevocable (*D.E.* 1.1). Augustine likewise precluded the Jews, as Jews—that is, while living under Judaism—from finding God's salvation (*C.D.* 18.46; 20.29). For Aphrahat, the entire Jewish nation, the "entire branch," was given over to destruction by God (*Dem.* 23.20).

## The Causes

What factors led to the strong anti-Jewish bias in early Christian literature that has continued to influence Christian thought well into the current century? The most obvious reasons for the separation of the two religious communities were a difference in their understanding of the person of Jesus and a difference in their understanding of the nature and role of the Torah. From the very beginnings of the Christian movement, the Jews stumbled over the notion of a crucified Messiah (1 Cor 1:23), and that did not change with time.[121] The chris-

---

117. E.g., Ignatius, *Magn.* 9:1-2; *Ep. Diog.* 3, 4; Origen, *In Ex. Hom.* 5:1; *In Joh. Comm.* 10:24; *In Num. Comm.* 23:1.

118. According to Justin, the Holy Spirit and all of the gifts of the Spirit now belong to the Christians (*Dial.* 82, 87); this includes the Jews' Scriptures (*1 Apol.* 1.28; cf. also Clement of Alexandria, *Strom.* 6.28.1, and Irenaeus, *Demonstr.* 95, 99; *Adv. Haer.* 4.6.1; 4.7.4; 4.18.4) and their antiquities (Justin, *Dial.* 11, 119, 135, 139). Irenaeus emphasizes that the church has become the "new Israel" (*Adv. Haer.* 4.8.1, and *Demonstr.* 95).

119. Origen, *In Jerem. Hom.* 5 (GCS 3.31.26–28); *In Rom. Comm.* 8:9 (*PG* 14.1187B).

120. Trans. from NPNF 23.334. In one passage on Eph 2:14, however, Chrysostom seems to acknowledge that a Jew can become a Christian, thereby ceasing to be a Jew and becoming one who is now "united to the Gentile when he becomes a believer" (see *Ephesians,* Homily 5 [NPNF 23.73]).

121. In Justin, *Dial.* 10.3, Trypho objects to the Christians' hope of the blessing of God because they were "resting their hopes on a man that was crucified." Justin overcomes that objection with

tological formulations about Jesus, namely, that he was Lord and Christ, were also considered incompatible with the Jewish understanding of the person and role of the Messiah.[122] It was also impossible for the Jews to square the gentile Christian attitude toward the Law with their own understanding of Torah and the responsibility of living within God's covenant.[123] All of this, of course, makes the eventual separation of Christianity from Judaism seem inevitable, even though a significant number of Jewish Christians who were called Ebionites, Elkasaites, Cerinthians, and Nazoreans did not see that as necessary.[124] It is hard to imagine how the two groups could have stayed together long given their differences on these major issues, but this still does not account for the level of vindictive rhetoric and eventual hostilities that existed between them nor for their negative preoccupation with each other for hundreds of years.[125] Wilken, Simon, and Moore have correctly observed that the *adversus Judaeos* literature did not occur in a vacuum, but in the context of a vigorous debate that continued between Jews and Christians for centuries.[126] But what moved the relations from debate to open hostilities?

## The Failure of the Jews to Convert to Christianity

There were three major expectations of the early Christians that did not materialize in the way they had hoped: (1) that Jesus would soon return to the earth

---

an argument on the resurrection and the second advent of Jesus (see 32.1–3). For a more complete discussion of this and also for the possibility of a suffering Messiah in Jewish theology, see Simon, *Verus Israel,* 158–59, and 461 nn. 14–16.

122. A. F. Segal, *Rebecca's Children: Judaism and Christianity in the Roman World* (Cambridge, Mass.: Harvard Univ. Press, 1986) 154–60, and Lazare, *Anti-Semitism,* 31, stress the importance of Christology as a significant factor in the separation of Christianity from Judaism, even though it does not take the prominent place in the polemic, as Simon, *Verus Israel,* 157, correctly observes. David Flusser's discussion of the problem that a high or divine Christology posed for Judaism is worth careful consideration. See his *Judaism and the Origins of Christianity* (Jerusalem: Magnes, 1988) 620–25, in which he stresses that even those Jews who were prepared to accept Jesus' messiahship were less prepared to accept him as the divine Son of God.

123. Segal, *Rebecca's Children,* 143, 156, 161.

124. The best source for determining the theology of early Jewish Christianity is, of course, the New Testament—e.g., Matthew, James, Hebrews—but one should also consider the *Didache.* Callan, *Root,* 40–43, argues that John's Gospel comes from a conservative Jewish Christianity. These groups of Jewish Christians survived the first century but were clearly in the minority of the Christian community in the second century. The fourth-century Clementine *Homilies and Recognitions,* which depend on the late second-century *Preaching of Peter,* provide us with the best post–second-century understanding of conservative Jewish Christianity. Those are the Jewish Christians who eventually survived the first century, but their theological stance is much debated. Most agree that their christological formulations were incompatible with gentile orthodox positions on the divinity of Jesus. See Callan, *Root,* 27–52 and 65–66, for a summary of the Jewish-Christian theological stance.

125. Notice in the *Didascalia Apostolorum* 5.14.23 (third century) that the chief reason for celebrating Easter was not only to observe the passion of Jesus, but also "to obtain forgiveness for the guilty and unfaithful Jews."

126. Wilken, "Judaism," 327. Simon, *Verus Israel,* 135–41, and Moore, "Christian Writers on Judaism," 197ff., also agree.

and establish his kingdom, (2) that the city of Jerusalem would become the religious capital for the Christian faith, and (3) that the nation of Israel would soon
come to accept Jesus as the promised Messiah.[127] The last of these unfulfilled
expectations eventually proved to be quite frustrating for the early church and
preoccupied it with concern for the Jews for centuries. How could those who
had received the promises of God, who were the interpreters of the Law and
the Prophets, and who were the heirs of Israel's traditions—how could they have
failed to recognize that Jesus was the promised Messiah? Paul shared this frustration but was convinced that the Jews would eventually come to faith in Christ
(Romans 9–11). No one in the earliest church believed that Israel's rejection of
Jesus as Messiah would continue for long.

The church attempted to deal with this problem in two ways: (1) It made
many attempts to convert the Jews, believing that God had not rejected them;[128]
those efforts, however, did not prove successful; as time went on, fewer and
fewer Jews became Christians, and the Gentiles became a majority of the Christian community.[129] (2) After those developments, many Christians, as we have
already seen, began to raise the question of whether the Jews had been rejected
by God; the evidence of this rejection was that the Jews were no longer able
either to interpret the Scriptures because of their spiritual blindness and hardness of heart or to understand God's salvation in Christ. It was further argued,
as we have already seen, that the church took the place of Israel and indeed had
become the new Israel. The problem facing those who held this view was that
the "old Israel" not only continued to exist some four hundred years after the
formation of the church, but that it was also prospering and offered a viable
alternative to the Christian faith. Therefore, the failure of the Jews to convert
constituted a major theological problem for the early Christians who called into
question Israel's existence and religious heritage. The church's claim to have
inherited Israel's promises and traditions could only bring it into sharp conflict
with the Jews, who continued to have a vibrant and influential community of
faith for centuries after the church had announced this claim.

---

127. See S. Neill, *Jesus through Many Eyes* (Philadelphia: Fortress, 1976) 32–37, who discusses
these disappointments and their consequences in the Christian community.

128. See, e.g., the Petrine sermons of Acts 2:38-41; 3:17-26, and Paul's argument in Rom 1:16;
10:1; 11:1-2, 23-32, but also the thrust of many of the early and late dialogues that call upon the
Jews to convert to Christ.

129. The dialogue genre, which purported to convince the Jews to convert to faith in Christ,
continued in the churches well into the Middle Ages. There are numerous examples of a call for
the Jews to convert to faith in Christ throughout the patristic period and even later. See Clement
of Alexandria in *Strom.* 2 (c.1); Hippolytus, *Demonstrations to the Jews* (*PG* 10.787-94), who gives
a call but sees no hope for it; so also Origen, *In Jerem. Hom.* 5 (GCS 3.31.26) and *In Rom. Comm.*
8:9 (*PG* 14.1187a) and his *Didascalia* 5.14.15, whose goal is the conversion of the Jews. Evagrius's
dialogue between Simon and Theophilus (ca. 400) shows continued interest in the conversion of
the Jews and like Justin evidences more respect to the Jew (Simon) than do some of the other
dialogues, even though the Jew is still a straw man in the discussion. Ruether fails to take sufficient
notice of these references in her comments in *Faith and Fratricide*, 148.

## Christian Apologetic Needs

The Christian apologies to the pagans as well as the Christian attacks on the various heresies and heretics within the church, for example, Marcion, often cast aspersions on the Jews. It has already been noted that Tertullian has more criticism of the Jews in his treatment of Marcion and other heretics than he does when dealing specifically with the Jews in his *Adversus Judaeos*.[130] Their pagan opponents asked the Christians why they did not obey the Law, practice circumcision, or observe the Sabbath if they truly had accepted the Hebrew Scriptures as their own. How can the Hebrew Scriptures be normative for the church when the church does not obey the Law the Scriptures promote? The Christian response came once again at the expense of the Jews. It was because of the Jews' hardness of heart and their many crimes that God first instituted the Law and because of their continuing obduracy that God changed the whole scene of redemption including doing away with the necessity for the Law. God's new people, the church, are now under a new dispensation of God's grace and are therefore no longer under the Law. The cause for its institution in the first place was the hardness of the Jews' hearts. When the Jews were removed as the people of God and the church was made the new Israel, a new day in God's economy began. The Hebrew Scriptures could no longer be understood literally, but only spiritually since the Spirit was now resident in the new community of faith.[131] These and other criticisms against Christianity were raised by Celsus, and they were answered at the Jews' expense.[132] Porphyry wrote some fifteen books against the Christians severely criticizing their religion and denouncing them for their having abandoned their religious heritage—Judaism.[133]

## The Attractiveness of Judaism to the Christians

Many Christians in the fourth and fifth centuries were anguished over the fact that gentile Christians and many pagan Gentiles were finding Judaism more attractive than Christianity. Many were attending Jewish festivals regularly and even converting to Judaism. Large numbers of them sought physical healing from the Jews through their prayers, incantations, and the wearing of Jewish amulets. The successes of the Jewish missionary efforts can be seen in the fact that Chrysostom felt obliged to warn Christians against converting to Judaism some twenty-three years after the death of Julian, near the end of the fourth

---

130. See, e.g., *De Prescript.* 8 and his *Adv. Marc.* 3.23.1–2; 4.14, 15.

131. Simon, *Verus Israel,* 189–213, gives a summary of the Christian responses to the pagan community. See also Wilken, "Judaism," 318.

132. See, e.g., Origen,. *C. Cels.* 1.55; 2.76–78; 3.10; 4.77, etc. Wilde, *Treatment of the Jews,* 99–101, offers evidence of these kinds of argument in Justin's *1 Apology*.

133. These books are discussed in Eusebius, *Praep. Ev.* 1.2.1–4; 1.3.1.

century.[134] Consider also how the author of the *Apostolic Constitutions*, writing near the end of the fourth century and probably from the region of Syria, shows that not just the laity but also the church's leaders were tempted toward Judaism. He stipulates what treatment should come to those who follow Jewish practices and orders that "if any bishop, or any other of the clergy, fast with the Jews, or keeps the festivals with them, or accepts of the presents from their festivals, as unleavened bread or some such thing, let him be deprived; but if he be one of the laity, let him be suspended" (8.47:70).[135] In another place, after he has enumerated the crimes of the Jews including their blindness and hardness of heart, he commands that the Christians no longer "keep the feast with the Jews, for we have now no communion with them" (5.3.16–17).[136] The appeal of Judaism in the third and fourth centuries was not new. It was present from the earliest beginnings of the church[137] and was still attested among Christians in the ninth century when such a fear of Christians converting to Judaism caused Agobard, archbishop of Lyons (ca. 824–28), not only to warn Christians against being led astray into Judaism but also to chastise those who had.[138] He charged that the Jews "dare to preach to Christians what they ought to believe and hold, blaspheming in their presence our Lord God and Saviour, Jesus Christ," but in anguish and exasperation he acknowledged that "uneducated Christians say that Jews preach better to them than our priests."[139]

It is hard to believe that all of these conversions to Judaism, or even Christian participation in Jewish festivals and other religious activities, could have taken place without significant missionary activity on the part of the Jews. Jewish proselytizing appears to have played a major role in producing some of the church's strongest invective against the Jews well into the Middle Ages. This polemic was most intense in places where Jewish missionary activity was having considerable success among the Christians. Although the evidence is not conclusive, it does appear that the intimidation by the Jews and their successful proselytizing of Christians were factors behind Melito's strong polemic against the Jews. He attacked the Jews of Sardis in a message to Christians, whom he reminded that

---

134. See Meeks and Wilken, *Jews and Christians*, 83–126, for a translation of the first and eighth of these homilies. Eusebius reports that around 200 CE a certain Domnus had also "fallen away from the faith of Christ, at the time of the persecution, to Jewish will-worship" (*Hist. Eccl.* 6.12.1).

135. ANF trans. 7.504. Saldarini, "Jews and Christians," suggests that even the liturgical prayers of the third-century *Didascalia* and the fourth-century *Apostolic Constitutions* were probably of second- or even third-century Jewish origins. He argues that because of the many parallels between them and the continuing attractiveness of Judaism to the Christian community, the once held rigid boundaries between Judaism and early Christianity can no longer be maintained.

136. ANF trans. 7.446–47.

137. See, for example, the paraenetic passages of Hebrews, especially in 6:6; 8:1-13; and 10:29, in which the author gives a warning to the Christians who were seeking security in Judaism and not in Christ.

138. See Epistle C, *De Insolentia Judaeorum* (Migne, *PL*, cols. 69–76) and *Ep. D* in *Epistola Agobardi, Bernardi, et Eaof de Judaicis superstitionibus* (Migne, cols. 77–100).

139. Epistle C, *De Insolentia Judaeorum* (Migne, cols. 71, 74). See Williams, *Adversus Judaeos*, 348–55.

"he who hung the earth is hanging; he who fixed the heavens has been fixed; he who fastened the universe has been fastened to a tree; the God has been murdered; the King of Israel has been put to death by an Israelite hand."[140] Sardis contained many Jews, and they had built not only the largest synagogue known in ancient times, but also owned and operated one of the largest and most impressive gymnasiums. Jewish accomplishments in Sardis were impressive and no doubt attracted many persons to Judaism. Marc Saperstein has stressed this and has rightly claimed that the Christians were in an inferior position in Sardis and, far from being the oppressors of the Jews in Sardis, were in fact trying to deal with the problem of the impressive presence of the Jews in that city at a time when Christians were supposed to have superseded them.[141] In similar circumstances, and here we are on more sure ground, John Chrysostom in 387 warned the Christians against being attracted to Judaism and to do all that was necessary to bring a "defector" (one who had left the church and converted to Judaism) back to the Christian fold, even if it involved the use of force. He supported these measures by focusing on the enormity of the crimes of the Jews and told his audience to ask the defector: "Tell me, do you agree with the Jews who crucified Christ and who blaspheme him to this day and call him a transgressor of the law? Surely he will not dare say—if he is a Christian, and even if he has been judaizing countless times—'I agree with the Jews.' "[142] Such invective reveals that Judaism, far from vanishing from the scene, was in fact flourishing in the latter half of the fourth century. See also the similar alarm found in another text from Chrysostom:

"If [the Jews] are ignorant of the Father, if they crucified the Son, and spurned the aid of the Spirit, cannot one declare with confidence that the synagogue is a dwelling place of demons? God is not worshiped there. Far from it! Rather, the synagogue is a temple of idolatry.... A synagogue is less honorable than any inn. For it is not simply a gathering place for thieves and hucksters, but also of demons. Indeed, not only the synagogue, but the soul of the Jews are also the dwelling places of demons.[143]

---

140. Melito, *Peri Pascha* 55; trans. from C. M. Williamson and R. J. Allen, *Interpreting Difficult Texts: Anti-Judaism and Christian Preaching* (London: SCM Press, 1989) 11. See also *Peri Pascha* 21, which details the crimes of the Jews.

141. M. Saperstein, *Moments of Crisis in Jewish-Christian Relations* (Philadelphia: Trinity Press Int., 1989) 6. Saperstein's work is excellent in his assessment of the church's role in continuing the anti-Judaistic sentiment from ancient times and even into the present; however, he unfortunately overlooks the role that the Jews may have played in that continuing invective in antiquity and gives little attention to it in the present. His solution to the problem toward the end of his book appears honest and deals with problems within the Christian community, but again little stress is placed on how there can be give-and-take on both sides of the equation—that is, he fails to address Jewish responsibility and obligation regarding the problem (see pp. 59–64).

142. Chrysostom, *Against the Jews*, Homily 8 (*PG* 48.934); trans. from Meeks and Wilken, *Jews and Christians*, 115.

143. I owe this quote from *Discourse* 1.3.3 and 1.4.2 to Marc Saperstein, *Moments of Crisis*, 6, who depends on the translation in Meeks and Wilken, *Jews and Christians*, 90, 92.

The criticisms of the Jews reached new heights in the sermons of John Chrysostom, which perhaps also reveal the critical situation of the church in the latter half of the fourth century following the death of Constantine and the attempted reversal of Christian ascendency by Julian the Apostate, Constantine's successor. Simon has observed that as late as 691 CE, the Trullan Synod, meeting at Justinian II's palace in Constantinople, reenacted several disciplinary decrees against Christian Judaizers who ate unleavened bread with the Jews, resorted to the synagogue for cures of their illnesses accepting their sundry prescriptions, and attended their ritual ablutions.[144] What this points to, of course, is the continuing influence of Judaism upon Christianity—or, perhaps the Jews' successful proselytizing of the Christians and how the church chose to deal with it.[145] Simon rightly asks whether this continuing appeal of Judaism to Christians, which was met by a strong negative Christian response, could have happened without the Jewish community actively proselytizing the Christians with considerable success.[146] Wilken is right when he concludes that "the virulence of Christian anti-Semitism is a sign of the vitality of Judaism in the later empire."[147]

### The Intimidation Factor

Another factor that may help us to understand the Christians' strong negative stance against the Jews and Judaism is the vast difference in the size of their religious bodies. By the turn of the first century, those who counted themselves among the Christians were probably fewer than 100,000 throughout the Roman Empire,[148] but at the same time, the Jewish population was somewhere between six and seven million, which was approximately one seventh to one tenth of the entire population of the Roman Empire. Of that number, it is estimated that between one and two million Jews lived in Palestine.[149] By any estimates, the Christians in their first two hundred years and probably longer were greatly outnumbered and quite possibly intimidated not only by the number of Jews in the empire, but also by their large buildings, like those at Sardis, and their long-standing influence and protected privileges in the Greco-Roman world. Further,

---

144. Simon (*Verus Israel*, 369–70) has taken this example from Hefele and Leclerq, *Histoire des Conciles* 3.564.

145. Simon, *Verus Israel*, 369–70.

146. Ibid., 145–46.

147. Wilken, "Judaism," 328.

148. L. T. Johnson, "The New Testament's Anti-Jewish Slander and the Conventions of Ancient Polemic," *JBL* 108 (1989) 423, gives this count of the Christians.

149. Scholars give various estimates of the size of the Jewish community in the first century CE, but generally speaking, the above numbers are considered valid. All scholars agree that the Jews were a large community and significantly outnumbered the Christians in the first three centuries. See H. G. Perelmuter, *Siblings: Rabbinic Judaism and Early Christianity at Their Beginnings* (New York: Paulist, 1989) 18, and W. A. Meeks, *The First Urban Christians* (New Haven: Yale Univ. Press, 1983) 34, who estimate that there were five to six million Jews in the first century; and Poliakov, *History of Anti-Semitism*, 5, puts the figure at three to four million Jews living in the Diaspora and one million in Palestine.

there is no certain evidence that the Christians significantly outnumbered the Jews in the century following the conversion of Constantine.

Besides this, there were many Gentiles (called "God-fearers") who had converted to Judaism and accepted its basic tenets, and an even larger number who accepted many aspects of Judaism but did not generally convert to it.[150] Conversion to Judaism essentially involved accepting the God and Torah of the Israelites as well as being accepted into the Jewish community, though some rabbis believed that a convert could never become an Israelite (*Bik.* 1.4). Before the destruction of the Temple in 70 CE, conversion to Judaism involved circumcision, sacrifice, and keeping the Law, but afterwards it always stressed the essential tenets of Torah as taught by Judaism's teachers of the Law.[151] Many Gentiles throughout the empire had adopted some of the most common Jewish practices such as Sabbath and holiday observance, attendance at the synagogue, and the veneration of God. Cohen has noted that John Chrysostom condemned Christians in Antioch who were observing with the Jews the first two of these practices.[152]

So powerful was the influence of the Jews in the empire that the Christians could not be certain even in the fourth and fifth centuries that the gains they had acquired under Constantine would not be overturned. In order to understand the Christians' fear at that point in time, one need only recall the actions of the emperor Julian, who tried to return the empire to its former pagan ways. After rejecting his Christian upbringing, he attempted to reverse the gains of the Christians partly by promoting the welfare of the Jews over the Christians but also by trying to rebuild the Temple in Jerusalem. Twice earlier, during the reigns of Hadrian and Constantine, the Jews attempted to rebuild their Temple, but were unsuccessful. Had Julian's attempt been successful, one of the Christians' most enduring arguments against Judaism would have been blunted. They had long claimed that the destruction of the Temple and the expulsion of the Jews from Jerusalem under Hadrian were evidence of God's rejection of the Jews and proof of the consequent election of the Christians to take their place. So common was this claim that one can scarcely believe that Julian, who was raised in the Christian religion, was unaware of it.[153] Understandably, the failure of

---

150. Cohen, *From the Maccabees to the Mishnah*, 55. Wilken, "Judaism," 313–18, notes that many of the impressive gains by the Jews in the Roman Empire were made between 135–425 CE, the very years during which the polemical language by the Christians was most intense.

151. Cohen, *From the Maccabees to the Mishnah*, 50–59. Cohen also indicates that women converted to Judaism by marriage to a Jew, but that there were no generally accepted guidelines for a woman to convert (pp. 53, 54).

152. Ibid., 57.

153. Examples of this argument in the Christian tradition are found in Justin, *1 Apology* 1.47, 53; *Dial.* 117; Irenaeus, *Adv. Haer.* 4.4.1–2 and 4.13.4; Origen, *C. Cels.* 7.20 and *In Jer. Hom.* 14.13. The Jews themselves even gave this as evidence of God's judgment of them, but not, of course, as evidence that God had replaced them in favor of the Gentiles (see *Dial.* 16, 40, 92). In the introduction to his *Historia Ecclesiastica*, Eusebius indicates that one of the purposes of his work is to "add the fate which has beset the whole nation of the Jews from the moment of their plot

Julian's attempt to rebuild the Temple was disheartening for the Jews but encouraging to the church in its polemic against the Jews. Socrates, the church historian (ca. 380–450 CE), tells of Julian's promotion of and financial support for the Jews to rebuild the Temple in Jerusalem and describes in detail the supernatural intervention of God by an earthquake and fire to prevent it from happening. He also emphasizes that Cyril, bishop of Jerusalem, had predicted the demise of the structure, thereby denoting divine intervention in the matter. Socrates says that as a consequence of this divine activity, many Jews "confessed that Christ is God: yet they did not his will" even after a cross miraculously appeared on their garments afterward![154] Whatever happened in Jerusalem to terminate Julian's plan, his early death from wounds received in battle in the East brought a cessation to any further plans for rebuilding the Temple. Christians saw that all of this was proof of God's rejection of the Jews and validation of the Christian claims. Sozomen (ca. 425–430), emphasizing the divine role in this event, claims that after the destruction of Julian's Temple in Jerusalem, "many [Jews] were hence led to confess that Christ is God, and that the rebuilding of the temple was not pleasing to Him."[155] Whether or not there is any truth to this part of the story—there is a tendency in ancient histories to be self-serving—one can at least see the importance of the failure to rebuild the Temple for the Christian apologetic.

The Christians were ill-prepared for the successes of Judaism both among gentile pagans and Christians. Wilken is right when he concludes that

> the fathers thought Judaism was dying, that the victory of the church signified the demise of Judaism. They created a caricature to meet their expectations and refused to look at Judaism for what it really was. But the problem of Judaism arose as a theological issue because Judaism had not died. It had not come to an end in Jesus, and it was still a force to be reckoned with in the Roman empire.[156]

Ruether has shown not only that the Judaism of the patristic period was *not* benign, but that it also "refused to be obsolete and threatened, again and again, to become compellingly relevant in a way that could call into question the very foundations of the Christian claim."[157] She goes on to state that this Judaism posed a threat to Christianity because it became a viable alternative to it regarding itself as the "true and legitimate successor and fulfillment of the Hebrew Scriptures."[158] Adella Yarbro Collins adds that not only did Christianity and

---

against our Saviour" (*Hist. Eccl.* 1.1.2 [LCL 1.7]), and he goes into considerable detail describing the destruction of Jerusalem and the Temple (2.6.3–7 and 3.5–6), concluding that "such was the reward of the iniquity of the Jews and of their impiety against the Christ of God" (3.7.1). Ruether, *Faith and Fratricide*, 144–45, gives several other examples of this argument.

154. Socrates "Scholasticus," in his *Hist. Eccl.* 3.20.
155. Eusebius, *Hist. Eccl.* 5.22.
156. Wilken, *Judaism*, 229.
157. Rosemary Ruether, *Faith and Fratricide*, 63.
158. Ibid.

Judaism compete for the same heritage; they also competed for the same adherents, which often brought them into sharp conflict with one another.[159] It is therefore not surprising that the church took seriously its most persistent and oldest foe.[160]

### Jewish Polemic and Hostilities against Christians

Given the level of Christian anti-Judaic rhetoric, it is inconceivable that the Jews did not respond in some way to the Christian polemic against them. But therein lies a major problem. There are very few Jewish sources from the earliest days of the church to document such a response from the Jews. This dearth is acknowledged by all scholars of ancient Judaism and Christianity, but not all agree on how to account for it. Leonhard Goppelt concedes that the "inner-Jewish, rabbinic tradition speaks only rarely and in veiled terms about Jesus or the Nazarenes" and that it is difficult to tell if any specific references are directed toward Christianity at all.[161] Marcel Simon, who says the Christian polemical literature is a response to Jewish hostilities toward the Christian community, asks: "How could Christians even conceive the idea of directing these treatises [vindictive and polemical texts] against the Jews if they had not on some occasions had experience of attacks from that quarter?"[162] David Flusser, in contrast, believes that the polemic was one-sided and that the Christians alone—out of "historical necessity," in order to become a viable religion in the pagan world—were responsible for the tension between themselves and Judaism.[163]

If the Jews did produce polemical writings against the church, how is it that so few of them currently exist? G. F. Moore suggests that the answer probably lies in the fact that such literature was expunged from the Jewish community after the Christian triumph over the empire,[164] but John C. Meagher argues that the infrequency of a vilification of Jesus in Jewish writings shows that the real issue against the Christians for the Jews had to do with the matter of the Law and not with Jesus himself.[165] He argues that Christians, like Stephen in Acts, were persecuted because they abused the Law, not for their views about Jesus' messiahship. He further adds that when the Christians retaliated against Jewish persecution, they eventually gained the upper hand.[166] Whatever the reason(s)

---

159. Collins, "Vilification," 314.

160. See Simon, *Verus Israel*, 98–100, for a discussion of this perceived threat to the church.

161. L. Goppelt, *The Theology of the New Testament*, trans. J. Alsup (Grand Rapids, Mich.: Eerdmans, 1981) 1.19.

162. Simon, *Verus Israel*, 138.

163. Flusser, *Judaism and the Origins of Christianity*, 142–44.

164. Moore, "Christian Writers on Judaism," 200, makes this point. See also Segal, *Rebecca's Children*, 147.

165. J. C. Meagher, "As the Twig was Bent," in *Anti-Semitism and the Foundations of Christianity*, 19–20.

166. Ibid., 20–21.

for the scarcity of the Jewish rhetoric against the Christians, the Christian writings themselves offer abundant evidence for the circulation of Jewish polemic against the church in the Roman Empire. In Origen's *Contra Celsum*, a Jew—an unknown, thoroughly conservative Jewish figure who shows a considerable awareness of the Christian faith—feeds Celsus with many substantial objections to the Christian faith.[167] Porphyry was also aware of similar Jewish criticisms against the Christians and made wide use of them in his arguments against the Christian religion.

When Ambrose attempted to persuade the emperor Theodosius that Christians should not be forced to rebuild the Jewish synagogue destroyed by the Christians in Callinicum, part of his argument was that the Jews themselves had destroyed several Christian churches and nothing was done about reparations. Complaining about the Roman laws that required that Christians assume responsibility for the rebuilding of the synagogue, Ambrose asks, "Where were those laws when they [the Jews] set fire to the domes of the sacred basilicas [Christian churches]?" (*De ob. Theo.* 40). Similar evidence comes from Cyril of Alexandria, who tried to have the Jews expelled from the city because of their hostilities against the church that resulted in the death of several Christians.[168]

Although it has been quite popular since Harnack to question whether the Christian treatises against the Jews reflect a genuine attempt to deal with real objections by the Jews against the Christians, more recently some scholars are concluding that there were many contacts between the Jewish and Christian communities throughout the first five centuries and that the Christian writings do reflect many of the actual issues raised by the Jews, though not, of course, in an unprejudicial manner.[169]

The Jews' evidence for their polemic against the Christians is slim, but worth noting. The first is found in the *Birkath ha-Minim*, namely, the benediction (or malediction) against heretics found in the twelfth of the Eighteen Benedictions, or the *Shemonah Esrey*, which forms the basic prayer of the Jewish liturgy. It reads:

> And for the separatists and for the heretics [*minim*] let there be no hope; and let all wickedness perish as in an instant; and let all thy enemies be cut off quickly; and mayst thou uproot and break to pieces and cast down and humble the arrogant kingdom quickly and in our days. Blessed art thou, O Lord, who breakest enemies and humblest the arrogant.[170]

---

167. See *C. Cels.* 2.4.1–2; 2.9.1; 2.13.1ff.; 2.18, 26, 28, 34, 39, 41, and elsewhere.

168. Socrates, *Hist. Eccl.* 7.13, relates this story, but not without prejudice against the Jews. He does not hesitate to criticize Cyril for his behavior either, but the Jews receive severe prejudicial treatment. This is reflected elsewhere in his history; see 3.20 and 5.22. Wilken, *Judaism*, 54–57, has a good summary of the events in Alexandria that led up to this crisis.

169. See Wilken, *Judaism*, 35–53 and 229, and idem, "Judaism," 327–28, and Simon, *Verus Israel*, 143ff.

170. *Prayer Book* 50 (48). This translation is from H. Maccoby, *Early Rabbinic Writings* (Cambridge: Cambridge Univ. Press, 1988) 208, and it shows a reference to *Tos. Ber.* 3:25.

The question here is whether the *Birkath ha-Minim* makes a direct reference to the Christians. Undoubtedly it was not so intended in its earliest formulations, but the issue is whether *minim* became a normal Jewish designation for the Christians by the fourth century. There are some versions of the twelfth benediction dating from the fourth century that contain the word *noserim*, "Nazoreans." It is possible that this was strictly a reference to Jewish Christians,[171] but more likely it refers to all Christians. Tertullian, for example, indicates that this term was used by the Jews as a reference to all Christians. Explaining the meaning of the word, he states that "the Christ of the Creator had to be called a *Nazarene* according to prophecy; whence the Jews also designate us, on that very account, *Nazarenes* after Him."[172] Flusser, who offers a detailed and helpful history of the origin and use of the *Birkath ha-Minim*, rejects the notion that it was ever used against all Christians, claiming that it was instead directed first against the Essenes and then only much later against "Nazoreans," whom he believes were *Jewish* Christians.[173] Segal is probably more correct when he says that the term *minim* was a reference in the benedictions that included, but was not limited to, all Christians.[174] Justin appears to substantiate this when he refers to a curse directed against all Christians. Explaining for Trypho some of the reasons for the calamities that had befallen the Jews (probably the events surrounding 66–70 and 132–35 CE), he wrote: "Accordingly, these things have happened to you in fairness and justice, for you have slain the Just One, and His prophets before him; and now you reject those who hope in Him, and in Him who sent Him—God the Almighty and Maker of all things—*cursing in your synagogues those that believe on Christ*." Adding a reference to actual persecutions of the Christians, Justin continued: "For you have not the power to lay hands on us, on account of those who now have the mastery, *but as often as you could, you did so*."[175]

Along with the *Birkath ha-Minim*, there are a number of anti-Christian references in the Palestinian Talmud and the subsequent *Toldoth Yeshu*, which offers an anthology of talmudic references put together for use against the Christians. Craig A. Evans has collected a sample of texts in the talmudic literature that gives clear indication of the tensions between the Jews and the Christians. He has shown that the Babylonian Talmud casts aspersions on Mary, the mother of Jesus, who is sometimes also confused with Mary Magdalene.[176] Evans notes

---

171. So argues Maccoby, *Early Rabbinic Writings*, 209.

172. Tertullian, *Adv. Jud.* 4.8.1 (ANF trans).

173. Flusser, *Judaism and the Origins of Christianity*, 637–43.

174. Segal, *Rebecca's Children*, 150.

175. Justin, *Dial.* 16.4 (ANF trans.; italics mine). See also 16, 47, 96, 137. Origen, *H. Jerem.* 10.8.2; Epiphanius, *Panarion* 29.9.1; and Jerome, *Ep. August.* 112.13 all saw the *Birkath ha-Minim* as a curse against the Christians. See also Justin, *1 Apol.* 131, in which he accuses the Jews of cruel punishments and even of killing the Christians.

176. I think it is important to note that I am indebted here to Craig A. Evans's work, *Noncanonical Writings and New Testament Interpretation* (Peabody, Mass.: Hendrickson, 1992). He has

that Mary is described as "one who was the descendent of princes and governors, [yet] played the harlot with carpenters [Joseph]" (*b. Sanh.* 106a). On the matter of Jesus' death, the Babylonian Talmud states that he was excommunicated and condemned for worshiping an idol (*b. Sanh.* 107b; *Soṭa* 47a). In regard to his ministry, Jesus' practice of healing is described as sorcery: "Jesus the Nazarene practiced magic and led Israel astray" (*b. Sanh.* 107b; see the interesting parallel in Mark 3:22). Jesus' crucifixion is described in similarly negative terms in both the Babylonian and Jerusalem Talmuds:

> On the eve of Passover they hanged Jesus the Nazarene. And a herald went out before him for forty days, saying: "He is going to be stoned, because he practiced sorcery and enticed and led Israel astray. Anyone who knows anything in his favor, let him come and plead in his behalf." But, not having found anything in his favor, they hanged him on the eve of Passover. (*b. Sanh.* 43a; cf. *t. Sanh.* 10.11; *y. Sanh.* 7.16; 67a)

Even the reports of Jesus' resurrection are spoken of disparagingly and in terms of him being a magician: "He then went and raised Jesus by incantation" (*b. Giṭ.* 57a, MS M). "Woe to him who makes himself alive by the name of God" (*b. Sanh.* 106a).[177] Alan Segal and Marcel Simon also have excellent summaries of this literature,[178] and both have shown that the vituperative language found in the early Christian writings was not so one-sided as others have suggested.[179] David Rokeah's conclusion that "the Jews clearly had no hand in the persecutions of Christians by the imperial authorities: Jews neither informed on Christians nor turned Christians over to the Roman authorities"[180] cannot be substantiated by any fair treatment of the primary sources, both Jewish and Christian.[181] Equally unfounded is his contention that the Christian polemic and persecutions directed against the Jews were caused only by Christian frustration over the failure of the Jews to convert to Christianity.[182] He does not give sufficient weight to the long list of references in the patristic writers that gives ample evidence not only of Jewish rhetoric against the Christians, but also of their persecution of them.[183] If Jewish participation in the Christian suffering

---

included many other references to Jesus in ancient rabbinic literature that are also illustrative of the point being made here.

177. Ibid., 143–46.

178. Segal, *Rebecca's Children*, 147–58, and Simon, *Verus Israel*, 178–201.

179. Parkes, *Conflict*, 121–50, has an excellent discussion of the sources depicting Jewish persecution of the Christians. His conclusions about that literature on pp. 148–50 are unrealistic, but his collection and discussion are worth examining. In Appendix 5 (pp. 402–4), he also includes a helpful list of martyrs reportedly killed by the Jews in the first century.

180. D. Rokeah, "Behind the Appearances," *Explorations* 3 (1989) 2–3.

181. See, e.g., the references in the *Martyrdom of Polycarp* to the Jews' participation in exciting the crowds to kill Polycarp and even desecrate his body by not allowing a proper burial (see *Mart. Pol.* 12.2; 13.1; 17.2; 18.1). There are no good reasons to reject the essential reliability of this report that the Jews incited the crowds against the Christian community.

182. D. Rokeah, "Behind the Appearances," 4.

183. See, for example, Justin, *Dial.* 16, 17, 32, 34, 117, 131, 133, 136, 137; Irenaeus, *Adv.*

did not occur, as Rokeah argues, then we are without an adequate cause for the hateful intensity of the Christian polemic against the Jews. Luke T. Johnson has shown that Jewish polemic against the pagans was quite common in ancient times and that some of the very language later used by Christians against the Jews was used earlier by the Jews in reference to their pagan enemies.[184] He lists numerous references in Josephus to Jewish violence and hostilities, including Josephus's own use of malicious terms to describe his opponents and the enemies of the Jews, which are plentiful in his *Against Apion*.[185] He makes another interesting observation that even though there is very little surviving literature of the Jewish polemic against the Samaritans, its presence in the ancient world is still regarded as axiomatic.[186]

Johnson is right when he says that in today's world, perhaps to overcompensate for past injustices, theologians treat the first-century Jews as if they were pacific in their relations to Jesus or to the early Christian church and treat the Pharisaic traditions' self-portrayal "uncritically" and "dismiss any possibility of frailty."[187] As proof of Jewish culpabilities, he lists twenty-one references from Josephus that show that the Jews were often fanatical and violent.[188] He concludes that all parties from the ancient world made use of such language and that understanding this can rob the polemic of much of its disproportionate force.[189] All of this is not to relieve the Christians from any responsibility for their own actions, of course, but rather to balance the picture somewhat and state that the Jews were not beyond irresponsible and unkind acts in ancient times anymore than were the Christians.

In fairness we should stress that the Christian teachings on the Law, the demise and rejection of the Jews, and the replacement of the Jews by the Christians (supersession) could not expect to receive favorable responses from the Jewish community. Indeed similar arguments would have inflamed any ancient or modern religious community.[190]

---

*Haer.* 4.21.3; Hippolytus, *In Gen.* 49.86, who also says that Jews joined with pagans against the Christians (*In Dan.* 1.29.21). Cf. *Mart. Pol.* 13.2, 17.2, and 18.1, which tells of the Jews' complicity in the death of Polycarp; Origen, *Gen. Hom.* 13.3; Parkes, *Conflict*, 121–50.

184. L. T. Johnson, "New Testament's Anti-Jewish Slander," 434–41. Johnson notes that in *Embassy to Gaius*, Philo describes his Alexandrian neighbors as "promiscuous and unstable rabble" (18.120) and later refers to the Egyptians as a "seedbed of evil in whose souls both the venom and temper of the native crocodiles and wasps are reproduced" (26.166)! Other similar examples are found in his *The Contemplative Life*, as well as in the earlier author of Wisdom of Solomon (ca. first century BCE in Alexandria).

185. See Johnson, "New Testament's Anti-Jewish Slander," 422 and 434–35, for several of these references.

186. Ibid., 437–38.

187. Ibid., 421–22.

188. Ibid. On p. 439 he also cites examples of the Essenes' hostilities against all outsiders.

189. Ibid., 441.

190. Flusser, *Judaism and the Origins of Christianity*, 625–26, correctly raises this issue.

# Conclusion

Robert Wilde has made the observation that Marcion's work was the first well-reasoned advocacy of anti-Semitism/anti-Judaism in the church, but it was deemed heretical and ruled out of court by such major contributors as Justin, Irenaeus, Melito, Tertullian, and Origen.[191] The church went to great lengths in its earliest years to maintain the unity of the God of the Hebrew Scriptures with the God of Jesus and the apostles and also to stress that Christianity's roots are firmly in the Jewish religious tradition. Unfortunately, the recognition of Christian indebtedness to the Jewish heritage did not prevent the Christians and the Jews from extreme and sometimes hostile competition over who was the rightful heir to that heritage. There is no question that a large body of angry anti-Jewish rhetoric exists in the writings of the early church fathers, and that rhetoric became even more pronounced in the fourth and fifth centuries. It can be debated whether this was in response to persecution by the Jews and their polemic against the church, or whether the Christian polemic against the Jews led to Jewish persecution and the rise of the Jewish polemic against the Christians; however, there can be no debate over the fact that the Jews opposed Christianity: that opposition is seen first in the New Testament[192] and then in the church fathers. Jewish opposition to Christianity, as we have argued, came both because of the church's christological perspective[193] and because of its teaching on the role of the Law and its ritual.[194] When Christianity was small, Judaism could largely ignore it (though there is no evidence that it did), but with the church's significant growth in the second and subsequent centuries, the Christian faith was seen as a threat to Judaism and drew serious Jewish reaction to it. In contrast, the survival of Judaism posed a threat to the Christian's argument that the church had replaced Judaism and had become heir to its antiquity and Scriptures.

There can be no lasting solution to the problem of anti-Semitism if we fix all of the blame for its existence on the Christian community, largely ignoring the possibility of Jewish culpability.[195] Both groups at various times in their histories

---

191. Wilde, *Treatment of the Jews*, 150.

192. While J. Gager, *The Origins of Anti-Semitism: Attitudes toward Judaism in Pagan and Christian Antiquity* (New York: Oxford Univ. Press, 1983) 117–20, is correct in arguing that much of the New Testament focus that has been brought against the Jews and Judaism was in fact references to gentile Judaizers, this still does not account for all of the anti-Jewish bias (e.g., 1 Thess 2:14-16; Acts 28:17-31).

193. Flusser, *Judaism and the Origins of Christianity*, 619–25, makes a good case for this. See also Segal, *Rebecca's Children*, 154–60, for a discussion of the christological issues that divided Christianity and Judaism.

194. Meagher, "As the Twig Was Bent," 19–21, acknowledges the significance of the christological issue, but contends that the primary reason for Jewish opposition to Christianity was its trivialization of the Law.

195. It seems to me that this is exactly what Ruether, Flusser, and Rokeah have done and what makes their works in these areas of less value.

have been guilty of shameful acts toward each other. An unfortunate example of this on the church's side was its practice of imposing baptism upon the Jews whether in Spain, Antioch, France, or elsewhere, hoping to bring about by force what it could not accomplish through evangelism and argument, namely the conversion of the Jews.[196] Just as unsatisfying as trying to fix the blame for all anti-Judaistic sentiment squarely on the church's shoulders is the tendency today for Christians, possibly out of a sense of guilt because of the Holocaust, to downplay their sense of mission to the Jews. Such a practice in effect denies the validity of the Christian understanding that the Hebrew Scriptures find their ultimate fulfillment in Jesus. The continuation of Israel's election and place in the final plan of God need not be lost sight of, but, at the same time, the Christian has good news to share that is important for both Jews and Gentiles alike. Donald Bloesh, in commenting on the tendency today toward theological reductionism that seeks some convergence of the two great religions into one syncretistic creation, cautions that this could undermine the integrity of both religions and ignore the power of the gospel of God revealed in Jesus Christ.[197]

Whether or not some Jewish religious leaders participated in the decision to crucify Jesus—and there is no good reason to deny that as a possibility—Christians do not have sufficient grounds thereby to condemn the whole nation and hold all Jews of every generation responsible for the deed. Further, Christians should reexamine the level and intensity of the ancient anti-Jewish rhetoric in the Christian community, knowing that regardless of one's views on the acceptance of the basic tenets of Judaism as a means of attaining the salvation of God, the Jews are not beyond God's love and grace and should not be beyond the love of Christians. Thus, on the one hand, the very level of hatred and bitterness on the lips of Chrysostom, for instance, cannot be allowed to go unchallenged in the court of Christian opinion. It is clearly wrong! On the other hand, there is no evidence that suggests that the Jews of antiquity would have treated the Christians more humanely had they, instead of the church, triumphed over the Roman Empire. By their actions and in their polemic both religious communities give evidence in their religious histories of having betrayed some of the essentials of their faith, denying through spiteful deeds the universal love and forgiveness of God. We can understand the Christians' disappointment over the Jews' failure to recognize Jesus as their Messiah, or their cry of despair in the midst of persecution, and even their fears due to their comparatively small numbers when facing such overwhelming odds in the early stages of their development, but

---

196. Parkes, *The Conflict,* documents this unfortunate practice in medieval times (see pp. 245, 250, 334–35, etc.).

197. D. Bloesh, "'All Israel Will Be Saved': Supersessionism and the Biblical Witness," *Int* 43 (1989) 130–42, discusses the tendency of Christians to shy away from their mission to the Jews today and advocates that a more humane treatment of the Jews and a more defensible theological understanding of their role in the plan of God do not mitigate against the Christian mission (see p. 138).

the church cannot sanction in any age hatred and bitterness in the heart of the child of God. Whenever that occurs, or whenever it is welcomed as acceptable behavior for Christians, then the very character of the Christian faith itself is undermined, and the church ceases to be the community of Jesus. When such feelings or actions are generated within the church, a major shift has taken place with serious and lasting consequences that affect the integrity and vitality of the religious life of the church. When adherents of Judaism and Christianity express hostile attitudes or negative suspicions toward each other, then the very nature of that which each faith seeks to establish is called into question. It is preferable that both Jews and Christians acknowledge their past failures in their relations with each other, and, as Adella Yarbro Collins encourages, take "the opportunity to relate as adult siblings, respecting differences and rejoicing in a common origin."[198] This seems to be the least that we all could do to insure the continuing viability of our faiths in today's pluralistic world.

---

198. Collins, "Vilification," 320.

# -*12*-

# Anti-Judaism in the
# New Testament Apocrypha:
# A Preliminary Survey

## *James R. Mueller*

It is both surprising and not surprising how little work has been done on anti-Judaism[1] in the early Christian apocryphal literature.[2] Over the past several decades, the period after the Holocaust, innumerable studies have been published dealing with anti-Judaism and anti-Semitism from every conceivable angle and in every time period.[3] We now have a much better grasp of pagan views,

---

1. Throughout this essay I will generally use the term "anti-Judaism," as distinct from "anti-Semitism," to describe the material in the literature, following J. Gager's definitions in *The Origins of Anti-Semitism* (New York: Oxford Univ. Press, 1985) 7–9. Gager distinguishes between the terms as follows: anti-Judaism is "a matter of religious and theological disagreement"; and anti-Semitism is "hostile statements about Jews and Judaism on the part of Gentiles.... They are expressed by complete outsiders, betray very little knowledge of Jews or Judaism, and tend to be sweeping generalizations." It will become clear that some of the manifestations of anti-Judaism in the New Testament Apocrypha may crowd the line that separates anti-Judaism from anti-Semitism.

2. The limits of this category of literature are notoriously slippery. For a recent attempt to define the limits, see J. H. Charlesworth with James R. Mueller, *The New Testament Apocrypha and Pseudepigrapha: A Guide to Publications with Excursuses on Apocalypses* (Metuchen, N.J.: Scarecrow, 1987) 1–11. Although nearly every definition of the literature, including the one just mentioned, provides a place for some of the gnostic, or at least some of the Nag Hammadi, documents, and nearly every recent edition of the New Testament Apocrypha includes them (see E. Hennecke and W. Schneemelcher, eds., *Neutestamentliche Apocryphen* [2 vols.; 5th ed.; Tübingen: J. C. B. Mohr (Paul Siebeck), 1987, 1989]; English trans. of German 5th edition: *New Testament Apocrypha*, ed. R. McL. Wilson [Louisville: Westminster/John Knox, 1991, 1992] [hereafter Hennecke-Schneemelcher-Wilson, *New Testament Apocrypha*]), I will not deal with that material in order to avoid overlap with another essay in this volume (see below). Several other important writings, including the Apostolic Fathers, caught betwixt and between in the various definitions of early Christian literature will also not be included in what follows.

3. To begin to list all the publications would require more space than can be allotted here. For a good review of the literature on the subject see Gager, *Origins*, 13–34.

both positive and negative, of Judaism;[4] we have attacks on, and defenses of, the New Testament writers' widely varying views on their Jewish opponents;[5] and we have a growing appreciation of the diversity of opinions expressed by the church "fathers."[6] Yet even the most cursory review of the secondary literature reveals very little discussion of any of the New Testament Apocrypha.[7] What becomes clear is that nearly one hundred documents from the first several centuries of the church have rarely been examined and have not been a part of the study of Jewish-Christian polemic and relations. Surprising.

However, this lack of attention is also not overly surprising. First, the "corpus" is not easy to access, for it is in reality an ill-defined modern categorization that brings together a wide array of documents that span several centuries and many religious orientations.[8] Sometimes the same material will be identified in both ancient and modern literature by different titles, such as the *Gospel of Nicodemus* and the *Acts of Pilate*, which can be confusing to the newcomer. The documents are difficult to date or to locate precisely, and often there are

---

4. See especially the three-volume work by M. Stern, *Greek and Latin Authors on Jews and Judaism* (Jerusalem: Israel Academy of Sciences and Humanities, 1974, 1980, 1984). Stern's work superseded the work of Th. Reinach, *Textes d'auteurs grecs et romains relatifs au Judaïsme* (1895; repr., Hildesheim: Georg Olms, 1963). For a more accessible anthology of texts, see M. Whittaker, *Jews and Christians: Graeco-Roman Views* (Cambridge Commentaries on Writings of the Jewish and Christian World 200 BC–AD 200, no. 6; Cambridge: Cambridge Univ. Press, 1984) 3–130. For an interesting analysis of the data from a social and cultural perspective, see Gager, *Origins*, 35–112.

5. See in addition to the older work by S. Sandmel (*Anti-Semitism in the New Testament?* [Philadelphia: Fortress, 1978]), the more recent essay collections, especially P. Richardson with D. Granskou, eds., *Anti-Judaism in Early Christianity*, vol. 1: *Paul and the Gospels* (Studies in Christianity and Judaism, no. 2; Waterloo, Ont.: Wilfrid Laurier Univ. Press, 1986).

6. See, for example, S. G. Wilson, ed., *Anti-Judaism in Early Christianity*, vol. 2: *Separation and Polemic* (Studies in Early Judaism and Christianity, no. 2; Waterloo, Ont.: Wilfrid Laurier Univ. Press, 1986); H. Schreckenberg, *Die christlichen Adversus-Judaeos-Texte und ihr literarisches und historisches Umfeld (1.-11. Jh.)* (Europäische Hochschulschriften, no. 23, Theologie 172; Frankfurt am Main: Peter Lang, 1982). Still helpful is the treatment of M. Simon, *Verus Israel: A Study of the Relations between Christians and Jews in the Roman Empire (135–425)*, trans. H. McKeating (Oxford: Oxford Univ. Press, 1986).

7. For example, in looking through the citation indices of several recent publications, one is hard pressed to find much related to this corpus of literature. In the whole volume of articles edited by Wilson (*Separation and Polemic*) on anti-Judaism in the early church, only the *Acts of Pilate* appear (although one does discover upon closer examination that the *Dialogue of Timothy and Aquila* is discussed, but not indexed). The only remark remotely applicable in Gager's *Origins* is that there is "no trace of anti-Jewish polemic" in the Pseudo-Clementines (p. 124). Gager does mention other apocryphal texts, but not in terms of their anti-Jewish tendencies (cf. the *Acts of Paul and Thecla* regarding asceticism and the *Dialogue of Timothy and Aquila* regarding the dialogue form in Christian anti-Jewish texts). The only somewhat substantial treatments of the corpus I was able to locate are A. L. Williams's discussion of the *Dialogue of Timothy and Aquila* (*Adversus Judaeos: A Bird's Eye View of Christian Apologiae until the Renaissance* [Cambridge: Cambridge Univ. Press, 1935] 67–78); and R. Wilde's discussion of only a few texts (*The Treatment of the Jews in the Greek Christian Writers of the First Three Centuries* [Catholic University of America Patristic Studies, no. 81; Washington, D.C.: Catholic Univ. of America Press, 1949] 216–24).

8. See the various attempts to define the New Testament Apocrypha, such as those by M. R. James, *The Apocryphal New Testament* (Oxford: Clarendon, 1924) xi–xxvii; Hennecke-Schneemelcher-Wilson, *New Testament Apocrypha*, 1.50–61; and Charlesworth with Mueller, *New Testament Apocrypha and Pseudepigrapha*, 6–11.

numerous recensions, versions, and epitomes of a particular document, each exhibiting its own peculiar theology. Pertinent to the discussion at hand is the *Acts of Andrew and Matthias in the City of the Cannibals,* a very entertaining tale of the evangelization of Myrmidonia (according to Gregory, the late sixth-century bishop of Tours). In the *Acts* the residents capture Matthias, gouge out his eyes, and begin to fatten him for slaughter and consumption. Andrew is sent by God to rescue his fellow apostle and complete the work of converting the residents. In the earliest traditions the villagers are described variously as savage, bloodthirsty, and wilder than beasts, but as the story is retold by the ninth-century monk Epiphanius, the residents, while retaining their ferocity, also become identified as "Jews": "There was a large population of Jews in that city, splintered into several parties, men of barbarous and savage habits, who for this reason are called cannibals."[9] Although it seems that we have in this particular case a fairly clear example of a reworking of a text in the ninth century, it would be fair to ask (but probably impossible to answer) whether Epiphanius created the identification of the Myrmidonians as Jews. Was he using as his base text some earlier, now lost, manuscript witness, or was he relying on an oral tradition?[10] Given that the original *Acts of Andrew* have not survived and that all modern editions must reconstruct the text from hagiographies such as the one produced by Gregory of Tours and Epiphanius, what if all that had been preserved of the *Acts* had been Epiphanius's version? Would the identification of the Jews as cannibals have been thought to have originated early in the Christian era, at the time of the composition of the original *Acts,* thus totally warping our views on early Christian anti-Judaism? What we can know is that Epiphanius at least supported the identification, thus including it in his version of the story, but without a clear textual history of a document, we can know little else.

This confusion of titles, contents, and manuscript and versional evidence leads to the second, related problem in trying to examine the New Testament Apocrypha—the lack of reliable critical editions of the texts.[11] Again to use the *Acts of Andrew* as an example, two recent editions of the material reconstruct the

---

9. Translation and brief synopsis are from D. R. MacDonald, *The Acts of Andrew and the Acts of Andrew and Matthias in the City of the Cannibals* (SBLTT, Christian Apocrypha Series 1; Atlanta: Scholars Press, 1990).

10. The reason that the evidence is fairly clear for this particular case is that there are many places in the earlier witnesses to the story where the inhabitants are clearly to be understood as pagans (see esp. their conversion to the God of Andrew [MacDonald, *Acts of Andrew,* 155–69]).

11. This situation has begun to change thanks to the work of the joint Swiss-French team that is producing the Series Apocryphorum of the Corpus Christianorum. See their excellent new editions of the *Acts of John* (E. Junod and J. D. Kaestli, eds., *Acta Iohannis* [2 vols.; Turnhout: Brepols, 1983]), the *Armenian Acts of the Apostles* (L. Leloir, ed., *Acta Apostolorum Armenica* [1986]), and the *Acts of Andrew* (J.-M. Prieur, ed., *Acta Andreae* [2 vols.; 1989]). In North America the Early Christian Apocryphal Literature Group of the Society of Biblical Literature (chaired by D. MacDonald) has also begun to publish critical texts and translations of the documents. The first volume in that series, not coincidentally, was also an edition of the *Acts of Andrew and Matthias.*

text of the *Acts* using numerous sources from various time periods that appear in a variety of languages. As D. R. MacDonald so clearly states in his edition:

> Certainly one must not confuse the ancient Acts with the content of this volume, which is, of necessity, a conjectural reconstruction based on literary debris: quotations, epitomes, fragments, and expansions in Greek, Latin, Coptic, Anglo-Saxon, and Armenian.... Most materials printed here are textual offspring, more or less resembling their parents but not to be mistaken for them.[12]

Because of the nonexistence of a single reliable witness (or family of witnesses) to the text of the original *Acts*, and despite very careful analyses of the available texts, the two recent editions even differ significantly in terms of their views on the extent of the original *Acts*. MacDonald includes in his edition the story of *Andrew and Matthias in the City of the Cannibals*, while J.-M. Prieur does not.[13] Should, therefore, an examination of anti-Judaism in the New Testament apocryphal literature include the cannibalistic Myrmidonians as part of the *Acts of Andrew* (probably second century) or in a separate category? Or is the best that we can do is deal with the material as it is represented in the hagiographical literature—that is, as evidence of Gregory's or Epiphanius's views on the Jews? This is not to say that the textual tradition is as murky for all the documents as it is for the *Acts of Andrew*, but it is not uncommon that even after intensive study of transmission histories we are left with major differences of opinion regarding nearly every critical issue ranging from date to provenance to theological outlook.

A third, related problem one encounters when looking at the early Christian apocryphal literature for evidence of anti-Jewish polemic is that it is not always clear whether the characters identified in the stories as "Jews" are meant to be understood as such. Take for example another scene in the *Acts of Andrew* where Jesus, disguised as a boat captain, asks Andrew:

> Why did the faithless Jews not believe in him [Jesus] and say that he was not God but a human? How could a human do the miracles of God and his great wonders? Make it clear to me, disciple of the one called Jesus, for we heard that he revealed his divinity to his disciples.[14]

The rest of the dialogue centers on the miracles of Jesus, including some that are not recorded in the canonical Gospels, as proof of his divinity. Andrew answers the boat captain: "He [Jesus] did indeed reveal to us that he is God, so do not suppose he is a human, for he himself created human beings."[15]

---

12. MacDonald, *Acts of Andrew*, ix.

13. For a presentation of the opposing views, see D. MacDonald, "The Acts of Andrew and Matthias and the Acts of Andrew," in D. MacDonald, ed., *The Apocryphal Acts of the Apostles* (*Semeia* 38 [1986], 9–26); see also the response by Prieur in the same volume, pp. 27–33; and a further response by MacDonald, pp. 35–39.

14. MacDonald, *Acts of Andrew*, 91.

15. Ibid., 93.

Although the divinity of Jesus is an issue between Jews and Christians (though rarely in connection with his miraculous deeds),[16] it is also a major issue between rival Christian groups in early Christianity.[17] On the one hand, in the early Jewish-Christian polemic, as evidenced in the Gospels and other early Jewish and Christian texts, the debates in which the miracles play a major role tend to revolve around the source of Jesus' power and/or the designation of Jesus as either a miracle worker or a sorcerer, not around his divinity.[18] On the other hand, it is not uncommon for early Christian writers to characterize their own Christian opponents as "Jews."[19] Is that possibly the case in the excerpt cited above from the *Acts of Andrew*? Is the author arguing with a "Jewish" position regarding the person of Christ, or an alternative Christian position? Again, though the *Acts of Andrew* may not be completely typical of all early Christian apocryphal literature, the document raises another important issue that needs to be kept in mind as one studies the various texts' anti-Judaism, namely the referent of the term "Jews."

It is not surprising then that so little has been written about anti-Judaism in the New Testament Apocrypha. The nonexhaustive list of the difficulties encountered in working with the early Christian apocryphal material enumerated above makes it obvious that it is almost impossible to present definitive state-

---

16. See, for example, Justin's rather lukewarm defense of the divinity of Jesus (*Dialogue with Trypho* 48), where Justin is content to "prove" that Jesus is the Christ, the prophesied Messiah, and to allow the possibility that "He has become Christ by election," as some Christians he is aware of claim (ANF 1.217). For a good discussion of Justin's position with regard to Judaism, see H. Remus, "Justin Martyr's Argument with Judaism," in *Anti-Judaism in Early Christianity*, 2.59–80.

17. See the excellent review of the treatment of the miracles of Jesus in the early church, including the New Testament Apocrypha, by P. J. Achtemeier, "Jesus and the Disciples as Miracle Workers in the Apocryphal New Testament," in E. Schüssler Fiorenza, ed., *Aspects of Religious Propaganda in Judaism and Early Christianity* (Univ. of Notre Dame Center for the Study of Judaism and Christianity in Antiquity 2; Notre Dame, Ind.: Univ. of Notre Dame Press, 1976) 149–86. Achtemeier notes that there is little emphasis in the apocryphal literature on the miracles performed by Jesus (which he calls a continuing mystery [p. 177]), but a great deal of emphasis on the miracle working of the disciples "in the name of Jesus." It is the ability of the disciples to perform miracles by the power of the name of Jesus (in contrast to the magicians of the Jews and the pagans) that attests to the divinity of Jesus in second- and third-century apologetics, not the actual miracles performed by Jesus.

18. Cf. Mark 3.22 (and par.), *Gospel of Nicodemus* 1.1. For a summary of the Jewish evidence, see J. Klausner, *Jesus of Nazareth* (London: George Allen, 1929) 17–54. There is a growing consensus that the primary divisive element in the early period was not the person of Jesus, but instead the abandonment of the practice of the Law (see L. Schiffman, "At the Crossroads: Tannaitic Perspectives on the Jewish-Christian Schism," in E. P. Sanders et al., eds., *Jewish and Christian Self-definition* [Philadelphia: Fortress, 1981], 2.115–56). See also the recent thorough treatment by J. D. G. Dunn, *The Partings of the Ways* (London: SCM; Philadelphia: Trinity, 1991). For a more general picture of the Jewish response to Christianity, see Simon, *Verus Israel*, 179–201; and E. Urbach, *The Sages, Their Concepts and Beliefs*, trans. I. Abrahams (2 vols.; Jerusalem: Magnes, 1975).

19. That this is the case has long been recognized in the discussions of Jewish Christianity; see W. Bauer, *Orthodoxy and Heresy in Earliest Christianity*, ed. R. Kraft and G. Krodel (Philadelphia: Fortress, 1971); H. Koester, *Introduction to the New Testament*, vol. 2: *History and Literature of Early Christianity* (Philadelphia: Fortress, 1982); and Hennecke-Schneemelcher-Wilson, *New Testament Apocrypha*, 1.134–78 (see esp. the bibliography on p. 134).

ments about the anti-Judaism in the texts. Given the uncertainties of the dating of the various documents (including the assessment of the faithfulness of the witnesses to any original apocryphal work), it is not really possible to survey the chronological development of anti-Judaism within the corpus. Since it is equally difficult, given the present state of research, to describe accurately the provenance of the texts, it is also not possible to survey the anti-Jewish traditions in the texts as representative of the views held in specific locales. In fact, the whole enterprise may even be called into question because the New Testament Apocrypha is a modern category made up of distinct, often unrelated ancient works. The texts should be treated within the general framework of early Christian anti-Judaism, beside the widely studied, more easily accessible *adversus Judaeos* treatises.

So why attempt such a survey? I hope that this preliminary survey will serve as both an invitation and an encouragement to further study, not just the study of anti-Judaism in the texts, but also the intensive study of each of the documents individually. It is also the goal of this study to demonstrate a certain level of continuity (perhaps intertextuality) between the other more "official" literature of the early church and the apocryphal literature in the hopes that future discussions of early Christian anti-Jewish polemic will include the New Testament Apocrypha. In order to illustrate the commonalities and the differences, and also to avoid the problems listed above regarding chronological and geographical uncertainties, the anti-Jewish material in the apocryphal texts will be presented under five general headings often used to characterize patristic anti-Judaism: (1) the proper text of Scripture (Greek versus Hebrew); (2) the role of the ritual Law; (3) the messiahship of Jesus (often argued in terms of whether messianic prophecies had been fulfilled by Jesus); (4) the death of Jesus (often termed deicide); and (5) the rejection of Israel.[20]

## The Proper Text

One of the intriguing aspects of the Jewish-Christian debate is the existence of two divergent forms of the "Old Testament," the Hebrew and the Greek. The church apologists based their arguments on the Greek while the Jews tended to argue from the Hebrew (and sometimes from the Greek).[21] In fact, those Christians who studied the Hebrew text, most notably Origen and Jerome, were criticized as "Judaizers" because they seemed to make the church dependent on the Jews for the "true" Scriptures, an intolerable situation in a polemical

---

20. See Simon, *Verus Israel,* 135–78.

21. This representation is, of course, a vast oversimplification of the situation, but serves our purpose in terms of delineating anti-Jewish texts.

context.[22] On the other side of the coin, the Jews responded to the Christian appropriation of the Septuagint by commissioning new translations, such as Aquila's version, which were more literal translations of the Hebrew text than the Septuagint, and which did not contain, or offered alternate translations of, many of the passages Christians relied on to prove that Jesus was the Messiah foretold in Scripture. Justin Martyr even accuses Jewish teachers of having erased certain parts of Scripture that the Christians claimed prophesied the coming of Christ.[23]

This dispute over the proper text is the least represented aspect of the Jewish-Christian debate in the apocryphal literature. In the *Dialogue of Timothy and Aquila*, the Christian Timothy attacks Aquila's claim that the Christians have manipulated Scripture to suit their own needs.[24] Timothy's response consists of an assault on the Jewish translation of Scripture by Aquila (the namesake of the character in the dialogue) and a defense of the Septuagint. The Greek version is to be preferred because it, in contrast to Aquila's version, was inspired by the Holy Spirit. In a reworking of the legend contained in the *Letter of Aristeas*,[25] Timothy claims that the seventy-two translators, each dwelling in separate rooms, gave exactly identical translations of the Hebrew text. Thus, while not following exactly the line of argumentation employed by Justin, the author of the *Dialogue of Timothy and Aquila* does attempt to accomplish the same goal, that is, to establish the trustworthiness of the Greek Christian Old Testament over against any other version.

Also in the *Dialogue of Timothy and Aquila*, a slightly different claim is made against the Jewish Scriptures. The Christian interlocutor argues that the book of Deuteronomy is not to be used in the debate because it "was not dictated by the mouth of God but [one MS adds 'deuteronomized'] by Moses. This is why it was not deposited in the *'aron*, that is to say, the ark of the covenant."[26] Thus

---

22. For a discussion of Origen's relationship with the Jews, see N. de Lange, *Origen and the Jews: Studies in Jewish-Christian Relations in Third-century Palestine* (Cambridge: Cambridge Univ. Press, 1976). A good summary of the knowledge of Hebrew in the early Christian writers is C. J. Elliot, "Hebrew Learning among the Fathers," in *Dictionary of Christian Biography*, 2.851–72.

23. Justin Martyr, *Dialogue with Trypho* 71–73: "And from the ninety-fifth (ninety-sixth) Psalm they have taken away this short saying of the words of David: 'From the wood.' For when the passage said, 'Tell ye among the nations, the Lord hath reigned from the wood,' they have left, 'Tell ye among the nations, the Lord hath reigned'" (ANF 1.234–35). For a full discussion of this passage in Justin, see O. Skarsaune, *The Proof from Prophecy: A Study in Justin Martyr's Proof-text Tradition: Text-type, Provenance, Theological Profile* (NovTSup 56; Leiden: Brill, 1987) 35–46.

24. For a full discussion of the dialogue, see Williams, *Adversus Judaeos*, 67–78. For the text, see F. C. Conybeare, *The Dialogues of Athanasius and Zacchaeus and of Timothy and Aquila* (Oxford: Clarendon, 1898) 65–104. For bibliography on all the apocryphal works discussed in this essay, see Charlesworth with Mueller, *New Testament Apocrypha and Pseudepigrapha*.

25. See R. J. H. Shutt, "Letter of Aristeas," in J. H. Charlesworth, ed., *The Old Testament Pseudepigrapha* (2 vols.; Garden City, N.Y.: Doubleday, 1983, 1985) 2.7–34. For a discussion of Christian reworking of the legend, see S. Jellicoe, *The Septuagint and Modern Study* (1968; repr., Winona Lake, Ind.: Eisenbrauns, 1978) 41–47.

26. Fol. 77r; quoted from Simon, *Verus Israel*, 90 (see also p. 150). The passage is also dealt with in Williams, *Adversus Judaeos*, 72. This same theme is also developed in the *Didascalia Apostolorum* 26, and in slightly different terms by Maximus.

Timothy, while recognizing the extra books modern Protestants call the Old Testament Apocrypha, does not accept one of the books of the Pentateuch as canonical because of its "human" origin. In general it seems that this position was not taken up by many writers because, as Simon correctly argues, "it placed in question the unity of scripture, and this was regarded as dangerous."[27]

A related argument is made in the *Kerygmata Petrou*, where the author asserts that:

> The prophet Moses having by the order of God handed over the law with the elucidations to seventy chosen [men] that they might prepare those who were willing among the people, after a short time the law was committed to writing. At the same time some false pericopes intruded into it. These defamed the only God, who made heaven and earth and all that is in them.[28]

The "wicked one" placed these false pericopes in the text to lead believers away from God, and only those who know how to ferret out the true from the false will understand God's will and plan. The obvious claim here is that the Jews cannot separate truth from falsehood and thus stand condemned, whereas the Christians are able to discern the difference.

As regards this debate about the proper text, there is both continuity and discontinuity with the patristic writings. The patristic and apocryphal texts share a common defense of the Greek version of the Scriptures over against the Hebrew and later more literal Jewish translations into Greek. The apocryphal texts are somewhat distinct in that they also contain attacks on portions of the biblical text that the patristic texts do not generally dispute, namely Deuteronomy and isolated pericopes within the Pentateuch.


## The Ritual Law


Clearly one of the major disputes between emerging Christianity and Judaism was whether or not Christians were obligated to observe the Mosaic Law (and later, the rabbinic elaboration of it). As the "Pauline" position that Christians (especially Gentiles) were not required to observe the Law came to dominate, the patristic writers searched for ways to explain the place of the Law to their Christian audiences. In the Apostolic Fathers, the *Epistle of Barnabas* gives two reasons why the Law is not to be understood as the Jews understand it: (1) the Jews forfeited the Sinai covenant when Moses threw down the two tablets he had brought down from the mountain because the people had turned to idols by fashioning the golden calf (chap. 4);[29] and (2) the Jews misunderstood the

---

27. Simon, *Verus Israel*, 90.

28. Homily 2.38; quoted from Hennecke-Schneemelcher-Wilson, *New Testament Apocrypha*, 2.533. See also Wilde, *Treatment of the Jews*, 214–16.

29. See also *Sibylline Oracles* 8.299-301.

true spiritual and christocentric intent of the Law and interpreted it literally (see chap. 10). Barnabas explains the dietary laws to illustrate his point:

And now for that saying of Moses, *You are not to eat of swine, nor yet of eagle, hawk, or crow; nor of any fish that has not got scales.* In this there are three distinct moral precepts which he had received and understood. (For God says in Deuteronomy, *I will make a covenant with this people that will embody my rules for holiness;* so, you see, the Divine command is no sense a literal ban on eating, and Moses was speaking spiritually.) The meaning of his allusion to swine is this: what he is really saying is, "you are not to consort with the class of people who are like swine, inasmuch as they forget all about the Lord while they are living in affluence, but remember Him when they are in want.[30]

Melito of Sardis, Tertullian, and others also argue that the Law was not eternal, but only a preliminary sketch or model of what was to come.[31]

The situation is not nearly so clear in the apocryphal literature because of the presence of Jewish-Christian Gospels, works that maintained a fairly high regard for the Law and for the Christian's responsibility to uphold it. However, it is not possible to supply a comprehensive picture of these works' positive evaluation of the Law because of their suppression by the "orthodox."[32] Only fragments survive, and they do not contain prolonged defenses of the position that Christians should observe the Law, but there are some portions that hint at such a view. In a reworking of the story of the rich young man (Matt 19:16-24), the *Gospel of the Nazaraeans*, as reported by Origen, relates the following:

The other of the two rich men said to him: Master, what good thing must I do that I may live? He said to him: Man, fulfil the law and the prophets. He answered him: That I have done. He said to him: Go and sell all that you possess and distribute it among the poor, and then come and follow me. But the rich man then began to scratch his head and it [*the saying*] pleased him not. And the Lord said to him: How can you say, I have fulfilled the law and the prophets? For it stands written in the law: Love your neighbor as yourself; and behold, many of your brothers, sons of Abraham, are begrimed with dirt and die of hunger—and your house is full of many good things and nothing at all comes forth from it to them. (*Comm. on Matt.* 15.14 on 19:16-24)[33]

Though not a general endorsement of the whole of the ritual Law, the story does explicitly connect the familiar saying of Jesus about selling all and giving the proceeds to the poor as a requirement of discipleship with the fulfillment of the Law and the Prophets, a connection not made in the canonical Gospels.

---

30. Quoted from M. Staniforth, trans., *Early Christian Writings* (New York: Penguin, 1968) 206. See M. B. Shukster and P. Richardson, "Temple and Bet Ha-midrash in the Epistle of Barnabas," in *Anti-Judaism in Early Christianity*, 2.17-31.

31. For Melito's argument, see S. G. Wilson, "Melito and Israel," in *Anti-Judaism in Early Christianity*, 2.81-102.

32. See the discussion in Hennecke-Schneemelcher-Wilson, *New Testament Apocrypha*, 1.134–52. Almost all that we know of these Gospels is found in citations in the church fathers.

33. Quoted, with slight alterations to eliminate archaisms, from Hennecke-Schneemelcher-Wilson, *New Testament Apocrypha*, 1.161.

More often than not, though, what has survived in the apocryphal Gospels mirrors the attitudes about the Law reflected in the canonical Gospels. Jesus is presented as a disputant with the Pharisees over the true intent of the Law. Oxyrhyncus Papyrus 840 preserves just such a dispute. In the pericope Jesus and his disciples enter the place of purification and are accosted by a "Pharisaic chief priest" who asks Jesus:

> Who allowed you to [trea]d this place of purification and to look upon [the]se holy utensils without having bathed yourself and even without your disciples having [wa]shed their f[eet]? On the contrary, being defi[led], you have trodden the Temple court, this clean p[lace], although no [one who] has [not] first bathed [himself] or [chang]ed his clot[hes] may tread it and [venture] to vi[ew] [these] holy utensils!

Jesus asks the priest if he considers himself to be clean, and the priest replies that he is because he has bathed himself in the pool of David. Jesus then responds to the priest's purity claim:

> Woe unto you blind that see not! You have bathed yourself in water that is poured out, in which dogs and swine lie night and day and you have washed yourself and have chafed thine outer skin, which prostitutes also and flute-girls anoint, bathe, chafe, and rouge, in order to arouse desire in men, but within they are full of scorpions and of [bad]ness [of every kind]. But I and [my disciples], of whom you say that we have not im[mersed] ourselves, [have been im]mersed in the liv[ing . . . ] water which comes down from [ . . . B]ut woe unto them that. . . .[34]

Reminiscent of several Synoptic scenes Jesus here emphasizes the relative unimportance of outward allegiance to the Law, and pronounces woes on those who concern themselves only with the strict adherence to the Law. It is not surprising then that in the *Gospel of Nicodemus (Acts of Pilate)* we find the chief priests and scribes standing before Pilate and accusing Jesus of breaking the Law by healing on the Sabbath.[35] Again the Jewish characters are represented as overly concerned with the letter of the Law.

The gnostic *Acts of John* condemns not only those who cling to the Law, but also the one who gave the Law, claiming that the "lawgiver is the lawless serpent."[36] Such an overtly negative attitude toward the Law is not to be found elsewhere in the corpus. Instead there is nearly always an attempt to link Moses and Jesus positively, either by maintaining that the Law was to be kept or by demonstrating that the Law's original intent had been misunderstood by its recipients. In the second alternative, the problem is not with God's Law, but with those who practice it with blinders on.

---

34. Quoted, with slight alteration, from Hennecke-Schneemelcher-Wilson, *New Testament Apocrypha*, 1.94–95. The brackets denote reconstructed words and phrases.

35. *Gospel of Nicodemus* 1.1; see Hennecke-Schneemelcher-Wilson, *New Testament Apocrypha*, 1.506. The Jews also make the claim in this scene, as they do in the canonical Gospels, that Jesus is a sorcerer and that he casts out demons by the power of Beelzebub. Pilate (who generally comes off favorably in the apocryphal works) defends Jesus from this attack by making the alternate claim that Jesus does such works "by the god Asclepius."

36. Chap. 94; quoted from Hennecke-Schneemelcher-Wilson, *New Testament Apocrypha*, 2.181.

# Messiahship of Jesus

Early Christian writers expend a lot of energy trying to demonstrate that the Hebrew Scriptures foretold the birth, life, death, and resurrection of Jesus. Although certain key passages such as Isa 7:14, the prediction of the virgin birth, are frequently the subject of debate between Jews and Christians, each writer approaches the task of proving Jesus is the Messiah in a slightly different way. All, however, share the hermeneutical principle that Christ is to be found on every page of the biblical text. Such christocentric readings often play havoc with any type of traditional Jewish reading of a text and are often strained, but it must be kept in mind that they are intended not to convert those who do not believe, but to confirm those who come to the texts already committed to a faith in Jesus as the Messiah. As Justin says in the *Dialogue with Trypho,* the things the prophets spoke "cannot be perceived or understood by all, but only by the man to whom God and His Christ have imparted wisdom."[37]

Once again the form of the debate is different in the apocryphal works, but the points at issue are the same. While Trypho and Justin argue over whether or not Isa 7:14 says that a virgin shall conceive (Trypho counters that the Hebrew text says "a young woman"), the *Gospel of Nicodemus (Acts of Pilate)* presents a scene in which some Jewish officials charge Jesus before Pilate of three things: "Firstly, that you were born of fornication; secondly, that your birth meant the death of the children in Bethlehem; thirdly, that your father Joseph and your mother Mary fled into Egypt because they counted for nothing among the people."[38] The accusations do not reflect any of the charges brought against Jesus in the canonical trial narratives, but they do reflect points about Jesus that were in dispute between Jews and Christians in the first few centuries. Each point relates to the Gospel birth narratives, the location of a large number of messianic proof texts, and the place, along with the passion narratives, where Jewish objections to Christian claims are most prevalent.[39] It is interesting to note that in the *Gospel of Nicodemus,* other Jewish officials defend Jesus against the charge that he is an illegitimate child, but the other charges go unanswered as Annas and Caiaphas accuse Jesus of threatening to destroy the Temple. Such a defense may indicate that the issue of the virgin birth was the most hotly debated of the messianic proof texts. Regardless, the whole scene, set within the trial of Jesus before Pilate and culminating with the Jews demanding that Jesus be cru-

---

37. *Dialogue with Trypho* 7 (ANF 1.198).

38. *Gospel of Nicodemus* 2.3; quoted from Hennecke-Schneemelcher-Wilson, *New Testament Apocrypha,* 1.508.

39. In the *Dialogue of Timothy and Aquila* (fol. 93r), the Jewish participant is presented as arguing that even the Gospel of Matthew (1:16, in a reading also found in the Old Syriac) presents Joseph as the father of Jesus: "Jacob begat Joseph, the husband of Mary, of whom was born Jesus who is called Christ, and Joseph begat the Jesus who is called Christ." Therefore, he claims, even the Christian texts do not uphold the virgin birth. For other Jewish tales about the parentage of Jesus, see Klausner, *Jesus of Nazareth.*

cified, seems to reflect in narrative form the same concerns found in Justin, and others, regarding the messianic prophecies.

Another way the apocryphal writers defend Jesus' messianic status is by the addition of proof texts not found in the canonical Gospels. One good example of this strategy is found in the *Gospel of Pseudo-Matthew* (a late compilation of several infancy Gospels), where Mary takes the three-day-old Jesus and places him in a manger where

> an ox and an ass worshiped him. Then was fulfilled that which was said through the prophet Isaiah: "The ox knows his owner and the ass his master's crib" (Isa 1:3). Thus the beasts, ox and ass, with him between them, unceasingly worshiped him. Then was fulfilled that which was said through the prophet Habakkuk: "Between two beasts are you known" (Hab 3:2 LXX).[40]

One could argue that since this text is not overtly anti-Jewish, it does not really belong in this survey; however, the excerpt does point out that Christians continued to feel the need to defend their messianic claims by appeal to as many proof texts as they could find. It is likely that this is a response to continuing counterclaims by Jews that Jesus did not fulfill the messianic prophecies; this text thus rightly has a place in a survey of Jewish-Christian polemics.[41]

## The Death of Jesus

As the early church separated from Judaism and came to be dominated by Gentiles, one charge against the Jews became very popular. Christian writers increasingly came to blame the Jews for the death of Jesus and to exculpate the Romans. This tendency is already apparent in the canonical Gospels, but it becomes even more apparent in other early Christian writings. In Melito's paschal homily the Jews are pictured as accepting the blame for Jesus' death: " 'I did,' says Israel, 'kill the Lord.' "[42] Melito also charges that the Jews

> prepared for him sharp nails and false witnesses
> > and ropes and scourges
> > and vinegar and gall
> > and sword and forceful restraint as against a murderous robber.
>
> For you brought both scourges for his body
> > and thorn for his head:

---

40. Quoted from Hennecke-Schneemelcher-Wilson, *New Testament Apocrypha*, 1.462.

41. That Jewish legends and tales about Jesus, often defamatory, continued to circulate in the eighth and ninth centuries (the approximate date of the *Gospel of Pseudo-Matthew*) is certain; see the various talmudic stories as well as the medieval compilation known as the *Toledoth Yeshu*, the "Life of Jesus" (summarized in Klausner, *Jesus of Nazareth*; see also the article "Toledoth Yeshu" in *Encyclopedia Judaica*, vol. 15, cols. 1208–9).

42. Quoted from S. G. Hall, *Melito of Sardis on Pascha and Fragments* (Oxford and New York: Clarendon, 1979) 41. For other examples of the charge that the Jews were directly responsible for Jesus' death, see Tertullian, *An Answer to the Jews* 8, 10; Origen, *Contra Celsum* 2.34.

> and you bound his good hands,
>> which formed you from earth:
> and that good mouth of his which fed you with life
>> you fed with gall. And you killed your Lord at the great feast.
>
> (*On Pascha* 79)

As can be seen from this quotation, the Jews are presented as no longer merely initiators or manipulators of the trial against Jesus, but they are active participants in the crucifixion.

Nowhere is this tendency to blame the Jews more evident than in the surviving portions of the *Gospel of Peter,* a second-century retelling of the passion narrative. The Akhmimic fragment begins with Herod and the judges refusing to wash their hands at the trial of Jesus, an obvious literary play on the Matthean scene (Matt 27:24) in which Pilate washes his hands and proclaims his innocence with regard to Jesus' blood. Herod, not Pilate, then orders his own troops to take Jesus away to be crucified. Jesus then undergoes many of the torments known from the canonical Gospels (mocking, the crown of thorns, scourging, etc.), but the text makes it clear that it is the Jewish soldiers who act against Jesus, not the Roman soldiers. As Jesus is on the cross, the soldiers command that his legs should not be broken "so that he might die in torments."[43] They give Jesus gall with vinegar and "fulfilled all things and completed the measure of their sins on their heads." After Jesus' death the Jews are even pictured as drawing the nails from his hands.[44]

After Jesus' burial, the scribes and the Pharisees and elders ask Pilate for soldiers to guard the tomb (see Matt 27:62-66, 28:11-15). The *Gospel of Peter* makes clear that not only were the soldiers at the tomb at the moment of the resurrection, but the elders of the Jews were there also. The soldiers confess Jesus as "Son of God," but the Jews convince Pilate that it would be better for the soldiers to be kept quiet about what they have witnessed. Pilate agrees and commands the soldiers to say nothing.

Although the *Gospel of Peter* provides the fullest account of the Jews' responsibility for the death of Jesus, there are at least two significant variations on this theme in other apocryphal works. In a fragment of the Jewish-Christian *Gospel of the Nazaraeans* the Jews are not said to have actually crucified Jesus, but instead they are pictured as having bribed the Roman soldiers: "The Jews

---

43. All quotations from the Gospel taken from Hennecke-Schneemelcher-Wilson, *New Testament Apocrypha,* 1.223–26. This material is also included in the brief summary by Wilde, *Treatment of the Jews,* 216–18. For a unique, yet full treatment of the *Gospel of Peter,* see J. D. Crossan, *The Cross That Spoke: The Origins of the Passion Narrative* (San Francisco: Harper and Row, 1988).

44. See also the *Legend of Abgar* (King Abgar says that he would have taken a force and destroyed "the Jews who crucified him" if Roman sovereignty had not restrained him); *Acts of Peter* 32 (Simon Magus challenges Peter to prove that faith in Jesus, "whom the Jews destroyed," is of God); *Apocalypse of Peter* (Eth.) 2 (the work refers to Christ whom the Jews crucified); and *Apocalypse of Paul* 48 (Moses tells Paul that he is weeping because on the day that the people hanged Jesus, God wept for him).

bribed four soldiers to scourge the Lord so severely that the blood might flow from every part of his body. They had also bribed the same soldiers to the end that they crucified him."[45]

In two other apocryphal works, the devil is said to be responsible for the actions of the Jews against Jesus. In a long indictment of Satan in the *Acts of Peter*, the apostle charges that: "You did harden the heart of Herod . . . and did give Caiaphas the boldness to hand over our Lord Jesus Christ to the cruel throng" (*Acts of Peter* 8).[46]

Similarly, in the *Acts of Thomas*, the serpent relates to Thomas: "I am he who inflamed Herod and kindled Caiaphas to the false accusation of the lie before Pilate; for this was fitting for me; I am he who kindled Judas and bribed him to betray Christ to death" (*Acts of Thomas* 32).[47] It is hard to tell whether this second charge actually heightens or diminishes the guilt of the Jews for the death of Jesus. In one sense they are associated with the adversaries of God, the devil and his cohorts, but in another sense they are in some way excused from some of the responsibility because they had been used by Satan to accomplish his purpose.

It is clear that the apocryphal works share with many other early Christian writings the tendency to make the Jews more directly responsible for the death of Jesus. It is also clear that the noncanonical material develops some new twists to the theme, and thus provides additional insight into the continuing early Christian claim that it was the Jews who really killed the Lord, not the Romans.

## The Rejection of Israel

To many Christian writers it is clear that God has rejected his people for their having rejected his Messiah. Having witnessed the miraculous deeds of Jesus and heard his teachings, the Jews refused to believe in him.[48] As a result, God has now turned to the Gentiles and brought them into the church, and God has allowed the holy city of Jerusalem, along with the Temple, to be destroyed by the Romans. But to the surprise of many authors, even those events have not persuaded the Jews to repent and believe in Jesus: "Even when your city is captured, and your land ravaged, you do not repent, but dare to utter imprecations

---

45. Quoted from Hennecke-Schneemelcher-Wilson, *New Testament Apocrypha*, 1.164.

46. Quoted, with slight alteration, from Hennecke-Schneemelcher-Wilson, *New Testament Apocrypha*, 2.295. See also Wilde, *Treatment of the Jews*, 221–22.

47. Quoted from Hennecke-Schneemelcher-Wilson, *New Testament Apocrypha*, 2.352. See also the *Ascension of Isaiah* 11.19, where it is said that the adversary envied Jesus and roused the children of Israel against him (Knibb, in *OTP* 2.175).

48. See *Acts of Andrew and Matthias* 13–15, where Jesus, in the presence of the high priests, turns two sphinxes into living beings so that they might prove that Jesus is indeed God; Jesus also brings Abraham, Isaac, and Jacob into the high priests to refute their claims that Jesus is not God; see also the *Gospel of Nicodemus* 1, where the Roman standards, even when improperly held by Jews, bow down before Jesus.

on Him and all who believe in Him."[49] The Jewish opponents of these writers continue in their ways despite God's clear movement away from them.

In the New Testament Apocrypha there is little explicit mention of the destruction of the Temple as God's punishment on the Jews, but there is one notable exception. In book 1 of the *Sibylline Oracles,* immediately after a particularly venomous anti-Jewish account of the passion of Jesus, the destruction is "foretold":

> Then when the Hebrews reap the bad harvest,
> a Roman king will ravage much gold and silver....
> But when the temple of Solomon falls in the illustrious land
> cast down by men of barbarian speech
> with bronze breastplates, the Hebrews will be driven from their land;
> wandering, being slaughtered, they will mix much darnel in their wheat.
> There will be evil strife for all men;
> and the cities, violated in turn,
> will weep for each other on receiving the wrath of the great
> God in their bosom, since they committed an evil deed.[50]

But the Jews should have known earlier that the Temple was no longer the abode of God. Playing on the Gospel account of the rending of the Temple veil, the *Gospel of the Nazaraeans* tells of the collapse of the wondrously large lintel of the Temple at the moment of Jesus' death (frag. 21, 36), indicating that God was no longer present in the Temple (see Josephus, *J.W.* 6.5.3 §293–300).

God has now abandoned Israel and begun to call the Gentiles to faith. The apocryphal writers see this as part of God's plan from the beginning, made known before the birth of Jesus to Mary, who in the *Protevangelium of James* alternately weeps and laughs because she sees two peoples, "one weeping and lamenting and one rejoicing and exulting."[51] In *5 Ezra* 1:24-26, God says emphatically:

> I will turn to other nations and give to them my name, that they may keep my statutes. Since you have forsaken me, I will also forsake you. When you implore me for mercy, I will have no mercy upon you. When you call on me, I will not hear. For you have defiled your hands with blood and your feet are swift to commit acts of murder.[52]

And in another passage in *5 Ezra,* God gives what once belonged to Israel to the nations (2:10). The old covenant is no longer valid; the new covenant (Christianity) is in force.[53]

---

49. Justin Martyr, *Dialogue with Trypho* 108 (quoted from ANF 1.253).

50. *Sibylline Oracles* 1.387-400 (quoted from Collins, in *OTP* 1.344). See also *5 Ezra* 2:7 for the theme of the scattering of Israel because of their disbelief.

51. *Protevangelium of James* 17.2 (quoted from Hennecke-Schneemelcher-Wilson, *New Testament Apocrypha,* 1.433).

52. Quoted from Hennecke-Schneemelcher-Wilson, *New Testament Apocrypha,* 2.643.

53. See *Kerygma Petri:* "A new one has he made with us. For what has reference to the Greeks

# Conclusion

To continue the idea of surprise: it is somewhat surprising, given the sheer volume of material generally associated with the label "New Testament Apocrypha," that there is not a greater amount of explicit anti-Judaism in these texts. Instead the texts seem to relate more to the intramural arguments among the various factions of the early church (see the disputes mirrored in the *Acts of Thomas* and the *Epistle of Titus* over whether extreme asceticism is the proper Christian life-style), with only occasional swipes at Judaism. There are not, as there are among the patristic writers, whole narratives devoted to the "Jews" (except perhaps the *Dialogue of Timothy and Aquila*). It is as if the Jews stand outside many of the authors' direct vision, and are picked up only by their peripheral vision. The Jews often appear as historical figures when the drama of the life (and death) of Christ is told, but only rarely as the contemporary opponents of these Christian writers.

It probably should not be surprising that much of what can be found in a survey of anti-Judaism in the New Testament Apocrypha looks very much like what is found in the other early Christian writings. The charges against the Jews tend to revolve around only a few points, thus some overlap is to be expected. But it is also true, as evident from this survey, that although the apocryphal literature takes up many of the same themes of the more official literature of the church, it does not mirror the approach of those authors completely. There are several interesting twists and variations to what we find in the patristic writers' treatises. I hope that the adaptations outlined here will serve to bring more attention to the New Testament Apocrypha and will encourage further work on the corpus as more light is shed on the dimensions of anti-Judaism in early Christianity.[54]

---

and Jews is old. But we are Christians, who as a third race worship him in a new way" (quoted from Hennecke-Schneemelcher-Wilson, *New Testament Apocrypha*, 2.39).

54. I would like to thank the members of my graduate seminar on the New Testament Apocrypha at the University of Florida for their help in discovering many of the texts discussed in the chapter.

# -13-

# Anti-Semitism in Gnostic Writings

## R. McL. Wilson

"Once hostility has been aroused against a class of people and taken root, whatever the reason, everything in the object of the hatred becomes hateful; preconceived opinion gives birth or credit to fables and to calumnies, which in their turn contribute to strengthening it and spreading it more widely, and sometimes even outlive its real causes. The Jew ... did not escape this fatal law." These words, in their original French, were not written with reference to the Holocaust, or to any pogroms, or to hostility toward the Jews in medieval Christendom. They appear in the introduction to a collection of texts from Greek and Roman authors relating to Judaism, as the words omitted above would have at once made clear: "The Jew in the ancient world."[1] Nevertheless, they deserve to be borne in mind in any investigation of anti-Semitism, or more accurately of anti-Judaism, because they help to set things in a true perspective. Christianity is frequently saddled with the blame for anti-Semitism, and it has to be confessed that Christians have often been guilty; but the Jews were no more popular in the ancient world, even before the rise of Christianity, and outside of it, than they have been in later periods. Philo for example bears witness to gentile assaults upon the Jews in Alexandria, and there is other evidence. From some points of view it may be legitimate enough to classify all such phenomena under the general head of "anti-Semitism"; but it may also be important to note not only the similarities but the differences, and in addition the reasons for such outbreaks of hostility, for these reasons were not always the same. As Th. Reinach observes, "The opinions of the ancients regarding Judaism ... have passed in part, along with the whole legacy of ancient civilization, to the Christian church

---

1. Th. Reinach, *Textes d'auteurs grecs et romains relatifs au Judaisme* (Paris: E. Leroux, 1895) xvi.

and to modern states."[2] Yet in certain respects anti-Semitism in the Christian era is of a different character.

In approaching a topic such as this, it is vitally important that we should be clear from the outset as to what it is that we are looking for. Nothing would be easier than to search the documents, extract every passage that voices criticism of the Jews or Judaism, and claim the whole dossier as evidence for anti-Semitism. But is it in fact such evidence? Does criticism of the Jews or Judaism *ipso facto* constitute anti-Semitism? Or is it possible that a more nuanced position might be more true to the facts? Is this dossier, for example, evidence for anti-Semitism on a large scale, or only sporadically? Was the hostility general, or only shown by some group or other? Was it consistent and sustained, or does it only appear here and there in the literature? Again, what do we actually mean by the term "anti-Semitism"? The *Concise Oxford Dictionary* has under "anti-Semite" the entry "[person] hostile to Jews," but under "Semite" we find the definition "[member] of any of the races supposed to be descended from Shem, son of Noah (Gen 10:21ff.), including esp. the Jews, Phoenicians, Arabs, and Assyrians." Not so very long ago the strongest hostility toward the Jews, and in particular the state of Israel, was manifested by Arab nations—so here we have anti-Semitism practiced by Semites! There is also the understandable antipathy of Palestinian Arabs to the Jewish settlers who have occupied lands in what once was Palestinian Arab territory. Clearly "anti-Semitism" is one of those terms that call for careful definition if any discussion is to be meaningful.

Indeed, a further refinement may be necessary: in the paragraph above, reference has been made to "criticism of the Jews or Judaism" as one of the characteristics associated with anti-Semitism, but it is perfectly possible for an author to voice criticism of Judaism as an institution, or of the ordinances and institutions of the Jewish religion, without being hostile to the Jews. A salient example is provided by the apostle Paul, who has some severe criticism of the Jewish Law and thus provides ammunition for those who find anti-Semitism in the New Testament; but at the same time and in the same letters this same Paul also voices his concern for the conversion and salvation of the Jewish people. He was after all a Jew himself, as indeed were many, if not most, of the New Testament writers. It is in fact possible to trace several gradations, from outright hostility to the Jews and Judaism, and everything connected with them, through milder degrees of criticism that do not of necessity involve hostility, to a criticism that cannot in any real sense be called anti-Semitic. The *Gospel of Peter*, for example, may fairly be claimed as anti-Semitic, since a part of the author's

---

2. Reinach, *Textes*, ix. S. Sandmel (*Anti-Semitism in the New Testament?* [Philadelphia: Fortress, 1978] 5) objects to the view that Christian anti-Semitism "is merely a legacy left to Christendom from the pagan world," affirming that there is no relationship between Christian and pagan anti-Semitism. In that connection it should be observed that Reinach remarks (pp. xv–xvi) that neither racial nor economic anti-Semitism nor religious intolerance played any appreciable role in the Greco-Roman period. The whole question is somewhat more complex than is sometimes allowed.

purpose is to shift the onus for the crucifixion from Pilate and the Romans to Herod and the Jews. But is all criticism of the Jews or Judaism anti-Semitic to that degree or in that sense? This is a question that must be borne in mind as we approach the gnostic texts.

A further point is the need for some historical perspective. We must recognize the possibility that the situation was different at different periods, and that this is reflected in the evidence at our disposal. In the Fourth Gospel "the Jews" is "the title regularly given by John to Judaism and its official leaders, who stand over against Jesus." As C. K. Barrett notes, "John's use of the title shows that he (like most Christian writers at and later than the end of the first century A.D.) was well aware of the existence of the Church as a distinct entity, different from and opposed by Judaism, which it claimed to have supplanted."[3] One question that immediately arises is: How much further back can this awareness be traced? Is it always present, or only from the time of the separation of church and synagogue? Samuel Sandmel notes that Matthew rewrites freely, "openly expressing anti-Semitism that was not explicit in Mark," but that the invective is usually addressed to scribes and Pharisees rather than to "the Jews."[4] From this he deduces that "for Matthew the scribes and Pharisees represent what we would today call 'the establishment' and that Matthew is appealing, as it were, over the heads of 'the establishment' to the ordinary Jews, inviting them into the new movement."[5] In that respect there is already some difference between Matthew and the Fourth Gospel, which in Sandmel's words "is widely regarded as either the most anti-Semitic or at least the most overtly anti-Semitic of the Gospels."[6] The gnostic texts for the most part belong to a later period, into the second century, and one might naturally assume that here the process would have developed further; but that is not something that may be taken for granted.[7] We need to examine the texts and see what they actually have to say.

One feature of many gnostic systems is the inversion of values brought about by the downgrading of the Old Testament Creator to the status of an inferior Demiurge, often depicted as hostile to the human race. Is that to be considered a fruit of anti-Semitism, or is it merely the logic of the gnostic repudiation of this world and all that belongs to it? It may be that in the case of Marcion we do have a touch of anti-Semitism, since he expressly made a point of purging his

---

3. C. K. Barrett, *The Gospel according to John* (London: SPCK, 1958) 143.

4. Sandmel, *Anti-Semitism*, 68.

5. Ibid., 69. At the beginning of the *Apocryphon of John* (Codex II, 1.5-17) John is upset by a Pharisee named Arimanius, who declares: "With deception did this Nazarene deceive you." In the *Testimony of Truth* (Codex IX, 29.20) the scribes and Pharisees "belong to the archons who have authority over them." These passages take a negative view of the Pharisees, but whether this implies hostility to Jews is quite another matter.

6. Sandmel, *Anti-Semitism*, 101.

7. Cf. H. Jonas, in *The Bible in Modern Scholarship*, ed. J. P. Hyatt (Nashville: Abingdon, 1965) 289: "The more archaic the source, the more vehement the anti-Semitism. The comparatively conciliatory, mitigating views of a Valentinus are clearly second thoughts, and not first thoughts."

"New Testament" of every Jewish element; but it has long been a moot point whether Marcion is to be thought of as a Gnostic, and even if he is, there remains the other question: Did all Gnostics manifest such an anti-Jewish attitude? In that connection there is the further point of the presence of Jewish elements and Jewish influences in many gnostic systems—so much so that some scholars have argued for a Jewish origin for the whole gnostic movement. A quarter of a century ago Hans Jonas made some penetrating observations on this question, which still merit attention: "On one point there can surely be no quarrel: the Gnostics, as a matter of plain fact, made liberal use of Jewish material; they must therefore have been acquainted with it."[8] But at the same time "the nature of the relation of Gnosticism to Judaism—in itself an undeniable fact—is defined by the *anti-Jewish animus* with which it is saturated."[9] For Jonas, therefore, Gnosticism is clearly and beyond question anti-Jewish; but that was before the Nag Hammadi codices became fully accessible. It remains to be seen whether examination of the evidence that they provide will confirm that judgment or entail some nuancing of it.

In regard to the figure of the Demiurge, it should be noted that the earliest Christian Gnostics "do not *expressly* name the God of the Old Testament as creator of the world; either they speak of angels who made the world, or they ascribe the creation to a 'power.' The Church Fathers would probably have mentioned it, had they either named or intended the God of the Old Testament."[10] Such details may be pointers to stages of development within the gnostic theology, which ought not to be ignored. One of the problems in tracing the history of that development is precisely that of determining where and when some element was first introduced; for example, where and when the characteristic gnostic fusion of Greek and Jewish ideas first took place: some aspects cannot be documented before the second century, but others may well be older.

Reference has already been made to the presence of Jewish elements and Jewish influences in many gnostic systems. We need only recall, on the most superficial level, that one of the Nag Hammadi texts bears the title the *Paraphrase of Shem*, a second the *Second Treatise of the Great Seth*, a third the *Three Steles of Seth*, and a fourth *Melchizedek*; several include the term "apocalypse" in their titles. This does not even begin to take account of the very considerable amount of Jewish material of one kind or another in the texts. (Although it must be noted that insofar as the material was drawn from the Old Testament, the LXX version was also the Bible of the early church, so that this material, while ultimately Jewish, could have been derived through the medium of Christianity. Here as in other cases the problems are more complex than is sometimes realized.) Alexander Böhlig[11] long ago pointed to the *Umdeutung* that has taken

---

8. Jonas, *The Bible*, 286.
9. Ibid., 288.
10. W. Foerster, *Gnosis* I (New York and Oxford: Oxford Univ. Press, 1972) 1.34.
11. A. Böhlig, *Mysterion und Wahrheit* (Leiden: Brill, 1968) 90–101. "If pieces of tradition from

place in the taking over of these Jewish elements, a revision and reinterpretation to adapt them and make them suitable for gnostic purposes. We need to consider whether such adaptation should also be regarded as anti-Jewish: in such cases as the use of Isa 45:5; 46:9 LXX as the boast of the Demiurge[12] that may be so, if the downgrading of the God of the Old Testament is to be so regarded; but there are other cases in which it is difficult to see any kind of an anti-Jewish slant. The Nag Hammadi *Exegesis on the Soul,* for example, contains a cluster of Old Testament and other quotations that do not seem to present any anti-Jewish bias: indeed at one point the text says, "Concerning the harlotry of the soul the Holy Spirit prophesies in many places," and then follow citations of Jer 3:1-4 LXX; Hos 2:4-9; and Ezek 16:23-26a LXX.[13] Here the prophetic material is quite clearly given a positive assessment. In the introduction to this text in the Coptic Gnostic Library edition, W. C. Robinson writes: "*ExSoul* is important in that it reflects a simple form of the androgyne myth without any anti-Jewish aspects."[14] It remains to be seen whether the same holds true for other gnostic texts.

Gnostic knowledge of the Old Testament has been described as "meagre and truncated," and indeed has sometimes been said to be limited to the early chapters of Genesis. The latter statement, of course, has in view the reinterpretation in gnostic cosmogonies of the narratives of the creation and the Fall: with the repudiation of this world and all that belongs to it, and the downgrading of the Creator into the Demiurge, the story of the Fall in particular has to be stood on its head. This may perhaps account for Jonas's reference to "the massive evidence of anti-Jewish use of Jewish material,"[15] but it has to be remembered once again that Jonas wrote before the Nag Hammadi material became fully available. In point of fact the text most frequently quoted in a fairly wide range of material is not from Genesis; it is the verse from Isaiah cited above (45:5), the boast of the Demiurge. Moreover the range of the Old Testament books quoted is quite extensive. The evidence points rather to a selective use: the

---

Judaism, and also from Jewish Christianity, may have filtered into it [Gnosticism] in large numbers, it yet creates something entirely new; to speak of Jewish Gnosis can only mean that the material here disseminated is Jewish, but not that these circles still either could or wished to make any claim to be Jews" (p. 83). H. G. Bethge (in B. Layton, ed., *Nag Hammadi Codex II, 2-7* [NHS 20-21; 2 vols.; Leiden: Brill, 1989] 2.14) notes that Jewish influence and background are "a dominant and especially characteristic element in *OnOrgWld,*" and that the gnostic interpretation of the material varies considerably, from a total revaluation to relatively unaltered adoption of given Jewish ideas and motifs.

12. E.g., in *Hyp. Arch.* (NHC II, 4) 86.30; see J. M. Robinson, ed., *The Nag Hammadi Library in English* (3rd ed., San Francisco: Harper and Row; Leiden: Brill, 1988) 162. Cf. also W. Foerster, *Gnosis* (New York and Oxford: Oxford Univ. Press, 1974) 2.44, and the references for these texts in the index, p. 352. F. Siegert (*Nag-Hammadi-Register* [Tübingen: Mohr (Siebeck), 1982] 3) refers to Exod 20:5 and Isa 45:5 for the boast, and lists the passages under the rubric ANOK PE PNOYTE.

13. Robinson, ed., *Nag Hammadi Library,* 193; Foerster, *Gnosis,* 2.104.

14. Layton, ed., *Nag Hammadi Codex II, 2-7,* 140.

15. Jonas, *The Bible,* 289.

Gnostics chose those passages that suited their purpose and reinterpreted them in accordance with their own ideas.[16]

In this connection it should be noted that reinterpretation of the early chapters of Genesis does not at first sight appear to be so prominent in the Nag Hammadi texts as in the patristic reports, although some texts may simply presuppose it without entering into detail. The index to Foerster's anthology presents a striking contrast, in that it lists only thirty-three references to Genesis for volume 2, containing eight Nag Hammadi texts, against more than a hundred for volume 1, which presents the patristic material.[17] Moreover, twenty-four of the thirty-three references in the second volume relate to pages 45–48 (the *Hypostasis of the Archons*). To keep things in proper perspective, however, it should be added that pages 105–20 of volume 1 strictly belong with the Nag Hammadi material: here the *Apocryphon of John* is brought together with a passage in Irenaeus that runs parallel to the first part of it. That reduces the number of entries for the first volume by some thirteen, but the disparity is still considerable.

These findings are confirmed by examination of *The Nag Hammadi Library in English* (hereafter *NHLE*) since here the reinterpretation appears predominantly in three texts, the *Apocryphon of John*, the *Hypostasis of the Archons*, and *On the Origin of the World*, each of which incidentally focuses attention on a different section of the Genesis narrative.[18] The *Tractatus Tripartitus* appears to present a special case, since the reinterpretation seems to be less prominent than in the other cases, and is largely confined to the section on anthropogony (104.4–108.12). The question is complicated by the fact that the Valentinian system has here undergone some revision: Attridge and Pagels in their commentary note that the author "revises the major themes of Valentinian theology more radically than any other extant source and approximates more closely than any other Valentinian thinker to the positions taken by more orthodox theologians of the third and fourth centuries."[19] They therefore suggest a date in the first half of the third century, or even later.[20] Moreover the Demiurge "is not

---

16. For a cursory survey, based on Foerster's *Gnosisbuch* and therefore not a complete conspectus, see "The Gnostics and the Old Testament," in G. Widengren, ed., *Proceedings of the International Colloquium on Gnosticism* (Stockholm: Almqvist and Wiksell; Leiden: Brill, 1977) 164–68. The vast preponderance of the quotations does indeed come from the first six chapters of Genesis, but there are numerous references also to Exodus, the Psalms, and Isaiah. Seventeen Old Testament books in all are represented, but we must also pay due regard to the question of distribution: some schools may have been much more biblically oriented than others.

17. Since only eight texts are included, this could convey a misleading impression. For a more complete list see Siegert, *Nag-Hammadi-Register*, 335ff., which lists over a hundred for the first six chapters. The scope of this study does not permit examination in detail.

18. Cf. also the *Testimony of Truth* (Codex IX, 45.23–48.15) (Robinson, ed., *Nag Hammadi Library*, 454–55).

19. H. W. Attridge, ed., *Nag Hammadi Codex I* (NHS 22-23; 2 vols.; Leiden: Brill, 1985) 1.177. See also E. Thomassen (*Le traité tripartite* [Bibliothèque Copte de Nag Hammadi: section "textes" 19; Quebec: Laval Univ. Press, 1989]), who takes a different view on some points.

20. Attridge, ed., *Nag Hammadi Codex I*, 1.178.

characterized by negative attributes, except that he is unaware that 'the movement within him is from the spirit' " (101.3-4).[21] The anti-Jewish use of Jewish material would thus seem to have been less massive than would appear from our patristic sources; or possibly the development was in the direction of a gradual phasing out of such reinterpretation. Certainly some of the other texts would seem to contain little or no specifically Jewish material—which should not be taken to imply any diminution of the Jewish contribution to the development of Gnosis and Gnosticism.

There is one passage in the *Tractatus*, in some respects rather obscure, that might seem to contain criticism of the Jews: it refers to "the things which came forth from the <race> of the Hebrews, things which are written by the hylics who speak in the fashion of the Greeks" (110.23-25), and includes a reference to "many heresies which exist to the present among the Jews" (112.20-22). This is, however, part of a longer discussion beginning at 108.13, which contains criticism of Greek philosophy as well. As Attridge and Pagels note,[22] three stages of revelation are distinguished: the hylic wisdom of the Greek, the psychic of the Hebrews, and the perfect revelation conveyed by Christ. This is a gnostic version of the position found in some "orthodox" documents also, which sees Christianity as superior both to the wisdom of the Greeks and to that of the Hebrews. Christians indeed are sometimes described as "a third race," distinct from both Jews and Greeks. Similarly W. Foerster notes with reference to the book *Baruch* by the gnostic Justin that "Judaism and heathenism were incapable of receiving the message of salvation and spreading it further afield." Only with Jesus did the angel Baruch at last find success.[23] The passage in the *Tractatus* is thus not so anti-Semitic as might perhaps appear at first sight.

The *Gospel of Philip* presents a number of cases that may serve to illustrate something of the range of possibilities, although it shows no overt and explicit anti-Semitism. Its generally Valentinian character fits well, as indeed does the *Tractatus Tripartitus*, with Jonas's comment about the "comparatively conciliatory" views of a Valentinus.[24] At 62.26, for example, we find the words:

> If you (sing.) say "I am a Jew," no-one will be moved. If you say "I am a Roman," no-one will be disturbed. If you say "I am a Greek, a barbarian, a slave, a free man," no-one will be troubled. If you say "I am a Christian" [ . . . ] will tremble.

---

21. Ibid., 1.184.

22. Ibid., 2.417, 424; see also 1.185. Thomassen (*Le traité tripartite,* 412ff.) sees three groups: the Greeks and barbarians (109.24–110.22); a mixed group, a fusion of the Jewish and Hellenistic traditions (110.22–111.5); and the prophecies (111.6–112.9); but he notes that the author distinguishes between the prophecies as such, deriving from the spiritual sphere, and their interpretation by the prophets and the Jews (112.9ff.); see his note on 111.17-23 on p. 416. We may perhaps recall the discussion of the origins of the Law in the *Epistle of Ptolemy to Flora.* Criticism of other views, not necessarily Jewish only, is voiced in *On the Origin of the World, Eugnostos,* and the *Sophia of Jesus Christ,* to name a few.

23. Foerster, *Gnosis I,* 51.

24. See n. 7 above.

The lacuna in the final sentence is unfortunate, but quite clearly Christians are being contrasted as a people apart, distinct from other groups in society, just as in the passage mentioned in the preceding paragraph. Here anti-Semitism obviously does not come into question, or we should have to assume hostility to Greeks, Romans, and the rest as well!

At 75.30 the original *NHLE* translation (1977) ran:

> No Jew [was ever born] to Greek parents [as long as the world] has existed. And [as a] Christian [people] we [ourselves do not descend] from the Jews. [There was] another [people and] these [blessed ones] are referred to as "the chosen people of [the living God]" and "the true man" and "the Son of man" and "the seed of the Son of man."

The restorations here could be justified as reflecting the separation of church and synagogue and the Christians' consciousness of their status as now the true Israel; but even so there are problems. We need only compare the reconstruction offered by J. E. Ménard:

> There was not [again] any Jew [coming] from the [Greeks, so long as the Law] was in force. And [we ourselves were begotten] from the Jews [before we became] Christians.[25]

In support of Ménard's reconstruction of the second sentence, it may be noted that there are two earlier points (52.21ff.; 62.5-6) where "Hebrews" appear to be contrasted with Christians: they represent a lower level from which Christians have now passed. The lacunae here however are such as to make any reconstruction precarious, and the latest *NHLE* frankly recognizes the fact:

> No Jew [ ... ] [ ... ] has existed. And [ ... ] from the Jews. [ ... ] Christians, [ ... ] these [ ... ] are referred to as "the chosen people of [ ... ]" and "the true man."

The point is that on earlier reconstructions (of which several might have been quoted) there might be grounds for detecting an element of anti-Semitism here. However, with half of the text missing for the last ten lines of the page, restoration cannot be other than conjectural and affords no firm foundation on which to build. This passage must therefore be left out of consideration.

Of the two other passages mentioned above, 52.21ff. runs: "When we were Hebrews, we were orphans and had (only) our mother, but when we became Christians we obtained a father and a mother." As R. M. Grant observed long ago, these words are close to the Basilidian statement, recorded by Irenaeus, that they were "no longer Jews, but not yet Christians" (*Adv. Haer.* 1.24).[26] This certainly places the Jews on a lower level, but whether it should be interpreted as evidence for anti-Semitism is quite another question. The statement at 62.5-6,

---

25. J. E. Ménard, *L'évangile selon Phillipe* (Strasbourg: Univ. of Strasbourg Press, 1967) 95 (the page of the codex is here numbered 77, not 75).

26. R. M. Grant, "Two Gnostic Gospels," *JBL* 79 (1960) 6.

"He who has not received the Lord is still a Hebrew," is probably to be understood along the same lines. The strangest reference to Jews or to Hebrews in this document is however at 55.27ff.: "Mary is the virgin whom no power defiled. She is a great anathema to the Hebrews, who are the apostles and apostolic men." If as elsewhere the "Hebrews" represent an earlier and less advanced stage from which the Gnostic has emerged, then here he appears to be superior even to the apostles (cf. Carpocrates ap. Irenaeus 1.25). We may perhaps recall the view of F. C. Burkitt that Valentinus and others were Christians who sought "to set forth the living essence of their Religion in a form uncontaminated by the Jewish envelope in which they had received it."[27] Whether this implies an anti-Semitic bias remains open to question; there was polemic also against the "orthodox," and on occasion against other gnostic groups.[28]

There is reference to Hebrews and proselytes in the opening words of the *Gospel of Philip:* "A Hebrew makes another Hebrew, and such a person is called 'proselyte.' But a proselyte does not make another proselyte." That is a simple statement of fact and cannot be claimed in evidence, unless there was something in the fragmentary following lines to make the whole anti-Semitic. What emerges from the document as a whole is the gnostic consciousness of superiority to the nongnostic, including other Christians as well as "Hebrews," but there is no real evidence here for anti-Semitism. Indeed the interest in the Hebrew language shown at 62.13 (cf. the references to Syriac [=Aramaic][29] at 56.8 and 63.22) might point in the opposite direction, unless it is merely a piece of learned decoration.

Two logia in the *Gospel of Thomas* recall Sandmel's comment, cited above, about Matthew appealing over the heads of "the establishment," the scribes and Pharisees, to the ordinary Jew. These are logia 39, about their hiding the keys of knowledge, and 102, the fable of the dog in the manger. Logion 53, about the true circumcision, recalls Rom 2:25ff., and if Paul's words there are classed as anti-Semitic the same should probably be said of this logion.[30] Logion 43 contains the words: "From what I say to you, you do not understand who I am, but

---

27. F. C. Burkitt, *Church and Gnosis* (Cambridge: Cambridge Univ. Press, 1932) 27ff.

28. Cf. K. Koschorke, *Die Polemik der Gnostiker gegen das kirchliche Christentum* (NHS 12; Leiden: Brill, 1978) 148 n. 67: "The reproach of Judaism plays a fundamental role...in the debates between Gnosis and the church.... 'Jew' in gnostic usage is not a historical but a theological category" (see also his index, p. 274). He remarks that in Valentinian exegesis of Romans what Paul describes as the marks of the "Jews" rank as characteristics of the psychic Christians. Attridge and Pagels (*Nag Hammadi Codex I*, 2.424) note that some Valentinians identify the Jews with the psychic church, while other Gnostics "saw a correspondence between the Jews who persecuted Christ and the leaders of orthodoxy who persecuted Gnostics"; on the whole topic they refer to Koschorke, *Die Polemik*, 148–51. It is thus sometimes necessary to ask whether what on the surface refers to the Jews may not actually refer to another group for which they stand as a symbol. In the latter case such polemic is scarcely to be called anti-Semitic in the ordinary sense of the term.

29. Cf. A. Böhlig, *Gnosis und Synkretismus* (Tübingen: Mohr [Siebeck], 1989) 2.418ff. The article (pp. 414–53, originally in *Studien zu Sprache und Religion Ägyptens* [Göttingen: Vandenhoeck and Ruprecht, 1984]) is concerned with the question of Aramaic elements in the Nag Hammadi texts.

30. Cf. *The Concept of Our Great Power* 45.17-22: "Then those men who follow after him (i.e.,

you have become like the Jews; for they love the tree and hate its fruit, and they
love the fruit and hate the tree." However this is to be understood, it is at least
somewhat disparaging with regard to the Jews. Finally, logion 65 contains the
parable of the Wicked Husbandmen, concerning which Mark (12:12) remarks
that the Jewish authorities recognized that it was aimed at them; but in *Thomas*
it does not have the "allegorizing" embellishments that appear in the canonical
Gospels and make the application more specific. Does *Thomas* present a more
primitive version, or a condensation of the canonical parable? Assessment of
this Gospel presents problems similar to those that arise in connection with the
canonical Gospels: there are sayings of Jesus, with canonical parallels, that voice
criticism of the Jews or of Jewish institutions, of the scribes and Pharisees, and
so on. How far are these authentic sayings of Jesus, how far do they reflect a later
stage in the history of the early church? And for our present purposes: How far
are they to be considered anti-Jewish? If Jesus challenged some current Jewish
custom or practice, was he *ipso facto* guilty of anti-Semitism? It is not difficult
to see how much depends upon our definition of the term.

A more obvious case for consideration appears in the *Second Treatise of the
Great Seth* (*NHLE* 1988, 368), where Adam, Abraham, Isaac and Jacob, David
and Solomon, the prophets and even Moses are all described as laughingstocks.[31]
"Neither he [the Hebdomad, i.e., the Demiurge] nor those before him, from
Adam to Moses and John the Baptist, none of them knew me and my brothers"
(63.31–64.1). A few lines further down (64.18ff.) we read: "The Archon was a
laughing-stock because he said, 'I am God, and there is none greater than I. I
alone am the Father, the Lord, and there is no other beside me. I am a jealous
God.'" The echoes of the boast of the Demiurge, although they are not exact
quotations, make it clear that it is he who is in question. This passage thus is
to be included with others of the kind. Insofar as the Creator God of the Old
Testament is degraded to the status of an archon hostile to humanity, there is
possibly an anti-Jewish element here; but it is by no means clear that this also
involved an outright hostility toward the Jews.

In the early years of the church's life, its members, in particular those who
had grown up as Jews and then became followers of "the Way," had to face opposition, hostility, and even persecution at the hands of the Jews who adhered to
their ancestral traditions. Naturally the Christians reacted and sought to defend
themselves; and in the process they sometimes drew analogies between their
own situation and the opposition encountered by Jesus in the course of his ministry. This is reflected at various points in the New Testament, and particularly

---

the imitator) will introduce circumcision. And he will pronounce judgment on those who are from
the uncircumcision, who are the (true) people" (Robinson, ed., *Nag Hammadi Library*, 313).

31. Cf. *Testimony of Truth* 70.2ff. (Robinson, ed., *Nag Hammadi Library*, 458), where David
and Solomon are associated with the demons. See S. Giversen, "Solomon und die Dämonen," in
M. Krause, ed., *Essays on the Nag Hammadi Texts in Honour of Alexander Böhlig* (NHS 3; Leiden:
Brill, 1972) 16–21.

in the Gospels. One problem here is to determine how far the evidence relates to the historical ministry of Jesus, and how far it is colored by the later experience of Christian communities, for example at the time of the separation of church and synagogue. A second problem is to decide whether, or how far, the defense passed over into attack, to polemic and hostility, to anti-Judaism. Reference has already been made to passages in the *Gospel of Thomas* that have parallels in the canonical Gospels and present us with just these problems. Our difficulties are only increased by the fact that the Gnostics quite often took over such material, but used it in their own way and for their own purposes. We are therefore confronted with the further problem: Does this material in a gnostic context reflect (1) the historical events of the life of Jesus, or (2) the Christian understanding of these events in the light of the later experience of the church, or (3) a gnostic reinterpretation of the material for gnostic ends and gnostic purposes?

The *Gospel of Truth* (Codex I, 19.18-30) presents an example for consideration:

> In the place of instruction he came in the midst, he spoke the word as a teacher. There came to him those who were wise in their own estimation, putting him to the proof; but he confounded them, for they were foolish. They hated him, for they were not truly wise. After all these there came to him the little children, those to whom belongs the knowledge of the Father.

Here we have allusion rather than explicit quotation, although the reference is clearly enough to Jesus (mentioned on the preceding page, although not named in the present context). The "wise in their own estimation" would then be the Pharisees (and perhaps the Sadducees), who are often introduced in the Gospels as putting Jesus to the test.[32] The last sentence, with its reference to the "little children," recalls the "Johannine thunderbolt" of Matt 11:25; Luke 10:21; indeed K. Grobel notes: "19.21-28 looks very much like a dramatization of this synoptic passage."[33] These words could thus be taken as a generalizing summary of the teaching ministry of Jesus and of the Pharisaic reaction; but are they anti-Jewish? The little children who came to Jesus in the course of his earthly ministry were presumably also Jewish! In a gnostic context, however, the whole

---

32. Cf. the New Testament echoes and allusions identified by Puech in E. Hennecke and W. Schneemelcher, eds., *New Testament Apocrypha* (Philadelphia: Westminster, 1963) 1.237. The references suggested for the first sentence are, however, somewhat problematic, as the question marks show. L. Cerfaux ("De Saint Paul à l'évangile de la Vérité," *NTS* 5 [1958–59] 106–7) noted long ago that both in Luke 2:42-52 and in the quotation in Irenaeus (cf. the *Infancy Gospel of Thomas* 6, in Hennecke and Schneemelcher, eds., *New Testament Apocrypha*, 1.394) the context is very different. He plausibly suggests that the "place of instruction" might be simply the synagogue; cf. also K. Grobel, *The Gospel of Truth* (London: A. and C. Black; Nashville: Abingdon, 1960) 57. For discussion, cf. Ménard, *L'évangile de Vérité* (NHS 2; Leiden: Brill, 1972) 92–94; Attridge, *Nag Hammadi Codex I*, 2.55; both retain the suggestion that the first sentence "is possibly an allusion to Luke 2:46-49 or to a non-canonical infancy gospel." It would seem more likely that it is nothing of the sort. At the gnostic stage such precise identification appears no longer to be significant, or we should have exact quotation and not generalizing allusion.

33. Grobel, *Gospel of Truth*, 59.

is generalized: the revealer comes and proclaims the saving word of Gnosis, but those who are wise in their own estimation reject him, thereby revealing their own ignorance and folly. The little children are then the Gnostics, those who are willing to hear and to receive, to whom belongs the knowledge of the Father. In this case it is open to question whether any recollection of the original context remains, and therefore whether there is any anti-Semitism here at all.

One passage in the *Authoritative Teaching* might conceivably be claimed as evidence (33.4–34.34; *NHLE* 309–10). It refers to those without knowledge, who do not seek after God nor inquire about their dwelling place, which is in rest, but go about in bestiality. They are more wicked than the pagans (33.10); indeed they are sons of the devil (33.25-26). George MacRae remarks: "One is tempted to think of a Christian berating the Jews for their failure to heed the message which they have heard preached to them, but again there is no unambiguous allusion to either Christian or Jewish belief or practice."[34] He earlier notes that there is no trace of "the heavy dependence on Jewish speculation which we find in so many other Nag Hammadi tractates." A reference to the Jews is therefore at most a possibility, but it is a possibility that may perhaps be strengthened if we compare John 8:44, when Jesus says to the Jews: "You are of your father the devil."[35] However, even if this Johannine verse may lie somewhere in the background, the reference in the *Authoritative Teaching* is not specifically to the Jews; in this context it may mean only that those who reject the gnostic message are worse than pagans. In that case there may have been an element of anti-Semitism at some earlier stage, but in its present form and in the present context the words are scarcely to be classed as anti-Semitic.

There is a similar case in the *Second Apocalypse of James* (59.12ff.), where we find:

> You have passed judgment on yourselves (cf. Matt 27:25?) and because of this will remain in their fetters. You have burdened yourselves and will repent, (and yet) you will in no way profit.[36]

A few lines further on we read:

> Therefore I say to you <in the name of the Lord>: "See, I have given you your house—this of which you say that God made it, (and) in which he who dwells in

---

34. Robinson, *Nag Hammadi Library*, 304–5; also in D. M. Parrott, ed., *Nag Hammadi Codices V, 2-5 and VI* (NHS 11; Leiden: Brill, 1979) 258.

35. Cf. 1 John 3:8, 10. Curiously, John 8:31 at the beginning of this section refers to "the Jews who had believed in him." R. Bultmann (*The Gospel of John: A Commentary* [Philadelphia: Westminster, 1971] 314) considers vv. 30-40 as "addressed to people who have declared their faith in Jesus—however valueless that faith might be," and vv. 41-47 as "addressed to those who reject his word from the very outset." Barrett (*John*, 285) notes that "the only believers in this chapter are highly unsatisfactory," and later that v. 37 follows oddly after v. 31; but Johannine problems cannot be entered into here.

36. Translation after W. P. Funk, in W. Schneemelcher, ed., *NT Apocrypha* (rev. ed.; Cambridge: James Clarke; Louisville, Ky.: Westminster/John Knox Press, 1991) 1.338. Cf. C. W. Hedrick, in Parrott, ed., *Nag Hammadi Codices*, 139, and Robinson, ed., *Nag Hammadi Library*, 274–75.

it has promised to give you an inheritance. This I will tear down, to the ruin and derision of those who are in ignorance." (60.13-22)[37]

This is, however, part of a speech by James in which he appeals to the people to change their ways:

Abandon this difficult way, which has (such) a multitude of forms, [and] walk according to him who desires [that] you may become free men [with] me, after you have overcome every dominion! For he will not [judge] you on account of the things which you have done, but he will have mercy upon you. [For] it was not you who did them, but it was [your] lord (who did them). He (scil. Jesus) was [not] a wrathful one, but he was a kind father. (59.1-11)

The whole passage thus has a somewhat more irenic tone, presenting an appeal rather than outright condemnation, although it is still critical, and in the sequel the people show that they are not persuaded (61.4). The martyrdom (61.12–62.12) follows on the lines of the report in Hegesippus,[38] with some verbal similarities,[39] but is not overtly anti-Jewish.[40] A considerable place is given to James's dying prayer (62.16–63.28).

What is important here is that insofar as there is an element of anti-Judaism in the document it probably goes back to an earlier stage, to the Jewish-Christian tradition that has been taken over. In other words, it reflects the struggle between Jewish Christians and unbelieving Jews, not a conflict between Gnostics and Jews. It is not a piece of gnostic polemic against the Jews or Judaism, but a reinterpretation of older material for gnostic purposes. In Funk's words, the chief aim of this document

is not the denunciation of the ignorant, but the provision of a literary basis for a cultic reverence for James—a James who is appointed for the purpose of opening

---

37. The restoration follows Funk, in Schneemelcher, ed., *NT Apocrypha*, 338 and n. 9. Hedrick (in Parrott, ed., *Nag Hammadi Codices*, 140-41 and notes) offers another solution. In his commentary (*Die zweite Apokalypse des Jakobus aus Nag-Hammadi Codex V* [TU 119; Berlin: Akademie, 1976] 170) Funk links this passage with the Josephus quotation in Eusebius (*Eccl. Hist.* 2.23.20ff.), according to which the siege of Jerusalem was in requital for the martyrdom of James (not in the extant text of Josephus); see further below (n. 43).

38. Ap. Eusebius, *Eccl. Hist.* 2.23. On the martyrdom, cf. Böhlig, *Mysterion und Wahrheit*, 111–18. On the whole question of the traditions about James the Lord's brother see W. Pratscher, *Der Herrenbruder Jakobus und die Jakobustradition* (FRLANT 139; Göttingen: Vandenhoeck and Ruprecht, 1987) 177: "The James of Gnosis has become a completely different person compared with that of the nomistic Jewish Christianity."

39. Hedrick, in Parrott, ed., *Nag Hammadi Codices*, 108.

40. Cf. Funk, in Schneemelcher, ed., *NT Apocrypha*, 331: "The pointed contrasting of the known and the unknown father, of the earthly and the heavenly promise (small and great, evil and good), of might and mercy etc. not infrequently leads in this document to antithetic formulations which come very close to some antitheses of Marcion—yet without any polemic against the Jews." For C. Scholten, however (*Martyrium und Sophiamythos im Gnostizismus nach den Texten von Nag Hammadi* [JAC 14; Münster: Aschendorff, 1987] 51), this document "stands in direct confrontation with the Judaism which slew Jesus. Just because of its Jewish motifs the portrayal of the martyrdom takes on for the reader the value of a testimony against the Jews, such as would rather be expected from a non-Jewish Christianity." In his commentary Funk (*Die zweite Apokalypse*, 94, 170, 203) notes anti-Jewish tendencies and polemic.

the gates of heaven to those returning home, and distributing the reward (p. 55), who is envied by the creator (p. 55.25f.), "the first who will unclothe himself" (p. 56.9f.), indeed the one for whose sake redemption is bestowed on those to be redeemed (p. 56.2-7).[41]

In the *First Apocalypse of James* (25.7-9), Jesus tells James, "They will arrest me the day after tomorrow, but my deliverance will be near," and then bids him, "Depart from Jerusalem! For this (city) always gives the cup of bitterness to the children of light; it is a dwelling-place for many archons."[42] Further on we read, "This (people) existed [as] a type of the archons, and it deserved to be destroyed through them" (31.23-26; *NHLE* 265). Later on (36.16-19) Jesus says, "When you go away, then immediately war will be made with this land—therefore [weep?] for him who dwells in Jerusalem." If the injunction to weep is a correct restoration (so too Schoedel), this can hardly be considered hostile to the Jews. In this document there are clear similarities to the quotations from Hegesippus and "Josephus" in Eusebius, already mentioned,[43] but Schoedel notes, "It is often difficult to identify Jewish-Christian elements clearly, and no theme in our apocalypse can be assigned a Jewish-Christian provenance without reservation."[44] What is striking is the way in which the material has been transmuted by identification of the Jews with the archons. Thus at 33.2-5 James is warned, "When you are arrested and exposed to these sufferings, a multitude will arm themselves against you, in order that they may lay hold of you" (cf. *2 Apoc. Jas* 45.9-12, where "a multitude" is reported to be angry with James); but in the following lines (33.5-11) we find, "But especially three will lay hold of you, who sit as toll collectors. Not only do they demand tribute, but they also take away souls by stealth." As the immediate sequel shows, these three are among the keepers of the heavenly gates through which the soul must pass on its way to its true abode; this would be only the more clear if Schoedel's suggestion is correct "that in 34.26 there begins some variant of the formula in Iren. *Haer.* I.21.5 (Epiph. *Pan.* 36.3.4-5)" to be used by the soul confronting "the powers about the Demiurge."[45] In that case what might originally have been Jewish-Christian polemic against the Jews has been thoroughly gnosticized. As Schoedel notes, "The passion serves as a visible symbol of a cosmic struggle centered in Jerusalem, a 'dwelling-place of a great number of archons' (25.18-19), from which James must flee. Since both the Lord and James function as prototypes of the

---

41. Funk, in Schneemelcher, ed., *NT Apocrypha*, 331.

42. Translations after Funk, in Schneemelcher, ed., *NT Apocrypha*, 313–26, except as noted. See also W. R. Schoedel, in Parrott, ed., *Nag Hammadi Codices*, and Robinson, *Nag Hammadi Library*, 260–68.

43. Cf. above, n. 37. See also Pratscher, *Der Herrenbruder Jakobus*, 189–90, 229 n. 3, 251.

44. Schoedel, in Parrott, ed., *Nag Hammadi Codices*, 66. On p. 67 he writes: "Perhaps 1 Apoc. Jas. may be best understood as a product of Syrian Jewish Christianity penetrated by a variety of forms of Gnosticism." Scholten (*Martyrium und Sophiamythos*) expresses reservations about links with Jewish Christianity.

45. Schoedel, in Parrott, ed., *Nag Hammadi Codices*, 88.

Gnostic, the crucifixion and its aftermath become a representation of the agony through which every Gnostic must pass at death."[46]

In the *Apocryphon of James* in Codex I the disciples plead "not to be tempted by the devil, the evil one" (4.28-30). In the rebuke that follows they are told that they have not yet been abused, accused unjustly, shut up in prison, condemned unlawfully, "and crucified <without> reason, and buried <shamefully>,[47] as I was, by the evil one" (5.9-20). Here again there is reference to persecution, and it is linked with the passion of Jesus, but the Jews are not mentioned.[48] The "as I was" obviously refers to the passion of Jesus, and an allusion to the Jews could therefore be seen in the background; but the responsibility is placed on the shoulders of "the evil one."

One final reference to persecution appears in the *Second Treatise of the Great Seth:*

> After we went forth from our home, and came down to this world, and came into being in the world in bodies, we were hated and persecuted, not only by those who are ignorant, but also by those who think that they are advancing the name of Christ, since they were unknowingly empty, not knowing who they are, like dumb animals. They persecuted those who have been liberated by me, since they hate them. (Codex VII, 59.19-29; *NHLE* 366)

Here "those who are ignorant" could refer to the Jews, but it might also refer to non-Christians in general. What is significant in this passage is the reference to "those who think that they are advancing the name of Christ," which must clearly refer to "orthodox" Christians. This is a note that recurs in other documents also, testifying to gnostic polemic against orthodox Christianity. There are also indications of a polemic against other gnostic groups.

It has long been noted that the Gnostics gave little if any place to the crucifixion of Jesus: it was not the cross but the gnosis that he brought that was the vehicle of salvation. It was therefore a matter of some surprise when the Nag Hammadi texts were found to contain many references, some veiled but

---

46. Ibid., 66. Scholten (*Martyrium und Sophiamythos*) presents a detailed survey of the attitudes to suffering and martyrdom revealed in various Nag Hammadi texts. For *1 Apoc. Jas.*, see pp. 68–80, for *2 Apoc. Jas.*, pp. 47–61.

47. The *editio princeps*, with reservations, followed the MS reading, translating "in sand" or "in the sand"; see M. Malinine, et al., *Epistula Jacobi Apocrypha* (Zurich and Stuttgart: Rascher, 1968) 51. But, for one thing, the only person in the Bible said to have been buried in the sand is the Egyptian slain by Moses (Exod 2:12), which is not exactly helpful to understanding. Quispel noted that in *2 Apoc. Jas.* (62.7-12) James is buried up to the middle at his stoning, but this too seems rather remote.

48. F. E. Williams (in Attridge, ed., *Nag Hammadi Codex I*, 21) notes that this document "is less obviously Gnostic than many Nag Hammadi tractates," but thinks it "presupposes the existence of a small, elect community, who possess a secret, superior revelation communicated by Jesus." He also notes "a clarion call to martyrdom" at 4.22–6.21, "the extreme form of the Christian response to persecution" (p. 24). Scholten (*Martyrium und Sophiamythos*, 35) regards it as "a nongnostic preliminary stage in regard to gnostic interpretation of suffering," and notes that Old Testament or Jewish themes have left no recognizable traces (p. 47, referring to S. Pétrement, *Le Dieu séparé* [Paris: Cerf, 1984] 646–48, who thinks it could be directed against Jewish Christianity).

others quite explicit, to the passion story. For example, one of the first texts to be published, the *Gospel of Truth*, speaks of Jesus enlightening "those who were in darkness by reason of oblivion," giving them a way that was "the truth which he taught them"; the text continues: "Because of this, Error was wroth with him, persecuted him, was distressed at him, (and) brought to naught.[49] He was nailed to a tree, and became a fruit of the knowledge of the Father" (Codex I, 18.17-26). As in the *Apocryphon of James* the responsibility is assigned to "the evil one," so here it is given to "Error." Further on we find the words: "For this reason the merciful and faithful Jesus was patient in accepting sufferings until he took that book, since he knew that his death is life for many" (20.10-14). "He was nailed to a tree; he published the edict of the Father on the cross" (20.25-27). At first sight this second passage could be taken as a straightforward summary of the orthodox doctrine of the atonement, with an echo of Col 2:14, which on the evidence available prior to the Nag Hammadi discovery would be unusual in a gnostic text. The whole section, however, is a gnostic reinterpretation in which, as Attridge and Pagels put it, the text holds two poles in tension: "It does not, in a docetic fashion, deny the reality of Christ's suffering and death, nor is it unaware of the deeper, 'spiritual' significance of the crucifixion event."[50] Further on, they add: "The physical reality of the passion of Jesus is not ignored.... Its significance is, however, seen as revelatory, not atoning."[51] In the light of Scholten's study there may be another factor: its significance by way of encouragement for the facing of trials and tribulations.[52]

For our present purpose, however, what is significant is that in these texts the crucifixion is clearly a reality and not explained away; but there is no reference to the Jews or to Jewish responsibility. In other texts, in addition to those already mentioned above, that responsibility is clearly and unambiguously transferred to archons. Thus in the *Concept of our Great Power* we find:

---

49. Attridge and MacRae, in Robinson, ed., *Nag Hammadi Library*, construe the last two verbs here as intransitive and referring to the destruction of Error (see Attridge, *Nag Hammadi Codex I*, 2.50). The *editio princeps* and J. Ménard (*L'évangile de Vérité*, 88) take them as transitive, which makes the whole refer to Error's assault upon Jesus: "Error was wroth with him, persecuted him, oppressed him, brought him to naught." This makes perfectly good sense from an "orthodox" point of view, but at the expense of the Coptic usage. As to how Error could be "brought to naught" by Jesus, Grobel (*Gospel of Truth*, 51-53) answers, "In the same way implied in 1 Cor. 2:8: 'None of the *archontes* of this age understood this; for if they had, they would not have crucified the Lord of glory'—his crucifixion meant their downfall." As Attridge and Pagels note (*Nag Hammadi Codex I*, ad loc.), that archontic powers were responsible for the crucifixion "is a frequent theme in Gnosticism" (see further below).

50. Attridge and Pagels, *Nag Hammadi Codex I*, 2.51.

51. Ibid., 58.

52. Cf. Scholten, *Martyrium und Sophiamythos*, 102: "The given fact of the Passion of Christ, thus seen, is itself sufficient of a shock, and in any case requires an interpretation from the gnostic side, which certainly can come into play particularly when physical suffering of the disciples demands an aid to understanding." A footnote refers to *Gos. Truth* 18.21-27; 20.23-21.2; and *Gos. Phil* 63.21-24. Two of these are passages with which we are concerned.

> He opened the gates of the heavens with his words. And he put to shame the ruler of Hades; he raised the dead, and he destroyed his dominion. Then a great disturbance took place. The archons raised up their wrath against him. They wanted to hand him over to the ruler of Hades. Then they recognized one of his followers. A fire took hold of his (i.e. Judas') soul. He handed him over, since no one knew him. They acted and seized him. They brought judgment upon themselves.[53]

It is not difficult to see links with the passion narratives in the Gospels: "one of his followers" is naturally identified as Judas, who gave the mob he led a sign by which to identify Jesus (Matt 26:48; Mark 14:44); nobody else in that crowd knew him. The archons who "raised up their wrath against him" might originally have been the *archontes tōn Ioudaiōn*, the rulers of the Jews, but this has long been forgotten. It might be objected that such an interpretation entails the identification of the ruler of Hades as Pilate, but this might perhaps be explained by the Jews' hatred of the Roman domination of their country; or more probably it is simply part of the reinterpretation that has taken place. There are possible links also with the apocryphal *Gospel of Nicodemus* or *Acts of Pilate*,[54] although they are scarcely such as to suggest dependence. For present purposes the point is that once again what might at one stage have been directed against the Jews is now in its gnostic context completely transformed.

There is something similar in the *Second Treatise of the Great Seth*, but this time with a docetic element explaining away the reality of the passion:

> I was in the mouths of lions. And the plan which they devised about me to release their Error and their senselessness—I did not succumb to them as they had planned. But I was not afflicted at all. Those who were there punished me. And I did not die in reality but in appearance, lest I be put to shame by them because these are my kinsfolk. I removed the shame from me and I did not become faint-hearted in the face of what happened to me at their hands. I was about to succumb to fear, and I <suffered> according to their sight and thought, in order that they may never find any word to speak about them. For my death which they think happened, (happened) to them in their error and blindness, since they nailed their man unto their death. For their Ennoias did not see me, for they were deaf and blind. But in doing these things, they condemn themselves. Yes, they saw me; they punished me. It was another, their father, who drank the gall and the vinegar; it was not I. They struck me with the reed; it was another, Simon, who bore the cross on his shoulder. It was another upon whom they placed the crown of thorns. But I was rejoicing in the height over all the wealth of the archons and the offspring of their error, of their empty glory. And I was laughing at their ignorance.[55]

Here there are links with the theory attributed to Basilides, that it was Simon of Cyrene who was crucified and not Jesus; also with the laughing Jesus of the

---

53. Codex VI, 41.7-25; see Robinson, ed., *Nag Hammadi Library*, 314, and F. Wisse and F. E. Williams, in Parrott, ed., *Nag Hammadi Codices, V, 2-5 and VI*, 291-323 (this passage appears on pp. 306-7).

54. For this document see Schneemelcher, ed., *NT Apocrypha*, 1.501-536.

55. Codex VII, 55.9-56.19; cf. Robinson, ed., *Nag Hammadi Library*, 365.

following text in the Codex, the *Apocalypse of Peter* (83.3-24; *NHLE* 377).[56]
Reading with the Gospel story in mind, it is not difficult to see elements that
might refer to the Jews, in particular the words "these are my kinsfolk"; but
the Jews are never mentioned, and in the present context it is more likely that
the archons are intended. Once again, material that at some stage might have
reflected the struggle between Jewish Christians and the unbelieving Jews has
been converted into a vehicle for gnostic theology.

The *Apocalypse of Peter* (VII,3; *NHLE* 372-78) "is organized around three
vision reports attributed to Peter."[57] In the first of them Peter sees the priests and
people "running up to us with stones, as if they would kill us," but is told that
they are "blind ones who have no guide" (72.5-13; cf. 73.10-12: "these [people]
are blind and deaf"). The Jews are not explicitly mentioned, but anyone familiar with the canonical Gospels would naturally think of them at certain points,
particularly in view of the Gospel echoes that occur in this text; but as Brashler
notes, the vision is interpreted in terms of several groups, some of which seem
to belong to the orthodox church while others are better understood as rival
gnostic sects. "The apocalyptic form... has been employed to present a gnostic understanding of Christian tradition about Jesus. The traditional material is
skilfully interpreted in accordance with gnostic theology."[58] The polemic is directed primarily at orthodox Christians and rival gnostic groups, but Koschorke
remarks, "It is fascinating to see how the portraits of the Jews and those of the
heretics become merged in one another."[59] The Jews have become, as it were,
the prototypes for opponents of various kinds.

The unfortunately fragmentary *Testimony of Truth* (IX,3; *NHLE* 448-59)
begins with a reference to the old leaven of the Pharisees and the scribes of the
Law: "And the leaven is [the] errant desire of the angels and the demons and the
stars. As for the Pharisees and the scribes, it is they who belong to the archons
who have authority [over them]. For no one who is under the Law will be able
to look up to the truth, for they will not be able to serve two masters."[60] The
following lines present criticism of the Law from an ascetic and encratite point
of view ("the defilement of the Law is manifest"–it commands procreation). Further on (45.23-48.4) the author recounts the paradise story from Genesis, and
asks, "What sort of a God is this?" The answer is: "He has shown himself to

---

56. For discussion of this text see Koschorke (*Die Polemik*, 11-90), who sees here polemic against
orthodox Christianity. J. Brashler in his introduction (in Robinson, ed., *Nag Hammadi Library*,
376) notes: "The persecution of Jesus is used as a model for understanding early Christian history
in which a faithful gnostic remnant is oppressed by those 'who name themselves bishop and also
deacons.'" The statement "they will cleave to the name of a dead man, thinking that they will
become pure" (74.13-15) is obviously directed against orthodox Christian teaching (cf. Koschorke,
*Die Polemik*, 37-39).

57. Brashler, in Robinson, ed., *Nag Hammadi Library*, 372.

58. Ibid., loc. cit.

59. Koschorke, *Die Polemik*, 12.

60. Robinson, ed., *Nag Hammadi Library*, 450.

be a malicious grudger." The treatise, however, is not directed against the Jews at all; the author's chief opponents are "catholic Christians of the ecclesiastical establishment."[61] The purpose of the document is "to bolster the convictions of the author's fellow Gnostics and to warn them against the errors of (catholic) Christian opponents."[62] One element here, as Koschorke notes, is the opposition between the God of the Jews, whom the catholics serve (48.14-15), and Christ, whom the Gnostics follow.[63] In the author's eyes the orthodox, by retaining the Old Testament, were still bound to the old dispensation and were not truly living in "the freedom with which Christ has set us free."[64]

It is time to bring this discussion to a close, to draw the threads together and try to formulate the conclusions that seem to emerge. The focus of attention has been concentrated mainly on the Nag Hammadi texts, since the situation with regard to the patristic evidence is adequately summed up in the views expressed by Jonas a quarter of a century ago. How does the picture now appear?

Three points in particular may be singled out from Jonas's discussion of the alleged Jewish origins of Gnosticism: (1) his argument that the Gnostics made abundant use of Jewish material and must therefore have been acquainted with it; (2) his reference to the anti-Jewish animus with which Gnosticism is saturated; and (3) his reference to "the massive anti-Jewish use of Jewish material."

Of these, the first remains unchallenged, and indeed is confirmed by the evidence of the Nag Hammadi library. In fact, these texts provide attestation for gnostic use of some Old Testament books that in our patristic sources are not reported to have been used by the Gnostics. The other two points, however, now require some qualification: the anti-Jewish use of Jewish material is rather less massive than might appear, except where the figure of the Demiurge is concerned, and even here the reinterpretation of the Genesis narratives is not always specifically directed against the Jews. We have seen evidence in some texts of a gnostic reinterpretation of Jewish material for gnostic ends and gnostic purposes, with no sign of an anti-Jewish bias. Indeed, some material that might originally have had its *Sitz im Leben* in conflict between Jewish Christians and non-Christian Jews has been so reworked as to leave but little sign of its original setting: it now serves a gnostic purpose. In the same way, the Nag Hammadi texts do not suggest that Gnosticism is "saturated" with an anti-Jewish animus.

---

61. B. A. Pearson, in Robinson, ed., *Nag Hammadi Library*, 448.

62. Ibid., 448.

63. Koschorke, *Die Polemik*, 149. This document is discussed on pp. 91–174.

64. Many years ago J. Munck ("Jewish Christianity in Post-Apostolic Times," *NTS* 6 [1959–60] 110) quoted Macaulay's description, in his *History of England*, of the Earl of Crawford (who happened to be a Scot): "He had a text from the Pentateuch or the Prophets ready for every occasion. He filled the despatches with allusions to Ishmael and Hagar, Hannah and Eli, Elijah, Nehemiah, and Zerubbabel, and adorned his oratory with quotations from Ezra and Haggai. It is a circumstance strikingly characteristic of the man, and the school in which he had been trained, that, in all the mass of the writing which has come down to us, there is not a single word indicating that he had ever in his life heard of the New Testament."

There is admittedly a background of hostility, but there are few specific attacks
except in the *Gospel of Thomas*, which presents much the same problems in this
respect as do the canonical Gospels: If sayings of Jesus are critical of the Jews
or Jewish institutions, or of the scribes and Pharisees, are they thereby anti-
Semitic? Here it might perhaps be important to make a distinction, and here
the texts of Greek and Roman authors relating to Judaism could be of some
significance. These writers were looking on the Jews and Judaism from without,
often disparagingly and in condemnation, and hence it is legitimate to speak of
their anti-Semitism, although this anti-Semitism was not in all respects identical
with the anti-Semitism of later centuries. Jesus, however, was challenging from
within, as did prophets like Jeremiah, Amos, and Hosea. There is therefore a
very real question whether criticism from the lips of Jesus ought to be classified
as anti-Semitism at all. The situation is, however, different at a later stage, when
these sayings are seen and reinterpreted in the light of the experience of early
Christian communities, particularly at the time of the split between church and
synagogue. This is the stage represented, for example, by Matthew and the
Fourth Gospel, and by the *Gospel of Thomas*. Here we may find vindication of
another of Jonas's dicta: "The more archaic the source, the more vehement the
anti-Judaism." When such material is taken over by the Gnostics, it is sometimes
reinterpreted in a thoroughly gnostic fashion for gnostic ends.

Jean Daniélou in his *Théologie du Judéo-Christianisme* suggests among
other definitions of "Jewish Christianity" that it is "a form of Christian thought
which does not imply any link with the Jewish community, but finds expression in categories borrowed from Judaism."[65] Whatever the criticisms brought
against this definition, and the problems that it raises for the discussion and
investigation of Jewish Christianity, it does have a certain validity, for as he
says, following Goppelt, "Down to the middle of the second century, Christianity, spread throughout the Mediterranean basin, remains Jewish in structure."
What is important for our purposes is a further point: "This Jewish Christianity
was evidently that of the Christians who came from Judaism, but also that of
the converted pagans." For this means that Jewish elements in this period may
not necessarily have come from Judaism. They could already have become part
of the Christian tradition. The Jewish War, the fall of Jerusalem in 70 CE, the reconstruction at Jamnia—all had the effect of widening the gap, and at least from
the time of the Bar Kokhba revolt the Christian church was predominantly gentile. This could provide an explanation for some of the phenomena noted: the
reinterpretation of material possibly reflecting conflict between Jews and Jewish Christians, the gradual phasing out of "Jewish" material, and so on. What
emerges very often from the texts is the gnostic consciousness of superiority, not
only to the Jews, who are sometimes not mentioned, but to all non-Gnostics, in-

---

65. J. Daniélou, *Théologie du Judéo-Christianisme* (Tournai: Desclée and Co., 1958); English
trans.: *The Theology of Jewish Christianity* (London: Darton, Longman and Todd, 1964).

cluding other Christians. The equation of "Hebrews" with psychic Christians, as contrasted with Valentinians, may be disparaging to the Jews, as are some other items in our evidence, but disparagement does not always amount to hostility.

To sum up: if by anti-Semitism we mean hostility and antagonism, or material likely to provoke such hostility, there is little in the Nag Hammadi texts. Disparagement there is, to some extent, but we have to bear in mind Koschorke's comment about the reproach of "Judaismus" in gnostic polemic against orthodox Christians: in gnostic eyes, Christians who held to the Old Testament were little better than Judaizers. On occasion there is material that could be construed as reflecting the conflicts of Jews and Jewish Christians, but in a gnostic context this material is often reinterpreted in such a way as to yield a completely different significance. If we leave aside the downgrading of the Creator into the Demiurge, real evidence for an anti-Jewish animus is generally hard to come by.

# Epilogue

## *Joel Marcus*

It is not a denigration of the preceding essays to say that their purpose seems to be partly apologetic. They aim to show that, while the books of the New Testament and some other early Christian writings have harsh things to say about certain Jews and Jewish institutions, they do not demonstrate the sort of racial anti-Semitism, the hatred of Jews simply because they are Jews, that has so tragically characterized many Christians in the subsequent centuries. The New Testament writers and their earliest successors are thus at least partially absolved of responsibility for the bloody history of persecution that reached its climax in the Nazi Holocaust. The chief means to this apologetic end is the placement of the early Christian writings within particular historical contexts that explain their anti-Jewish polemic without recourse to the hypothesis of anti-Semitic prejudice.

In this historical approach the essays stand apart from any tendency to treat the Scriptures as artistic creations that should be literarily analyzed without reference to the historical conditions out of which they arose. Some of the essays, to be sure, use the methods and terminology of secular literary criticism in an attempt to lay bare the internal dynamics of the texts they investigate, but they do not do so in a way that divorces literary from historical investigation.

This consideration of the historical dimension of the texts, it seems to me, is absolutely required by the problem under investigation, and the best of all possible methods to study it is probably a combination of literary and historical inquiry. Robert Kysar's essay on the Fourth Gospel may serve as a model in this regard. It begins with a straight "literary" analysis of the texts in John that have to do with the Jews and Jewish institutions; the driving question of this portion of his essay is what impression "the reader," that is, *any* reader, would derive of Jews and Judaism from the sequence of John's narrative. Kysar then moves on, however, to a survey of recent attempts to reconstruct the history of

291

the Johannine community, implicitly recognizing that "the reader's" response to the portrayal of Judaism finally depends on exactly *who* that reader is, and that the readers about whom the exegete must first and foremost be concerned are the earliest ones within the Johannine community itself. Were they Jews or Gentiles, or was the community a mélange of both groups? What sorts of relationships had they had with non-Christian Jews, with Jewish Christians, with gentile Christians, and with non-Christian Gentiles before they heard John's Gospel? What knowledge had they previously had of traditions about Jesus and his relationships with various kinds of Jews? Asking these sorts of vital historical questions, and attempting to answer them, begins to turn the literary phantom called "the reader" into something more substantial.

The subject under investigation is no joking matter, but an analogy from the realm of humor may help to illuminate the importance of asking such historical questions. In the telling of "ethnic jokes," it makes a great deal of difference who is telling the joke, and to whom. To take the case most relevant to our subject, a "Jewish joke" takes on a very different valence depending on whether it is told by a Jew to other Jews, by a Gentile to other Gentiles, or in some other combination of teller and audience. The words may be the same, but the impact becomes radically different in each instance. In the first case, that of a Jew telling a Jewish joke to other Jews, the joke remains in the family, and the derision to which the Jewish characters in the story may be subjected is cushioned by the shared participation of both the teller and the audience in the Jewish people. In the second case, that of a Gentile entertaining other Gentiles with a Jewish joke, there is no such cushion, the joker is talking not about "us" but about "them," and the joke may subtly or overtly reflect anti-Semitic prejudice. The situation becomes a bit more complicated if the teller is Jewish but his audience is gentile, if the audience is a mixed group of Jews and Gentiles, and so on.

Similarly, the very same New Testament polemics against Jews could be construed as either anti-Semitic or not depending on the ethnic identity and sociological setting of the narrator and his audience. The central theme of this volume is that the polemic against Jews and Jewish institutions found within the New Testament is primarily an in-house phenomenon, analogous, *mutatis mutandis*, to the case of a Jew telling a Jewish joke to other Jews. It is mostly, in other words, a criticism formulated by Jews (i.e., Jewish Christians) against other Jews, and the audience for whose benefit the criticism is enunciated also includes a sizeable number of Jews (Jewish Christians). Hence, in the eyes of the scholars represented here, the New Testament's anti-Jewish polemic cannot rightly be labeled anti-Semitism, a term they would reserve for a "racial" prejudice against Jews as Jews. In my opinion, they make a convincing case for this contention.

The historical distance between the first-century and twentieth-century situations, then, makes a big difference in interpreting the anti-Jewish polemics of the New Testament. "Jew" and "Christian" then were not necessarily opposites, as they are for most people today; all of the very earliest Christians were both. Two other examples of this distance that have a profound impact on our subject are as follows:

1. In the New Testament era, the relative strengths of the synagogue and the church were vastly different from what they are today. Whereas in our time most Jews live in nominally Christian countries and their total number world-wide is a fraction of the total number of Christians, in the New Testament era the number of adherents, and hence the political power, of the Jewish commu-nity was far greater than that of the nascent Christian sect. Judaism was an old and, at least in some quarters, a respected religion, officially recognized by the Roman Empire and boasting well-known cultural heroes such as Abraham and Moses; Christianity, in contrast, was an upstart movement whose adherents worshiped a crucified criminal and were accused of undermining the empire with their atheism. Although the subject is steeped in controversy and the ev-idence is fragmentary, it appears that in some instances Jewish authorities or mobs exploited their relatively strong political position and their considerable autonomy to persecute Christians; as Lee McDonald points out in his essay on the early church fathers, the existence of such persecution is supported by, and at the same time helps to explain, the intensity of early Christian polemic against Jews. The balance of forces, then, differed greatly from the one that has prevailed in Christendom since the time of Constantine; from that time on, of course, the record of Jewish-Christian relations has been in great measure a sordid tale of Christian persecution of Jews.

2. Their relatively strong position, then, provided non-Christian Jews with the opportunity to persecute Christians; and the competition between the Chris-tian mission and a Jewish mission to Gentiles may have provided part of the motivation. The existence of a Jewish mission, to be sure, is also a point that is much debated in contemporary scholarly literature, and even the authors of the essays collected in this volume disagree about it. Whereas both James Dunn and Lee McDonald argue that it was a vital factor in the early Christian era, Scot McKnight's essay anticipates the results of his monograph in asserting its unim-portance and even nonexistence. I incline to the opinion of Dunn and McDonald on the basis of evidence such as the grudging acknowledgment of Pharisaic pros-elytizing in Matt 23:15. If there was such a Jewish mission competing with the Christian one, however, that was another way in which the first-century situa-tion differed from the twentieth-century one, and this difference is an important part of the historical background of early Christian polemic against Jews and Judaism. Rival evangelists can say some pretty nasty things about each other, as we have seen in our own time. In the particular case under discussion, early Christians would have thought that some non-Christian Jews, by their competing mission and their hostility to Jesus, were keeping Gentiles who might otherwise be kindly disposed from coming to a knowledge of God's definitive revelation of eschatological truth, the only "name under heaven given among human be-ings by which we must be saved" (Acts 4:12). This reconstruction makes the

intensity of their anti-Jewish polemic more understandable, although some aspects of that polemic may still—and perhaps should—make modern Christians uncomfortable.

Historical investigation, then, is an absolutely vital component of responsible study of anti-Judaism in the early Christian writings. We may add in passing that the contemporary upsurge in interest in this subject—an interest expressed for example in the publication of this volume—is itself a historical phenomenon worthy of note, reflecting in large measure the impact of that most shattering of recent historical events, the Holocaust, on Jew and Gentile alike.

Of course, merely acknowledging the historical factors behind early Christian polemic against Jews does not totally erase the problem that such polemic poses when it becomes part of the church's sacred Scripture. Here I would both agree and disagree with something Craig Evans says in an illuminating section of his introduction. Evans compares the New Testament polemic against Jews and Judaism with that of the Qumran sect against its enemies, concluding that the New Testament criticism is mild in comparison with that of Qumran. He then speculates that, had the Qumran sect survived and become more and more gentile over the centuries, its vituperation of its enemies would have come to be seen as an expression of anti-Semitism. It is not so seen, he adds, because we interpret the Dead Sea Scrolls, as we should, in their original context.

These are excellent points, but I wonder whether they acknowledge sufficiently the complicating factor that the New Testament writings have been canonized by the Christian church, whereas the Dead Sea Scrolls have been canonized by no group at all. As James Sanders's foreword and Robert Kysar's essay on John in particular recognize, this canonization, the attribution of divine authority that goes along with it, the historical distance caused by the intervening centuries, and the persistent friction between Christians and Jews have all led to a situation in which the New Testament polemics have often been read as timeless and eternally valid denunciations of the Jewish people. Such a hermeneutic is still very much alive today; in some Christian circles "Pharisee" is still a derogatory term for a self-righteous prig, "Judaism" is equated with legalistic works-righteousness, and there is little recognition that there is even a problem involved in New Testament statements such as the Johannine one that Jesus' Jewish opponents are of their father, the devil (John 8:44).

I do not see, however, why it should be *inevitable* that the anti-Jewish polemic in the New Testament should function canonically in this destructive, ahistorical way, as Robert Kysar seems to assume that it must. His assertion that the historical origin of such polemic becomes less and less knowable with the passing of centuries appears to me to be overly pessimistic in view of the solid exegetical gains to which he and others have contributed. Is it not arguable that exegetes in the latter part of the twentieth century understand better the factors behind John's depiction of the Jews than did, say, their counterparts in the Middle Ages? Is it really true that, because of its canonization as Holy Scripture, the Fourth Gospel now "stands on its own in isolation from the situation that occasioned its writing"? On the contrary, is it not possible to view the advent of historical criticism and its slow penetration of even some parish churches as part of a providential divine initiative to reverse this dehistoricizing process and bring the church's canonical Scriptures back into historical context? Indeed, contrary to Kysar's pessimism, might not historical criticism come to play a larger and larger role in the church in the coming years, especially by throwing light on such vital questions as the New Testament attitude toward Judaism and other religions, toward Jews and other "others"? " 'Tis a consummation devoutly to be wished."

It would be naive, however, to think that historical criticism can solve all of the hermeneutical problems arising out of the polemical references to Jews and Judaism in the New Testament and other early Christian literature. Some of the difficulty remains even when the historical setting of this polemic is taken into consideration, and this is partly because the New Testament attitude toward Judaism and the Jewish people is a subset of the peculiar New Testament eschatology. As Donald Hagner observes, for example, Paul's "anti-Judaism," so far as the Law is concerned, flows out of his conviction that in the crucifixion and resurrection of Jesus the new age has dawned, and that with its dawning the Mosaic Law as conceived in Judaism has passed away. As Paul expresses this certainty of accomplished eschatological change, "There is a new creation; old things have passed away; behold, new things have come into being!" (2 Cor 5:17). The difficulty is that most of the Jewish people did not share this certainty, so that they were unable to agree with Paul and the other New Testament writers when the latter drew corollaries concerning the eschatological transformation of central religious categories such as the Law and the people of God.

This Jewish reticence is understandable; Christians should not let their habituation to New Testament eschatology obscure the fact that it is extremely paradoxical. Probably some Jews were prepared to accept the proposition that the Law would be drastically transformed with the arrival of the messianic age; they may even have been willing to grant that, on "that day," when the Lord became one and his name one (Zech 14:9), Torah would become superfluous as an external commandment engraved on stone because it would now be written on human hearts (Jer 31:33; cf. 2 Cor 3:3). They might, moreover, have been willing to entertain the further possibility that, when this happened, the dividing wall of hostility between Jew and Gentile would be broken down, and Jews and righteous Gentiles would walk together in the eschatological light of the Lord (cf. Isa 2:2-5). But where was the evidence that that time had arrived, that the new age had indeed dawned in Jesus' death and resurrection? Had Jesus confirmed his messiahship by redeeming Israel? Had not his messianic claims, on the contrary, been thoroughly discredited by his ignoble death on a cross, a mode of death not only held in abhorrence throughout the Greco-Roman world but also seemingly cursed by God in the Torah (cf. Deut 27:26)? And in the absence of support for the Christians' extravagant eschatological claims, was it not an act of blasphemy to turn one's back on the everlasting covenant that God had given for as long as sun and moon should remain (cf. 2 Sam 23:5; Ps 89:30-37) and deny the distinctiveness of the nation whom he had chosen, in spite of all their failings, to be his special people forever (Exod 19:5-6)? Such denials struck at the very heart of Jewish identity, since they challenged what Jews had always seen as their raison d'être—their conviction of salvation-historical priority and eternal calling.

Of course, early Christian eschatology includes not only a strong sense that redemption has already begun but also a recognition that it is not yet complete. This characteristic Christian tension between the "already" and the "not yet" has major ramifications for the subject of Christian anti-Judaism. Because Paul, for example, believes that the Law-created boundaries between Jew and non-Jew have already begun to crumble under the explosive impact of Jesus' resurrection, he denies the final significance of Jewish and every other ethnic identity, along with the ultimacy of class and gender differences (see, e.g., Gal 3:28). But because he also knows that he lives in a world that has not yet experienced the final redemption in its fullness and thinks that until that consummation the distinctions built into creation by God will retain some sort of penultimate significance, he recognizes the continuing force of the commitment made by God to Israel at its birth and the unique nature of their reciprocal relationship (see, e.g., Rom 3:1-2; 9:4-5).

Paul is a central figure for the question investigated in this volume, and it is appropriate to close it with a reflection on the distance he traveled on the Damascus Road. Before his conversion to faith in Jesus, he seems to have felt in a visceral way the challenge to the centrality of the Law, and hence to Jewish self-understanding, that was posed by the Christian claim that the Messiah had died a salvific death while under the curse of the Law. He undoubtedly interpreted this claim as an insolent rebuke of the covenant God himself. It was only a blinding revelation, what he calls "an apocalypse of Jesus Christ" (Gal 1:12), that caused him to reevaluate that challenge and to proclaim the apocalyptic death of the Law and the consequent evaporation of the salvific distinction between Jew and Gentile. The distance between Paul the Pharisee and Paul the follower of Jesus, then, is an eschatological chasm that probably cannot be bridged by historical criticism or even by Jewish-Christian dialogue. It encapsulates, moreover, the entire problem this volume discusses, since Paul eventually arrived at a position that relativized Jewish religious claims and in that sense was "anti-Jewish" by definition. But Paul's stance, and the similar positions of other Christians in the earliest period, were not anti-Semitic, as the historical analysis deployed in this volume demonstrates; and that is a conclusion that may be productively explored in future attempts at dialogue between Christians and Jews.

# Index of Ancient Writings

## OLD TESTAMENT

**Genesis**
| | |
|---|---|
| 1:27 | 91 |
| 2:24 | 91 |
| 3 | 91 |
| 10:21ff. | 270 |
| 12–25 | 10 |
| 14:17-20 | 177 |
| 15:6 | 13 |
| 21:10 | 142 |
| 25:27 | 21 n.1 |
| 27:30-40 | 172 |
| 28:12 | 231 n.87 |

**Exodus**
| | |
|---|---|
| 1:8-14 | 63 n.29 |
| 1:15-22 | 63 |
| 2:1-10 | 64 |
| 2:11-22 | 64 |
| 2:12 | 283 n.47 |
| 3 | 23 n.4, 36 n.15 |
| 4:18-20 | 64 |
| 4:19 (LXX) | 64 |
| 7:11 | 162 |
| 7:22 | 162 |
| 13:1-16 | 210 |
| 19:5-6 | 296 |
| 19:5 | 163 |
| 19:6 | 158, 208 |
| 20:5 | 273 n.12 |
| 32–34 | 23 n.4 |
| 33:20 | 161 |

**Leviticus**
| | |
|---|---|
| 12:6-8 | 48 |
| 19:18 | 91 |

| | |
|---|---|
| 23:33-43 | 45 |
| 23:40 | 45 |
| 23:41 | 45 |
| 26:11-12 | 158 |

**Numbers**
| | |
|---|---|
| 12:5-8 | 175 |
| 12:7 | 175 |
| 16:5 | 162 |
| 24:17 | 46 |
| 25:1-9 | 202 |
| 25:1ff. | 202 |
| 25:6-9 | 206 |
| 25:14 | 203 |
| 26:9 | 205 |
| 31:16 | 202 |

**Deuteronomy**
| | |
|---|---|
| 6:4-9 | 210 |
| 6:4-5 | 91 |
| 6:4 | 157, 161 |
| 7:1-6 | 224 |
| 7:6 | 163 |
| 9:5 | 163 |
| 10:16 | 13, 155 |
| 10:17 | 161 |
| 11:13-21 | 210 |
| 13:1-11 | 207 |
| 14:2 | 163 |
| 16:13-15 | 45 |
| 16:13 | 45 |
| 16:15 | 45 |
| 18:15-20 | 108 |
| 21:23 | 231 n.87 |
| 24:1-4 | 91 |
| 27:26 | 296 |

**Deuteronomy** (*continued*) _____

| | |
|---|---|
| 28:28 | 9 |
| 29:1-3 [2-4E] | 5 |
| 29:3 | 144 |
| 29:4 (LXX) | 144 |
| 30:14 | 140 |
| 32:15 | 164 |
| 32:39 | xv |

**Joshua** _____

| | |
|---|---|
| 10:6-14 | 10 |

**Judges** _____

| | |
|---|---|
| 13:5 | 63 n.30 |

**1 Samuel** _____

| | |
|---|---|
| 15:22 | 182 |

**2 Samuel** _____

| | |
|---|---|
| 5 | 11 |
| 5:17-21 | 10 |
| 5:20 | 10 |
| 5:22-25 | 10 |
| 12:25 | 231 n.87 |
| 14 | xi |
| 23:5 | 296 |

**1 Kings** _____

| | |
|---|---|
| 18–19 | 36 n.16 |
| 19:10 | 135 |
| 19:14 | 135 |
| 22 | 36 n.16 |

**2 Kings** _____

| | |
|---|---|
| 17:20 | 6 |
| 22–23 | 36 |

**1 Chronicles** _____

| | |
|---|---|
| 14:13-16 | 10 |
| 23:31 | 156 n.21 |

**2 Chronicles** _____

| | |
|---|---|
| 2:4 | 156 n.21 |
| 31:3 | 156 n.21 |
| 36:11-16 | 4 |

**Nehemiah** _____

| | |
|---|---|
| 10:33 | 156 n.21 |

**Job** _____

| | |
|---|---|
| 1:21 | 161 |

**Psalms** _____

| | |
|---|---|
| 4:22-24 | 159 |
| 8:4-6 | 177 n.28 |
| 8:5-7 (LXX) | 177 n.28 |
| 8:6 | 159 |
| 22 | 97 |
| 24:5 | 164 |
| 31:21 | 163 |
| 34:14 | 161 n.46 |
| 34:19 | 163 |
| 35:8 | 11 |
| 39:7-9 (LXX) | 179, 181 |
| 40:4-8 | 179 |
| 40:6-8 | 172 n.16, 177, 181, 182, 184 |
| 40:6 | 182 |
| 50:8-10 | 182 |
| 51:16-17 | 182 |
| 62:12 | 163 |
| 68:22-23 (LXX) | 144 |
| 69:22-23 | 11, 144 |
| 79:6 | 152 |
| 88:23 (LXX) | 153 |
| 89:30-37 | 296 |
| 95:4 (LXX) | 204 |
| 95:7b-11 | 172 n.16 |
| 96:4 | 204 |
| 110:1 | 95 |
| 110:4 | 175, 177, 178, 184 |
| 119:98 | 163 |
| 130:8 | 63 n.30, 163 |

**Proverbs** _____

| | |
|---|---|
| 2:6 | 162 |
| 3:4 | 161 n.46 |
| 3:7 | 161 n.46 |
| 22:21 | 191 |
| 24:12 | 163 |

**Ecclesiastes** _____

| | |
|---|---|
| 5:15 | 161 |
| 12:10 | 191 |

**Isaiah**

| | |
|---|---|
| 1–39 | 37 |
| 1:2-4 | 227 |
| 1:3 | 26 |
| 1:4 | 3 |
| 1:9-10 | 205 |
| 1:10-13 | 182 |
| 1:13-14 | 156 n.21 |
| 1:21-23 | 27 |
| 1:21 | 4 |
| 2:2-5 | 295 |
| 2:6 | 6 |
| 2:9 | 5 |
| 5:1-7 | 26 |
| 5:8-9 | 24 |
| 5:18 | 23 |
| 5:21 | 161 n.46 |
| 6 | 36 n.15 |
| 6:1-3 | 231 n.87 |
| 6:9-10 | 8, 9, 84 n.15, 216, 234 n.108 |
| 7:14 | 231 n.87, 263 |
| 8:14 | 144 |
| 10:5 | xii |
| 13 | 201 |
| 14:12-14 | 153 |
| 18:23 | 5 |
| 25:4 (LXX) | 153 |
| 26:13 | 162 |
| 26:20-21 | 29 |
| 27:6 | xii |
| 27:9 | 148 |
| 28:7-8 | 28 |
| 28:14 | 10 |
| 28:16 | 144, 158, 162 |
| 28:21 | 10 |
| 28:22 | 10 |
| 29:9-10 | 9, 28 |
| 29:10 | 11, 144 |
| 29:13 | 156 |
| 30:9-11 | 3 |
| 40–55 | 36 |
| 40:3 | 12 |
| 42:18-19 | xvi |
| 45:1 | xi |
| 45:5 | 273, 273 n.12 |
| 46:9 (LXX) | 273 |
| 47 | 201 |

| | |
|---|---|
| 51:17 | 28 |
| 51:22 | 28 |
| 53 | 97 |
| 56:7 | 92, 93 |
| 57:3-5 | 4 |
| 57:3 (LXX) | 153 |
| 59:5 | 26 |
| 59:20-21 | 154 |
| 59:20 (LXX) | 154 |
| 65:2 | 144 |
| 66:2-4 | 182 |

**Jeremiah**

| | |
|---|---|
| 1 | 36 n.15 |
| 2–3 | 27 |
| 2:4-13 | 24 |
| 2:5 | 25 |
| 2:7 | 25 |
| 2:9 | 24 |
| 2:12 | 24 |
| 2:20b | 27 |
| 2:21 | 26 |
| 2:23-24 | 27 |
| 2:25 | 32 |
| 3:1-4 (LXX) | 273 |
| 3:6 | 4 |
| 4:4 | 13, 155 |
| 4:22 | 32 |
| 5:21-23 | 9 |
| 7 | 25 |
| 7:11-14 | 92 |
| 7:11 | 31, 92, 93 |
| 7:16 | 5 |
| 7:21-24 | 182 |
| 7:25-26 | 5 |
| 8:6-7 | 26 |
| 8:8-12 | 33 |
| 9:25-26 | 155 |
| 9:26 | 4, 13 |
| 10:10 | 161 |
| 10:25 | 152 |
| 11 | 32 |
| 11:7-8 | 5 |
| 11:14 | 5 |
| 12:7 | 35 |
| 13:23 | 236 |
| 14:11-12 | 5 |

**Jeremiah (*continued*)** ⎯⎯⎯⎯⎯⎯

| | |
|---|---|
| 14:12-14 | 28 |
| 14:19 | 6 |
| 18:21 | 5 |
| 20:1-2 | 36 n.16 |
| 24:7 | 180 n.33 |
| 25:15-16 | 28 |
| 26 | 29, 30, 36 n.16 |
| 27:2-4 | 32 |
| 29:7 | 161 |
| 31:31-34 | 177, 179, 179 n.30, 180, |
| | 181, 183, 184, n.102 |
| 31:33 | 295 |
| 36 | 36 |
| 37–38 | 36 n.16 |
| 38:4 | 30 |
| 38:31-34 (LXX) | 179 |
| 50 | 201 |
| 51 | 201 |
| 52 | 201 |

**Ezekiel** ⎯⎯⎯⎯⎯⎯

| | |
|---|---|
| 2–3 | 36 n.15 |
| 12:1-3 | 9 |
| 13:10-11 | 8 |
| 16 | 27 |
| 16:23-26a (LXX) | 273 |
| 16:45b | 28 |
| 19 | 28 |
| 21:24-25 | 153 |
| 23 | 27 |
| 23:31-34 | 28 |
| 28:2 | 153 |
| 33:23-29 | 31 |
| 37:23 | 163 |
| 37:27 | 158 |
| 44:9 | 13, 155 |

**Daniel** ⎯⎯⎯⎯⎯⎯

| | |
|---|---|
| 2:19 | 154 |
| 2:28 | 154 |
| 4 | 201 |
| 5 | 201 |
| 7:13 | 95 |
| 11:31 | 153 |
| 11:36 | 153 |
| 12:11 | 153 |

**Hosea** ⎯⎯⎯⎯⎯⎯

| | |
|---|---|
| 1:2 | 4 |
| 1:6 | 5 |
| 1:9 | 10 |
| 1:10 | 10 |
| 2 | 27 |
| 2:2-3 | 28 |
| 2:4-9 | 273 |
| 2:11 | 156 n.21 |
| 4:6 | 6, 32 |
| 5:4 | 32 |
| 6:6 | 32, 182 |

**Joel** ⎯⎯⎯⎯⎯⎯

| | |
|---|---|
| 2:28 | 163 |

**Amos** ⎯⎯⎯⎯⎯⎯

| | |
|---|---|
| 1:1–9:5 | 55 |
| 2:9-11 | xi |
| 3:1-2 | xi |
| 4:4-5 | 29 |
| 5:18-20 | 31 |
| 5:21-27 | 182 |
| 6:12 | 26 |
| 7:10-15 | 36 n.16 |
| 7:10-13 | 30 |
| 9:7-8 | 31 |
| 9:7 | 159 |

**Micah** ⎯⎯⎯⎯⎯⎯

| | |
|---|---|
| 4:10 | 201 |
| 6:1-5 | 24 |
| 6:1-2 | 24 |
| 6:3-4 | 24 |
| 6:10-12 | 25 |
| 6:13-14 | 25 |
| 7:7 | 164 |

**Habukkuk** ⎯⎯⎯⎯⎯⎯

| | |
|---|---|
| 2:15-17 | 28 |
| 3:2 (LXX) | 264 |

**Zephaniah** ⎯⎯⎯⎯⎯⎯

| | |
|---|---|
| 3:3 | 26 |

**Haggai** ⎯⎯⎯⎯⎯⎯

| | |
|---|---|
| 2:26-27 | 177 n.28 |

**Zechariah**
| | |
|---|---|
| 2:7ff. | *201* |
| 14:9 | *45, 295* |
| 14:16 | *45* |

## APOCRYPHA

**Baruch**
| | |
|---|---|
| 1:11 | *161* |

**4 Ezra**
| | |
|---|---|
| 2:7 | *55* |
| 7:22-25 | *55* |
| 7:26 | *201 n.8* |
| 12:36-38 | *154* |
| 14:5 | *154* |
| 15:1ff. | *201* |
| 15:43ff. | *201* |

**1 Maccabees**
| | |
|---|---|
| 2:16 | *163* |
| 4:30 | *164* |

**2 Maccabees**
| | |
|---|---|
| 1:24-25 | *161* |
| 2:17 | *208* |
| 12:15 | *161* |

**3 Maccabees**
| | |
|---|---|
| 5:35 | *161* |

**Sirach**
| | |
|---|---|
| 7:34 | *161 n.46* |
| 43:26 | *191* |

**Wisdom**
| | |
|---|---|
| 1:6 | *163* |
| 5:16 | *163* |
| 14:12 | *154* |
| 14:22-27 | *154* |
| 16:7 | *164* |
| 18:15 | *191* |

## NEW TESTAMENT

**Matthew**
| | |
|---|---|
| 1:1-17 | *60, 62, 67* |
| 1:1 | *67* |
| 1:2 | *67* |
| 1:16 | *263 n.39* |
| 1:18–2:23 | *63* |
| 1:18-21 | *63* |
| 1:21 | *63, 66, 70* |
| 1:23 | *65* |
| 2:1-12 | *64, 67, 75, 77* |
| 2:6 | *65* |
| 2:13-15 | *64* |
| 2:15 | *65* |
| 2:16-18 | *63, 64* |
| 2:18 | *65* |
| 2:19-21 | *64* |
| 2:20 | *64* |
| 2:23 | *65* |
| 3:2 | *70* |
| 3:3 | *12* |
| 3:7 | *70 n.56, 74* |
| 3:7-10 | *1, 59, 70* |
| 3:10 | *70 n.56* |
| 3:11 | *70 n.57* |
| 3:11-12 | *70* |
| 3:13-17 | *70* |
| 4:1-11 | *70* |
| 4:12–26:1 | *73* |
| 4:12–11:1 | *71* |
| 4:12-17 | *70* |
| 4:12-16 | *67* |
| 4:12 | *71 n.62, 72* |
| 4:17 | *69* |
| 4:18-22 | *67, 68, 70* |
| 4:23-25 | *67, 70* |
| 4:23 | *61* |
| 5:1–7:29 | *68, 70* |
| 5:1-2 | *63* |
| 5:3-12 | *68, 71* |
| 5:6 | *68* |
| 5:10 | *68* |
| 5:11-12 | *68* |
| 5:13-16 | *67* |
| 5:17-48 | *67* |
| 5:17-28 | *65* |

**Matthew (*continued*)** _____

| | |
|---|---|
| 5:17-20 | *62, 63, 65, 66 n.40* |
| 5:17 | *65* |
| 5:18 | *65, 65 n.38* |
| 5:19-20 | *65* |
| 5:19 | *65* |
| 5:20 | *65, 65 n.38, 68, 71, 74* |
| 5:21-48 | *68, 192* |
| 5:43-48 | *75* |
| 5:43 | *192* |
| 5:44 | *xiv, 6, 191* |
| 5:48 | *71, 191* |
| 6:1-18 | *59, 68, 71, 74* |
| 6:1 | *68* |
| 6:7-8 | *67* |
| 6:10 | *68* |
| 6:14-15 | *6* |
| 6:30 | *68* |
| 6:33 | *67* |
| 7:6 | *71* |
| 7:12 | *71, 75* |
| 7:13-27 | *71* |
| 7:15-27 | *68* |
| 7:21-27 | *66, 67* |
| 7:21 | *68* |
| 8:1–9:34 | *63, 70* |
| 8:4 | *71* |
| 8:5-13 | *39 n.3, 71, 75, 77* |
| 8:11 | *39 n.2, 44 n.27, 45* |
| 8:12 | *44 n.27, 45* |
| 8:18-22 | *67, 71* |
| 8:23-34 | *71* |
| 8:25 | *63* |
| 9:1-8 | *71* |
| 9:3 | *72* |
| 9:9-13 | *67, 68, 71, 72* |
| 9:14-17 | *71, 72* |
| 9:17 | *66* |
| 9:21-22 | *63* |
| 9:32-34 | *71, 72* |
| 9:35–11:1 | *71* |
| 9:35 | *61* |
| 9:36 | *68* |
| 10:1-15 | *68* |
| 10:2-4 | *69* |
| 10:5-6 | *66, 67, 67 n.45, 71, 75* |
| 10:12-15 | *74* |
| 10:14 | *73* |
| 10:15 | *74* |
| 10:16-38 | *68* |
| 10:17-20 | *71* |
| 10:18 | *67, 67 n.45* |
| 10:23 | *71, 75, 75 n.74* |
| 10:24-25 | *71* |
| 10:24 | *68* |
| 10:34-36 | *71* |
| 10:41 | *69* |
| 11:2-19 | *72* |
| 11:2-9 | *60* |
| 11:7-15 | *71* |
| 11:12 | *71 n.62* |
| 11:16-19 | *71* |
| 11:16 | *71 n.59, 74* |
| 11:19 | *71, 89* |
| 11:20-24 | *60, 74* |
| 11:25-30 | *63, 67, 68* |
| 11:25-27 | *60* |
| 11:25 | *279* |
| 11:28-30 | *75* |
| 12 | *39 n.2* |
| 12:1-14 | *72* |
| 12:6 | *64* |
| 12:11-12 | *59, 74* |
| 12:18 | *67* |
| 12:21 | *67* |
| 12:22-37 | *72* |
| 12:28 | *64, 71* |
| 12:31-32 | *64, 74* |
| 12:38-42 | *74* |
| 12:39-45 | *71 n.59* |
| 12:41 | *64* |
| 12:42 | *64* |
| 12:46-50 | *67* |
| 12:50 | *68* |
| 13:1-9 | *72* |
| 13:10-17 | *72* |
| 13:18-23 | *72* |
| 13:24-30 | *67* |
| 13:31-32 | *67* |
| 13:36-43 | *67* |
| 13:44-46 | *43 n.20* |
| 13:52 | *69* |
| 13:54-58 | *72* |
| 14:3-12 | *71, 72* |

| | | | |
|---|---|---|---|
| 14:30 | *63* | 22:16 | *87* |
| 15:1-20 | *59, 74* | 22:18 | *74* |
| 15:7 | *74* | 22:34-40 | *75* |
| 15:21-28 | *39 n.3, 77* | 22:41-46 | *76* |
| 15:24 | *67, 67 n.45* | 23 | *76 n.81* |
| 16:2-3 | *59* | 23:1–26:2 | *59* |
| 16:4 | *71 n.59* | 23:1–25:46 | *61* |
| 16:13-20 | *69* | 23:1–24:36 | *76* |
| 16:17-20 | *66* | 23:1-39 | *74* |
| 16:18 | *62, 66, 68* | 23:1-36 | *76* |
| 16:21 | *72* | 23:8-12 | *69* |
| 16:24-28 | *67* | 23:13-33 | *60, 74* |
| 17:2-9 | *63* | 23:15 | *74, 293* |
| 17:17 | *71 n.59* | 23:16-22 | *48* |
| 17:22-23 | *72* | 23:16 | *216* |
| 17:24-27 | *51 n.48, 68* | 23:23 | *74* |
| 18 | *69* | 23:25 | *74* |
| 18:11 | *63* | 23:27-33 | *2* |
| 18:12-14 | *43 n.20, 69* | 23:27 | *74* |
| 18:15-20 | *69* | 23:29-36 | *216* |
| 18:17 | *62, 66, 68* | 23:29 | *74* |
| 19:3 | *91 n.39* | 23:34-39 | *60, 68* |
| 19:16-24 | *261* | 23:34-36 | *2* |
| 19:28 | *68* | 23:34 | *69* |
| 20:18-19 | *72* | 23:36 | *71 n.59* |
| 21:1-19 | *76* | 23:37-39 | *76, 76 n.81* |
| 21:9 | *73 n.64* | 23:37-38 | *2* |
| 21:12 | *47* | 23:37 | *135* |
| 21:12a | *51* | 23:38 | *75* |
| 21:12b | *51* | 24 | *76 n.81* |
| 21:12c | *51* | 24:1-36 | *76* |
| 21:13 | *47, 51* | 24:1-3 | *76 n.81* |
| 21:18-19 | *75* | 24:2 | *76 n.81* |
| 21:23–22:40 | *72, 76* | 24:3 | *76 n.81* |
| 21:25 | *72* | 24:8 | *76 n.81* |
| 21:28-32 | *67, 71, 71 n.62* | 24:9-14 | *67, 68* |
| 21:31-32 | *71* | 24:14 | *77, 77 n.85* |
| 21:32 | *72* | 24:29-31 | *67 n.45* |
| 21:33–22:14 | *76* | 24:31 | *77, 77 n.85* |
| 21:33-46 | *59, 62, 67 n.45, 74, 77* | 24:33 | *76 n.81* |
| 21:43 | *61, 66, 67, 68, 75–77* | 24:34 | *60, 76 n.81* |
| 21:45 | *59* | 24:45-51 | *78* |
| 21:46 | *73 n.64* | 25:31-46 | *43 n.20, 67* |
| 22:1-14 | *39 n.2, 67, 67 n.45, 74, 77* | 26:3-5 | *72* |
| 22:1-10 | *43 n.20* | 26:5 | *73 n.64* |
| 22:7 | *75* | 26:6-13 | *67* |
| 22:11-14 | *43 n.20* | 26:14-16 | *73* |

**Matthew (continued)** _____

| | |
|---|---|
| 26:14 | 72 |
| 26:17-30 | 68 |
| 26:20-25 | 73 |
| 26:25 | 40 n.4 |
| 26:30-35 | 72 |
| 26:36-46 | 72 |
| 26:47-56 | 73 |
| 26:48 | 285 |
| 26:49 | 40 n.4 |
| 26:57-75 | 72 |
| 26:57 | 74, 83 n.12 |
| 27:1-2 | 72 |
| 27:2 | 72 |
| 27:11-14 | 72 |
| 27:20 | 72 |
| 27:22-23 | 72 |
| 27:24-25 | 59, 72 n.64, 74 |
| 27:24 | 265 |
| 27:25 | 40, 58, 60, 72, 72 n.64, 73 n.64, 76 n.79, 280 |
| 27:27-31 | 72 |
| 27:33-44 | 72 |
| 27:42 | 63 |
| 27:51 | 77 |
| 27:54 | 77 |
| 27:62-66 | 72, 265 |
| 28:11-15 | 60, 265 |
| 28:15 | 40 |
| 28:16-20 | 63, 67, 67 n.45, 69, 77 |
| 28:19 | 76 |
| 28:20 | 68 |

**Mark** _____

| | |
|---|---|
| 1:1 | 81, 82 n.8, 89, 97, 100, 101 |
| 1:3 | 12 |
| 1:4-8 | 82 n.8 |
| 1:11 | 97 |
| 1:14-15 | 89, 100, 101 |
| 1:14 | 97 |
| 1:16–8:26 | 83 |
| 1:16-20 | 82 n.8, 83, 83 n.14 |
| 1:21-28 | 100 |
| 1:22 | 85, 85 n.23 |
| 1:23-28 | 82 |
| 1:34 | 97 |
| 1:40-45 | 99 |

| | |
|---|---|
| 1:44 | 91 |
| 2:1–3:6 | 94 |
| 2:1–3:5 | 94 |
| 2:1-12 | 89, 100 |
| 2:5 | 90 |
| 2:6-7 | 94 |
| 2:6 | 85, 85 n.23, 86 |
| 2:13-17 | 82 n.8, 89 |
| 2:13-14 | 83 n.14, 84 n.18 |
| 2:13 | 84 |
| 2:16 | 85, 85 n.23, 86, 86 nn.24-25; 89, 94 n.48 |
| 2:17 | 89, 90 |
| 2:18-22 | 89 |
| 2:18 | 86, 86 n.24 |
| 2:20 | 94 |
| 2:23-28 | 88, 100 |
| 2:23-24 | 88 |
| 2:24 | 86 nn.24, 25 |
| 2:25-26 | 89 |
| 2:27-28 | 89 |
| 3:1-6 | 89 |
| 3:4 | 89 |
| 3:5 | 84, 87, 89 |
| 3:6 | 86, 86 n.24, 87, 89, 94, 96, 97 |
| 3:7-12 | 84 |
| 3:11-12 | 97 |
| 3:11 | 85, 97 |
| 3:13-19 | 82 n.8, 83, 84 |
| 3:14 | 83 |
| 3:20 | 94 n.48 |
| 3:22 | 85 n.23, 86, 94 n.47, 248, 257 n.18 |
| 3:28-30 | 87 |
| 3:28-29 | 94 n.47 |
| 4:1 | 84 |
| 4:11-12 | 12 |
| 4:11 | 84 |
| 4:12 | 84 |
| 4:13-20 | 83, 84 n.18 |
| 4:13 | 83 |
| 4:26-29 | 43 n.20 |
| 4:33-34 | 83, 84 n.18 |
| 4:41 | 83 |
| 5:1-20 | 82 |
| 5:7 | 82 n.11 |
| 5:21-43 | 100 |

| | |
|---|---|
| 5:21-24 | 82 n.8 |
| 6:6 | 84 |
| 6:7-13 | 83 |
| 6:17-29 | 82 |
| 6:30-44 | 83 |
| 6:34 | 84 |
| 6:37 | 83 |
| 6:52 | 83, 84 |
| 7 | 90, 91, 99 |
| 7:1-23 | 85, 90, 232 |
| 7:1-13 | 90, 90 n.38, 99 |
| 7:1-2 | 90 n.38 |
| 7:1 | 85, 85 n.23, 86 nn.24-25; 94 n.48 |
| 7:3-4 | 99 |
| 7:3 | 40, 85, 86, 86 n.24, 87 n.28, 98 |
| 7:4 | 40 |
| 7:5 | 85, 85 n.23, 86 nn.24-25, 86 n.25, 87 n.28, 90 |
| 7:5a | 90 n.38 |
| 7:5b | 90 n.38 |
| 7:6 | 86 |
| 7:6-13 | 90 |
| 7:9-13 | 90 n.38 |
| 7:14-23 | 90, 90 n.38 |
| 7:15 | 90 n.38 |
| 7:16-18 | 90 n.38 |
| 7:17-23 | 83 |
| 7:18-23 | 90 |
| 7:18 | 83 |
| 7:19 | 90, 99 |
| 7:24-30 | 39 n.3 |
| 7:26 | 98 |
| 7:27-28 | 83 n.11 |
| 7:31-37 | 82 n.10 |
| 8:1-9 | 83 |
| 8:11-13 | 100 |
| 8:11 | 86, 86 n.24 |
| 8:14-21 | 83 |
| 8:15-21 | 232 |
| 8:15 | 86, 86 n.24 |
| 8:17 | 84 |
| 8:18 | 84 |
| 8:26–16:8 | 83 |
| 8:27–13:37 | 83 |
| 8:27–10:52 | 83, 96 |
| 8:27-29 | 83, 96 |
| 8:27-28 | 96 |
| 8:29-31 | 98 |
| 8:29 | 97 |
| 8:31-33 | 83 |
| 8:31 | 85 n.23, 86 n.27, 87 n.28, 96, 97, 100 |
| 8:33 | 84, 164 |
| 9:2-9 | 97, 98 |
| 9:5 | 40 n.4 |
| 9:7 | 97 |
| 9:9 | 97 |
| 9:11-13 | 85, 97 |
| 9:11 | 85 n.23 |
| 9:14 | 85, 85n.23 |
| 9:19 | 84 |
| 9:31 | 96, 97 |
| 9:34-38 | 83 n.14 |
| 9:38-40 | 83 |
| 10:1 | 84 |
| 10:2-12 | 90 |
| 10:2-9 | 88 |
| 10:2 | 86, 86 nn.24-25 |
| 10:3-4 | 91 |
| 10:5 | 84 |
| 10:19 | 91 |
| 10:20-21 | 91 |
| 10:33-34 | 100 |
| 10:33 | 85 n.23, 86 n.27, 96, 97 |
| 10:45 | 100 |
| 10:46-52 | 82 n.8 |
| 10:51 | 40 n.4 |
| 11:1–13:37 | 83 |
| 11:1-11 | 96 |
| 11:11 | 92 |
| 11:12-14 | 92, 93 |
| 11:15-17 | 47, 92, 95, 99 |
| 11:15-16 | 93 |
| 11:15 | 92 |
| 11:15a | 51 |
| 11:15b | 51 |
| 11:15c | 51 |
| 11:16 | 51 |
| 11:17 | 51, 86, 92, 93 |
| 11:17b | 92 |
| 11:17c | 92 |
| 11:18 | 84, 85, 85 n.23, 86, 86 n.27, 92, 94, 99, 100 |

**Mark** *(continued)* _____

| | |
|---|---|
| 11:20-23 | 92 |
| 11:20-22 | 92 |
| 11:20 | 92 |
| 11:21 | 40 n.4 |
| 11:27–12:40 | 95 |
| 11:27–12:34 | 87 |
| 11:27-33 | 100 |
| 11:27 | 85 n.23, 86, 86 n.27, 87, 87 n.28, 92, 95 |
| 11:28 | 85 |
| 12:1-12 | 96 n.50, 97 |
| 12:1 | 86 |
| 12:9 | 158 |
| 12:12 | 84, 86, 95, 278 |
| 12:13 | 86, 86 n.24, 87 |
| 12:18 | 87 |
| 12:28-34 | 85, 88, 91, 99, 100 |
| 12:28 | 85 n.23 |
| 12:32 | 85 n.23, 91 |
| 12:34 | 91 |
| 12:35-37 | 85, 97 |
| 12:35 | 85 n.23, 92 |
| 12:37-40 | 216 |
| 12:38-40 | 85, 87 |
| 12:38 | 85 n.23 |
| 12:43 | 82 n.8 |
| 13 | 43 n.21 |
| 13:1 | 92 |
| 13:2 | 92, 93, 94, 99 |
| 13:3-37 | 93 |
| 13:3 | 92 |
| 13:9a | 99 |
| 13:14 | 153 |
| 14 | 97 |
| 14:1 | 85, 85 n.23, 86, 86 n.27, 95 |
| 14:10-11 | 95 |
| 14:10 | 86 n.27 |
| 14:21 | 97 |
| 14:27 | 97 |
| 14:36 | 97, 100 |
| 14:39 | 97 |
| 14:43-44 | 95 |
| 14:43 | 85, 85 n.23, 86, 86 n.27, 87, 87 n.28 |
| 14:44 | 285 |
| 14:45 | 40 n.4 |
| 14:47 | 87 n.29 |
| 14:49 | 92 |
| 14:50 | 83 |
| 14:53-65 | 100 |
| 14:53 | 85, 85 n.23, 86, 86 n.27, 87, 87 n.28 |
| 14:54 | 87 n.29 |
| 14:55-65 | 95, 97 |
| 14:55-59 | 96, 98 |
| 14:55 | 86, 87, 95 |
| 14:58 | 92, 93 |
| 14:60 | 87 |
| 14:61-65 | 97, 98, 100 |
| 14:61-62 | 96, 97 |
| 14:61 | 87, 95 |
| 14:63-64 | 95 |
| 14:63 | 87 |
| 14:64 | 94, 95, 96 |
| 14:65 | 98 |
| 14:66-72 | 83 |
| 14:66 | 87 n.29 |
| 14:71 | 84 |
| 15:1-15 | 82 |
| 15:1 | 85, 85 n.23, 86, 86 n.27, 87, 87 n.28, 95, 97, 98 |
| 15:2-11 | 100 |
| 15:2 | 85, 95, 96, 98 |
| 15:3 | 86, 86 n.27, 95 |
| 15:6-14 | 82 |
| 15:6 | 82 n.8 |
| 15:7 | 82, 96 |
| 15:8-15 | 84 |
| 15:9-10 | 95 |
| 15:9 | 85, 97, 98 |
| 15:10 | 86 n.27, 95, 98 |
| 15:11-14 | 84 |
| 15:11 | 85, 86, 86 n.27 |
| 15:12 | 85, 95, 97, 98 |
| 15:14 | 96, 98 |
| 15:18 | 85, 98 |
| 15:21 | 82 n.8 |
| 15:24 | 100 |
| 15:26 | 85, 95-98, 100 |
| 15:27 | 82, 96 |
| 15:29-32 | 93, 94 |
| 15:29 | 92, 93 |
| 15:31-32 | 93, 97, 98, 100 |

| | |
|---|---|
| 15:31 | *85, 85 n.23, 86, 86 n.27* |
| 15:32-39 | *100* |
| 15:32 | *85, 96-98, 100* |
| 15:37-38 | *93* |
| 15:37 | *93* |
| 15:38 | *93, 93 n.45, 99* |
| 15:39 | *82, 83 n.11, 93, 97, 98* |
| 15:40 | *82 n.8* |
| 15:42-46 | *101* |
| 15:43 | *82 n.8* |
| 15:47 | *83* |
| 16:1 | *82 n.8, 83* |
| 16:8 | *83* |

**Luke**

| | |
|---|---|
| 1:1 | *105* |
| 1:4 | *112* |
| 1:75 | *12* |
| 2:1 | *156 n.20* |
| 2:29-35 | *107* |
| 2:34 | *108* |
| 2:42-52 | *279 n.32* |
| 2:46-49 | *279 n.32* |
| 3:4-6 | *12* |
| 4:14-30 | *108* |
| 4:16-30 | *40* |
| 6:16 | *108* |
| 7:1-10 | *39 n.3* |
| 7:34 | *90* |
| 7:36-50 | *13* |
| 9:51-56 | *6* |
| 10:21 | *279* |
| 13:28 | *39 n.2, 44 n.27, 45* |
| 13:29 | *39 n.2, 44 n.27, 45* |
| 13:34 | *6, 135* |
| 14:15-24 | *39 n.2, 43 n.20* |
| 15:1-2 | *13* |
| 15:4-7 | *43 n.20* |
| 16:22-24 | *39 n.2* |
| 17:20 | *45, 51* |
| 17:21 | *45* |
| 17:21a | *51* |
| 17:21b | *51* |
| 17:22-27 | *51* |
| 19:41-44 | *6* |
| 19:44 | *107* |
| 19:45 | *47, 51* |

| | |
|---|---|
| 19:46 | *47, 51* |
| 21:21 | *106* |
| 21:24 | *106* |
| 22:3-6 | *108* |
| 23:28-31 | *6, 107* |
| 23:34 | *6* |
| 24:44-47 | *230* |
| 24:47 | *107* |

**John**

| | |
|---|---|
| 1:1-18 | *123* |
| 1:9 | *117* |
| 1:16 | *51* |
| 1:17 | *117* |
| 1:23 | *12* |
| 1:31 | *124* |
| 1:38 | *40 n.4, 115 n.6* |
| 1:47 | *117* |
| 1:49 | *40 n.4, 124* |
| 2:1-10 | *117* |
| 2:6 | *115* |
| 2:13-17 | *47* |
| 2:13 | *114* |
| 2:14 | *51* |
| 2:15 | *49 n.36* |
| 2:15a-c | *51* |
| 2:15d | *51* |
| 2:17 | *49, 51* |
| 2:18 | *115* |
| 2:19-22 | *117* |
| 2:20 | *115* |
| 3:1-15 | *115* |
| 3:1-4 | *115* |
| 3:2 | *40 n.4* |
| 3:25 | *115* |
| 4:1 | *116* |
| 4:9 | *115* |
| 4:21 | *117* |
| 4:22 | *115, 123, 123 n.28, 144 n.5* |
| 4:31 | *40 n.4* |
| 4:39-42 | *117* |
| 4:43-45 | *115* |
| 5:1 | *114* |
| 5:10-18 | *216* |
| 5:16-18 | *115* |
| 5:18 | *162* |
| 5:37-47 | *232* |

**John (*continued*)**

| | |
|---|---|
| 5:39-40 | *115* |
| 5:39 | *117, 122* |
| 5:45 | *117* |
| 6:4 | *114* |
| 6:25 | *40 n.4* |
| 6:32 | *117* |
| 6:37 | *116* |
| 6:39 | *116 n.7* |
| 6:41-59 | *216* |
| 6:41 | *115* |
| 6:45 | *117* |
| 6:52 | *115* |
| 6:58 | *117* |
| 7:1 | *115, 216* |
| 7:2 | *114* |
| 7:10-13 | *216* |
| 7:13 | *115* |
| 7:14ff. | *117* |
| 7:15 | *115* |
| 7:19 | *115, 172 n.15* |
| 7:25-27 | *168* |
| 7:25 | *115* |
| 7:28 | *117* |
| 7:32-35 | *115* |
| 7:32 | *116* |
| 7:35 | *115* |
| 7:50-52 | *115* |
| 8:13 | *116* |
| 8:29-41a | *223* |
| 8:30-40 | *280 n.35* |
| 8:31-59 | *168* |
| 8:31 | *115, 117, 280 n.35* |
| 8:37 | *280 n.35* |
| 8:39-44 | *115* |
| 8:41-47 | *280 n.35* |
| 8:42-47 | *2* |
| 8:44 | *224 n.49, 280, 294* |
| 8:48-59 | *216* |
| 8:48 | *115* |
| 8:56 | *117* |
| 8:57 | *115* |
| 8:58 | *117* |
| 9:2 | *40 n.4* |
| 9:13-17 | *124* |
| 9:13-16 | *116* |
| 9:13 | *115* |

| | |
|---|---|
| 9:18 | *115, 124* |
| 9:22 | *13, 40, 115, 117-119, 168* |
| 9:40-41 | *116* |
| 10:1-18 | *116* |
| 10:1-15 | *122* |
| 10:24 | *115, 168* |
| 10:31-39 | *115* |
| 10:31 | *115* |
| 10:33 | *162* |
| 10:34 | *117* |
| 10:36 | *168* |
| 11:8 | *40 n.4, 115* |
| 11:19 | *115* |
| 11:31 | *115* |
| 11:36 | *115* |
| 11:45 | *115* |
| 11:46-53 | *116* |
| 11:54 | *115* |
| 11:55 | *114* |
| 11:57 | *116* |
| 12:9 | *115* |
| 12:10 | *116* |
| 12:11 | *115* |
| 12:13 | *124* |
| 12:17 | *115* |
| 12:24 | *13* |
| 12:37-43 | *116 n.8* |
| 12:42-43 | *168* |
| 12:42 | *40, 116, 117, 119* |
| 14:6 | *117* |
| 16:1-2 | *206* |
| 16:2 | *13, 40, 117, 119* |
| 17 | *122* |
| 18:3 | *116* |
| 18:3-19 | *116* |
| 18:12 | *116* |
| 18:13 | *83 n.12* |
| 18:31 | *116* |
| 18:37 | *117* |
| 18:38-40 | *116* |
| 18:38 | *116* |
| 18:41 | *115* |
| 19:4-8 | *116* |
| 19:4 | *116* |
| 19:6 | *116* |
| 19:7 | *168* |
| 19:12-16 | *116* |

| | |
|---|---|
| 19:12 | *116* |
| 19:15 | *115, 116* |
| 19:16 | *116* |
| 19:21 | *116* |
| 19:38 | *115* |
| 19:39 | *115* |
| 20:19 | *115, 118* |

**Acts**

| | |
|---|---|
| 1:8 | *105* |
| 1:18 | *108* |
| 2:23 | *135* |
| 2:36 | *102, 107, 190* |
| 2:38-41 | *238* |
| 3:17-26 | *108, 238* |
| 3:17-18 | *107* |
| 3:19-21 | *112* |
| 3:26 | *107* |
| 4:1-31 | *206* |
| 4:2 | *109* |
| 4:12 | *294* |
| 4:17 | *109* |
| 4:27-28 | *108* |
| 5 | *13, 110* |
| 5:1-11 | *105* |
| 5:16 | *110* |
| 5:17-42 | *206* |
| 5:17 | *11 n.14, 109* |
| 5:19 | *110* |
| 5:28 | *109* |
| 5:30-32 | *107* |
| 5:33-40 | *110* |
| 5:34 | *86 n.26* |
| 5:38 | *110* |
| 5:39 | *110* |
| 5:41 | *110* |
| 5:42 | *110* |
| 6 | *105* |
| 6:7 | *11 n.14* |
| 6:8–8:3 | *206* |
| 7:38 | *172 n.15* |
| 7:51-53 | *2* |
| 7:53 | *172 n.15* |
| 8:9-24 | *105* |
| 9 | *105* |
| 9:1-29 | *107* |
| 9:2 | *12* |

| | |
|---|---|
| 9:5 | *107* |
| 9:15-16 | *107* |
| 9:15 | *110* |
| 9:27-29 | *110* |
| 10 | *105, 110* |
| 10:9-16 | *90* |
| 10:14 | *110* |
| 10:28 | *110* |
| 10:39-43 | *107* |
| 10:39 | *135* |
| 10:45 | *163* |
| 10:47 | *111* |
| 11:2 | *163* |
| 11:17 | *111* |
| 11:18 | *111* |
| 11:19–12:19 | *206* |
| 13 | *40 n.8* |
| 13:27 | *107* |
| 13:28 | *135* |
| 13:32-38 | *107* |
| 13:46-48 | *2* |
| 13:46 | *103* |
| 15 | *105* |
| 15:1-5 | *108* |
| 15:1 | *13* |
| 15:5 | *11 n.14, 109* |
| 15:19-21 | *166* |
| 15:28 | *111* |
| 16:4 | *156 n.20* |
| 17:1-10 | *206* |
| 17:7 | *156 n.20* |
| 17:11 | *112* |
| 18:6 | *2, 103* |
| 18:12-17 | *206* |
| 18:15 | *110* |
| 19:23 | *12* |
| 19:33 | *162* |
| 21:27-36 | *206* |
| 22:4 | *12* |
| 23:1-5 | *109* |
| 23:6-9 | *13* |
| 23:6 | *86 n.26, 109* |
| 23:9 | *86 n.26* |
| 23:12-22 | *206* |
| 24:5 | *11 n.14* |
| 24:14 | *11 n.14, 12* |
| 24:22 | *12* |

**Acts (*continued*)** _____
| | |
|---|---|
| 26:5 | *11 n.14* |
| 26:19-23 | *107* |
| 26:26 | *105* |
| 28:17-31 | *250 n.192* |
| 28:22 | *11 n.14* |
| 28:23-28 | *107* |
| 28:25-29 | *2, 216* |
| 28:28 | *103* |

**Romans** _____
| | |
|---|---|
| 1:3-4 | *162* |
| 1:5 | *153* |
| 1:7 | *154 n. 16* |
| 1:16 | *140, 147, 238* |
| 1:18–3:20 | *157 n.30* |
| 1:18 | *133* |
| 2:12-16 | *161* |
| 2:13 | *137* |
| 2:16 | *137* |
| 2:18-20 | *160* |
| 2:20 | *137* |
| 2:21 | *137* |
| 2:25ff. | *277* |
| 2:25 | *137* |
| 2:28-29 | *13* |
| 3:1-2 | *147, 296* |
| 3:9-20 | *140* |
| 3:9 | *147* |
| 3:11 | *137* |
| 3:19-20 | *147* |
| 3:20–4:6 | *157* |
| 3:20 | *137* |
| 3:21-26 | *148* |
| 3:21 | *137* |
| 3:22-24 | *140, 147* |
| 3:23-25 | *137* |
| 3:25 | *154* |
| 3:28-29 | *144* |
| 3:28 | *137* |
| 3:29-30 | *147, 159* |
| 3:31 | *137* |
| 4 | *13* |
| 4:1-18 | *224* |
| 4:1-15 | *40* |
| 4:6-8 | *139* |
| 4:14 | *137* |

| | |
|---|---|
| 4:16 | *144* |
| 4:22-25 | *144* |
| 5:2 | *158* |
| 5:4 | *137* |
| 5:20 | *140* |
| 6:4-6 | *155 n.19* |
| 6:13 | *138 n.38* |
| 6:14-15 | *137* |
| 6:15 | *138 n.38* |
| 6:22 | *138 n.38* |
| 7:6 | *137* |
| 7:7 | *154 n. 17* |
| 7:10 | *140* |
| 7:12-13 | *161* |
| 7:12 | *137* |
| 8:3 | *154* |
| 8:4 | *138 n.38, 141* |
| 8:33 | *154 n. 16* |
| 9–11 | *11, 75 n.70, 144, 145 n.57, 146 n.60, 147* |
| 9 | *10, 145 n.57* |
| 9:1ff. | *144* |
| 9:2-3 | *150* |
| 9:4-5 | *147, 296* |
| 9:5 | *147 n.63, 150* |
| 9:6-7 | *144* |
| 9:11 | *157* |
| 9:22-26 | *10* |
| 9:27-29 | *144* |
| 9:27 | *12* |
| 9:30-33 | *144* |
| 9:31-32 | *138* |
| 9:32 | *157* |
| 10:1 | *147, 238* |
| 10:3 | *138* |
| 10:4 | *137, 140* |
| 10:5 | *138* |
| 10:9 | *148* |
| 10:9-13 | *140* |
| 10:9-10 | *148* |
| 10:12-13 | *148* |
| 10:14-21 | *153* |
| 10:17 | *148* |
| 10:18-19 | *148* |
| 10:21 | *144, 145* |
| 11 | *131, 133* |
| 11:1-6 | *146* |

| | |
|---|---|
| 11:1-2 | *238* |
| 11:1 | *6, 145 n.57* |
| 11:2-5 | *12* |
| 11:3 | *135* |
| 11:5 | *144* |
| 11:6 | *157* |
| 11:8-10 | *136, 144* |
| 11:8 | *11* |
| 11:9 | *11* |
| 11:11-12 | *145* |
| 11:11 | *145, 217 n.12* |
| 11:12 | *145* |
| 11:13 | *160* |
| 11:15 | *145, 217 n.12* |
| 11:17-30 | *216* |
| 11:18 | *103, 150* |
| 11:20 | *145* |
| 11:23-32 | *238* |
| 11:23-24 | *217 n.12* |
| 11:23 | *135, 145, 148* |
| 11:24 | *145* |
| 11:25-27 | *224* |
| 11:25-26 | *145, 146 n.58, 160* |
| 11:25 | *145* |
| 11:26 | *135, 147* |
| 11:28-29 | *146, 224 n.51* |
| 11:28 | *3, 144, 144 n.56, 145* |
| 11:30 | *145* |
| 11:31 | *135, 148* |
| 12:15-21 | *161 n.46* |
| 13:3-4 | *161* |
| 13:8-10 | *141* |
| 14 | *160 n.43* |
| 14:6 | *160* |
| 15:8-12 | *150* |
| 16:18 | *136* |

**1 Corinthians**

| | |
|---|---|
| 1:23 | *103, 236* |
| 1:24 | *140* |
| 2:8 | *216, 235 n.115, 284 n.49* |
| 3:16-17 | *154* |
| 6:11 | *207* |
| 6:19 | *154* |
| 7 | *160* |
| 8–10 | *160* |
| 8:1ff. | *160* |

| | |
|---|---|
| 9:19-23 | *140* |
| 10:20 | *204* |
| 10:26 | *160* |
| 11:25 | *142* |
| 12 | *189* |
| 12:13 | *155* |
| 15:9 | *133 n.22* |

**2 Corinthians**

| | |
|---|---|
| 3 | *143 n.54* |
| 3:3-6 | *232* |
| 3:3 | *295* |
| 3:6-17 | *143* |
| 3:6-11 | *141* |
| 3:6 | *142* |
| 4:3 | *143* |
| 4:6 | *143* |
| 5:10 | *162* |
| 5:17 | *295* |
| 5:21 | *154* |
| 6:16 | *154* |
| 11:13-15 | *136, 164* |
| 11:23-26 | *206* |
| 11:24-26 | *133 n.22* |

**Galatians**

| | |
|---|---|
| 1:8-9 | *8 n.7* |
| 1:12 | *296* |
| 1:13-14 | *160* |
| 1:13 | *133 n.22* |
| 1:15-16 | *160* |
| 2:1-10 | *168* |
| 2:7-10 | *166* |
| 2:8 | *160* |
| 2:9 | *168* |
| 2:11-21 | *39* |
| 2:11-14 | *90* |
| 2:12 | *155, 163* |
| 2:15–3:14 | *157* |
| 2:16 | *140* |
| 3–4 | *216* |
| 3:6-9 | *40, 224* |
| 3:10-12 | *138* |
| 3:13-14 | *224* |
| 3:13 | *50 n.47* |
| 3:15-29 | *139* |
| 3:15-18 | *138* |

**Galatians** (*continued*)

| 3:19 | 156, 172 n.15 |
| 3:21 | 137, 140 |
| 3:23-29 | 138 |
| 3:23-25 | 156 |
| 3:28 | 155, 189, 296 |
| 4:2-3 | 156 |
| 4:5 | 140, 142 |
| 4:9-10 | 156 |
| 4:11 | 155 |
| 4:21-31 | 142, 142 n.50, 143 n.53, 232 |
| 4:26 | 154 n. 15 |
| 5:1 | 140, 142 |
| 5:6 | 155 |
| 5:11 | 206 |
| 5:12 | 136 |
| 5:13-14 | 138 n.38 |
| 6:15 | 155 |
| 6:18 | 224 n.51 |

**Ephesians**

| 1:1 | 156 |
| 1:4 | 156 |
| 1:9 | 156 |
| 1:11-14 | 157 n.28 |
| 1:14 | 156 |
| 1:15 | 156 |
| 1:18 | 156 |
| 1:22 | 159 |
| 2:1 | 157 |
| 2:2 | 157 |
| 2:3 | 157 |
| 2:5 | 157 |
| 2:8-9 | 157 |
| 2:11-22 | 157 nn.27-28 |
| 2:11 | 157, 159 |
| 2:14 | 158, 236 n.120 |
| 2:15 | 156 n.20, 159 |
| 2:17-19 | 158 |
| 2:18-22 | 158 |
| 2:20 | 158 |
| 3:1 | 157 |
| 3:3-4 | 156 |
| 3:6 | 158 |
| 3:9 | 156 |
| 3:36 | 160 |

| 4:6 | 157 |
| 4:17-19 | 157 |
| 4:20 | 157 |
| 5:5 | 156, 157 |
| 5:6 | 157 |
| 5:8 | 157 |
| 5:21–6:9 | 125 |
| 5:32 | 156 |
| 6:19 | 156 |

**Philippians**

| 3:2 | 136 |
| 3:5-6 | 12 |
| 3:9 | 138 |
| 3:18-19 | 136 |

**Colossians**

| 1:2 | 154 |
| 1:4 | 154 |
| 1:12 | 154 |
| 1:26-27 | 154 |
| 1:26 | 154 |
| 1:27 | 158, 160 |
| 2:2 | 154 |
| 2:8 | 156 |
| 2:11-13 | 155 |
| 2:11 | 155 |
| 2:13 | 155 |
| 2:14-17 | 155 |
| 2:14 | 284 |
| 2:15 | 156 |
| 2:16-19 | 210 |
| 2:16-18 | 156 |
| 2:16-17 | 156 |
| 2:17 | 156 |
| 2:20-23 | 155, 156 |
| 2:20-21 | 156 |
| 2:20 | 156 |
| 2:21 | 156 |
| 2:22 | 156 |
| 3:5 | 154, 157 |
| 3:9 | 155 n.19 |
| 3:10 | 155 |
| 3:11 | 155 |
| 3:12 | 154 |
| 3:18–4:1 | 125 |
| 3:24 | 154 |

| | |
|---|---|
| 4:3 | *154* |
| 4:10-14 | *105* |
| 4:11 | *155, 163* |

**1 Thessalonians** ⎯⎯⎯⎯⎯⎯

| | |
|---|---|
| 1 | *131* |
| 2:1-12 | *131* |
| 2:12-17 | *131* |
| 2:13-16 | *132* |
| 2:13 | *131* |
| 2:14-16 | *3, 130, 130 n.8, 131, 133, 133 n.19, 134 nn.27-28; 136, 145, 216, 236, 250 n.192* |
| 2:14-15 | *133 n.22* |
| 2:15-16 | *134 n.24, 135 n.32* |
| 2:16 | *131, 132, 145* |
| 2:16c | *135* |

**2 Thessalonians** ⎯⎯⎯⎯⎯⎯

| | |
|---|---|
| 1:5ff. | *152* |
| 2 | *153, 154* |
| 2:3-4 | *153* |
| 2:8-10 | *153* |
| 2:8 | *153* |
| 3:2 | *153* |

**1 Timothy** ⎯⎯⎯⎯⎯⎯

| | |
|---|---|
| 1:1 | *164* |
| 1:4 | *160* |
| 1:6-7 | *161* |
| 1:7-9 | *161* |
| 1:7 | *161 n.45* |
| 1:8 | *161* |
| 1:9 | *161* |
| 1:11 | *161* |
| 1:12-14 | *160* |
| 1:14 | *160* |
| 1:20 | *160* |
| 2:2 | *161* |
| 2:3 | *164* |
| 2:5 | *161* |
| 2:7 | *160* |
| 2:10 | *160* |
| 3:1 | *160* |
| 3:9 | *160* |
| 3:15 | *161* |
| 3:16 | *160* |

| | |
|---|---|
| 4:7 | *160* |
| 4:10 | *164* |
| 4:15 | *160* |
| 5:10 | *160* |
| 5:25 | *160* |
| 6:7 | *161* |
| 6:15-16 | *161* |
| 6:18 | *160* |
| 6:20 | *160* |

**2 Timothy** ⎯⎯⎯⎯⎯⎯

| | |
|---|---|
| 1:3 | *162* |
| 1:9 | *162* |
| 1:10 | *164* |
| 1:15 | *162* |
| 2:7 | *162* |
| 2:8 | *162* |
| 2:10 | *162* |
| 2:14 | *162* |
| 2:16 | *162* |
| 2:17-18 | *162* |
| 2:19 | *162* |
| 2:21 | *162* |
| 2:23 | *162* |
| 3:8 | *162* |
| 3:11 | *162* |
| 3:15-16 | *162* |
| 3:15 | *163* |
| 3:17 | *162* |
| 4:8 | *163* |
| 4:10 | *162* |
| 4:14 | *162, 163* |
| 4:17 | *163* |

**Titus** ⎯⎯⎯⎯⎯⎯

| | |
|---|---|
| 1:1 | *163* |
| 1:3 | *164* |
| 1:10-11 | *163* |
| 1:10 | *164* |
| 1:14 | *151, 160, 163, 164* |
| 2:10 | *164* |
| 2:13 | *164* |
| 2:14 | *163* |
| 3:4-7 | *163* |
| 3:4 | *164* |
| 3:5-7 | *164* |
| 3:6 | *164* |
| 3:9 | *163* |

| Hebrews | |
|---|---|
| 1:1–2:18 | 174 |
| 1:1-2a | 173, 174 |
| 1:4–2:16 | 175 |
| 2:1-4 | 173, 174 |
| 2:2-4 | 176 |
| 2:2 | 172 |
| 2:3-4 | 172 |
| 2:3 | 180 n.34 |
| 2:5-9 | 173, 177 n.28 |
| 2:10 | 182 |
| 2:14 | 182 |
| 2:17 | 182 |
| 3:1-6 | 175 |
| 3:2 | 175 |
| 3:3-6a | 176 |
| 3:5 | 175 |
| 3:7b–4:13 | 173 |
| 3:7b–4:11 | 173 |
| 3:7b-14 | 172 n.16 |
| 3:12-15 | 184 |
| 3:12-13 | 184 |
| 4:5–10:31 | 174 |
| 4:15-16 | 184 |
| 5:4-10 | 176 |
| 5:6 | 177 |
| 5:7 | 182 |
| 5:10 | 177 |
| 5:11 | 173 |
| 6:4-8 | 184 |
| 6:6 | 240 n.137 |
| 6:20 | 177 |
| 7:1-28 | 177 |
| 7:11-25 | 178 n.29 |
| 7:11-19 | 179 n.31 |
| 7:11-12 | 178, 181 |
| 7:12 | 178 |
| 7:14 | 180 n.34 |
| 7:18-19 | 176 |
| 7:18 | 178 |
| 7:19 | 175 |
| 7:22 | 175 |
| 7:24-25 | 184 |
| 8:1-13 | 240 n.137 |
| 8:5 | 156 |
| 8:6-13 | 173, 179, 179 n.31 |
| 8:6-7 | 175 |
| 8:6 | 180 |
| 8:7-13 | 183 |
| 8:7-8a | 179 |
| 8:7 | 176 |
| 8:8-12 | 179, 233 n.102 |
| 8:8-9 | 179 |
| 8:8 | 181 |
| 8:8a | 180 |
| 8:10 | 180 |
| 8:13 | 176, 179, 180 |
| 9:8-10 | 176 |
| 9:11-28 | 184 |
| 9:13 | 172 |
| 10:1-4 | 176 |
| 10:1 | 156 |
| 10:5-10 | 173, 179, 181 |
| 10:5-7 | 172 n.16, 182 |
| 10:5 | 182 |
| 10:7 | 183 |
| 10:8-10 | 182 |
| 10:8 | 182 |
| 10:8b | 183 |
| 10:9 | 176 |
| 10:9b | 182, 183 |
| 10:10 | 182, 183 |
| 10:15-18 | 173 |
| 10:16-17 | 180 n.34 |
| 10:19-25 | 184 |
| 10:23 | 173 |
| 10:26-31 | 184 |
| 10:27-28 | 176 |
| 10:28-29 | 172 |
| 10:29 | 240 n.137 |
| 10:35-39 | 173, 184 |
| 11:11 | 173 |
| 12:14-17 | 184 |
| 12:14 | 184 |
| 12:17 | 172 |
| 12:18-29 | 175, 181, 184 |
| 12:18-24 | 174 |
| 12:22 | 154 n. 15 |
| 12:24 | 176 |
| 12:25-29 | 184, 185 |
| 12:25-26 | 172 |
| 12:25 | 176 |
| 12:25a | 173 |
| 12:26-29 | 173, 177 n.28 |

| | |
|---|---|
| 13:7 | *172* |
| 13:12-14 | *185* |
| 13:15-16 | *184* |
| 13:20 | *180 n.34* |

**James** ——————
| | |
|---|---|
| 1:1 | *187, 188 n.50* |
| 1:2-8 | *194* |
| 1:2-4 | *197* |
| 1:5-8 | *197* |
| 1:15 | *154 n. 17* |
| 1:17-21 | *194, 197* |
| 1:17-18 | *190* |
| 1:18 | *191* |
| 1:22–2:26 | *189* |
| 1:22–2:6 | *191* |
| 1:22-27 | *197* |
| 1:22-25 | *194* |
| 1:27 | *194* |
| 1:27a | *189* |
| 1:27b | *189* |
| 1:27c | *189* |
| 2:1-11 | *197* |
| 2:1-7 | *187, 189, 191* |
| 2:1 | *187, 188 n.50, 190, 192, 193* |
| 2:1b | *188* |
| 2:5 | *190* |
| 2:8-26 | *189* |
| 2:8 | *189, 194* |
| 2:8b | *194* |
| 2:12-13 | *189, 190, 194, 196, 197* |
| 2:14-26 | *196, 197* |
| 2:19 | *189 n.52* |
| 2:19a | *196* |
| 2:19b | *196* |
| 3:1-18 | *191, 197* |
| 3:9-12 | *196* |
| 4:1–5:6 | *191* |
| 4:1-6 | *198* |
| 4:7-12 | *197* |
| 4:11-12 | *196* |
| 4:13–5:6 | *187* |
| 4:13-17 | *198* |
| 5:1-6 | *198* |
| 5:7-9 | *190, 196* |
| 5:10-11 | *189* |
| 5:14 | *190* |
| 5:17-18 | *189* |

**1 Peter** ——————
| | |
|---|---|
| 2:13–3:7 | *126* |

**1 John** ——————
| | |
|---|---|
| 1:1-4 | *169* |
| 2:19 | *168* |
| 2:22 | *168* |
| 2:23 | *168* |
| 3:8 | *280 n.35* |
| 3:10 | *280 n.35* |
| 4:2-3 | *168* |
| 4:2 | *169* |

**2 John** ——————
| | |
|---|---|
| 7 | *168, 169* |

**Revelation** ——————
| | |
|---|---|
| 1:5-6 | *208, 208 n.25* |
| 2:9 | *3, 41, 199, 200, 204, 205, 209* |
| 2:10 | *206* |
| 2:14-16 | *204* |
| 2:14 | *203, 211* |
| 2:20 | *203, 211* |
| 3:9 | *3, 41, 199, 200, 204-6, 209* |
| 3:12 | *154 n. 15, 201, 205* |
| 5:9-10 | *207, 208* |
| 7:1-8 | *207* |
| 7:4-8 | *209* |
| 7:9ff. | *207* |
| 7:9-14 | *209* |
| 7:9 | *207* |
| 7:14 | *207, 208* |
| 11:1-3 | *205* |
| 11:8 | *205, 205 n.17* |
| 14:1 | *201* |
| 14:8 | *201* |
| 16:19 | *201* |
| 17:5 | *201* |
| 18:2-3 | *201* |
| 18:2 | *201* |
| 18:3 | *201* |
| 18:9 | *201* |
| 18:10 | *201* |
| 18:21-23 | *201* |
| 18:21 | *201* |
| 21:2 | *154 n. 15, 201, 205* |
| 21:12 | *201* |
| 21:24-25 | *201* |

# OT PSEUDEPIGRAPHA

| | |
|---|---|
| *2 Apoc. Bar.* 81:4 | 154 |
| *2 Bar.* | |
|   4:2-6 | 201 n.8 |
|   32:2-4 | 201 n.8 |
| *2 Enoch* 24:3 | 154 |
| *Apoc. Abr.* 24:10 | 154 n.17 |
| *Apoc. Mos.* 19:3 | 154 n.17 |
| *1 Enoch* | |
|   41:1 | 154 |
|   103:2 | 154 |
|   106:19 | 154 |
| *Ep. Arist.* | |
|   132 | 161 |
|   142 | 156 |
|   305 | 85 |
| *Joseph and Asenath* 14:12-17 | 207 |
| *Jub.* | |
|   12:12-14 | 13 |
|   15:31 | 157 n.29 |
|   16:18 | 208 |
| Ps.-Philo *Bib. Ant.* 6:1-18 | 13 |
| *Pss. Sol.* 4:23 | 163 |
| *Sib. Or.* | |
|   1:360-71 | 9 |
|   1:387-400 | 267 n.50 |
|   5:143 | 201 |
|   8:299-301 | 260 n.29 |
| *T. Dan* 5:12 | 201 n.8 |
| *T. Levi* 6:11 | 132 |
| *T. Mos.* | |
|   7 | 156 |
|   7:9-10 | 156 n.25 |
| *T. Naph.* 8:3–9:5 | 13 |

# DEAD SEA SCROLLS

| | |
|---|---|
| CD | |
|   4:14-18 | 204 |
|   4:19 | 8 |
|   8:12 | 8 |
| 1QH | |
|   1:21 | 154 |
|   2:13 | 154 |
|   2:18 | 155 |

| | |
|---|---|
|   4:6-8 | 6 |
|   4:9-11 | 6 |
|   4:13-14 | 7 |
|   4:27-28 | 154 |
|   18:20 | 155 |
| 1QM 3:9 | 134 |
| 1QpHab | |
|   2:1-2 | 8 |
|   5:3-5 | 8 |
|   5:11 | 8 |
|   7:4-5 | 154 |
|   8:8-13 | 205 |
|   8:8 | 8 |
|   8:16–9:2 | 205 |
|   9:9 | 8 |
|   10:9 | 8 |
|   10:10 | 205 |
|   11:4-8 | 205 |
|   11:4 | 8 |
|   11:12-15 | 205 |
|   11:13 | 155 |
|   12:2-6 | 205 |
|   12:2 | 8 |
|   12:7-10 | 205 |
|   12:8 | 8 |
| 1QS | |
|   2:4-9 | 8 |
|   2:15 | 134 |
|   5:5 | 155 |
|   5:10-13 | 7 |
|   8:14 | 12 |
|   9:16-18 | 7 |
|   9:18 | 12, 154 |
|   9:19-20 | 12 |
|   9:21-22 | 8 |
|   11:3-8 | 154 |
|   11:13-15 | 158 |
| 4QpIsa^c | |
|   23 ii 10 | 8 |
|   30 i 3 | 8 |
| 4QpNah | |
|   1-2 ii 7 | 8 |
|   3-4 i 7 | 8 |
|   3-4 ii 4 | 8 |
| 4QpPs^a | |
|   1-10 ii 5 | 205 |
|   1-10 ii 9-11 | 204 |

| | |
|---|---|
| 1-10 ii 10-11 | *204* |
| 1-10 iii 5 | *205* |
| 1-10 iv 8 | *8* |

# RABBINIC WRITINGS

**Midrashim** _____

*Mek.*
| | |
|---|---|
| Exod 17:14 | *45 n.31* |
| Exod 19:6 | *208* |
| *Mek. Rabbi Simon* 96–97 | *208* |
| *Midr. Ps.* 100:1 | *209 n.27* |
| *Lam. Rab.* 2.2.4 | *46* |
| *Sipre Deut* §354 (on 33:18) | *209 n.27* |
| *Sipre Num* §103 (on 12:1-16) | *175 n.24* |
| *Sipre Zuta* to Num 12:6-8 | *175 n.24* |
| Tanhuma Buber, | |
| *Debarim* §2 | *209 n.27* |

**Mishnah** _____

*Abot*
| | |
|---|---|
| 3:9 | *42 n.17* |
| 3:10 | *42 n.17* |
| *Ber.* 9:5 | *49 n.42* |
| *Ker.* 1:7 | *48* |
| *Sanh.* 11:2 | *50 n.46* |
| *Šeqal.* | |
| 1:1 | *51* |
| 1:3 | *50 n.45, 51* |
| 2:1 | *50 n.45* |
| 4:7 | *49 n.42* |
| 5:4 | *50 n.44* |
| 5:6 | *50 n.43* |
| 6:1 | *50 n.43* |
| 6:5 | *50 n.43* |
| 7:1 | *50 n.43* |
| 7:2 | *48 n.35* |
| *Sukk.* 4:2 | *45* |

**Tosefta** _____
| | |
|---|---|
| *Ber.* 3:25 | *246 n.170* |
| *Hag.* 2:11 | *47 n.33* |
| *Sanh.* 10.11 | *248* |

**Talmud Babli** _____
| | |
|---|---|
| *'Abod. Zar.* 8b | *49 n.38* |

*Beṣa*
| | |
|---|---|
| 20a | *47* |
| 20a, b | *47 n.33* |
| *Git.* 57a | *248* |
| *Pesaḥ.* 26a | *50 n.46* |
| *Šabb.* | |
| 15a | *49 n.38* |
| 153a | *44* |
| *Sanh.* | |
| 41a | *49 n.38* |
| 43a | *248* |
| 106a | *248* |
| 107b | *248* |
| *Soṭa* 47a | *248* |
| *Yoma* 39b | *93 n.46* |

**Talmud Yerushalmi** _____
| | |
|---|---|
| *Beṣa* 2:4 | *47 n.33* |
| *Ḥag.* 2:33 | *47 n.33* |
| *Sanh.* 7:16, 67a | *248* |
| *Ta'an.* 4:7 | *46* |

**Targumim** _____
| | |
|---|---|
| *Tg. Ps.-J.* Gen 11:28 | *13* |
| *Tg. Ps.-J.* Exod 1:15 | *64* |
| *Tg. Isa* | |
| 24:23 | *39* |
| 25:6-8 | *39* |
| *Tg. Zech* 14:1-15 | *45* |
| 14:16-21 | *45* |
| 14:16 | *45* |
| 14:18 | *45* |
| 14:19 | *45* |

**Liturgical Texts** _____
| | |
|---|---|
| *Shem. Es.* §12 | *246 n.170* |

# PHILO

*Abr.*
| | |
|---|---|
| 56 | *208* |
| 98 | *208* |
| *Conf.* 190 | *156* |
| *Decal.* | |
| 142 | *154 n.17* |
| 150 | *154 n.17* |
| 153 | *154 n.17* |
| 173 | *154 n.17* |

**PHILO** (*continued*)

| | |
|---|---|
| *Leg. ad Gaium* 18.120 | *249 n.184* |
| *Migr.* 89-93 | *211* |
| *Mos.* 1.149 | *208* |
| *Mut. nom.* 12 | *63 n.30* |
| *Sobr.* 66 | *208* |
| *Spec. Leg.* | |
| 1.52 | *208 n.22* |
| 1.54-57 | *202, 204* |
| 1.305 | *155* |
| 1.315 | *203* |
| 1.315ff. | *204* |
| *Virt.* 102–3 | *208 n.22* |

## JOSEPHUS

| | |
|---|---|
| *Ag. Ap.* | |
| 2.10 §121 | *135 n.31* |
| 2.14 §148 | *135 n.31* |
| *Ant.* | |
| 2.9.1-3 §201-16 | *63* |
| 2.9.1 §201-4 | *63 n.29* |
| 2.9.2 §205-9 | *63* |
| 2.9.2 §205 | *64* |
| 2.9.3 §216 | *63* |
| 2.9.4 §217-27 | *64* |
| 2.9.6-7 §228-37 | *64 n.32* |
| 2.11.1 §254-57 | *64* |
| 4.6.6 §126-30 | *203* |
| 4.6.7 §130 | *203* |
| 4.6.8 §137-38 | *203, 204* |
| 4.6.11 §145-49 | *203* |
| 4.6.11 §148-49 | *203* |
| 12.3.2 §125-26 | *204* |
| 18.1.4 §16 | *87 n.31* |
| 18.2.2 §33-35 | *49 n.40* |
| 18.4.3 §90-95 | *49 n.41* |
| 18.9.1 §312 | *51* |
| *J.W.* | |
| 2.1.5 §28 | *156* |
| 2.8.14 §165 | *87 n.31* |
| 3.8.3 §351-53 | *93 n.46* |
| 6.5.3 §293-300 | *267* |
| 7.6.6 §218 | *51* |

## GRECO-ROMAN LITERATURE

| | |
|---|---|
| Dio Cassius, *History of Rome* | |
| 37.16-17 | *222 n.43* |
| Dio Chrysostom, *Corp. Pap. Judaic.* | |
| 152.23-25 | *222 n.40* |
| Diodorus, *World History* | |
| 4.3.8-9 | *222 n.41* |
| Juvenal, *Satires* | |
| 1.3.10-16 | *220 n.30* |
| 1.3.296 | *220 n.30* |
| 2.6.542-47 | *220 n.31* |
| 5.14.96-106 | *220 n.30* |
| 5.14.96-101 | *223 n.44* |
| Plutarch, *Quaest. Conv.* | |
| 4.4.4–5.3 | *222 n.43* |
| Suetonius, *Claud.* 5.25.4 | *221 n.34* |
| Tacitus, *Ann.* 15.44.5 | *135 n.31* |
| Tacitus, *Hist.* | |
| 5.5.2 | *135 n.31* |
| 5.1-13 | *220 n.32, 222 n.41* |

## EARLY CHRISTIAN LITERATURE

**New Testament Pseudepigrapha** ____

| | |
|---|---|
| *Acts of Andr. Matt.* 13–15 | *266 n.48* |
| *Acts of John* 94 | *262 n.36* |
| *Acts of Peter* | |
| 8 | *266* |
| 32 | *265 n.44* |
| *Acts of Thom.* 32 | *266* |
| *Apoc. Paul* 48 | *265 n.44* |
| *Apoc. Peter* (Eth.) 2 | *265 n.44* |
| *Apos. Const.* | |
| 5.3.16-17 | *240* |
| 8.47.70 | *240* |
| *Barn.* | |
| 2–3 | *218 n.18* |
| 3:6 | *160* |
| 4 | *260* |
| 4:6-8 | *218 n.18* |
| 4:6-7 | *157, 231 n.88* |
| 4:13 | *157* |
| 4:14 | *157, 230 n.82* |
| 5:11 | *235* |
| 6:6-8 | *218 n.18* |

*Dial. Tim. Aq.*

| | |
|---|---|
| fol. 77r | *259 n.26* |
| fol. 93r | *263 n.39* |

*Didasc. Apos.*

| | |
|---|---|
| 5.14.23 | *237 n.125* |
| 26 | *259 n.26* |

*Ep. Diog.*

| | |
|---|---|
| 3-4 | *218 n.19, 236 n.117* |
| 4:6 | *218 n.19* |

*5 Ezra*

| | |
|---|---|
| 1:24-26 | *267* |
| 2:7 | *267 n.50* |
| 2:10 | *267* |

*Gos. Naz.*

| | |
|---|---|
| 21 | *267* |
| 36 | *267* |

*Gos. Nicod.*

| | |
|---|---|
| 1 | *266 n.48* |
| 1.1 | *257 n.18, 262 n.35* |
| 2.3 | *263 n.38* |

*Gos. Thom.*

| | |
|---|---|
| §39 | *277* |
| §43 | *40, 277* |
| §55 | *277* |
| §65 | *277* |
| §102 | *277* |

| | |
|---|---|
| *Inf. Gos. Thom.* | *279 n.32* |
| *Keryg. Pet.* Hom. 2.38 | *260 n.28* |

*Mart. Pol.*

| | |
|---|---|
| 12.2 | *248 n.181* |
| 13.1 | *248 n.181* |
| 13.2 | *249 n.183* |
| 17.2 | *248 n.181, 249 n.183* |
| 18.1 | *248 n.181, 249 n.183* |

| | |
|---|---|
| *Protev. Jas.* 17.2 | *267 n.51* |

**Church Fathers** _____

Agobard

| | |
|---|---|
| *Ep.* C | *240 nn.138, 139* |
| *Ep.* D | *240 n.138* |

Ambrose

| | |
|---|---|
| *De ob. Theo.* 40 | *246* |

*Ep.*

| | |
|---|---|
| 40 | *218 n.16* |
| 41 | *218 n.16* |

Aphrahat

| | |
|---|---|
| *Dem.* 23.20 | *236* |

*Homilies*

| | |
|---|---|
| 12.7 | *227 n.73* |
| 17.1 | *227 n.73* |
| 21.1-7 | *227 n.73* |

Augustine, *Civ. Dei*

| | |
|---|---|
| 12.7 18.46 | *236* |
| 20.29 | *236* |

Chrysostom

*Against the Jews*

| | |
|---|---|
| Homily 1 | *234 n.109* |
| Homily 8 | *217 n.10, 241 n.142* |

*Discourse*

| | |
|---|---|
| 1.3.3 | *241 n.143* |
| 1.4.2 | *241 n.143* |
| *Ephesians*, Homily 5 | *236 n.120* |
| *Or. C. Jud.* 1.7 | *232 n.93* |

Clement of Alexandria

| | |
|---|---|
| *Paed.* (col. 5) 19.4 | *235 n.111* |

*Strom.*

| | |
|---|---|
| 2 | *238 n.129* |
| 6.28.1 | *223 n.47, 236 n.118* |

Cyprian, *Testimonies*

| | |
|---|---|
| Treatise 5 | *235 n.112* |
| Treatise 10 | *227 n.70, 230 n.83* |
| Treatise 12 | *217 n.12, 231 n.88* |

| | |
|---|---|
| Cyril, *In Lucam*, Homily 101 | *217 n.9* |

Ephraem the Syrian, *Rhy. C. Jud.*

| | |
|---|---|
| 15 | *229 n.78* |

Epiphanius, *Panarion*

| | |
|---|---|
| 29.9.1 | *247 n.175* |

Eusebius

| | |
|---|---|
| *Dem. Ev.* 1.1 | *236* |

*Hist. Eccl.*

| | |
|---|---|
| 1.1.2 | *244 n.153* |
| 2.3.5-6 | *244 n.153* |
| 2.6.3-7 | *244 n.153* |
| 2.17.2 | *218 n.14* |
| 2.23 | *281 n.38* |
| 2.23.20ff. | *281 n.37* |
| 3.7.1 | *244 n.153* |
| 5.22 | *244 n.155* |
| 6.12.1 | *240 n.134* |

*Praep. Ev.*

| | |
|---|---|
| 1.2.1-4 | *239 n.133* |
| 1.3.1 | *239 n.133* |

Hippolytus
  *Demonstrations to the*
    *Jews*      238 n.129
  *In Dan.* 1.29.21      249 n.183
  *In Deut.* 24–26      235 n.111
  *In Gen.*
    49.6      235 n.114
    49.86      249 n.183
  *In Prov.* 1.11      235 n.114
Ignatius
  *Eph.*
    inscrip.      162
    18:2      162
  *Magn.*
    8–10      160, 218 n.17
    9:1-2      236 n.117
  *Phld.*
    5–6      218 n.17
    5:2      223 n.46, 230 n.81
    6:1      235 n.110
  *Rom.* inscrip.      162
  *Trall.* 7:1      162
Irenaeus
  *Adv. Haer.*
    1.24      276
    1.25      277
    2.35.4      233 n.103
    3.31.1      233 n.103
    3.4.1      233 n.103
    4.4.1-2      243 n.153
    4.6.1      236 n.118
    4.7.4      236 n.118
    4.8.1      236 n.118
    4.13.4      243 n.153
    4.14.2      235 n.111
    4.15.2      235 n.111
    4.16.4      235 n.111
    4.17.2      235 n.111
    4.18.4      235 n.114, 236 n.118
    4.21.3      249 n.183
  *Demonst.*
    95      235 n.114, 236 n.118
    99      236 n.118
Isidore of Spain, *C. Jud.* 1.18      236
Jerome, *Ep. August.*
  112.13      247 n.175

Justin
  *1 Apol.*
    1.28      236 n.118
    1.47      243 n.153
    1.53      243 n.153
    36      235 n.111
    131      247 n.175
  *Dial.*
    7      263 n.37
    9      235 n.111
    10.3      236 n.121
    11      223 n.48, 224 n.51, 236 n.118
    12      223 n.48
    16      243 n.153, 247 n.175, 248 n.183
    16.4      247 n.175
    17      248 n.183
    29.2      231 n.88
    32      248 n.183
    32.1-3      237 n.121
    34      248 n.183
    39      235 n.111
    40      243 n.153
    47      247 n.175
    47.4      160
    48      275 n.16
    71–73      259 n.23
    92      243 n.153
    96      247 n.175
    98      235 n.114
    112–14      232 n.94
    114      231 n.90
    117      243 n.153, 248 n.183
    119      224 n.49, 236 n.118
    123      224 n.51
    126      231 n.90, 235 n.111
    131      248 n.183
    133      248 n.183
    135      224 n.51, 236 n.118
    136      248 n.183
    137      247 n.175, 248 n.183
    139      236 n.118
    141      235 n.114
Melito, *Peri Pascha*
  21      241 n.140
  55      241 n.140

| | |
|---|---|
| 72–99, lines 567–84 | *235* |
| 72–99, lines 693–716 | *235* |
| 79 | *265* |
| 259–79 | *218 n.20* |
| 732–47 | *218 n.20* |

Origen

*Comm. in Ep. ad Rom.*

| | |
|---|---|
| 2.14 | *231 n.90, 232 n.96* |
| 6.12 | *231 n.92* |

*Comm. in Matt.* 15.14      *261*

*Contra Celsum*

| | |
|---|---|
| 1.14–16 | *225 n.58* |
| 1.55 | *239 n.132* |
| 1.61 | *231 n.90* |
| 2.4.1–2 | *246 n.167* |
| 2.9.1 | *246 n.167* |
| 2.13.1ff. | *246 n.167* |
| 2.18 | *246 n.167* |
| 2.26 | *246 n.167* |
| 2.28 | *246 n.167* |
| 2.34 | *246 n.167, 264 n.42* |
| 2.39 | *246 n.167* |
| 2.41 | *246 n.167* |
| 2.75-78 | *239 n.132* |
| 3.10 | *239 n.132* |
| 4.73 | *225 n.58* |
| 4.77 | *239 n.132* |
| 5.8 | *225 n.58* |
| 7.20 | *243 n.153* |

| | |
|---|---|
| *Didascalia* 5.14.15 | *238 n.129* |
| *Gen. Hom.* 13.3 | *249 n.183* |
| *Hom. Jerem.* 10.8.2 | *247 n.175* |
| *In Ex. Hom.* 5:1 | *236 n.117* |
| *In Isaiam. Hom.* 6.7 | *235 n.111* |

*In Jerem. Hom.*

| | |
|---|---|
| 5 | *225 n.58, 236 n.119, 238 n.129* |
| 9.2 | *224 n.58* |
| 14.13 | *243 n.153* |

| | |
|---|---|
| *In Joh. Comm.* 10:24 | *236 n.117* |
| *In Levit. Hom.* 6.1 | *231 n.92* |

*In Lib. Jud. Hom.*

| | |
|---|---|
| 8.2 | *223 n.45, 231 n.91* |
| 18.2 | *231 n.90, 235 n.111* |

| | |
|---|---|
| *In Luc. Hom.* 12 | *231 n.92* |
| *In Num. Comm.* 23:1 | *236 n.117* |

| | |
|---|---|
| *In Rom. Comm.* 8:9 | *236 n.119, 238 n.129* |

Socrates, *Hist. Eccl.*

| | |
|---|---|
| 3.20 | *244 n.154, 246 n.168* |
| 5.22 | *246 n.168* |
| 7.7 | *217 n.7* |
| 7.13 | *217 n.8, 246 n.168* |

Tertullian

*Adv. Jud.*

| | |
|---|---|
| 4.8 | *247 n.172* |
| 5 | *232 n.93* |

*Adv. Marc.*

| | |
|---|---|
| 2.19.1 | *218 n.21* |
| 3.23.1ff. | *218 n.21* |
| 3.23.1-2 | *239 n.130* |
| 4.14 | *239 n.130* |
| 4.15 | *239 n.130* |
| 5.4.1ff. | *218 n.21* |

*Answer to the Jews*

| | |
|---|---|
| 8 | *264 n.42* |
| 10 | *264 n.42* |
| 13 | *217 n.11* |

| | |
|---|---|
| *Apology* 21.16-17 | *9* |
| *De Prescript.* 8 | *239 n.130* |

# NAG HAMMADI

*Apocryph. Jas.*

| | |
|---|---|
| I 4.22–6.21 | *283 n.48* |
| I 4.28-30 | *283* |
| I 5.9-20 | *283* |

*Gos. Truth*

| | |
|---|---|
| I 18.17-26 | *284* |
| I 18.21-27 | *284 n.52* |
| I 19.18-30 | *279* |
| I 19.21-28 | *279* |
| I 20.10-14 | *284* |
| I 20.23–21.2 | *284 n.52* |
| I 20.25-27 | *284* |

*Tract. Tripart.*

| | |
|---|---|
| I 52.21ff. | *276* |
| I 55.27ff. | *277* |
| I 56.8 | *277* |
| I 62.5-6 | *276* |
| I 62.13 | *277* |
| I 62.26 | *275* |

**NAG HAMMADI**

*Tract. Tripart. (continued)*

| | |
|---|---|
| I 63.22 | 277 |
| I 75.30 | 276 |
| I 101.3-4 | 275 |
| I 104.4–108.12 | 274 |
| I 108.13 | 275 |
| I 109.24–110.22 | 275 n.22 |
| I 110.22–111.5 | 275 n.22 |
| I 110.23-25 | 275 |
| I 111.6–112.9 | 275 n.22 |
| I 111.17-23 | 275 n.22 |
| I 112.9ff. | 275 n.22 |
| I 112.20-22 | 275 |

*Gos. Phil.* II 63.21-24 — 284 n.52

*1 Apoc. Jas.*

| | |
|---|---|
| V 25.7-9 | 282 |
| V 25.18-19 | 282 |
| V 31.23-26 | 282 |
| V 33.2-5 | 282 |
| V 33.5-11 | 282 |
| V 34.26 | 282 |
| V 36.16-19 | 282 |

*2 Apoc. Jas.*

| | |
|---|---|
| V 45.9-12 | 282 |
| V 55 | 282 |
| V 55.25f. | 282 |
| V 56.2-7 | 282 |
| V 56.9f. | 282 |
| V 59.1-11 | 281 |
| V 59.12ff. | 280 |
| V 60.13-22 | 281 |
| V 61.4 | 281 |
| V 61.12–62.12 | 281 |
| V 62.7-12 | 283 n.47 |
| V 62.16–63.28 | 281 |

*Auth. Teach.*

| | |
|---|---|
| VI 33.4–34.34 | 280 |
| VI 33.10 | 280 |
| VI 33.25-26 | 280 |

*Conc. Great Power*

| | |
|---|---|
| VI 41.17-22 | 285 n.53 |
| VI 45.17-22 | 277 n.30 |

*2 Treat. Great Seth*

| | |
|---|---|
| VII 55.9–56.19 | 285 n.55 |
| VII 59.19-29 | 283 |
| VII 63.31–64.1 | 278 |
| VII 64.18ff. | 278 |

*Apoc. Pet.*

| | |
|---|---|
| VII 72.5-13 | 286 |
| VII 73.10-12 | 286 |
| VII 74.13-15 | 286 n.56 |
| VII 83.3-24 | 286 |

*Test. Truth*

| | |
|---|---|
| IX 45.23–48.15 | 274 n.18 |
| IX 45.23–48.4 | 286 |
| IX 48.14-15 | 287 |

## QUR'AN

| | |
|---|---|
| 2:88 | 224 |
| 3:110 | 224 |
| 4:46 | 224 |
| 4:52 | 224 |
| 5:13 | 224 |
| 5:60 | 224 |
| 5:64 | 224 |
| 5:78 | 224 |
| 33:40 | 224 |
| 59:3 | 224 |

# Index of Modern Authors

Achtemeier, P. J., 257 n.17
Allison, D. C., Jr., 69 n.53
Attridge, H. W., 106, 274–75, 277 n.28, 279 n.32, 284
Aune, D. E., 203 n.13

Baarda, T., 130 n.8
Bammel, E., 132 n.16
Barrett, C. K., 142 n.51, 271, 280 n.35
Barth, M., 128 n.1
Bauer, W., 257 n.19
Baum, G., 14, 78 n.88, 137 n.36
Baur, F. C., 132, 166, 167
Beck, N. A., 15, 59 nn.12, 13; 81 n.6, 120 n.18, 125 n.32, 143 n.55, 157 n.30, 162 n.50
Beker, J. C., 126–27, 146 n.59
Ben-Chorin, S., 133 n.22
Bethge, H. G., 273 n.11
Bloesch, D., 251
Böhlig, A., 272–73, 277 n.29
Brashler, J., 286
Broer, I., 133 n.19, 134, 134 n.29, 135 n.31
Brouwer, G., 142 n.50
Brown, R. E., 119–20, 121 n.23, 123 nn.26, 28; 167 n.3, 169, n.8
Bruce, F. F., 133 n.19, 135 n.32
Brueggemann, W., 34
Buchanan, G. W., 144 n.55
Bultmann, R., 123 n.28, 280 n.35
Burchard, C., 189 n.52
Burkitt, F. C., 277
Burnett, F. W., 58 n.9, 59 nn.12, 13; 60 n.16

Callan, T., 16, 219 n.27, 237 n.124
Cerfaux, L., 279 n.32
Charlesworth, J. H., 14, 200
Childs, B. S., 36, 187 n.47
Cohen, S. J. D., 12 n.16, 59 n.12, 216 n.6, 222, 243
Collins, A. Y., 200, 244–45, 252
Cook, M. J., 56 n.3, 59 n.1, 61 n.19, 134 n.25
Cranfield, C. E. B., 147 n.63, 148 n.65
Crossan, J. D., 73 n.64, 265 n.43
Culpepper, R. A., 116 n.7

Daniel, J. L., 59 n.11
Daniélou, J., 288
Davids, P., 185 n.42, 189 n.53, 190, 191, 194 n.72
Davies, W. D., 11 n.13, 64, 69 n.53, 78, 79, 128 n.1, 132 n.13, 134 n.29, 150 n.69
Dentan, R., xi
Dibelius, M., 188, 190 n.61
Donfried, K. P., 133 n.20, 134 n.28
Dunn, J. D. G., 78 n.88, 139 n.46, 143 n.53, 166 n.1, 193 n.71, 195 n.74, 293

Elliott, J. H., 168 n.6
Eppstein, V., 49
Evans, C. A., 92 n.43, 234 n.108, 247–48, 294

Feldman, L. H., 58 n.8
Fiorenza, E. S., 200
Fisher, E. J., 16 n.41
Fitzmyer, J. A., 73 n.64

Flusser, D., 58 n.8, 59 n.12, 129 n.4,
    237 n.122, 245, 247, 249 n.190, 250
    nn.193, 195
Foerster, W., 272 n.10, 274, 275
Fortna, R. T., 123 n.28
Fraikin, D., 134 n.27
Francis, F. O., 187 n.46
Frend, W. H. C., 221
Freyne, S., 42 n.13, 55 n.1, 74 n.68
Fuller, R. H., 125 n.32
Funk, R. W., 281

Gager, J. G., 16, 59 n.11, 80, 96 n.50,
    98, 101, 143 n.54, 147 n.62, 149 n.67,
    250 n.192, 253 n.1, 254 nn.4, 7
Garland, D., 74 n.67
Gaston, L., 58–59, 74 n.70, 122 n.24,
    136 n.36, 143 nn.53, 54
Geertz, C., 105 n.12
Gilliard, F. D., 134 n.24
Gnilka, J., 66 n.42
Goppelt, L. 133 n.19, 245, 288
Granskou, D., 16
Grant, R. M., 276
Grobel, K., 279, 284 n.49
Grundmann, W., 52 n.49
Gundry, R. H., 63 n.30, 139 nn.42, 44

Haas, P., 103
Haenchen, E., 103
Haering, T., 173 n.19
Hagner, D. A., 56 n.3, 58 n.8, 295
Hamerton-Kelly, R. G., 50
Hare, D. R. A., 57 n.4, 59 nn.12, 13; 61
    n.20, 62 n.23, 66 n.41, 74 n.70, 80,
    81, 99, 100
Harnack, A., 246
Harrington, D. J., 58 n.8, 61 n.19
Harrisville, R. A., 180 n.32
Harvey, A. E., 41 n.10
Heinlein, R. A., x
Heschel, A. J., 34
Holtz, T., 132 n.14, 133 n.19, 136 n.34
Hulen, A. B., 227
Hurtado, L. W., 62 n.23

Isaac, J., 14

Jervell, J., 104 n.9, 149 n.66, 192 n.69
Jewett, R., 132 n.16
Jodock, D., 126 n.33
Johnson, E. E., 58 n.9, 130 n.6
Johnson, L. T., 8, 55 n.2, 134 n.27, 189
    n.53, 242 n.148, 249
Johnson, S., 132 n.16
Jonas, H., 195 n.75, 271 n.7, 272, 273,
    275, 288
Juel, D., 61 n.21, 64 n.33, 92 n.43

Kampling, R., 72 n.64
Katz, S. T., 13
Kingsbury, J. D., 64 n.34, 73 n.64, 83
    n.13
Klassen, W., 175 n.26, 176 n.27, 216 n.6,
    220, 224
Klausner, J., 129 n.2
Klein, C., 14, 113 n.2
Klenicki, L., 16 n.41
Koenig, J., 60 n.15, 120 n.18
Koester, H., 200
Koschorke, K., 277 n.28, 286, 287, 289
Kosmala, H., 72 n.64
Kraft, H., 200
Krentz, E., 69 n.54
Kristeva, J., xiv
Kuhn, K. G., 157 n.26
Kysar, R., 291–92, 294–95

Lake, K., 223 n.46
Lane, W. L., 93 n.44, 95 n.49
Langmuir, G. I., 170
Lapide, P., 129 n.3
Laws, S., 190 n.54, 191
Lazare, B., 220, 221 n.33, 224 n.53, 233,
    237 n.122
Légasse, S., 76 n.82
Lemcio, E. E., 166 n.1
Levenson, J. D., 149 n.67
Levine, A.-J., 61 n.19, 69 n.55, 71 n.60,
    76 n.83, 77
Lindeskog, G., 129 n.2
Littell, F. H., 224
Loew, H., 208 n.22

Lowe, M., 61 n.19
Lüdemann, G., 143 n.52, 149 n.68
Lührmann, D., 93 n.45
Luz, U., 66 n.42, 146 n.58

MacDonald, D. R., 255 n.10, 256
Mack, B. L., 52 n.49
MacRae, G., 280, 284 n.49
Maier, P. L., 72 n.64
Malamat, A., 22 n.3
Malina, B. J., 55 n.1, 121 n.23
Marshall, I. H., 132 n.17
Martin, R. P., 188 n.48
Martyn, J. L., 13, 119–20, 121 n.23,
   123–24
McDonald, L. M., 293
McKnight, E. V., 113 n.3
McKnight, S., 67 nn. 43, 44; 103 n.7,
   163 n.54, 293
Meade, D. G., 187 n.47
Meagher, J. C., 245, 250 n.194
Meeks, W. A., 121 n.23, 242 n.149
Ménard, J. E., 276, 279 n.32, 284 n.49
Michel, O., 133 n.21, 173 n.19
Minear, P. S., 120 n.22
Montefiore, C. G., 208 n.22
Moore, G. F., 226 n.61, 227, 234, 237,
   245
Mounce, R. H., 205 n.17
Munck, J., 287 n.64
Mussner, F., 14, 134 n.27, 137 n.36, 147
   n.62

Neill, S., 238 n.127
Neusner, J., 89 n.36, 106, 107, 228, 233
Newman, B. M., 200
Neyrey, J. H., 55 n.1, 121 n.23
Niebuhr, Reinhold, x
Niedner, F. A., Jr., 58 n.9

Oepke, A., 173 n.20

Pagels, E., 274–75, 277 n.28, 284
Parkes, J., 14, 55 n.2, 218 n.16, 219
   n.24, 221 n.35
Patte, D., 57 n.5
Pawlikowski, J. T., 146 n.60

Pearson, B., 131, 132, 217 n.14, 287
   nn.61, 62
Perelmutter, H. G., 242 n.149
Perrin, N., 43–44
Pétrement, S., 283 n.48
Poliakov, L., 216 n.4, 242 n.149
Pratscher, W., 281 n.38
Prieur, J.-M., 256
Pritz, R. A., 193 n.71
Przybylski, B., 12 n.17, 61 n.19

Quispel, G., 283 n.47

Räisänen, H., 147 n.62
Reinach, Th., 269–70
Reinhartz, A., 57 n.5
Richardson, P., 16, 62 n.24, 163 n.53
Robinson, W. C., 273
Rokeah, D., 248–49, 250 n.195
Ruether, R. R., 14–15, 61 n.21, 129 n.5,
   149 n.67, 215 n.1, 216, 219 n.26,
   224–25, 225 n.57, 227, 229, 232, 235
   nn.113, 114; 238 n.129, 244, 250
   n.195

Saldarini, A. J., 224 n.51, 240 n.135
Sanders, E. P., 15, 43, 137 n.36, 138,
   138 n.39, 139, 195 n.73
Sanders, J. A., 9, 170 n.11, 197, 294
Sanders, J. T., xix, 16–17
Sandmel, S., x, xix, 3, 15, 57 nn. 4, 5; 59
   nn.12, 13; 60 n.18, 72 n.64, 81 n.6,
   84 n.17, 100, 113, 128 n.1, 129 n.2,
   149 n.67, 151 n.5, 200, 271, 277
Saperstein, M., 16 n.41, 241
Sayler, G. B., 106
Schierse, F. J., 183 n.39
Schiffman, L., 257 n.18
Schmidt, D., 131
Schnackenburg, R., 114 n.5, 123 n.28
Schoedel, W. R., 282–83
Schoeps, H. J., 142 n.50, 150, 166 n.2
Scholten, C., 281 n.40, 282 n.44, 283
   n.48, 284
Schreiner, T. R., 139 n.47
Segal, A. F., 237 n.122, 247, 248
Seland, T., 206

Senior, D. P., 73 n.65
Sevenster, J. N., 224
Sheppard, A. R. R., 209 n.30
Siker, J. S., 16, 224
Simon, M., 215, 216 n.6, 218 n.23, 219
    nn.25, 26; 226, 227, 228, 229, 232,
    234, 237, 239 n.131, 242, 245, 248,
    260
Sloyan, G. S., 15
Smith, D. M., 118, 120 n.18, 125 n.32,
    200
Spitta, F., 185 n.42
Staley, J. L., 115 n.6
Stanton, G. N., 58 n.9
Stern, M., 254 n.4
Stonehouse, N. B., 73 n.64
Stuhlmacher, P., 129 n.3, 133 n.22

Talbert, C. H., 143 n.55
Taylor, V., 95 n.49
Terrien, S., xi
Thyen, H., 172 n.17
Trachtenberg, J., 199
Trilling, W., 72 n.64, 75 n.74

Van Voorst, R. E., 186 n.43
Vasholz, R. I., 57 n.4
Vermes, G., 42, 43
von Wahlde, U. C., 118, 123 n.28

Walker, R., 68 n.50
Wanamaker, C. A., 132 n.14, 133 n.19,
    134 n.27
Whittaker, M., 222 n.43, 254 n.4
Wilckens, U., 129 n.4
Wilde, R., 217 n.14, 221 nn.33, 35; 227,
    239 n.132, 250, 254 n.7, 265 n.43
Wilken, R. L., 217 n.7, 219 n.26, 221
    n.35, 222 n.42, 237, 242, 243 n.150,
    244
Williams, A. L., 226 n.61, 228, 230, 254
    n.7
Williams, F. E., 283 n.48
Williamson, C. M., 57 n.4
Wilson, R., 29
Wilson, S. G., 16, 254 n.7
Wolff, H. W., xi, 179 n.30
Wuellner, W. H., 187 n.46